Handbook of Early
Literacy Research

Volume 3

D1572980

Handbook of
Early Literacy
Research

Volume 3

Edited by

Susan B. Neuman
David K. Dickinson

THE GUILFORD PRESS
New York   London

KH

© 2011 The Guilford Press
A Division of Guilford Publications, Inc.
72 Spring Street, New York, NY 10012
www.guilford.com

Paperback edition 2011

Printed in the United States of America

This book is printed on acid-free paper.

Last digit is print number: 9   8   7   6   5   4   3   2

Library of Congress Cataloging-in-Publication Data is available from the Publisher.

ISBN 978-1-60918-027-0 (hardcover)

ISBN 978-1-4625-0335-3 (paperback)

9/19/12

About the Editors

Susan B. Neuman, EdD, is Professor in Educational Studies at the University of Michigan. A former U.S. Assistant Secretary for Elementary and Secondary Education, Dr. Neuman established the Early Reading First program, developed the Early Childhood Educator Professional Development Program, and was responsible for all activities in Title I of the Elementary and Secondary Education Act. Her research and teaching interests include early literacy development, early childhood policy, curriculum, and early reading instruction. She has published over 100 articles and 11 books.

David K. Dickinson, EdD, is Professor and Chair of the Department of Teaching and Learning at Vanderbilt University's Peabody College of Education and Human Development. His major research interests include the role of language in literacy, the contributions of homes and preschools to language and literacy development, professional development interventions, and challenges associated with enhancing program quality. He has published numerous articles and books and is coauthor of a preschool curriculum, Opening the World of Learning.

Contributors

Dorit Aram is head of the Special Education Program at Tel Aviv University, Israel. Her research focuses on parent–child literacy interactions and their implications for early literacy and socioemotional development. She has conducted early interventions aimed at improving kindergarten and preschool teachers' as well as parents' mediation and children's literacy.

Erica M. Barnes is a doctoral student in the Department of Teaching and Learning at Vanderbilt University's Peabody College of Education and Human Development. Her research interests include early literacy and language development. She has been a special education teacher and consultant in Michigan and Massachusetts.

W. Steven Barnett is Board of Governors Professor and Co-Director of the National Institute for Early Education Research at Rutgers University. His research includes studies of the economics of early care and education, long-term effects of preschool programs on children's learning and development, and the distribution of educational opportunities.

Samantha B. Berkule-Silberman is a developmental psychologist, Assistant Professor of Psychology at Manhattanville College, Assistant Professor of Pediatrics at New York University School of Medicine, Director of the Video Interaction Project 0–3, and a Fellow of Zero to Three Leader for the 21st Century. Her research interests include infant and child development, specifically parent–child interactions, maternal sensitivity, attachment, early reading, and parenting interventions.

Clancy Blair is Professor in the Department of Applied Psychology at New York University. His research focuses on school readiness and self-regulation, particularly the development of executive functions in early childhood.

Kristen Paratore Bock holds a Certificate of Advanced Educational Specialization from the Lynch School of Education at Boston College and a master's degree in International Education Policy from Harvard Graduate School of Education. Her research interests include home–school connections, language and literacy acquisition among English language learners, and federal education policy.

Carolyn A. Brockmeyer is a developmental psychologist and a postdoctoral research fellow at New York University School of Medicine, as well as Director of the Bellevue Project for Early Language, Literacy, and Education Success. Her research focuses on the roles of narrative and play in promoting literacy and social cognition. She has significant experience with using narrative interventions in preschool and primary-care settings to promote school readiness for low-income children.

Margaret Burchinal is Professor in the Department of Education at the University of California, Irvine. She is interested in determining how child care experiences can help children, especially children from low-income families, succeed in school and in identifying effective teaching practices and instructional programs for preschoolers and children in elementary school. As an applied statistician, she has served as the primary data analyst for many large child care and evaluation projects and as an advisor for programs such as Head Start.

Adriana Bus is Professor in the Department of Learning Problems and Impairments, Institute of Education and Child Study, Leiden University, The Netherlands. Her research examines the impact of (electronic) storybook reading on children's language and literacy skills, and how early literacy is tied to attachment, executive functions, and genetics. She has published in leading journals in education, educational psychology, and child development.

Lydia L. S. Chan is a postdoctoral researcher at the University of Oxford. Her thesis examined the development of emergent literacy in Chinese children learning English as a second language. Prior to graduate studies at Oxford, she explored Law and Economics at the University of Cambridge as an Overseas Honorary Scholar.

Carol McDonald Connor is Associate Professor at Florida State University and the Florida Center for Reading Research. A recipient of the U.S. Presidential Early Career Award, her research examines the links between young children's language and literacy development with the goal of illuminating reasons for the perplexing difficulties that children who are atypical and diverse learners have in developing basic and advanced literacy skills.

Anne E. Cunningham is Professor of Cognition and Development at the University of California, Berkeley. Known for her research on reading development, she examines the cognitive and motivational processes that underlie reading ability and the interplay of context, development, and literacy instruction.

Megan Dunn Davison is Assistant Professor of Communication Sciences and Disorders at Temple University and a certified speech–language pathologist. Her research areas include language and literacy development and disorders in at-risk populations. She has completed work on bilingual preschool early language and literacy development and has also conducted research on written language outcomes in bilingual school-age children as well as children identified with language and learning disabilities.

Karen E. Diamond is Professor of Developmental Studies in the Department of Child Development and Family Studies at Purdue University. She is past Editor of the *Early Childhood Research Quarterly*. Her research focuses on classroom interventions to improve outcomes for preschool children from lower-income families and for children with disabilities.

David K. Dickinson (see "About the Editors").

Benard P. Dreyer is Professor of Pediatrics, Director of the Division of Developmental–Behavioral Pediatrics at New York University School of Medicine, and president-elect of the Academic Pediatric Association. His research has concentrated on the assessment of the home learning environment, the promotion of health literacy, and the effectiveness of primary-care interventions in enhancing parenting and school readiness for low-income families.

Mary Ann Evans is Professor of Psychology and Director of Clinical Training at the University of Guelph. A recipient of the President's Distinguished Faculty Award and the Psychology Teaching Award, she primarily studies literacy, communication development, shyness, and shared book reading.

Anne Fernald is Josephine Knotts Knowles Professor of Human Biology in the Department of Psychology at Stanford University, where she also runs the Center for Infant Studies on campus as well as a community laboratory for research with Spanish-learning children from immigrant Latino families. Her research has focused on how differences in the quantity and quality of children's early language experience results in differences in infants' speech processing efficiency, with cascading consequences for later language learning.

Nina Forestieri is a research assistant at the FPG Child Development Institute at the University of North Carolina at Chapel Hill. Her research interests include early childhood education, development, and school readiness, particularly among at-risk populations.

Ellen C. Frede, a developmental psychologist specializing in research to inform policy and practice, is Co-Director of the National Institute for Early Education Research. Her numerous studies have primarily investigated the relationship of program quality to child outcomes. Most recently, she coedited the book *Developing the Research Agenda for Young English Language Learners*.

Jill B. Freiberg is a doctoral student in the Department of Teaching and Learning at Vanderbilt University's Peabody College of Education and Human Development. Her research interests include early childhood language and literacy development and teacher education and development. She is particularly focused on improving educational opportunities for children from low-income backgrounds.

Roberta Michnick Golinkoff holds the H. Rodney Sharp Chair in the School of Education at the University of Delaware and is also a member of the Departments of Psychology and Linguistics. She conducts research in language acquisition and playful learning. Among her awards are a Guggenheim Fellowship and the Urie Bronfenbrenner Lifetime Achievement Award. She has authored 12 books and numerous journal articles.

Tamara Halle is Co-Director of Early Childhood Research at Child Trends in Washington, D.C. Her research interests include children's early cognitive and social development, early care and education, family and community supports for school readiness, and school characteristics associated with ongoing achievement and positive development. Her recent work focuses especially on

early literacy development among English language-learning children, and evaluations of early childhood curricula, programs, and professional development aimed at supporting children's school readiness.

Carol Scheffner Hammer is Professor of Communication Sciences and Disorders at Temple University. Her research focuses on cultural and environmental influences on children's language and literacy development and on school readiness interventions, with an emphasis on dual-language learners.

Justin Harris is a graduate student studying developmental psychology at Temple University. His research interests primarily focus on the role of play in early learning, but also include spatial cognition in early childhood.

Anne E. Henry is a postdoctoral fellow in the National Institute of Mental Health Children's Mental Health Services Training Program at the Johns Hopkins Bloomberg School of Public Health. Her research interests include the measurement and improvement of teacher quality and effectiveness in the context of school- and classroom-level interventions.

Annemarie H. Hindman is Assistant Professor in the College of Education at Temple University. Her research aims to identify how parents and teachers can, independently and in collaboration, support the development of children's early literacy skills during the transition to school. Her work is particularly focused on supporting positive outcomes for educators, families, and young children in underresourced communities.

Kathy Hirsh-Pasek is Lefkowitz Professor in the Department of Psychology at Temple University. A recipient of the American Psychological Association's (APA) Urie Bronfenbrenner Award for lifetime contribution to the science of developmental psychology and the APA Award for Distinguished Service to Psychological Science, her research in the areas of early language development, literacy, and infant cognition resulted in 11 books and over 100 publications.

Laura M. Justice is Professor in the School of Teaching and Learning at The Ohio State University. Her current research interests concern issues related to classroom composition in preschool settings and how this may affect children's learning and development. She is a certified speech–language pathologist and Editor of the *American Journal of Speech–Language Pathology*. She is the principal investigator of several large-scale trials of intervention approaches in early childhood settings, and publishes frequently on this topic.

Ann P. Kaiser is Susan W. Gray Professor of Education and Human Development at Vanderbilt University's Peabody College of Education and Human Development. Her primary area of research is early language interventions for children with developmental disabilities and children at risk due to poverty. Her research has investigated the effects of social communication interventions implemented by early childhood educators, parents, siblings, and peers.

Cornelia A. T. Kegel is a doctoral student at Leiden University, The Netherlands. Her research focuses on early literacy interventions, regulatory skills, and behavioral genetics.

Iris Levin is a Professor in the School of Education at Tel Aviv University, Israel. Her studies focus on the development and enhancement of early literacy and language, especially of alphabetic skills, phonological/morphological awareness, spelling, and vocabulary. She headed the committee that developed the national program for literacy of young children in Israel.

Ragan H. McLeod is completing her doctoral training in Early Childhood Special Education at Vanderbilt University. While at Vanderbilt, she has served as a teacher coach on two federally funded research projects. Her research interests include teacher professional development and best practices in vocabulary instruction for at-risk preschoolers.

Edward Melhuish is Professor of Human Development at Birkbeck, University of London. He has undertaken funded research projects in 12 countries, including the Effective Pre-school and Primary Education Project, the Effective Pre-school Provision in Northern Ireland, and the National Evaluation of Sure Start projects. He has over 200 publications. He has contributed to the formulation of social policy for young children

and is a scientific advisor in Norway, Finland, Portugal, Australia, and Chile.

Alan L. Mendelsohn is Associate Professor of Pediatrics at New York University School of Medicine; Director of Clinical Research for the Divisions of General and Developmental–Behavioral Pediatrics; Principal Investigator of the Bellevue Project for Early Language, Literacy, and Education Success; and a Graduate Fellow of Zero to Three. His research focuses on pediatric primary-care interventions aiming to promote parenting and school readiness for low-income children.

Jamie L. Metsala is Associate Professor in Educational Psychology at the University of Western Ontario. Her research interests include the development of spoken word recognition and reading-related processes in young children and linguistic/cognitive processes in children with learning disabilities. She is a registered clinical psychologist and has worked in clinical and school settings with children and families affected by learning disabilities.

Lesley Mandel Morrow is Professor of Literacy at Rutgers University's Graduate School of Education and a past president of the International Reading Association (IRA). Her research deals with early literacy development for children from diverse backgrounds. She has received IRA's lifetime award for scholarship and service; Rutgers' Excellence in Research, Teaching and Service Awards; Fordham University's Alumni Award for Outstanding Achievement; and was elected into the Reading Hall of Fame, also serving as their president. Dr. Morrow has published more than 300 articles and book chapters.

Susan B. Neuman (see "About the Editors").

Soojin S. Oh is a doctoral candidate at the Harvard Graduate School of Education. Her research primarily focuses on advancing theory and innovative methods to examine the educational experiences of young children in immigrant families. She also examines the causal impact of early childhood interventions on various developmental outcomes. She has conducted evaluations of various early childhood instruments and developmental literacy assessments.

Mariela M. Páez is Associate Professor in the Lynch School of Education at Boston College. Her research focuses on bilingualism, children's language and literacy learning, and early childhood education. She has conducted two longitudinal studies on the language development acquisition and literacy of Spanish-speaking children, currently focusing on developing intervention programs for this population. She is coeditor of *Latinos: Remaking America* and has published widely on language and literacy development.

Barbara Alexander Pan, recently retired from the Harvard Graduate School of Education, was trained as a developmental psychologist and studies the language and literacy development of young monolingual and bilingual children. Her work focuses particularly on factors affecting the development of children from low-income families.

Scott G. Paris is Professor at Nanyang Technological University and Head of the Centre for Research in Pedagogy and Practice at the National Institute of Education in Singapore. His research examines the development of reading skills, strategies, and comprehension with a focus on formative assessments in primary classrooms.

Robert C. Pianta is Dean of the Curry School of Education at the University of Virginia, Novartis Professor of Education, Professor of Psychology, and Director of the Center for Advanced Study of Teaching and Learning. His work in teacher and classroom quality is nationally recognized.

Shayne Piasta is Visiting Assistant Professor in the School of Teaching and Learning and Assistant Director of the Children's Learning Research Collaborative, both at The Ohio State University. Her areas of expertise include early literacy development and empirical validation of educational practices.

Lianna Pizzo is a doctoral candidate in the Lynch School of Education at Boston College. Her work focuses on bilingual language development specific to native Spanish speakers and deaf children using American Sign Language.

Douglas R. Powell is Distinguished Professor in Purdue University's Department of Child Development and Family Studies. His research focuses on interventions to improve young children's school readiness. He is a Consulting Editor of *Child Development* and former Editor of the *Early Childhood Research Quarterly*.

John Protzko is a student of Developmental Psychology at New York University. His main interests are in intelligence, reasoning, and psychological methodology.

Megan Y. Roberts, a licensed speech–language pathologist, is completing her doctoral training in Early Childhood Special Education at Vanderbilt University. She is currently the project director of a randomized clinical trial examining the efficacy of using the KidTalk program with toddlers with language delays. Her research interests include parent-implemented language interventions and observational language assessments for children with language delays.

Jean Saint-Aubin is Associate Professor at the University of Moncton in New Brunswick, Canada. His research is in the field of experimental psychology, with a special emphasis on short-term memory and reading processes highlighted by the missing-letter effect and eye movements.

Pam Sammons is Professor of Education in the Department of Education at the University of Oxford. Her research interests include educational effectiveness and improvement, leadership, and equity. She has conducted many studies of primary and secondary schools and their influence on pupils' educational outcomes, including longitudinal research on preschool effects.

Shelley Scarpino is Assistant Professor at the Richard Stockton College of New Jersey and is a doctoral candidate at The Pennsylvania State University. Her research focuses on phonological acquisition and disorders in monolingual and bilingual children and the relationship between language and emergent literacy skills, particularly in dual-language learners.

Monique Sénéchal is Professor in the Department of Psychology at Carleton University, Ottawa, Canada. She is a cognitive developmentalist interested in how young children learn from normally occurring activities. Her research focuses on language development and literacy acquisition.

Iram Siraj-Blatchford is Professor of Early Childhood Education in the Institute of Education at the University of London. She is Principal Investigator of major longitudinal studies in England, Ireland, and Australia. She has published extensively on the processes and practices associated with appropriate early childhood pedagogies and curriculum development.

Catherine E. Snow is Patricia Albjerg Graham Professor at the Harvard Graduate School of Education. She has published widely on language and literacy development, currently focusing on academic language skills of urban and language-minority youth.

Rebecca Starr is Research Scientist at Child Trends in Minneapolis, Minnesota, where she works on projects examining the quality of early care and education settings and the effects on children's developmental outcomes.

Kathy Sylva is Professor of Educational Psychology at the University of Oxford. A dominant theme throughout her work is the impact of education on children's problem solving, social skills, and self-regulation, as well as academic skills. A related theme is the impact of early interventions on combating social disadvantage. She was Specialist Adviser to the House of Commons Committee on Education (2000–2010).

Brenda Taggart worked in primary education as a teacher, deputy and acting principal, and teacher trainer. She has conducted research for both governmental and nongovernmental departments exploring the impact of educational initiatives. She works with practitioners on issues of quality and effective pedagogy.

Kathryn Tout is Co-Director of Early Childhood Research at Child Trends in Minneapolis, Minnesota. Her research focuses on policies and programs to improve the quality of early care and education and families' access to quality settings. She also conducts research on programs to improve the quality and effectiveness of the early childhood workforce.

Alexandra Ursache is a doctoral student in Developmental Psychology at New York University. She received her undergraduate degree from McGill University and her MEd from the Harvard Graduate School of Education.

Verna van der Kooy-Hofland, a former teacher and staff developer in primary education, is a doctoral student at Leiden University, The Netherlands. Her research focuses on the efficacy of computer programs to stimulate alphabetic knowledge in groups of young learners at risk for reading impairments.

Marina Vasilyeva is Associate Professor of Applied Developmental Psychology in the Lynch School of Education at Boston College. Her research interests encompass cognitive development and language acquisition in young children. Her work explores sources of individual differences, focusing on the role of learning environments in explaining variability among children across development.

Barbara A. Wasik is Professor and PNC Endowed Chair in Early Childhood Education at Temple University. She has extensive experience in curriculum development and has developed and evaluated a research-based language and literacy professional development program for early childhood teachers titled Exceptional Coaching for Early Language and Literacy (ExCELL), funded through the U.S. Department of Education Early Reading First grants.

Heidi Waterfall is a postdoctoral associate in Developmental Psychology at Cornell University. She is also a researcher in Developmental Psychology at the University of Chicago. Her research investigates the role of the linguistic environment, specifically caregiver–child interaction, in child language development.

Adriana Weisleder is a doctoral student in the Department of Psychology at Stanford University. She is interested in how early language experience contributes to individual differences in infants' language processing skills and language development. In her dissertation research, she is conducting a longitudinal study of the home language environments of low-socioeconomic-status (SES) Latino children living in the United States.

She is particularly interested in language learning by bilingual children, and hopes that her research will contribute to the development of language-enriching interventions with low-SES children.

Martha Zaslow, a developmental psychologist, is Director of the Office for Policy and Communications of the Society for Research in Child Development and a Senior Scholar at Child Trends in Washington, D.C. Her research focuses on utilization of early childhood care and education, and approaches to measuring and strengthening quality in these settings.

Jamie Zibulsky is Assistant Professor of Psychology at Fairleigh Dickinson University. As a school psychologist, she focuses on collaborating with teachers and parents to support children's reading acquisition. Her research focuses on the interaction between early reading skills and behavioral development.

Preface

This third volume of the *Handbook of Early Literacy Research* gives testimony to the vibrancy and diversity of the research being done with relevance to understanding the origins of literacy. Consistent with prior volumes, we retain our focus on the years from birth to the beginning of formal literacy instruction and include chapters that focus primarily on theoretical issues, others that describe and evaluate interventions, and still others that examine policy-relevant topics. Core theoretical constructs related to the reading process—including language, phonological awareness, and alphabetic knowledge and skills—receive attention in some chapters, while others take more of a setting-specific approach as they examine parents and parenting, classrooms, or community-based delivery. This volume accords greater prominence to certain topics than in previous volumes, including reviews of observational studies with very large samples, discussion of the early roots of language, phonological awareness and self-regulation, and interventions and issues associated with delivering effective interventions.

For this volume we have divided chapters into five parts. These groupings roughly reflect a convergence of certain core issues; however, there are cross-cutting themes throughout the volume. To help navigate your way between sections, we provide cross-references from one chapter to the next. We also briefly review key points of each section and the chapters within them.

Contents of This Volume

In Part I, Basic Developmental Processes, chapters present theory and developmental research that spans infancy to the early primary grades, providing a tapestry of findings that illustrate the interwoven nature of early development and the powerful continuities between the earliest years and later literacy.

In Chapter 1, Fernald and Weisleder set the tone for the first section by discussing the tensions that have surrounded efforts to understand persistent differences in academic success that are associated with social and economic class and using results of their groundbreaking work to demonstrate how understanding the environmental sources of differences can help guide interventions designed to address these issues. They review results of elegant experiments that assess how fast children can relate the sounds of words to meanings and show how early differences measured in fractions of a second are related to later language growth and, most important for those interested in early intervention research, to early language exposure.

In Chapter 2, Blair, Protzko, and Ursache examine the behavioral and cognitive research on self-regulation development and the neuroscience of self-regulation and its relationship to early literacy development. In particular they discuss how early stress-inducing experiences, often associated with poverty, set in motion patterns of neural response that affect brain development and emerging self-regulatory abilities that later play an important role in literacy development. They examine, in a sensitive manner, the differences in how children experience and respond to stress, and consider implications of these differences for educators.

Vasilyeva and Waterfall, in Chapter 3, extend discussion of variation in language development, noting that study of environmental influences on language, especially with respect to syntax, is contrary to the perspective of linguists such as Chomsky who view language development as primarily genetically determined. While acknowledging the role of genetically based contributions, they review evidence of socioeconomic status in multiple facets of language and discuss their own elegant studies that provide causal evidence of the impact of adult input on syntactic growth, one of the language strands related to later reading success.

In Chapter 4, Harris, Golinkoff, and Hirsh-Pasek also trace the early emergence of language, but take a different approach as they focus on vocabulary and discuss six principles that determine rate of acquisition of new words. Drawing on those principles, they argue that we need more playful approaches to teaching vocabulary. While acknowledging the urgent need to help some children rapidly acquire new words, they stress that direct instruction methods, the approach that often seems to be most expedient and fastest, are not the best for learning language or for children as emerging learners.

Metsala's Chapter 5, on lexical reorganization and phonological awareness, reinforces the potency of early experience on early reading as the author traces the emergence of phonological awareness from the early establishment of phonological representation of words into the primary grades. Metsala describes results of experimental studies that shed light on the relationship between vocabulary growth, receptive and productive measures of phonological representations, and children's ability to access these representations. She reviews literature that updates the influential lexical reorganization hypothesis, including a timeframe that extends into the early primary grades.

In Part II, Development among Diverse Populations, we review the development of language and literacy from the preschool years through the early elementary grades in two countries, the United States and England, with special attention given to children who are learning English as a new language and children with disabilities.

Burchinal and Forestieri provide a broad backdrop for understanding normative development in Chapter 6, as they review the results of multiple large-scale studies of early development, focusing in particular on environmental factors related to language and early literacy development. Their review reveals the consistency of findings pointing to the importance of high-quality early care environments and establish beyond a doubt that children at risk by virtue of poverty or other factors stand to gain the most from receiving high-quality services. Of particular interest is the intriguing finding that there may be thresholds in quality, such that the effect of improvements in quality may not appear until a certain minimal threshold level is achieved.

Chapter 7, by Sylva, Chan, Melhuish, Sammons, Siraj-Blatchford, and Taggart, describes findings from the Effective Pre-school and Primary Education (EPPE) Project, a nationally representative longitudinal study of literacy development of children in England from ages 3 to 11. This project was designed to identify enduring and interacting effects of family and preschool influences on children's literacy development. Particularly interesting, their findings indicate that variation in quality has educationally important implications for growth in code-related skills and in nonverbal intelligence, but not for language development.

In Chapter 8, the first of two chapters on dual-language learners, Hammer, Scarpino, and Davison focus on the results of a large longitudinal study that followed children from the preschool years into the early primary grades. This work examines children in terms of when they first were exposed to English, at home or in their Head Start classroom, and tracks lexical and syntactic growth. They report that language growth during preschool predicted later reading and that, by the middle of the primary grades, children in both groups had caught up with their monolingual peers' language scores. Reading performance of dual-language learners was strong, with scores approaching national norms at the end of kindergarten and both groups' reading comprehension scores above average by the end of first grade.

Another perspective on second-language learners is provided in Chapter 9 by Páez, Bock, and Pizzo, who report results from a longitudinal study of children whose first language is Spanish. Their study found considerable variability in home support for language and literacy and in home and classroom influences on language growth. They also describe encouraging early results from an intervention designed to help parents better support language development by introducing words and books in Spanish at home that are linked to books being used in the classrooms. Particularly encouraging is evidence of substantially improved depth of knowledge of word meanings.

Kaiser, Roberts, and McLeod, in Chapter 10, review the extensive literature linking language-based problems across multiple aspects of language functioning to early reading and describe a range of conditions that disrupt typical language development. They point out that the timing and severity of these disruptions affect children's success in learning to read, emphasizing the need for intervention for children's conditions associated with persistent delay. Language disorders often co-occur with behavioral challenges, and this combination places children at particular risk of failure in school. After reviewing the extensive literature that links developmental disabilities to reading, they provide a number of recommendations for practice that have implications for policy developers, programs, and teachers.

The field of intervention research has burgeoned in the last 5 years. This research has led to building a stronger knowledge base on code-related knowledge and interventions, as you will find in Part III, and curriculum and professional development, in Part IV. The chapters in Part III, Supporting Code-Related Abilities, begin with a focus on the family and the important home supports that characterize effective parental influence on children's readiness skills.

Monique Sénéchal, in Chapter 11, examines the power of joint attention between parent and child and its relation to outcomes. She reviews a series of longitudinal studies, elaborates on a home literacy model that distinguishes between informal literacy activities and more formal literacy activities, and tests the model's influence on children's outcomes.

In a complementary chapter (Chapter 12), Aram and Levin take a look at how parents may mediate a different joint activity in the home—writing. They use the term "writing mediation" to refer to the different levels of guidance that caregivers provide children in writing words, thereby teaching them about the written system. The authors' work shows some exciting new advances in the field of writing for young children and those with special needs. Through a series of studies described in the chapter, their findings indicate that writing mediation can be improved through intervention for children from different backgrounds and with specific needs, and that such trainings can enhance school readiness skills.

Alphabetic knowledge is, of course, indispensable to early reading and of central concern to teachers of young children. In Chapter 13, Justice and Piasta discuss prior studies that demonstrate the centrality of letter knowledge to early reading development. They examine promising results from studies that use an approach to book reading devised to enable teachers to make adjustments in how they read books aloud in order to draw children's attention to print and build their print knowledge. The authors describe a specific instructional practice—"print referencing"—that can be used to increase a specific set of skills that relate to print knowledge, and they provide a rich set of recommendations that can support letter knowledge in early childhood classrooms.

Van der Kooy-Hofland, Kegel, and Bus, in Chapter 14, explore new roles that computers can play to assist and support teachers in helping children develop related skills, focusing their attention particularly on phonological awareness. Noting the computer's ability to tailor the format and content to individual differences, they argue that computer programs can be used as an attractive tool for providing additional home-like experiences in literacy, especially for young children at risk. Their studies and multiple replications provide convincing evidence that such programs can be effectively scaled up to promote children's early literacy development.

In Chapter 15, Paris focuses on the distinctions among early reading skills and suggests ways that reading skills may be related longitudinally. His groundbreaking work makes the important distinction between constrained skills and unconstrained skills and their implications for statistical analyses and interpretations of reading skills. He argues that constraints explain the different developmental trajectories of reading components and why some components should not be treated as normally distributed variables. These constraints illustrate differences between (1) temporary developmental delays and enduring developmental differences and (2) necessary and sufficient conditions for learning to read.

Evans and Saint-Aubin, in Chapter 16, provide a highly sensitive technique for examining children's attention to print when looking at books. Using eye-tracking technology, they look at the features of books themselves that may affect children's learning about print, and at how parents may modify children's attention to print when interacting with books. The evidence suggests that certain features in books may spark children's attention to print, which parents might then use during shared book reading to promote children's learning.

The final chapter in the section offers the most appropriate caveat: Connor, in Chapter 17, on aptitude–treatment interactions, argues that *one size doesn't fit all*. It is highly unlikely that researchers and practitioners will find *the* perfect reading intervention that will work for all students. Rather, multicomponent interventions are more likely to be effective for greater numbers of students. Her work, however, beautifully details that we can predict, with a fairly high degree of precision, what mix of reading instructional activities (using a multidimensional view of instruction) is going to be effective for particular students if we know enough about their profile of language, literacy, and other skills and aptitudes.

Part IV, Interventions: Curriculum and Professional Development, addresses curriculum and professional development in multiple settings. In a fascinating series of studies detailed in Chapter 18, Mendelsohn, Dreyer, Brockmeyer, Berkule-Silberman, and

Morrow, describe the Video Interaction Project (VIP) an innovative pediatric program for bolstering parent–child interactions. Based on a three-part intervention, a child development specialist first models ideas and provides the mother with suggestions for interacting with her child. The specialist creates a videotape of the mother and child interacting for 5–7 minutes, then uses the video for a period of review and reflection and provides additional materials. Evidence from two randomized controlled trials is reviewed, showing strong support that the VIP significantly impacts both parenting and child development.

The next three chapters in this section highlight both the challenges and successes in professional development for early childhood educators. This area of research, in particular, has shown tremendous growth and vitality in the past 5 years, resulting from our understanding that teachers make an extraordinary difference in children's growth and development in literacy.

Powell and Diamond, in Chapter 19, and Henry and Pianta, in Chapter 20, have turned toward Web-based interventions as a strategy for scaling up professional development. Technology holds great potential to extend the reach of professional development. Using a case-based hypermedia resource, Powell and Diamond show how video illustrations of instruction linked with descriptive and explanatory text and other video exemplars can be a powerful intervention for teachers who traditionally have lacked access to professional development. Summarizing their randomized trials, they demonstrate the effects on teacher practices with concomitant effects on children's alphabetic and print concepts.

Henry and Pianta describe their program of research on MyTeachingPartner, a Web-mediated system of professional development to improve teacher–child interactions in preschool programs. Using a consultant model that is similar to the coaching approach of Powell and Diamond, their results suggest that it is possible to impact teacher practice at a scale only previously envisioned before. Their work is highly promising and has implications for how states, universities, and private providers may design professional development systems and for the kind and focus of supports teachers need to be effective in classrooms.

In Chapter 21, Wasik and Hindman provide yet another model of coaching for professional development, *Exceptional Coaching for Early Language and Literacy* (ExCELL). The chapter works particularly well in this context because it focuses on isolating the aspects or "active ingredients" of the model that appear to make it effective. Furthermore, their model targets vocabulary development and the role of the teacher in the process of helping children develop these important language skills.

Dickinson, Freiberg, and Barnes, in Chapter 22, raise the provocative question that has stymied many policymakers who wish to support early childhood: Why are so few interventions really effective? They answer the question by arguing that, although we know that classrooms can foster growth, we lack the kind of detailed information about them that is needed to effectively make changes in classroom instruction. The authors suggest that we need a more fine-grained approach, which can allow us to identify some of the traditional barriers to effective implementation and improvements in language and literacy instruction.

In Chapter 23, Neuman makes a case for placing vocabulary at the forefront of early literacy instruction. She first reviews what we know about quality vocabulary training for children in the early years, and then highlights why vocabulary training has proven to be especially complex in instructional programming. Finally, she examines the potential of quality instruction for children, using evidence from the World of Words (WOW), a highly effective vocabulary intervention that has been shown to accelerate word learning.

Part V, Social Policy and Early Literacy, begins with the important topic of assessment. Chapter 24, by Snow and Oh, draws heavily on the report of the National Academy of Sciences Committee on Developmental Assessment and Outcomes for Young Children and examines early childhood assessment across domains. It first highlights the debacle of the National Reporting System, an effort by the federal government to collect data on all Head Start children. It then reviews what we know about assessing early language and literacy skills, considering to what extent our procedures for conducting assessments are research based and usable in research undertakings. The authors focus on what kinds of considerations should be brought to bear when selecting assessments or when evaluating the quality of research that relies on assessments, which should provide a useful framework for making decisions.

Cunningham and Zibulsky, in Chapter 25, review the substantial research on reading aloud. They first describe the common techniques associated with shared book reading and then describe a meta-analysis conducted as part of the National Early Literacy Panel report. Their findings indicate that shared book reading has a moderate impact on children's oral language development, but that more formal instruction in alphabet knowledge and decoding will be necessary to facilitate early reading development.

In Chapter 26, Pan turns to the important issue of literacy development in the very early years. She reviews findings from Early Head Start Research and Evaluation Project, a study that provides a longitudinal, developmental look at the trajectories of children's language development and their emergent literacy skills through prekindergarten. This research shows the enormous variability in language skills and literacy environments of children from low-income U.S. homes as early as the second year of life and identifies key factors associated with that variability. However, it also demonstrates the promise of a highly effective intervention for children's language skills by age 3, even though the intervention is not focused specifically or exclusively on language or literacy.

Zaslow, Tout, Halle, and Starr begin Chapter 27 by describing some of the long-held beliefs about professional development for early childhood educators. They go on to describe the new conceptualizations that are emerging from multiple projects funded by the U.S. Department of Education to improve access to and quality of professional development for early educators working in low-income communities—the Early Childhood Educator Professional Development programs. These projects provide a valuable source for recent thinking on how professional development can strengthen educational practices and improve gains in children's early achievement, especially in the area of emergent literacy.

The final chapter of the *Handbook* addresses the quality of early care and education and, in this respect, offers a most fitting conclusion to the volume. Most children in the United States today attend a preschool or child care center prior to kindergarten. Federal and state governments subsidize millions of children so that they can attend programs that better meet their needs for early learning and development. Yet many children make such inadequate progress in language and literacy prior to kindergarten that they are poorly prepared to succeed in school. In Chapter 28, Barnett and Frede investigate the reasons for this perplexing problem and find a disparity between the characteristics of the programs children attend and characteristics of programs that have produced large gains in language and literacy. From a policy perspective, their chapter provides important new directions for research and planning designed to improve the effectiveness of preschool participation in promoting the language and literacy development of America's children.

Contents

III. SUPPORTING CODE-RELATED ABILITIES

IV. INTERVENTIONS: CURRICULUM AND PROFESSIONAL DEVELOPMENT

V. SOCIAL POLICY AND EARLY LITERACY

Handbook of Early Literacy Research

Volume 3

I
BASIC DEVELOPMENTAL PROCESSES

1

Early Language Experience Is Vital to Developing Fluency in Understanding

ANNE FERNALD
ADRIANA WEISLEDER

In this chapter we argue that early experience with language, beginning in infancy, promotes fluency in understanding and growth in vocabulary, building the foundation for later literacy. One of our conclusions is that speech directed to the young child in an engaging way is essential for the optimal development of vocabulary knowledge, but we know a lot about that already from previous studies. The exciting new theme in this story is that early experience with child-directed speech matters in another way as well: Infants who hear more and richer language from their caregivers also develop *stronger processing skills*, which in turn enable them to learn more language more quickly.

The chapter is organized in three sections. First, we consider the long history of research on sources of variability in the development of children's verbal abilities. This overview shows that insightful studies conducted decades ago were the first to reveal links between early experience and later language outcomes, important discoveries that are now often ignored. We discuss why this issue has been sidelined in current discussions of language learning and argue that it is central to understanding the development of linguistic proficiency. Second, we describe recent studies exploring new ways to characterize developmental gains in verbal ability,

by assessing infants' fluency in interpreting spoken language in real time. Third, we present research investigating how it is that early experience with language benefits language development. Our results show that having more opportunities to engage with language increases processing efficiency, while also increasing vocabulary. We conclude by suggesting that gains in processing efficiency affect growth in other cognitive capacities—a developmental cascade starting in infancy that contributes to building skills essential for language learning and later literacy.

A Historical Overview of Research on Sources of Variability in Children's Verbal Abilities

The long history of research exploring sources of variability in children's verbal abilities, going back to the beginning of the last century. Here we trace back to the origins of the insight that early language experience plays an important role in the development of verbal skills, then address a puzzling question: If studies over 60 years have shown that differences in the amount and quality of language experienced by a child can have enduring consequences for the development of language proficiency, why is this not a more central topic in current research on language acquisition? For a variety of reasons, ranging from theoretical biases to ideological convictions and a concern for political correctness, this extensive and revealing literature has largely been ignored in language development research since the 1980s. Our goal in reviewing this earlier literature is to highlight its historical significance and also its current relevance, providing a foundation for more recent discoveries about experiential sources of variability in young children's language proficiency.

IQ Testing and the View That Verbal Abilities Are Genetically Determined

Scientific research on individual differences in cognitive capacities began with the development of psychometric instruments for assessing intelligence. When Binet introduced the first IQ test in France in 1905, his goal was to use this instrument to identify children who needed extra help in school, and his view was that mental abilities are influenced by environmental as well as genetic factors (Siegler, 1992). However, when Terman (1916) transformed this test for use in the United States, he had strong convictions about the inherited intellectual superiority of some ethnic groups. The Stanford–Binet IQ Test was soon put to use in hundreds of studies purporting to provide objective measures of innate differences in mental ability related to race and ethnicity (e.g., Brigham, 1923; Goddard, 1917), consistent with theories of genetic determinism and views on eugenics that were popular at the time (Degler, 1991).

The racial and ethnic groups represented in these early studies of IQ obviously differed in many potentially influential ways that were not taken into account. White Americans were compared to black Americans and to recent immigrants from Italy, Germany, Poland, Mexico, and elsewhere, although white Americans were much less likely to live in poverty than these other ethnic groups, and much more likely to have access to education. Terman (1916) had rejected a priori the notion that social class differences could explain differences in intelligence, arguing that "the children of successful and cultured parents test higher

than children from wretched and ignorant homes for the simple reason that their heredity is better" (Gould, 1981, p. 117). Following similar logic, the correlation observed between years of schooling and IQ was interpreted as clear evidence that innate intelligence enables individuals of higher IQ to be academically more successful and thus to continue longer in school. Faith in the premise of genetic determinism was so strong at this time that there was little interest in the possibility that experiential factors might also influence mental development.

Searching for Mediating Variables in the Link between Ethnicity and IQ

In the 1930s, research on IQ differences began to move in a new direction, stimulated by serendipitous findings from studies that included other information about individuals besides ethnicity. When Klineberg (1935) investigated whether selective migration could account for cognitive differences between southern (rural) blacks and northern (urban) blacks, he found that IQ scores were correlated with length of residence in New York City. Klineberg's tentative conclusion was that the more stimulating urban environment might have increased the mental abilities of southern-born children who moved up north at an earlier age. In another study from this period, Sherman and Key (1932) compared Appalachian children living in isolated "hollows" in the Blue Ridge Mountains with others who had migrated to a nearby small town with a more regular school. They found that the IQ scores of all the children *declined* between the ages of 6 and 16 years, and that the decrease was substantially greater in the isolated mountain children from the hollows who had less access to education. Moreover, as the mountain children grew older, they spent even fewer hours in school overall, and the IQ difference between groups widened with age. Here too, the authors offered a tentative conclusion, suggesting that "the only plausible explanation of the increasing difference [in IQ] . . . is that children develop only as the environment demands development" (Sherman & Key, 1932, p. 288).

The idea that mental stimulation in early childhood could influence the development of intelligence gradually began to take hold. Freeman (1934) examined the effects of continuity in education on children in London, some of whom attended school only intermittently because they had itinerant parents. He also found a decrease in IQ with increasing age, inconsistent with the view that intelligence is predetermined and stable. Freeman concluded that "without the opportunity for mental activity of the kind provided by the school—though not restricted to it—intellectual development will be seriously limited or aborted" (p. 115). Interest in disentangling ethnicity and socioeconomic status (SES) also began to increase. Brown and Cotton (1941) compared Italian and Polish school children in "deteriorated" and "non-deteriorated" areas of Chicago, using a nonverbal IQ task to reduce the influence of differences in English language proficiency. They also found that IQ declined with age, concluding that this drop "may be due to lack of stimulative influence in the community" (p. 23). The contribution of SES to cognitive outcomes was unclear in this research given that age, gender, and first- versus second-generation immigrant status also played a role, but the results clearly indicated that many factors beyond ethnicity were associated with differences in IQ.

Parenting Practices as Mediating Variables in the Relation between SES and IQ

By the 1940s, more and more evidence indicated that SES differences were influential beyond genetic differences, predicting children's mental abilities. But what was it about growing up in a middle-class family that fostered more positive outcomes? There is obviously no simple answer given that myriad factors—such as nutrition, sanitation, access to medical care, family stability, noise level, exposure to toxins and dangerous conditions, and many other circumstances of everyday life—differ dramatically for children in lower- and higher-SES families, and that these environmental factors are known to be associated with differences in cognitive and social outcomes (e.g., Evans, 2004). The finding in several studies that some children's IQ tended to decline with age, especially those living in more disadvantaged conditions, suggested that lack of cognitive

stimulation over time might have negative consequences.

This possibility was also examined in studies of young children living in orphanages or hospitals, whose language development was substantially delayed when compared to home-reared children (e.g., Brodbeck & Irwin, 1946; Goldfarb, 1945). Research with institutionalized infants provided compelling evidence that verbal ability was not simply an inherited trait that remains stable over time, and strongly suggested that lack of opportunity for verbal interaction with an attentive caregiver could have detrimental effects on language development. By this time there were numerous reports of correlations between SES differences and measures of verbal IQ (e.g., Brown, 1944; McCarthy, 1930). These findings converged to reframe the question in a way that went beyond genetic determinism to explain how differences in language abilities arise: To the extent that the absence of consistent attentive mothering available to institutionalized infants resembles the care a child receives in an impoverished family, where crowded conditions and other hardships can make it difficult for the caregiver to meet the needs of the child, could it be that a lack of cognitive stimulation contributes to language delay in lower-SES children, as well as in those who are institutionalized?

Milner (1951) was among the first to examine the benefits of early language experience from this perspective, comparing reading readiness in first graders from higher- and lower-SES black families. She noted that higher-scoring children came from more advantaged families, consistent with many previous findings. But by gathering qualitative as well as quantitative data on verbal interactions between parents and child in the home, Milner was also able to show that children in higher-SES families typically experienced a more warm and positive family atmosphere that offered more opportunities to interact verbally with adults. Studies in orphanages also continued in the 1950s, with several focusing specifically on language development. Observing the extreme "backwardness in language" in institutionalized children, Kellmer Pringle and Bossio (1958) concluded that early social and cognitive deprivation are more detrimental to a child's linguistic development than to nonverbal IQ. These authors speculated that because institutionalized children fall so far behind in language, they may "give the impression of lacking ability, when in many cases they have lacked mainly appropriate stimulation and opportunity" (p. 163).

Early Research Linking Parental Speech to Children's Language Development

By the late 1950s, many studies had reported relations between children's early experience with a responsive caregiver and their later language abilities, motivating a new wave of research designed to identify specific factors in parents' verbal behavior that could enhance or inhibit language development (Raph, 1965). Basil Bernstein (1961), a British sociologist and educator, attempted to explain how language use is shaped by experience in a particular social class and is powerfully influential in maintaining SES differences. Although debate in the United States had focused on the relative contribution of genetic and environmental factors to cognitive differences related to SES, this dichotomy was of little interest to Bernstein. Instead, he asked how young children internalize various influences of the social conditions experienced early in life An important claim in Bernstein's theory was that children's experience of learning how language is used in a particular social class affects the skills in speaking and reasoning they will have as adults, with significant consequences for future academic and professional success.

The developmental process proposed by Bernstein (1961, 1971) involved children's differential exposure to two distinct *language codes*, or typical modes of language use. *Restricted code*, consisting of structurally simple, shorter utterances, is the kind of speech commonly used among friends and family members, with topics of discussion are highly predictable. In contrast, *elaborated code* consists of structurally more complex utterances in which detail and explanation are required because the speaker cannot assume that extensive background knowledge is shared by others in the conversation. Elaborated code is more explicit, abstract, and nuanced in meaning; thus, it "facilitates the verbal elaboration of subjective intent" (Bernstein, 1961, p. 292). According to Bern-

stein, elaborated code is the dominant mode of speech in middle-class families, although in this group both codes are used frequently in the appropriate circumstances; however, in working-class families, restricted code is used almost exclusively, while elaborated code is rarely used. An important corollary in Bernstein's theory is that the middle-class child develops skill in using both codes effectively, flexibly switching between them, while the working-class child learns only to use restricted code, a mode of language that "discourages the speaker from verbally elaborating subjective intent, and progressively orients him to descriptive rather than analytic concepts" (p. 292).

To provide evidence for Bernstein's predictions, Hess and Shipman (1965) examined how mothers' teaching styles would differ as a function of SES, and how their use of restricted and elaborated codes would affect children's responses and behavior. Black mothers in four SES categories were observed interacting with their 4-year-old children in structured tasks, such as sorting toys by color and function. Mothers in different SES groups varied in both the quantity and quality of their language. Higher-SES mothers spoke more overall and used longer utterances, with more complex syntax and abstract words, consistent with Bernstein's (1961) distinction between elaborated and restricted code. From a pragmatic perspective, higher-SES mothers also offered more explanation and elaboration, while lower-SES mothers used more imperatives to control the child's behavior, and such differences in "cognitive style" were correlated with differences in children's performance. Hess and Shipman concluded that there are "large differences among the status groups in the ability of the mothers to teach and the children to learn" (p. 881). Their speculations about the potential consequences of these SES differences were consistent with Bernstein's theory that variability in academic success is grounded in early language experience: Those children with more exposure to maternal teaching using elaborated speech would develop a cognitive style that made them adept at problem solving and abstract reflection, while those whose mothers used a less effective teaching style with mainly restricted speech would have limitations in these abilities.

The "Culturally Deprived" Child: Verbal Deficits or Verbal Differences?

In the tumultuous aftermath of the 1954 Supreme Court decision on *Brown v. Board of Education*, the new view that SES differences in children's academic accomplishments resulted from cultural differences in early experience rather than from inherent genetic differences was first viewed as cause for celebration. The idea of "cultural deprivation" as an explanatory construct caught on with educators in the late 1950s and was elaborated in Reissman's popular book, *The Culturally Deprived Child* (1962). To liberals of the Kennedy–Johnson era, this seemed a plausible rationale for the poor school performance of low-SES minority children. It also offered hope that solutions were possible, if appropriate interventions could be provided in the early years—a national goal in the War on Poverty that led to the establishment of Operation Head Start in 1965, along with other preschool intervention programs.

But characterizing the early home environment of minority children as "deficient" in linguistic and cognitive stimulation was a double-edged sword. On the one hand, this notion rallied political support for early intervention efforts in education and research in the 1960s. On the other hand, designating low-SES children as "culturally deprived" clearly had negative connotations. Although there was now agreement that the academic difficulties of minority children were environmentally induced, the effects of cultural deprivation were often compared to mental retardation (Barksdale, 1970), a negative stereotype that resonated with earlier theories of the genetic basis of low IQ in some racial groups. And even the most sympathetic portrayals of the difficulties faced by low-SES families tended to characterize minority children in ways that seemed demeaning. For example, Hess and Shipman (1965) concluded that "the meaning of deprivation is the deprivation of meaning" (p. 885), implying that children who grow up in "deprived" circumstances have no experience of meaning in their home life at all.

By the early 1970s, opposition to the "deficit model" among academics was coming from several directions (Cole & Bruner, 1971). Some blamed the ineffectiveness of teachers and schools for the poor performance of disadvantaged children (Clark, 1965; Friedman, 1978). The deficit model was also passionately denounced within the field of linguistics. Bernstein's (1961) views on the importance of early language experience, which a decade earlier had seemed so relevant to understanding language and cognitive development, were now associated with a deficit model and widely rejected. Although Bernstein had focused on British social class differences, his insights were misconstrued when applied to educational problems in the racially divided society of the United States. For example, his theory was endorsed by educational psychologists (e.g., Jensen, 1968) who were strong proponents of racially based differences in IQ. Although Bernstein had never advocated hereditary differences in intelligence, his arguments for class differences in language use were assimilated to arguments for racial deficiencies (Bolander & Watts, 2009). Another attack on Bernstein's theory came in a scathing critique by the sociolinguist Labov (1970), who argued that nonstandard dialects of English, such as the Black English Vernacular (BEV), are structurally as complex as Standard English and should not be characterized as a "deficient" means of communication. Labov criticized the view that "lower-class Negro children have no language at all," claiming that this position was "first drawn from Basil Bernstein's writings" (p. 4). However, Bernstein had never written about particular minority groups in the United States, and his views on communicative codes used by different SES groups certainly did not equate the use of restricted code with having "no language at all."

Despite these misunderstandings, Labov's critique was hailed by Cole and Bruner (1971, p. 868) as "the most coherent denial of the deficit position" in part because it shifted the debate from a focus on disadvantage to a more positive appreciation of cultural differences:

> From this point of view, cultural *deprivation* represents a special case of cultural *difference* that arises when an individual is faced with demands to perform in a manner inconsistent with his past (cultural) experience. In the present social context of the U.S., the greater power of the middle class has rendered differ-

ences into deficits because middle-class behavior is the yardstick of success. (Cole & Bruner, 1971, p. 874, original emphasis)

This conclusion reflected new perspectives from anthropology and cross-cultural psychology emerging in developmental research at this time (Cole, Gay, Glick, & Sharp, 1971). One influential study that exemplified this view was Heath's (1983) ethnographic research on the language development of children in two rural communities in Appalachia. Heath argued persuasively that educators need to understand and value the rich oral traditions of language use in black communities, celebrating rather than condemning differences in the home environments in which children in different subcultures learn language.

From Differences to Universals: Chomsky's Influence on Research on Early Language Experience

Debate about the role of early experience in language learning was intensified by the widely recognized need for educational reform in the 1960s. However, by the 1970s, some social scientists began to argue that discussion of SES differences in children's language outcomes had become so racially charged and politically divisive that it was morally irresponsible to continue research on this topic (Sroufe, 1970; Tulkin, 1972). Such political concerns were one factor leading to the gradual suppression of open debate about whether and how children's language exposure in advantaged and disadvantaged families might contribute to later gaps in academic achievement. But another powerful factor that killed interest in this question, for quite different reasons, was the intellectual revolution gaining force in the field of linguistics. Chomsky's (1957) theory of universal grammar proposed that an innately specified maturational bioprogram specific to language made language learning possible. His famous assertion that adult speech available to children was a degraded form unsuitable as a model for language learning (Chomsky, 1965) strongly implied that variation in caregivers' speech to infants was unimportant in language development.

Although research on early language experience continued, the questions motivating

this research began to change in important ways, reflecting Chomsky's influence. Challenging his claims about the ungrammatical and fragmented nature of speech to children, detailed corpus analyses showed that mothers' speech to children learning English was simplified in ways that might be beneficial to the inexperienced listener, especially when contrasted with speech among adults (Phillips, 1973; Snow, 1972). But rather than investigating differences in the language experience of children in socially relevant groups, the main question of interest had shifted to how the child-directed speech (CDS) register differs from adult-directed speech (ADS), and whether CDS could provide an adequate model for learning syntax (Newport, Gleitman, & Gleitman, 1977; Snow & Ferguson, 1977). Since the development of grammatical knowledge was the central mystery to be explained in Chomsky's theory, this emphasis on syntax dominated the emerging field of child language research. Roger Brown's seminal book *A First Language* (1973) represented a new paradigm informed by linguistic theory, in which detailed analyses of longitudinal language samples of just three children documented universal patterns in syntactic development. Although Brown was careful to include both white and black children from different SES levels in this small sample, and although these children achieved various developmental milestones at substantially different rates, the focus was squarely on their common patterns of language growth. Differences among them were no longer of interest.

Reframing the "Deficits-versus-Differences" Debate

As the field of language acquisition expanded and flourished over the next 25 years, the emphasis on universal patterns in language growth remained dominant, while interest in variability in language outcomes receded. Although hundreds of studies over this period explored word learning by infants and young children (Bloom, 2000), almost all of this research focused on children from middle-class families, with very few studies including children from more diverse backgrounds, and even fewer examining potential sources of variability in word-learning success. This imbalance reflects an unstated assumption that variability in universal developmental patterns is of little theoretical significance, and that findings based on middle-class infants can be generalized to all children (Arnett, 2008; Fernald, 2010). Yet the extensive research on SES differences in language experience and academic outcomes from 1940 to 1970 suggests that these more recent studies might have led to different results if they had included children from a wider range of backgrounds. However, this older literature is rarely cited, and the question of experiential causes of early differences in verbal proficiency has now moved to the sidelines in research on language learning.

But there are also prominent exceptions. By carefully circumventing many of the problems that aroused such hostility toward earlier studies of SES differences in children's language, social scientists working in two different traditions have continued to deepen our understanding of the influence of early experience on the development of language skills. One of these traditions is centered in education research, with a focus on understanding the conditions that support the development of skills essential for literacy (Dickinson & McCabe, 2001; Snow, Burns, & Griffin, 1998). This research area is well represented by other contributors to this volume, so we mention it only briefly here. Because oral language proficiency is widely recognized as critical to success in learning to read, many early literacy researchers have been interested in experiential factors that influence lexical and syntactic growth before children enter kindergarten (e.g., Dickinson & Tabors, 2001). Research in this tradition has explored the benefits of book reading at home (Scarborough & Dobrich, 1994), as well as exposure to rich and varied vocabulary in daily conversations (Weizman & Snow, 2001), and variability among children from different SES backgrounds is a central concern. However, given the goal of helping teachers prepare young children more effectively for literacy, these studies have focused on children's language experience in the preschool years rather than in infancy.

The second tradition is centered in psycholinguistic research, where studies of variability in young children's early language experience have been few since the 1980s. Although this research is high in both theoretical and social significance, it represents just a tiny fraction of the thousands of studies on early language development published in the past three decades. The few examples described here are studies based on fine-grained analyses of mothers' interactions with infants in the home environment, using longitudinal designs to determine which features of maternal speech predict outcome measures such as vocabulary development. In one seminal longitudinal study, Huttenlocher, Haight, Bryk, Seltzer, and Lyons (1991) recorded maternal speech to infants from 14 to 26 months of age. Mothers differed substantially in how much they talked to their infants, and variation in the amount of CDS predicted children's trajectories of vocabulary growth. Although a link between the sheer amount of speech to toddlers and their later academic outcomes had been reported previously by Wells (1981), Huttenlocher and colleagues were the first to integrate detailed linguistic measures with growth curve analyses to document the relation between early language exposure and vocabulary growth within a middle-class sample.

In 1995, Hart and Risley published their landmark study of "meaningful differences" in children's exposure to language and vocabulary growth in three SES groups. Following 42 families with infants over age 3 years, they recorded interactions in the home every month. By 36 months, the higher-SES children knew twice as many words as the lower-SES children, but the most striking finding was the variation in amounts of CDS among families at different SES levels, which correlated with children's vocabulary differences. Hart and Risley estimated that children in professional families heard some 30 million more words over the first 3 years than did children living in poverty, a stunning difference that was also predictive of children's academic achievement years later in elementary school (Walker, Greenwood, Hart, & Carta, 1994). Higher-SES mothers were also more likely to use affirmatives and conversation-eliciting utterances, while lower-SES mothers used more directives and prohibitions, consistent with observations made many years earlier (Hess & Shipman, 1965; Milner, 1951). Research by Hoff has also documented SES differences both in the quantity of CDS across a range of communicative contexts and in features of maternal speech that support vocabulary learning (Hoff, 2006; Hoff-Ginsberg, 1991, 1998). Another of Hoff's (2003) noteworthy findings is that the well-established relation between SES and children's vocabulary knowledge is actually *mediated* by differences among mothers in the lexical diversity and grammatical complexity of their speech to children.

Looking Back over a Century of Research on Variability in Children's Verbal Abilities

To summarize, in this historical overview we have focused on four main points: First, there is a long history of research linking variation in SES to substantial differences in verbal IQ and academic success, relations originally attributed to genetic factors. However, by the 1950s it was gradually becoming clear that cognitive and social stimulation in childhood are critical for intellectual development, and that early language experience is especially influential. Second, although the idea that differences in early language experience might contribute to the achievement gap was initially viewed in a positive light, SES differences were increasingly conflated with racial differences in the turbulent times of the 1960s, and the "language deficit" hypothesis was renounced as racist and culturally insensitive. Third, by the end of 1970s two quite different revolutionary forces had converged to silence the debate about experiential sources of variability in children's language development. One revolutionary force was the political aftershock of the civil rights movement, which aroused intense opposition to any implicitly negative evaluation of cultural differences among children's home environments. The other was the intellectual revolution in linguistics, with the rise of a powerful new theory of language development in which early experience played only a minor role. As a consequence of these disparate converging forces, research on the contribution of early language exposure to variability in children's verbal proficiency and academic success was no longer seen as central to understanding language development. Yet despite declining interest in this question since the 1980s, several more recent studies have greatly expanded our understanding of the importance of early language experience to language learning and readiness for literacy.

Our next goal is to bring new evidence to bear on this critical issue, based on recent discoveries about how children learn to make sense of spoken language from moment to moment, an essential skill in the development of language proficiency. But before presenting this evidence, we need to lay the groundwork. Thus, the next section describes a new approach to assessing real-time speech processing by infants and young children, one that provides us with powerful tools to investigate links between early language experience and language growth.

Using Real-Time Measures to Assess the Development of Fluency in Understanding

Over the first year of life infants become attuned to sound patterns in the ambient language (Kuhl, 2004; Werker, 1989), and attend to speech patterns relevant to language structure (Jusczyk, 1997; Saffran, 2003). Studies show how infants begin to become skilled listeners, able to make distributional analyses of phonetic features of speech and to form some kind of acoustic–phonetic representation for frequently heard sound patterns. Between the ages of 10 and 14 months, children typically start to show signs of associating sound patterns with meanings, to produce a few words, and to appear to understand many more. And by the end of the second year, they reveal progress in understanding through increasingly differentiated verbal and behavioral responses to speech. Yet because understanding is a mental event that can only be inferred indirectly from a child's behavior in a particular context, the early development of receptive language competence has been less accessible to observation than developmental gains in speech production.

Many studies of comprehension in young children have relied on *offline* measures, responses made *after* the offset of the speech stimulus that do not capture the real-time dynamics of interpreting spoken language. One widely used instrument for assessing infants' early understanding is the MacArthur–Bates Communicative Development Inventory (CDI), a vocabulary checklist on which parents judge that a child does or does not "understand" a word such as *dog* or *cup*, based on interactions with the child in many different contexts (Fenson et al., 1994). While offline measures do provide evidence that a child responds systematically in a way that indicates understanding, they do not tap into the dynamic nature of language understanding; thus, they reveal little about the child's developing efficiency in interpreting familiar words in fluent speech. In contrast, studies of adult speech processing rely on *online* measures that monitor the time course of the listener's response to spoken words in relation to key points in the speech signal. Because comprehension happens quickly and automatically, it is revealing to study the listener's interpretation *during* processing of the speech signal rather than waiting until processing is complete.

Studying the Development of Speech Processing Efficiency in Infants and Children

Here we describe recent research using the "looking-while-listening" (LWL) paradigm (Fernald, Zangl, Portillo, & Marchman, 2008), an experimental procedure for monitoring the time course of comprehension by very young language learners. In the LWL procedure, infants look at pairs of pictures while listening to speech naming one of the pictures, and their gaze patterns are videorecorded as the sentence unfolds in time. In terms of stimulus presentation, this is similar to the intermodal, preferential-looking procedure originally developed by Golinkoff, Hirsh-Pasek, Cauley, and Gordon (1987). The main difference lies how the data are analyzed, since our focus has been on maximizing the precision and stability of real-time measures of eye movements in relation to relevant points in the speech signal. Using this paradigm, we have shown that speed and efficiency in infants' recognition of familiar words increase substantially over the second year for English- and Spanish-learning children (Fernald, Pinto, Swingley, Weinberg, & McRoberts, 1998; Hurtado, Marchman, & Fernald, 2007), that young children make use of linguistic information at multiple levels in real-time processing (Lew-Williams & Fernald, 2007; Swingley, Pinto, & Fernald, 1999), and that individual differences in early processing efficiency are related to

lexical and grammatical development, both concurrently and at later ages (Fernald, Perfors, & Marchman, 2006; Marchman & Fernald, 2008). These findings validate the LWL paradigm as a valuable method for exploring how very young children develop fluency in understanding the speech they hear in relation to information in the visual world as they learn to find meaning in spoken language.

In research on real-time speech processing by adults, reaction time (RT) is a common measure used to explore the influence of linguistic and nonlinguistic factors on speed of lexical access and sentence interpretation. Because studies with adults often require participants to make voluntary behavioral responses, the task demands are high. For this reason, RT measures have not been widely used with infants, who have a limited repertoire of voluntary behaviors that can serve as reliable response measures. However, moving the eyes to an interesting stimulus is a behavior with which infants have extensive experience, and developmental researchers have found many ways to use infant gaze as a revealing experimental measure. In the LWL procedure, RT is assessed by calculating the latency of the infant's first shift away from the distracter toward the target picture as the target word is spoken, measured from a critical point in the stimulus sentence. Figure 1.1 shows the results of the first study using RT measures of spoken word recognition by infants at 15, 18, and 24 months of age (Fernald et al., 1998). These results revealed that over the second year of life, when most infants show a "vocabulary spurt" in speech production, they also make dramatic gains in receptive language skill by increasing the speed with which they can identify familiar words and match them with the appropriate referent. These cross-sectional findings have been replicated in longitudinal studies with infants learning English (Fernald et al., 2006) and infants from Latino families in the United States learning Spanish as their first language (Hurtado et al., 2007).

What Is Fluency in Understanding?

To follow a conversation, adults process 10–15 phonemes per second as they continuously integrate acoustic information with linguistic and conceptual knowledge. If the

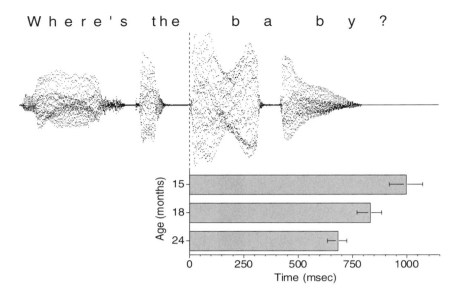

FIGURE 1.1. Reaction time analysis: Mean latencies to initiate a shift in gaze from the distracter to the target picture, measured from the beginning of the spoken target word, in a cross-sectional study of infants at 15, 18, and 24 months. This analysis included only trials on which the infant was initially looking at the incorrect picture then shifted to the correct picture within 1,800 milliseconds of the target-word onset. Fernald, A., Pinto, J., Swingley, D., Weinberg, A., & McRoberts, G. Rapid gains in speed of verbal processing by infants in the 2nd year. *Psychological Science, 9*(3), 72–75, May 1998, Association for Psychological Science. Adapted with permission from Wiley-Blackwell.

listener could only process one phoneme at a time, recognizing words in fluent speech would be impossible. Similarly, a listener who interprets words one by one would have difficulty following the meaning of fluently spoken sentences, since a word easily understood in isolation may be unintelligible when embedded in fluent speech. This discouraging experience is familiar to anyone who has studied a second language by learning many words but has little experience hearing them strung together meaningfully in speech. Fluent understanding of a speaker's meaning requires the ability to listen *predictively*, anticipating what is coming next in the speech stream by integrating different sources of linguistic knowledge with nonlinguistic information from the context in which the words are spoken. Many studies show that adult listeners exploit linguistic and nonlinguistic knowledge on multiple levels in anticipating upcoming words, and that these predictions are made continuously and instantaneously as the speech signal unfolds.

Two examples illustrate how very young children, like adults, are already able to make use of potentially informative sources of contextual information, processing speech incrementally from moment to moment. The first example illustrates incremental processing at the *lexical* level, when the listener identifies a word based on partial phonetic information, without waiting to hear the whole word. When Allopenna, Magnusen, & Tanenhaus (1998) presented adults with objects that included candy and a candle, and asked them to "Pick up the can-," participants waited to hear the next speech sound before orienting to the appropriate object, postponing their response until the final syllable of the target word made it clear which object was the intended referent. The child who hears "Where's the dog?" in the presence of a dog and a doll is also faced with a temporary ambiguity, since the words *dog* and *doll* overlap phonetically and are thus indistinguishable for the first 300 msec or so. In this situation, 24-month-olds in the LWL procedure also delayed their response by about 300 msec, until disambiguating information became available (Swingley et al., 1999). Even when they heard *only* the initial phonemes in a familiar word (e.g., the isolated first syllable of *baby* or *kitty*), 18-month-olds were able to use this limited information to identify the appropriate referent (Fernald, Swingley, & Pinto, 2001). Thus, infants in the second year are already able to use their rudimentary lexical knowledge to identify familiar words more rapidly.

The second example illustrates incremental processing at a *morphosyntactic* level. In languages such as Spanish, all nouns have grammatical gender, with obligatory gender-marking on preceding articles (e.g., $la_{[f]}$, $el_{[m]}$, *the*). This morphosyntactic information can also be useful in incremental processing. Adult native speakers of languages with grammatical gender exploit this cue in online sentence interpretation (Dahan, Swingley, Tanenhaus, & Magnuson, 2000). Although in English the article *the* reveals little about the following noun, hearing *la* or *el* in Spanish can inform the listener about the upcoming noun and in some contexts can enable identification of the referent before the noun is spoken. To explore the early development of this ability, Lew-Williams and Fernald (2007) tested children learning Spanish in the LWL procedure. Children saw pairs of pictures with names of either the same (e.g., *la pelota, ball$_{[f]}$, la galleta, cookie$_{[f]}$*) or different grammatical gender (e.g., *la pelota, el zapato, shoe$_{[m]}$*), as they heard sentences referring to one of the pictures (e.g., *Encuentra la pelota*, "Find the ball"). On same-gender trials, the article could not be used to identify the referent before the noun was spoken; however, on different-gender trials, the gender-marked article was potentially useful in predicting the subsequent noun. If young Spanish-learning children can take advantage of gender agreement in interpreting speech, they should shift to the target picture more quickly on different-gender than on same-gender trials. Indeed, children were reliably faster to identify the referent on different-gender trials, as were native Spanish-speaking adults tested in the same procedure (see Figure 1.2). Although they were slower than adults in interpreting spoken language, young children learning Spanish as their first language already demonstrated a processing advantage that is typical of adult native speakers but not of second language learners (Guillelmon & Grosjean, 2001). With only a few hundred words in their vocabulary, 2- to 3-year-old Spanish learners were able to identify familiar nouns almost 100 msec faster when a gender-marked article gave them an edge. This ability to exploit morphosyntactic information in incremental processing reveals another dimension of fluency in understanding.

Stability and Predictive Validity of Online Processing Measures

In the experiments on children's speech processing described so far, measures from the LWL procedure were used to make *between-group* comparisons, tracking age-related differences in RT and accuracy in cross-sectional designs (Fernald et al., 1998; Hurtado et al., 2007), or examining condition differences in children of the same age (Swingley et al., 1999) or between age groups (Lew-Williams & Fernald, 2007). Using such between-group designs, we have shown that children become much more efficient in recognizing familiar words over the second and third year of life, and that their ability to interpret more complex sentence structure also improves dramatically over this period (Fernald, Thorpe, & Marchman, 2010). These results using real-time measures provide new insights into the early development of fluency in understanding, complementing research based on more traditional measures of lexical and grammatical growth over the first 3 years.

But characterizing age differences is just one perspective in developmental research; another central goal is to characterize *variation* among children. For example, young children vary widely in the size of their expressive vocabulary, and one 18-month-old may produce more than 100 words, while another has not yet started to speak at all, with substantial variability in both grammatical and lexical growth over the first few years (Bates, Dale, & Thal, 1995). Research using online processing measures of language understanding can also address important questions about differences among children at any given age. Is speed of lexical processing a *stable* measure across age for individual children? That is, do those 18-month-olds who respond more quickly on average in identifying familiar words also respond relatively more quickly at later ages?

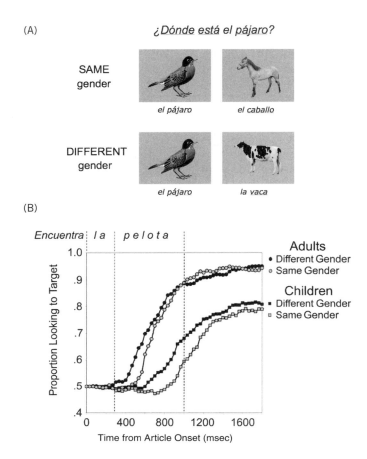

FIGURE 1.2. (A) Examples of stimuli on same-gender and different-gender trials in Spanish. (B) Curves depict changes in the proportion shifts from distracter to target picture by Spanish-speaking 3-year-olds and adults as the article and noun unfold, measured from article onset (in milliseconds). Filled squares show responses on different-gender trials, when the article was potentially informative; open squares show responses on same-gender trials, when the article was not informative. Vertical dashed lines indicate offsets of article and target word. Lew-Williams, C., & Fernald, A. (2007). Young children learning Spanish make rapid use of grammatical gender in spoken word recognition. *Psychological Science, 18*(3), 193–198, March 2007, Association for Psychological Science. Adapted with permission from Wiley-Blackwell.

And if so, how do individual differences in early speech processing efficiency relate to later language growth, as assessed by standardized measures of lexical and grammatical knowledge? Does processing efficiency in infancy actually predict language and cognitive outcomes at later ages?

We first addressed these questions in a longitudinal study of 59 English-learning infants who were tested four times in the LWL procedure between 15 and 25 months (Fernald et al., 2006). Children's efficiency in identifying familiar words increased significantly over this period, consistent with

earlier cross-sectional results. Moreover, measures of early processing skill were moderately stable from one age to the next. Parental reports of vocabulary and grammar on the MacArthur–Bates CDI were also gathered across the second year, along with a standardized test of lexical knowledge at 25 months, enabling us to explore the relation of online measures of speech processing skill to more traditional measures of linguistic development. Speed and accuracy in speech processing at 25 months were robustly related to lexical and grammatical development across a range of measures from

12 to 25 months. Growth curve analyses showed strong relations between differences in speech processing efficiency and trajectories of vocabulary growth. As shown in Figure 1.3, those children who were relatively faster in mean RT at 25 months had also shown more accelerated vocabulary growth across the second year.

Given the stability and short-term predictive validity of these online measures in the infancy period, the obvious next question was to what extent individual differences in early processing efficiency predict *long-term* language and cognitive outcomes. In a follow-up study, 30 children from the original Fernald and colleagues (2006) longitudinal sample were tested at 8 years of age on two standardized assessments of cognitive and language skills (Marchman & Fernald, 2008). Multiple regression analyses were used to evaluate the long-term predictive validity of two measures in infancy—expressive vocabulary and mean RT at 25 months—in relation to school-age outcomes. Relations between processing speed in infancy and performance on a working memory task were also examined in light of links between efficiency of spoken language comprehension and working memory in older children and adults (e.g., Gathercole & Baddeley, 1993). Vocabulary size at 25 months was correlated with later cognitive and language skills, but knowing mean RT in addition to CDI *doubled* the predictive power, accounting for 58% of the variance in working memory at 8 years. This prospective longitudinal study was the first to reveal the long-term predictive validity of early measures of real-time processing efficiency, showing that individual differences in fluency of understanding at 2 years predict children's cognitive and language outcomes in later childhood.

How Early Language Experience Influences Processing Efficiency and Vocabulary Learning

These findings on real-time processing efficiency suggest that children who are faster to identify familiar words in fluent speech are also better word learners, with long-term benefits for the development of cognitive skills in later childhood. How then do these results relate to the literature reviewed earlier on variability in CDS (Hart & Risley, 1995; Hoff, 2003; Huttenlocher et al., 1991), which showed that infants who hear more and richer speech from caregivers are also more advanced in vocabulary development? To explore this question, we used a combination of observational and experimental methods to assess Latina mothers' interactions with their Spanish-learning infants, linking these

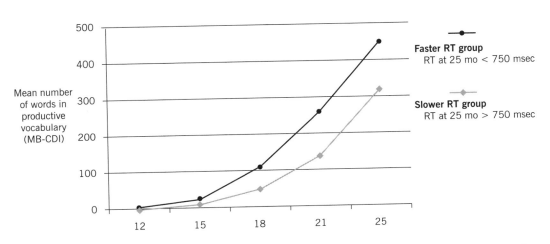

FIGURE 1.3. Mean trajectories of growth in vocabulary production across the second year as a function of reaction time in spoken word recognition at 25 months of age. Groupings are based on a median split of mean RT at 25 months to shift from the distracter to the named target picture. Fernald, A., Perfors, A., & Marchman, V. (2006). Picking up speed in understanding: Speech processing efficiency and vocabulary growth across the 2nd year. *Developmental Psychology, 42*(1), 98–116, January 2006, American Psychological Association. Adapted with permission.

children's early language experience to both vocabulary growth and the development of efficiency in real-time processing (Hurtado, Marchman, & Fernald, 2008) (see Figure 1.4). The first question was whether mothers' CDS at 18 months predicted their children's vocabulary at 18 and 24 months, an association that had been documented previously in English-learning infants (Huttenlocher et al., 1991) but not before in Spanish-learning infants. Next, we asked whether children's vocabulary size would also relate to their efficiency in identifying familiar nouns in fluent speech, to determine whether variation in speech processing efficiency, like variation in vocabulary knowledge, is also linked to early language experience. In a series of multiple regression models, we then assessed the proposal that children's processing speed and vocabulary knowledge work together to allow more efficient uptake of the information that is available in caregiver talk.

This research was conducted in a community-based laboratory in a low-income Latino neighborhood staffed by bicultural/bilingual Spanish-speaking researchers. Twenty-seven mother–child dyads participated when the children were ages 18 and 24 months. Most parents were recent immigrants from Mexico and native Spanish speakers with low English proficiency. At the 18-month visit, mothers were recorded as they played with their children for 20 minutes. From transcriptions of maternal and child utterances, several measures of mothers' speech were assessed, including total number of utterances, word tokens, and word types, as well as mean length of utterance. Children's efficiency in online comprehension was assessed in the LWL procedure at 18 and at 24 months, and parents reported on their child's productive vocabulary at these ages as well.

This longitudinal study of mothers' speech to Spanish-learning children revealed four main findings: First, there was considerable variability in maternal talk within this low-SES sample, and differences in amount of CDS were associated with differences in children's vocabulary outcomes. Children of mothers who talked relatively more heard on average seven times more words, five times more utterances, three times more different

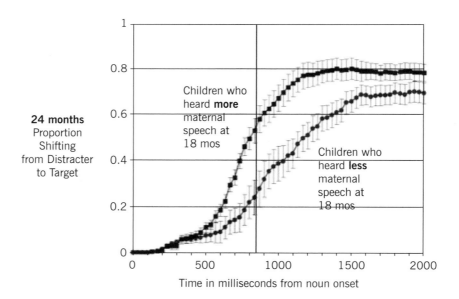

FIGURE 1.4. Mean proportion of trials on which 24-month-olds shifted correctly from distracter to target picture as a function of amount and quality of maternal speech to the child at 18 months. Solid vertical line represents target noun offset; error bars represent *SE*s over participants. Hurtado, N., Marchman, V. A., & Fernald, A. (2008). Does input influence uptake?: Links between maternal talk, processing speed and vocabulary size in Spanish-learning children. *Developmental Science, 11*(6), 31–39, November 2008, Association for Psychological Science. Adapted with permission from Wiley-Blackwell.

words, and sentences that were longer than those heard by children of less engaged mothers. Those children who had heard more maternal speech at 18 months had larger vocabularies at 24 months and made greater gains in vocabulary, links that remained strong after researchers controlled for vocabulary differences at 18 months. Second, children with larger vocabularies at 24 months were also faster to identify familiar words in fluent speech at that age. As in the Fernald and colleagues (2006) longitudinal study with English-learning children, Spanish-learning children who had faster mean RTs at the age of 2 years made greater gains in vocabulary from ages 18 to 24 months compared to children with slower RTs.

Third, we discovered a link between early language experience and the development of speech processing efficiency by the child. The quantity and quality of mothers' speech at 18 months predicted children's efficiency in understanding at 24 months. Controlling for differences in mean RT at 18 months, those children whose mothers spoke more words and used more complex utterances during the play session at 18 months were significantly faster in online comprehension 6 months later than those who had heard less maternal talk. This finding offered the first evidence that variability in infants' language experience in day-to-day interactions is related to differences in their early speed and efficiency in language processing. Thus, maternal talk is associated not only with children's vocabulary learning but also with the development of fluency in understanding spoken language in real time.

These relations between mothers' speech and both vocabulary growth and processing efficiency in the child can be modeled in two ways. Maternal speech may facilitate vocabulary development because children who hear more talk get more practice in skills directly implicated in word learning, such as parsing speech, accessing semantic representations, or monitoring distributional cues to meanings or grammatical categories. According to this scenario, early efficiency in speech processing is strengthened by infants' early experiences with caregiver speech, accounting for the relation between input and vocabulary knowledge reported in earlier studies. Or it could be that vocabulary knowledge mediates the relation between language input and processing speed, in that the experience of

hearing more maternal speech exposes children to more varied exemplars of words in context, yielding a richer database of lexical and morphosyntactic cues to meaning. The findings of this research are consistent with both of these models, suggesting that early language experience affects both processing efficiency and vocabulary knowledge, which are mutually influential in a synergistic fashion. An increase in processing efficiency may enable faster word learning, while an increase in lexical knowledge may further sharpen the processing skills required to interpret increasingly complex and diverse strings of words.

We can conclude that the frequent experience of engaging with rich and varied language from an attentive caretaker provides the infant not only with *models* for language learning, but also with crucial opportunities for *practice* in interpreting language in real time, thus tuning and strengthening the processing skills used during real-time language comprehension. And as in building any skill, the amount of exercise a child experiences in language processing has enduring consequences for the optimal development of brain mechanisms underlying verbal fluency. By using gradient measures of efficiency in moment-to-moment processing that are robustly related to a range of long-term language and cognitive outcomes, we can now begin to get a few steps closer to understanding the mechanisms underlying the association between early language experience and the development of verbal proficiency that were discovered half a century ago.

Acknowledgments

We are especially grateful to Virginia Marchman, Nereyda Hurtado, Ana Luz Portillo, Dan Swingley, Casey Lew-Williams, Renate Zangl, and the staff of the Center for Infant Studies at Stanford University for major contributions to the research presented here. This work was supported by Grant Nos. HD 42235 and DC 008838 from the National Institutes of Health to Anne Fernald.

References

Allopenna, P., Magnuson, J., & Tanenhaus, M. (1998). Tracking the time course of spoken word recognition using eye movements: Evidence for continuous mapping models. *Journal of Memory and Language, 38,* 419–439.

Arnett, J. J. (2008). The neglected 95%: Why American psychology needs to become less American. *American Psychologist, 63*, 602–614.

Barksdale, M. W. (1970). Mentally retarded and culturally deprived children: Some parallels. *Phylon, 31*, 48–53.

Bates, E., Dale, P., & Thal, D. (1995). Individual differences and their implications for theories of language development. In P. Fletcher & B. MacWhinney (Eds.), *Handbook of Child Language*. Oxford, UK: Blackwell.

Bernstein, B. (1961). Social class and linguistic development: A theory of social learning. In A. H. Halsey, J. Floyd, & C. A. Anderson (Eds.), *Education, economy and society*. Glencoe, IL: Free Press.

Bernstein, B. (1971). *Class, codes and control: Vol. 1. Theoretical studies towards a sociology of language*. New York: Schocken Books.

Bloom, P. (2000). *How children learn the meanings of words: Learning, development, and conceptual change*. Cambridge, MA: MIT Press.

Bolander, B., & Watts, R. J. (2009). Re-reading and rehabilitating Basil Bernstein. *Multilingua - Journal of Cross-Cultural and Interlanguage Communication, 28*, 143–173.

Brigham, C. C. (1923). *A Study of American intelligence*. Princeton, NJ: Princeton University Press.

Brodbeck, A. J., & Irwin, O. C. (1946). The speech behavior of infants without families. *Child Development, 17*, 145–156.

Brown, A. W., & Cotton, C. B. (1941). A study of the intelligence of Italian and Polish school children from deteriorated and non-deteriorated areas of Chicago as measured by the Chicago Non-Verbal Examination. *Child Development, 12*, 21–30.

Brown, F. (1944). An experimental and critical study of the intelligence of Negro and White kindergarten children. *Journal of Genetic Psychology, 65*, 161–175.

Brown, R. (1973). *A first language: The early stages*. Cambridge, MA: Harvard University Press.

Chomsky, N. (1957). A review of B. F. Skinner's *Verbal Behavior. Language, 35*, 26–58.

Chomsky, N. (1965). *Aspects of the theory of syntax*. Cambridge, MA: MIT Press.

Clark, K. B. (1965). *Dark ghetto: Dilemmas of social power*. New York: Harper & Row.

Cole, M., & Bruner, J. S. (1971). Cultural differences and inferences about psychological processes. *American Psychologist, 26*, 867–876.

Cole, M., Gay, J., Glick, J., & Sharp, D. W. (1971). *The cultural context of learning and thinking*. New York: Basic Books.

Dahan, D., Swingley, D., Tanenhaus, M. K., & Magnuson, J. S. (2000). Linguistic gender and spoken-word recognition in French. *Journal of Memory and Language, 42*, 465–480.

Degler, C. N. (1991). *In search of human nature*. New York: Oxford University Press.

Dickinson, D. K., & McCabe, A. (2001). Bringing it all together: The multiple origins, skills, and environmental supports of early literacy. *Learning Disabilities Research and Practice, 16*, 186–202.

Dickinson, D. K., & Tabors, P. O. (2001). *Beginning literacy with language: Young children learning at home and school*. Baltimore: Brookes.

Evans, G. W. (2004). The environment of childhood poverty. *American Psychologist, 59*, 77–92.

Fenson, L., Dale, P. S., Reznick, J. S., Bates, E., Thal, D. J., Pethick, S. J., et al. (1994). Variability in early communicative development. *Monographs of the Society for Research in Child Development, 59*(5).

Fernald, A. (2010). Getting beyond the "convenience sample" in research on early cognitive development. *Behavioral and Brain Sciences, 33*, 91–92.

Fernald, A., Perfors, A., & Marchman, V. (2006). Picking up speed in understanding: Speech processing efficiency and vocabulary growth across the second year. *Developmental Psychology, 42*, 98–116.

Fernald, A., Pinto, J. P., Swingley, D., Weinberg, A., & McRoberts, G. W. (1998). Rapid gains in speed of verbal processing by infants in the second year. *Psychological Science, 9*, 72–75.

Fernald, A., Swingley, D., & Pinto, J. P. (2001). When half a word is enough: Infants can recognize spoken words using partial phonetic information. *Child Development, 72*, 1003–1015.

Fernald, A., Thorpe, K., & Marchman, V. A. (2010). Blue car, red car: Developing efficiency in online interpretation of adjective–noun phrases. *Cognitive Psychology, 20*, 190–217.

Fernald, A., Zangl, R., Portillo, A. L., & Marchman, V. A. (2008). Looking while listening: Using eye movements to monitor spoken language comprehension by infants and young children. In I. A. Sekerina, E. M. Fernández, & H. Clahsen (Eds.), Developmental psycholinguistics: Online methods in children's language processing (pp. 97–135). Amsterdam: Benjamins.

Freeman, E. (1934). *Individual differences*. New York: Holt.

Friedman, N. L. (1978). Cultural deprivation: A commentary on the sociology of knowledge. In J. Beck, C. Jenks, & N. Keddie (Eds.), *Toward a sociology of education*. Piscataway, NJ: Transaction.

Gathercole, S. E., & Baddeley, A. D. (1993). *Working memory and language*. Hillsdale, NJ: Erlbaum.

Goddard, H. H. (1917). Mental tests and the immigrant. *Journal of Delinquency, 2*, 243–277.

Goldfarb, W. (1945). Effects of psychological deprivation in infancy and subsequent stimulation. *American Journal of Psychiatry, 102*, 18–33.

Golinkoff, R. M., Hirsh-Pasek, K., Cauley, K. M., & Gordon, L. (1987). The eyes have it: Lexical and syntactic comprehension in a new paradigm. *Journal of Child Language, 14*, 23–45.

Gould, S. J. (1981). *Mismeasure of man*. New York: Norton.

Guillemon, D., & Grosjean, F. (2001). The gender marking effect in spoken word recognition: The case of bilinguals. *Memory and Cognition, 29*, 503–511.

Hart, B., & Risley, T. (1995). *Meaningful differences in the everyday experience of young American children*. Baltimore: Brookes.

Heath, S. B. (1983). *Ways with words: Language, life, and work in communities and classrooms*. New York: Cambridge University Press.

Hess, R. D., & Shipman, V. C. (1965). Early experience and the socialization of cognitive modes in children. *Child Development, 36,* 869–886.

Hoff, E. (2003). The specificity of environmental influence: Socioeconomic status affects early vocabulary development via maternal speech. *Child Development, 74,* 1368–1878.

Hoff, E. (2006). How social contexts support and shape language development. *Developmental Review, 26,* 55–88.

Hoff-Ginsberg, E. (1991). Mother–child conversation in different social classes and communicative settings. *Child Development, 62,* 782–797.

Hoff-Ginsberg, E. (1998). The relation of birth order and socioeconomic status to children's language experience and language development. *Applied Psycholinguistics, 19,* 603–629.

Hurtado, N., Marchman, V. A., & Fernald, A. (2007). Spoken word recognition by Latino children learning Spanish as their first language. *Journal of Child Language, 37,* 227–249.

Hurtado, N., Marchman, V. A., & Fernald, A. (2008). Does input influence uptake?: Links between maternal talk, processing speed and vocabulary size in Spanish-learning children. *Developmental Science, 11,* F31–F39.

Huttenlocher, J., Haight, W., Bryk, A., Seltzer, M., & Lyons, T. (1991). Early vocabulary growth: Relation to language input and gender. *Developmental Psychology, 27,* 236–248.

Huttenlocher, J., Vasilyeva, M., Cymerman, E., & Levine, S. (2002). Language input and child syntax. *Cognitive Psychology, 45,* 337–374.

Jensen, A. (1968). Social class and verbal learning. In M. Deutsch, I. Katz, & A. Jensen (Eds.), *Social class, race, and psychological development.* New York: Holt.

Jusczyk, P. (1997). *The discovery of spoken language.* Cambridge, MA: MIT Press.

Kellmer Pringle, M. L., & Bossio, V. (1958). A study of deprived children: Part II. Language development and reading attainment. *Vita Humana, 1,* 142–170.

Klineberg, O. (1935). *Negro intelligence and selective migration.* New York: Columbia University Press.

Kuhl, P. K. (2004). Early language acquisition: Cracking the speech code. *Nature Reviews Neuroscience, 5,* 831–843.

Labov, W. (1970). The logic of non-Standard English. In F. Williams (Ed.), *Language and poverty.* Chicago: Markham Press.

Lew-Williams, C., & Fernald, A. (2007). Young children learning Spanish make rapid use of grammatical gender in spoken word recognition. *Psychological Science, 18,* 193–198.

Marchman, V. A., & Fernald, A. (2008). Speed of word recognition and vocabulary knowledge in infancy predict cognitive and language outcomes in later childhood. *Developmental Science, 11,* F9–F16.

McCarthy, D. A. (1930). *The language development of the preschool child* (Institute of Child Welfare, Monograph Series No. 4). Minneapolis: University of Minnesota Press.

Milner, E. (1951). A study of the relationship between reading readiness in grade one school children and patterns of parent–child interaction. *Child Development, 22,* 95–122.

Newport, E. L., Gleitman, H., & Gleitman, L. R. (1977). Mother, I'd rather do it myself: Some effects and non-effects of maternal speech style. In C. Snow & C. Ferguson (Eds.), *Talking to children: Language input and acquisition.* Cambridge, UK: Cambridge University Press.

Raph, J. B. (1965). Language development in socially disadvantaged children. *Review of Educational Research, 35,* 389–400.

Phillips, J. R. (1973). Syntax and vocabulary of mothers' speech to young children: Age and sex comparisons. *Child Development, 44,* 182–185.

Reissman, F. (1962). *The culturally deprived child.* New York: Harper & Row.

Saffran, J. R. (2003) Statistical language learning: Mechanisms and constraints. *Trends in Cognitive Science, 12,* 110–114.

Scarborough, H. S., & Dobrich, W. (1994). On the efficacy of reading to preschoolers. *Developmental Review, 14,* 245–302.

Sherman, M., & Key, C. (1932). The intelligence of isolated mountain children. *Child Development, 3,* 279–290.

Siegler, R. S. (1992). The other Alfred Binet. *Developmental Psychology, 28,* 179–190.

Snow, C. E. (1972). Mothers' speech to children learning language. *Child Development, 43,* 549–565.

Snow, C. E., Burns, M. S., & Griffin, P. (1998). *Preventing reading difficulties in young children.* Washington, DC: National Academy Press.

Snow, C., & Ferguson, C (1977). *Talking to children: Language input and interaction.* Cambridge, MA: Cambridge University Press.

Sroufe, L. A. (1970). A methodological and philosophical critique of intervention-oriented research. *Developmental Psychology, 2,* 140–145.

Swingley, D., Pinto, J. P., & Fernald, A. (1999). Continuous processing in word recognition at 24 months. *Cognition, 71,* 73–108.

Terman, L. M. (1916). *The measurement of intelligence.* Boston: Houghton Mifflin.

Tulkin, S. R. (1972). An analysis of the concept of cultural deprivation. *Developmental Psychology, 6,* 326–339.

Walker, D., Greenwood, C., Hart, B., & Carta, J. (1994). Prediction of school outcomes based on early language production and socioeconomic factors. *Child Development, 65,* 606–621.

Weizman, Z. O., & Snow, C. E. (2001). Lexical input as related to children's vocabulary acquisition: Effects of sophisticated exposure and support for meaning. *Developmental Psychology, 37,* 265–279.

Wells, G. (1981). Some antecedents of early educational attainment. *British Journal of Sociology of Education, 2,* 181–200.

Werker, J. F. (1989). Becoming a native listener: A developmental perspective on human speech perception. *American Scientist, 77,* 54–59.

2

Self-Regulation and Early Literacy

CLANCY BLAIR
JOHN PROTZKO
ALEXANDRA URSACHE

This chapter examines the role of self-regulation in the development of reading ability in terms of both the behavioral and cognitive research on self-regulation development and the neuroscience of self-regulation development in early childhood. There is a good deal of interest in the application of neuroscience to topics in educational research such as the promotion of literacy development and prevention of reading disability. This integration of research on neuroscience and education is a priority for neuroscientists and educators alike as both look to develop dialogue and collaborative endeavors that can capitalize on an interdisciplinary approach (*www.sfn.org/index. aspx?pagename=neuroed_summit*). The study of self-regulation represents a potentially useful and relatively straightforward example of how current knowledge about the ways the brain processes information is relevant to and can be integrated with knowledge about the ways young children learn to read. There are important gaps in knowledge on both the neuroscience and educational sides of early literacy research; however, by examining what is known, and by identifying some of these gaps, it is likely that the path toward improving literacy development and enhancing educational practice and child educational achievement will become clearer.

General Background

Early literacy development occurs as children become increasingly proficient in cognitive processes that support skilled reading. Prominent among these is the development of phonological knowledge. In terms of phonological development, early reading is characterized by a process through which spoken language is mapped onto phonological primitives that are associated with alphabetic characters and assembled into larger units of meaning. Therefore, in terms of neuroscience research, one aspect of understanding the development of reading ability involves understanding how the brain becomes proficient at phonological processing.

At a general level, from the perspective of neuroscience, the question of how children develop proficiency in phonological ability involves some understanding of the processes through which the brain transforms unfamiliar and potentially confusing information into familiar and readily accessible information; that is, one aspect of early reading from a neurobiological perspective concerns identifying areas of the brain that support the process of acquiring and using phonological information. Having identified such a link between neuroscience and education research, the empirical process for this aspect of reading research is to determine how and when phonological information can be introduced in ways that appropriately optimize the potential for the individual to begin processing that information efficiently and automatically to promote the development of skilled reading. Importantly, making previously effortful processing of information automatic frees cognitive resources previously dedicated to deliberate and effortful processing of phonological information to acquire new and increasingly elaborate information and to consolidate that information with prior information.

Developmental Neuroanatomy of Reading

Using the methods of neural imaging, neuroscientists have identified brain areas and neural circuitry in cross-sectional studies associated with increasing proficiency in reading ability (Schlaggar & McCandliss, 2007). Generally speaking, the picture is one which two broad, primarily posterior brain regions are associated with increases in skilled reading. The first of these, the dorsal temporoparietal system, includes the angular gyrus and supramarginal gyrus of parietal and temporal cortex, and an area of frontal cortex in the inferior frontal gyrus. This first system, shown in Figure 2.1, is associated with pho-

nological processing, word decoding, and symbol processing, and is relatively slow and effortful. The second system, a ventral occipitotemporal system, includes the visual word form area. This second system, also shown in Figure 2.1, is a relatively fast and automatic system associated with rapid, skilled reading. Both of these systems demonstrate change with age that is correlated in cross-sectional studies with reading ability. Specifically, younger, less proficient readers show greater activity than do older, more skilled readers in the first system, the dorsal temporoparietal system. This is thought to reflect increased effortful processing of phonological information, decoding of new words, and mapping of visual information from print onto the semantic structure of language in younger, less skilled readers relative to older, more skilled ones. In contrast, older readers demonstrate less activation in the first system and greater activity in the second, the ventral occipitotemporal system, associated with fast and automatic processing of words (Pugh, Sandak, Frost, Moore, & Mencl, 2006). Overall, the inference from cross-sectional studies is that the neural basis for the development of reading ability is characterized by a general slow to fast anterior dorsal to posterior ventral shift in neural activity (Schlaggar et al., 2002).

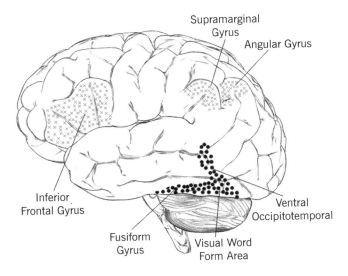

FIGURE 2.1. Neural systems involved in reading. The dorsal temporoparietal system includes inferior frontal gyrus, supramarginal gyrus, and angular gyrus. The ventral occipitotemporal system includes the visual word form area located in fusiform gyrus.

The anterior dorsal to posterior ventral shift in the neural basis for reading development is perhaps a good example of a general characteristic of the learning brain. This shift in activity with increasing skill is more or less common across a range of cognitive abilities studied (Johnson, 2001; Sakai et al., 1998) and reflects the shift from effortful, deliberate processing associated with learning to more automatic processing associated with learned information. Importantly, in demonstrating this shift in neural activity, researchers who study reading development have identified and addressed a key methodological issue in brain imaging research, namely, the need to equate performance in younger and older participants when coming to conclusions about patterns of change in activation (Schlaggar et al., 2002). Studies of cognitive development that have appropriately attended to this methodological point demonstrate the general anterior to posterior shift in the process of making new information automatic in studies of the development of mathematical ability (Rivera, Reiss, Eckert, & Menon, 2005), the development of reasoning ability (Eslinger et al., 2009), and development of the ability to inhibit responding (Durston et al., 2002).

Self-Regulation and Executive Functions

In the areas of cognitive ability in which the functional neuroanatomy of development has been studied, including reading results suggest that neural activations in frontal regions are indicative of the role of the control of attention and *executive functions* (EFs) in the process of making new information familiar and automatic. EFs refer to cognitive processes associated with holding information in mind in working memory, inhibiting automatic responses to stimulation, and flexibly shifting attention between distinct but related pieces of information or aspects of a given task. EFs are particularly relevant to performance and ability when information is novel and potentially confusing, and new associations have to be established and/or prior associations and responses overridden.

Brain Imaging of EFs

As seen in a number of brain imaging studies, EF tasks reliably activate anterior brain regions, primarily frontal cortex, but also cingulate cortex and the striatum (Chudasama & Robbins, 2006; Robbins, 2000) as well as parietal cortex (Klingberg, 2006; Olesen, Nagy, Westerberg, & Klingberg, 2003). These activations represent the role of neural circuitry centered in prefrontal cortex in representing goals and orchestrating processes in numerous brain regions to meet those goals (Duncan, 2001; Miller & Cohen, 2001). There are, of course, a number of caveats in the interpretation of findings from brain imaging research that examines the development of complex behaviors such as reading and executive functions. In particular, interpretation of patterns of brain activation that are presumed to change with age and ability in neuroimaging studies can be difficult primarily due to the issue of comparability of performance between older and younger groups noted earlier, as well as the fact that most, if not all, developmental imaging studies are cross-sectional rather than longitudinal. As well, it is inappropriate to conclude that if a brain region associated with a specific cognitive ability is active in a given task, then that task must necessarily involve that cognitive ability (Poldrack, 2006). Differences in brain activations associated with age may reflect variations in strategies and approaches to a given task, leading to distinct patterns of activity at younger versus older ages (Brown, Petersen, & Schlaggar, 2006).

EF and Reading

Keeping these caveats in mind, however, the findings that demonstrate increased frontal activations in areas associated with EFs in early readers do converge with the findings of behavioral research on cognitive abilities associated with reading development. Study of the development of EFs and of the relation of EFs to school readiness and early academic achievement is the focus of a number of research programs, including my own. For example, in one study with children from low income homes, Blair and Razza (2007) demonstrated that measurement of EF ability with a task that makes demands on the ability to maintain rule-based information while inhibiting a prepotent response, the peg tapping task (Diamond & Taylor, 1996; Luria, 1966), was a good predictor of both phonemic awareness and letter knowledge in kindergarten (Blair & Razza, 2007). In fact, in this study, and in subsequent analyses of the data, Blair and Razza found that EF ability was a better predictor of phonemic awareness than were measures of receptive vocabulary and general fluid intelligence.

In a follow-up to these findings, Welsh, Nix, Blair, Bierman, and Nelson (2010) obtained similar results in a separate sample of children, also from low-income homes. In this study, they measured EF ability using the peg-tapping task and also a measure of working memory, the backward word span task (Carlson, 2005), and a measure of attention set-shifting ability, the dimensional change card sort (DCCS) task (Zelazo, 2006). In the backward word span task, children hold successively longer strings of words in mind and are asked to repeat the strings in reverse order. In the DCCS, children sort cards containing red and blue boats and rabbits by one dimension (e.g., shape), and are then asked to shift attentional set and sort the cards by a second dimension (e.g., color). In this follow-up study, we also collected data at an additional time point, at the beginning of preschool, as well as at the end of preschool and kindergarten. Here we found that a composite of the measures of EF predicted early literacy development, as assessed by measures of letter–word knowledge, story recall, and reading efficiency, at the end of both preschool and kindergarten. In fact, in this analysis, EF at both time points accounted for significant variation in literacy development even when controlling for earlier literacy ability. Furthermore, in this study, EF at the beginning of preschool predicted later literacy ability when controlling for early literacy ability, but the converse was not true; literacy ability at the beginning of preschool was unrelated to later EF ability.

Early Literacy and EFs

Results described above are similar to those observed by a number of investigators indicating the relation of various measures of EF and self-regulation to early literacy. For example, another study using a response inhibition task similar to peg tapping with children in both the fall and the spring of their preschool year also found that the ability to maintain a rule-based response while inhibiting a prepotent response is related to both fall and spring phonemic awareness and vocabulary ability. Furthermore, as in the studies (Blair & Razza, 2007; Welsh et al., 2010) with low-income preschoolers, this study found that the increase in EF ability was positively associated with increases in early literacy abilities even when researchers controlled for initial levels of child literacy ability (McClelland et al., 2007). Similarly, a longitudinal study of first through fourth graders showed the importance of inhibition and switching in predicting literacy outcomes (Altemeier, Abbott, & Berninger, 2008). A measure of rapid automatic switching and a combined switching–inhibition measure predicted all literacy skills, including efficiency of phonemic decoding, efficiency of word reading, pseudoword decoding, word reading, spelling, and written expression. Inhibition predicted all of the outcomes except for written expression, and in a combined model of all three measures, inhibition had the highest correlation with literacy outcomes. Moreover, this study also showed that students with greater increases in EF throughout the first 4 years of schooling had better literacy outcomes at the end of fourth grade. Additional evidence indicating the role of self-regulation in early academic ability is found in studies measuring aspects of temperament such as inhibitory control, and the ability to focus attention and to regulate emotion (Howse, Calkins, Anastopoulos, Keane, & Shelton, 2003; Trentacosta & Izard, 2007). In combination, these results are generally consistent with a model of early school readiness that focuses on processes of self-regulation and ways the regulation of emotion and attention underlie the development of self-directed learning and academic achievement (Blair, 2002; Raver, 2002).

EFs, Academic Achievement, and Intelligence

The studies reviewed briefly earlier demonstrate that EFs and self-regulation are important for the development of early literacy ability. As aspects of cognition that are important for dealing with new and unfamiliar information and organizing that information in goal-directed tasks, EFs are relevant to a variety of academic outcomes. For example, several of the studies described earlier examining the relation of EFs to reading development also demonstrated the relevance of EFs to mathematics achievement. If anything, relations between EFs and mathematics achievement are somewhat stronger than those for reading achievement. The reason for this concerns the relation of EFs to the fluid as opposed to crystallized dimension of intelligence (Blair, 2006). *Fluid intelligence* refers to reasoning ability and processing of novel information, and is therefore closely associated with EFs and activity in frontal cortex systems (Carpenter, Just, & Shell, 1990; Lee et al., 2006; Wendelken, Nakhabenko, Donohue, Carter, & Bunge, 2008). In contrast, *crystallized intelligence* refers to acquired and acculturated aspects of intelligence, such as factual information and general knowledge, and is associated primarily with specific posterior cortical regions (Choi et al., 2008).

Generally speaking, much of the focus in early literacy is on the acquisition of crystallized knowledge associated with reading ability, such as alphabetic knowledge, phonological knowledge, and vocabulary knowledge. In the process of acquiring knowledge in early childhood, EFs play an important role. Once this crystallized knowledge is acquired, however, it may be that it, more than executive functioning, is most essential for continued reading success. Similarly, in mathematics, aspects of crystallized knowledge are central to the development of ability, such as the acquisition of the number sense and various aspects of procedural knowledge. Mathematics, however, more explicitly than reading, makes consistent and ongoing demands on reasoning ability and conceptual knowledge of relations among problem elements. Consequently, throughout development, measures of EF are more likely to demonstrate relations to measures of mathematics ability than to measures of reading ability. This inherent reasoning demand of mathematics assessment may in part underlie the intriguing result of an analysis of six longitudinal datasets in which early achievement in mathematics better predicted later

achievement in reading, as well as later achievement in math, than did early reading achievement (Duncan et al., 2007).

When considering the relative contribution of EFs to reading and mathematics achievement, however, it is necessary to consider the child's developmental level, as well as the type of academic skill that is being assessed. Aspects of reading, such as vocabulary knowledge, and aspects of mathematics, such as the times tables, are expected to be crystallized aspects of ability for typically developing children in the early to midelementary grades. In contrast, aspects of reading that require comprehension and integration of information, and aspects of mathematics that require the flexible use of and switching between algorithms largely reflect the ongoing contributions of EFs to achievement. For example, after accounting for knowledge-based aspects of reading comprehension, such as decoding skills and vocabulary, measures of working memory are important contributors to reading comprehension abilities (Sesma, Mahone, Levine, Eason, & Cutting, 2009; Swanson & Berninger, 1995).

Overall, the fluid versus crystallized distinction in the study of mental ability indicates that for reading development, EFs are important for the initial acquisition of phonological information in the preschool and early elementary school years that supports skilled reading. Once acquired, these crystallized abilities plus executive abilities support skilled reading and the development of reading comprehension (Ferrer et al., 2007). As the child gains experience with reading, the cognitive demand for reading words and sentences lightens as more taxing processes, such as those requiring comprehension and drawing inferences, are needed. Around middle childhood, the typical reader has developed a vocabulary of hundreds, if not thousands, of words, so that reading the bulk of sentences a normal developing 8-year-old encounters does not require sounding out words or trying to figure out what they mean. However, to comprehend a sentence, or series of sentences, and to draw inferences for what may come next, or for subtext unstated in the information, require EFs. They require one to understand the principal actors in an event and to discern who is doing what to whom, and how it may affect later interactions, while remembering previous information. EFs also coordinate the retrieval of information from long-term memory, integrate this previously acquired information with what is currently being input, and anticipate what comes next (Swanson & Sáez, 2003). The greater the executive capacity individuals have, the greater their abilities at text comprehension (Dixon, LeFevre, & Twilley, 1988), even when controlling for word reading ability, vocabulary, and verbal intelligence (Cain, Oakhill, & Bryant, 2004). This association has been confirmed in longitudinal studies that have shown working memory to contribute uniquely to reading growth that is separate from the effects of phonological awareness (Swanson & Jerman, 2007; see also Gathercole, Alloway, Willis, & Adams, 2006).

EF Development and Early Literacy Development

Research on early literacy development suggests that EFs are important for the acquisition of abilities that support the initial development of skilled reading, and that continue to contribute to advanced reading ability due to their role in reading comprehension. Therefore, an important priority in the research process is demarcation of where difficulties in the process of acquiring and maintaining literacy skills originate. It is necessary to determine the extent to which early or later deficits in reading development are due to problems with EF processes that are important for the initial acquisition of abilities that support skilled reading and for ongoing comprehension as reading continues to develop, and the extent to which problems are indicative of difficulty not in executive processes but in processes related to storing and accessing automatized information, such as phonological and alphabetic knowledge. The literature on reading disability has clearly shown that deficits in executive processes are one aspect of reading disability (Swanson, Jerman, & Zheng, 2009). However, a variety of aspects of cognition distinguish typical readers from readers with learning disabilities. EF deficits in some instances might co-occur with difficulties in storing and accessing phonological information. In other instances, however, EFs might serve a compensatory role

through which individuals with difficulty in the rapid and automatic processing of phonological information, and word and letter knowledge, may rely more heavily on executive processes for reading.

Problems with EF development, although only one aspect of early reading difficulty, may be of specific interest, however, in that they likely play a role in early reading problems in a large number of children for whom reading delays are due to poverty. EF and self-regulation problems are more prevalent in children from low-income homes (Blair et al., in press; Evans, 2003; Noble, Norman, & Farah, 2005) and represent a potential causal mechanism linking poverty with delays in reading development and academic achievement. Therefore, an important research goal is to understand the causal influences on EF development. A number of studies have shown that a primary pathway through which the conditions of poverty affect school readiness and early academic ability is disruptions of early caregiving relationships, leading to reduced support and opportunity for learning and self-regulation (McLoyd, 1998). An additional pathway through which the environment of poverty affects school readiness is increased stress leading to poor EF and self-regulation. Research has increasingly demonstrated that poverty is stressful for children, and adversities that are more prevalent in households in poverty, such as higher levels of crowding, increased family turmoil, and increased noise and chaos, are related to higher levels of stress hormones and lower levels of self-regulation abilities (Blair et al., in press; Evans, 2003; Fernald & Gunnar, 2009; Lupien & Lepage, 2001). As a consequence, children growing up in poverty are less likely than children in more advantaged environments to receive support for the regulation of attention, emotion, and physiological reactivity to stress in ways that promote self-regulation and EF development (Blair et al., in press; Evans & English, 2002; McLoyd, 1990). In fact, it may be that the environment of poverty is more likely to promote reactive and less flexible responses to stimulation rather than reflective responses associated with EF and effortful control (Blair, in press). This is due to the ways in which environments affect stress physiology and the idea that experience alters physiology to potentiate behaviors and responses to stimulation that are likely to be beneficial within a given environment.

Effects of Stress Physiology on Neural Functioning and Development

Environmentally induced alteration in stress physiology, such as that documented in children in poverty, is referred to as *allostasis*, or *adaptive homeostasis*. With repeated exposure to stressors, resting levels or set points for physiological stress response systems are altered to ranges that are less conducive to the flexible regulation of stress reactivity (McEwen, 1998) and to EF abilities (Ramos & Arnsten, 2007; Robbins, 2005). The process of allostasis under conditions of stress is an adaptive and protective response to uncertainty and lack of predictability in low-resource environments; that is, in lower-resource environments it is beneficial to be more reactive to stimulation and less reflective, and to maintain a vigilant state associated with increased levels of neuroendocrine hormones. Such a response, however, when stress is chronic, comes at a cost, leading to poor longer-term physical and mental health outcomes (McEwen & Wingfield, 2003; Shonkoff, Boyce, & McEwen, 2009) and shorter-term problems with EFs and self-regulation. In fact, the shorter-term effects of chronic stress on EF and self-regulation development may be one mechanism linking chronic stress with poor physical health outcomes through poor health-related decision making and behavior.

Evidence from Animal Models

Ongoing and persistent stress in children's lives can be expected to contribute to problems with EF development that in combination with reduced language stimulation and learning opportunities in low-income environments can lead to problems with reading ability and academic achievement. To understand the relation between environmental effects on stress physiology and the development of self-regulation and EFs important for early literacy and school readiness, it is useful to review literature examining the influence of early experience on stress physiology in animal models. Relations between early experience and stress physiology, including the expression of genes associated with the regulation of stress physiology, have been clearly demonstrated in rats and to some extent in monkeys.

Animal models, primarily with rats, have shown that early experience can substantially influence brain development and stress physiology in areas important for EF (Braun, Lange, Metzger, & Poeggel, 2000; Kinnunen, Koenig, & Bilbe, 2003; Lemaire, Koehl, Le Moal, & Abrous, 2000). These studies have demonstrated that chronic early stress affects the development of stress physiology by altering the functioning and connectivity of brain areas associated with emotional and stress reactions to stimulation, namely, structures in the limbic system and areas of prefrontal cortex important for regulating the stress response and emotion, and most importantly for present purposes, for coordinating information and planning and monitoring responses to stimulation through EFs (Barbas & Zikopoulos, 2007; Holmes & Wellman, 2009). In a number of studies of rat models, early stress results in disruptions of the neural connections between the limbic areas of the brain and the prefrontal cortical areas. As well, these changes in the brain are accompanied by performance decrements on tasks requiring EF abilities (Cerqueira, Mailliet, Almeida, Jay, & Sousa, 2007; Collins, Roberts, Dias, Everitt, & Robbins, 1998; Floresco, Seamans, & Phillips, 1997; Goldstein, Rasmusson, Bunney, & Roth, 1996; Mizoguchi, Ishige, Takeda, Aburada, & Tabira, 2004; Seamans, Floresco, & Phillips, 1998).

A particularly illuminating example of the way early experience can affect the development of stress physiology is provided by research on maternal behavior in the rat. This line of research indicates that early experience essentially programs the development of stress response systems in ways that make them more or less sensitive to stress (Meaney, 2001). The study of typically occurring variation in maternal behavior in rats has demonstrated that high levels of maternal licking and grooming, and a style of nursing referred to as arched back nursing during the first 8 postnatal days, have meaningful consequences for the development of the hypothalamic–pituitary–adrenal (HPA) axis component of the physiological response to stress. The HPA axis controls levels of the glucocorticoid hormone cortisol (corticosterone in rodents) and as such is a relatively slow-acting arm of the stress response that enables the organism to deal with sustained challenge in the environment. Offspring of rat mothers that engage in more licking and grooming behavior are better at regulating HPA reactivity to stress as adults and perform at higher levels on complex learning and memory tasks (Liu et al., 1997; Liu, Diorio, Day, Francis, & Meaney, 2000).

Remarkably, research on the development of the HPA axis in rats has shown that the effect of maternal behavior on the development of the stress response extends to the level of the genome (Weaver, Diorio, Seckl, Szyf, & Meaney, 2004). High levels of licking and grooming behavior in rat mothers lead to the modification of gene expression, in this instance, in a gene that codes for the density of receptors for corticosteroid stress hormones in key areas of the brain associated with regulation of the stress response. A greater number of receptors means that the organism is better able to respond to stress and to regulate cortisol, and is therefore better able to regulate behavior. The association between maternal behavior and development of the HPA axis in rats is one example of the way experience affects the development of the stress response, with implications for EF development and early reading.

Experiential Canalization

The alteration of stress physiology by experience represents a process of adaptation referred to as *biological embedding* (Boyce & Ellis, 2005) or the *experiential canalization of development* (Gottlieb, 1991). In the process of experiential canalization, information about the quality of the environment shapes development to enhance the potential for optimal functioning in that environment. In terms of stress physiology and EF, an example of experiential canalization occurs when prenatal stress or stress in the early postnatal environment influences development to make the individual more reactive and less reflective. Increased reactivity to stimulation in unpredictable environments

in which resources and support are low is a beneficial response that can promote survival. In supportive and resource-rich environments, however, stress response physiology and neural systems develop (i.e., are canalized) so that the reactivity of physiological stress response systems is well regulated and therefore conducive to effortful processing of information and reflective self-regulation associated with EFs.

The pathway through which stress physiology is understood to canalize development concerns the way in which stress hormones influence neural activity in prefrontal cortex (PFC). In both human and animal studies, levels of stress hormones, including the corticosteroid hormone cortisol produced by the HPA axis, and catecholamines (dopamine, norepinephrine) associated with the sympathetic response to stress, have an inverted U-shaped relation with EFs. At very high or very low levels of cortisol and catecholamines, EF ability is low; at moderate increases, however, EF ability is improved (Arnsten & Li, 2005; Lupien, Gillin, & Hauger, 1999; Mizoguchi et al., 2004; Vijayraghavan, Wang, Birnbaum, Williams, & Arnsten, 2007). This inverted U-shaped relation between stress hormone levels and EFs is in part a function of the types of neural receptors present in PFC and the relative sensitivity of these receptors to stress hormones. For example, moderate increases in norepinephrine (NE) result in increased occupation of a specific type of neural receptor that has a high affinity for NE and is predominantly located in PFC and associated with EFs (Ramos & Arnsten, 2007). As levels of NE increase beyond a moderate level, however, this type of receptor becomes saturated, and neural receptors with a lower affinity for NE become active. These receptors are predominantly located in limbic and posterior brain regions associated with reflexive and reactive responses to stimulation. In this way, levels of NE act to influence the neural response to stimulation, promoting neural activity in PFC associated with reflective and reasoned responses to stimulation at moderate levels of arousal, while at high levels, NE reduces neural activity in PFC and increases neural activity in brain areas associated with reactive, more automatic responses to stimulation (Arnsten, 2000).

Similarly, of the two types of corticosteroid receptors in the brain, glucocorticoid receptors (GR) and mineralocorticoid receptors (MR), the GR is less sensitive to cortisol than the MR, and therefore remains largely unoccupied at low levels of stress arousal. However, with increasing stress and moderate cortisol increase, GR occupation increases, supporting sustained neural activity. Increases in cortisol with stress arousal beyond a moderate level, indicating increasingly high GR occupation, however, are associated with reduced neural activity (de Kloet, Oitzl, & Joëls, 1999; Erickson, Drevets, & Schulkin, 2003). The inverted U-shaped relation between stress levels and EFs is a manifestation at the neural level of the relation between arousal and performance first described by Yerkes and Dodson (1908). In the Yerkes–Dodson principle, arousal at moderate levels increases performance on complex tasks, but at very high or very low levels it impairs performance. In this relation between stress and performance, however, the inverted U-shaped relation is specific to complex tasks. For more reactive aspects of cognition and behavior, arousal is positively and linearly related to performance (Diamond, Campbell, Park, Halonen, & Zoladz, 2007). As such, in keeping with the idea of biological embedding and experiential canalization, the key point concerning early experience and self-regulation development is the ability to regulate the stress response. It is not simply that high levels of stimulation early in life are necessarily detrimental or beneficial. In supportive contexts, stimulation results in an increased ability to regulate physiology that is conducive to self-regulation. In unsupportive, less predictable contexts, however, stimulation leads to patterns of physiological responding that are conducive to high behavioral reactivity and to lower effortful self-regulation.

Early Childrearing, Stress, and Self-Regulation

As with the rat model of the effect of early experience on the development of stress physiology and learning and memory, the primary source of information about the quality of the environment early in human development would seem to be communicated through maternal care. Maternal effects on stress physiology and what are termed *defensive responses* important for longer-term success in favorable versus unfavorable environments are seen across a wide range of species, ranging from plants to insects to birds to mammals (Cameron et al., 2005). The association of poverty with self-regulation development and academic achievement in young children reflects to a considerable extent the influence of poverty on parental caregiving behavior. Parents in lower-income homes face a variety of challenges associated with what can be considered less prototypically supportive parenting practices (McLoyd, 1998). A number of studies with young children have demonstrated, not surprisingly, that the development of the ability to effortfully regulate attention, emotion, and stress physiology is very much influenced by parent–child interaction (Calkins, 2004; Sroufe, 1996). Experimental demonstrations of correlational associations have been confirmed in studies in which parenting interventions have increased sensitive and responsive caregiving lead to increased cognitive ability, socioemotional self-regulation, and academic achievement in children (Landry, Smith, & Swank, 2006; van den Boom, 1994). Indeed, the effect of caregiving and self-regulation on socioemotional outcomes appears to be largest for children who are initially temperamentally predisposed to higher levels of behavioral and physiological reactivity to stimulation (Belsky, Bakermans-Kranenburg, & van IJzendoorn, 2007).

The relations of early experience to stress physiology and of stress physiology to self-regulation are theoretically strong and bolstered by a wide variety of studies. None, however, had previously examined relations among early experience, stress physiology, and EF development in young children in poverty. Therefore, in a longitudinal study of children and families in predominantly low-income and rural communities in two high-poverty regions in the United States, my colleagues and I found that poverty indicators, including income-to-need ratio, maternal education, household crowding and safety, and, in this sample, African American ethnicity (an indicator of deep and persistent poverty) were associated with lower levels of prototypically supportive parenting in the primary caregiver (the mother in 97% of the sample) and higher typical levels of the stress hormone cortisol in children between ages 7 months and 24 months. Furthermore, as expected, we found that prototypically supportive parenting mediated the effects of poverty on cortisol, and that cortisol was itself a significant mediator of effects of parenting on child EF ability at age 3 years (Blair et al., in press); that is, consistent with the process of experiential canalization outlined earlier, poverty impacts parenting behavior, which in turn leads to elevations in child stress physiology, as indicated by the stress hormone cortisol, and thereby to lower EF levels.

These findings, like those in the literature reviewed earlier, indicate that the early experience of children in poverty may be influencing the development of neural and endocrine systems associated with self-regulation in ways not conducive to the development of cognitive abilities, such as EFs that are important for early reading. Whether such effects of early care on stress physiology and EFs are associated with alterations in gene expression and changes to frontal cortex in terms of both size and connectivity, as seen in animal models, are interesting questions that will be important to address in future studies using experimental designs. Most important here is the need to assess stress physiology and self-regulation development within the context of experimental evaluations of early intervention programs designed to promote school readiness and early school achievement. Such studies can definitively address the behavioral, physical, and mental health consequences of alterations to stress physiology resulting from early experience and the potential reversibility of early experience effects on stress physiology and EFs important for early literacy development and school readiness. Studies in rats indicate that environmental enrichment (larger cages, lots of stimulation) in the peripubertal period following early stress exposure is associated with positive behavioral, learning, and memory changes. These changes, however, are not necessarily associated with a reversal at the neural and physiological level of the effects of early stress, suggesting a compensatory mechanism (Bredy, Humpartzoomian, Cain, & Meaney, 2003; Francis, Diorio, Plotsky, & Meaney, 2002).

Early Intervention for Children at Risk for School Failure

Studies of the reversibility of the effects of pre- and perinatal stress on development in rats are very much consistent with the widely cited evidence of the effectiveness of early care and educational interventions for children in poverty. Data from early intervention programs, including the Abecedarian Project (Ramey & Campbell, 1991) and Perry Preschool Study (Schweinhart et al., 2005), both of which used randomized designs, and the Chicago Parent–Child Centers (Reynolds & Temple, 2006), a quasi-experimental follow-up study, demonstrate that high-quality care that begins early and is of sufficient duration and intensity (i.e., care that occurs at least several days per week over several years) improves educational outcomes, including reading abilities, as well as occupational and life event outcomes for program recipients. An initial finding for these early intervention programs was an advantage in favor of the treated groups on standardized measures of intelligence. These gains in intelligence were sustained to some extent over time after the programs ended (Barnett, 1995; Campbell, Pungello, Miller-Johnson, Burchinal, & Ramey, 2001); however, advantages on longer-term outcomes, such as academic achievement, job and relationship stability, and reductions in criminality and judicial involvement, became perhaps a more important indicator of program effects (Reynolds, Temple, Robertson, & Mann, 2001). These results perhaps suggest that a primary mechanism of the programs' beneficial effects on participants' lives was through gains in self-regulation rather than the observed increase in intelligence as such. Of course, the pattern of findings does not necessarily suggest that effects were either on intelligence or on self-regulation; the two types of outcomes are not mutually exclusive. It may be that program-related advantages in self-regulation helped to boost performance on intelligence tests at earlier ages, but that this advantage became less apparent in terms of measured mental ability and more apparent in terms of life outcomes over time. For example, as demonstrated in a recent reanalysis of the Perry Preschool Study data, a primary benefit of the program was improvement of participants' self-regulation skills, and benefits to self-regulation were a primary mechanism of the program's effects (Heckman, Malofeeva, Pinto, & Savelyev, 2008).

Conclusion and Implications

This chapter has reviewed literature on the development of self-regulation, particularly EFs, and considered the influence of EFs on reading development and school readiness. It considered the association between early experience, particularly parenting behavior, and EF development as an aspect of poverty-related gaps in school readiness and academic achievement. This association is one, however, that requires further examination in a variety of studies designed clearly to examine mechanisms through which these associations transpire. At one level, these associations would appear to be quite straightforward and essentially to boil down to the idea that children who have difficulty paying attention, holding information in mind, and effortfully regulating behavior are more likely to have difficulty learning to read and to do well in school. This much is intuitively obvious and clear. At another level, however, to the extent that these associations reflect larger and overarching processes relating early experience to neural and endocrine systems, and to self-regulation development, they indicate that some children are not socialized, biologically and psychologically, for schooling and the types of cognitive abilities and behaviors that are demanded in school settings. Here it is important to recognize a potential match or mismatch between types of early experience and development of the types of abilities required for success in formal schooling. Too often the association of poverty with problems in early school achievement has been couched only in terms of a deficit model: that children are not receiving enough exposure to learning opportunities and to information needed to learn to read and to do well in school. The implication of such a deficit approach is that the provision of learning opportunities and specific information needed for school success is perhaps all that is required to make up for the deficit and redress the achievement gap. To some extent, of course, this logic is correct and represents an important goal

for early childhood education. As we stated earlier, however, in less favorable and prototypically unsupportive contexts, such as those that occur more frequently in the environment of poverty, early experience can lead to patterns of physiological responding that are not conducive to the development of self-regulation that to some extent underlies early learning. Again, it is not simply that high levels of reactivity are necessarily good or bad for development. In supportive contexts, stimulation results in an increased ability to regulate physiology that is conducive to self-regulation. In unsupportive, less predictable contexts, however, stimulation leads to patterns of physiological responding that are conducive to high behavioral reactivity and to lower self-regulation.

Given the overarching importance of promoting school readiness and early academic ability, particularly early literacy, approaches to the elimination of socioeconomic status (SES) gaps in academic achievement can profitably focus on self-regulation development, as well as the provision of content information (e.g., knowledge of phonics, the alphabet). Doing so is very much consistent with the emphasis in early childhood education on educating the whole child, and the need to find innovative ways to assist children in becoming proficient in using attention and EFs to process academic information and engage in learning activities, in addition to exposure to and experience with letters and numbers, and opportunities for learning.

To this end, a particularly innovative early education program known as Tools of the Mind (Bodrova & Leong, 2007) focuses on the development of academic abilities by enhancing self-regulation development. Tools of the Mind is innovative in that it explicitly focuses on the role of self-regulation in learning and academic ability by integration of self-regulation–promoting activities with instructional activities designed to build foundational skills in literacy, mathematics, and socioemotional competence. In doing so, the program is grounded in a Vygotskian theory of development, in which teachers scaffold children's learning with the aim of improving self-regulation, particularly EFs, as a means to increase academic learning. For example, teachers have children engage in learning plans in which children reflect on their prior experience in the activity and integrate that prior experience with planned future actions. Another example of the ways Tools of the Mind promotes self-regulation and academic achievement simultaneously is activities in which children alternate roles as "doers" and "checkers" using visual symbols (a picture of lips for a reader and a picture of an ear for a listener in a reading exercise) assigned to each role. In what is termed "buddy reading," the child in the role of the doer, the lips, reads or otherwise describes what is on the page, while the child in the role of the checker, the ear, observes and follows along. The children then switch roles, so that each child has multiple turns practicing doing and checking. By taking on doing and checking roles individually rather than simultaneously in activities such as this one, children are able to develop proficiency in each role and increased cognitive set-shifting ability. This assists children in integrating these skills later in development and promotes reading and comprehension abilities.

By designing cooperative activities around different roles, thus engaging children in a shared activity, Tools of the Mind maximizes children's engagement in the context of large-group or small-group activities. Children do not wait for the teacher's help but help each other or work as much as they can on their own. In addition, by assuming strategically identified roles, children learn to monitor and reflect on their own and others' actions, eventually internalizing criteria they will be able to apply to their own work. In respect to the development of self-regulation and EF, such activities build cognitive and social competencies that are central to self-regulated learning (Schunk, 1999), as well as provide optimal contexts for children to practice perspective taking and develop insights into theory of mind associated with the development of EF and self-regulation (Carlson, 2005; Hughes & Ensor, 2007).

Although promising, to date, the Tools of the Mind program has not yet been evaluated in a large experimental study to document potential effects on self-regulation and early achievement. The need for a high-quality experimental evaluation of Tools of the Mind is indicated by the strong theoretical basis of the program in its focus on self-regulation and the fact that a previous small-scale, limited, randomized controlled

evaluation of the prekindergarten (PreK) version of the curriculum found mixed effects on child outcomes and classroom processes. Positive child effects were observed for executive functions (Diamond, Barnett, Thomas, & Munro, 2007); behavior problems reported by teachers; receptive vocabulary and oral language; and classroom environment and process, including global quality, support for literacy acquisition, and scaffolding of learning activities (Barnett et al., 2008). However, no child effects were observed on a set of math and reading measures, such as the applied problems and Letter–Word subscales of the Woodcock–Johnson Tests of Academic Achievement. Importantly, this evaluation faced numerous limitations, in that the study was underpowered, with only 85 children in the treatment condition and 120 children in the control condition. Also, the generalizability of the study is limited, in that it took place in only one school with 18 classrooms. Accordingly, a number of evaluations of the Tools of the Mind program are underway in well-designed, adequately powered studies to determine unequivocally the extent to which the curriculum promotes academic achievement in young children.

In conclusion, close examination of the role of self-regulation in early literacy development, in descriptive studies such as those describe earlier, and in experimental evaluations of programs such as Tools of the Mind can expand the knowledge base on the best ways to promote early literacy development and prevent school failure. The idea that self-regulation skills and early knowledge acquisition combine to promote academic achievement is one aspect of the widely recognized need to focus on the education of the whole child (Scarr & Weinberg, 1986; Zigler, 1969). In combination with reduced opportunities for early learning, increased stress in lower-resource home environments affects the development of attention and behavior in ways that are likely to undermine EF development and early school achievement. When coupled with the fact that children from low-resource, more stressful homes almost invariably attend low-resource, lower-quality preschools and early elementary schools, this potent combination conspires to perpetuate an achievement gap. By focusing on self-regulation as one aspect of high-quality early childhood and early elementary education, it is likely that socioeconomic disparities in achievement can be substantially reduced.

References

Altemeier, L. E., Abbott, R. D., & Berninger, V. W. (2008). Executive functions for reading and writing in typical literacy development and dyslexia. *Journal of Clinical and Experimental Neuropsychology, 30*(5), 588–606.

Arnsten, A. F., & Li, B. M. (2005). Neurobiology of executive functions: Catecholamine influences on prefrontal cortical functions. *Biological Psychiatry, 57*(11), 1377–1384.

Arnsten, A. F. T. (2000). Through the looking glass: Differential noradenergic modulation of prefrontal cortical function. *Neural Plasticity, 7,* 133–146.

Barbas, H., & Zikopoulos, B. (2007). The prefrontal cortex and flexible behavior. *Neuroscientist, 13*(5), 532–545.

Barnett, W. S. (1995). Long term effects of early childhood programs on cognitive and school outcomes. *The Future of Children, 5,* 25–50.

Barnett, W. S., Jung, K., Yarosz, D. J., Thomas, J., Hornbeck, A., Stechuk, R., et al. (2008). Educational effects of the tools of the mind curriculum: A randomized trial. *Early Childhood Research Quarterly, 23*(3), 299–313.

Belsky, J., Bakermans-Kranenburg, M. J., & van IJzendoorn, M. H. (2007). For better *and* for worse: Differential susceptibility to environmental influences. *Current Directions in Psychological Science, 16*(6), 300–304.

Blair, C. (2002). School readiness: Integrating cognition and emotion in a neurobiological conceptualization of children's functioning at school entry. *American Psychologist, 57*(2), 111–127.

Blair, C. (2006). How similar are fluid cognition and general intelligence?: A developmental neuroscience perspective on fluid cognition as an aspect of human cognitive ability. *Behavioral and Brain Sciences, 29*(2), 109–160.

Blair, C. (in press). Stress and the development of self-regulation in context. *Child Development Perspectives.*

Blair, C., Granger, D., Willoughby, M., Mills-Koonce, R., Cox, M., Greenberg, M. T., et al. (in press). Salivary cortisol mediates effects of poverty and parenting on executive functions in early childhood. *Child Development.*

Blair, C., & Razza, R. P. (2007). Relating effortful control, executive function, and false belief understanding to emerging math and literacy ability in kindergarten. *Child Development, 78*(2), 647–663.

Bodrova, E., & Leong, D. J. (2007). Play and early literacy: A Vygotskian approach. In K. A. Roskos & J. F. Christie (Eds.), *Play and literacy in early childhood: Research from multiple perspectives* (2nd ed., pp. 185–200). Mahwah, NJ: Erlbaum.

Boyce, W. T., & Ellis, B. J. (2005). Biological sensitivity to context: I. An evolutionary-developmental theory of the origins and functions of stress reactivity. *Development and Psychopathology, 17,* 271–301.

Braun, K., Lange, E., Metzger, M., & Poeggel, G. (2000). Maternal separation followed by early social deprivation affects the development of monoaminergic fiber systems in the medial prefrontal cortex of *Octodon degus. Neuroscience, 95*(1), 309–318.

Bredy, T. W., Humpartzoomian, R. A., Cain, D. P., & Meaney, M. J. (2003). Partial reversal of the effect of maternal care on cognitive function through environmental enrichment. *Neuroscience, 118*(2), 571–576.

Brown, T. T., Petersen, S. E., & Schlaggar, B. L. (2006). Does human functional brain organization shift from diffuse to focal with development? *Developmental Science, 9*(1), 9–11.

Cain, K., Oakhill, J., & Bryant, P. E. (2004). Children's reading comprehension ability: Concurrent prediction by working memory, verbal ability, and component skills. *Journal of Educational Psychology, 95,* 31–42.

Calkins, S. D. (2004). Early attachment processes and the development of emotional self-regulation. In R. F. Baumeister & K. D. Vohs (Eds.), *Handbook of self-regulation: Research, theory, and applications* (pp. 324–339). New York: Guilford Press.

Cameron, N. M., Champagne, F. A., Parent, C., Fish, E. W., Ozaki-Kuroda, K., & Meaney, M. J. (2005). The programming of individual differences in defensive responses and reproductive strategies in the rat through variations in maternal care. *Neuroscience and Biobehavioral Reviews, 29*(4–5), 843–865.

Campbell, F. A., Pungello, E. P., Miller-Johnson, S., Burchinal, M., & Ramey, C. T. (2001). The development of cognitive and academic abilities: Growth curves from an early childhood educational experiment. *Developmental Psychology, 37*(2), 231–242.

Carlson, S. M. (2005). Developmentally sensitive measures of executive function in preschool children. *Developmental Neuropsychology, 28*(2), 595–616.

Carpenter, P. A., Just, M. A., & Shell, P. (1990). What one intelligence test measures: A theoretical account of the processing in the Raven Progressive Matrices Test. *Psychological Review, 97*(3), 404–431.

Cerqueira, J. J., Mailliet, F., Almeida, O. F., Jay, T. M., & Sousa, N. (2007). The prefrontal cortex as a key target of the maladaptive response to stress. *Journal of Neuroscience, 27*(11), 2781–2787.

Choi, Y. Y., Shamosh, N. A., Cho, S. H., DeYoung, C. G., Lee, M. J., Lee, J. M., et al. (2008). Multiple bases of human intelligence revealed by cortical thickness and neural activation. *Journal of Neuroscience, 28*(41), 10323–10329.

Chudasama, Y., & Robbins, T. W. (2006). Functions of frontostriatal systems in cognition: Comparative neuropsychopharmacological studies in rats, monkeys and humans. *Biological Psychology, 73*(1), 19–38.

Collins, P., Roberts, A. C., Dias, R., Everitt, B. J., & Robbins, T. W. (1998). Perseveration and strategy in a novel spatial self-ordered sequencing task for non-human primates: Effects of excitotoxic lesions and dopamine depletions of the prefrontal cortex. *Journal of Cognitive Neuroscience, 10*(3), 332–354.

de Kloet, E. R., Oitzl, M. S., & Joëls, M. (1999). Stress and cognition: Are corticosteroids good or bad guys? *Trends in Neurosciences, 22*(10), 422–426.

Diamond, A., Barnett, W. S., Thomas, J., & Munro, S. (2007). Preschool program improves cognitive control. *Science, 318,* 1387–1388.

Diamond, A., & Taylor, C. (1996). Development of an aspect of executive control: Development of the abilities to remember what I said and to "do as I say, not as I do." *Developmental Psychobiology, 29*(4), 315–334.

Diamond, D. M., Campbell, A. M., Park, C. R., Halonen, J., & Zoladz, P. R. (2007). The temporal dynamics model of emotional memory processing: A synthesis on the neurobiological basis of stress-induced amnesia, flashbulb and traumatic memories, and the Yerkes–Dodson law. *Neural Plasticity.*

Dixon, P., LeFevre, J. A., & Twilley, L. (1988). Word knowledge and working memory as predictors of reading skill. *Journal of Educational Psychology, 80*(4), 465–472.

Duncan, G. J., Dowsett, C. J., Claessens, A., Magnuson, K., Huston, A. C., Klebanov, P., et al. (2007). School readiness and later achievement. *Developmental Psychology, 43*(6), 1428–1446.

Duncan, J. (2001). An adaptive coding model of neural function in prefrontal cortex. *Nature Reviews Neuroscience, 2*(11), 820–829.

Durston, S., Thomas, K. M., Yang, Y., Ulug, A. M., Zimmerman, R. D., & Casey, B. J. (2002). A neural basis for the development of inhibitory control. *Developmental Science, 5*(4), F9–F16.

Erickson, K., Drevets, W., & Schulkin, J. (2003). Glucocorticoid regulation of diverse cognitive functions in normal and pathological emotional states. *Neuroscience and Biobehavioral Reviews, 27*(3), 233–246.

Eslinger, P. J., Blair, C., Wang, J., Lipovsky, B., Realmuto, J., Baker, D., et al. (2009). Developmental shifts in fMRI activations during visuospatial relational reasoning. *Brain and Cognition, 69*(1), 1–10.

Evans, G. W. (2003). A multimethodological analysis of cumulative risk and allostatic load among rural children. *Developmental Psychology, 39*(5), 924–933.

Evans, G. W., & English, K. (2002). The environment of poverty: Multiple stressor exposure, psychophysiological stress, and socioemotional adjustment. *Child Development, 73,* 1238–1248.

Fernald, L. C., & Gunnar, M. R. (2009). Poverty-alleviation program participation and salivary cortisol in very low-income children. *Social Science and Medicine, 68*(12), 2180–2189.

Ferrer, E., McArdle, J. J., Shaywitz, B. A., Holahan, J. M., Marchione, K., & Shaywitz, S. E. (2007). Longitudinal models of developmental dynamics between reading and cognition from childhood to adolescence. *Developmental Psychology, 43*(6), 1460–1473.

Floresco, S. B., Seamans, J. K., & Phillips, A. G. (1997). Selective roles for hippocampal, prefrontal cortical, and ventral striatal circuits in radial-arm maze tasks with or without a delay. *Journal of Neuroscience, 17*(5), 1880–1890.

Francis, D. D., Diorio, J., Plotsky, P. M., & Meaney, M. J. (2002). Environmental enrichment reverses the effects of maternal separation on stress reactivity. *Journal of Neuroscience, 22*(18), 7840–7843.

Gathercole, S. E., Alloway, T. P., Willis, C., & Adams, A. M. (2006). Working memory in children with reading disabilities. *Journal of Experimental Child Psychology, 93*(3), 265–281.

Goldstein, L. E., Rasmusson, A. M., Bunney, B. S., & Roth, R. H. (1996). Role of the amygdala in the coordination of behavioral, neuroendocrine, and prefrontal cortical monoamine responses to psychological stress in the rat. *Journal of Neuroscience, 16*(15), 4787–4798.

Gottlieb, G. (1991). Experiential canalization of behavioral development: Results. *Developmental Psychology, 27*(1), 35–39.

Heckman, J. J., Malofeeva, L., Pinto, R., & Savelyev, P. (2008). *The effect of the Perry Preschool Program on cognitive and noncognitive skills: Beyond treatment effects.* Unpublished manuscript, University of Chicago, Department of Economics, Chicago.

Holmes, A., & Wellman, C. L. (2009). Stress-induced prefrontal reorganization and executive dysfunction in rodents. *Neuroscience and Biobehavioral Reviews, 33*(6), 773–783.

Howse, R. B., Calkins, S. D., Anastopoulos, A. D., Keane, S. P., & Shelton, T. L. (2003). Regulatory contributors to children's kindergarten achievement. *Early Education and Development, 14*(1), 101–19.

Hughes, C., & Ensor, R. (2007). Executive function and theory of mind: Predictive relations from ages 2 to 4. *Developmental Psychology, 43*(6), 1447–1459.

Johnson, M. H. (2001). Functional brain development in humans. *Nature Reviews Neuroscience, 2,* 475–483.

Kinnunen, A. K., Koenig, J. I., & Bilbe, G. (2003). Repeated variable prenatal stress alters pre- and postsynaptic gene expression in the rat frontal pole. *Journal of Neurochemistry, 86*(3), 736–748.

Klingberg, T. (2006). Development of a superior frontal-intraparietal network for visuo-spatial working memory. *Neuropsychologia, 44*(11), 2171–2177.

Landry, S. H., Smith, K. E., & Swank, P. R. (2006). Responsive parenting: Establishing early foundations for social, communication, and independent problem-solving skills. *Developmental Psychology, 42*(4), 627–642.

Lee, K. H., Choi, Y. Y., Gray, J. R., Cho, S. H., Chae, J. H., Lee, S., et al. (2006). Neural correlates of superior intelligence: Stronger recruitment of posterior parietal cortex. *NeuroImage, 29*(2), 578–586.

Lemaire, V., Koehl, M., Le Moal, M., & Abrous, D. N. (2000). Prenatal stress produces learning deficits associated with an inhibition of neurogenesis in the hippocampus. *Proceedings of the National Academy of Sciences USA, 97*(20), 11032–11037.

Liu, D., Diorio, J., Day, J. C., Francis, D. D., & Meaney, M. J. (2000). Maternal care, hippocampal neurogenesis, and cognitive development in rats. *Nature Neuroscience, 3*, 799–806.

Liu, D., Diorio, J., Tannenbaum, B., Caldji, C., Francis, D., Freedman, A., et al. (1997). Maternal care, hippocampal glucocorticoid receptors, and hypothalamic–pituitary–adrenal responses to stress. *Science, 277*, 1659–1662.

Lupien, S. J., Gillin, C. J., & Hauger, R. L. (1999). Working memory is more sensitive than declarative memory to the acute effects of corticosteroids: A dose–response study in humans. *Behavioral Neuroscience, 113*(3), 420–430.

Lupien, S. J., & Lepage, M. (2001). Stress, memory, and the hippocampus: Can't live with it, can't live without it. *Behavioural Brain Research, 127*(1–2), 137–158.

Luria, A. R. (1966). *Higher cortical functions in man.* New York: Basic Books.

McClelland, M. M., Cameron, C. E., Connor, C. M., Farris, C. L., Jewkes, A. M., & Morrison, F. J. (2007). Links between behavioral regulation and preschoolers' literacy, vocabulary, and math skills. *Developmental Psychology, 43*(4), 947–959.

McEwen, B. S. (1998). Stress, adaptation, and disease: Allostasis and allostatic load. *Annals of the New York Academy of Sciences, 840*, 33–44.

McEwen, B. S., & Wingfield, J. C. (2003). The concept of allostasis in biology and biomedicine. *Hormones and Behavior, 43*, 2–15.

McLoyd, V. C. (1990). The impact of economic hardship on black families and children: Psychological distress, parenting, and socioemotional development. *Child Development, 61*(2), 311–346.

McLoyd, V. C. (1998). Socioeconomic disadvantage and child development. *American Psychologist, 53*(2), 185–204.

Meaney, M. J. (2001). Maternal care, gene expression, and the transmission of individual differences in stress reactivity across generations. *Annual Review of Neuroscience, 24*(1), 1161–1192.

Miller, E. K., & Cohen, J. D. (2001). An integrative theory of prefrontal cortex function. *Annual Review of Neuroscience, 24*, 167–202.

Mizoguchi, K., Ishige, A., Takeda, S., Aburada, M., & Tabira, T. (2004). Endogenous glucocorticoids are essential for maintaining prefrontal cortical cognitive function. *Journal of Neuroscience, 24*(24), 5492–5499.

Noble, K. G., Norman, M. F., & Farah, M. J. (2005). Neurocognitive correlates of socioeconomic status in kindergarten children. *Developmental Science, 8*(1), 74–87.

Olesen, P. J., Nagy, Z., Westerberg, H., & Klingberg, T. (2003). Combined analysis of DTI and fMRI data reveals a joint maturation of white and grey matter in a fronto-parietal network. *Brain Research: Cognitive Brain Research, 18*(1), 48–57.

Poldrack, R. A. (2006). Can cognitive processes be inferred from neuroimaging data? *Trends in Cognitive Sciences, 10*(2), 59–63.

Pugh, K. R., Sandak, R., Frost, S. J., Moore, D. L., & Mencl, W. E. (2006). Neurobiological investigations of skilled and impaired reading. In D. K. Dickinson & S. B. Neuman (Eds.), *Handbook of early literacy research* (Vol. 2, pp. 64–74). New York: Guilford Press.

Ramey, C. T., & Campbell, A. F. (1991). Poverty, early childhood education, and academic competence: The Abecedarian Experiment. In A. C. Huston (Ed.), *Children in poverty: Child development and public policy* (pp. 190–221). Cambridge, UK: Cambridge University Press.

Ramos, B. P., & Arnsten, A. F. T. (2007). Adrenergic pharmacology and cognition: Focus on the prefrontal cortex. *Pharmacology and Therapeutics, 113*(3), 523–536.

Raver, C. C. (2002). Emotions matter: Making the case for the role of young children's emotional development for early school readiness. *Society for Research in Child Development Social Policy Report, 16*, 1–19.

Reynolds, A., Temple, J., Robertson, D., & Mann, E. (2001). Long-term effects of an early childhood intervention on educational achievement and juvenile arrest. *Journal of the American Medical Association, 285*, 2339–2346.

Reynolds, A. J., & Temple, J. (2006). Cost-effective early childhood development programs from preschool to third grade. *Annual Review of Clinical Psychology, 4*, 109–139.

Rivera, S. M., Reiss, A. L., Eckert, M. A., & Menon, V. (2005). Developmental changes in mental arithmetic: Evidence for increased functional specialization in the left inferior parietal cortex. *Cerebral Cortex, 15*(11), 1779–1790.

Robbins, T. W. (2000). From arousal to cognition: The integrative position of the prefrontal cortex. *Progress in Brain Research, 126*, 469–483.

Robbins, T. W. (2005). Chemistry of the mind: Neurochemical modulation of prefrontal cortical function. *Journal of Comparative Neurology, 493*, 140–146.

Sakai, K., Hikosaka, O., Miyauchi, S., Takino, R., Sasaki, Y., & Putz, B. (1998). Transition of brain activation from frontal to parietal areas in visuomotor sequence learning. *Journal of Neuroscience, 18*(5), 1827–1840.

Scarr, S., & Weinberg, R. (1986). The early childhood enterprise: Care and education of the young. *American Psychologist, 41*, 1140–1146.

Schlaggar, B. L., Brown, T. T., Lugar, H. M., Visscher, K. M., Miezin, F. M., & Petersen, S. E. (2002). Functional neuroanatomical differences between adults and school-age children in the processing of single words. *Science, 296*, 1476–1479.

Schlaggar, B. L., & McCandliss, B. D. (2007). Development of neural systems for reading. *Annual Review of Neuroscience, 30*, 475–503.

Schunk, D. H. (1999). Social-self interaction and achievement behavior. *Educational Psychologist, 34*(4), 219–227.

Schweinhart, L. J., Montie, J., Xiang, Z., Barnett, W. S., Belfield, C. R., & Nores, M. (2005). *Lifetime effects: The HighScope Perry Preschool Study through age 4* (Monographs of the HighScope Educational Research Foundation, 14). Ypsilanti, MI: HighScope Press.

Seamans, J. K., Floresco, S. B., & Phillips, A. G. (1998).

D1 receptor modulation of hippocampal–prefrontal cortical circuits integrating spatial memory with executive functions in the rat. *Journal of Neuroscience, 18*(4), 1613–1621.

Sesma, H. W., Mahone, E. M., Levine, T., Eason, S. H., & Cutting, L. E. (2009). The contribution of executive skills to reading comprehension. *Child Neuropsychology, 15*(3), 232–246.

Shonkoff, J. P., Boyce, W. T., & McEwen, B. S. (2009). Neuroscience, molecular biology, and the childhood roots of health disparities: Building a new framework for health promotion and disease prevention. *Journal of the American Medical Association, 301*(21), 2252–2259.

Sroufe, L. A. (1996). *Emotional development: The organization of emotional life in the early years*. New York: Cambridge University Press.

Swanson, H. L., & Berninger, V. W. (1995). The role of working memory in skilled and less skilled readers' comprehension. *Intelligence, 21*, 83–108.

Swanson, H. L., & Jerman, O. (2007). The influence of working memory on reading growth in subgroups of children with reading disabilities. *Journal of Experimental Child Psychology, 96*(4), 249–283.

Swanson, H. L., Jerman, O., & Zheng, X. (2009). Math disabilities and reading disabilities: Can they be separated? *Journal of Psychoeducational Assessment, 27*, 175–196.

Swanson, H. L., & Sáez, L. (2003). Memory difficulties in children and adults with learning disabilities. In H. L. Swanson, K. R. Harris, & S. Graham (Eds.), *Handbook of learning disabilities* (pp. 182–198). New York: Guilford Press.

Trentacosta, C. J., & Izard, C. E. (2007). Kindergarten children's emotion competence as a predictor of their academic competence in first grade. *Emotion, 7*(1), 77–88.

van den Boom, D. C. (1994). The influence of temperament and mothering on attachment and exploration: An experimental manipulation of sensitive responsiveness among lower-class mothers with irritable infants. *Child Development, 65*(5), 1457–1477.

Vijayraghavan, S., Wang, M., Birnbaum, S. G., Williams, G. V., & Arnsten, A. F. (2007). Inverted-U dopamine D1 receptor actions on prefrontal neurons engaged in working memory. *Nature Neuroscience, 10*(3), 376–384.

Weaver, I. C., Diorio, J., Seckl, J. R., Szyf, M., & Meaney, M. J. (2004). Early environmental regulation of hippocampal glucocorticoid receptor gene expression: Characterization of intracellular mediators and potential genomic target sites. *Annals of the New York Academy of Sciences, 1024*, 182–212.

Welsh, J., Nix, R., Blair, C., Bierman, K., & Nelson, K. (2010). The development of cognitive skills and gains in academic school readiness for children from low-income families. *Journal of Educational Psychology, 102*(1), 43–53.

Wendelken, C., Nakhabenko, D., Donohue, S. E., Carter, C. S., & Bunge, S. A. (2008). "Brain is to thought as stomach is to ?": Investigating the role of rostrolateral prefrontal cortex in relational reasoning. *Journal of Cognitive Neuroscience, 20*(4), 682–693.

Yerkes, R. M., & Dodson, J. D. (1908). The relation of strength of stimulus to rapidity of habit-formation. *Journal of Comparative Neurology and Psychology, 18*, 459–482.

Zelazo, P. D. (2006). The dimensional change card sort (DCCS): A method of assessing executive function in children. *Nature Protocols, 1*(1), 297–301.

Zigler, E. (1969). Developmental versus differences theories of mental: Retardation and the problem of motivation. *American Journal on Mental Deficiency, 73*, 536–556.

3

Variability in Language Development: Relation to Socioeconomic Status and Environmental Input

MARINA VASILYEVA
HEIDI WATERFALL

The development of oral language and the acquisition of literacy skills are linked together by strong bidirectional ties. On the one hand, reading provides an excellent resource for language enrichment. Once acquired, literacy skills can serve as instrumental tools for the learning of new words and new ways of organizing diverse sentence structures to convey meaning in a variety of contexts (Echols, West, Stanovich, & Zehr, 1996). On the other hand, the ability to read itself depends in large part on the language skills of a young reader. A considerable body of research has documented the role of various aspects of oral language in the emerging literacy (Beron & Farkas, 2004; Scarborough, 1989; Sénéchal, Ouellette, & Rodney, 2006; Snow, 1983; Whitehurst & Lonigan, 1998). Children who have large vocabularies and who can map complex sentence structures onto corresponding meanings have a clear advantage in reading compared to those with poorer language proficiency.

By the time children start acquiring literacy skills, large individual differences already exist in the level of their language mastery (e.g., Hart & Risley, 1992; Hoff, 2003; Huttenlocher, Vasilyeva, Cymerman, & Levine, 2002; Vasilyeva, Waterfall, & Huttenlocher, 2008). In order to develop effective strategies for improving children's readiness for literacy instruction, it is critical to understand the nature of variability in their early language development and to identify malleable factors associated with the growth of language skills.

Sources of Variability in Language Skills

Much of the earlier work on language development has focused on commonalities observed across children rather than on individual differences (Braine, 1976; Brown, 1973; Chomsky, 1965; De Villiers & De Villiers, 1978). Indeed, language acquisition in a typical course of development reveals common patterns in vocabulary growth, order of emergence of major sentence structures, and types of errors characteristic of young children's speech. Yet despite these commonalities in the overall patterns, later empirical investigations have demonstrated substantial variability among children in language skills achieved at any given age (Bates, Bretherton, & Snyder, 1988; Farkas & Beron, 2004; Fenson et al., 1994; Hart & Risley, 1995; Hoff, 2003; Jackson & Roberts, 2001). This variability is salient at a group level, with children from lower socioeconomic backgrounds at a disadvantage, but it is also prominent at an individual level within particular socioeconomic groups.

Searching for the sources of variability in the growth of language skills, investigators have considered both biological and environmental explanations. Although all language researchers acknowledge that environmental input plays a role in language development, there is considerable disagreement concerning its centrality. This is especially true for the domain of *syntax*—the aspect of language concerned with organizing individual words into phrases and sentences. It has been suggested that the speech input children receive may function as a trigger, allowing them to set the syntactic parameters of their language within a constrained set of possibilities (Baker, 2001; Chomsky, 1981; Hyams, 1994; Lidz & Gleitman, 2004). In this view, syntactic development is based largely on innate structures, and differences among individuals are attributed to variations in their genetic predispositions rather than in their language environments (Pinker, 1994; Pinker & Bloom, 1990). Behavioral genetic studies have provided empirical support for these claims, implicating genetic factors in the level of language skill individuals achieve (Dale, Dionne, Eley, & Plomin, 2003; Oliver & Plomin, 2007; Stromswold, 2001).

While acknowledging these findings, in this chapter we turn our attention to the body of literature that has examined children's linguistic environment as a potential source of variability in their language skills. In so doing, we focus on malleable rather than relatively fixed factors associated with language development. Clearly, the fact that biological factors explain a portion of variability in language skills does not exclude the possibility that environmental factors also play a role in explaining individual differences. The evidence we review in this chapter suggests that the amount and composition of the input are in fact related to the level of language skills individual children achieve. We begin by examining the evidence of the relation between children's language mastery and the socioeconomic status (SES) of their family. We then address the role of environmental input in the development of language skills. In considering the significance of input, we discuss vocabulary and, especially, syntactic skills, which for a long time have been at the center of the debate about the role of environmental factors in language development.

SES-Related Differences in Language Development

There is a growing body of research indicating that parents from different SES groups provide their children with very different linguistic experience. Specifically, parents with a higher level of education have more diverse vocabularies, and their sentences tend to be longer and more complex than those of parents with a lower level of education (Hammer & Weiss, 1999; Hoff, 2003; Hoff-Ginsberg, 1991; Huttenlocher, Vasilyeva, Waterfall, Vevea, & Hedges, 2007). Parents from middle-SES backgrounds include more language-teaching speech during play with children than do low-SES parents (Hammer & Weiss, 1999). Furthermore, the amount of spontaneous parental speech addressed to children and the amount of book reading show striking differences across SES groups (Fletcher & Reese, 2005; Hart & Risley, 1995; Heath, 1990). If the amount and type of language to which children are exposed affect their language development, one would expect to see differences in children's skills corresponding to SES-related differences in their linguistic input.

Examining Variability in Children's Vocabulary and Syntax

STUDIES OF SES DIFFERENCES IN VOCABULARY

Researchers have accumulated a substantial body of evidence documenting SES-related differences in children's vocabulary knowledge (Arriaga, Fenson, Cronan, & Pethick, 1998; Dollaghan et al., 1999; Hart & Risley, 1995; Hoff-Ginsberg, 1998; Huttenlocher, Haight, Bryk, Seltzer, & Lyons, 1991; Oller & Eilers, 2002; Pan, Rowe, Singer, & Snow, 2005). These differences concern both *receptive vocabulary*, which refers to children's ability to recognize and understand word meanings, and *productive vocabulary*, which refers to children's ability to use words appropriately in different contexts. A detailed examination of the trajectory of vocabulary knowledge from toddler age through middle school has revealed that differences among children as a function of their socioeconomic background persist throughout childhood (Farkas & Beron, 2004).

Similar to prior investigations (e.g., Hart & Risley, 1995), the study by Farkas and Beron (2004) showed that an SES gap is apparent even at the earliest stages of word learning. Furthermore, during preschool years, children from higher-SES families show a greater rate of vocabulary growth, which results in a further increase of the initial SES gap. Starting at kindergarten age, SES differences in vocabulary, while remaining large, become relatively stable; that is, during school years, the rate of vocabulary growth is similar across SES groups, which suggests a possible equalizing effect of school experience on language development in children from different family backgrounds. Yet despite similar growth rates, low-SES students who start school at a disadvantage continue to lag behind their higher-SES counterparts.

It should be noted that the magnitude of reported SES differences in children's vocabulary at a given age varies substantially across studies. This is most likely due to the difference in the SES range of participants (Hoff, 2006). Not surprisingly, studies that include participants with similar socioeconomic characteristics tend to report that SES effects are quite small. For example, Fenson and colleagues (1994) obtained data on the growth of toddlers' vocabulary from a middle-class sample with a restricted range of variability in parental income and education. In this study, SES accounted for only about 1% of the variance in children's vocabularies. In those studies that include a broader range of socioeconomic backgrounds, SES has been shown to play a major role in predicting differences among children. For example, the investigation by Hart and Risley (1995), which involved families ranging from low-SES (public assistance) to high-SES (professionals), showed that SES accounted for more than one-third of variance in children's vocabulary.

STUDIES OF SES DIFFERENCES IN SYNTAX

The question of whether there are systematic differences in the growth of children's language skills associated with SES appears to be particularly relevant to our understanding of the nature of syntax acquisition. One of the main arguments for the existence of common, innate mechanisms of syntactic development was based on early studies demonstrating an apparent lack of a significant variability in the mastery of syntax in children from different families (e.g., Brown, 1973; Chomsky, 1981). Yet it has been pointed out that the lack of variability reported in earlier investigations may be due, in part, to the use of small samples of participants recruited from relatively homogeneous socioeconomic backgrounds. Thus, it is important to examine whether children who come from diverse SES groups and who most likely receive very different exposure to language, demonstrate significant differences in their syntactic skills.

The evidence concerning a potential association between children's SES and their syntactic skills is more complex than that concerning vocabulary skills. Several studies have reported a significant link between SES and syntactic mastery (Dollaghan et al., 1999; Huttenlocher et al., 2002; Snow, 1999). In particular, researchers have documented that high-SES children have, on average, greater MLU (mean length of utterance) than their low-SES peers (Arriaga et al., 1998; Snow, 1999). Generally, the length of utterance can be increased by the use of optional syntactic elements, such as adjectives and adverbs (e.g., "Your *red* dress is *really* pretty"), and by combining simple clauses into more complex, multiclause sentences (e.g., "It's raining but the sun is out").

Thus, findings of MLU differences across SES groups indicate that high-SES children produce more complex syntactic structures than low-SES children of the same age. Studies that have directly examined children's production and comprehension of complex sentences confirm these findings (e.g., Huttenlocher et al., 2002). They show that, while children across SES groups eventually produce a variety of syntactic structures, high-SES children tend to use complex sentences more frequently than their low-SES peers. Furthermore, high-SES children perform significantly better on the tests assessing the understanding of complex sentences.

In contrast to the studies implicating SES as a significant factor related to syntactic skill, several studies did not find such a link (e.g., Hoff & Tian, 2005; Jackson & Roberts, 2001; Noble, Norman, & Farah, 2005). One possible reason for not detecting an association with SES is a limited amount of variability in socioeconomic backgrounds of participants. As indicated earlier, studies of vocabulary growth that involved a limited range of SES groups also tended to find only a weak relation between SES and children's skills. Similarly, constraining the socioeconomic characteristics of the sample makes it difficult to find differences in syntactic skills associated with SES. For example, Jackson and Roberts (2001) found no relationship between the number of complex syntax forms children produced and maternal education in a study that involved participants from primarily low-SES groups. Hoff-Ginsberg (1998) reported no difference in MLU associated with SES in a study that involved middle-SES and high-SES families.

In examining other possible explanations, we have recently suggested that the contrasting SES findings on syntax may have to do with the nature of syntactic measures examined (Vasilyeva et al., 2008). Consider, for example, the findings of a large-scale study by Feldman and colleagues (2000), in which parent-reported data on children's language were collected using MacArthur Communicative Development Inventories. In this study, a different pattern of SES-related variability was observed for the measures of basic simple syntax and complex syntactic structures. Compared to high-SES parents, low-SES parents tended to report higher levels of mastery for children's understanding of simple syntactic forms but lower levels of mastery for more complex syntactic forms.

Because of the potentially subjective nature of parental reports, such discrepancies have been often discussed in the context of differential bias that parents from low- and high-SES groups may have had in filling out the questionnaires (Feldman et al., 2000; Fenson et al., 2000). However, it is also possible that basic and complex syntactic skills indeed show a different relation to SES. In the work we discuss below, we address this possibility by looking directly at children's spontaneous speech.

Different Patterns of SES Findings for Basic and Complex Syntax

In a recent study (Vasilyeva et al., 2008), we have examined longitudinal changes in syntactic characteristics of children's speech between ages 14 and 42 months in participants from diverse socioeconomic backgrounds. The extensive time span of the study allowed us to examine syntactic skills systematically, starting at the age when children begin to combine words into simple sentences, and continuing through the emergence of complex sentences. One group of measures employed in this study tapped the early mastery of basic syntactic rules, namely, the accuracy of word orders corresponding to the three main types of simple English sentences (questions, declaratives, and imperatives) and the use of obligatory syntactic elements. For example, if a child produced a sentence that lacked one of the required verb arguments (e.g., "I find" or "Give it"), then this sentence was coded as syntactically incomplete. The other group of measures concerned the mastery of complex sentences (i.e., sentences that include more than one clause). English, as well as most other languages, offers a variety of ways in which simple sentences can be combined into complex sentences, including *coordination* (e.g., "We went to the store and then we came home") and *complementation* ("I think I want a cookie now"). We measured the diversity and frequency of use of complex sentences in children's speech.

Our results showed a striking similarity among children from different SES groups on the measures of basic syntax. The order of emergence and the relative frequency of usage for the basic sentence structures corresponding to declaratives, imperatives, and questions were virtually identical across SES groups. There was no systematic variability in the age at which children from different SES backgrounds started producing simple sentences, nor were there SES differences at any given age in the proportion of simple sentences that contained all required arguments of the verb and followed the correct word order. In summary, the mastery of the obligatory aspects of language that are essential for achieving native language speaker proficiency appears to be very similar across SES groups.

It is possible, then, that the acquisition of these aspects of language relies on common mechanisms that are available to all typically developing individuals. Such mechanisms could be biological, as originally suggested, but they also could be environmental; that is, the mastery of obligatory elements of syntax may rely on the universal environmental supports available across a wide range of socioeconomic contexts. After all, basic aspects of simple sentences appear very frequently in everyday conversations: Simple sentences and phrases make up the majority of caregiver speech (Huttenlocher et al., 2007). Because of the ubiquity of basic syntactic structures, the amount of verbal input provided in lower-SES environments may be sufficient for acquisition, and variations beyond that amount may not confer any additional advantages.

The picture emerging from the analysis of complex syntactic structures calls for a very different explanation of the acquisition process. In contrast to the findings with simple sentence production, the acquisition of complex sentences revealed significant differences across SES groups. These differences appeared at the earliest stages of complex sentence production, when most of the children in our sample using such sentences were from high-SES groups. Not only did these children begin to produce complex sentences earlier but they also had a significantly higher frequency and diversity of such sentences throughout the period of the study. Furthermore, the shape of the growth trajectories suggests that children from different SES groups may be moving further apart in frequency and diversity of complex sentences as they grow older (Vasilyeva et al., 2008). In the next section, we examine to what extent the observed differences in children's early skills and subsequent growth can be explained by the differences in their linguistic experiences.

Relation between Child Language Development and Caregiver Input

The evidence from prior research, as well as recent findings from our own studies, indicates that many aspects of children's language, including vocabulary and complex syntax, consistently show SES-related variability. Establishing the existence of such variability is an important step toward a better understanding of the nature of individual differences. Findings that indicate SES-related differences in language exposure correspond to SES-related differences in children's own skills are consistent with the view that language input may play an instrumental role in language development. Yet these findings do not eliminate an alter-

native interpretation positing that parents and children from a particular SES group may have similar ability levels, and it is the ability rather than exposure to language that drives the association between SES and language performance. In other words, the studies that examine SES-related variability in language skills provide only indirect evidence pointing to a possibility that differences in children's experience may cause differences in their language development. In order to take the next step in exploring this possibility, it is important to study directly the relation between the language input individual children receive from their caregivers and the level of language skill they achieve.

Investigating Effects of Experience on Language Development: Findings and Challenges

STUDIES OF PARENTAL INPUT

Among the studies examining the role of input in children's language, a large body of research has focused on home environment and parental input. The findings indicate that the overall amount of speech parents provide at home predicts language skills of their children (Goodman, Dale, & Li, 2008; Hart & Risley, 1995; Huttenlocher et al., 1991). Furthermore, certain parenting practices, such as reading to children and playing games that involve intensive verbal interactions, have been directly linked to the development of early language skills, especially to the growth of children's vocabulary (Frijters, Barron, & Brunello, 2000; Payne, Whitehurst, & Angell, 1994; Raikes et al., 2006).

Investigators have also shown that children's language skills are specifically related to many linguistic characteristics of parents' speech, including the sophistication of parental vocabulary (Weizman & Snow, 2001), length and complexity of parents' utterances (Hoff, 2003; Hoff-Ginsberg, 1991; Huttenlocher et al., 2002), and the frequency of specific grammatical constructions (Naigles & Hoff-Ginsberg, 1998; Newport, Gleitman, & Gleitman, 1977). This work has provided important insights into the nature of variability in children's language and its relation to the environment. However, since correlations between parents and their children may reflect genetic commonalities, as well as environmental input effects, further work, especially with biologically unrelated input providers, is needed to tease apart biological and environmental factors.

STUDIES OF TEACHER INPUT

Teachers constitute an important source of language input to school-age children, as well as preschoolers attending day care and preschool programs. A number of research studies have explored the role of teacher input in children's language growth. For example, a large-scale National Institute of Child Health and Human Development (NICHD) investigation, which examined multiple indicators of child-care quality in relation to child development, revealed that the amount of teacher speech directed at young children predicts their early vocabulary skills, as well as later performance on standardized language tests (NICHD Early Child Care Research Network, 2000, 2002). Furthermore, the amount of verbal interactions between teachers and students largely accounted for the effects of broad indicators of child-care quality on language development.

In addition to studies looking at the amount of verbal interaction between teachers and their students, several studies examined more global indicators of classroom environment in relation to children's language skills (Barnett, Young, & Schweinhart, 1998; Peisner-Feinberg et al., 2001; Pianta, La Paro, Payne, Cox, & Bradley, 2002). For example, Peisner-Feinberg and colleagues (2001) reported that a composite measure of preschool quality predicted children's receptive vocabulary in kindergarten. The indicators of child-care quality used in this study included measures of teacher sensitivity and responsiveness. These measures may reflect the amount and richness of verbal interactions with students, although the researchers did not look directly at the relation between global measures of child-care quality and specific features of linguistic input provided by teachers.

In summary, accumulating evidence from large-scale investigations of classroom effects suggests that variability in children's language growth is related to variability in their classroom experiences (NICHD Early Child Care Research Network, 2000; Peisner-Feinberg et al., 2001; Pianta et al., 2002). It should be noted, though, that these

investigations, while providing information about the general role of educational context in child development, are somewhat limited in their ability to identify specific features of classroom environment that are related to language growth. Due to the large scale of the investigations, the measures of teacher input employed in these studies are generally very broad and not sufficiently specific. For example, in the NICHD Early Child Care Research Network (2000) study, the key indicator of linguistic input was the frequency of language stimulation, which encompassed a variety of caregiver behaviors, such as asking questions, providing contingent responses to children's vocalizations, non-negative talk, and so forth. Perhaps, partly due to the crudeness of the language input measure, the effect size reported in this study was quite small. A more focused investigation of the specific features of teachers' verbal behavior may reveal a stronger relation between input and language growth.

Indeed, in-depth examinations of the nature of teacher–student interactions have provided more direct and robust evidence of a positive association between certain characteristics of teachers' input and the language skills of their students (Connor, Morrison, & Slominski, 2006; Dickinson & Smith, 1994; Dickinson & Tabors, 2001; Girolametto & Weitzman, 2002; Wasik, Bond, & Hindman, 2006). In particular, it has been shown that language skills of preschool and school-age children are linked to the teachers' use of specific strategies during classroom activities. For example, the use of cognitively challenging analytic talk by teachers during book reading predicts better vocabulary and story comprehension scores in kindergarten students (Dickinson & Smith, 1994). Similarly, teachers' use of interaction-promoting and language-modeling strategies during play activities predicts the overall amount of speech and vocabulary level in preschoolers (Girolametto & Weitzman, 2002). Studies examining teachers' interactions with older students (e.g., Elley, 1989) also report that involving children in word-related discussions and providing them with repeated exposure to unfamiliar words in different contexts facilitate students' acquisition of low-frequency vocabulary.

Note that most of the reviewed studies exploring a potential impact of classroom experience on language development have focused on children's vocabulary skills. Similarly, much of the intervention work with school-age children has involved programs and curricular materials designed to improve children's vocabulary (e.g., Hargrave & Sénéchal, 2000; Lonigan & Whitehurst, 1998; Stahl & Fairbanks, 1986). Much less work has explored parallel issues with respect to syntactic skills. In particular, there has been a lack of systematic research on how syntactic skills can be fostered in educational settings. In our own program of research presented below, we address the questions of whether and how the development of children's syntactic skills is related to the syntactic features of the speech of their caregivers.

The Role of Caregiver Speech in the Growth of Children's Syntax

THE SIGNIFICANCE OF UNDERSTANDING
THE ROLE OF ENVIRONMENT
IN SYNTACTIC DEVELOPMENT

The issues related to understanding the extent of malleability of syntactic skills and identifying conditions conducive to their development are relevant to educational practice. As noted earlier, while all typically developing children acquire basic syntax early in life, the acquisition of complex syntax has a more prolonged developmental course (Vasilyeva et al., 2008). The mastery of complex syntax varies systematically across language environments. Many children, especially from low-SES backgrounds, show incomplete mastery of complex syntactic structures well into their school years (e.g., Loban, 1976; Scott, 1984). This may present a serious obstacle to their academic achievement. For example, when reading a textbook or listening to the teacher's explanation, a child with relatively low-level mastery of syntax must focus additional cognitive resources on processing and understanding complex sentence structures.

Low skills levels may prevent children from not only acquiring new knowledge but also revealing their existing knowledge during assessments. Achievement tests in different subject areas often involve questions that are complex in form, and children must be able to decipher the form to determine the essence of the question. Consider, for example, a question from a second-grade math test: "Tommy had five marbles, two of which were taken by Harry. How many marbles does Tommy have left?" Children who have not fully mastered passive or complex sentence forms may fail (even if they have considerable understanding of number), especially if the test is timed and they have to answer each question quickly. The importance of understanding complex syntax in speech, reading, and writing increases over the school years as subject matter becomes more sophisticated. In summary, a lack of skill with complex syntax may prevent accurate and efficient online processing of oral and written texts in all subject areas, including social studies, the sciences, and mathematics. Thus, it is critical to understand what factors in children's environment may be related to their mastery of complex syntax and how this mastery can be further improved in educational settings.

EXPLORING THE ROLE OF INPUT: A CLOSER LOOK
AT PARENTAL SPEECH

In a series of studies, we, along with our colleagues, have examined children's comprehension and production of multiclause sentences in relation to parental speech. The first study (Huttenlocher et al., 2002) involved 4- to 5-year-old children and their mothers. Each mother–child dyad was videotaped at home during a single 90-minute visit. On the basis of the analysis of naturally occurring interactions, we calculated the percentage of complex sentences (i.e., sentences containing more than one verb) in mothers' and children's speech. The children were also given a comprehension test that targeted a variety of complex syntactic constructions. The results were parallel for production and comprehension measures. Specifically, both the percentage of complex sentences children produced and their comprehension scores were significantly linearly related to the proportion of complex sentences in parents' speech.

This study has provided the first piece of evidence of a close relation between parents' and children's complex syntax. Yet it was clear to us that the design of the study, similar to other studies of parental input, limited our ability to interpret this relation as a causal one; that is, the observed correlations might be driven by variations in input, language ability, or both. Furthermore, correlations between caregivers and children based on observations at a single time point might reflect temporary factors, such as shared topics of conversation during a single session.

In a subsequent investigation of parent–child interactions, we have taken several steps to address some of the difficulties arising in earlier correlational studies. Rather than examining parental input at a single time point, the study examined parent and child speech longitudinally, over an extended period of time (Huttenlocher, Waterfall, Vasilyeva, Vevea, & Hedges, in press). The families were visited and videotaped during spontaneous interactions at home every 4 months between children's ages of 14 and 46 months. A key focus of this study was the production of complex sentences by the speakers.

Our previous work has shown that children vary significantly in the diversity of complex syntactic constructions they produce (Vasilyeva et al., 2008). While many young children use primarily two types of complex sentences, referred to as *object complements* (e.g., "He made me do this") and *coordinate sentences* ("Let's go outside and play in the sandbox"), some produce a much greater diversity of complex sentences, using different kinds of structural relations between clauses (e.g., "The one I want is over there"; "I like the picture that we made for Daddy"; "Before we get outside, we have to put on our coats"). We examined the diversity of complex sentence structures used by parents and their children at different ages.

To explore enduring relations between parents' and children's speech, we used a lagged regression analysis, in which the speech of parents and children was examined at different time points (4 months apart). First, we examined whether characteristics of parent speech at an earlier time point predicted characteristics of child speech at a later time point, then we examined the reversed relation between child speech at an earlier time and caregiver speech at a later time. The findings indicated a unidirectional relation between the syntactic diversity of parent and child speech; that is, over the period of the longitudinal study, parent speech at an earlier time was a significant predictor of child speech at later time points; yet child speech at an earlier time did not predict later parent

speech. Note that if the longitudinal relation between parent and child speech were bidirectional, it could reflect either biological similarity or reciprocal influences between the characteristics of their speech, or both. However, a unidirectional relation from the parent to the child strongly suggests that parent input is a source of growth for children's acquisition of complex sentences.

EXPLORING THE ROLE OF INPUT: NATURALISTIC OBSERVATIONS OF TEACHER SPEECH

In addition to using methodological tools that allowed us to explore the direction of causal flow in the relation between parents and children, we investigated the sources of variability in children's language by looking at nonbiological input providers. In a series of studies in collaboration with our colleagues from the University of Chicago and Boston College, we examined the role of specific characteristics of teacher speech in language growth of their students (Bowers & Vasilyeva, in press; Huttenlocher et al., 2002). One of these investigations (Huttenlocher et al., 2002) involved examining the growth of complex syntactic skills in preschoolers. The children were given a comprehension test that included a diverse sampling of complex sentences; they were tested in the beginning and at the end of the school year to determine the change in their comprehension of complex syntax over an academic year. The teachers were videotaped during interactions with their students in the middle of the school year; their recorded speech was transcribed to calculate both the amount of input provided during an observation session and the complexity of speech (percentage of complex sentences out of all utterances).

Unlike investigations of parental input, there is neither a biological relation between the teacher and the students nor, at the beginning of the school year, a history of prior input from the teacher. This provides us with a basis for arguing that a potential relation between caregiver speech and children's growth may be indicative of input effects. Yet one could argue that higher-ability parents may tend to send their children to classrooms with higher-ability teachers, or teachers may provide better input to children who come to school with a higher language ability level. To address this possibility, we examined whether children's skills at the beginning of the school year predicted teachers' speech characteristics assessed in the middle of the year. Our results showed that children's initial skills levels were uncorrelated with teacher speech characteristics.

At the same time, the growth of children's syntactic skills over the school year was significantly related to teacher measures. In particular, the frequency of teacher use of various complex sentences in interactions with children was the best predictor of children's growth on the syntactic comprehension test. When the complexity of teacher speech was entered into a regression equation predicting students' growth, other characteristics of classroom environment, such as the overall amount of speech addressed to students, general quality of teaching, availability of books in the classroom, were rendered nonsignificant. This pattern of findings strongly suggests that variations in the composition of language input per se affect syntactic growth over a school year.

Interestingly, the pattern of findings was quite different with respect to children's SES: We found that children's performance on a syntax comprehension test at the beginning of the school year was highly correlated with their SES. Yet the growth of children's syntactic comprehension over the school year was not related to SES. Thus, the type of input provided by the teacher, rather than the student's SES background, predicted improvements in the mastery of complex syntactic devices over a school year in preschool children.

EXPLORING THE ROLE OF INPUT:
EXPERIMENTAL RESEARCH

Studies of spontaneous interactions between children and their caregivers provide important insights concerning the extent to which input is implicated in language development. A limitation, however, is that this approach does not allow for the systematic manipulation of input variables. Consequently, we carried out a series of experiments that allowed us to obtain even stronger evidence of the causal relation between input and child's syntax. In our laboratory studies, we systematically manipulated the characteristics of speech the child heard from the experimenter to determine how this manipulation might affect the child's own language production (Huttenlocher, Vasilyeva, & Shimpi, 2004; Shimpi, Gámez, Huttenlocher, & Vasilyeva, 2007; Vasilyeva et al., 2010).

In these studies, we examined whether presenting children with a particular syntactic form increases the likelihood that they would subsequently produce that form themselves. Children's ages varied between 3 and 6 years. To determine whether the experimenter's input affected children's sentence production, we used a game-like procedure in which experimenter and child took turns describing different pictures. The pictures presented simple events that could be described in alternative ways. For example, the scenes depicting transitive actions could be described using either the active voice (e.g., "The ball broke the window") or the passive voice (e.g., "The window was broken by the ball"). After the experimenter described a picture (using an active or a passive sentence, depending on the experimental condition), children were asked to describe a different picture.

The results indicated that children were more likely to produce the target structure (e.g., the passive) when the experimenter had previously used that form. Furthermore, the effect persisted even when children's productions did not immediately follow the input; that is, when children were given a block of 10 pictures to describe, their use of the target structure still varied, reflecting the input provided earlier by the experimenter. The youngest children (3-year-olds) increased their production of target structures only when they were first asked to repeat the experimenter's sentence before describing a subsequent picture, which suggests that very young children benefit either from actively producing the form themselves or from hearing more exposures. The findings, especially those obtained with younger participants, are particularly interesting given the fact that English-speaking children typically do not produce full passive sentences in spontaneous speech until age 4 or 5 years (Harris & Flora, 1982). We have shown that the use of this infrequent form can be increased by exposure to relevant input.

The results of our experimental studies suggest a possibility that children's mastery of syntactic forms may be improved through short interventions. To test this possibility in a classroom context, we used an intervention design aimed at increasing children's mastery of the passive voice, a challenging syntactic form that is not common in verbal exchanges between children and their caregivers (Vasilyeva, Huttenlocher, & Waterfall, 2006). Although they occur infrequently in everyday speech, passives are more common in scientific texts; they appear in textbooks, as well as in questions included in the assessment batteries. Children should be able to process this form quickly and efficiently so that they can focus cognitive resources on understanding the relevant concept rather than deciphering the form of a sentence. Yet the passive voice presents difficulties to children in elementary school, as evidenced by low comprehension scores on test items that include passives (Huttenlocher & Levine, 1990). Thus, we set out to determine whether children's skills levels with the passive form could be increased prior to kindergarten.

We presented a group of preschool students with stories containing a very high proportion of passives. A control group of preschoolers was presented with similar stories in which the passive versions of sentences were replaced with active versions. All stories involved simple plots portraying children or animal characters engaged in various adventures. Some of the sentences in the stories were illustrated. Children heard two stories a day over a period of 2 weeks, and their mastery of passives was tested before and after the intervention. To test children's production of passives, we used a task in which they were asked to describe a picture without any experimenter input (e.g., "What's happening here?"). To test children's comprehension of passives, we used a task in which the experimenter presented two pictures, read a passive sentence, and asked the children to select the picture that corresponded to the sentence (e.g., "Point to the picture I tell you about: The bird was carried by the mouse").

Our results showed significant differences between children who participated in the passive story condition and those in the active story condition. The children who received a concentrated exposure to passives showed better results on both production and comprehension tasks. In terms of pro-

duction, they were able to produce more sentences containing the passive, and they made fewer structural errors in their passives. In terms of comprehension, the average performance of the control group was not statistically different from chance, whereas the performance of the intervention group was significantly above chance. Children were tested at different time intervals following the intervention. There was no decrease in the performance on either task over the testing period, suggesting that the effect of temporarily increasing children's exposure to a particular form may have lasting consequences for learning. These results clearly indicate that syntactic skills of preschoolers can be improved through classroom intervention.

Conclusions and Future Directions

The evidence accumulated over the past decades of educational and psychological research indicates that individual variability in children's language skills is driven in part by the variability present in their linguistic environments. Our research in collaboration with our colleagues at the University of Chicago and Boston College has contributed to this body of literature by increasing the understanding of malleable factors associated with the development of syntactic skills. While prior work on the relation between input and the mastery of syntax has focused primarily on simple correlations between parents and their children, we have utilized designs that increase the validity of causal inferences.

In exploring a potential role of parental input, we have used longitudinal designs examining a predictive relation between parental input and subsequent growth of syntactic skills in children. The statistical treatment of the longitudinal data, using reverse-lag analysis, allowed us to determine that the relation between parent speech at an earlier time point and child's syntax at a later time point is stronger than the relation between the child's earlier syntax and the parent's later speech. These findings strongly suggest that caregiver speech serves as a source of later growth of child syntax. In addition to longitudinal studies of parent–child interactions, we have examined language input from biologically unrelated caregivers. The design of these studies has minimized the possibility that the observed relation is due to biological factors, thus indicating that variation in language input impacts language growth.

Finally, our experimental work and, in particular, intervention research provide the strongest evidence of the sensitivity of syntactic development to environmental input. To be sure, whereas environmental variability explains only part of the variance in children's skills, another part of the variance can be accounted for by biological predispositions. Nevertheless, the studies establishing a connection between children's language development and the specific characteristics of their experience have important educational implications. Our findings suggest the possibility of incorporating material designed to increase children's syntactic mastery into early education programs. The intervention can be done in a simple, naturalistic manner by presenting children with stories or scenarios that provide multiple examples of syntactic forms that generally present difficulties for young children.

Currently, there is a large body of work exploring and documenting factors associated with vocabulary learning in classroom settings (Connor et al., 2006; Dickinson & Smith, 1994; Dickinson & Tabors, 2001; Wasik et al., 2006). Because the mastery of complex syntax presents another challenging area for children, particularly, for students from lower socioeconomic backgrounds, it is essential to get a deeper understanding of classroom-level factors associated with better learning of complex syntax forms. While our findings indicate a possibility of improving children's syntactic skills through classroom interventions, future research may do well to explore the conditions that increase the effectiveness of such interventions.

Further investigations are needed to determine whether and how different parameters of input affect the outcomes. Potential aspects of input to consider include the number (or proportion) of target forms presented to children during teaching sessions, the diversity of those forms, and the length of intervention to be conducted. In addition, the nature of the presentation of target syntactic forms can be manipulated to examine the role of pictorial stimuli in facilitating the mapping of the form onto meaning and to compare the effectiveness of embedding target forms in the verbal exchanges between caregivers and children (e.g., during mealtime) versus story reading. Finally, future studies will have to explore the long-term effects of classroom-level interventions on later language growth and, more generally, on academic achievement in later school years.

References

Arriaga, R. I., Fenson, L., Cronan, T., & Pethick, S. J. (1998). Scores on the MacArthur Communicative Developmental Inventory of children from low- and middle-income families. *Applied Psycholinguistics, 19*(2), 209–223.

Baker, M. (2001). *The atoms of language.* New York: Basic Books.

Barnett, W. S., Young, J. W., & Schweinhart, L. J. (1998). How preschool education influences long-term cognitive development and school success. In W. S. Barnett & S. S. Boocock (Eds.), *Early care and education for children in poverty: Promises, programs, and long-term results* (pp. 167–184). Albany: State University of New York Press.

Bates, E., Bretherton, I., & Snyder, L. (1988). *From first words to grammar: Individual differences and dissociable mechanisms.* Cambridge, UK: Cambridge University Press.

Beron, K. J., & Farkas, G. (2004). Oral language and reading success: A structural equation modeling approach. *Structural Equation Modeling, 11*(1), 110–131.

Bowers, E., & Vasilyeva, M. (in press). The relation between teacher input and language growth of preschoolers. *Applied Psycholinguistics.*

Braine, M. D. S. (1976). Children's first word combinations. *Monographs of the Society for Research in Child Development, 41*(1), 1–104.

Brown, R. (1973). *A first language: The early stages.* Cambridge, MA: Harvard University Press.

Chomsky, N. (1965). *Aspects of the theory of syntax.* Cambridge, MA: MIT Press.

Chomsky, N. (1981). *Lectures on government and binding.* Dordrecht: Foris.

Connor, C. M., Morrison, F. J., & Slominski, L. (2006). Preschool instruction and children's emergent literacy growth. *Journal of Educational Psychology, 98*(4), 665–689.

Dale, P. S., Dionne, G., Eley, T. C., & Plomin, R. (2003). Lexical and grammatical development: A behavioral genetic perspective. *Journal of Child Language, 27*, 619–642.

De Villiers, J. G., & De Villiers, P. A. (1978). *Language acquisition.* Cambridge, MA: Harvard University Press.

Dickinson, D. K., & Smith, M. W. (1994). Long-term effects of preschool teachers' book readings on low-income children's vocabulary and story comprehension. *Reading Research Quarterly, 29*, 105–122.

Dickinson, D. K., & Tabors, P. O. (2001). *Beginning literacy with language*. Baltimore: Brookes.

Dollaghan, C. A., Campbell, T. F., Paradise, J. L., Feldman, H. M., Janosky, J. E., Pitcairn, D. N., et al. (1999). Maternal education and measures of early speech and language. *Journal of Speech, Language, and Hearing Research, 42*, 1432–1443.

Echols, L. D., West, R. F., Stanovich, K. E., & Zehr, K. S. (1996). Using children's literacy activities to predict growth in verbal cognitive skills: A longitudinal investigation. *Journal of Educational Psychology, 88*(2), 296–304.

Elley, W. B. (1989). Vocabulary acquisition from listening to stories. *Reading Research Quarterly, 24*, 174–187.

Farkas, G., & Beron, K. (2004). The detailed age trajectory of oral vocabulary knowledge: Differences by class and race. *Social Science Research, 33*(3), 464–497.

Feldman, H. M., Dollaghan, C. A., Campbell, T. F., Kurs-Lasky, M., Janosky, J. E., & Paradise, J. L. (2000). Measurement properties of the MacArthur Communicative Development Inventories at ages one and two years. *Child Development, 71*, 310–322.

Fenson, L., Bates, E., Dale, P., Goodman, J., Reznick, J. S., & Thal, D. (2000). Measuring variability in early child language: Don't shoot the messenger. *Child Development, 71*(2), 323–328.

Fenson, L., Dale, P., Reznick, J. S., Bates, E., Thal, D., & Pethick, S. (1994). Variability in early communicative development. *Monographs of the Society for Research in Child Development, 59*, 1–173.

Fletcher, K. L., & Reese, E. (2005). Picture book reading with young children: A conceptual framework. *Developmental Review, 25*(1), 64–103.

Frijters, J. C., Barron, R. W., & Brunello, M. (2000). Direct and mediated influences of home literacy and literacy interest on prereaders' oral vocabulary and early written language skills. *Journal of Educational Psychology, 92*(3), 466–477.

Girolametto, L., & Weitzman, E. (2002). Responsiveness if child care providers in interactions with toddlers and preschoolers. *Language, Speech, and Hearing Services in Schools, 33*, 268–281.

Goodman, J. C., Dale, P. S., & Li, P. (2008). Does frequency count?: Parental input and the acquisition of vocabulary. *Journal of Child Language, 35*(3), 515–531.

Hammer, C. S., & Weiss, A. L. (1999). Guiding language development: How African-American mothers and their infants structure play interactions. *Journal of Speech, Language, and Hearing Research, 42*, 1219–1233.

Hargrave, A. C., & Sénéchal, M. (2000). Book reading interventions with language-delayed preschool children: The benefits of regular reading and dialogic reading. *Early Childhood Research Quarterly, 15*, 75–90.

Harris, F. N., & Flora, J. A. (1982). Children's use of get passives. *Journal of Psycholinguistic Research, 11*, 297–311.

Hart, B., & Risley, T. R. (1992). American parenting of language-learning children: Persisting differences in family–child interactions observed in natural home environments. *Developmental Psychology, 28*(6), 1096–1105.

Hart, B., & Risley, T. R. (1995). *Meaningful differences in the everyday experience of young American children*. Baltimore: Brookes.

Heath, S. B. (1990). The children of Trackton's Children: Spoken and written language in social change. In J. W. Stigler, R. A. Shweder, & G. Herdt (Eds.), *Cultural psychology: Essays on comparative human development* (pp. 496–519). New York: Cambridge University Press.

Hoff, E. (2003). Causes and consequences of SES-related differences in parent-to-child speech. In M. H. Bornstein & R. H. Bradley (Eds.), *Socioeconomic status, parenting, and child development* (pp. 147–160). Mahwah, NJ: Erlbaum.

Hoff, E. (2006). How social contexts support and shape language development. *Developmental Review, 26*, 55–88.

Hoff, E., & Tian, C. (2005). Socioeconomic status and cultural influences on language. *Journal of Communication Disorders, 38*, 271–278.

Hoff-Ginsberg, E. (1991). Mother–child conversation in different social classes and communicative settings. *Child Development, 62*, 782–796.

Hoff-Ginsberg, E. (1998). The relation of birth order and socioeconomic status to children's language experience and language development. *Applied Psycholinguistics, 19*, 603–629.

Huttenlocher, J., Haight, W., Bryk, A., Seltzer, M., & Lyons, T. (1991). Early vocabulary growth: Relation to language input and gender. *Developmental Psychology, 27*(2), 236–248.

Huttenlocher, J., & Levine, S. C. (1990). *Primary Test of Cognitive Skills*. Monterey, CA: MacMillan/McGraw-Hill.

Huttenlocher, J., Vasilyeva, M., Cymerman, E., & Levine, S. (2002). Language input and child syntax. *Cognitive Psychology, 45*, 337–374.

Huttenlocher, J., Vasilyeva, M., & Shimpi, P. (2004). Syntactic priming in young children. *Journal of Memory and Language, 50*, 182–195.

Huttenlocher, J., Vasilyeva, M., Waterfall, H. R., Vevea, J. L., & Hedges, L. V. (2007). The varieties of speech to young children. *Developmental Psychology, 43*(5), 1062–1083.

Huttenlocher, J., Waterfall, H., Vasilyeva, M., Vevea, J., & Hedges, L. (in press). Sources of variability in children's language growth. *Cognitive Psychology*.

Hyams, N. (1994). Nondiscreteness and variation in child language: Implications for principle and parameter models of language development. In Y. Levy (Ed.), *Other children, other languages: Issues in the theory of language acquisition* (pp. 11–40). Hillsdale, NJ: Erlbaum.

Jackson, S. C., & Roberts, J. E. (2001). Complex syntax production of African-American preschoolers. *Journal of Speech, Language, and Hearing Research, 44*, 1083–1096.

Lidz, J., & Gleitman, L. R. (2004). Yes, we still need Universal Grammar: Reply. *Cognition, 94*, 85–93.

Loban, W. (1976). *Language development: Kindergarten through grade twelve.* Urbana, IL: National Council of Teachers of English.

Lonigan, C. J., & Whitehurst, G. J. (1998). Relative efficacy of a parent and teacher involvement in a shared-reading intervention for preschool children from low-income backgrounds. *Early Childhood Research Quarterly, 13,* 262–290.

Naigles, L., & Hoff-Ginsberg, E. (1998). Why are some verbs learned before other verbs?: Effects of input frequency and structure on children's early verb use. *Journal of Child Language, 25,* 95–120.

Newport, E. L., Gleitman, H., & Gleitman, L. (1977). Mother, I'd rather do it myself: Some effects and noneffects of maternal speech style. In C. E. Snow & C. A. Ferguson (Eds.), *Talking to children: Language input and acquisition* (pp. 109–150). Cambridge, MA: Cambridge University Press.

NICHD Early Child Care Research Network. (2000). The relation of child care to cognitive and language development. *Child Development, 71*(4), 960–980.

NICHD Early Child Care Research Network. (2002). Child-care structure–process–outcome: Direct and indirect effects of child-care quality on young children's development. *Psychological Science, 13,* 199–206.

Noble, K., Norman, F., & Farah, M. (2005). Neurocognitive correlates of socioeconomic status in kindergarten children. *Developmental Science, 8,* 74–87.

Oliver, B. R., & Plomin, R. (2007). Twins' Early Development Study (TEDS): A multivariate, longitudinal genetic investigation of language, cognition and behavior problems from childhood through adolescence. *Twin Research and Human Genetics, 10*(1), 96–105.

Oller, D. K., & Eilers, R. E. (Eds.). (2002). *Language and literacy in bilingual children.* Clevedon, UK: Multilingual Matters.

Pan, B. A., Rowe, M. L., Singer, J. D., & Snow, C. E. (2005). Maternal correlates of growth in toddler vocabulary production in low-income families. *Child Development, 76*(4), 763–782.

Payne, A. C., Whitehurst, G. J., & Angell, A. L. (1994). The role of home literacy environment in the development of language ability in preschool children from low-income families. *Early Childhood Quarterly, 9,* 427–440.

Peisner-Feinberg, E. S., Burchinal, M. R., Clifford, R. M., Culkin, M. L., Howes, C., Kagan, S. L., et al. (2001). The relation of preschool child-care quality to children's cognitive and social developmental trajectories through second grade. *Child Development, 72*(5), 1534–1553.

Pianta, R. C., La Paro, K. M., Payne, C., Cox, M. J., & Bradley, R. (2002). The relation of kindergarten classroom environment to teacher, family, and school characteristics and child outcomes. *Elementary School Journal, 102*(3), 225–238.

Pinker, S. (1994). *The language instinct.* New York: Morrow.

Pinker, S., & Bloom, P. (1990). Natural language and natural selection. *Behavioral and Brain Sciences, 13,* 707–784.

Raikes, H., Pan, B., Luze, G., LeMonda, C. S., Gunn, J., & Constantine, J. (2006). Mother–child book reading in low-income families: Correlates and outcomes during the first three years of life. *Child Development, 77,* 924–253.

Scarborough, H. S. (1989). Prediction of reading disability from familial and individual differences. *Journal of Educational Psychology, 81*(1), 101–108.

Scott, C.M. (1984). Adverbial connectivity in conversations with children 6–12. *Journal of Child Language, 11,* 423–452.

Sénéchal, M., Ouellette, G., & Rodney, D. (2006). The misunderstood giant: On the predictive role of early vocabulary in future reading. In D. K. Dickinson & S. B. Neuman (Eds.), *Handbook of early literacy research* (Vol. 2, pp. 173–182). New York: Guilford Press.

Shimpi, P. M., Gámez, P. B., Huttenlocher, J., & Vasilyeva, M. (2007). Syntactic priming in 3- and 4-year-old children: Evidence for abstract representations of transitive and dative forms. *Developmental Psychology, 43*(6), 1334–1346.

Snow, C. E. (1983). Literacy and language: Relationships during the preschool years. *Harvard Educational Review, 53,* 165–189.

Snow, C. E. (1999). Social perspectives on the emergence of language. In B. MacWhinney (Ed.), *The emergence of language* (pp. 257–276). Mahwah, NJ: Erlbaum.

Stahl, S. A., & Fairbanks, M. M. (1986). The effects of vocabulary instruction: A model-based meta-analysis. *Review of Educational Research, 56,* 72–110.

Stromswold, K. (2001). The heritability of language: A review and meta-analysis of twin, adoption, and linkage studies. *Language, 77,* 647–723.

Vasilyeva, M., Huttenlocher, J., & Waterfall, H. (2006). Effects of language intervention on syntactic skill levels in preschoolers. *Developmental Psychology, 42*(1), 164–174.

Vasilyeva, M., Waterfall, H., Gámez, P., Gómez, L., Bowers, E., & Shimpi, P. (2010). Cross-linguistic syntactic priming in bilingual children. *Journal of Child Language, 37,* 1037–1064.

Vasilyeva, M., Waterfall, H., & Huttenlocher, J. (2008). Emergence of syntax: Commonalities and differences across children. *Developmental Science, 11*(1), 84–97.

Wasik, B. A., Bond, M. A., & Hindman, A. (2006). The effects of a language and literacy intervention on Head Start children and teachers. *Journal of Educational Psychology, 98*(1), 63–74.

Weizman, Z. O., & Snow, C. E. (2001). Lexical output as related to children's vocabulary acquisition: Effects of sophisticated exposure and support for meaning. *Developmental Psychology, 37*(2), 265–279.

Whitehurst, G. J., & Lonigan, C. J. (1998). Child development and emergent literacy. *Child Development, 69*(3), 848–872.

4

Lessons from the Crib for the Classroom: How Children Really Learn Vocabulary

JUSTIN HARRIS
ROBERTA MICHNICK GOLINKOFF
KATHY HIRSH-PASEK

January 2010: Nine years after the enactment of No Child Left Behind, prekindergarten (PreK) through third-grade classrooms across America have become narrowly focused on reading and math outcomes. A recent report from the Alliance for Childhood (Miller & Almon, 2009) offers a portrait of kindergarten teachers in Los Angeles and New York. Thirty percent claim to have no time for student-chosen activities or play. These changes in school structure arose in an attempt to narrow the achievement gap and to raise the emergent literacy scores of disadvantaged children. Roughly 80% of the teachers interviewed suggest that they spend 20 minutes each day in test preparation. Furthermore, teachers often follow scripted learning plans designed to build language skills. Students, for example, are taught a stack of vocabulary words—along with their definitions—before they hear those same words used in a story. To further underscore the lack of developmental appropriateness, young children, using techniques developed to help high-school students memorize Scholastic Aptitude Test (SAT) words like *syzygy* and *synergy*, practice learning new words for the upcoming test.

The *motives* behind these techniques are sound. Hart and Risley (1995) report that by age 3, children from disadvantaged homes hear roughly 25% of the words that pass the ears of their more advantaged peers. And this lack of input has consequences for both quick language processing (see Fernald & Weisleder, Chapter 1, this volume) and trajectories of language and literacy acquisition (Dickinson & Freiberg, 2009; Dickinson, Golinkoff, & Hirsh-Pasek, 2010; National Institute of Child Health and Human Development [NICHD] Early Child Care Research Network, 2005) through elementary school. The *methods* used to increase the vocabularies of these young children, however, are antithetical to 40 years of research on early word learning.

This chapter merges the language and literacy literatures by examining how lessons from the crib can teach us about strategies for enhancing vocabulary in the PreK–third-grade classroom. Six well-tested principles of word learning emerge in the language domain (Dickinson, Hirsh-Pasek, & Golinkoff, under review). After discussing each, and the evidence that supports them, we suggest that vocabulary development can be enhanced not by scripted SAT-type memorization, but by classroom conversations and playful engagement. We demonstrate how playful learning flows from the language-learning principles to enhance vocabulary development for all children.

Flashback: How Vocabulary Learning Begins

Infants and toddlers learn vocabulary not from explicit instruction but in the course of their everyday interactions with parents and caregivers. By the time children arrive at preschool, they have honed some amazing processes for vocabulary learning. Capitalizing on these processes can only enhance vocabulary teaching.

Baby Steps: Finding the Sounds and Words in Language

Infants face two daunting tasks that are prerequisite to learning vocabulary (Golinkoff & Hirsh-Pasek, 1999; Saffran, Werker, & Werner, 2006): *segmentation* and *storing the sounds* that comprise words. Word learning cannot begin until babies segment or isolate words from the sound stream. Uncovering how babies do this is an active research goal (e.g., Blanchard, Heinz, & Golinkoff, 2010; Myers, Blumstein, Walsh, & Eliassen, 2009). To find the words, babies utilize a number of cues, among which are *statistical* cues (*transitional probabilities*) between syllables (Aslin, Saffran, & Newport, 1998; Saffran, Aslin, & Newport, 1996) and *highly frequent and familiar words* (e.g., their own names or "Mommy") (Bortfeld, Morgan, Golinkoff, & Rathbun, 2005). By 6 months of age, babies recognize a novel word that comes after their *own* names, but not a novel word after someone else's name. Babies also use *word stress* to help them find words. The syllables of each language follow a characteristic stress pattern, and by 9 months, infants recognize their language's dominant stress pattern. A French baby, for example, considers a syllable pattern with weak–strong stress (*iambic*) to be a two-syllable word ("guiTAR") (Polka, Sundara, & Blue, 2002), while a baby hearing English looks for strong–weak or *trochaic* stress (as in "TAble") (Jusczyk, Houston, & Newsome, 1999). By the time children are learning to read, they have segmented literally thousands of words from the speech stream, even if they do not know what all the words mean.

Infants must also store the individual sound segments that comprise words that emerge from the segmentation process. Consider the frequently heard word *Mommy*. When can babies recognize that *Tommy* sounds different than *Mommy*? Apparently, even 6-month-old babies do more than store holistic representations of frequently heard words (Bortfeld et al., 2005) because they can tell the difference between *Mommy* and *Tommy*.

These early processes continue to be useful to children in vocabulary building and reading. In the sentence "Turn on the spigot," children cannot ask what *spigot* means if they cannot segment it from the sentence. Sensitivity to common stress patterns helps children to pronounce unfamiliar words found in text correctly. Statistical capabilities come into play when children recognize which letter patterns are commonly found together in print. For example, the ability to note that the letter clusters *ch* and *ea* often appear together correlates with children's reading scores in second grade (Golinkoff & Gibson, 1974).

Sound Patterns Turn into Words: The Earliest Vocabulary

When do babies invest frequently heard sound patterns with meaning? Tincoff and Jusczyk (1999) showed that by 6 months of age, babies already know some frequent words and their meanings—words like *Mommy* and *Daddy*. Thus, even in the first year, babies find words in the language stream and store word forms both with and without meanings. Table 4.1 indicates children's progress in early word learning (Fenson et al., 1994). Comprehension leads production dramatically in the first year of life, suggesting that it is easier to store frequently heard word forms than to produce them. The variability observed is enormous, with productive vocabularies at 24 months ranging from 56 to 520 words (Fenson et al., 1994)! Interestingly, these enormous differences in vocabulary have their roots partly in the nonverbal *gestural* interactions that take place between babies as young as 14 months of age and their mothers. More maternal gestures predict more gestures by children, which in turn predicts children's school-entry vocabulary at 54 months of age (Rowe & Goldin-Meadow, 2009; Rowe, Özçaliskan, & Goldin-Meadow, 2008). Pointing things out in the environment and honoring chil-

TABLE 4.1. Median Number of Words (and Ranges) in the Comprehension and Production Vocabularies of Children Ages 10, 12, 18, 24, and 30 Months, According to Parental Report from the MacArthur Communicative Development Inventory

Age (months)	Comprehension		Production	
	Median	Range	Median	Range
10	42	11–154	2	0–10
12	74	31–205	6	2–30
18	—	—	75	14–220
24	—	—	308	56–520
30	—	—	555	360–630

Note. Data from Fenson et al. (1994).

dren's communicative bids feed into vocabulary learning.

Yet learning the meaning of words is a lengthy process. An initial "fast mapping" (Carey & Bartlett, 1978; Golinkoff, Hirsh-Pasek, Bailey, & Wenger, 1992) must be augmented with more exposure to words in varied contexts. Discerning a word's range of application and the nuances of its meaning allows children to use the word generatively in new situations (Golinkoff, Mervis, & Hirsh-Pasek, 1994; Maguire, Hirsh-Pasek, & Golinkoff, 2006; Maguire, Hirsh-Pasek, Golinkoff, & Brandone, 2008). This is an important point: The flashcard, SAT style of vocabulary memorization often presents isolated words without context and fails to invite children to learn how a word is used in a range of linguistic and environmental contexts. Embedding words in sentences is crucial to illustrate word meaning and at the same time influences the learning of grammar. Vocabulary learning and grammatical learning are reciprocal processes.

Many Word Types Are Needed for Vocabulary, Grammar, and Narrative

While nouns make a good entry point for lexical and grammatical learning because they label many concrete and nonrelational concepts (Maguire, Hirsh-Pasek, & Golinkoff, 2006; Waxman & Lidz, 2006), other parts of speech are needed to talk about relations and events (Bloom, Tinker, & Margulis, 1993; Nelson, 1988). Verbs, for example, are the architectural centerpieces of sentences because they encode the event the sentence describes and dictate the

players involved (Golinkoff & Hirsh-Pasek, 2008; Imai et al., 2008). While verbs and spatial–relational terms are more difficult than concrete nouns for children to acquire (Golinkoff & Hirsh-Pasek, 2008; Hirsh-Pasek & Golinkoff, 2006), they are necessary if children are to comprehend and produce complex sentences. Children learn verbs and spatial terms best when these are presented in sentences that are typical of their language (Imai et al., 2008) and in the context of real-world events (e.g., Tomasello & Kruger, 1992). For children to combine vocabulary into sentences and narratives, relational words (verbs, adverbs, adjectives, and spatial prepositions) need to be taught in the preschool classroom and populate children's vocabularies.

Word Learning in the Wild: How Vocabulary Learning Continues

What can we learn from the crib that transfers to teaching vocabulary in the classroom? For one thing, vocabulary learning takes place in the course of natural interaction as children indicate their interests either vocally or through gestures. When parents and caregivers build on children's interest by offering information, vocabulary comes alive. Kemler-Nelson, Egan, and Holt (2004) report that young children do not just want to hear a *name* of a new object (e.g., "It's a toaster") when they say, "What's that?" What children want is information about what the object is used for and where it is found (e.g., "It's a toaster—a kind of machine that cooks our bread"). Children insist until they are offered more information. As Kemler-Nelson and colleagues write, "when young children ask, "What is it?" . . . they are more concerned with knowing what kind of thing it is—that is, what its intended function is—than what it is called" (p. 388). These findings indicate that from the child's perspective, vocabulary learning is not about learning words in isolation but about acquiring the *concepts* for which the words stand.

Take, for example, a case borrowed from Chase-Lansdale and Takanishi (2009, p. 4) in which they present what Hunter referred to as "three mothers and an eggplant." They write:

> The first mother wheels her shopping cart down the produce aisle, where her kindergartner spots an eggplant and asks what it is. The mother shushes her child, ignoring the question. A second mother, faced with the same question, responds curtly, "Oh, that's an eggplant, but we don't eat it." The third mother coos, "Oh, that's an eggplant. It's one of the few purple vegetables." She picks it up, hands it to her son, and encourages him to put it on the scale. "Oh, look, it's about two pounds!" she says. "And it's $1.99 a pound, so that would cost just about $4. That's a bit pricey, but you like veal parmesan, and eggplant parmesan is delicious too. You'll love it. Let's buy one, take it home, cut it open. We'll make a dish together."

The first mother ignores the child, as well as the question. The second mother at least shares the child's eye gaze, then offers the name of the new food. The third mother not only engages the child in a conversation but also comments on the eggplant, explains that it is a kind of vegetable, and builds on the child's query. When parents talk about their children's focus of attention, they offer vocabulary *and* rich information (e.g., Callanan, Siegel, & Luce, 2007; Gelman, Coley, Rosengren, Hartman, & Pappas, 1998).

Analogously, similar patterns characterize storybook reading. Reading builds vocabulary most when it is *dialogic* (e.g., Zevenbergen, Whitehurst, & Zevenbergen, 2003). Dialogic reading occurs when adults prompt children with questions, evaluate and expand upon children's verbalizations, and reward children's efforts to tell the story and label objects in the book. Numerous intervention studies with diverse populations have found that engaging with an adult in dialogic reading causes children to use more words, to speak in longer sentences, to score higher on vocabulary tests, and to demonstrate overall improvement in expressive language skills (Doyle & Bramwell, 2006; Hargrave & Sénéchal, 2000; Huebner, 2000a, 2000b; Huebner & Meltzoff, 2005). Consistent with these findings, a comprehensive meta-analysis revealed that shared dialogic reading is especially beneficial to the expressive language of young preschoolers (Mol, Bus, de Jong, & Smeets, 2008).

The third mother's treatment of her child's eggplant query and episodes of dialogic reading have features in common that nurture vocabulary. Notably they motivate children to want to learn new words by capitalizing on children's focus of attention. These episodes in the wild serve as a model for how to foster vocabulary learning in the classroom. Six principles of word learning (see Table 4.2) emerge from the study of word learning in the crib, as well as from the vocabulary instruction seen in preschool and kindergarten. First, children learn the words that they hear most; frequency matters. Second, they learn words for things and events that interest them. Third, they learn best in interactive and responsive rather than in passive contexts. Fourth, they learn words in meaningful contexts that exemplify the meanings of the words. Fifth, they are able to learn words from definitions when those definitions are presented in a "child-friendly" way that takes into account children's prior knowledge. And finally, vocabulary learn-

TABLE 4.2. Six Principles of Word Learning

1. Frequency matters: Children learn the words that they hear the most.
2. Make it interesting: Children learn words for things and events that interest them.
3. Make it responsive: Interactive and responsive contexts rather than passive contexts favor vocabulary learning.
4. Focus on meaning: Children learn words best in meaningful contexts.
5. Be clear: Children need clear information about word meaning.
6. Beyond the word: Vocabulary learning and grammatical development are reciprocal processes.

Note. Data from Dickinson, Hirsh-Pasek, and Golinkoff (under review).

ing and grammatical learning are reciprocal processes. Offering definitions or using words in sentences during interaction always includes a surrounding linguistic context.

The rest of this chapter reviews the empirical support for these principles. There is little disembodied SAT-type "direct instruction" that takes place between parents and children; that is, parents typically do not offer children words to memorize without context. Instead, vocabulary is offered in a natural way as part of the conversation, or specifically, prompted by children's queries (e.g., "What's that?"). The principles of vocabulary learning offered below invite their transfer to the preschool classroom.

Six Principles of Vocabulary Learning

As Neuman and Dywer (2009) concluded after conducting a review of the limited literature on vocabulary instruction in preschool, "pedagogical principles for teaching vocabulary to young children are sorely needed. There appears little consensus on developmentally effective strategies for teaching vocabulary" (p. 391). Perhaps by examining the literature on early vocabulary learning in toddlers and preschool environments, the principles suggested below can fill that gap.

Children Learn the Words That They Hear Most

As Neuman and Dwyer (2009) suggest, "Talk may be cheap but it is priceless for young developing minds" (p. 384). The fact that children learn words that are used in their ambient environment has long been known. The classic study by Hart and Risley (1995) found that a key variable distinguishing more and less educated parents is the sheer *amount* of vocabulary addressed to children. This is best exemplified in the differences in the amount of speech that the third mother used relative to the others in the eggplant encounter (Chase-Lansdale & Takanishi, 2009). These findings on language frequency have been echoed in a number of correlational studies (Hoff, 2006a; Hoff & Naigles, 2002; Hoff-Ginsberg, 1991; Tamis-LeMonda & Bornstein, 2002) and seem to have long-range consequences for later language and reading levels (Walker, Greenwood, Hart, & Carta, 1994; Weizman & Snow, 2001; Fernald & Weisleder, Chapter 1, this volume).

The relationship between adult input and child output appears not only in home environments but also in studies of child care and early schooling (Hoff, 2006a; Hoff & Naigles, 2002; Hoff-Ginsberg, 1991; McCartney, 1984; NICHD Early Child Care Research Network, 2000, 2002, 2005). In a beautifully designed study by Huttenlocher, Vasilyeva, Cymerman, and Levine (2002), the relation between a teacher's input and children's language growth was evaluated by examining the average growth of that class over the school year, controlling for parental language, child's starting language, and socioeconomic status (SES). Results suggest that the complexity and variety of the teacher's language relate to the children's language levels, above and beyond the language accounted for by parent language or SES. Given that prior research strongly suggest that young children are very sensitive to statistical patterns in the language input, this finding is not surprising (Saffran et al., 1996). When children hear varied and complex language, they have more opportunities to discover the grammatical patterns. In fact, research finds that children learn not only language that is directed to them but also profit from overheard speech (Akhtar, 2005; Weizman & Snow, 2001).

Increased levels of exposure to vocabulary are particularly likely to have beneficial effects when the input includes a relatively high density of novel words relative to total words (i.e., type:token ratio) because the density of novel words children hear is a better predictor of vocabulary growth than is a simple count of word types (Hoff, 2003; Hoff & Naigles, 2002; Huttenlocher, Haight, Bryk, Seltzer, & Lyons, 1991; Pan, Rowe, Singer, & Snow, 2005). But even more critical than a good ratio of novel relative to repeated words may be the inclusion of sophisticated words that children are less likely to know (Dickinson, Flushman, & Freiberg, 2009; Malvern, Richards, Chipere, & Durán, 2004).

Frequency of exposure to vocabulary also has been found to be an important determiner of word learning in experimental studies in classrooms using book reading to build vocabulary knowledge. While book-reading researchers have found learning that is associated with a single reading, most intervention studies employ between two and four rereadings. Some evidence suggests that younger children (i.e., kindergartners) benefit more from additional exposure, but the number of words children are *taught* may be an even more potent predictor of total learning gains (Biemiller & Boothe, 2006). Thus, book reading provides repeated exposure to words that children are not likely to know, a second reason why book experiences have been linked to stronger vocabulary (Dickinson & Tabors, 2001; Weizman & Snow, 2001).

Children Learn Words for Things and Events That Interest Them

The classic work here comes from vocabulary learning in young children acquiring their first words. In what Lois Bloom (2000) dubbed the "principle of relevance," she wrote, "Language learning is enhanced when the words a child hears bear upon and are pertinent to the objects of engagement, interest and feelings" (p. 19). A significant body of research in the joint attention literature attests to the fact that children of parents who talk about what their children are looking at have more advanced vocabularies (Akhtar, Dunham, & Dunham, 1991; Masur, 1982; Tomasello & Farrar, 1986). A corollary finding is that children of parents who try to redirect children's attention and label objects not of interest learn fewer words (e.g., Dunham, Dunham, & Curwin, 1993; Golinkoff, 1981; Hollich, Hirsh-Pasek, Tucker, & Golinkoff, 2000). In the eggplant story, one would expect the third child to learn and remember the word *eggplant* because the mother capitalized on the child's interest.

In addition to the role of parents and teachers, playful peer interactions feed into vocabulary development. Dickinson (2001a) noted that the amount of time 3-year-olds spend talking with peers while pretending is positively associated with the size of their vocabularies 2 years later, when they begin kindergarten. Bergen and Mauer (2000) found that 4-year-olds' play, in the form of making shopping lists and "reading" storybooks to stuffed animals, predicted both language and reading readiness after the children entered kindergarten. Nicolopoulou, McDowell, and Brockmeyer (2006) also found that children who engage in sociodramatic play build the language skills required for literacy. As in other areas of pedagogy, piquing a child's interest in language through playful activities increases attention, motivation, and real learning (Hirsh-Pasek & Golinkoff, 2003; Hirsh-Pasek, Golinkoff, Berk, & Singer, 2009; Singer, Golinkoff, & Hirsh-Pasek, 2006). These are ripe contexts for children to pick up new vocabulary from their peers.

The effect of free play among peers on language appears to have a universal quality. An analysis of early education settings across 10 countries found that small-group free play at age 4 was positively associated with multiple measures of oral language ability at age 7 (Montie, Xiang, & Schweinhart, 2006). The unique demands of communicating meaning during sociodramatic play is likely one of the reasons for vocabulary growth associated with such episodes. Children work at duplicating the talk associated with particular roles (e.g., talking like a doctor). They also use language to negotiate the play itself, covering topics such as how the play will progress, what roles each child will take, and what is allowable for those roles (i.e., what is acceptable behavior for a doctor) (Vedeler, 1997). Pellegrini and Galda (1990) and Pellegrini, Galda, Dresden, and Cox (1991) also reported that preschoolers participate in much commentary *about* language when creating make-believe scenes, even using complex mental state verbs such as *say, talk, tell, write,* and *explain.*

Interactive and Responsive Rather Than Passive Contexts Favor Vocabulary Learning

Adults who take turns, share periods of joint focus, and express positive affect when interacting with young children provide children with the scaffolding needed to facilitate language and cognitive growth (Bradley et al., 1989; Bronfenbrenner & Morris, 1998; Clarke-Stewart, 1973; Howes, 2000; Katz, 2001; Tomasello & Farrar, 1986). The third mother in the eggplant vignette clearly built on the child's interest and encouraged more conversation rather than shutting it down. Stimulating and responsive parenting in early childhood are among the strongest predictors of children's later language, cognitive, and social skills (Bronfenbrenner & Morris, 1998; Sameroff, 1983; Shonkoff & Phillips, 2000). Children's language skills are strongly related to proximal measures of quality in parent–child interaction such as sensitivity, cooperation, acceptance, and responsiveness (Hirsh-Pasek & Burchinal, 2006; Landry, Smith, Swank, Assel, & Vellet, 2001; Tamis-LeMonda & Bornstein, 2002; Wakschlag & Hans, 1999). Parental warmth, demonstrated as open displays of affection, physical or verbal reinforcement, and sensitivity to children's requests and feelings, are also significantly associated with academic achievement and cognitive growth (Bornstein & Tamis-LeMonda, 1989; Burchinal, Campbell, Bryant, Wasik, & Ramey, 1997; Clark, 2003; Cunningham & Stanovich, 1997; Howes, Phillips, & Whitebook, 1992; Howes & Smith, 1995; Landry et al., 2001; Landry, Smith, & Swank, 2006; Landry, Swank, Smith, Assel, & Gunnewig, 2006; Morrison & Cooney, 2002).

While the role of sensitive input has been more extensively explored in the parenting literature, responsive and stimulating behavior by caregivers also relates independently to child outcomes (Burchinal, Roberts, Nabors, & Bryant, 1996; Burchinal et al., 2000; Hirsh-Pasek & Burchinal, 2006; Howes et al., 1992; Love et al., 2003; NICHD Early Child Care Research Network, 2000; NICHD Early Child Care Research Network & Duncan, 2003; Peisner-Feinberg & Burchinal, 1997; Zill, Resnick, & McKey, 1999). Even smaller studies (Burchinal et al., 1996, 2000; Dunn, 1993; Kontos, 1991; McCartney, 1984; Schliecker, White, & Jacobs, 1991) find a direct relationship between environmental sensitivity and cognitive and language outcomes. This link has been observed in child-care homes and relative care, as well as center care (Clarke-Stewart, Vandell, Burchinal, O'Brien, & McCartney, 2002; Kontos, Howes, Shinn, & Galinsky, 1997).

Sensitive interactions are especially beneficial when accompanied by rich lexical input. In a longitudinal study researchers examined teacher–child conversations when children were 4, controlling at age 3 for children's language ability (i.e., the mean length of their utterances), parental income, education, and home support for literacy (e.g., reading), and found that higher-quality conversations and richer vocabulary exposure during free play and group book reading were related to children's language, comprehension, and print skills at the end of kindergarten (Dickinson, 2001b; Tabors, Snow, & Dickinson, 2001) and fourth grade (Dickinson, 2001b; Dickinson & Porche, under review; Tabors et al., 2001).

Finally, three studies examined this relationship over time. Two held that parental sensitivity across time relates to changes in child outcomes (see Bornstein & Tamis-LeMonda, 1989; Landry, Smith, Swank, & Miller-Loncar, 2000; Landry et al., 2001; NICHD Early Child Care Research & Duncan, 2003; Tamis-LeMonda & Bornstein, 2002). Landry and colleagues (2001), for example, found that children with highly sensitive parents in the first 3 years of life, followed by lower sensitivity, did not perform as well as children who had consistently highly sensitive parents across early childhood. Hirsh-Pasek and Burchinal (2006) noted similar relationships with children in childcare settings. To the best of our knowledge, this dimension of language learning has not been directly explored in intervention studies within the preschool or early elementary school setting. However, the frequency of warmth and sensitivity in teacher–child conversations in preschool classrooms was found to be correlated with the same teachers' tendency to engage in cognitively and linguistically enriching conversations with children (Densmore, Dickinson, & Smith, 1995).

Children Learn Words Best in Meaningful Contexts

After their review of how vocabulary is taught in preschool, Neuman and Dwyer (2009) concluded: "Strategies that introduce young children to new words and entice them to engage in meaningful contexts through semantically related activities are much needed" (p. 384). This insight is completely in line with research on memory: People learn best when information is presented in integrated contexts rather than as a set of isolated facts (Bartlett, 1932/1967; Bransford & Johnson, 1972; Bruner, 1972; Neisser, 1967; Tulving, 1968). The same is true for children. A set of words connected in a grocery list is better remembered than the same list of words without context. Meaningful connections between words are also fostered in studies that use thematic play as a prop for language development. Christie and Roskos (2006), for example, find that children who learn connected vocabulary for categories of objects such as hammers, hard hats, screwdrivers, and tool belts (the category of building) better remember and use these words than do children who do not learn in this more integrative way. Additional support for children learning vocabulary in meaningful contexts comes from the work of Neuman and Roskos (1992), who found that enriching play centers with literacy-related objects increased the frequency, duration, and complexity of peer verbal exchanges around literacy objects and literacy themes.

New research by Han, Moore, Vukelich, and Buell (in press) finds that children given an opportunity to use vocabulary in a playful context learn it better than those who learn only under explicit instruction. By way of example, low-income children in the explicit instruction group heard a reading of *Warthogs in the Kitchen*. Following the reading, they heard the word *bake* while being shown a picture of the word in the storybook. They were then offered a "child-friendly" definition of the word *bake* and asked to repeat it and point to an instance of the concept. This group spent a full 30 minutes on the book and on receiving the explicit vocabulary instruction. The playgroup spent 20 minutes on the book and the associated definitions, and so forth, but had 10 minutes to engage in guided play with props. Subsequent vocabulary tests revealed that the group that played remembered the target vocabulary better and included more children who reached vocabulary benchmark levels on the standardized Peabody Picture Vocabulary Test (PPVT).

As Neuman and Dwyer (2009) pointed out, experimental research comparing vocabulary learning in meaningful versus less meaningful contexts is scant. Yet correlational studies in language, play, and memory research converge to suggest that teaching vocabulary in integrated and meaningful contexts enriches and deepens children's background knowledge and, hence, their mental lexicons (Hirsh-Pasek et al., 2009). Since parents and teachers provide the input

that makes vocabulary learning possible, it is crucial to understand the guided play contexts that support parents and teachers in the production of new words for children (Christie & Roskos, 2006; Fisher, Hirsh-Pasek, Golinkoff, Singer, & Berk, in press).

Educational theory and research suggest that guided play approaches promote superior learning, retention, and academic achievement compared to direct instruction (Burts, Hart, Charlesworth, & Kirk, 1990; Burts et al., 1992; Hirsh-Pasek, 1991; Lillard & Else-Quest, 2006; Love, Ryer, & Faddis, 1992; Marcon, 1993, 2002; Roskos, Tabors, & Lenhart, 2004, 2009; Schweinhart & Weikart, 1988; Schweinhart, Weikart, & Larner, 1986). In guided play contexts, educators structure an environment around a general curricular goal by encouraging children's natural curiosity, exploration, and play with learning-oriented objects/materials (Fein & Rivkin, 1986; Hirsh-Pasek et al., 2009; Marcon, 2002; Schweinhart, 2004). Conversations that take place between adults and children in the context of a playful activity, and that build on children's interests, offer children new lexical concepts that are more likely to be retained than unbidden verbal explanations (e.g., Golinkoff, 1986).

In a study in which children and parents were asked to build block structures together (Ferrara, Shallcross, Hirsh-Pasek, Golinkoff, & Newcombe, in preparation), the nature of the task influenced the quantity and richness of the spatial language parents offered. For example, when the task was structured, with the goal of reproducing a figure from a picture, parental spatial language was richer (e.g., "Put the big one on the little one") than when the task was more open-ended and dyads built without a model. Play is the ideal context for word learning because the child is actively engaged in a meaningful and pleasurable activity, eager to participate with an interested adult, and the language used often has instrumental purposes the child wants to achieve. Of course, children can also learn vocabulary from didactic instruction (e.g., Biemiller, 2006). In the Han and colleagues (in press) study, the didactic group and the playgroup did not differ significantly in the *particular* words upon which they were trained. However, the performance of children in the playgroup, who had experienced guided pretend-play vocabulary-learning episodes, exceeded that of the didactic group on the PPVT months later.

Children Need Clear Information about Word Meaning

Words can be understood in different ways and to different degrees. For many words, a *fast mapping* (Carey & Bartlett, 1978) comes first. This is when the child might be offered the meaning of a word ostensively or infer that the novel, unnamed object or action is the one to which the new label should be attached (Golinkoff et al., 1992, 1994; Golinkoff, Jacquet, Hirsh-Pasek, & Nandakumar, 1996). Fast mapping, however, yields a relatively cursory understanding of word meaning; repeated exposures to a new word in varied contexts, or the provision of definitions to which children can relate (Booth, 2009), lead to a deeper, more nuanced understanding of word meaning. The field knows a great deal about factors that influence fast mapping, such as perceptual factors or what a child finds attractive (Hollich et al., 2000; Pruden, Hirsh-Pasek, Golinkoff, & Hennon, 2006), grammatical contexts in which a word is embedded (Gleitman, 1990; Hirsh-Pasek & Golinkoff, 1996), and social cues speakers offer about what they are discussing (Hollich et al., 2000; Tomasello, 1999). Observation of parent–child conversations revealed that children benefited when parents provided quick explanations about the meanings of words, and suggested that young children may not require elaborated, decontextualized word definitions to gain some understanding of the meaning of a word (Weizman & Snow, 2001). Weizman and Snow (2001) also found that adults are often sensitive to those words a child might not understand and can therefore support understanding by providing additional hints as to word meaning. Such was the case with the third mother's explanation of the eggplant; the word was couched in familiar routines, such as eating veal parmesan.

The field knows less about how to foster conceptual understanding and decontextualized word meanings. Most efforts have used book reading as the instructional context, and one suggested way is to offer explicit definitions. Work with kindergarten and early primary grade children has revealed that while children learn some

words simply from hearing them in a story (De Jong & Bus, 2002; Elley, 1989; Elley & Mangubhai, 1983), telling children the definitions of words consistently increases word learning substantially (Biemiller, 2006; Biemiller & Boote, 2006; Brabham & Lynch-Brown, 2002; Elley, 1989; Penno, Wilkinson, & Moore, 2002). Children with weaker language skills seem to be especially likely to benefit from such explicit information (Penno et al., 2002), perhaps because they have more difficulty making inferences about word meaning. However, there is evidence that older children benefit more than younger children from explicit language-based information (Dickinson, 1984), possibly reflecting the greater metalinguistic abilities of older children. If book reading devolves into an extended vocabulary lesson, the highly explicit teaching that results in the greatest gains in short-term interventions with older children could paradoxically have a negative long-term impact on children's enjoyment of books and teacher's use of books to deepen comprehension.

Research by Booth (2009) represents an attempt to uncover those factors in explicit definitions that foster retention and extension of newly learned word meanings. Booth reports that providing definitions to 3-year-olds about what one can *do* with an object or action promotes better vocabulary learning than providing static, noncausal definitions. These findings dovetail with the prior principle that word learning takes place best in a meaningful context. Seeing objects and actions embedded in a causal sequence appears to be a powerful impetus to word learning. Even acting out the meanings of words with props in pretend play (Han et al., in press) contributes to children's understanding of word meaning.

Vocabulary Learning and Grammatical Development Are Reciprocal Processes

The amount and diversity of verbal stimulation fosters earlier and richer language outcomes in terms of both vocabulary and grammar (Beebe, Jaffee, & Lachman, 1992; Hart & Risley, 1995, 1999; Huttenlocher et al., 1991; Snow, 1986; Tamis-LeMonda, Bornstein, & Baumwell, 2001). Importantly, in these and many more recent studies, vocabulary and grammar are not divorced.

They feed one another. Dixon and Marchman (2007), for example, based on a large sample of children ages 16–30 months (N = 1,461), argue that words and grammar are "developing in synchrony across the first few years of life" (p. 209). This relationship between grammar and vocabulary learning is also celebrated in research with bilingual children. Conboy and Thal (2006) found that toddlers' English vocabulary predicted their English grammar and the reverse, and their Spanish vocabulary predicted their Spanish grammar.

Children learn vocabulary through grammar and grammar through vocabulary in two ways: By noting the linguistic context in which words appear, children gain information about a word's part of speech (Imai et al., 2008) and, once a word is known, children detect nuances in word meaning by observing the diverse linguistic contexts in which words are used (Gillette, Gleitman, Gleitman, & Lederer, 1999; Naigles, 1990). Furthermore, oral language measured as *both* vocabulary and grammar (NICHD Early Child Care Research Network, 2005) is crucial for early literacy. Building vocabulary is not a matter of learning words in isolation but one of hearing words in sentences. Research shows that exposure to complex language throughout a school year can improve the syntactic comprehension of 4-year-old children (Huttenlocher et al., 2002), a finding supported by an experimental study that employed books to foster syntactic development (Vasilyeva, Huttenlocher, & Waterfall, 2006).

An important extension of this language-learning principle is that children's current language abilities condition their ability to learn new words. This premise is central to the *emergent coalitionist perspective* (Golinkoff & Hirsh-Pasek, 2006; Hirsh-Pasek & Golinkoff, 1996; Hollich et al., 2000), which posits that children use multiple available cues when learning words, and that employed cues shift as children become more competent language learners. The impact of current language status on word learning has been seen in studies in which children are taught new words by reading stories. Children with stronger language skills are more apt to gain more from the stories, unless there are special efforts to provide redundant and explicit information

about word meanings (Elley, 1989; Penno et al., 2002; Robbins & Ehri, 1994).

To summarize, word learning requires that children learn the sounds of the word, the word's part of speech, and the word's meaning. However, memorization of these facts is not enough. To claim that children *really* know a word, we must show that they have not only acquired a minimal grasp of the word but can also *transfer* the word to new contexts, and *retain* the word and its meaning over time. Too few studies hold word learning to these high standards. However, the literature does permit us to extract six principles about vocabulary learning that can guide our research in the future.

Unfortunately, children who are at risk for reading problems are likely to have limitations in the language skills on which reading draws. For example, children from lower-SES backgrounds are at risk due to a substantially decreased vocabulary size (see Hoff, 2006a, 2006b, 2009). Therefore, to the extent that we understand the processes that contribute to vocabulary learning, the more effective will be our interventions for children who lag behind. Ironically, while the research shows that word learning takes place best in meaningful and playful contexts where child engagement is high, the educational system appears to be moving in the opposite direction, increasing the amount of definition memorization required of children.

Back to Basics: Natural Interaction and Playful Learning as the Platform for Vocabulary Learning

Taken collectively, the six principles of vocabulary development derived from the crib and the classroom in effect dictate the kind of pedagogical approach that will yield optimal vocabulary development. Although children can learn definitions, relatively passive memorization will not yield the depth and long-term retention needed to allow children to recognize the appropriateness of a word for a range of situations. The six principles of vocabulary learning encourage a combination of pedagogical approaches that offer clear and easily digestible definitions and that allow children to explore the meaning of words via playful interaction.

Thus, research suggests that vocabulary acquisition occurs most effectively in preschool classrooms that mimic the way vocabulary learning takes place in the home—through events that spark children's motivation to learn new words and heighten their engagement. Often, though not always, these interactions occur in a playful context—between children and adults or between peers (Hirsh-Pasek et al., 2009). In fact, many of these principles point in the direction of playful learning—both free play and guided play—as they describe how presenting words in meaningful contexts, in which children are engaged, enhances vocabulary development. Representing a broad array of activities, including object play, pretend and socio-dramatic play, and rough-and-tumble play, free play has been notoriously difficult to define (see Hirsh-Pasek et al., 2009). Contemporary play researchers generally agree that free-play activities are fun, voluntary, flexible, have no extrinsic goals, involve active engagement of the child, and often contain an element of make-believe (Johnson, Christie, & Yawkey, 1999; Pellegrini, 2009; Sutton-Smith, 2001). Guided play, on the other hand, is seen when teachers (1) provide materials in the classroom to spur children's engagement and discovery, and (2) comment or query children about their play by providing the words to describe it. Thus, adults who interact with children use the vocabulary demanded by the children's situation. There is no disembodied memorization of vocabulary words under a guided play approach. Play that is adult-supported leads to more conversation (Levy, 1992) and, when combined with book reading, helps to direct children's attention to specific vocabulary words. Wasik and Bond (2001) embedded concrete vocabulary-related objects into story reading and subsequent play. This combination allowed the adults to subtly shape the children's play to support the mastery of specific, important vocabulary words. Wasik and Bond attribute the positive impact of this vocabulary intervention to the meanings children understood as a function of the play context they created.

Note what these playful contexts do, whether in the context of storybook reading, conversation between parents or teachers and children, guided play with adults, or free play between children or children and adults: They instantiate the six principles of vocabulary learning. Take the case of a pair of children pretending to play doctor and baby. When children are at play they not only hear words for topics that interest them (e.g., *stethoscope*) (Principle 2) but they also frame *sentences* to convey meanings and comprehension of the sentences of others (e.g., when the stethoscope is brought to the baby's chest) (Principle 6). They are involved as active, constructive participants (Principle 3), making the meaning of words clear by them acting out and using their bodies to reflect their understanding (Principle 4) or to infer meaning of words they might not know by watching how their co-players bring those meanings to life (Principle 5). Crucially, and perhaps most important of all, they are deeply engaged in the co-constructed narrative, learning words for things and events they are keenly interested in representing (Principle 2). And when children repeatedly engage in such make-believe play, they hear some of the same words over again, heightening their opportunity to learn them (Principle 1). Play heightens engagement and enjoyment, increasing the likelihood that new learning will occur. This situation is very different from an adult offering words in a way that does not explicitly link to children's experiences. Various learning theories (e.g., information processing, constructivism, Vygotskian scaffolding) suggest that new learning occurs best when it builds on and expands what children (or adults) already know.

Conclusions

Early language development—including both vocabulary and syntax—is crucial for children's school success and acquisition of literacy. There is no doubt that the new focus on language and vocabulary is important and has serious implications for later communication skills and literacy outcomes throughout a child's school years. As we move to more academically rich curricula, however, we must be mindful that *how* one learns is as important as *what* one learns. A considerable bank of scientific data exists to guide us in knowing how children learn words and master their native tongue. Indeed, the literature here is sizable enough to formulate principles for how to optimize vocabulary and language learning. It is time that we use what we know in evidence-based practice.

Although additional research is sorely needed, research points us in the direction of natural interactions as the source of vocabulary learning. Whether through free play between peers arguing about who plays what role in sociodramatic play or an adult introducing literacy terms (e.g., *sentence, word*), as children engage in play with literacy tools, the likelihood that vocabulary will "stick" is heightened when children's engagement and motivation for learning new words is high. Embedding new words in activities that children want to do recreates the conditions by which vocabulary learning takes place in the crib.

Given the data, we strongly suggest that didactic SAT learning formats will not produce good speakers or good readers. Just as we quickly forgot the meaning of *syzygy* after the test, children who memorize meaningless words and definitions will not retain these words or be able to use them in new contexts. When words are presented frequently in contexts meaningful to children, and with clear information about their meaning, children really learn—even complex words like *eggplant*. As we translate the lessons of vocabulary learning in the crib to the classroom, we create more playful and conversational contexts for learning. While children may outgrow their cribs, the principles that govern vocabulary learning in young children, based on playful interaction and capitalizing on children's interests and proclivities, remain useful.

Acknowledgments

This research was funded by joint grants to Roberta Michnick Golinkoff and Kathy Hirsh-Pasek: from the National Science Foundation, Grant No. SBR9615391, and from the National Institutes of Health, Grant No. R01HD050199.

References

Akhtar, N. (2005). The robustness of learning through overhearing. *Developmental Science, 8*, 199–209.

Akhtar, N., Dunham, F., & Dunham, P. J. (1991). Directive interactions and early vocabulary development: The role of joint attentional focus. *Journal of Child Language, 18*, 41–49.

Aslin, R. N., Saffran, J. R., & Newport, E. L. (1998). Computation of conditional probability statistics by 8-month-old infants. *Psychological Science, 9*, 321–324.

Assel, M. A., Landry, S. H., Swank, P. R., & Gunnewig, S. (2007). An evaluation of curriculum, setting, and mentoring on the performance of children enrolled in pre-kindergarten. *Reading and Writing, 20*, 463–494.

Bartlett, F. C. (1967). *Remembering: A study in experimental and social psychology*. Cambridge, UK: Cambridge University Press. (Original work published 1932)

Beebe, B., Jaffee, J., & Lachman, F. M. (1992). A dyadic systems view of communication. In N. Skolnick & S. Warshaw (Eds.), *Relational perspectives in psychoanalysis* (pp. 61–81). Hillsdale, NJ: Analytic Press.

Bergen, D., & Mauer, D. (2000). Symbolic play, phonological awareness, and literacy skills at three age levels. In K. Roskos & J. F. Christie (Eds.), *Play and literacy in early childhood: Research from multiple perspectives* (pp. 45–62). Mahwah, NJ: Erlbaum.

Biemiller, A. (2006). Vocabulary development and instruction: A prerequisite for school learning. In D. K. Dickinson & S. B. Neuman (Eds.), *Handbook of early literacy research* (Vol. 2, pp. 41–51). New York: Guilford Press.

Biemiller, A., & Boote, C. (2006). An effective method for building meaning vocabulary in primary grades. *Journal of Educational Psychology, 98*, 44–62.

Blanchard, D., Heinz, J., & Golinkoff, R. M. (2010). Modeling the contribution of phonotactic cues to the problem of word segmentation. *Journal of Child Language, 37*, 487–511.

Bloom, L. (2000). The intentionality model of word learning: How to learn a word, any word. In R. M. Golinkoff, K. Hirsh-Pasek, N. Akhtar, L. Bloom, G. Hollich, L. Smith, et al. (Eds.), *Becoming a word learner: A debate on lexical acquisition* (pp. 19–50). Oxford, UK: Oxford University Press.

Bloom, L., Tinker, E., & Margulis, C. (1993). The words children learn: Evidence against a noun bias in early vocabularies. *Cognitive Development, 8*(4), 431–450.

Booth, A. E. (2009). Causal supports for word learning. *Child Development, 80*, 1243–1250.

Bornstein, M. H., & Tamis-LeMonda, C. S. (1989). Maternal responsiveness: Characteristics and consequences. *New Directions for Child and Adolescent Development, 43*, 31–47.

Bortfeld, H., Morgan, J. L., Golinkoff, R. M., & Rathbun, K. (2005). Mommy and me: Familiar names help launch babies into speech-stream segmentation. *Psychological Science, 16*, 298–304.

Brabham, E. G., & Lynch-Brown, C. (2002). Effects of teachers' reading-aloud styles on vocabulary acquisition and comprehension of students in the early elementary grades. *Journal of Educational Psychology, 94*(3), 465–473.

Bradley, R. H., Caldwell, B. M., Rock, S. L., Ramey, C. T., Barnard, K. E., Gray, C., et al. (1989). Home environment and cognitive development in the first 3 years: A collaborative study involving six sites and three ethnic groups in North America. *Developmental Psychology, 25,* 217–235.

Bransford, J. D., & Johnson, M. K. (1972). Contextual prerequisites for understanding. *Journal of Verbal Learning and Verbal Behavior, 11,* 717–726.

Bronfenbrenner, U., & Morris, P. A. (1998). The ecology of developmental processes. *Handbook of Child Psychology, 1,* 993–1028.

Bruner, J. (1972). Nature and uses of immaturity. *American Psychologist, 27,* 687–708.

Burchinal, M. R., Campbell, F. A., Bryant, D. M., Wasik, B. H., & Ramey, C. T. (1997). Early intervention and mediating processes in cognitive performance of children of low-income African American families. *Child Development, 68,* 935–954.

Burchinal, M. R., Roberts, J. E., Nabors, L. A., & Bryant, D. M. (1996). Quality of center child care and infant cognitive and language development. *Child Development,* 606–620.

Burchinal, M. R., Roberts, J. E., Riggins, R., Jr., Zeisel, S. A., Neebe, E., & Bryant, D. (2000). Relating quality of center-based child care to early cognitive and language development longitudinally. *Child Development, 71,* 338–357.

Burts, D. C., Hart, C. H., Charlesworth, R., Fleege, P. O., Mosley, J., & Thomasson, R. (1992). Observed activities and stress behaviors of children in developmentally appropriate and inappropriate kindergarten classrooms. *Early Childhood Research Quarterly, 7,* 297–318.

Burts, D. C., Hart, C. H., Charlesworth, R., & Kirk, L. (1990). A comparison of frequencies of stress behaviors observed in kindergarten children in classrooms with developmentally appropriate versus developmentally inappropriate instructional practices. *Early Childhood Research Quarterly, 5,* 407–423.

Callanan, M., Siegel, D., & Luce, M. (2007). Conventionality in family conversations about everyday objects. In C. Kalish & M. Sabbagh (Eds.), *Conventionality in cognitive development: How children acquire shared representations in language, thought, and action. New Directions in Child and Adolescent Development, 115,* 83–97.

Carey, S., & Bartlett, E. (1978). Acquiring a single new word. *Papers and Reports on Child Language Development, 15,* 17–29.

Chase-Lansdale, P. L., & Takanishi, E. (2009, October). *How do families matter?: Understanding how families strengthen their children's educational achievement.* New York: Foundation for Child Development.

Christie, J., & Roskos, K. (2006). Standards, science, and the role of play in early literacy education. In D. Singer, R. Galinkoff, & K. Hirsh-Pasek (Eds.), *Play = learning: How play motivates and enhances children's cognitive and social-emotional growth* (pp. 57–73). Oxford, UK: Oxford University Press.

Clark, E. V. (2003). *First language acquisition.* Cambridge, UK: Cambridge University Press.

Clarke-Stewart, K. A. (1973). Interactions between mothers and their young children: Characteristics and consequences. *Monographs of the Society for Research in Child Development, 38*(Serial No. 153).

Clarke-Stewart, K. A., Vandell, D. L., Burchinal, M., O'Brien, M., & McCartney, K. (2002). Do regulable features of child-care homes affect children's development? *Early Childhood Research Quarterly, 17,* 52–86.

Conboy, B. T., & Thal, D. J. (2006). Ties between the lexicon and grammar: Cross-sectional and longitudinal studies of bilingual toddlers. *Child Development, 77,* 712–735.

Cunningham, A. E., & Stanovich, K. E. (1997). Early reading acquisition and its relation to reading experience and ability 10 years later. *Developmental Psychology, 33,* 934–945.

De Jong, M. T., & Bus, A. G. (2002). Quality of book-reading matters for emergent readers: An experiment with the same book in a regular or electronic format. *Journal of Educational Psychology, 94,* 145–155.

Densmore, A., Dickinson, D. K., & Smith, M. W. (1995, April). *The socioemotional content of teacher–child interaction in preschool settings serving low-income children.* Paper presented at the annual conference of the American Educational Research Association, San Francisco.

Dickinson, D., Golinkoff, R. M., & Hirsh-Pasek, K. (2010). Speaking out for language: Why language is central for reading development. *Educational Researcher, 39,* 305–310.

Dickinson, D., Hirsh-Pasek, K., & Golinkoff, R. M. (under review). Increasing vocabulary in preschools: Using cognitive science to guide pedagogy: Proposal to Institute for Education Science.

Dickinson, D. K. (1984). First impressions: Children's knowledge of words after a single exposure. *Journal of Applied Psycholinguistics, 5,* 359–373.

Dickinson, D. K. (2001a). Large-group and free-play times: Conversational settings supporting language and literacy development. In D. K. Dickinson & P. O. Tabors (Eds.), *Beginning literacy with language: Young children learning at home and school* (pp. 223–255). Baltimore: Brookes.

Dickinson, D. K. (2001b). Putting the pieces together: The impact of preschool on children's language and literacy development in kindergarten. In D. K. Dickinson & P. O. Tabors (Eds.), *Beginning literacy with language: Young children learning at home and school* (pp. 257–287). Baltimore: Brookes.

Dickinson, D. K., Flushman, T. R., & Freiberg, J. B. (2009). Language, reading and classroom supports: Where we are and where we need to be going. In B. Richards, M. H. Daller, D. D. Malvern, P. Meara, J. Milton, & J. Trefers-Daller (Eds.), *Vocabulary studies in first and second language acquisition: The interface between theory and application* (pp. 23–38). Hampshire, UK: Palgrave-MacMillan.

Dickinson, D. K., & Freiberg, J. G. (2009). *Preschool language development and later academic success.* Paper presented at the Workshop on the Role of Language in School Learning: Implications for Closing the Achievement Gap, National Academy of Sciences, Menlo Park, CA.

Dickinson, D. K., & Porche, M. (under review). The relationship between teacher–child conversations with low-income four-year-olds and grade four language and literacy development.

Dickinson, D. K., & Tabors, P. O. (2001). *Beginning literacy with language: Young children learning at home and school*. Baltimore: Brookes.

Dixon, J. A., & Marchman, V. A. (2007). Grammar and the lexicon: Developmental ordering in language acquisition. *Child Development, 78*, 190–212.

Doyle, B. G., & Bramwell, W. (2006). Promoting emergent literacy and social-emotional learning through dialogic reading. *Reading Teacher, 59*, 554–564.

Dunham, P. J., Dunham, F., & Curwin, A. (1993). Joint attentional states and lexical acquisition at 18 months. *Developmental Psychology, 29*, 827–831.

Dunn, L. (1993). Proximal and distal features of day care quality and children's development. *Early Childhood Research Quarterly, 8*, 167–192.

Elley, W. B. (1989). Vocabulary acquisition from listening to stories. *Reading Research Quarterly, 24*, 174–187.

Elley, W. B., & Mangubhai, F. (1983). The impact of reading on second language learning. *Reading Research Quarterly, 19*, 53–67.

Fein, G., & Rivkin, M. (1986). *The young child at play: Reviews of research (Vol. 4)*. Washington, DC: National Association for the Education of young Children.

Fenson, L., Dale, P., Reznick, S., Bates, E., Thai, D., & Pethick, S. (1994). Variability in early communicative development. *Monographs of the Society for Research in Child Development, 59*(Serial No. 242).

Ferrara, K., Shallcross, W. L., Hirsh-Pasek, K., Golinkoff, R. M., & Newcombe, N. (under review). Block talk: Parental use of spatial language during block play.

Fisher, K., Hirsh-Pasek, K., Golinkoff, R. M., Singer, D., & Berk, L. E. (in press). Playing around in school: Implications for learning and educational policy. In A. Pellegrini (Ed.), *The Oxford handbook of play*. New York: Oxford University Press.

Gelman, S. A., Coley, J. D., Rosengren, K., Hartman, E., & Pappas, A. (1998). Beyond labeling: The role of maternal input in the acquisition of richly-structured categories. *Monographs of the Society for Research in Child Development, 63*(Serial No. 253).

Gillette, J., Gleitman, H., Gleitman, L., & Lederer, A. (1999). Human simulations of vocabulary learning. *Cognition, 73*, 135–176.

Gleitman, L. (1990). The structural sources of verb meanings. *Language Acquisition, 1*, 3–55.

Golinkoff, R., & Hirsh-Pasek, K. (2008). How toddlers learn verbs. *Trends in Cognitive Science, 12*, 397–403.

Golinkoff, R. M. (1981). The influence of Piagetian theory on the study of the development of communication. In I. E. Sigel, D. M. Brodzinsky, & R. M. Golinkoff (Eds.), *New directions in Piagetian theory and practice* (pp. 127–142). Hillsdale, NJ: Erlbaum.

Golinkoff, R. M. (1986). "I beg your pardon?": The preverbal negotiation of failed messages. *Journal of Child Language, 13*, 455–476.

Golinkoff, R. M., Bailey, L., Wenger, N., & Hirsh-Pasek, K. (1992). Young children and adults use lex-

ical principles to learn new nouns. *Developmental Psychology, 28*, 99–108.

Golinkoff, R. M., & Gibson, E. J. (1974, March). *Children's judgments of spelling patterns relate to reading achievement in second grade*. Presented at the annual meeting of the American Educational Research Association, Chicago.

Golinkoff, R. M., & Hirsh-Pasek, K. (1999). *How babies talk: The magic and mystery of language development in the first three years of life*. New York: Plume.

Golinkoff, R. M., & Hirsh-Pasek, K. (2006). Baby wordsmith: From associationist to social sophisticate. *Current Directions in Psychological Science, 15*, 30–33.

Golinkoff, R. M., Jacquet, R., Hirsh-Pasek, K., & Nandakumar, R. (1996). Lexical principles may underlie the learning of verbs. *Child Development, 67*, 3101–3119.

Golinkoff, R. M., Mervis, C., & Hirsh-Pasek, K. (1994). Early object labels: The case for a developmental lexical principles framework. *Journal of Child Language, 21*, 125–155.

Han, M., Moore, N., Vukelich, C., & Buell, M. (in press). Does play make a difference?: Effects of play intervention on at-risk preschoolers' vocabulary learning. *American Journal of Play*.

Hargrave, A. C., & Sénéchal, M. (2000). A book reading intervention with preschool children who have limited vocabularies: The benefits of regular reading and dialogic reading. *Early Childhood Research Quarterly, 15*, 75–90.

Hart, B., & Risley, T. R. (1995). *Meaningful differences in the everyday experience of young American children*. Baltimore: Brookes.

Hart, B., & Risley, T. R. (1999). *The social world of children learning to talk*. Baltimore: Brookes.

Hirsh-Pasek, K. (1991). Pressure or challenge in preschool?: How academic environments affect children. In L. Rescorla, M. C. Hyson, & K. Hirsh-Pasek (Eds.), *New directions in child development: Academic instruction in early childhood: Challenge or pressure?* (No. 53, pp. 39–46). San Francisco: Jossey-Bass.

Hirsh-Pasek, K., & Burchinal, M. (2006). Mother and caregiver sensitivity over time: Predicting language and academic outcomes with variable- and person-centered approaches. *Merrill–Palmer Quarterly, 52*, 449–485.

Hirsh-Pasek, K., & Golinkoff, R. (1996). *The origins of grammar: Evidence from early language comprehension*. Cambridge, MA: MIT Press.

Hirsh-Pasek, K., & Golinkoff, R. (2003). *Einstein never used flashcards: How our children really learn and why they need to play more and memorize less*. Emmaus, PA: Rodale Press.

Hirsh-Pasek, K., & Golinkoff, R. (2006). *Action meets word: How children learn verbs*. New York: Oxford University Press.

Hirsh-Pasek, K., Golinkoff, R. M., Berk, L. E., & Singer, D. G. (2009). *A mandate for playful learning in preschool: Presenting the evidence*. New York: Oxford University Press.

Hoff, E. (2003). The specificity of environmental influence: Socioeconomic status affects early vocabulary development via maternal speech. *Child Development, 74,* 1368–1378.

Hoff, E. (2006a). Environmental supports for language acquisition. In D. K. Dickinson & S. B. Neuman (Eds.), *Handbook of early literacy research* (Vol. 2, pp. 163–172). New York: Guilford Press.

Hoff, E. (2006b). How social contexts support and shape language development. *Developmental Review, 26,* 55–88.

Hoff, E. (2009). *Do vocabulary differences explain achievement gaps and can vocabulary-targeted interventions close them?* Unpublished manuscript, Florida Atlantic University.

Hoff, E., & Naigles, L. (2002). How children use input to acquire a lexicon. *Child Development, 73,* 418–433.

Hoff-Ginsberg, E. (1991). Mother–child conversation in different social classes and communicative settings. *Child Development, 62,* 782–796.

Hollich, G., Hirsh-Pasek, K., Tucker, M. L., & Golinkoff, R. M. (2000). A change is afoot: Emergentist thinking in language acquisition. In P. Anderson, C. Emmeche, N. O. Finnemann, & P. V. Christiansen (Eds.), *Downward causation* (pp. 143–178). Oxford, UK: Aarhus University Press.

Howes, C. (2000). Social-emotional classroom climate in childcare, child–teacher relationships and children's second grade peer relations. *Social Development, 9,* 191–204.

Howes, C., Phillips, D., & Whitebook, M. (1992). Thresholds of quality: Implications for the social development of children in center-based child care. *Child Development, 63,* 449–460.

Howes, C., & Smith, E. W. (1995). Relations among child care quality, teacher behavior, children's play activities, emotional security, and cognitive activity in child care. *Early Childhood Research Quarterly, 10,* 381–404.

Huebner, C. E. (2000a). Community-based support for preschool readiness among children in poverty. *Journal of Education for Students Placed at Risk, 5,* 291–314.

Huebner, C. E. (2000b). Promoting toddlers' language development through community-based intervention. *Journal of Applied Developmental Psychology, 21,* 513–535.

Huebner, C. E., & Meltzoff, A. N. (2005). Intervention to change parent–child reading style: A comparison of instructional methods. *Journal of Applied Developmental Psychology, 26,* 296–313.

Huttenlocher, J., Haight, W., Bryk, A., Seltzer, M., & Lyons, T. (1991). Early vocabulary growth: Relation to language input and gender. *Developmental Psychology, 27,* 236–248.

Huttenlocher, J., Vasilyeva, M., Cymerman, E., & Levine, S. (2002). Language input and child syntax. *Cognitive Psychology, 45,* 337–374.

Imai, M., Li, L., Haryu, E., Hirsh-Pasek, K., Golinkoff, R. M., & Shigematsu, J. (2008). Novel noun and verb learning in Chinese, English, and Japanese children: Universality and language-specificity in novel noun and verb learning. *Child Development, 79,* 979–1000.

Johnson, J. E., Christie, J. R., & Yawkey, T. D. (1999). *Play and early childhood development* (2nd ed.). New York: Addison-Wesley/Longman.

Jusczyk, P. W., Houston, D., & Newsome, M. (1999). The beginnings of word segmentation in English-learning infants. *Cognitive Psychology, 39,* 159–207.

Katz, J. R. (2001). Playing at home: The talk of pretend play. In D. K. Dickinson & P. O. Tabors (Eds.), *Beginning literacy with language* (pp. 53–73). New York: Brookes.

Kemler-Nelson, D. G., Egan, L. C., & Holt, M. (2004). When children ask *What is it?*: What do they want to know about artifacts? *Psychological Science, 15,* 384–389.

Kontos, S., Howes, C., Shinn, M., & Galinsky, E. (1997). Children's experiences in family child care and relative care as a function of family income and ethnicity. *Merrill–Palmer Quarterly, 43,* 386–403.

Kontos, S. J. (1991). Child care quality, family background, and children's development. *Early Childhood Research Quarterly, 6,* 249–262.

Landry, S. H., Smith, K. E., & Swank, P. R. (2006). Responsive parenting: Establishing early foundations for social, communication, and independent problem-solving skills. *Developmental Psychology, 42,* 627–642.

Landry, S. H., Smith, K. E., Swank, P. R., Assel, M. A., & Vellet, S. (2001). Does early responsive parenting have a special importance for children's development or is consistency across early childhood necessary? *Developmental Psychology, 37,* 387–403.

Landry, S. H., Smith, K. E., Swank, P. R., & Miller-Loncar, C. L. (2000). Early maternal and child influences on children's later independent cognitive and social functioning. *Child Development, 71,* 358–375.

Landry, S. H., Swank, P. R., Smith, K. E., Assel, M. A., & Gunnewig, S. B. (2006). Enhancing early literacy skills for preschool children: Bringing a professional development model to scale. *Journal of Learning Disabilities, 39,* 306–324.

Levy, A. K. (1992). Sociodramatic play as a method for enhancing the language performance of kindergarten age students. *Early Childhood Research Quarterly, 7,* 245–262.

Lillard, A., & Else-Quest, N. (2006). The early years: Evaluating Montessori education. *Science, 313,* 1893–1894.

Love, J., Ryer, P., & Faddis, B. (1992). *Caring environments: Program quality in California's publicly funded child development programs.* Portsmouth, NH: RMC Research.

Love, J. M., Harrison, L., Sagi Schwartz, A., Van IJzendoorn, M. H., Ross, C., Ungerer, J. A., et al. (2003). Child care quality matters: How conclusions may vary with context. *Child Development, 74,* 1021–1033.

Maguire, M., Hirsh-Pasek, K., & Golinkoff, R. (2006). A unified theory of word learning: Putting verb acquisition in context. In K. Hirsh-Pasek & R. Golinkoff (Eds.), *Action meets word: How children learn verbs* (pp. 364–392). New York: Oxford University Press.

Maguire, M. J., Hirsh-Pasek, K., Golinkoff, R. M., & Brandone, A. C. (2008). Focusing on the relation: Fewer exemplars facilitate children's initial verb learning and extension. *Developmental Science, 11,* 628–634.

Malvern, D., Richards, B., Chipere, N., & Durán, P. (2004). *Lexical diversity and language development: Quantification and assessment.* Palgrave-Macmillan.

Marcon, R. A. (1993). Socioemotional versus academic emphasis: Impact on kindergartners' development and achievement. *Early Child Development and Care, 96,* 81–91.

Marcon, R. A. (2002). Moving up the grades: Relationship between preschool model and later school success. *Early Childhood Research and Practice, 4,* 1–20.

Masur, E. F. (1982). Mothers' responses to infants' object-related gestures: Influences on lexical development. *Journal of Child Language, 9,* 23–30.

McCartney, K. (1984). Effect of quality of day care environment on children's language development. *Developmental Psychology, 20,* 244–260.

Miller, E., & Almon, J. (2009). *Crisis in the kindergarten: Why children need to play in school.* College Park, MD: Alliance for Childhood.

Mol, S. E., Bus, A. G., De Jong, M. T., & Smeets, D. J. H. (2008). Added value of dialogic parent–child book readings: A meta-analysis. *Early Education and Development, 19,* 7–26.

Montie, J. E., Xiang, Z., & Schweinhart, L. J. (2006). Preschool experience in 10 countries: Cognitive and language performance at age 7. *Early Childhood Research Quarterly, 21,* 313–331.

Morrison, F. J., & Cooney, R. R. (2002). Achievement: Multiple paths to early literacy. In J. G. Borkowski, S. L. Ramey, M. Bristol-Power, & the Robert Wood Johnson Foundation, National Institute of Child Health and Human Development (Eds.), *Parenting and the child's world: Influences on academic, intellectual, and social–emotional development* (pp. 141–160). Mahwah, NJ: Erlbaum.

Myers, E. B., Blumstein, S., Walsh, E., & Eliassen, J. (2009). Inferior frontal regions underly the perception of phonetic category invariance. *Psychological Science, 20,* 895–903.

Naigles, L. (1990). Children use syntax to learn verb meanings. *Journal of Child Language, 17,* 357–374.

Neisser, U. (1967). *Cognitive psychology.* New York: Appleton–Century–Crofts.

Nelson, K. (1988). Constraints on word learning? *Cognitive Development, 3,* 221–246.

Neuman, S. B., & Dwyer, J. (2009). Missing in action: Vocabulary instruction in pre-K. *Reading Teacher, 62,* 384–392.

Neuman, S. B., & Roskos, K. (1992). Literacy objects as cultural tools: Effects on children's literacy behaviors in play. *Reading Research Quarterly, 27,* 203–225.

NICHD Early Child Care Research Network. (2000). The relation of child care to cognitive and language development. *Child Development, 71,* 960–980.

NICHD Early Child Care Research Network. (2002).

Early child care and children's development prior to school entry: Results from the NICHD Study of Early Child Care. *American Educational Research Journal, 39,* 133–164.

NICHD Early Child Care Research Network. (2005). Pathways to reading: The role of oral language in the transition to reading. *Developmental Psychology, 41,* 428–442.

NICHD Early Child Care Research Network, & Duncan, G. (2003). Modeling the impacts of child care quality on children's preschool cognitive development. *Child Development, 74,* 1454–1475.

Nicolopoulou, A., McDowell, J., & Brockmeyer, C. (2006). Narrative play and emergent literacy: Storytelling and story-acting meet journal writing. In D. G. Singer, R. M. Golinkoff, & K. Hirsh-Pasek (Eds.), *Play = Learning: How play motivates and enhances children's cognitive and social–emotional growth* (pp. 124–144). New York: Oxford University Press.

Pan, B. A., Rowe, M. L., Singer, J. D., & Snow, C. E. (2005). Maternal correlates of growth in toddler vocabulary production in low-income families. *Child Development, 76,* 763–782.

Peisner-Feinberg, E. S., & Burchinal, M. R. (1997). Relations between preschool children's child-care experiences and concurrent development: The Cost, Quality, and Outcomes Study. *Merrill–Palmer Quarterly, 43,* 451–477.

Pellegrini, A. D. (2009). *The role of play in human development.* New York: Oxford University Press.

Pellegrini, A. D., & Galda, L. (1990). Children's play, language, and early literacy. *Topics in Language Disorders, 10,* 76–88.

Pellegrini, A. D., Galda, L., Dresden, J., & Cox, S. (1991). A longitudinal study of the predictive relations among symbolic play, linguistic verbs, and early literacy. *Research in the Teaching of English, 25,* 219–235.

Penno, J. F., Wilkinson, I. A. G., & Moore, D. W. (2002). Vocabulary acquisition from teacher explanation and repeated listening to stories: Do they overcome the Matthew effect? *Journal of Educational Psychology, 94,* 23–33.

Polka, L., Sundara, M., & Blue, S. (2002). *The role of language experience in word segmentation: A comparison of English, French, and bilingual infants.* Paper presented at the 143rd Meeting of the Acoustical Society of America: Special Session in Memory of Peter Jusczyk, Pittsburgh, PA.

Pruden, S. M., Hirsh-Pasek, K., Golinkoff, R. M., & Hennon, E. A. (2006). The birth of words: Ten-month-old learn words through perceptual salience. *Child Development, 77,* 266–280.

Robbins, C., & Ehri, L. C. (1994). Reading storybooks to kindergartners helps them learn new vocabulary words. *Journal of Educational Psychology, 86,* 54–64.

Roskos, K., Tabors, P. O., & Lenhart, L. A. (2004). *Oral language and early literacy in preschool: Talking, reading, and writing.* Newark, DE: International Reading Association.

Roskos, K., Tabors, P. O., & Lenhart, L. A. (2009). *Oral language and early literacy in preschool: Talk-*

ing, reading, and writing (2nd ed.). Newark, DE: International Reading Association.

Rowe, M. L., & Goldin-Meadow, S. (2009). Differences in early gesture explain SES disparities in child vocabulary size at school entry. *Science, 323,* 951–953.

Rowe, M. L., Özçaliskan, S., & Goldin-Meadow, S. (2008). Learning words by hand: Gesture's role in predicting vocabulary development. *First Language, 28,* 182–199.

Saffran, J. R., Aslin, R. N., & Newport, E. L. (1996). Statistical learning by 8-month-old infants. *Science, 274,* 1926–1928.

Saffran, J. R., Werker, J., & Werner, L. (2006). The infant's auditory world: Hearing, speech, and the beginnings of language. In R. Siegler & D. Kuhn (Eds.), *Handbook of child development* (pp. 58–108). New York: Wiley.

Sameroff, A. (1983). Resilient children and how they grew. *PsycCRITIQUES, 28,* 11–12.

Schliecker, E., White, D. R., & Jacobs, E. (1991). The role of day care quality in the prediction of children's vocabulary. *Canadian Journal of Behavioural Science, 23,* 12–24.

Schweinhart, L. (2004). *The High/Scope Perry Preschool Study through age 40.* Ypsilanti, MI: High/Scope Educational Research Foundation.

Schweinhart, L. J., Weikart, D., & Larner, M. B. (1986). Consequences of three preschool curriculum models through age 15. *Early Childhood Research Quarterly, 1,* 15–45.

Schweinhart, L. J., & Weikart, D. P. (1988). The High/Scope Perry Preschool Program. In R. H. Price, E. L. Cowen, R. P. Lorion, & J. Ramos-McKay (Eds.), *Fourteen ounces of prevention: A casebook for practitioners* (pp. 53–66). Washington, DC: American Psychological Association.

Shonkoff, J., & Phillips, D. (2000). *From neurons to neighborhoods: The science of early childhood development.* Washington, DC: National Academy Press.

Singer, D., Golinkoff, R., & Hirsh-Pasek, K. (Eds.). (2006). *Play = learning: How play motivates and enhances children's cognitive and social–emotional growth.* New York: Oxford University Press.

Snow, C. E. (1986). Conversations with children. In P. Fletcher & M. Garman (Eds.), *Language acquisition: Studies in first language development* (2nd ed., pp. 69–89). Cambridge, UK: Cambridge University Press.

Sutton-Smith, B. (2001). *The ambiguity of play.* Cambridge, MA: Harvard University Press.

Tabors, P. O., Snow, C. E., & Dickinson, D. K. (2001). Homes and schools together: Supporting language and literacy development. In D. K. Dickinson & P. O. Tabors (Eds.), *Beginning literacy with language: Young children learning at home and school* (pp. 313–334). Baltimore: Brookes.

Tamis-LeMonda, C. S., & Bornstein, M. H. (2002). Maternal responsiveness and early language acquisition. *Advances in Child Development and Behavior, 29,* 89–127.

Tamis-LeMonda, C. S., Bornstein, M. H., & Baumwell, L. (2001). Maternal responsiveness and children's achievement of language milestones. *Child Development, 72,* 748–767.

Tincoff, R., & Jusczyk, P. W. (1999). Some beginnings of word comprehension in 6-month-olds. *Psychological Science, 10,* 172–175.

Tomasello, M. (1999). *The cultural origins of human cognition.* Cambridge, MA: Harvard University Press.

Tomasello, M., & Farrar, J. (1986). Joint attention and early language. *Child Development, 57,* 1454–1463.

Tomasello, M., & Kruger, A. (1992). Joint attention on actions: Acquiring verbs in ostensive and nonostensive contexts. *Journal of Child Language, 19,* 311–333.

Tulving, E. (1968). When is recall higher than recognition? *Psychonomic Science, 10,* 53–54.

Vasilyeva, M., Huttenlocher, J., & Waterfall, H. (2006). Effects of language intervention on syntactic skill levels in preschoolers. *Developmental Psychology, 42,* 164–174.

Vedeler, L. (1997). Dramatic play: A format for "literate" language? *British Journal of Educational Psychology, 67,* 153–167.

Wakschlag, L. S., & Hans, S. L. (1999). Relation of maternal responsiveness during infancy to the development of behavior problems in high-risk youths. *Developmental Psychology, 35,* 569–579.

Walker, D., Greenwood, C., Hart, B., & Carta, J. (1994). Prediction of school outcomes based on early language production and socioeconomic factors. *Child Development, 65,* 606–621.

Wasik, B. A., & Bond, M. A. (2001). Beyond the pages of a book: Interactive book reading and language development in preschool classrooms. *Journal of Educational Psychology, 93,* 243–250.

Waxman, S. R., & Lidz, J. (2006). Early word learning. In D. Kuhn & R. Siegler (Eds.), *Handbook of child psychology* (6th ed., Vol. 2, pp. 299–335). Hoboken, NJ: Wiley.

Weizman, Z. O., & Snow, C. E. (2001). Lexical input as related to children's vocabulary acquisition: Effects of sophisticated exposure and support for meaning. *Developmental Psychology, 37,* 265–279.

Zevenbergen, A. A., Whitehurst, G. J., & Zevenbergen, J. A. (2003). Effects of a shared-reading intervention on the inclusion of evaluative devices in narratives of children from low-income families. *Journal of Applied Developmental Psychology, 24,* 1–15.

Zill, N., Resnick, G., & McKey, R. H. (1999, April). *What children know and can do at the end of Head Start and how it relates to program quality.* Presentation at the annual meeting of the Society for Research in Child Development, Albuquerque, NM.

5

Lexical Reorganization and the Emergence of Phonological Awareness

JAMIE L. METSALA

Over the last several decades, the role of phonological awareness in learning to read has been well documented. Phonological awareness has a strong association with later word-reading skills (Adams, 1990; Stanovich, 2000), and individuals with reading disabilities display severe and persistent deficits in phonological awareness (Snowling, 2000). Perhaps most importantly, training in phonological awareness coupled with systematic phonics instruction improves children's early reading achievement (Bus & van IJzendoorn, 1999; Ehri et al., 2001). A relatively more recent goal of research has been to delineate the developmental processes underlying the origins and growth of phonological awareness (e.g., Elbro & Jensen, 2005; Fowler, 1991; Lonigan, 2007; McBride-Chang, 1995; Metsala, 1999; Swan & Goswami, 1997; Walley, 1993). Within this context, the emergence of the phoneme as a unit of representation for speech processing and as the organizing unit of the mental lexicon is relevant to research on reading acquisition.

Just over a decade ago, we proposed the lexical restructuring model to explain developmental advances in spoken word recognition across childhood, and the relationship between these advances and phonological awareness/reading acquisition (Metsala & Walley, 1998; see also Fowler, 1991; Walley,

1993). In this chapter, I examine claims of the lexical restructuring model that directly concern emerging phonological awareness and reading acquisition. A change in emphasis in the model from lexical restructuring to lexical reorganization is highlighted. To provide a context for considering the importance of developmental changes in lexical representations to phonological awareness, aspects of research on spoken language processing in infancy and childhood are briefly discussed, as is adult spoken word recognition.

The Emergence and Growth of Phonological Awareness

As stated, one goal of research has been to delineate the developmental origins of phonological awareness. This endeavor seems very appropriate given several recent advances in our understanding of this ability in preschool children. Whereas phonological awareness was once thought to be largely a consequence of reading instruction, there appears to be a growing consensus that phonological awareness/sensitivity "is a skill that is acquired during the preschool period, prior to formal reading instruction" (Lonigan, 2007, p. 21; but see Foy & Mann, 2003). As well, phonological awareness has been shown to be a stable individual-difference trait across this period and from preschool into the earliest school years (Lonigan, Burgess, & Anthony, 2000; see also Lonigan, Burgess, Anthony, & Barker, 1998). Importantly, the structure of three frequently identified, reading-related phonological processing skills appears invariant over the preschool period (Lonigan et al., 2009), similar to findings concerning school-age children (e.g., Wagner, Torgesen, Laughon, Simmons, & Rashotte, 1993; Wagner, Torgesen, & Rashotte, 1994). Finally, phonological awareness is consistently a front-runner among early reading-related skills in predicting reading achievement (e.g., Lonigan et al., 1998, 2000, 2009; Storch & Whitehurst, 2002; for review, see the National Early Literacy Panel, 2008).

In addition to addressing spoken word recognition development in childhood, the lexical restructuring model proposes that the gradual segmental reorganization of words in the mental lexicon makes access to the sublexical structure of spoken words possible (see also Fowler, 1991). Predictions or claims that follow from this proposal include (1) the size of the listener's vocabulary should be related to, and play a causal role in, phonological awareness development; (2) the ease of phonological analysis for individual words should be related to properties proposed to drive segmental reorganization; and (3) individual differences in spoken word recognition should be related to phonological awareness given that both are proposed to depend on the representational properties of items in the mental lexicon. Evidence pertaining to the first of these claims is discussed next, followed by an examination of more basic processes involved in the perception and recognition of spoken language. A review of evidence pertaining to the second and third claims of the model that bear directly upon the emergence of phonological awareness is then presented.

Association between Vocabulary and Phonological Awareness

One line of research has focused on delineating the role of vocabulary in the development of phonological awareness. Studies have generally found that vocabulary knowledge (measured by receptive or expressive tasks) contributes unique variance to concurrent and subsequent phonological awareness (e.g., Carroll & Snowling, 2001; Cooper, Roth, Speece, & Schatschneider, 2002; Foy & Mann, 2001, 2003; Lonigan et al., 2000; Sénéchal & LeFevre, 2002; Sénéchal, Ouellette, & Rodney, 2006; Silvén, Niemi, & Voeten, 2002). One longitudinal study in Finland found that vocabulary measures at 3.5 years were strongly associated with later phonological awareness, beyond variance accounted for by letter knowledge; furthermore, the effects of the home literacy environment (HLE) on later phonological awareness were indirect, through the impact of the HLE on vocabulary (Torppa et al., 2007; see also, Chaney, 1994; Cooper et al., 2002; Sénéchal & LeFevre, 2002). While Burgess (2002) did not find that oral language predicted unique variance in phonological awareness, grammatical rather than vocabulary knowledge was measured. McDowell, Lonigan, and Goldstein (2007) found that among a sample of 700 2- to 5-year-olds, measures of speech-sound accuracy and vocabulary each contributed unique variance to growth in phonological awareness. Rvachew (2006) also found that for children with speech-sound disorders, preschool receptive vocabulary predicted kindergarten phonological awareness after accounting for speech perception and autoregressive effects; the converse relationship between preschool phonological awareness and kindergarten vocabulary was not significant (see also Rvachew & Grawburg, 2006). In a sample of children with reading disabilities, second and third graders' receptive vocabulary scores were associated with phonological awareness (Wise, Sevcik, Morris, Lovett, & Wolf, 2007). Some have suggested that the impact of vocabulary on phonological awareness is mediated by articulation skills for native speakers (e.g., Carroll, Snowling, Stevenson, & Hulme, 2003) and for English language learners (Roberts, 2005); however, others have not found this to be the case (e.g., Rvachew, 2006; Rvachew & Grawburg, 2006).

The strong association between vocabulary and phonological awareness has been demonstrated for children from both more and less privileged economic backgrounds (e.g., McDowell et al., 2007). Initial receptive vocabulary predicted variance in later measures of phonological awareness beyond that accounted for by age and initial phonological awareness skills in samples of 4-year-olds from middle-class backgrounds (e.g., Burgess & Lonigan, 1998) and 4-year-olds enrolled in Head Start programs (e.g., Lonigan, 2007).

The considerable body of evidence linking vocabulary knowledge to growth in phonological awareness has to this point been correlational. One recent reanalysis of data sought to test directly the proposed causal link between these two variables (Lonigan, 2007). Within a larger intervention study, two groups of preschool children received training in either phonological awareness or oral language/vocabulary for one academic year (for the larger sample at study onset, mean age was about 4.5 years and mean Peabody Picture Vocabulary Test—Revised [PPVT-R] standard score was 76.9; SD = 15.75). The group that received the vocabulary intervention improved on postintervention vocabulary and phonological awareness compared to a control group. Compared to a control group, the group that received the phonological awareness intervention improved on posttest awareness but not vocabulary. As noted by Lonigan (2007), this is one of the first studies to show an effect on phonological awareness without direct training (see also Elbro & Jensen, 2005), and it provides strong evidence for a causal link from vocabulary knowledge to phonological awareness skills.

Such a link from vocabulary to phonological awareness could contribute to the increased risk for reading failure in children from lower socioeconomic status (SES) backgrounds. Preschoolers from disadvantaged economic backgrounds show less well-developed vocabularies (e.g., Lonigan, 2007; Storch & Whitehurst, 2002; Zevenbergen, Whitehurst, & Zevenbergen, 2003). For example, McDowell and colleagues' (2007) samples, classified on the basis of a preschool funding source, showed staggering differences in vocabulary knowledge; middle SES (N = 505; average PPVT-R standard score = 101.45; SD = 15.93) and low SES (N = 195; average PPVT-R standard score 74.73; SD = 16.01). Sizable group differences concerning both language input and vocabulary knowledge are apparent across different SES backgrounds early in development (e.g., Hoff, 2003; Rowe, 2008). One illuminating example comes from the families observed by Hart and Risley (1995; as reported in Rowe, 2008). They estimated that the children in families from high-SES backgrounds heard about 11,000 utterances per day; the children in families from low-SES backgrounds heard about 700 utterances per day. Such differences in amount and style of child-directed speech are related to variability in vocabulary knowledge in toddlers/young children (e.g., Pan, Rowe, Singer, & Snow, 2005; Rowe, 2008). The notion that such early differences in vocabulary knowledge increase risk for reading difficulties is underscored by findings from a Finnish study. Silvén and colleagues (2002) found that variation in vocabulary knowledge in infancy (measured at 12 and 24 months) was related to phonological awareness at 3 and 4 years of age. Additionally, differences in aspects of the HLE (e.g., shared reading, book exposure, teaching about reading/writing) that are predictive of phonological awareness may also exert their influence through children's vocabulary knowledge (Torppa et al., 2007; see also Cooper et al., 2002; Sénéchal & LeFevre, 2002).

Vocabulary is thus potentially implicated in several causal pathways associated with an increased risk for reading failure in children from disadvantaged SES backgrounds. Within this context, further examination of a causal link between vocabulary and phonological awareness is warranted. Implications for early interventions also need to be explored; for example, what components of shared reading experiences and oral language interventions can be added or amplified to maximize impact on vocabulary development for toddlers and young children at risk for future reading failure (see Fischel & Landry, 2008; Lonigan, Shanahan, & Cunningham, 2008)?

Lexical Development and Organization

Before examining the remaining claims of the model that directly relate to phonological awareness, aspects of the literature related to the development of phonological representations and lexical organization, foundational to the lexical restructuring model, are discussed. Toward this end, prominent features of models of adult spoken word recognition are mentioned because these provide the goal or end state of development. Second, speech perception and word recognition in infancy comprise one focus of study, and the impressive developments across this period have implications for later development. Finally, continued lexical development across early childhood, the period of emergence of phonological awareness, is examined.

Spoken Word Recognition in Adults

Spoken word recognition refers to processes involved in matching the speech input to words' sound patterns or phonological forms stored in the listener's mental dictionary. In models of adult spoken word recognition and the mental lexicon, words are organized into phoneme-based similarity neighborhoods (Goldinger, Luce, & Pisoni, 1989; Luce, Goldinger, Auer, Vitevitch, 2000; Luce & Pisoni, 1998). *Similarity neighborhoods* have most often been defined as the number of words that vary from the target word by a one-phoneme addition, substitution, or deletion. Thus, *cat*, which overlaps with many words (about 30–35 word neighbors; e.g., *pat, hat, rat, cut, curt, cap*) is said to reside in a dense neighborhood; *fudge* has only a few neighbors (about six word neighbors; e.g., *judge, fun, fuss*) and can be said to reside in a sparse neighborhood.[1]

In the process of word recognition, the spoken input activates a neighborhood of similar-sounding words in lexical memory, and these activated candidates compete for recognition. Words with many similar-sounding neighbors have more competition; thus, word recognition is expected to be less efficient than for words with few similar-sounding neighbors. Indeed, adult performance across a variety of spoken word recognition tasks demonstrates this *competition effect* because recognition is quicker and sometimes more accurate for words from sparse versus dense neighborhoods (e.g., Goldinger et al., 1989; Luce et al., 2000).

The competition effect in spoken word recognition tasks is one strand of evidence that supports assumptions concerning the primacy of the phonemic/segmental level of representation, processing, and organization in the adult lexicon. Additional assumptions encompassed within adult models of the mental lexicon that are important to examine across development are that phonemic organization does not vary as a function of similarity neighborhood or position of the information within a word (Storkel, 2002).

Speech Perception and Spoken Word Recognition in Infancy

Examinations of phonological development in infancy are important for understanding continued changes in processing spoken language across early childhood, a period of critical importance to phonological awareness and reading. One view is that phonological development and principles of lexical organization are complete by late infancy (e.g., Swingley & Aslin, 2000, 2002, 2007; White & Morgan, 2008). An implication of this position is that the challenge for the young child learning to read is primarily metacognitive; that is, the young child's task is to gain conscious access to the phonemic units used in speech processing (e.g., Gleitman & Rozin, 1977). An alternative view is that basic developmental processes in spoken word recognition and lexical organization continue into early childhood and beyond (e.g., Beckman, Munson, & Edwards, 2007; Bonte & Bloomert, 2004; Fowler, 1991; Hazan & Barrett, 2000; Nittrouer, Studdert-Kennedy, & McGowan, 1989; Vihman, 1996). Given this view, young children's emerging phonological awareness is, in part, dependent on the very nature of phonological representations and organizational development in the mental lexicon (e.g., Fowler, 1991; Munson, Kurtz, & Windsor, 2005; Walley, 1993).

Extensive research has concerned the development of basic perceptual processing of speech and spoken word recognition across infancy. Studies of speech perception focus on the processes involved in the discrimination and categorization of speech sounds, whereas studies of spoken word recognition focus on processes involved in matching the spoken input to words in lexical memory. Innate processing predispositions influence infants' earliest processing of spoken language, and exposure to the native language brings with it impressive accomplishments within the first year of development (for a review, see Werker & Tees, 1999). For example, by 5 months of age, infants can discriminate their native language from those within the same rhythmic category (and from a different dialect of their native language) but fail to distinguish unfamiliar languages within the native or non-native rhythmic class (e.g., Nazzi, Jusczyk, & Johnson, 2000). In an experimental study, 8-month-olds quickly became sensitive to transitional probabilities of the presented speech input and could use this knowledge to segment the speech stream (e.g., Saffran, Aslin, & Newport, 1996). Importantly, while infants are initially sensitive to phonetic distinctions that are not present in their native language, by 10 to 12 months of age, they no longer attend to these distinctions (e.g., Werker & Tees, 1984).[2] These and many similar developments demonstrate the finely tuned perceptual abilities of infants and the vast development across the first year of life.

Although very young infants can discriminate phonemic contrasts in tasks that do not require attention to meaningful aspects of speech, there is currently debate about whether they are as attuned to such phonological detail when tasks require processing spoken words (i.e., meaningful units; White & Morgan, 2008). For example, 14-month-olds failed to learn novel label–object pairings for minimal contrast pairs (e.g., *bih* and *dih*; Stager & Werker, 1997), although they are able to discriminate such contrasts that do not require learning the label of an object (as can younger infants) and can learn such object–label pairings for phonologically dissimilar pairs. Further research suggests that infants' phonological sensitivity may be somewhat dependent on the familiarity of a word. At 14 months of age, infants can detect small phonetic changes in familiar object–label pairings to which they have been habituated, but fail to detect such a change in the label of a novel object (Fennell & Werker, 2003). As can be seen, examinations of findings from studies on infants' ability to perceive differences in speech sounds have sometimes contradicted findings from studies on phonological processing for tasks requiring attention to the meaning of words (Walley, 2005; Werker & Curtin, 2005). It may be that the demands of word processing lead infants to analyze (and consequently represent) speech input differently than they do for basic speech perception tasks that do not require linking meaning to the input.

Toward explaining contradictory findings concerning the properties of the speech input that infants use and/or have access to across different tasks, Werker and Curtin (2005) proposed the developmental framework PRIMIR (processing rich information from multidimensional interactive representations). Within this model, the interaction of innate processing biases, the developmental level of the infant, and the demands of the language-learning task determine the plane of representation to which an infant attends. Initial representations of words consist of phonetic details stored in a highly context-sensitive manner. Phonemes emerge once the number and density of word representations are adequate.

Consistent with this model, and with an increasing focus on what Saffran et al. (1996) refer to as *experience-dependent mechanisms* in infant speech perception, there appears to be substantial support for the view that phonemes are units that emerge with language experience rather than innate perceptual processing units (e.g., Beckman et al., 2007; Ferguson & Farwell, 1975; Jusczyk, 1993, 1997; Vogel-Sosa & Stoel-Gammon, 2006; Werker & Curtin, 2005). Perhaps a more contentious issue, and one central to the study of phonological awareness and reading acquisition, is whether the development of lexical representations based on phonemes is complete or close to complete at or near the outset of the vocabulary growth spurt (Swingley & Aslin, 2000, 2002; Werker & Yeung, 2005; White & Morgan, 2008), or is a protracted process with continued vocabulary learning (e.g., Beckman et al., 2007; Ferguson, 1986; Fowler, 1991; Metsala & Walley, 1998; Vihman, 1981). For example, an alternative to phoneme organization in infancy is Jusczyk's (1986, 1993) proposal of an initial word recognition system organized around phonetic characteristics of syllable onsets. Clustering around onsets would reduce the number of lexical items to be searched, making recognition efficient, and is consistent with the salience of word initial information in infants' vocabularies (e.g., Zamuner, 2009) and the temporal nature of speech. As more and more unfamiliar and similar-sounding words are learned, segmental structure would come to predominate. The controversy concerning the completeness of lexical representations in late infancy is ongoing (e.g., McLeod & Hewett, 2008; Swingley & Aslin, 2007; Vogel-Sosa & Stoel-Gammon, 2006; White & Morgan, 2008). Although beyond the scope of the current volume, this debate has important implications for examinations of continued lexical development across the years encompassing the emergence of phonological awareness.

Continued Development in Spoken Word Recognition and Lexical Organization

There are relatively fewer data concerning the development of speech perception and spoken word recognition for children than for infants and adults (e.g., Nittrouer, 2002a, 2002b; Walley, 2005). Significant changes in lexical knowledge and continued exposure to one's native language over this period, however, may cause substantial changes in these processes. Learning to read in an alphabetic orthography might also be expected to affect phonological representation and/or processing (e.g., Bonte & Blomert, 2004; Goswami, 2000). The lexical restructuring model focuses on development during this early childhood period and is consistent with other models that propose an instrumental role for vocabulary growth in driving spoken word processing toward the segmentally based recognition observed in adults (Metsala & Walley, 1998; see also Ferguson & Farwell, 1975; Fowler, 1991; Nittrouer et al., 1989; Walley, 1993).

If rapid vocabulary growth continues beyond the initial vocabulary growth spurt, then the context within which words are being stored and recognized across childhood would be constantly changing. The lexical restructuring model proposes that changes in segmental representation and/or processing happen gradually on an item-by-item basis, as a function of such changes in the absolute size and rate of expansion in the listener's lexicon, in the familiarity of words, and in the sound–similarity relations among words in the listener's lexicon (i.e., neighborhood structure; Metsala & Walley, 1998). Thus, for the youngest listeners, only relatively familiar words and those with many neighbors may be composed of sharply defined and less context-dependent phonemic segments, and be primarily organized into phonemic-based neighborhoods. With increasing familiarity and neighborhood crowding across early childhood, more and more words come to be represented and organized as such.

Indeed, research has shown that the lexicon is undergoing rapid expansion during the early childhood period (e.g., Anglin, 1993; Bates & Carnevale, 1993). This continued development may be as impressive as the growth spurt identified in late infancy. Based on computational modeling that examines knowledge from birth through early adulthood, Moore and ten Bosch (2009) concluded that "the rate of growth of the acquired vocabulary increases steadily with a peak of acquisition rate at about five years of age and with no evidence of an earlier growth spurt" (p. 8; see also Granger & Brent, 2004). With this growth, the lexical restructuring model proposes that as particular areas of the lexicon become more crowded, lexical representations become restructured or reorganized—that is, more segmental representations emerge or become more salient (see also Storkel, 2002; Walley, 2005, 2006). Computational analyses of lexical databases corresponding to 1- to 7-year-olds show that similarity neighborhoods do increase with development across this period and are less dense than those for adult listeners (e.g., Charles-Luce & Luce, 1990, 1995; Logan, 1992; see also Vincente, Castro, & Walley, 2003). Logan (1992) found that neighborhoods based on alternative phonetic characteristics (manner class) across lexical databases corresponding to those of 1- to 5-year-olds did not significantly increase density counts compared to those based on phonemes. It was suggested that for the developing lexicon, alternative representations to those based on phonemic units may be adequate for efficient discrimination. More recent data suggest that young children's vocabularies may consist primarily of short, relatively high-frequency and high-density words (Storkel, 2004; see also Dollaghan, 1994), suggesting that for many early acquired words, movement from more holistic to segmental representation and/or processing may take place relatively early.

Taken together, findings from studies on *speech perception* in early childhood suggest that young listeners' speech processing is less segmental (i.e., segments more tied to phonetic context); that there are significant changes in phonemic representations even into late childhood; and that how sharply defined phonemic categories are may be somewhat dependent on lexical knowledge. For example, Hazan and Barrett (2000) reported substantial increases in how sharply phonemic categories were defined across a range of consonant contrasts for 6- to 12-year-olds, and 12-year-olds were still less consistent in their categorization than adults (see also Nittrouer & Studdert-Kennedy, 1987). Similarly, perception of vowels has been shown to be more influenced by the acoustic–phonetic context for 3-year-olds (Murphy, Shea, & Aslin, 1989) and for 5- to 11-year-olds than for adults (Ohde, Haley, & McMahon, 1996). Walley and Flege (1999) reported that boundaries between phonemic categories became increasingly steeper across groups of 5-year-olds, 9-year-olds, and adults for native language and non-native language vowel contrasts presented in a nonword context. When these same native language contrasts were presented in highly familiar words, young children's phonemic categories were much more similar to those of older listeners.

Research findings that address another aspect of development in childhood, spoken word recognition, suggest that continued development may be especially pronounced for both less familiar words and words from sparse neighborhoods. Early studies on spoken word recognition suggested that recognition for the most familiar words is similar across children (about ages 5–8 years) and adults, but that important developmental changes are still taking place for recognition of less familiar words (e.g., Cole & Perfetti, 1980; Walley, 1988; Walley & Metsala, 1990, 1992). With respect to familiarity, we found robust word age-of-acquisition (AOA) effects on children's spoken word recognition (see also Walley & Metsala, 1990, 1992), but minimal effects of frequency when AOA was controlled (Garlock, Walley, & Metsala, 2001). In these examinations, children and adults differed most for later acquired words. With respect to neighborhood density, in two studies using a task that measured how much of the speech input was needed

to recognize a spoken word (speech gating tasks), we found that developmental differences between preschoolers and/or early elementary students and adults were greater for words from sparse versus dense neighborhoods (Garlock et al., 2001; Metsala, 1997a). These findings on group differences support the proposal that increasing neighborhood density prompts segmental, adult-like processing in order to avoid confusion with many similar-sounding word neighbors (see also Storkel, 2002).

Recall that in adult models of spoken word recognition, the effect of competing neighbors on word recognition is one indicator of the primacy of phonemic processing and organization. If there are changes across early childhood in terms of the salience of phonemic organization, then it would be expected that competition based on neighborhood structure may not be as salient for younger children. In the first year of a longitudinal study, Garlock and colleagues (2001) compared performance on word repetition and speech-gating tasks across groups of preschoolers/kindergartners, first- and second-graders, and adults. The older group of children displayed a competition effect similar to that of adults, but stronger for familiar words. Young children showed a competition effect only for the most familiar words, and only for the word repetition task. One year later, these youngest children did demonstrate a competition effect on the gating task, but only for the most familiar words (Metsala, Stavrinos, & Walley, 2009). Similarly, for a group of adult English language learners, a competition effect was found only for the most familiar words (Imai, Walley, & Flege, 2005), further supporting the notion that segmental organization may vary as a function of word familiarity.

Munson, Swenson, and Manthei (2005) found a competition effect in older (7-year-olds), but not younger (4-year-olds) children. For even younger children, the opposite effect has been observed. Pitrat, Logan, Cockell, and Gutteridge (1995) found that 2-year-olds identified high-frequency words with more neighbors better. This effect was smaller for 3-year-olds and absent for 4-year-olds. Overall, these developmental findings support the conclusions of Munson, Swenson, and colleagues (2005; see also

Garlock et al., 2001; Metsala et al., 2009), that competition based on phonemic neighborhoods emerges with development. This emergence may reflect both changes in the representation of phonemes, as attested to in speech perception studies (e.g., Hazan & Barrett, 2000; Walley & Flege, 1999), and a gradual reorganization of similarity neighborhoods to membership based on phoneme similarity (see also Storkel, 2002). Bonte and Blomert (2004) examined electrophysiological responses for 5- to 6-year-olds' and 7- to 8-year-olds' performance on spoken word recognition tasks, and came to similar conclusions. They suggested that "the lexical system undergoes substantial restructuring at the level of phonological representations and processing" and that "vocabulary growth and the acquisition of reading may critically contribute to the formation of a fully segmental lexical system" (p. 409).

Storkel (2002) noted that findings from her structural analysis of young children's neighborhoods were consistent with the lexical restructuring model. For words from dense neighborhoods, 3- to 6-year-olds classified neighbors based on phoneme similarity regardless of overlap position. For words in sparse neighborhoods, similarity was based on phoneme similarity for the onset nucleus position but an alternate clustering for the rhyme position (i.e., manner similarity; see also Gerken, Murphy, & Aslin, 1995; Treiman & Breaux, 1982; Walley, Smith, & Jusczyk, 1986). Storkel suggested that her "results along with past results indicate that the type of similarity used to structure the lexicon changes from manner class similarity to phoneme similarity (Jusczyk et al., 1999)" (p. 266), and that the lexical restructuring model accounts for the observed asymmetry across dense and sparse neighborhoods. Neighborhood density was thus identified as critical in promoting restructuring, and these findings extended the model in terms of the importance of the position of information within a word in relation to restructuring (see also Jusczyk, 1986, 1993, 1997; Walley, 1987, 1988; Walley et al., 1986).

The lexical restructuring model was proposed to fill a gap in research concerning children's word recognition, having recognized the impressive perceptual abilities accomplished in infancy. In order to recognize and emphasize better that developmental change may be primarily in attention, processing, and organizational aspects of the mental lexicon, we will emphasize lexical *reorganization* rather than restructuring in the future (see also Walley, 2006). Reorganization may principally concern changing neighborhood structure, prompted by new words entering the listener's lexicon, and accompanying changes in the salience of, and attention to, segments. Consistent with adult models of the mental lexicon (e.g., Vitevitch, Luce, Pisoni, & Auer, 1999), two current models of lexical development invoke representations at the phonological and lexical levels (Beckman et al., 2007; Werker & Curtin, 2005). In these models, lexical representations comprised richly detailed and contextualized phonetic information. The phonemic level emerges from generalizations across these lexical representations either relatively early in development (e.g., Werker & Curtin, 2005; see also Werker & Yeung, 2005) or as a more protracted process, with continued vocabulary growth throughout childhood (e.g., Beckman et al., 2007). The Metsala and Walley (1998) model focused on this interaction between phonological and lexical processing throughout childhood. With increasing vocabulary, then, greater attention to the segmental level of representation becomes necessary to distinguish between words.

Reorganization into phoneme-based neighborhoods and increased segmental processing at the lexical level may be reciprocally related to the protracted emergence of more defined, adult-like phonemic units at the phonological level; it is not necessary to propose that increasing phonetic detail is added to lexical representations with development. In turn, increasingly more adult-like phonemes at the phonological level may direct attention in word recognition and word learning tasks, such that the phonetic segments within lexical representations continue to become less context-dependent with development (less holistic and more segmental) and more sharply defined and stable (e.g., Walley & Flege, 1999).

In summary, within the lexical restructuring model, development entails increasing attention to segments, reorganization into phoneme-based similarity neighborhoods, and progressively more context-independent and sharply defined segments within lexical representations (see also Walley, 2006). This development is prompted and sustained by young children's rapidly expanding vocabulary knowledge, and disperses throughout the lexicon as a function of the number of similar-sounding words in a child's lexicon and word familiarity.

Continued Examination of the Emergence of Phonological Awareness

A second claim of the lexical restructuring model that is directly related to the emergence of phonological awareness is that performance on phonological awareness tasks should be related to those variables driving segmental reorganization; that is, phonological awareness should be better for words with greater familiarity and neighborhood density. Across two studies preschoolers and early elementary school-age children performed better on phonological awareness tasks for more familiar versus less familiar words (i.e., high vs. low frequency; word vs. pseudoword; Metsala, 1999; Troia, Roth, & Yeni-Komshian, 1996). In terms of neighborhood density, young children were better at a rime oddity task for words from dense versus sparse rime neighborhoods (De Cara & Goswami, 2003). Children with higher scores on the receptive vocabulary test performed particularly well for the more difficult judgments involving final consonants (e.g., *meat, seat, weak*). Similarly, 3- to 4-year-olds performed better on a phoneme-blending, picture-matching task for words from dense versus sparse neighborhoods (there was no effect on an onset-rime task; Metsala, 1999; see also Hogan & Catts, 2004).

Not all studies have found this advantage for items from dense neighborhoods. Stadler, Watson, and Skahan (2007) failed to find an effect of density on a rhyme-matching task (although performance was strongly related to vocabulary). Garlock and colleagues (2001) also failed to find an effect of density for onset manipulation tasks. As well, children with speech and language impairments blended items better from sparse neighborhoods; however, this cell also had items of higher frequencies (Roth, Trioa, Worthing-

ton, & Handy, 2006). In one final study, an advantage for voice-onset time (but not accuracy) was reported for words with few versus many onset neighbors within overall dense neighborhoods (Foy & Mann, 2009). This reaction time advantage may reflect quicker recognition for words with few competing onset neighbors rather than an advantage in phonemically analyzing the sparse onsets per se. While findings from several studies support the claim that phonological analysis of words is related to the time course proposed for lexical reorganization (e.g., Metsala, 1999; Swan & Goswami, 1997), findings from other studies have not (e.g., Roth et al., 2006; Stadler et al., 2007). Studies that systematically vary the way neighborhoods are defined, the size of the linguistic unit being manipulated, and the position of these units within words should help to clarify the relationship between factors related to lexical reorganization and the development of phonological awareness.

Phonological Representation and Phonological Awareness

If the discussed developmental changes in lexical representation and organization make possible explicit access to sublexical information for phonological awareness tasks, then there should be a robust and causal relationship between performance on speech recognition tasks and phonological awareness tasks. As previously stated, this is the third claim in the lexical restructuring model that relates directly to phonological awareness. Findings from studies claiming to measure some aspect of representational quality have supported associations with phonological awareness and/or reading for normally achieving children (e.g., McBride-Chang, 1995; Metsala et al., 2009), preschool children (e.g., Claessen, Heath, Fletcher, Hogben, & Leitão, 2008), children with reading disabilities or language impairments (e.g., Elbro & Jensen, 2005; Rvachew, 2006; Swan & Goswami, 1997), children at-risk for reading disabilities (e.g., Elbro, Borstrom, & Petersen, 1998), and second language learners (e.g., Chiappe, Glaeser, & Ferko, 2007). This research is briefly reviewed to illustrate the many tasks used to measure representational quality and the findings across these different populations.

Phonological distinctiveness, a measure of precision in children's productions of lengthy complex words, predicted kindergartners' later, grade 2 phoneme awareness (Elbro et al., 1998) and is an area of difficulty for children and adults with reading disabilities (Elbro et al., 1998; Elbro, Nielsen, & Petersen, 1994). Both articulation and speech perception for a specific phoneme were found to predict unique variance in later phonological awareness for that same phoneme (Sénéchal, Oulette, & Young, 2004; see also Thomas & Sénéchal, 2004). From preschool to kindergarten, speech perception was uniquely related to growth in phonological awareness in children with speech-sound disorder (Rvachew, 2006; see also Rvachew & Grawburg, 2006). Identification functions in categorical phoneme perception tasks have been found to be less sharp and within-category identification more variable for children with reading disabilities (e.g., de Weirdt, 1988; Manis et al., 1997), and performance on these tasks predicted growth in phonological awareness for typically developing children (Boets, Wouters, van Wieringen, & Ghesquière, 2006; Chiappe et al., 2007; McBride-Chang, Wagner, & Chang, 1997). Word naming in noise predicted later phonological awareness in typically developing children (Metsala et al., 2009) and accounted for variance in phonological awareness for a group that included at-risk prereaders (Boets et al., 2006). Performance on speech-gating tasks has been found to be poorer in children with reading disabilities and predicts later phonological awareness and reading (Boada & Pennington, 2006; Metsala, 1997b; Metsala et al., 2009; but see Griffiths & Snowling, 2001; Wesseling & Reitsma, 2001). It has also been argued that nonword repetition measures individual differences in the quality of phonological representations (e.g., Bowey, 2001; Metsala & Chisholm, 2010), and performance predicts variance in concurrent and later phonological awareness (e.g., Chiappe et al., 2007; Metsala, 2010; Wesseling & Reitsma, 2001). Older children (11–13 years) with dyslexia performed more poorly than age- and reading-level control groups on a composite variable tapping implicit phonological representations (speech gating, lexical priming, and syllable similarity tasks; Boada & Pennington, 2006). This factor was strongly related to phonological awareness and to reading, and accounted for 63% of the overlapping variance between phonological awareness and reading.

While the relationship between phonological representation and awareness has been robust across many different tasks, not all researchers have come to the same conclusions (e.g., Foy & Mann, 2001, 2003; Griffiths & Snowling, 2001; see also Wesseling & Reitsma, 2001). For example, Foy and Mann (2001) argued that the relationship between multiple measures of phonological representation and phonological awareness is largely mediated by age, letter knowledge, and, most strongly, vocabulary. These researchers also argued that while rhyme awareness is closely related to phonological representation, phoneme awareness is better understood as an outcome of early literacy skills (Foy & Mann, 2003).

The overwhelming majority of research linking phonological representation and awareness/reading has been correlational; however, one study more directly speaks to the causal nature of this relationship. Grade 2 children underwent brief training for which they repeatedly imitated a maximally distinctive, synthetic vocal rendition for a set of words. Children then showed more distinctive pronunciations and better phonological awareness for these words on which they were trained (Elbro & Jensen, 2005). More research of this nature is clearly needed to support a causal role for advances in phonological representation on phonological awareness.

Findings from studies by our research group also suggest an interesting avenue for future research. We have found evidence that spoken word recognition for words from sparse neighborhoods is particularly related to phonological awareness and reading. If so, then measures of processing for words in sparse neighborhoods may provide the best early indicators of potential reading difficulties, and interventions might explore building up relatively less dense areas of the mental lexicon to enhance lexical reorganization. In an earlier study, children with reading disabilities showed a spoken word recognition deficit specific to words from sparse neighborhoods, and they did not show the competition effect for highly familiar words that was evident for normally achieving children (Metsala, 1997b). For the youngest children, recognition of words from sparse neighborhoods and phonological awareness each predicted unique variance in reading. In a second study, normally achieving children's spoken word recognition for early acquired words from sparse neighborhoods predicted concurrent phonological awareness (Garlock et al., 2001). Recognition for words from sparse but not dense neighborhoods predicted phonological awareness performance 1 year later, after age and autoregressive effects were taken into account (Metsala et al., 2009). Children in the lower half of the sample on Year 1 spoken word recognition for these words scored lower on year 2 decoding after researchers controlled for year 1 phonological awareness. In a final study (Metsala, 2010), nonword repetition was examined separately for items varying in wordlikeness because this measure is related to the number of real words that share similar sound patterns (e.g., Bailey & Hahn, 2001; Masterson, Laxon, Carnegie, Wright, & Horslen, 2005). For children in grade 1, fall nonword repetition only for items low in wordlikeness was related to spring reading beyond variance accounted for by initial reading, vocabulary, short-term phonological memory, and phonological awareness.

Why might lexical reorganization and segmental processing for words from sparse neighborhoods be delayed for some children, particularly for those who might experience reading problems? There are several possible explanations. These words are proposed to undergo reorganization later because they have few similar-sounding neighbors, and developmental differences in spoken word recognition are greatest for these items (e.g., Garlock et al., 2001). Thus, greater variation over a longer period of time may make recognition of these words particularly sensitive to individual differences in lexical reorganization and representation. Although less segmentally analyzed in young children (e.g., Storkel, 2002), it is assumed that segmental processing and representation do become salient even for these words as children learn more word neighbors.[3] A potential explanation for why some children may have particular difficulty with these words relates to overall vocabulary size. Children with smaller vocabularies or slower vocabulary growth know fewer word neighbors overall, disproportionately affecting reorganization

for less crowded areas of the mental lexicon.

While reorganization is thought to disperse throughout the lexicon in a protracted manner, there may be some critical point in vocabulary development at which all items become phonemically organized regardless of lexical characteristics. Consistent with this proposal, in 4-year-olds, performance was sensitive to lexical familiarity for onset rime and phoneme blending tasks, but in 5-year-olds, only for phoneme blending (Metsala, 1999). A developmental progression is suggested, such that segmental processing is tied to lexical characteristics but then becomes independent in typical development. Also consistent with this suggestion, vocabulary was negatively correlated with the magnitude of the advantage for repeating nonwords with higher versus lower frequency sequences (Munson, Edwards, & Beckman, 2005; see also Munson, Kurtz, & Windsor, 2005) and for repeating nonwords' constituent syllables from dense versus sparse neighborhoods (Metsala & Chisholm, 2010). Munson, Edwards, and colleagues (2005) suggested that with vocabulary growth, phoneme representations become more robust and autonomous (see also Beckman et al., 2007); such representations are needed for the repetition of infrequent phoneme sequences that are not as readily supported by larger sublexical units. Thus, for children with less rich vocabulary knowledge, phonemic analysis may remain tied to lexical characteristics for a longer period of time. Alternatively, it may be that a third variable, such as a lower-level processing deficit, is responsible for some children having more difficulty with processing the infrequent phonotactic sequences in sparse words and learning to read. For candidate processes, it would be interesting to determine how and why words in different areas of the mental lexicon are differentially affected.

There are many possible avenues for continued research on the links between vocabulary, phonological representation, phonological awareness, and reading. Given that several foundational issues concerning the measurement of phonological representation have not yet been adequately addressed, one path might be to follow the steps of those who laid out such groundwork with respect to phonological awareness (e.g., Lonigan et al., 1998, 2000, 2009; Stanovich, Cunningham, & Cramer, 1984; Wagner, Balthazor, Hurley, & Morgan, 1987; Wagner et al., 1993, 1994; Yopp, 1988). First, research is needed to determine whether the many tasks used as measures of phonological representation form a unitary construct; and if not, what measures together best capture reliable variance? Second, further exploration is needed to address whether such a construct (or constructs) represents a stable, individual-difference trait over the preschool period and across the early elementary school years. Finally, studies are needed to investigate whether such a phonological representations construct is in fact separable from phonological awareness, and how this might vary across developmental periods. Unlike findings for school-age children, Lonigan and his colleagues (2009) recently reported that phonological short-term memory and phonological awareness are not separable factors across the preschool period (tested in groups of 2- and 3-year-olds and 4- and 5-year-olds; see also Wagner et al., 1987, 1993). Lonigan and colleagues further noted that "the relationship between the Phonological Awareness/Memory factor and oral language skills was particularly strong in the older sample, suggesting common developmental origins of these skills" (p. 355). Along this same line of reasoning, and consistent with the theoretical orientation of this chapter, one suggestion is that future studies may reveal that phonological awareness is reducible to phonological representation and lexical organization. Regardless of the outcome of such future research, it is proposed that advancing our understanding in this area will be supported by theoretical grounding of the study of phonological representations in models addressing the development of spoken word recognition and lexical organization.

Acknowledgments

Preparation of this work was supported by a Discovery Grant from the Natural Sciences and Engineering Research of Council of Canada (No. 341588-2008). I would like to thank Amanda Walley for her contributions to this area of research and for the opportunity to collaborate over these past years on many aspects of the work presented in this chapter.

Notes

1. Neighborhoods calculated from the online database of the Washington University Speech and Hearing Lab, Neighborhood Database, Washington University in St. Louis. Retrieved October 1, 2009, from *neighborhoodsearch.wustl.edu/Neighborhood/Home.asp*.
2. Infants, as do adults, retain the ability to distinguish these foreign contrasts; furthermore, research indicates that differential event-related potential responses to the foreign contrast at 11 months of age predicted productive vocabulary size at 18 to 30 months (Rivera-Gaxiola, Klarman, Garcia-Sierra, & Kuhl, 2005).
3. Storkel (2002) suggested that this assumption should be tested more directly rather than assumed.

References

Adams, M. J. (1990). *Beginning to read: Thinking and learning about print.* Cambridge, MA: MIT Press.

Anglin, J. M. (1993). Vocabulary development: A morphological analysis. *Monographs of the Society for Research in Child Development, 58*(10, Serial No. 238), 1–186.

Bailey, T. M., & Hahn, U. (2001). Determinants of wordlikeness: Phonotactics or lexical neighborhood? *Journal of Memory and Language, 44,* 568–591.

Bates, E., & Carnevale, G. F. (1993). New directions in research on language development. *Developmental Review, 13,* 436–470.

Beckman, M. E., Munson, B., & Edwards, J. (2007). Vocabulary growth and developmental expansion of types of phonological knowledge. *Laboratory Phonology, 9,* 241–264.

Boada, R., & Pennington, B. F. (2006). Deficient implicit phonological representations in children with dyslexia. *Journal of Experimental Child Psychology, 95,* 153–193.

Boets, B., Wouters, J., van Wieringen, A., & Ghesquière, P. (2006). Auditory temporal information processing in preschool children at family risk for dyslexia: Relations with phonological abilities and developing literacy skills. *Brain and Language, 97,* 64–79.

Bonte, M., & Blomert, L. (2004). Developmental changes in ERP correlates of spoken word recognition during early school years: A phonological priming study. *Clinical Neurophysiology, 115,* 409–423.

Bowey, J. A. (2001). Nonword repetition and young children's receptive vocabulary: A longitudinal study. *Applied Psycholinguistics, 22,* 441–469.

Burgess, S. (2002). The influence of speech perception, oral language ability, the home literacy environment, and pre-reading knowledge on the growth of phonological sensitivity: A one-year longitudinal investigation. *Reading and Writing, 15,* 709–737.

Burgess, S. R., & Lonigan, C. J. (1998). Bidirectional relations between phonological awareness and reading extended to preschool letter knowledge: Evidence from a longitudinal investigation. *Journal of Experimental Child Psychology, 70,* 117–141.

Bus, A. G., & van IJzendoorn, M. H. (1999). Phonological awareness and early reading: A meta-analysis of experimental training studies. *Journal of Educational Psychology, 91,* 403–414.

Carroll, J. M., & Snowling, M. J. (2001). The effects of global similarity between stimuli on performance on rime and alliteration tasks. *Applied Psycholinguistics, 22,* 327–342.

Carroll, J. M., Snowling, M. J., Stevenson, J., & Hulme, C. (2003). The development of phonological awareness in preschool children. *Developmental Psychology, 39,* 913–923.

Chaney, C. (1994). Language development, metalinguistic awareness, and emergent literacy skills of 3-year-old children in relation to social class. *Applied Psycholinguistics, 15,* 371–394.

Charles-Luce, J., & Luce, P. A. (1990). Similarity neighborhoods of words in young children's lexicons. *Journal of Child Language, 17,* 205–215.

Charles-Luce, J., & Luce, P. A. (1995). An examination of similarity neighborhoods in young children's receptive vocabularies. *Journal of Child Language, 22,* 727–735.

Chiappe, P., Glaeser, B., & Ferko, D. (2007). Speech perception, vocabulary, and the development of reading skills in English among Korean- and English-speaking children. *Journal of Educational Psychology, 99,* 154–166.

Claessen, M., Heath, S., Fletcher, J., Hogben, J., & Leitão, S. (2008). Quality of phonological representations: A window into the lexicon? *International Journal of Language and Communication Disorders, 44,* 1–24.

Cole, R. A., & Perfetti, C. A. (1980). Listening for mispronunciations in a children's story: The use of context by children and adults, *Journal of Verbal Learning and Verbal Behavior, 19,* 297–315.

Cooper, D. H., Roth, F. P., Speece, D. L., & Schatschneider, C. (2002). The contribution of oral language skills to the development of phonological awareness. *Applied Psycholinguistics, 23,* 399–416.

De Cara, B., & Goswami, U. (2003). Phonological neighborhood density: Effects in a rhyme awareness task in five-year-old children. *Journal of Child Language, 30,* 695–710.

de Weirdt, W. (1988). Speech perception and frequency discrimination in good and poor readers. *Applied Psycholinguistics, 16,* 163–183.

Dollaghan, C. A. (1994). Children's phonological neighbourhoods: Half empty or half full? *Journal of Child Language, 21,* 257–271.

Ehri, L., Nunes, S., Willows, D., Schuster, B., Yaghoub-Zadeh, Z., & Shanahan, T. (2001). Phoneme awareness instruction helps children learn to read: Evidence from the National Reading Panel's meta-analysis. *Reading Research Quarterly, 36,* 250–287.

Elbro, C., Borstrom, I., & Petersen, D. K. (1998). Predicting dyslexia from kindergarten: The importance of distinctness of phonological representations of lexical items. *Reading Research Quarterly, 31,* 36–60.

Elbro, C., & Jensen, M. N. (2005). Quality of phonological representations, verbal learning, and phoneme awareness in dyslexic and normal readers. *Scandinavian Journal of Psychology, 46,* 375–384.

Elbro, C., Nielsen, I., & Petersen, D. K. (1994). Dyslexia in adults: Evidence for deficits in non-word reading and in the phonological representation of lexical items. *Annals of Dyslexia, 44,* 205–226.

Fennell, C. T., & Werker, J. F. (2003). Early word learners' ability to access phonetic detail in well-known words. *Language and Speech, 46,* 245–264.

Ferguson, C. A. (1986). Discovering sound units and constructing sound systems: It's child's play. In J. S. Perkell & D. H. Klatt (Eds.), *Invariance and variability in speech processes* (pp. 36–51). Hillsdale, NJ: Erlbaum.

Ferguson, C. A., & Farwell, C. B. (1975). Words and sound in early language acquisition: English initial consonants in the first fifty words. *Language, 51,* 419–439.

Fischel, J., & Landry, S. (2008). Impact of language enhancement interventions on young children's early literacy skills. In *Developing early literacy: Report of the National Early Literacy Panel* (pp. 211–227). Washington, DC: National Institute for Literacy.

Fowler, A. E. (1991). How early phonological development might set the stage for phoneme awareness. In S. A. Brady & D. P. Shankweiler (Eds.), *Phonological processes in literacy: A tribute to Isabelle Y. Liberman* (pp. 97–117). Hillsdale, NJ: Erlbaum.

Foy, J. G., & Mann, V. A. (2001). Does strength of phonological representations predict phonological awareness in preschool children? *Applied Psycholinguistics, 22,* 301–325.

Foy, J. G., & Mann, V. A. (2003). Home literacy environment and phonological awareness: Differential effects for phoneme awareness and rhyme awareness. *Applied Psycholinguistics, 24,* 59–88.

Foy, J. G., & Mann, V. A. (2009). Effects of onset density in preschool children: Implications for development of phonological awareness and phonological representation. *Applied Psycholinguistics, 30,* 339–361.

Garlock, V. M., Walley, A. C., & Metsala, J. L. (2001). Age-of-acquisition, word frequency and neighborhood density effects on spoken word recognition: Implications for the development of phoneme awareness and early reading ability. *Journal of Memory and Language, 45,* 468–492.

Gerken, L. A., Murphy, W. D., & Aslin, R. N. (1995). Three- and four-year-olds' perceptual confusions for spoken words. *Perception and Psychophysics, 57,* 475–486.

Gleitman, L. R., & Rozin, P. (1977). The structure and acquisition of reading: I. Relations between orthographies and the structure of language. In A. S. Reber & D. L. Scarborough (Eds.), *Toward a psychology of reading* (pp. 1–53). Hillsdale, NJ: Erlbaum.

Goldinger, S. D., Luce, P. A., & Pisoni, D. B. (1989).

Priming lexical neighbors of spoken words: Effects of competition and inhibition. *Journal of Memory and Language, 28,* 501–518.

Goswami, U. (2000). Phonological representations, reading development and dyslexia: Towards a cross-linguistic theoretical framework. *Dyslexia, 6,* 133–151.

Granger, J., & Brent, M. R. (2004). Reexamining the vocabulary spurt. *Developmental Psychology, 40,* 621–632.

Griffiths, Y. M., & Snowling, M. J. (2001). Auditory word identification and phonological skills in dyslexic and average readers. *Applied Psycholinguistics, 22,* 419–439.

Hazan, V., & Barrett, S. (2000). The development of phonemic categorization in children aged 6 to 12. *Journal of Phonetics, 28,* 377–396.

Hoff, E. (2003). The specificity of environmental influence: Socioeconomic status affects early vocabulary development via maternal speech. *Child Development, 74,* 1368–1378.

Hogan, T., & Catts, H. (2004, November). *Phonological awareness test items: Lexical and phonological characteristics affect performance.* Paper presented at the annual meeting of the American Speech–Language–Hearing Association, Philadelphia.

Imai, S., Walley, A. C., & Flege, J. E. (2005). Lexical frequency and neighborhood density effects on the recognition of native and Spanish-accented words by native English and Spanish listeners. *Journal of the Acoustical Society of America, 117,* 896–907.

Jusczyk, P. W. (1986). Toward a model of the development of speech perception. In J. S. Perkell & D. H. Klatt (Eds.), *Invariance and variability in speech processes* (pp. 1–33). Hillsdale, NJ: Erlbaum.

Jusczyk, P. W. (1993). From general to language-specific capacities: The WRAPSA model of how speech perception develops. *Journal of Phonetics, 21,* 3–28.

Jusczyk, P. W. (1997). *The discovery of spoken language.* Cambridge, MA: MIT Press.

Logan, J. S. (1992). *A computational analysis of young children's lexicons* (Research on spoken language processing, Technical Report No. 6). Bloomington: Indiana University Department of Psychology, Speech Research Laboratory.

Lonigan, C. J. (2007). Vocabulary development and the development of phonological awareness skills in preschool children. In R. K. Wagner, A. E. Muse, & K. R. Tannenbaum (Eds.), *Vocabulary acquisition: Implications for reading comprehension* (pp. 15–31). New York: Guilford Press.

Lonigan, C. J., Anthony, J. L., Phillips, B. M., Purpura, D. J., Wilson, S. B., & McQueen, J. D. (2009). The nature of preschool phonological processing abilities and their relations to vocabulary, general cognitive abilities, and print knowledge. *Journal of Educational Psychology, 101,* 345–358.

Lonigan, C. J., Burgess, S. R., & Anthony, J. L. (2000). Development of emergent literacy and early reading skills in preschool children: Evidence from a latent-variable longitudinal study. *Developmental Psychology, 36,* 596–613.

Lonigan, C. J., Burgess, S. R., Anthony, J. L., & Barker, T. A. (1998). Development of phonological sensitivity in 2- to 5-year-old children. *Journal of Educational Psychology, 90,* 294–311.

Lonigan, C. J., Shanahan, T., & Cunningham, A. (2008). Impact of shared-reading interventions on young children's early literacy skills. In *Developing early literacy: Report of the National Early Literacy Panel* (pp. 153–171). Washington, DC: National Institute for Literacy.

Luce, P. A., Goldinger, S. D., Auer, E. T., Jr., & Vitevitch, M. S. (2000). Phonetic priming and neighborhood activation, and PARSYN. *Perception and Psychophysics, 62,* 615–625.

Luce, P. A., & Pisoni, D. B. (1998). Recognizing spoken words in the mental lexicon: The neighborhood activation model. *Ear and Hearing, 19,* 1–36.

Manis, F. R., McBride-Chang, C., Seidenberg, M. S., Keating, P., Doi, L. M., Munson, B., et al. (1997). Are speech perception deficits associated with developmental dyslexia? *Journal of Experimental Child Psychology, 66,* 211–235.

Masterson, J., Laxon, V., Carnegie, E., Wright, S., & Horslen, J. (2005). Nonword recall and phonemic discrimination in four- to six-year-old children. *Journal of Research in Reading, 28,* 183–191.

McBride-Chang, C. (1995). What is phonological awareness? *Journal of Educational Psychology, 87,* 179–192.

McBride-Chang, C., Wagner, R. K., & Chang, L. (1997). Growth modeling of phonological awareness. *Journal of Educational Psychology, 89,* 621–630.

McDowell, K. D., Lonigan, C. J., & Goldstein, H. (2007). Relations among socioeconomic status, age, and predictors of phonological awareness. *Journal of Speech, Language, and Hearing Research, 50,* 1079–1092.

McLeod, S., & Hewett, S. R. (2008). Variability in the production of words containing consonant clusters by typical 2- and 3-year-old children. *International Journal of Phoniatrics, 60,* 163–172.

Metsala, J. L. (1997a). An examination of word frequency and neighborhood density in the development of spoken word recognition. *Memory and Cognition, 25,* 47–56.

Metsala, J. L. (1997b). Spoken word recognition in reading disabled children. *Journal of Educational Psychology, 89,* 159–169.

Metsala, J. L. (1999). Young children's phonological awareness and nonword repetition as a function of vocabulary development. *Journal of Educational Psychology, 91,* 3–19.

Metsala, J. L. (2010). *Repetition of less common sound patterns: A unique relationship to young children's phonological awareness and reading acquisition.* Manuscript submitted for publication.

Metsala, J. L., & Chisholm, G. M. (2010). The influence of lexical status and neighborhood density on children's nonword repetition. *Applied Psycholinguistics, 31,* 489–506.

Metsala, J. L., Stavrinos, D., & Walley, A. C. (2009). Children's spoken word recognition and contributions to phonological awareness and nonword repetition: A 1-year follow-up. *Applied Psycholinguistics, 30,* 101–121.

Metsala, J. L., & Walley, A. C. (1998). Spoken vocabulary growth and the segmental restructuring of lexical representations: Precursors to phonemic awareness and early reading ability. In J. L. Metsala & L. C. Ehri (Eds.), *Word recognition in beginning literacy* (pp. 89–120). Mahwah, NJ: Erlbaum.

Moore, R. K., & ten Bosch, L. (2009, September). Modelling vocabulary growth from birth to young adulthood. *Proceedings of Interspeech,* pp. 1727–1730.

Munson, B., Edwards, J., & Beckman, M. E. (2005). Relationships between nonword repetition accuracy and other measures of linguistic development in children with phonological disorders. *Journal of Speech, Language, and Hearing Research, 48,* 61–78.

Munson, B., Kurtz, B., & Windsor, J. (2005). The influence of vocabulary size, phonotactic probability, and wordlikeness on nonword repetitions of children with and without specific language impairment. *Journal of Speech, Language, and Hearing Research, 48,* 1033–1047.

Munson, B., Swenson, C. L., & Manthei, S. C. (2005). Lexical and phonological organization in children: Evidence from repetition tasks. *Journal of Speech, Language, and Hearing Research, 48,* 108–124.

Murphy, W. D., Shea, S. L., & Aslin, R. N. (1989). Identification of vowels in "vowelless" syllables by 3-year-olds. *Perception and Psychophysics, 46,* 375–383.

National Early Literacy Panel. (2008). *Developing early literacy: Report of the National Early Literacy Panel.* Washington, DC: National Institute for Literacy.

Nazzi, T., Jusczyk, P. W., & Johnson, E. K. (2000). Language discrimination by English learning 5-month-olds: Effects of rhythm and familiarity, *Journal of Memory and Language, 43,* 1–19.

Nittrouer, S. (2002a). *Learning to apprehend phonetic structure from the speech signal: The hows and whys.* Mahwah, NJ: Erlbaum.

Nittrouer, S. (2002b). Learning to perceive speech: How fricative perception changes, and how it stays the same. *Journal of the Acoustical Society of America, 112,* 711–719.

Nittrouer, S., & Studdert-Kennedy, M. (1987). The role of coarticulatory effects in the perception of fricatives by children and adults. *Journal of Speech and Hearing Research, 30,* 319–329.

Nittrouer, S., Studdert-Kennedy, M., & McGowan, R. S. (1989). The emergence of phonetic segments: Evidence from the spectral structure of fricative-vowel syllables spoken by children and adults. *Journal of Speech and Hearing Research, 32,* 120–132.

Ohde, R. N., Haley, K. L., & McMahon, C. M. (1996). A developmental study of vowel perception from brief synthetic consonant-vowel syllables. *Journal of the Acoustical Society of America, 100,* 3813–3824.

Pan, A. P., Rowe, M. L., Singer, J. D., & Snow, C. E. (2005). Maternal correlates of growth in toddler vocabulary production in low-income families. *Child Development, 76,* 763–782.

Pitrat, A., Logan, J., Cockell, J., & Gutteridge, M. E. (1995). *The role of phonological neighborhoods in the identification of spoken words by preschool children.* Poster presented at the annual meeting of the Canadian Society for Brain, Behaviour, and Cognitive Science, Halifax, Nova Scotia.

Rivera-Gaxiola, M., Klarman, L., Garcia-Sierra, A., & Kuhl, P. K. (2005). Neural patterns to speech and vocabulary growth in American infants. *NeuroReport, 16,* 495–498

Roberts, T. A. (2005). Articulation and vocabulary size contributions to phonemic awareness and word reading in English language learners. *Journal of Educational Psychology, 97,* 601– 616.

Roth, F. P., Troia, G. A., Worthington, C. K., & Handy, D. (2006). Promoting Awareness of Sounds in Speech (PASS): The effects of intervention and stimulus characteristics on the blending performance of preschool children with communication impairments. *Learning Disability Quarterly, 29,* 67–88.

Rowe, M. L. (2008). Child-directed speech: Relation to socioeconomic status, knowledge of child development and child vocabulary skill. *Journal of Child Language, 35,* 185–201.

Rvachew, S. (2006). Longitudinal predictors of implicit phonological awareness skills. *American Journal of Speech–Language Pathology, 15,* 165–176.

Rvachew, S., & Grawburg, M. (2006). Correlates of phonological awareness in preschoolers with speech sound disorders. *Journal of Speech, Language, and Hearing Research, 49,* 74–87.

Saffran, J. R., Aslin, R. N., & Newport, E. L. (1996). Statistical learning by 8-month-old infants. *Science, 274,* 1926–1928.

Sénéchal, M., & LeFevre, J. (2002). Parental involvement in the development of children's reading skill: A five-year longitudinal study. *Child Development, 73,* 445–460.

Sénéchal, M., Ouellette, G., & Rodney, D. (2006). The misunderstood giant: On the predictive role of early vocabulary to future reading. In D. K. Dickinson & S. B. Neuman (Eds.), *Handbook of early literacy research* (Vol. 2, pp. 173–182). New York: Guilford Press.

Sénéchal, M., Ouellette, G., & Young, L. (2004). Testing the concurrent and predictive relations among articulation accuracy, speech perception, and phoneme awareness. *Journal of Experimental Child Psychology, 89,* 242–269.

Silvén, M., Niemi, P., & Voeten, M. J. M. (2002). Do maternal interaction and early language predict phonological awareness in 3- to 4-year-olds? *Cognitive Development, 17,* 1133–1155.

Snowling, M. (2000). *Dyslexia* (2nd ed.). Malden, MA: Blackwell.

Stadler, M., Watson, M., & Skahan, S. (2007). Rhyming and vocabulary: Effects of lexical restructuring. *Communication Disorders Quarterly, 28,* 197–205.

Stager, C. L., & Werker, J. F. (1997). Infants listen for more phonetic detail in speech perception than in word-learning tasks. *Nature, 388*, 381–382.

Stanovich, K. E. (2000). *Progress in understanding reading: Scientific foundations and new frontiers.* New York: Guilford Press.

Stanovich, K. E., Cunningham, A., & Cramer, B. B. (1984). Assessing phonological awareness in kindergarten children: Issues of task comparability. *Journal of Experimental Child Psychology, 38*, 175–190.

Storch, S. A., & Whitehurst, G. J. (2002). Oral language and code-related precursors to reading: Evidence from a longitudinal structure model. *Developmental Psychology, 38*, 934–947.

Storkel, H. L. (2002). Restructuring of similarity neighborhoods in the developing mental lexicon. *Journal of Child Language, 29*, 251–274.

Storkel, H. L. (2004). Do children acquire dense neighborhoods?: An investigation of similarity neighborhoods in lexical acquisition. *Applied Psycholinguistics, 25*, 201–221.

Swan, D., & Goswami, U. (1997). Phonological awareness deficits in developmental dyslexia and the phonological representations hypothesis. *Journal of Experimental Child Psychology, 66*, 18–41.

Swingley, D., & Aslin, R. N. (2000). Spoken word recognition and lexical representations in very young children. *Cognition, 76*, 147–166.

Swingley, D., & Aslin, R. N. (2002). Lexical neighborhoods and the word-form representations of 14-month-olds. *Psychological Science, 13*, 480–484.

Swingley, D., & Aslin, R. N. (2007). Lexical competition in young children's word learning. *Cognitive Psychology, 54*, 99–132.

Thomas, E., & Sénéchal, M. (2004). Long-term association between articulation quality and phoneme sensitivity: A study from age 3 to age 8. *Applied Psycholinguistics, 25*, 513–541.

Torppa, M., Poikkeus, A. M., Laakso, M. L., Tolvanen, A., Leskinen, E., & Leppänen, P. H. T. (2007). Modeling the early paths of phonological awareness and factors supporting its development in children with and without familiar risk of dyslexia. *Scientific Studies of Reading, 11*, 73–103.

Treiman, R., & Breaux, A. (1982). Common phoneme and overall similarity relations among spoken syllables: Their use by children and adults. *Journal of Psycholinguistic Research, 11*, 569–598.

Troia, G. A., Roth, F. P., & Yeni-Komshian, G. H. (1996). Word frequency effects and age effects in normally developing children's phonological processing. *Journal of Speech and Hearing Research, 39*, 1099–1108.

Vihman, M. M. (1981). Phonology and the development of the lexicon. *Journal of Child Language, 8*, 239–264.

Vihman, M. M. (1996). *Phonological development: The origins of language in the child.* Cambridge, MA: Blackwell.

Vincente, S., Castro, S. L., & Walley, A. C. (2003). A developmental analysis of similarity neighborhoods for European Portuguese. *Journal of Portuguese Linguistics, 2*, 115–133.

Vitevitch, M. S., Luce, P. A., Pisoni, D. B., & Auer, E. T. (1999). Phonotactics, neighborhood activation, and lexical access for spoken words. *Brain and Language, 68*, 306–311.

Vogel-Sosa, A., & Stoel-Gammon, C. (2006). Patterns of intra-word phonological variability during the second year of life. *Journal of Child Language, 33*, 31–50.

Wagner, R. K., Balthazor, M., Hurley, S., & Morgan, S. (1987). The nature of prereaders phonological processing abilities. *Cognitive Development, 2*, 355–373.

Wagner, R. K., Torgesen, J. K., Laughon, P., Simmons, K., & Rashotte, C. A. (1993). Development of young readers' phonological processing abilities. *Journal of Educational Psychology, 85*, 83–103.

Wagner, R. K., Torgesen, J. K., & Rashotte, C. A. (1994). Development of reading-related phonological processing abilities: New evidence of bidirectional causality from a latent variable longitudinal study. *Developmental Psychology, 30*, 73–87.

Walley, A. C. (1987). Young children's detections of word-initial and -final mispronunciations in constrained and unconstrained contexts. *Cognitive Development, 2*, 145–167.

Walley, A. C. (1988). Spoken word recognition by young children and adults, *Cognitive Development, 3*, 137–165.

Walley, A. C. (1993). The role of vocabulary growth in children's spoken word recognition and segmentation ability. *Developmental Review, 13*, 286–350.

Walley, A. C. (2005). Speech perception in childhood. In D. B. Pisoni & R. E. Remez (Eds.), *Handbook of speech perception* (pp. 449–468). Oxford, UK: Blackwell.

Walley, A. C. (2006). Speech learning, lexical reorganization and the development of word recognition by native and non-native English speakers. In M. M. Munro & O. S. Bhon (Eds.), *Festshrift for James E. Flege* (pp. 315–330). Amsterdam: Benjamins.

Walley, A., & Flege, J. (1999). Effects of lexical status on children's and adults' perception of native and non-native vowels. *Journal of Phonetics, 27*, 307–332.

Walley, A. C., & Metsala, J. L. (1990). The growth of lexical constraints on spoken word recognition. *Perception and Psychophysics, 47*, 267–280.

Walley, A. C., & Metsala, J. L. (1992). Young children's age-of-acquisition estimates for spoken words. *Memory and Cognition, 20*, 171–182.

Walley, A. C., Smith, L. B., & Jusczyk, P. W. (1986). The role of phonemes and syllables in the perceived similarity of speech sounds for children. *Memory and Cognition, 14*, 220–229.

Werker, J. F., & Curtin, S. (2005). PRIMIR: A developmental framework of infant speech processing. *Language Learning and Development, 1*, 197–234.

Werker, J. F., & Tees, R. C. (1984). Cross-language speech perception: Evidence for perceptual reorganization during the first year of life. *Infant Behavior and Development, 7*, 49–63.

Werker, J. F., & Tees, R. C. (1999). Influences on infant speech processing: Toward a new synthesis. *Annual Review of Psychology, 50*, 509–535.

Werker, J. F., & Yeung, H. H. (2005). Infant speech perception bootstraps word learning. *Trends in Cognitive Sciences, 9*, 519–527.

Wesseling, R., & Reitsma, P. (2001). Preschool phonological representations and development of reading skills. *Annals of Dyslexia, 51*, 203–229.

White, K. S., & Morgan, J. L. (2008). Sub-segmental detail in early lexical representations. *Journal of Memory and Language, 59*, 114–132.

Wise, J. C., Sevcik, R. A., Morris, R. D., Lovett, M. W., & Wolf, M. (2007). The relationship among receptive and expressive vocabulary, listening comprehension, pre-reading skills, word identification skills, and reading comprehension by children with reading disabilities. *Journal of Speech, Language, and Hearing Research, 50*, 1093–1109.

Yopp, H. K. (1988). The validity and reliability of phonemic awareness tests. *Reading Research Quarterly, 23*, 159–177.

Zamuner, T. S. (2009). Phonological probabilities at the onset of language development: Speech production and word position. *Journal of Speech, Language, and Hearing Research, 52*, 49–60.

Zevenbergen, A. A., Whitehurst, G. J., & Zevenbergen, J. A. (2003). Effects of a shared-reading intervention on the inclusion of evaluative devices in narratives of children from low-income families. *Journal of Applied Developmental Psychology, 24*, 1–15.

II

DEVELOPMENT AMONG
DIVERSE POPULATIONS

6

Development of Early Literacy: Evidence from Major U.S. Longitudinal Studies

MARGARET BURCHINAL
NINA FORESTIERI

The acquisition of strong language and literacy skills is essential for children to succeed in today's information-based economy (Snow & Van Hemel, 2008). Researchers study this important issue with both descriptive and intervention studies. The intervention studies provide the strongest evidence regarding how children acquire these skills, but these programs rely on careful descriptive studies to understand the developmental processes involved in the acquisition of early literacy skills. Whereas other chapters describe the results of intervention studies designed to improve early literacy skills, this chapter focuses on the descriptive studies. Large, diverse longitudinal studies provide an opportunity to describe developmental patterns and identify factors that predict early development of literacy skills with more internal and external validity than smaller studies. These large studies have become more common, and their breadth and depth of measurement can be very useful in examining the development of early literacy skills in diverse populations. Almost all use an ecological model for studying early development and focus on the two primary contexts in early childhood—family and child care. For these reasons, our purpose in this chapter is to summarize the major findings from analyses of large longitudinal studies regarding the development of early literacy skills.

Overview

The acquisition of early literacy skills involves the development of many somewhat different skills (National Early Literacy Panel, 2008). Strong expressive and receptive language skills appear to underlie acquisition of the specific skills necessary to develop decoding skills and to be able to read with comprehension after the decoding skills are acquired (Snow, Burns, & Griffin, 1998). The specific skills necessary to acquire decoding skills include alphabetic knowledge, phonemic awareness and memory, and rapid automatic naming (National Early Literacy Panel, 2008). Almost all of the large studies have described early language acquisition, and few have examined early decoding skills. For this reason, this chapter focuses on decoding skills despite the importance of all of these other skills necessary for children to become competent readers.

During the past 30 years, developmentalists have increasingly focused on longitudinal studies that include substantial numbers of families from different ethnic/ racial backgrounds and incomes to describe developmental processes and outcomes (Brooks-Gunn, Berlin, Leventhal, & Fuligni, 2000). These studies include nationally representative samples such as the National Longitudinal Survey of Youth (NLSY), the Early Childhood Longitudinal Study—Kindergarten Cohort (ECLS-K), the Early Childhood Longitudinal Study—Birth Cohort (ECLS-B), and the Panel of Income Dynamics (PSID). All of these studies involve a complicated stratified sampling strategy that, when weights are appropriately applied, allow results to be generalized to children in the United States as a whole for the birth cohort involved in that study. The ECLS-B and ECLS-K recruited children and are most readily generalized to all U.S. children, whereas the NLSY and PSID follow the children born to randomly selected young adults. Nevertheless, findings from the sample to the population can be generalized to the general population in most cases for all four studies.

Many other large longitudinal studies have examined early childhood development. Many have focused on estimating the impact of child-care experiences on early development. These include the National Institute of Child Health and Human Development (NICHD) Study of Early Child Care and Youth Development (SECCYD), the Cost, Quality, and Outcomes (CQO) study, the National Center for Early Development and Learning 11-state PreK study (NCEDL), and Miami School Readiness Project. Children were recruited and their child-care experiences and developmental outcomes were documented in all of these studies. A few studies also extensively documented the family characteristics and home environment of the children. Each study is large and includes ethnically and economically diverse children but is not representative of the country at large. Findings can be generalized to the specific groups studied and the population in general to the extent that the observed developmental processes do not vary markedly across children from different backgrounds.

Developmental theory focuses on the young child's environment in shaping early development, including early literacy development. Bronfrenbrenner's ecological theo-

ry (Bronfenbrenner & Crouter, 1983) delineates four types of nested systems thought to influence young children's development directly and indirectly. The microsystem includes the most important and direct contexts for young children, the family, and child care. The mesosystem describes interactions among these immediate contexts, that is, parents and caregivers. The exosytem includes contexts in which people in the immediate contexts also interact, such as parental employment or social networks of friends. The macrosystem describes the larger sociocultural context. Each system contains roles, norms, and rules that can powerfully shape development. The young child's development depends on the frequency and complexity of interactions within the microsystem, and these interactions depend on interactions between caregivers at home relative to child care and other individuals, their beliefs about childrearing, and rules and norms of each system.

This chapter focuses on the role of the microsystem, the home and child-care environments, in the acquisition of early literacy skills. Other chapters in this volume describe the rich literatures that examine the many aspects of parenting and classroom instruction that contribute to the development of language, decoding, and phonemic skills. Our focus in this chapter is to discuss findings from the large, diverse studies that describe developmental patterns for children from diverse economic and ethnic backgrounds.

Parenting

Parenting practices appear to be the strongest predictors of early literacy skills (NICHD Early Child Care Research Network [ECCRN], 2003). While it is clear that demographic characteristics such as parental education, social class, family structure, and neighborhood safety are related, it appears the quality of interactions between young children and the adults in their family play the most crucial role (Snow et al., 1998). Specific dimensions of parenting have been examined, including the frequency with which young children experience positive, sensitive, and responsive interactions with parents; the extent to which the home environment includes age-appropriate cognitively stimulating books, toys, and activities; the frequency and complexity of parental language; and the frequency and responsiveness of book reading. Each of these aspects of the home environment has been studied longitudinally.

Parenting Practices

SENSITIVITY AND RESPONSIVENESS

Parental sensitivity and responsiveness play a crucial role for both social and cognitive development (NICHD ECCRN, 2002). Children acquire language skills more quickly when parents, typically the mother, provide prompt, contingent, and appropriate responses to infant behavior (Bornstein, 1989; Clarke-Stewart, 1973). These interactions often involve engaging the infant's attention with an object and using this joint attention to teach the infant about the world (Striano & Stahl, 2005). Mothers who create predictable and enjoyable interactions have children who show stronger language skills during the infant and preschool years (Landry, Smith, Swank, & Miller-Loncar, 2000). Mothers' responsiveness and sensitivity with their young children were strong predictors of children's language, decoding, and reading comprehension skills during the preschool and primary school years in the NICHD SECCYD (NICHD ECCRN, 2002; Belsky et al., 2007) and a moderate predictor in the NLSY (Bradley, Corwyn, Burchinal, McAdoo, & Garcia Coll, 2001) in analyses that adjusted for many of the potentially confounding demographic and schooling factors. In the SECCYD, a parenting composite was created from ratings of maternal sensitivity and responsiveness during mother–child free-play interactions and ratings on an observational measure, the Home Observation for Measurement of the Environment. Effect sizes were computed as the comparison of the lowest and highest quartiles. Adjusting for other demographic and child-care experiences yielded large parenting effect sizes for cognitive outcomes that ranged from $d = 0.40$ with a 15-month outcome to 1.23 with a 54-month outcome, and for social skills outcomes that ranged from 0.6 at 24 months to 0.8 at 54 months (NICHD ECCRN, 2006). Subsequent analyses indicated a pathway from early sensitive parenting through language skills at entry to school to reading skills through grade 3 in the NICHD SECCYD (NICHD ECCRN, 2004).

Some evidence has suggested that maternal sensitivity may operate differently depending on the background of the family. While maternal warmth appears to predict positive social and cognitive development for children of all ethnic and economic backgrounds, growing evidence suggests that maternal intrusiveness or harshness may have a more negative impact on white children than on African American or newly immigrated Mexican American children (Ispa et al., 2004). Using the large evaluation study of the Early Head Start project, Ispa and colleagues (2004) found that maternal intrusiveness was negatively related to child engagement during interactions with the mother only for white and native Hispanic families. Other large studies examined these factors as predictors of language skills. No evidence indicated that responsive and sensitive parenting predicted language and reading skills differently for children from diverse economic or ethnic backgrounds (Bradley et al., 2001).

STIMULATING HOME ENVIRONMENTS

Young children reared in homes with more stimulating books and objects also show faster acquisition of language skills (Bradley et al., 1989). These objects include age-appropriate books and cognitively stimulating toys (e.g., puzzles). Several evaluations of large datasets suggest that this factor provides the strongest prediction of early language reading skills among the various parenting practices typically examined. Such opportunities for learning provided the best prediction of language skills in the first 2 years (Fuligni, Hans, & Brooks-Gunn, 2004) and during preschool (Leventhal, Martin, & Brooks-Gunn, 2004) according to data from the NCLY and the NICHD SECCYD. Bradley and colleagues (1989) also demonstrated that the extent to which families provided such learning opportunities was a moderate predictor of language and reading skills from ages 2–13 years, and that these associations did not vary as a function of income or ethnic background. Furthermore, the presence of stimulating books and objects appeared to account, in part, for the treatment effects in a successful welfare-to-work intervention, Project New Hope (Huston et al., 2001).

Reading to young children has been widely advocated because it consistently is a predictor of early language and literacy skills (Scarborough & Dobrich, 1994). Reading appears to be important because it exposes children to vocabulary in context in interactions that are usually positive and provide children with scaffolded learning experiences. Young children are provided opportunities to learn a language when parents read bedtime stories or read aloud to children from highly engaging books that employ repetition and demonstrate language, syntax, and semantics (Daniels, 1994). Book reading is assumed to be important for all children, but whether parental book reading promotes language skills differently based on income or ethnicity does not appear to have been tested.

LANGUAGE

The complexity and frequency of language interactions between children and their parents also clearly play a critical role in language development (Snow, 1991). Mothers who provide more frequent and complex linguistic interactions with their infants have children who acquire language and linguistic skills more rapidly (Hoff, 2003; Huttenlocher, Haight, Bryk, Seltzer, & Lyons, 1991; Pan, Rowe, Singer, & Snow, 2005). Not surprisingly, none of the large datasets have included extensive analyses of the complexity of maternal language with young children due to the time and skill involved in coding maternal language.

PARENTING AS MEDIATOR OF POVERTY

Different aspects of parenting have been examined as mediators for the pathway between poverty and poorer child outcomes. Children raised in poverty scored substantially lower than children who never experienced poverty in the NICHD SECCYD, with a moderate effect size of $d = 0.52$ for academic and language skills through third grade (NICHD ECCRN, 2005a). Various studies have examined access to cognitively stimulating materials, maternal warmth and responsiveness in interactions with the child,

and maternal language skills. Children from low socioeconomic status (SES) families often have less access to cognitively stimulating materials, which accounts for ethnicity differences and at least some SES differences in language and literacy outcomes in early and middle childhood according to analyses of the NLSY (Bradley & Corwyn, 1999; Bradley et al., 2001), PSID (Duncan, Brooks-Gunn, & Klebanov, 1994), and NICHD SECCYD (NICHD ECCRN, 2005a, 2005b). Poverty is related to less warmth and responsiveness, and more withdrawal and harshness in mother–child interactions, which also accounts for at least some of the association between poverty and child outcomes in early and middle childhood according to analyses of the NLSY, NICHD SECCYD, and PSID (Brooks-Gunn & Duncan, 1997; Hoff, 2003; Linver, Brooks-Gunn, & Kohen, 2002; NICHD ECCRN, 2005a). Differences in maternal language input in early infancy and early childhood, including less elaborate vocabulary and syntax, have been implicated as explanatory factors for why low-income children have lower cognitive and language skills in early and middle childhood (Hart & Risley, 1995; Hoff, 2003). These conclusions have been supported with analyses of the NICHD SECCYD (Mistry, Vandewater, Huston, & McLoyd, 2002; NICHD ECCRN, 2005a, 2005b) and the NLSY (Linver et al., 2002; Yeung, Linver, & Brooks-Gunn, 2002).

In conclusion, there is extensive evidence that the sensitivity and responsiveness, cognitive stimulation, book reading, and quality of language interactions play an important role in young children's acquisition of early literacy skills. Little to no evidence suggests that these factors operate differently for low- and middle-income families or for families from diverse ethnic backgrounds.

Child Care

Numerous experimental and observational research studies document short-term and long-term benefits of attending preschool on language and early literacy development (Gormley, Gayer, Phillips, & Dawson, 2005; Lazar, Darlington, Murray, Royce, & Snipper, 1982; Magnuson, Meyers, Ruhm, & Waldfogel, 2004; NICHD ECCRN, 2003,

2006; Reynolds, Temple, Robertson, & Mann, 2001; Schweinhart et al., 2005). The extent to which child-care experiences are related to the acquisition of language and other literacy skills has been extensively examined in the child-care literature. These findings are summarized below, beginning with a discussion of the seminal intervention experiments, and including a discussion of findings on type and quality of child care.

Intervention Child Care

Early intervention projects such as the High/Scope Perry Preschool Study (Schweinhart et al., 2005; Nores, Barnett, Belfield, & Schweinhart, 2005) and the Abecedarian Project (Campbell, Ramey, Pungello, Sparling, & Miller-Johnson, 2002) demonstrated that sustained research-based child-care experiences can improve cognitive and social outcomes for children from low-income families. These improved outcomes translated into lifelong savings in terms of reduced criminal activities and increased education and occupational opportunities, with estimated costs–benefits associated with child-care programs ranging from $2.50 per $1 spent on Abecedarian Project children to $12.90 per $1 spent on Perry Preschool children (Belfield, Nores, Barnett, & Schweinhart, 2006).

Several meta-analyses have examined the magnitude of these early childhood intervention programs on children's short- and long-term development. Nelson, Westhues, and MacLeod (2003) estimated effect sizes for the 34 preschool intervention programs with at least one follow-up assessment. Moderately large effects for language and academic outcomes during preschool ($d = 0.52$) were still detectable at eighth grade ($d = 0.30$). Bigger cognitive effects were observed when programs had an intentional instruction component. Overall, programs that started at younger ages and provided more years of intervention had the largest effects. Similarly, in a RAND Corporation study, Karoly, Kilburn, and Cannon, (2005) examined 20 programs implemented in the United States that provide services to children and/or families during early childhood. They also reported that approximately two-thirds of the programs produced statistically significant benefits for children's outcomes,

with larger effects on IQ or standardized language or achievement test scores for intensive full-time early childhood education (ECE) interventions focused on improving school readiness, and smaller effects for parent ratings of socioemotional outcomes in typically less intensive programs focused on both mother and child.

Community and Public Child Care

Descriptive or quasi-experimental studies (i.e., studies that do not involve random assignment to ECE conditions) have provided further support for an association between higher-quality ECE and positive child outcomes in studies involving larger, more representative samples (Gormley et al., 2005; Howes et al., 2008; NICHD ECCRN, 2005b; Peisner-Feinberg et al., 2001; Reynolds, Temple, Robertson, & Mann, 2002). While the experimental studies were examining the impact of specific center-based ECE programs, many of the observational studies focused on the extent to which the quality of ECE that does not involve intervention predicts child outcomes during the preschool years or at entry to kindergarten.

In addition, growing evidence suggests that language and early literacy skills are enhanced when children receive community-based, center-based child care as preschoolers. The NICHD SECCYD followed over 1,000 infants from birth into high school. They found that more time in center-based child care was related to higher expressive language skills ($d = 0.09$) and reading skills from preschool through third grade in analyses that included a wide array of family and other child-care or school characteristics as covariates. Similarly, analyses of the nationally representative ECLS-K, using various approaches to account for possible biases related to family characteristics, found that children with center-based child-care experiences started kindergarten with higher early literacy skills (Loeb, Bridges, Bassok, Fuller, & Rumberger, 2005; Magnuson, Meyers, Ruhm, & Waldfogel, 2004). Effect sizes were not computed, and the apparent impact of center-based care is modest for most children, but appears to be greater for children from low-income families (Loeb et al., 2005; Magnuson et al., 2004). A welfare-to-work experiment that involved child-care subsidies also reported positive impacts on children's literacy skills that could be attributed to attending child-care centers (Huston et al., 2005).

The findings from the early intervention programs and other child-care research (Lamb, 1998) led to funding of large, federal child-care programs such as Head Start, and state programs such as public prekindergarten in an attempt to improve school readiness skills of children from low-income families. Evaluations of public PreK programs in Tulsa (Gormley et al., 2005), an 11-state evaluation of mature state PreK programs (Howes et al., 2008), and the nationally representative ECLS-K (Magnuson et al., 2005) also indicate that low-income children in these programs made moderate to large gains in language and early reading skills. Effect sizes apparently ranged from about $d = 0.12$ to $d = 0.86$, depending on the type of analyses used. Larger gains were observed for children from low-income families in the Tulsa evaluation and the ECLS-K.

Child-Care Quality

GLOBAL QUALITY MEASURES

Descriptive or quasi-experimental studies (i.e., studies that do not involve random assignment) have relatively consistently reported associations between child-care quality and both language and early reading outcomes (Lamb, 1998; Vandell, 2004). Three large child-care studies reported that children develop stronger language and early literacy skills when they attend higher-quality child-care settings (Howes et al., 2008; NICHD ECCRN, 2005b; Peisner-Feinberg et al., 2001; Reynolds et al., 2002). The NICHD SECCYD reported in its sample of over 1,000 children followed from birth that when children experienced higher-quality child care, their language skills were modestly higher at 36 months (NICHD ECCRN, 2000) and from entry to school through fifth grade (Belsky et al., 2007; NICHD ECCRN, 2003, 2006). Estimated effect sizes ($d = 0.09$) reflected the extent to which language scores were higher when children experienced quality that was one standard deviation higher. The CQO study related quality of care to children's language and reading outcomes in a study of 200 centers in four states. Children in higher-quality classrooms had better language (partial correlation $r_p = .19$) and reading skills ($r_p = .07$). Children in the 11-state PreK evaluation study also showed larger gains in their receptive and expressive language skills when they experienced higher-quality child care (standardized gains associated with a standard deviation gain in quality: $0.06 < d < 0.07$) (Howes et al., 2008; Mashburn et al., 2008). Studies of both low-income and middle-income children suggest that high-quality community child-care experiences promote short and long-term cognitive, academic, and social outcomes (NICHD ECCRN, 1999, 2000; 2005b; Peisner-Feinberg et al., 2001), but children from low-income families or families with other social risk factors showed larger gains in some studies of community child care (Burchinal, Peisner-Feinberg, Bryant, & Clifford, 2000; Burchinal, Roberts, Zeisel, Hennon, & Hooper, 2006; Peisner-Feinberg et al., 2001; Votruba-Drzal, Coley, & Chase-Lansdale, 2004). Indeed a recent analysis of the nationally representative ECLS-B indicated that preschool experiences appear to be beneficial for all children, especially for low-income African American, European American, and Hispanic children, and for middle-income African American children (Bassok, 2008).

While the relationship between quality and child outcomes is found quite consistently in these large, diverse studies, the association tends to be modest. Careful analyses with NICHD data concluded that the relationship was modest after researchers used different approaches to control for background characteristics of the children and families (NICHD ECCRN, 2006; NICHD ECCRN & Duncan, 2003). In a comprehensive examination of this issue, Burchinal, Kainz, and Cai (in press) conducted both a meta-analysis based on findings across individual early childhood studies and coordinated secondary analyses with multiple, large-scale early childhood datasets. Both research approaches resulted in the conclusion that measures of child-care quality consistently predict language and reading skills for 2- to 5-year-olds, but the strength of the relationship is modest (Burchinal et al., in press). Overall, the association between global quality and child outcomes ranged from a partial correlation of about .05 to about .15.

SPECIFIC QUALITY MEASURES

There is a growing sense that measures of child-care quality need to be more differentiated (Mashburn et al., 2008). Global quality measures combine all the quality indicators across all activities into a single composite score. Specific quality measures describe a specific aspect of the child-care experience (e.g., teacher sensitivity and responsiveness or quality of literacy instruction). Burchinal and colleagues' (in press) meta-analysis indicated that, while still modest, there were stronger associations when specific aspects of quality were examined. For example, associations were somewhat stronger when global quality predicted language skills at 3 years of age. The quality of the teacher's language predicted language skills at 4 years of age (partial correlation $r = .12$) more strongly than global quality predicted either language or reading skills (partial correlations $.08 < r < .09$).

THRESHOLDS

Recently, analyses of data from several large datasets indicated that these modest associations may be due to thresholds in the association between child-care quality and children's language and literacy skills. Thresholds exist when quality is more strongly related to child outcomes at some level of quality than at other levels. For example, many policymakers hoped to find thresholds suggesting that child outcomes would improve when quality improved, until quality reached a "good-enough" level. Alternatively, child-care advocates have argued that child outcomes might not improve with improvements in quality until quality reaches a moderately good-enough level. To test for threshold, analyses were conducted that allowed for nonlinear associations between child-care quality and child outcomes. Analyses of the 11-state PreK study (NCEDL) and Head Start evaluation (FACES) suggested that quality was a stronger predictor of language and reading skills when classrooms met conventional definitions of good quality, but was not related when classrooms met conventional definitions of poor quality. In lower-quality classrooms (e.g., classrooms with an Early Childhood Environment Rating Scale [ECERS] total score of less than

3), quality of teacher–child interactions did not predict language or reading skills. The quality of instruction was a much stronger predictor of language and reading when teachers provided moderate- to good-quality instruction and was not related when classrooms were deemed low quality (e.g., Classroom Assessment Scoring System [CLASS] Instruction score less than 2). These results are provocative in relation to further refinement of the association between quality and outcome gains, and have implications both for policies related to targeting the needs of children and teachers, and further refinement of measurement systems for assessing quality.

MODERATORS OF QUALITY

Questions have been raised about whether children from diverse racial/ethnic backgrounds require different types of experiences to develop cognitive and social skills during early childhood (Bowman, 2002; Rogoff, 2003). The potential disparity between educators' belief systems and socialization practices, and the family backgrounds of young children of color could mean that classroom practices more in line with home practices may be better at promoting acquisition of skills in these young children (Bowman, 2002; Garcia Coll et al., 1996). Several large studies have attempted to examine this issue. A secondary data analysis of SEC-CYD and CQO data tested whether widely used measures of quality predict children's acquisition of language and reading skills differently for European American, African American, and English-speaking Hispanic children (Burchinal & Cryer, 2003). Findings suggest that these widely used quality measures predict skills as well or better in the African American and Hispanic children than in European American children in analyses that also included many family characteristics. There was no evidence that alignment between home and family values enhanced child outcomes in that study, and recent analyses of NCEDL data (Barbarin et al., 2008) and an older analysis of SECCYD data (Burchinal & Cryer, 2003). Instead, it appears that all children benefited when they experienced caregiving at home or in child care from adults with more authoritative and less authoritarian attitudes. Indeed, recent analyses of the NICHD SECCYD suggest that experiencing higher-quality child care for low-income European American and African American children promoted academic success in elementary school by enhancing children's early language and other school readiness skills (Dearing, McCartney, & Taylor, 2009).

SPECIFIC ASPECTS OF CHILD-CARE QUALITY

Three specific aspects of child-care quality—the amount/quality of language interactions with caregivers, the quality of instruction, and the use of one-on-one or small-group instruction—appear to be especially important for development of literacy skills in child care. In addition, teacher education and training have been closely examined. These are discussed briefly below.

The extent to which young children engage in frequent scaffolded verbal interactions with their caregivers is almost universally accepted as the most critical aspect of early literacy development (Snow et al., 1998; Snow & Van Hemel, 2008). The Language and Interactions factor scores from the ECERS predicted gains in language skill in the NCEDL 11-state PreK evaluation (Howes et al., 2008; Jackson et al., 2007). Results from the NICHD SECCYD indicated that frequency of language interactions was the single best predictor of early cognitive, language, and reading skills at 2, 3, and 4.5 years-of-age (NICHD ECCRN, 2000, 2003). Follow-up analyses of a smaller sample indicated that the quality and quantity of language in preschool predict language and decoding skills in kindergarten and reading comprehension in fourth grade (Dickinson & Porche, in press). Frequency of inferential rather than literal questioning and of verbal interchanges in general have been linked to eliciting children's verbal responses (Zucker et al., 2010) and their acquisition of language skills (Huttenlocher et al., 1991). Head Start and state PreK programs increasingly focus on improving the language environment in child care because of its critical role in programs that serve as enrichment opportunities for young children (see Preschool Curriculum Evaluation Research Consortium [PCER], 2008, for review).

Instructional quality has also been implicated as being very important for early literacy acquisition in recent child-care studies. The CLASS (Pianta, La Paro, & Hamre, 2004) defines *instructional quality* as involving sequential and in-depth concept development, and differentiated and positive feedback to children. The NCEDL 11-state PreK evaluation reported that instructional quality is the best predictor of language and decoding skills from PreK (Howes et al., 2008) into kindergarten (Burchinal et al., 2008). Quality of instruction was a better predictor than sensitivity and responsiveness of the teacher, and the structural characteristics such as teacher education and adult–child ratios (Mashburn et al., 2008).

Growing evidence suggests that children learn literacy skills more quickly in one-on-one or small-group instruction than in whole-class or large-group instructional groups (National Early Literacy Panel, 2008). Both observational and intervention studies have suggested that homogeneous individualized instruction matched to the child's skills level is much more effective than large-group instruction.

Education and training are believed to give teachers the skills they need to provide high-quality care to young children. More education was related to higher-quality care and child outcomes in both large studies (Burchinal, Cryer, Clifford, & Howes, 2002; Clarke-Stewart, Vandell, Burchinal, O'Brien, & McCartney, 2002; Howes, Whitebook, & Phillips, 1992; Kontos & Wilcox-Herzog, 2001; NICHD ECCRN, 2000, 2002; Phillipsen, Burchinal, Howes, & Cryer, 1997; Scarr, Eisenberg, & Deater-Deckard, 1994; Vandell, 2004) and smaller ones (Burchinal et al., 2000; de Kruif, McWilliam, Ridley, & Wakely, 2000). Based on this research evidence and recommendations from early childhood advocates (Barnett, Hustedt, Robin, & Schulman, 2005; National Research Council, 2001; Trust for Early Education, 2004), state and federal policies have focused on requiring early childhood teachers to receive training and obtain college degrees. As of 2005, 17 of the 38 states with public PreK programs require that all lead teachers hold a bachelor's degree, and another 12 states require a bachelor's degree of some PreK teachers. Similarly, Improving Head Start for School Readiness Act of 2007 requires that at least 50% of Head Start teachers in center-based programs nationwide have a bachelor's degree.

A comprehensive reanalysis of data from large child-care studies examined the extent to which teacher education predicts preschool classroom quality and child outcomes. Early and colleagues (2007) reanalyzed data from seven large studies of the early care and education of 4-year-olds, using the same definitions of *teacher education* and *classroom quality*, and the same analytic methods across all major, large child-care study datasets. The datasets included three studies of public PreK programs, three studies that either exclusively or primarily examined Head Start classes, and one study that focused primarily on community child care. No consistent pattern of association was found between any index of teacher education and either classroom quality or child outcomes. The authors offered several possible explanations for this lack of association, focusing on newness and inadequate staffing of most early childhood education training programs, which has led to a lack of attention within those programs on issues especially pertinent to early childhood (Hyson, Tomlinson, & Morris, 2008).

Conclusions

Young children show more rapid acquisition of early language and literacy skills when they experience sensitive and cognitively stimulating care at home and in child care. Results from analyses of the large studies indicate that frequent warm, contingent, and scaffolded interactions during infancy, in which the caregiver engages the infant in joint attention, and warm, cognitively stimulating interactions during toddlerhood and preschool years promote these skills for all children regardless of economic or ethnic background. It is clear that parenting sensitivity, cognitive stimulation in the home environment, and parental language are stronger predictors of language skills than child-care experiences during early childhood (NICHD ECCRN, 2006). In contrast, intervention efforts to improve children's language skills have tended to be more successful when focused directly on the child, such as in child-care interventions, rather than on the parents, such as in home visits

or combined home and child-care interventions (Brooks-Gunn, 2003). The increased attention on developing linguistic skills in all early childhood interventions should help to promote these crucial skills for all children based on both descriptive studies from the large longitudinal studies and the intervention studies discussed in other chapters.

References

Barbarin, O. A., Frome, P., Early, D., Clifford, R., Bryant, D., Burchinal, M., et al. (2008). Parental conceptions of school readiness: Relation to ethnicity, socioeconomic status, and children's skills. *Early Education and Development, 19*(5), 671–701.

Barnett, W. S., Hustedt, J. T., Robin, K. B., & Schulman, K. L. (2005). *The state of preschool: 2005 state preschool yearbook*. New Brunswick, NJ: National Institute for Early Education Research.

Bassok, D. (2008, November). *Do Hispanic children benefit more from preschool?: Examining the role of differential selection processes in explaining the effects of early childhood interventions across racial and ethnic groups*. Paper presented at the annual conference of the Association for Public Policy Analysis and Management, Los Angeles.

Belfield, C. R., Nores, M., Barnett, S., & Schweinhart, L. (2006). The High/Scope Perry Preschool Program: Cost–benefit analysis using data from the age 40 follow-up. *Journal of Human Resources, 40*(1), 162–190.

Belsky, J., Vandell, D. L., Burchinal, M., Clarke-Stewart, A. K., McCartney, K., Owen, M. T., et al. (2007). Are there long-term effects of early child care? *Child Development, 78*(2), 681–701.

Bornstein, M. H. (1989). *Maternal responsiveness: Characteristics and consequences*. San Francisco: Jossey-Bass.

Bowman, B. (2002). Teaching young children well: Implications for 21st century educational policies. *Perspectives on Urban Education, 1*(1). Retrieved from *www.urbanedjournal.org/archive/issue%201/featurearticles/article0001.pdf*.

Bowman, B. T., Donovan, M. S., & Burns, M. S. (Eds.). (2001). *Eager to learn: Educating our preschoolers*. Committee on Early Childhood Pedagogy, Commission on Behavioral and Social Sciences and Education, National Research Council. Washington, DC: National Academy Press.

Bradley, R. H., Caldwell, B. M., Rock, S. L., Barnard, K., Gray, C., Hammond, M., et al. (1989). Home environment and cognitive development in the first 3 years of life: A collaborative study involving six sites and three cultural groups in North America. *Developmental Psychology, 25*, 217–235.

Bradley, R. H., & Corwyn, R. F. (1999). Parenting. In C. Tamis-LaMonda & L. Balter (Eds.), *Child psychology: A handbook of contemporary issues* (pp. 339–362). New York: Psychology Press.

Bradley, R. H., Corwyn, R. F., Burchinal, M., McAdoo, H. P., & Garcia Coll, C. (2001). The home environments of children in the United States: Part II. Relations with behavioral development through age thirteen. *Child Development, 72*, 1868–1886.

Bronfenbrenner, U., & Crouter, A. C. (1983). The evolution of environmental models in developmental research. In W. Kessen (Ed.), *Handbook of child psychology: Vol. 1. History, theory, and methods* (4th ed., pp. 357–414). New York: Wiley.

Brooks-Gunn, J. (2003). Do you believe in magic?: What we can expect from early childhood intervention programs. *Social Policy Report, 17*(1), 3.

Brooks-Gunn, J., Berlin, L. J., Leventhal, T., & Fuligni, A. S. (2000). Depending on the kindness of strangers: Current national data initiatives and developmental research. *Child Development, 71*(1), 257–268.

Brooks-Gunn, J., & Duncan, G. J. (1997). The effects of poverty on children. *The Future of Children, 7*(2), 55–71.

Burchinal, M., Kainz, K., & Cai, Y. (in press). How well are our measures of quality predicting to child outcomes?: A meta-analysis and coordinated analysis of data from large scale studies of early childhood settings. In M. Zaslow, I. Martinez-Beck, T. Halle, & K. Tout (Eds.), *Measuring quality in early childhood settings*. Baltimore: Brookes.

Burchinal, M. R., & Cryer, D. (2003). Diversity, child care quality, and developmental outcomes. *Early Childhood Research Quarterly, 18*, 401–426.

Burchinal, M. R., Cryer, D., Clifford, R. M., & Howes, C. (2002). Caregiver training and classroom quality in child care centers. *Applied Developmental Science, 6*(1), 2–11.

Burchinal, M. R., Peisner-Feinberg, E., Bryant, D. M., & Clifford, R. (2000). Children's social and cognitive development and child-care quality: Testing for differential associations related to poverty, gender, or ethnicity. *Applied Developmental Science, 4*, 149–165.

Burchinal, M. R., Roberts, J. E., Zeisel, S. A., Hennon, E. A., & Hooper, S. (2006). Social risk and protective child, parenting, and child care factors in early elementary school years. *Parenting: Science and Practice, 6*(1), 79–113.

Campbell, F. A., Ramey, C. T., Pungello, E., Sparling, J., & Miller-Johnson, S. (2002). Early childhood education: Young adult outcomes from the Abecedarian Project. *Applied Developmental Science, 6*(1), 42–57.

Clarke-Stewart, K. A. (1973). Interactions between mothers and their young children: Characteristics and consequences. *Monographs of the Society for Research in Child Development, 38*, 1–109.

Clarke-Stewart, K. A., Vandell, D. L., Burchinal, M., O'Brien, M., & McCartney, K. (2002). Do regulable features of child-care homes affect children's development? *Early Childhood Research Quarterly, 17*(1), 52–86.

Daniels, H. (1994). *Literature circles: Voice and choice in the student-centered classroom*. Markham, ON, Canada: Pembroke.

de Kruif, R. E. L., McWilliam, R. A., Ridley, S. M., & Wakely, M. B. (2000). Classification of teachers' interaction behaviors in early childhood classrooms. *Early Childhood Research Quarterly, 15*(2), 247–268.

Dearing, E., McCartney, K., & Taylor, B. A. (2009). Does higher quality early child care promote low-income children's math and reading achievement in middle childhood? *Child Development, 80*(5), 1329–1349.

Dickinson, D. K., & Porche, M. V. (in press). The relationship between teacher–child conversations with low-income four-year-olds and grade four languages and literacy development. *Child Development*.

Duncan, G. J., Brooks-Gunn, J., & Klebanov, P. K. (1994). Economic deprivation and early childhood development. *Child Development, 65*(2), 296–318.

Early, D. M., Maxwell, K. L., Burchinal, M., Alva, S., Bender, R. H., Bryant, D., et al. (2007). Teachers' education, classroom quality, and young children's academic skills: Results from seven studies of preschool programs. *Child Development, 78*(2), 558–580.

Fuligni, A. S., Han, W., & Brooks-Gunn, J. (2004). The Infant–Toddler HOME in the second and third years of life. *Parenting: Science and Practice, 4*, 139–159.

Garcia Coll, C., Lamberty, G., Jenkins, R., McAdoo, H. P., Crnic, K., Wasik, B. H., et al. (1996). An integrative model for the study of developmental competencies in minority children. *Child Development, 67*, 1891–1914.

Gormley, W. T., Gayer, T., Phillips, D., & Dawson, B. (2005). The effects of universal pre-K on cognitive development. *Developmental Psychology, 41*(6), 872–884.

Hart, B., & Risley, T. R. (1995). *Meaningful experiences in the everyday experiences of young American children*. Baltimore: Brookes.

Hoff, E. (2003). The specificity of environmental influence: Socioeconomic status affects early vocabulary development via maternal speech. *Child Development, 74*(5), 1368–1378.

Howes, C., Burchinal, M., Pianta, R., Bryant, D., Early D. M., & Clifford, R. (2008). Ready to learn?: Children's pre-academic achievement in prekindergarten programs. *Early Childhood Research Quarterly, 23*, 27–50.

Howes, C., Whitebook, M., & Phillips, D. (1992). Teacher characteristics and effective teaching in child care: Findings from the National Child Care Staffing Study. *Child and Youth Care Forum* [Special issue: Meeting the child care needs of the 1990s: Perspectives on day care: II], *21*, 399–414.

Huston, A. C., Duncan, G. J., Granger, R., Bos, J., McLoyd, V., Mistry, R., et al. (2001). Work-based antipoverty programs for parents can enhance the school performance and social behavior of children. *Child Development, 72*(1), 318–336.

Huston, A. C., Duncan, G. J., McLoyd, V. C., Crosby, D. A., Ripke, M. N., Weisner, T. S., et al. (2005). Impacts on children of a policy to promote employment and reduce poverty for low-income parents: New hope after 5 years. *Developmental Psychology, 41*(6), 902–918.

Huttenlocher, J., Haight, W., Bryk, A., Seltzer, M., &

Lyons, T. (1991). Early vocabulary growth: Relation to language input and gender. *Developmental Psychology, 27*(2), 236–248.

Hyson, M., Tomlinson, H. B., & Morris, C. (2008, April). *Does quality of early childhood teacher preparation moderate the relationship between teacher education and children's outcomes?* Paper presented at the annual neeting of the American Educational Research Association. New York, NY.

Ispa, J. M., Fine, M. A., Halgunseth, L. C., Harper, S., Robinson, J., Boyce, L., et al. (2004). Maternal intrusiveness, maternal warmth, and mother–toddler relationship outcomes: Variations across low-income ethnic and acculturation groups. *Child Development, 75*(6), 1613–1631.

Jackson, R., McCoy, A., Pistorino, C., Wilkinson, A., Burghardt, J., Clark, M., et al. (2007). *National evaluation of Early Reading First: Final report to Congress.* Washington, DC: Institute for Education Sciences.

Karoly, L. A., Kilburn, M. R., & Cannon, J. S. (2005). *Early childhood interventions: Proven results, future promise,* MG-341. Santa Monica, CA: RAND Corporation.

Kontos, S., & Wilcox-Herzog, A. (2001). How do education and experience affect teachers of young children? *Young Children, 52,* 4–12.

Lamb, M. (1998). Nonparental child care: Context, quality, correlates, and consequences. In W. Damon, I. E. Sigel, & K. A. Renninger (Eds.), *Handbook of child psychology: Child psychology in practice* (5th ed., Vol. 4, pp. 73–133). New York: Wiley.

Landry, S. H., Smith, K. E., Swank, P. R., & Miller-Loncar, C. L. (2000). Early maternal and child influences on children's later independent cognitive and social functioning. *Child Development, 71*(2), 358–375.

Lazar, I., Darlington, R., Murray, H., Royce, J., & Snipper, A. (1982). Lasting effects of early education: A report from the consortium for longitudinal studies. *Monographs of the Society for Research in Child Development, 47*(2–3, Serial No. 195).

Leventhal, T., Martin, A., & Brooks-Gunn, J. (2004). The EC-HOME across five national data sets in the third to fifth year of life. *Parenting: Science and Practice, 4,* 161–188.

Linver, M. R., Brooks-Gunn, J., & Kohen, D. E. (2002). Family processes in pathways from income to young children's development. *Developmental Psychology, 38,* 719–734.

Loeb, S., Bridges, M., Bassok, D., Fuller, B., & Rumberger, R. (2005). How much is too much?: The influence of pre-school centers on children's social and cognitive development. *Economics of Education Review, 26*(1), 52–66.

Magnuson, K. A., Meyers, M. K., Ruhm, C. J., & Waldfogel, J. (2004). Inequality in preschool education and school readiness. *American Educational Research Journal, 41*(1), 115–157.

Magnuson, K. A., Meyers, M. K., Ruhm, C. J., & Waldfogel, J. (2005). Inequality in children's school readiness and public funding. *Focus, 24*(1), 12–18.

Mashburn, A. J., Pianta, R. C., Hamre, B. K., Downer, J. T., Barbarin, O. A., Bryant, D., et al. (2008). Measures of classroom quality in pre-kindergarten and children's development of academic, language and social skills. *Child Development, 79*(3), 732–749.

Mistry, R. S., Vandewater, E. A., Huston, A. C., & McLoyd, V. C. (2002). Economic well-being and children's social adjustment: The role of family process in an ethnically diverse low-income sample. *Child Development, 73,* 935–951.

National Early Literacy Panel. (2008). *Developing early literacy: Report of the National Early Literacy Panel.* Washington, DC: National Institute for Literacy.

Nelson, G., Westhues, A., & MacLeod, J. (2003). A meta-analysis of longitudinal research on preschool prevention programs for children. *Prevention and Treatment, 6*(1). Retrieved from *journals.apa.org/prevention.*

NICHD Early Child Care Research Network (ECCRN). (1999). Child outcomes when child care center classes meet recommended standards for quality. *American Journal of Public Health, 89,* 1072–1077.

NICHD Early Child Care Research Network (ECCRN). (2000). The relation of child care to cognitive and language development. *Child Development, 71,* 958–978.

NICHD Early Child Care Research Network (ECCRN). (2002). Early child care and children's development prior to school entry: Results from the NICHD study of early child care. *American Educational Research Journal, 39,* 133–164.

NICHD Early Child Care Research Network (ECCRN). (2003). Does quality of child care affect child outcomes at age 4-½? *Developmental Psychology, 39,* 451–469.

NICHD Early Child Care Research Network (ECCRN). (2004, Spring). Multiple pathways to early academic achievement. *Harvard Educational Review,* pp. 1–29.

NICHD Early Child Care Research Network (ECCRN). (2005a). Duration and developmental timing of poverty and children's cognitive and social development from birth through third grade. *Child Development, 76*(4), 795–810.

NICHD Early Child Care Research Network (ECCRN). (2005b). Early child care and children's development in the primary grades: Follow-up results from the NICHD study of early child care. *American Educational Research Journal, 42*(3), 537–570.

NICHD Early Child Care Research Network (ECCRN). (2006). Child care effect sizes for the NICHD Study of Early Child Care and Youth Development. *American Psychologist, 61*(2), 99–116.

NICHD Early Child Care Research Network & Duncan, G. J. (2003). Modeling the impacts of child care quality on children's preschool cognitive development. *Child Development, 74,* 1454–1475.

Nores, M., Barnett, W. S., Belfield, C. R., & Schweinhart, L. J. (2005). Updating the economic impacts of the High/Scope Perry Preschool Program. *Educational Evaluation and Policy Analysis, 27*(3), 245–262.

Pan, B. A., Rowe, M. L., Singer, J. D., & Snow, C. E.

(2005). Maternal correlates of growth in toddler vocabulary production in low-income families. *Child Development, 76*(4), 763–782.

Peisner-Feinberg, E., Burchinal, M., Clifford, R., Culkin, M., Howes, C., Kagan, S., et al. (2001). The relation of preschool child-care quality to children's cognitive and social developmental trajectories through second grade. *Child Development, 72*(5), 1534–1553.

Phillipsen, L. C., Burchinal, M. R., Howes, C., & Cryer, D. (1997). The prediction of process quality from structural features of child care. *Early Childhood Research Quarterly, 12*(3), 281–303.

Pianta, R. C., La Paro, K. M., & Hamre, B. K. (2004). *Classroom Assessment Scoring System [CLASS] manual: Pre-K.* Baltimore: Brookes.

Preschool Curriculum Evaluation Research Consortium. (2008). *Effects of preschool curriculum programs on school readiness: Report from the Preschool Curriculum Evaluation Research Initiative.* Washington, DC: National Center for Education Research.

Reynolds, A. J., Temple, J. A., Robertson, D. L., & Mann, E. A. (2001). Long-term effects of an early childhood intervention on educational achievement and juvenile arrest: A 15-year follow-up of low-income children in public schools. *Journal of the American Medical Association, 285*(18), 2339–2346.

Reynolds, A. J., Temple, J. A., Robertson, D. L., & Mann, E. A. (2002). Age 21 cost–benefit analysis of the Title I Chicago Child–Parent Centers. *Education Evaluation and Policy Analysis, 24*(4), 267–303.

Rogoff, B. (2003). *The cultural nature of human development.* New York: Oxford University Press.

Scarborough, H. S., & Dobrich, W. (1994). On the efficacy of reading to preschoolers. *Developmental Review, 14*(3), 245–302.

Scarr, S., Eisenberg, M., & Deater-Deckard, K. (1994).

Measurement of quality in child care centers. *Early Childhood Research Quarterly, 9*(2), 131–151.

Schweinhart, L. J., Montie, J., Xiang, Z., Barnett, W. S., Belfield, C. R., & Nores, M. (2005). *Lifetime effects: The High/Scope Perry Preschool study through age 40.* Ypsilanti, MI: High/Scope Press.

Snow, C. E. (1991). The theoretical basis for relationships between language and literacy development. *Journal of Research in Childhood Education, 6,* 5–10.

Snow, C. E., Burns, M., & Griffin, P. (Eds.). (1998). *Preventing reading difficulties in young children.* Washington, DC: National Academies Press.

Snow, C. E., & Van Hemel, S. B. (Eds.). (2008). *Early childhood assessment: Why, what, and how?* Washington, DC: National Academies Press.

Striano, T., & Stahl, D. (2005). Sensitivity to triadic attention in early infancy. *Developmental Science, 8*(4), 333–343.

Trust for Early Education. (2004, Fall). *A policy primer: Quality pre-kindergarten.* Retrieved May 16, 2008 from *www.trustforearlyed.org/docs/tee-Primer4.pdf.*

Vandell, D. (2004). Early child care: The known and the unknown. *Merrill–Palmer Quarterly, 50,* 387–414.

Votruba-Drzal, E., Coley, R. L., & Chase-Lansdale, P. L. (2004). Child care and low-income children's development: Direct and moderated effects. *Child Development, 75*(1), 296–312.

Yeung, W. J., Linver, M. R., & Brooks-Gunn, J. (2002). How money matters for young children's development: Parental investment and family processes. *Child Development, 73,* 1861–1879.

Zucker, T. A., Justice, L. M., Piasta, S. B., & Kaderavek, J. N. (2010). Preschool teachers' literal and inferential questions and children's responses during whole-class shared reading. *Early Childhood Research Quarterly, 25*(1), 65–83.

7

Emergent Literacy Environments: Home and Preschool Influences on Children's Literacy Development

KATHY SYLVA
LYDIA L. S. CHAN
EDWARD MELHUISH
PAM SAMMONS
IRAM SIRAJ-BLATCHFORD
BRENDA TAGGART

The field of early literacy has enjoyed tremendous growth over the past two decades, as evidenced by the impressive body of work documented in the three volumes of this handbook. In line with contemporary trends in developmental science, as eloquently summarized by Morrison (2009), conceptual, methodological, and analytical advances have presented new research priorities and possibilities.

> Theoretical conceptualizations have adopted a more complex multilevel, interactive view of developmental change in which children are embedded in a larger context of influences spanning more distal (socioeconomic and sociocultural) to more proximal (parenting, schooling, individual) influences. . . . Laboratory based and largely cross-sectional experimental studies with relatively limited samples and few variables have given way to large, even national and international, longitudinal studies with samples that are more representative . . . . and incorporate many variables at different levels of analysis. . . . Fortuitously, development of analytic strategies, such as structural equation modeling (SEM) and hierarchical linear modeling, catalyzed the successful implementation of these more demand-

ing methodologies, providing statistical tools for responding to the increased complexity and sophistication of measurement. . . . Finally, there has been a subtler but nonetheless distinct shift in the focus of inquiry in recent years, from a universalist focus on abstract processes . . . to more applied areas of focus (schooling, parenting) where the interplay of child in context is more fruitfully revealed and the complex multilevel, interactive nature of developmental change can be fleshed out empirically. (pp. 361–362)

The broader conceptualization of emergent literacy, as proposed by Whitehurst and Lonigan (1998), has expanded the scope of inquiry to include not only the skills, knowledge, and attitudes that are developmental precursors to reading and writing but also the environments that support such developments (Whitehurst et al., 1999; Whitehurst & Lonigan, 2003). Thus, understanding the socialization of the child is now as important as understanding the structural aspects of developmental change (Evangelou, Sylva, Kyriacou, Wild, & Glenny, 2009). Although the empirical links between various preschool skills and later literacy outcomes have been modeled with increasing sophistication (Lonigan, Burgess, & Anthony, 2000; National Institute of Child Health and Human Development (NICHD) Early Child Care Research Network, 2005; Storch & Whitehurst, 2002), environmental influences are often neglected or addressed rather superficially in comparison. Apart from considering the typical sociodemographic variables and perhaps a selection of home literacy experiences (Payne, Whitehurst, & Angell, 1994; Storch & Whitehurst, 2001), predictive studies of developmental trajectories rarely take into account differences in children's preschool environments, especially in terms of the quality of curricular provision. There has indeed been extensive research on the long-term effects of early child-care quality on children's language development (Burchinal, Peisner-Feinberg, Bryant, & Clifford, 2000; NICHD Early Child Care Research Network, 2007); however, the quality assessments tend to focus mainly on the structural aspects of caregiving (e.g., group size, child–adult ratio, physical environment), caregivers' characteristics (e.g., formal education, specialized training, child-care experience, and beliefs about childrearing), and their interactions with children (NICHD Early Child Care Research Network, 2001), without a specific emphasis on pedagogy related to literacy exposure or instruction in the preschool center. Furthermore, the bulk of the research is either cross-sectional (Levy, Gong, Hessels, Evans, & Jared, 2006; Sénéchal, LeFevre, Thomas, & Daley, 1998) or spans relatively short time frames (e.g., from preschool to early elementary grades) (Burgess, 2002; Burgess, Hecht, & Lonigan, 2002; Hood, Conlon, & Andrews, 2008; Sénéchal & LeFevre, 2002), and often involves rather small and nonrepresentative samples (Evans, Shaw, & Bell, 2000; Foy & Mann, 2003; Frijters, Barron, & Brunello, 2000; Roberts, Jurgens, & Burchinal, 2005), such as disadvantaged segments of the population (Britto & Brooks-Gunn, 2001; Foster, Lambert, Abbott-Shim, McCarty, & Franze, 2005). Hence, the cumulative effects[1] of home and preschool environments on subsequent literacy achievement have yet to be fully explored.

This chapter contributes to the literature by presenting findings from the Effective Pre-School and Primary Education (EPPE) project, which demonstrate the enduring and interacting effects of family and preschool influences on children's literacy development from age 3 to 11. The focus is on two major influences: the early years home learning environment (HLE) and the quality of preschool provision, as measured by the Early Childhood Environment Rating Scale—Revised (ECERS-R; Harms, Clifford, & Cryer, 1998) and its British curricular extension, the ECERS-E (Sylva, Siraj-Blatchford, & Taggart, 2003).

Although the EPPE project is not primarily an early literacy study, it has collected much information on children's developmental trajectories in language and reading. A brief overview of the project appears below, outlining key features of the research design and characteristics of the sample. Only the analyses that pertain specifically to literacy development are presented (i.e., empirical models that predict children's language and literacy progress over the preschool years, and from middle to late primary school), the implications of which will also be discussed in relation to policy and practice, as well as future research directions.

Overview of the EPPE 3–11 Project

The EPPE project is Europe's largest longitudinal investigation into the effects of preschool and primary education on children's developmental outcomes.[2] It was commissioned by the U.K. government (Department of Children, Schools and Families) and adopts an "educational effectiveness" design using mixed methods. The main objective from the policy perspective was to identify the "value added" by preschool education and the effects of different types of provision (voluntary playgroup, local government preschool class or private nursery, etc.) on subsequent student attainment. Using multilevel modeling, the authors sought to establish, among other things, the contribution of child, family, home environment, and school characteristics to children's cognitive progress (including literacy) and their social/behavioral development from age 3–11 years. In other words, at the core of EPPE are questions about how the individual characteristics of children are shaped by the environments in which they develop. The view of reciprocal influences owes much to the work of Bronfenbrenner (1979), whose theory puts the child at the center of a series of nested spheres of social and cultural influence, including home and education (Sylva, Melhuish, Sammons, Siraj-Blatchford, & Taggart, 2010).

EPPE Sample

A total of 141 target preschool centers were drawn randomly from five regions across England,[3] selected to cover a range of socioeconomic and geographical areas, including ethnic diversity. Preschool centers were sampled from six types of provision: nursery classes in primary schools, voluntary playgroups, local government day nurseries, private day nurseries, and integrated or combined centers (i.e., centers combining education, health, and care, which are similar to nursery schools but provide extended services for parents and families). The study drew approximately equal numbers of target centers from each of the main types of provision.[4]

As illustrated in Figure 7.1, a nationally representative sample of more than 2,800 children was recruited at the start of preschool (around age 3) and followed until school entry (at age 5), when they were joined by an additional 310 "home" children with no preschool experience.[5] Approximately 2,700 of these children were then followed for a further 6 years until the end of primary school (age 11). Characteristics of the sample are summarized in Table 7.1.

This longitudinal sample consisted of roughly equal numbers of boys and girls, and in terms of ethnicity, 74% of the children were of white U.K. heritage. For 11% of the children, English was an additional language (EAL), but very few of them actually required extra EAL support by the end of primary schooling (only 1.9%). With respect to family structure, 14% of the children lived in large families (defined as those with three or more siblings), and the quality of the preschool HLE was quite varied (41% were in the good or very good categories, while 9% had rather poor provision). Family socioeconomic status (SES) was equally wide-ranging, with over 30% of the families classified in the two highest (professional) occupational categories and 16% reported as unemployed or not working. Furthermore, as a low-income indicator, 16% of the children were found to be eligible for free school meals (FSM) (Sammons, Sylva, Melhuish, Siraj-Blatchford, Taggart, & Hunt, 2008).

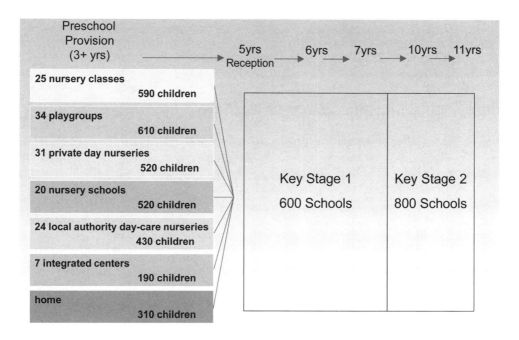

FIGURE 7.1. EPPE design.

TABLE 7.1. Selected Characteristics of EPPE 3–11 Sample (End of Primary School)

	n	%
Gender		
Male	1,375	50.9
Female	1,326	49.1
Ethnicity		
White U.K. heritage	1,974	73.1
White European heritage	84	3.1
Black Caribbean heritage	108	4.0
Black African heritage	59	2.2
Indian heritage	58	2.2
Pakistani heritage	158	5.9
Bangladeshi heritage	34	1.3
Mixed heritage	147	5.4
Any other ethnic-minority heritage	76	2.8
Family socioeconomic status		
Professional nonmanual	273	10.1
Other professional nonmanual	569	21.1
Skilled nonmanual	515	19.1
Skilled manual	558	20.7
Semiskilled	241	8.9
Unskilled	56	2.1
Unemployed/not working	423	16.0
Mother's highest qualification		
Other professional	39	1.5
Higher degree	87	3.4
Degree or equivalent	283	11.0
18 Academic	211	8.2
16 Academic	998	38.9
Vocational	388	15.1
None	562	21.9
Received free school meals[a]	344	16.2
English as an additional language	291	10.8
Three or more siblings	357	14.0
Preschool Home Learning Environment Index		
0–13 (very poor)	246	9.1
14–19 (poor)	585	21.6
20–24 (satisfactory)	629	23.3
25–32 (good)	815	30.2
33–45 (very good)	293	10.9

Note. N = 2,701.
[a]A proxy measure for poverty.

In addition to the collection of demographic data, a comprehensive developmental profile was established for each child, which included many cognitive verbal and nonverbal assessments (collected by trained researchers or by schoolteachers), social and emotional assessments (carried out by key preschool workers and primary schoolteachers), and self-reports completed by the children themselves. These longitudinal assessments at ages 3, 5, 6, 7, 10, and 11 form the core of the study, and are supplemented by parental interviews and questionnaires to collect information on family demographics and the HLE. The preschool settings and a subset of the primary schools were also studied through interviews, questionnaires, observations, and document scrutiny.[6]

This rich dataset enabled multiple research questions to be addressed, some of which are explored in this chapter, for example:

What is the contribution of the HLE to children's language and literacy development?

What is the impact of the amount or duration of preschool experience?

Does the quality of the preschool setting have a significant impact on children's language and literacy progress?

The relevant assessment measures are broadly outlined below.

Cognitive and Linguistic Measures

In terms of cognitive baseline measures, the children were assessed at the start of preschool on four subscales from the British Ability Scales–II[7] (BAS-II; Elliott, Smith, & McCulloch, 1996): Verbal Comprehension, Naming Vocabulary, Block Building, and Picture Similarities. The first two tests assess receptive and expressive verbal language skills, and the latter assess nonverbal reasoning and spatial awareness skills. Upon entry into primary school, these BAS-II measures were readministered (with BAS-II Pattern Construction replacing Block Building), and two additional code-related measures were included in the test battery to assess letter recognition and phonological awareness skills (Bryant & Bradley, 1985). In effect, both domains of children's emergent literacy were examined at age 5, resulting in two composite outcome measures, namely, code-related and oral language skills.

- Oral language skills
  - BAS-II Verbal Comprehension: receptive language; understanding of oral instructions involving basic language concepts.
  - BAS-II Naming Vocabulary: expressive language; knowledge of names.
- Code-related skills
  - Letter Recognition: identification of lowercase letters of the alphabet.
  - Phonological Awareness: two subscales designed by Bryant and Bradley (1985) on the detection of rhyme and alliteration; three words are presented at a time, and the child has to identify the odd one out (e.g., *bun/hut/sun*, or *pin/dog/pig*).
- Nonverbal skills
  - BAS-II Block Building: visual–perceptual matching, especially of spatial orientation, in copying block patterns.
  - BAS-II Picture Similarities: nonverbal reasoning shown by matching pictures that have a common element or concept.
  - BAS-II Pattern Construction: nonverbal reasoning and spatial visualization in reproducing designs with colored blocks.

For middle to late primary school literacy measures, children's results on the statutory National Curriculum Assessments in Years 2 (reading at age 7) and 6 (writing, spelling, and reading comprehension at age 11) were collected, which were subsequently internally standardized to a mean of 100 and a standard deviation of 15.[8]

Table 7.2 presents the intercorrelations, both concurrent and longitudinal, between the various assessment measures, computed as composite scores. Most were moderate in size (.40–.60) and, unsurprisingly, since prior attainment is a good predictor of later attainment, the strongest associations were found between the repeated preschool oral language measures (.75), and the primary school English literacy assessments (.73). Incidentally, children's achievement in literacy and mathematics was also highly intercorrelated (.69 in both Year 2 and Year 6).

TABLE 7.2. Intercorrelations between Preschool and Primary School Measures

	Age 5 oral language	Age 5 code-related	Age 7 reading	Age 11 literacy
Age 3 oral language	.747	.504	.489	.425
Age 5 oral language		.553	.543	.461
Age 5 code-related			.597	.536
Age 7 reading				.728

Note. All correlations are significant at the .01 level.

Home Environment Measure

Near initial recruitment to the study, the child's parents (or guardians) were interviewed (usually the mother), and a range of semistructured and open-ended questions were posed, some of which concerned learning and play activities in the home. The frequency with which the child engaged in the following 14 activities was later coded on an 8-point scale (0 = *not at all* to 7 = *very frequent*):

1. Being read to
2. Painting and drawing
3. Going to the library
4. Playing with letters/numbers
5. Learning activities with the alphabet
6. Learning activities with numbers/shapes
7. Learning activities with songs/poems/nursery rhymes
8. Playing with friends at home
9. Playing with friends elsewhere
10. Visiting relatives or friends
11. Shopping with parent
12. Watching television
13. Eating meals with the family
14. Having a regular bedtime

Note that for the preschool analyses, all of the above home environment items were included in the multilevel models independently. However, for the primary school analyses, only the first seven items relating to clear *learning* opportunities (as opposed to the rest that involve more social or daily routines) were considered, and a composite HLE index was formed. The index had a possible range of 0–49, and was normally distributed with a mean of 23.42 (*SD* = 7.71) (Melhuish et al., 2008). It was found to correlate .38 with children's total BAS-II score

at preschool entry, .32 with family SES, and .35 with parents' educational levels (Melhuish, Sylva, Sammons, Siraj-Blatchford, & Taggart, 2001). Despite these positive (yet moderate) correlations, it is worth emphasizing that consistent with findings from earlier studies (Christian, Morrison, & Bryant, 1998), there were well-educated parents of high SES who seemed to provide a poor HLE, and conversely, there were less well-educated parents of low SES who managed to provide a rich HLE.

Preschool Quality Measures

As previously mentioned, two environmental rating scales were used to assess the quality of all 141 preschool centers involved in the EPPE project. The American ECERS-R (Harms et al., 1998) is one of the most widely used observational measures for describing the characteristics of early childhood education and care. It provides an overview of the preschool environment, covering aspects of the center from furnishings to individuality of care and the quality of social interactions. There are 43 items divided into seven subscales: Space and Furnishings, Personal Care Practices, Language-Reasoning, Preschool Activities, Social Interaction, Organization and Routines, and Adults Working Together. Completion of the whole instrument usually involves approximately half a day of observation, as well as interviewing the staff about aspects of the routine that were not visible during the observation session (e.g., weekly swimming or seasonal outings). Each item is rated on a 7-point scale (1 = *inadequate*, 3 = *minimal/adequate*, 5 = *good*, 7 = *excellent*). For example, the subscale "Program structure" has an item titled "Schedule," which gives high ratings to a balance between adult-initiated and child-initiated activities. To score a 5, the center must achieve a balance between structure and flexibility, but a score of 7 requires variations to be made in the schedule to meet individual needs (e.g., a child working intensively on a project should be allowed to continue past the scheduled time) (Harms et al., 2005). The psychometric strength of this instrument has been demonstrated in past studies, and high interrater reliability was established between senior research officers in each of the five regions of the EPPE study (kappas ranging from .75 to .90).

The American ECERS-R was thought to be insufficiently focused on educational processes for assessing classroom practices in the English context. Although the notion of "developmentally appropriate practice" (Bredekamp & Copple, 1997), upon which the ECERS-R is based, applies in the United Kingdom, the English preschool curriculum concentrates more heavily on *emergent skills*, especially the emergence of literacy, numeracy, and scientific thinking (Soucacou & Sylva, 2010). An English "extension," the ECERS-E (Sylva et al., 2003; Sylva, Siraj-Blatchford, & Taggart, 2010), was therefore developed after wide consultation with experts in early childhood and piloting in the field, and serves as a supplement to the ECERS-R. The EPPE team created three curricular subscales—Literacy, Numeracy, and Science, one for each cognitive domain in the English curriculum (i.e., Communication, Language and Literacy, Numeracy, Knowledge and Understanding of the World),[9] and a fourth Diversity subscale to assess the extent to which the first three are implemented with respect to children of different genders, cultural/ethnic groups, and varying levels of ability (see Appendix 7.1). Like the ECERS-R, each of the four subscales comprises a range of items describing "quality" of the specific type of provision, and the same 7-point rating system is used (see Appendix 7.2). High interrater reliability was again established in all regions (kappas ranging from .83 to .97).

Together, the two observational measures assessed not only the structural elements (e.g., facilities and human resources) of the preschool centers but also the educational and care processes that children experience on a daily basis (Sylva et al., 1999). The total ECERS-R and ECERS-E scores were normally distributed and met parametric assumptions. They were found to correlate .78 with each other, and with the exception of Personal Care Routines, most of the subscales were also moderately intercorrelated, although scores on the ECERS-R tended to be higher than those on the ECERS-E (Sylva et al., 1999) (see Figure 7.2).

Although the ratings averaged across all types of provision were broadly satisfactory, closer inspection within types of provision revealed some striking differences. In this sample, many centers (e.g., nursery schools, combined centers, and nursery classes, all run by the local government) were found to be exciting places where children were challenged and supported in their learning, and where interactions between staff and children were sensitive and enabling. Unfortunately, other centers (e.g., playgroups and private day nurseries) were characterized by hasty planning and poor implementation of the curriculum. As an example, Figure 7.3 illustrates the mean ECERS-E Literacy subscale scores by preschool type.

Analytical Strategy

Two types of multilevel models were computed in the EPPE project: contextualized and value-added analyses of the predictors of children's literacy development. *Contextualized models* identify the unique (net) contribution of particular characteristics (e.g., family SES, parental education, ethnicity, HLE) to variation in children's outcomes, which is of policy interest to establish the nature and strength of such background influences. *Value-added models* investigate children's progress over time (i.e., cognitive gains) by controlling for their prior attainment, as well as a wide range of demographic and environmental influences. Although space constraints of this chapter preclude an extensive discussion of descriptive analyses, it is worth noting that significant subgroup differences in cognitive attainment have been identified since preschool entry and throughout primary schooling (relating to gender, ethnicity, and mother-tongue; family size; parental education; family SES; etc.), and these variables were all treated as covariates in the hierarchical models.

Value-added models predicting children's emergent literacy development over the pre-

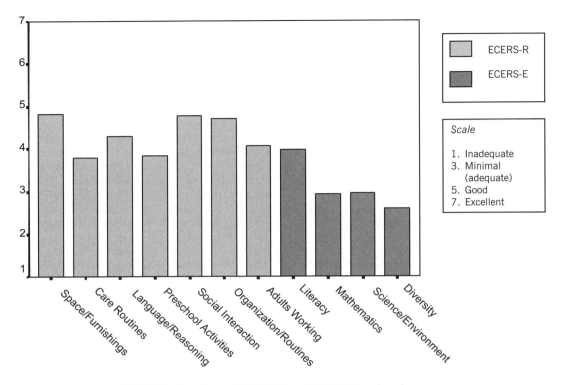

FIGURE 7.2. Mean ECERS-R and ECERS-E subscale scores.

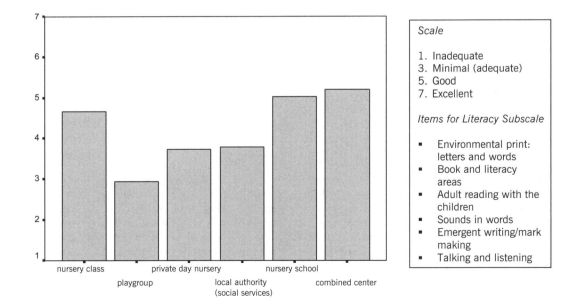

FIGURE 7.3. Mean ECERS-E Literacy subscale scores by preschool type.

school period are first discussed, followed by both contextualized and value-added models predicting literacy attainment and progress in primary school. For ease of interpretation, net effect sizes (ES) are reported in the relevant results tables, and the comparator is the second category within the parentheses next to the categorical variables. Also, only the significant predictors are presented, and for categorical variables, only the largest ESs are reported. Details of the full models can be found in other EPPE publications (Sammons et al., 2002, 2008).

Children's Emergent Literacy Development in Preschool (Age 3–5)

Home Factors Related to Code-Related Skills

Taking into account children's prior verbal and nonverbal attainment at age 3, girls were found to have made more progress by age 5 at developing code-related skills than boys (ES = 0.21; see Table 7.3). Children from ethnic/minority groups (e.g., black African, black Caribbean, Indian, and mixed heritage), who had significantly lower prior attainment scores at preschool entry, also made more progress than their white U.K.

counterparts (ES = 0.70), although they started from a lower base. The narrowing of the achievement gap was likewise found for children with EAL compared to native English speakers (ES = 0.34). Children from larger families (three or more siblings) made less progress than singletons (ES = −0.15), as well as those born with low birthweight compared to others of average or above average birthweight (ES = −0.19). In terms of family background factors, children who were eligible for free school meals (FSM) made less progress (ES = −0.12), as did those whose family SES was categorized as unskilled or semiskilled manual (ES = −0.27). However, children whose mothers held degrees made greater progress (ES = 0.25). In addition, two aspects of the HLE were reported to have a positive impact, namely, the extent to which children played with letters and numbers (ES = 0.36), or engaged in learning activities with the alphabet (ES = 0.51). Finally, both preschool duration (ES = 0.33) and the educational background of parents in the center (i.e., percentage of children whose mothers had a degree; ES = 0.24) were found to be influential predictors of children's progress in this code-related domain of emergent literacy development. This may stem from the

TABLE 7.3. Multilevel Analysis Predicting Progress in Code-Related Skills at Age 5 (Primary School Entry)

Factors	Effect size
Prior verbal attainment	0.89
Prior nonverbal attainment	0.34
Gender (girls vs. boys)	0.21
Ethnicity (minority group 3 vs. white UK)	0.70
No. of siblings (3+ vs. none)	−0.15
English as an additional language (EAL vs. English as mother tongue)	0.34
Birthweight (low vs. average/above average)	−0.19
Free school meal eligibility (eligible vs. not eligible)	−0.12
Mother's qualification level (degree vs. no degree)	0.25
Family SES (unskilled/semiskilled manual vs. professional nonmanual)	−0.27
HLE Item 4: Playing with letters/numbers (daily vs. never)	0.36
HLE Item 5: Learning activities with the alphabet (4–7 times per week vs. never)	0.51
Duration of preschool	0.33
% of children in center 1 *SD* below General Cognitive Assessment mean	0.19
% of children in center with mothers who have a degree or higher	0.24

Note. Impact of prior attainment, child, parent, home environment, and other composition of intake measures on code-related progress over the preschool period. Only the largest effect sizes are reported; comparison group in parentheses.

fact that a high or low proportion of "advantaged" children in a preschool center (in terms of the mother's educational level) will influence the intellectual level of peer play and interactions. Such a "parent status" effect may also influence staff behavior in ways likely to enhance children's development (perhaps through more challenging activities and higher expectations). The results indicate that more advantaged social grouping benefits all children, irrespective of the type of preschool attended.

Home Factors Related to Oral Language Skills

Unlike the development of code-related skills, there were no significant differences in receptive and expressive language progress (see Table 7.4) with regard to gender, birthweight, and eligibility for FSM (an indicator of poverty). Also, children from some ethnic/minority groups were found to have made smaller gains in language skills than the white U.K. group (ES = –0.59). Similarly, children with EAL struggled to catch up to their native speaker peers (ES = –0.24). However, in terms of family size (ES = –0.17), mother's education (ES = 0.24) and family SES measures (ES = –0.23), quite similar results to the previous code-related model

were obtained (i.e., children from larger or low SES families, or those whose mothers were less well-educated made less progress). In terms of the home environment, children who were read to daily (ES = 0.27); who visited the library often (ES = 0.18); or were encouraged to learn songs, poems, or nursery rhymes (ES = 0.20) improved more in their language acquisition. Interestingly, children who were reported to play very often with friends at home seemed to make less progress than others (ES = –0.13), perhaps due to reduced opportunities for interaction with adults. Again, the length of preschool had a positive effect (ES = 0.14), as did attending centers with a higher proportion of children whose mothers had higher levels of education (ES = 0.19). Overall, the combined impact of all these demographic and environmental influences on preschool oral language progress was weaker than for code-related development in the same period. This suggests that phonological awareness and letter knowledge are more "susceptible" to the instructed environment than is vocabulary.

Impact of Quality of Preschool on Cognitive Progress

Building upon the value added models, Table 7.5 presents a summary of the results on the

TABLE 7.4. Multilevel Analysis Predicting Progress in Oral Language Skills at Age 5 (Primary School Entry)

Factors	Effect size
Prior verbal attainment	1.52
Prior nonverbal attainment	0.34
Ethnicity (minority group 5 vs. white UK)	–0.59
No. of siblings (3+ vs. none)	–0.17
English as an additional language (EAL vs. English as mother tongue)	–0.24
Mother's qualification level (degree vs. no degree)	0.24
Family SES (semiskilled manual vs. professional nonmanual)	–0.23
HLE Item 1: Being read to (daily vs. rarely)	0.27
HLE Item 3: Going to the library (fortnightly vs. never)	0.18
HLE Item 7: Learning activities with songs/poems/nursery rhymes (3 times per week vs. never)	0.20
HLE Item 8: Playing with friends at home (3–7 times per week vs. never)	–0.13
Duration of preschool	0.14
% of children in center with mothers who have a degree or higher	0.19

Note. Impact of prior attainment, child, parent, home environment, and other composition of intake measures on oral language progress over the preschool period. Only the largest effect sizes are reported; comparison group in parentheses.

TABLE 7.5. Multilevel Analyses Predicting Impact of Quality of Provision (as Measured by ECERS-R and ECERS-E) on Children's Cognitive and Linguistic Progress over Preschool

	Code-related skills	Oral language	Nonverbal reasoning
ECERS-E			
Average total	Positive[b]		Positive
Literacy	Positive		
Math			Positive
Science/Environment			Positive[a]
Diversity	Positive[a]		Positive
ECERS-R			
Average total			
Space and Furnishings			
Personal Care Practices			
Language-Reasoning			
Preschool Activities			
Social Interaction			
Organization and Routines			
Adults Working Together	Positive[a]		

Note. Impact of prior attainment, child, parent, home environment, and other composition of intake measures controlled.
[a]Verging on significance.
[b]When change of center is not in model.

impact of quality of preschool provision on children's verbal and nonverbal cognitive progress. ECERS-R and ECERS-E scores were tested in the multilevel analysis of center effects, and only significant effects are reported (with *positive* denoting a positive significant effect after controlling for a wide range of child, parent, family, home environment and other preschool characteristics). The results show that there is no statistically significant relationship between children's expressive and receptive language progress and measures of preschool quality. However, there are significant positive associations between the preschool center's average total ECERS-E score and children's progress in developing code-related skills.

Further analyses revealed that children tended to make greater gains in code-related skills, other factors being controlled, if they attended preschool centers that scored higher on the ECERS-E Literacy subscale. Likewise, the ECERS-E Diversity subscale shows a positive relationship with code-related skills and nonverbal reasoning development. Note that the diversity scores reflect the degree to which the curriculum is implemented in ways that are appropriate to children of different abilities, cultures, and gender (i.e., "personalizing" the cur-

riculum). Interestingly, none of the ECERS-R subscales based on classroom observation predict verbal or nonverbal progress. Only the Adults Working Together subscale (provision for staff and parents) predicts code-related skills in the multilevel model. Moreover, as illustrated in Figure 7.4, the magnitude of the impact of preschool quality (as measured by ECERS-E) on children's achievement depends crucially upon their length of preschool attendance, as the effect sizes range from 0.25 (i.e., low quality and low duration) to above 0.60 (i.e., high quality and high duration).[10]

The interpretation of these findings is rather complex because it relates to issues of both measurement and classroom practice. Certain aspects of quality captured by the ECERS-E were associated with children's acquisition of code-related skills, but neither the ECERS-E nor the ECERS-R was able to account for children's oral language development. It could be that vocabulary and listening comprehension skills are much less amenable to the instructional practices measured by these two observational instruments, or that the rating scales are missing items that assess important aspects of language or literacy provision, which may differentially affect growth. It should be noted

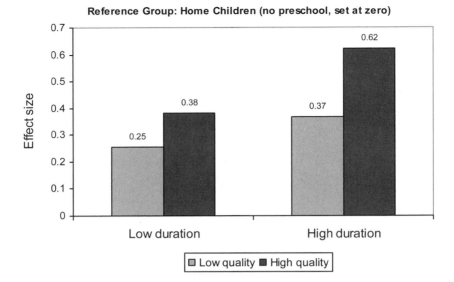

FIGURE 7.4. Impact of preschool duration and quality on code-related skills at age 5.

that center-level variance in children's oral language progress was lower than that of code-related variance. The intracenter correlation (which is the unexplained variance reflecting center influence) was 0.04 and 0.08 for oral language and code-related skills, respectively (Sammons et al., 2002). This implies that whereas some preschools were successful at improving children's letter knowledge and phonological awareness skills, others were much less successful in this respect. However, for oral language skills, all preschools had more or less the same effect on children's development. This limited variation between individual centers means that whatever differences in quality of provision that may have existed would be very difficult to establish.

Children's Literacy Development in Primary School (Age 7–11)

Having demonstrated the influence of the home environment and preschool quality on children's emergent literacy development during preschool, the next step was to explore whether the impact of such factors endures over the primary school years. The main analyses began with contextualized models predicting literacy attainment at ages 7 (Year 2) and 11 (Year 6), when children were tested on National Curriculum Assessments in English. The findings were generally in line with those reported earlier, as they confirm the importance of background influences (e.g., mother's education, family SES, low-income status, gender), including the preschool HLE, on children's literacy achievement (i.e., reading at age 7; writing, spelling, and reading comprehension at age 11), and provide additional evidence regarding the positive influence of preschool duration, quality (as measured by ECERS-E), and effectiveness, albeit with diminished effect sizes. The "home" children who had no preschool experience were therefore at a significant disadvantage.

Note that *preschool center effectiveness* is the value-added analysis of the cognitive attainment of all children in the EPPE sample who attended preschool, controlling for their prior attainment at entry and background influences. In other words, these effectiveness estimates are the value-added residuals, which measure relative gains over the preschool period after taking account of baseline scores. They reflect the unique contribution of each center in promoting different kinds of child outcomes.

This enables the identification of centers that are more or less effective (i.e., outliers),[11] and five different categories were created (Sammons et al., 2002). As shown in

Table 7.6, there is greater variation in preschool center effectiveness for children's development in code-related skills, and less variation for their oral language and nonverbal progress.

It is also worth noting that although children's HLE was measured again at age 7 using postal questionnaires, the early years HLE was found to explain more variance in primary school outcomes. This may be due to (1) the early learning at home being more powerful, or (2) face-to-face interviews conducted with parents when children were 3–4 years old yielding more accurate data. Regardless, it is clear that the influences of parenting upon children's literacy development are pervasive. Furthermore, since the quality of the early years HLE was found to be only moderately related with parents' social class or levels of education, what parents do is more important than who they are.

Significant net effects of preschool attendance on primary school achievement were consistently obtained (e.g., ES = 0.22 for predicting literacy attainment at age 11), and the interaction (or combined effects) between the HLE and preschool quality was further examined.[12] As shown in Figure 7.5, children with low HLE benefited from attending any preschool regardless of quality but, of course, high-quality preschools were ideal (ES = 0.44). Children with medium HLE also benefited from preschool attendance, but the extra boost of "high quality" was less substantial in comparison (ES = 0.36). Children who had high HLE and went to a medium- or high-quality preschool were found to have the strongest positive long-term benefit in English literacy attainment at the end of Year 6 (ESs = 0.61 and 0.58, respectively). Similarly, high HLE also acted as a protective mechanism against the lack of preschool experience or the attendance of low-quality centers (ES = 0.37) because these children performed better than their peers who had low (ES = 0.33) or medium (ES = 0.25) HLE and attended poor-quality preschools. Most noteworthy is that attending low-quality preschools did not result in enhanced progress for children with medium or high HLE.

So far we have discussed the ways in which the early home and preschool environments affect children's attainment at ages 5, 7, and 11 years. We turn now to examine factors associated with differential rates of growth between the ages of 7 and 11 (i.e., between Year 2 and Year 6 of primary school education). Do some children make more progress than others, i.e., demonstrating that they are better learners, and are more equipped to take advantage of instructional opportunities? In other words, did the HLE and preschool quality children experience in early childhood actually enhance their ability to acquire literacy skills in later years, and alter their developmental trajectory?

Using children's results on the age 11 (Year 6) National Curriculum Assessments in English as the outcome measure, the value-added model controlled for prior attainment at age 7 (Year 2), which accounted for approximately 53% of the total variance (see Table 7.7). The influence of background fac-

TABLE 7.6. Summary of Preschool Center Effects on Different Child Outcomes

Center effectiveness category	Code-related skills	Early number concepts	Oral language	Nonverbal reasoning	Spatial awareness/ reasoning
Above expectation (95% significance)	10 (7.1%)	7 (5.0%)	1 (0.7%)	1 (0.7%)	3 (2.1%)
Above expectation (68% significance)	18 (12.8%)	20 (14.2%)	16 (11.3%)	13 (9.2%)	8 (5.7%)
As expected	83 (58.9%)	95 (67.4%)	108 (76.6%)	113 (80.1%)	118 (84.3%)
Below expectation (68% significance)	24 (17.0%)	14 (10.0%)	14 (9.9%)	12 (8.5%)	9 (6.4%)
Below expectation (95% significance)	6 (4.3%)	5 (3.5%)	2 (1.4%)	2 (1.4%)	2 (1.4%)

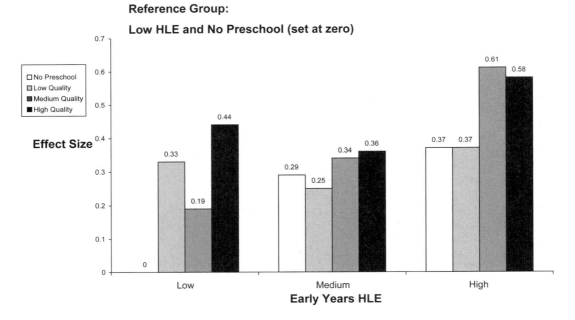

FIGURE 7.5. The combined impact of early years HLE and quality of preschool on literacy attainment at age 11.

tors (i.e., gender, mothers' education, family SES) was very much in line with past findings, and although ethnic differences remained, they were in favor of some minority groups that made better progress compared to their native-English-speaking peers (ES = 0.51).

Looking specifically at the HLE, children who enjoyed a rich environment made great-

er gains over the 4 years of primary school than those who experienced poorer environments (ES = 0.30). Most interestingly, the results indicate simply that the fact of having attended preschool was not sufficient for becoming a better learner, but that the critical factor was the *quality* of the preschool environment (as measured by the ECERS-E). Children who attended centers of medium

TABLE 7.7. Multilevel Analysis Predicting Literacy Attainment at Age 11 (Primary School Exit)

	Effect size
Prior reading attainment (Year 2; age 7)	2.12
Gender (girls vs. boys)	0.23
Ethnicity (minority group 6 vs. white UK)	0.51
Family SES (skilled manual vs. professional)	−0.22
Mother's qualification level (degree vs. no degree)	0.48
Early years HLE index (highest vs. lowest)	0.30
Preschool quality: ECERS-E (high and medium quality vs. no preschool)	0.23
Preschool effectiveness (high effectiveness vs. no preschool)	0.28
Primary school effectiveness (high effectiveness vs. low effectiveness)	0.37

Note. Impact of prior attainment, child, parent, home environment, and other composition of intake measures on literacy progress over the primary school period. Only the largest effect sizes are reported; comparison group in parentheses.

and high quality made greater progress than the "home" children (ES = 0.23). Similar findings were obtained for the measure of preschool effectiveness, which was only statistically significant when the highly effective group was compared to the group without preschool education (ES = 0.28). In addition, the impact of primary school academic effectiveness[13] was also examined and, as expected, children who attended highly effective primary schools made significantly greater progress than those who went to less effective institutions (ES = 0.37).

The joint effects of preschool experience and primary school effectiveness were further investigated. Due to smaller numbers, medium and highly effective primary schools were grouped together, and the reference group was the "home" children (i.e., no preschool) and those who attended low effective primary schools. As illustrated in Figure 7.6, children who did not attend any preschool had low literacy attainment, even if they went to a medium or highly effective primary school later on (ES = −0.13). Likewise, the negative impact of attending a low quality preschool was long-lasting because these children did not benefit from going to a medium or highly effective primary school. For children who attended a medium-quality

preschool, only those who went on to a medium or highly effective primary school showed enhanced attainment (albeit with a small ES of 0.07). Clearly, the ideal combination of attending a high-quality preschool and a highly effective primary school was best (ES = 0.23); however, even high-quality preschools alone could act as a protective or compensatory mechanism against possible adverse effects from attending less effective primary schools later on (ES = 0.12).

Summary of Main Findings and Future Directions

The EPPE study in England has shown that the development of literacy skills is shaped powerfully by the emergent literacy environments of both home and preschool. First and foremost, the empirical evidence demonstrates that experiencing a rich HLE and high-quality preschool (curricular) provision not only provides children with a stronger literacy "profile" at the start of school (i.e., better code-related and oral language skills), but also enables them to make more progress than their peers over the primary school years (e.g., greater gains in reading skills). In other words, the impact of these emergent

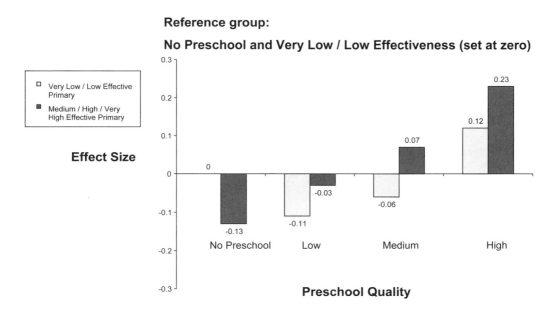

FIGURE 7.6. The combined impact of preschool and primary school effectiveness on literacy attainment at age 11.

literacy environments on literacy acquisition is long-lasting and cumulative, fundamentally changing children's developmental trajectories, and protecting them against less effective future schooling.

Second, EPPE sought to build upon past studies, often on smaller and less representative samples (Bracken & Fischel, 2008; Zill & Resnick, 2006), by attempting more refined measurement of both predictors and outcomes. Instead of relying on proxies of "instructional support" (e.g., parental education or number of books in the home), our HLE items were based on in-depth parental interviews. Similarly, rather than relying on global measures of child outcomes, more differentiated ones were used in EPPE to assess different domains of emergent literacy skills. Our results have confirmed that oral language development is promoted by parents through activities focused on meaning, such as book reading (Britto, Brooks-Gunn, & Griffin, 2006; Raikes et al., 2006), while acquisition of code-related skills is associated with specific home activities with letters (and sounds) (Foy & Mann, 2003).

Third, in terms of assessing the quality of the preschool environment, EPPE devised the ECERS-E as a complementary curricular rating scale to the ECERS-R, and found it to be a more sensitive measure of the classroom environment as it relates to literacy outcomes. However, it is important to acknowledge that unlike growth in code-related skills, neither the ECERS-E nor ECERS-R scores were related to children's oral language development over the pre-school period, which presents a challenge to both researchers and practitioners: Was this a failure of measurement or of practice? It is difficult to reach a definitive conclusion, but judging from the estimates of preschool effectiveness, it seems that the majority of centers (76.6%) have not made any difference to children's expected growth in vocabulary and listening comprehension skills (see Table 7.6). This does not imply that preschools do not have an impact on this domain of emergent literacy at all (because the "home" children have lower levels of language attainment than preschoolers as a whole, irrespective of the quality of provision), but that there is less variability between individual centers in the ways they support oral language. Perhaps the fact that *any* preschool center appears to support gains in language points to the importance of providing opportunities for peer play.

An area of future research may be experimental interventions to support parents in providing different kinds of learning experiences at home. Although most preschools and primary schools encourage parents to "share books" with their children (Department of Children, Schools, and Families, 2008), such activities are likely to be absent (or occur infrequently) in low-HLE households. Given the powerful protective effects of a rich HLE for children's later development, the benefits of reading with children, going to the library, and helping them discriminate the sounds of letters, and so forth, cannot be stressed too often with parents. Furthermore, our findings suggest that early childhood centers might explore more effective ways of supporting oral language. A second line of research would be classroom interventions in preschools (and perhaps the early primary grades), which might inform teachers about ways to improve their existing pedagogical practices, for example, daily group activities to enhance oral language, such as regular recall of shared experiences or collective storytelling. Experimental studies such as these would be a fine complement to longitudinal studies such as EPPE.

Acknowledgments

The EPPE 3-11 project is a major longitudinal study funded by the U.K. Department for Children, Schools and Families (DCSF). The research would not be possible without the support and cooperation of the six Local Authorities and the many preschool centers, primary schools, children, and parents participating in the research. EPPE is an associate project in the U.K. Economic and Social Research Council (ESRC) Teaching and Learning Research Programme.

Notes

1. Note that the term *effects* is used in this chapter to refer to statistical associations between predictor measures and developmental outcomes, with statistical control for confounding variables. It is understood that such correlational research does not allow strong inferences regarding causation.

2. Although the primary school phase of the EPPE

3–11 study came to an end in 2008, the research was extended into the Effective Pre-School, Primary and Secondary Education Project (EPPSE 16+), which follows the same children until their final year of compulsory schooling at age 16, and investigates their subsequent educational, training, and employment destinations. Please visit our website for further information at *eppe.ioe.ac.uk*.

3. The United Kingdom comprises four nations—England, Wales, Scotland, and Northern Ireland—with a population of over 60 million people. There are growing differences in curriculum and statutory provision across the country, and it is important to note that EPPE is focused solely on England, where an estimated 83% of the total U.K. population currently resides (Siraj-Blatchford, 2010).

4. Note that there were wide differences between the various types of provision. In general, state-maintained provision (e.g., nursery classes, nursery schools, and combined centers) had superior resources, training, professional facilities, and support, as well as better staff pay and conditions with lower rates of turnover compared to the private and voluntary sector (Siraj-Blatchford, 2010). However, all center-based preschool settings abide by the Early Years Foundation Stage (EYFS) curriculum and are regularly inspected by the government.

5. Note that early childhood education prior to the age of 5 is noncompulsory, and preschools usually cater to 3- and 4-year-olds. The term after the child's fifth birthday, he or she begins school and attends "Reception Class," which is similar in some ways to full-day kindergarten programs in the United States, except that it is mandatory and taught by teachers who have received the same training as other primary school (Years 1–6) teachers and are paid under the same conditions. Reception class is part of the EYFS curriculum from birth to age 5, and is distinct from the National Curriculum, which is subject-based and not play-based.

6. Further details of the study are available in various technical papers and reports, which are listed on the EPPE website (*eppe.ioe.ac.uk*).

7. The British Ability Scales (BAS) is the predecessor of the Differential Ability Scales (DAS) developed in the U.S. (Elliott, 2005). The BAS-II is a battery of individually administered tests of cognitive abilities and educational achievement. It is suitable for use with children and adolescents ages 2 years, 6 months, to 17 years, 11 months. The battery facilitates the psychological assessment of this age range by educational and clinical psychologists for a wide range of purposes, as well as providing researchers with a valuable research tool (Elliott, Smith, & McCulloch, 1997).

8. National assessments are usually reported in ordinal levels that are fairly broad and categorize children only into six attainment groups (e.g., for Year 2: working toward Level 1, Level 1, Levels 2a, 2b, 2c, and Level 3). Within each level there can be quite a range of ability; thus, EPPE collected data on individual test scores within levels, which allowed the creation of more finely differentiated outcomes measures (decimalized levels) for the multilevel analysis. See Technical Paper 11 for further elaboration of the decimalization procedure (Sammons et al., 2004). Furthermore, to ensure comparability over time, a complex internal standardization and normalization procedure was applied to the decimalized data (mean = 100; SD = 15). This effectively took account of age effects within 1 school year; hence, children's age does not feature as a significant predictor of attainment in the models.

9. The English curriculum was revised in 2000 and 2008. It has three additional areas of development (aside from the three included in the ECERS-E): Creative Development; Physical Development; and Personal, Social, and Emotional Development. These noncognitive domains were considered to be covered adequately by the ECERS-R.

10. Less than 12 months of preschool attendance at the target center (i.e., the center at which the child was recruited for the EPPE study) was considered "low duration," and attendance of 36 months or more was considered "high duration." For preschool quality, centers that received a mean score less than 4 were considered "low quality," 4–5 was considered "medium quality," and above 5 was "high quality."

11. Preschool center effects significantly above or below expectation at the 95% confidence level are identified by calculating confidence intervals for each value-added residual (value-added residual ± 1.96 standard error). If the confidence intervals for a value-added residual do not overlap zero (which is the average effect predicted for the whole sample based on child, parent, and home environment characteristics and prior attainment), the residual is identified as an outlier.

12. The EPPE sample was divided into groups of children with no preschool experience (i.e., home group, 10%), low-quality preschool (15%), medium-quality preschool (52%), and high-quality preschool (23%), based on ECERS-E scores.

13. Primary school academic effectiveness: Value-added academic effectiveness measures for primary schools were calculated using national assessment data for all primary schools in England linking age 7 and age 11 results, and separate indicators were calculated for the different

core curriculum subjects: English, mathematics, and science. These measures were thus independently derived and based on full national pupil cohorts. They provide indicators of the academic success of the school in promoting its pupils' progress for 3 consecutive years (2002–2004) (Melhuish et al., 2006).

References

Bracken, S. S., & Fischel, J. E. (2008). Family reading behavior and early literacy skills in preschool children from low-income backgrounds. *Early Education and Development, 19,* 45–67.

Bredekamp, S., & Copple, C. (Eds.). (1997). *Developmentally appropriate practice in early childhood programs.* Washington, DC: National Association for the Education of Young Children.

Britto, P. R., & Brooks-Gunn, J. (2001). Beyond shared book reading: Dimensions of home literacy and low-income African American preschoolers' skills. *New Directions for Child and Adolescent Development, 92,* 73–89.

Britto, P. R., Brooks-Gunn, J., & Griffin, T. M. (2006). Maternal reading and teaching patterns: Associations with school readiness in low-income African American families. *Reading Research Quarterly, 41,* 68–89.

Bronfenbrenner, U. (1979). *The ecology of human development.* Cambridge, MA: Harvard University Press.

Bryant, P., & Bradley, L. (1985). *Children's reading problems,* Oxford, UK: Blackwell.

Burchinal, M. R., Peisner-Feinberg, E., Bryant, D. M., & Clifford, R. (2000). Children's social and cognitive development and child-care quality: Testing for differential associations related to poverty, gender, or ethnicity. *Applied Developmental Science, 4,* 149–165.

Burgess, S. (2002). The influence of speech perception, oral language ability, the home literacy environment, and pre-reading knowledge on the growth of phonological sensitivity: A one-year longitudinal investigation. *Reading and Writing, 15,* 709–737.

Burgess, S. R., Hecht, S. A., & Lonigan, C. J. (2002). Relations of the home literacy environment (HLE) to the development of reading-related abilities: A one-year longitudinal study. *Reading Research Quarterly, 37,* 408–426.

Christian, K., Morrison, F. J., & Bryant, F. B. (1998). Predicting kindergarten academic skills: Interactions among child care, maternal education, and family literacy environments. *Early Childhood Research Quarterly, 13,* 501–521.

Department for Children, Schools and Families. (2008). *The Early Years Foundation Stage: Setting the standards for learning, development and care for children from birth to five.* London: Author.

Elliott, C. D. (2005). The Differential Ability Scales. In D. P. Flanagan & P. L. Harrison (Eds.), *Contemporary intellectual assessment: Theories, tests, and issues* (2nd ed., pp. 402–424). New York: Guilford Press.

Elliott, C. D., Smith, P., & McCulloch, K. (1996). *British Ability Scales–II administration and scoring manual.* Windsor, UK: nferNelson.

Elliott, C. D., Smith, P., & McCulloch, K. (1997). *British Ability Scales–II: Technical manual.* London: nferNelson.

Evangelou, M., Sylva, K., Kyriacou, M., Wild, M., & Glenny, G. (2009). *Early years learning and development: Literature review.* London: Department for Children, Schools and Families.

Evans, M. A., Shaw, D., & Bell, M. (2000). Home literacy activities and their influence on early literacy skills. *Canadian Journal of Experimental Psychology, 54,* 65–75.

Foster, M. A., Lambert, R., Abbott-Shim, M., McCarty, F., & Franze, S. (2005). A model of home learning environment and social risk factors in relation to children's emergent literacy and social outcomes. *Early Childhood Research Quarterly, 20,* 13–36.

Foy, J., & Mann, V. (2003). Home literacy environment and phonological awareness in preschool children: Differential effects for rhyme and phoneme awareness. *Applied Psycholinguistics, 24,* 59–88.

Frijters, J. C., Barron, R. W., & Brunello, M. (2000). Direct and mediated influences of home literacy and literacy interest on prereaders' oral vocabulary and early written language skill. *Journal of Educational Psychology, 92,* 466–477.

Harms, T., Clifford, R. M., & Cryer, D. (2005). *Early Childhood Environmental Rating Scale—Revised Edition (ECERS-R).* New York: Teachers College Press.

Hood, M., Conlon, E., & Andrews, G. (2008). Preschool home literacy practices and children's literacy development: A longitudinal analysis. *Journal of Educational Psychology, 100,* 252–271.

Levy, B. A., Gong, Z., Hessels, S., Evans, M. A., & Jared, D. (2006). Understanding print: Early reading development and the contributions of home literacy experiences. *Journal of Experimental Child Psychology, 93,* 63–93.

Lonigan, C. J., Burgess, S. R., & Anthony, J. L. (2000). Development of emergent literacy and early reading skills in preschool children: Evidence from a latent-variable longitudinal study. *Developmental Psychology, 36,* 596–613.

Melhuish, E., Romaniuk, H., Sammons, P., Sylva, K., Siraj-Blatchford, I., & Taggart, B. (2006). *The effectiveness of primary schools in England in Key Stage 2 for 2002, 2003 and 2004: Full Report.* London: Institute of Education, University of London.

Melhuish, E., Sylva, K., Sammons, P., Siraj-Blatchford, I., & Taggart, B. (2001). Technical Paper 7: The Effective Provision of Pre-School Education (EPPE) project: Social/behavioural and Cognitive development at 3–4 years in relation to family background. London: Department for Education and Employment/Institute of Education, University of London.

Melhuish, E. C., Phan, M. B., Sylva, K., Sammons, P., Siraj-Blatchford, I., & Taggart, B. (2008). Effects of the home learning environment and preschool center experience upon literacy and numeracy development in early primary school. *Journal of Social Issues, 64,* 95–114.

Morrison, F. J. (2009). Parenting and academic development. *Merrill–Palmer Quarterly, 55,* 361–372.

NICHD Early Child Care Research Network. (2001). Nonmaternal care and family factors in early development: An overview of the NICHD Study of Early Child Care. *Journal of Applied Developmental Psychology, 22,* 457–492.

NICHD Early Child Care Research Network. (2005). Pathways to reading: The role of oral language in the transition to reading. *Developmental Psychology, 41,* 428–442.

NICHD Early Child Care Research Network. (2007). Are there long-term effects of early child care? *Child Development, 78,* 681–701.

Payne, A. C., Whitehurst, G. J., & Angell, A. L. (1994). The role of literacy environment in the language development of children from low-income families. *Early Childhood Research Quarterly, 9,* 427–440.

Raikes, H., Pan, B. A., Luze, G., Tamis-Lemonda, C. S., Brooks-Gunn, J., Constantine, J., et al. (2006). Mother–child bookreading in low-income families: Correlates and outcomes during the first three years of life. *Child Development, 77,* 924–953.

Roberts, J., Jurgens, J., & Burchinal, M. (2005). The role of home literacy practices in preschool children's language and emergent literacy skills. *Journal of Speech, Language, and Hearing Research, 48,* 345–359.

Sammons, P., Sylva, K., Melhuish, E., Siraj-Blatchford, I., Taggart, B., & Elliot, K. (2002). *The Effective Provision of Pre-School Education (EPPE) project: Technical Paper 8a: Measuring the impact of pre-school on children's cognitive progress over the pre-school period.* London: Department for Education and Skills/Institute of Education, University of London.

Sammons, P., Sylva, K., Melhuish, E., Siraj-Blatchford, I., Taggart, B., & Hunt, S. (2008). *Effective Pre-school and Primary Education 3–11 Project (EPPE 3-11): Influences on children's attainment and progress in Key Stage 2: Cognitive outcomes in Year 6* (Research Report No. DCSF-RR048). Nottingham, UK: Department for Children, Schools and Families Publications.

Sammons, P., Sylva, K., Melhuish, E. C., Siraj-Blatchford, I., Taggart, B., Elliot, K., et al. (2004). *The Effective Provision of Pre-School Education (EPPE) Project: Technical Paper 11: Report on the continuing effects of pre-school education at age 7.* London: Department for Education and Skills/Institute of Education, University of London.

Sénéchal, M., & LeFevre, J. (2002). Parental involvement in the development of children's reading skill: A five-year longitudinal study. *Child Development, 73,* 445–460.

Sénéchal, M., LeFevre, J., Thomas, E. M., & Daley, K. E. (1998). Differential effects of home literacy experiences on the development of oral and written language. *Reading Research Quarterly, 33,* 96–116.

Siraj-Blatchford, I. (2010). The EPPE settings in the context of English pre-schools. In K. Sylva, E.

Melhuish, P. Sammons, I. Siragj-Blatchford, & B. Taggart (Eds.), *Early childhood matters: Evidence from the Effective Pre-school and Primary Education project.* London: Routledge.

Soucacou, E. P., & Sylva, K. (2010). Developing observation instruments and arriving at inter-rater reliability for a range of context and raters: The Early Childhood Environment Rating Scales. In E. Tucker, G. Walford, & M. Viswanathan (Eds.), *The Sage handbook of measurement* (pp. 61–85). London: Sage.

Storch, S. A., & Whitehurst, G. J. (2001). The role of family and home in the literacy development of children from low-income backgrounds. *New Directions For Child and Adolescent Development, 92,* 53–71.

Storch, S. A., & Whitehurst, G. J. (2002). Oral language and code-related precursors to reading: Evidence from a longitudinal structural model. *Developmental Psychology, 38,* 934–947.

Sylva, K., Melhuish, E., Sammons, P., Siraj-Blatchford, I., & Taggart, B. (Eds.). (2010). *Early childhood matters: Evidence from the Effective Pre-School and Primary Education project.* London: Routledge.

Sylva, K., Siraj-Blatchford, I., Melhuish, E., Sammons, P., Taggart, B., Evans, E., et al. (1999). *The Effective Provision of Pre-School Education (EPPE) project: Technical Paper 6: Characteristics of the centres in the EPPE sample: Observation profiles.* London: Department for Education and Employment/Institute of Education, University of London.

Sylva, K., Siraj-Blatchford, I., & Taggart, B. (2003). *Assessing quality in the early years: Early Childhood Environment Rating Scale Extension (ECERS-E): Four curricular subscales.* Stoke on Trent, UK: Trentham Books.

Sylva, K., Siraj-Blatchford, I., & Taggart, B. (2010). *Assessing quality in the early years: Curricular extension to the Early Childhood Environment Rating Scale—Revised.* Stoke on Trent, UK: Trentham Books.

Whitehurst, G. J., Crone, D. A., Zevenbergen, A. A., Schultz, M. D., Velting, O. N., & Fischel, J. E. (1999). Outcomes of an emergent literacy intervention from Head Start through second grade. *Journal of Educational Psychology, 91,* 261–272.

Whitehurst, G. J., & Lonigan, C. J. (1998). Child development and emergent literacy. *Child Development, 69*(3), 848–872.

Whitehurst, G. J., & Lonigan, C. J. (2003). Emergent literacy: Development from prereaders to readers. In S. B. Neuman & D. K. Dickinson (Eds.), *Handbook of early literacy research* (Vol. 1, pp. 11–29). New York: Guilford Press.

Zill, N., & Resnick, G. (2006). Emergent literacy of low-income children in Head Start: Relationships with child and family characteristics, program factors, and classroom quality. In D. K. Dickinson & S. B. Neuman (Eds.), *Handbook of early literacy research* (Vol. 2, pp. 347–371). New York: Guilford Press.

APPENDIX 7.1. Structure of the ECERS-E

I. Literacy	II. Mathematics	III. Science and environment	IV. Diversity
1. Environmental print: letters and words 2. Book and literacy areas 3. Adult reading with children 4. Sounds in words 5. Emergent writing/mark making 6. Talking and listening	7. Counting and application of counting 8. Reading and writing simple numbers 9a. Mathematical activities: shape and space 9b. Mathematical activities: sorting, matching, and comparing	10. Natural materials 11. Areas featuring science/science resources 12a. Science activities: nonliving 12b. Science activities: living processes and the world around us 12c. Science activities: food preparation	13. Planning for individual learning needs 14. Gender equality and awareness 15. Race equality and awareness

Note. Data from Sylva, Siraj-Blatchford, and Taggart (2010).

APPENDIX 7.2. Sample Items from the ECERS-E

Inadequate		Minimal		Good		Excellent
1	2	3	4	5	6	7

Item 3. Adult reading with the children

| 1.1 Adults rarely read to the children.* | 3.1 Adults read with children daily.*

3.2 There is some involvement of the children during reading times *(e.g., children are encouraged to join in with repetitive words and phrases in the text, adult shares pictures with the children or asks simple questions).* * | 5.1 Children take an active role during reading times, and the words and/or story are usually discussed.

5.2 Children are encouraged to use conjecture, and/or link the content of the book to other experiences. | 7.1 There is discussion about print and letters as well as content.*

7.2 There is support material for the children to engage with stories by themselves *(e.g., tapes, interactive displays, puppets, story sacks, computer games).*

7.3 There is evidence of one to one reading with some children.* |

Notes for clarification

1.1 Score yes if no reading with the children is seen during the observation and there is no daily reading time listed on the schedule.

3.1 Give credit if two or more examples of informal reading with groups or individual children should be seen during the observation. Alternatively, credit can be given if there is evidence of a planned daily reading time which includes all (or the majority of) the children even if this happens outside the observation time. This could be whole group reading, or planned small group reading times.

3.2 Reading with children must be observed on at least one occasion in order to score this indicator. If several reading times are observed, involvement of children should be a feature of the majority of sessions in order to give credit.

5.1 This must be observed at least once. If several reading sessions are observed, this should be true for most sessions.

5.2 Examples might include an adult asking: *"What do you think [the character] will do next?"* or *(when reading a factual book about pets)* *"Have any of you got a pet at home? How do you take care of them?"* If several reading sessions are observed, this should be true for most sessions.

7.1 This should be observed at least once to give credit.

7.3 Several examples should be observed. It should be clear that informal reading with individual children is a regular part of the daily routine.

(cont.)

APPENDIX 7.2. *(cont.)*

Item 4. Sounds in words

1.1 Few or no rhymes or poems are spoken or sung.*	3.1 Rhymes are often spoken or sung by adults to children.* 3.2 Children are encouraged to speak and/or sing rhymes.	5.1 The rhyming components of songs/rhymes are brought to the attention of children.* 5.2 The initial sounds in words are brought to the attention of children.*	7.1 Attention is paid to syllabification of words *(e.g., through clapping games, jumping etc.).* 7.2 Some attention is given to linking sounds to letters.*

Notes for clarification

Rhymes could include nursery rhymes and other rhyming songs, poems, rhyming games played on the computer, card games that involve rhymes, rhyming books, or phonics activities that include rhyme. Give credit for rhymes spoken or sung with small groups of children, as well as whole-group activities. If songs are used as evidence, credit can only be given if these are rhyming songs. Adults must be actively involved. For example, do not give credit if you see children listening to taped songs/rhymes by themselves.

Score "yes" if there is evidence that rhymes are spoken or sung fewer than two or three times per week (e.g., only one singing time scheduled per week and no evidence of informal singing during the session observed).

3.1 Often means daily. Give credit if there is evidence of a daily planned singing/rhyme session that includes all (or the majority of) the children, even if this occurs outside the observation period. If there is no daily group session planned, then at least two examples of informal use of rhyme (e.g., singing, rhyming books) with small groups or individual children should be seen during the observation.

3.2 It is not necessary for adults to draw explicit attention to rhyme to give credit at this level. For example, give credit if it is observed that children usually join in during singing sessions, or when reading a rhyming book.

5.1 At least one example must be observed.

5.2 At least two examples must be observed. Adults must draw explicit attention to the initial sounds in words and say the words out loud (e.g., drawing attention to the fact that *bat* and *ball* start with the same letter, by saying "Can you hear? They both begin with *b*. Can you think of anything else that starts with the same letter?").

7.1 Give credit if this is seen during the observation. If no examples are observed on the day, then at least two examples should be found in the sample of planning reviewed.

7.2 To give credit, observers should either see *two* examples of adults linking sounds to letters, or see *one* example and find two examples in the sample of planning reviewed. Examples might include phonics work that makes the link between letters and sounds explicit, or an adult helping a child to write down a particular spoken word.

8

Beginning with Language: Spanish–English Bilingual Preschoolers' Early Literacy Development

CAROL SCHEFFNER HAMMER
SHELLEY SCARPINO
MEGAN DUNN DAVISON

The number of children in the United States who speak a language other than English at home is increasing rapidly. From 1972 to 2007, the percentage of school-age children who spoke another language increased from 9 to 20%, making the total 10.8 million children (National Center for Education Statistics, 2009). This increase has been observed in preschool programs, such as Head Start, as well. Approximately, 30% of all children attending Head Start are bilingual. Of those children, nearly 85% speak Spanish at home.

Unfortunately, bilingual Latino children are at risk for poor academic outcomes. Statistics consistently show that Latinos enter kindergarten with lower emergent literacy abilities than their white, monolingual peers. Their abilities remain behind throughout their academic careers. They score below non-Hispanic whites in reading in grades 4, 8, and 12 (NCES, 2009) and are more likely than their white peers to drop out of high school (Federal Interagency Forum on Child and Family Statistics, 2007). Economic disadvantage is one factor that places Latino children at risk (August & Hakuta, 1997; Snow, Burns, & Griffin, 1998). Twenty-two percent of Latino families live in poverty

(DeNavas-Walt, Proctor, & Lee, 2005) and 75% of Latino children possess at least one sociodemographic risk factor when entering kindergarten (NCES, 2009). Having a home language other than English is a second major risk factor (Snow et al., 1998). According to the U.S. Department of Education, 27% of children from non-English-speaking homes have difficulty speaking English, with the vast majority coming from Spanish-speaking homes (NCES, 2009).

Given that Latino children living in the United States are at-risk for poor reading outcomes, it is essential that we understand their early development and its relationship to later abilities, as well as educational interventions that support children's development. In this chapter we discuss the findings of the longitudinal study Bilingual Preschoolers: Precursors to Literacy, which addressed this need. The chapter presents an overview of the study and research findings to date that focus on bilingual preschoolers' development and factors that impact later outcomes. The chapter also examines research on classroom interventions designed for bilingual preschoolers and concludes with a discussion of the implications of the research for educational practices.

Bilingual Preschoolers: Precursors to Literacy

Bilingual Preschoolers: Precursors to Literacy was a longitudinal study of the language and literacy development of bilingual Head Start children of Puerto Rican descent (Hammer & Miccio, 2000). The primary goals of the project were to (1) study the trajectories of bilingual children's oral language and literacy development during 2 years in Head Start through first grade and (2) determine individual differences in children's oral language and home environment that led to better reading outcomes. Before presenting the findings, we begin with a discussion of the framework that supported the research.

Theoretical Framework

The framework that guides our work on bilingual children is drawn from several areas of research, including emergent literacy, bilingualism, and ecological theory. The *model of emergent literacy development* proposed by Whitehurst and Lonigan (1998) served as the overall framework for the study. According to the model, the ability to read involves the acquisition of several component abilities categorized as outside-in and inside-out processes. *Outside-in processes* relate to children's understanding of the context, and involve language abilities and print knowledge. *Inside-out processes* include children's knowledge of rules for decoding the printed word, such as phonological awareness and letter knowledge, which do not require knowledge of the context.

This theoretical framework has been well supported by the literature on monolingual children. Strong relationships between the components of language (i.e., vocabulary, oral comprehension, morphosyntax) and reading outcomes have been consistently demonstrated (cf. Catts, Fey, Zhang, & Tomblin, 1999; McCardle, Scarborough, & Catts, 2001; Scarborough, 2001; Storch & Whitehurst, 2002). Additionally, significant relationships between inside-out skills, such as phonological sensitivity and letter knowledge, and reading abilities have been found (cf. Catts, Fey, Tomblin, & Zhang, 2002; Schatschneider, Fletcher, Francis, Carlson, & Foorman, 2004; Storch & Whitehurst, 2002). Given this empirical support, the

framework was applied to this investigation of bilingual children's development of language and emergent literacy.

Because the children we studied were learning two languages, we also drew from work in bilingualism. In particular, the study built on Cummins's *common underlying proficiency model*, which asserts that bilingual children's "experience with either language can promote development of the proficiency underlying both languages, given adequate motivation and exposure to both" (1981, p. 25). The model posits that bilingual children develop an underlying store of knowledge that they can access regardless of the language in which it was acquired (McSwan & Rolstad, 2005). This model is in contrast to the *separate underlying proficiency model*, which proposes that children's proficiency in their first language is separate from their proficiency in the second. According to the latter model, children's knowledge in one language is not accessed when acquiring knowledge in their other language (Cummins, 1981).

In addition, we built on the work of leading researchers who have argued that timing of exposure to English in relation to school entry is a key factor that needs to be considered (Butler & Hakuta, 2004; Genesee, 2004; Oller & Eilers, 2002). Differences may occur in children's outcomes depending on whether they are exposed to two languages before attending school or are exposed to their home language from birth and not expected to communicate in their second language until they enter school. Specifically, Oller and Eilers (2002) argued that "extent of English knowledge at entry to school could play a critical role in achievement of oral capacity and literacy and needs to be evaluated as an independent variable" (p. 8). Therefore, we hypothesized that differences may be observed among children whose exposure to Spanish and English varied early in their lives. In particular, we predicted that the development of Spanish-speaking children who were exposed to English at home from birth (i.e., home English communicators, or HECs) would differ from the development of Spanish-speaking children who were not exposed to and expected to communicate in English until they entered Head Start (i.e., school English communicators, or SECs).

The research was also guided by an ecological approach asserting that development does not occur in a vacuum, and that key systems impact children's outcomes (Bronfenbrenner, 1979). Therefore, we examined critical aspects of the home, such as maternal education, birthplace, and languages used by family members. Also, the home literacy environment was investigated given the evidence that home literacy activities support monolingual children's language and literacy abilities (cf. Beals, De Temple, & Dickinson, 1994; Britto & Brooks-Gunn, 2001; Burgess, Hecht, & Lonigan, 2002; Speece, Ritchey, Cooper, Roth, & Schatschneider, 2004).

The Children and Their Mothers

Eighty-six bilingual Head Start children from urban areas in central Pennsylvania took part in the study. All attended Head Start for 2 years, qualified financially for Head Start, and were typically developing. The children were 3 years, 8 months of age, on average, in the fall of their first Head Start year. All were from Spanish-speaking homes. During annual home visits in the middle of each school year, mothers reported the language(s) they used when speaking to their children. Approximately two-thirds of the children were exposed to English at home before they entered Head Start (i.e., HECs). The remaining one-third was not expected to communicate in English until the children entered Head Start (i.e., SECs). Most children were born on the U.S. mainland, although more children in the SEC group were born in Puerto Rico (35%) compared to children in the HEC group (6%). The children's mothers were Spanish-speaking and of Puerto Rican descent. At the beginning of the project, the mothers were on average 26 years of age, with 11 years of education. Approximately 50% of the mothers worked outside the home, and a large percentage were born in Puerto Rico (89% of the SEC mothers and 55% of the HEC mothers).

In general, mothers and children in the HEC group differed from mothers and children in the SEC group in the languages used when speaking to each other. During the first Head Start year, nearly 70% of the mothers of SEC children spoke mostly or all Spanish to their children. Less than 10% used primarily English. In contrast, over 33% of the mothers of HEC children used mostly or all English when interacting with their children. Nearly 50% used equal amounts of Spanish and English. Less than 20% used mostly or all Spanish.

Over 50% of the SEC children spoke predominantly Spanish when talking with their mothers. Thirty percent communicated to their mothers using more English than Spanish. In comparison, nearly 75% of the HEC children spoke to their mothers using mostly or all English. Few children in the HEC group used predominantly Spanish when talking with their mothers.

The children experienced a different language-learning environment when they went to Head Start, where they were placed in English immersion classrooms. Although children who did not understand or speak English were often assigned to classes with a Spanish-speaking assistant or on occasion a Spanish-speaking teacher, English was the language of instruction. At the beginning of the year, informal observations revealed that Spanish was used occasionally with individual children when they did not comprehend an instruction. As the year progressed, less and less Spanish was used. When in kindergarten and first grade, children continued to be instructed in English. Thus, children's language exposure at home varied among the children; however, when in school, they all had the common experience of being instructed in English.

Language and Literacy Development in Two Languages

Each year of the study, children's language abilities were assessed in both Spanish and English in the fall and spring. Assessment of their emerging literacy abilities began in the spring of the first year of Head Start and continued through the fall and spring of first grade.

Language Development

VOCABULARY DEVELOPMENT

During the early years, the size of young bilingual children's vocabulary is similar to that of monolinguals when the vocabularies in their two languages are combined (Conboy & Thal, 2006; Marchman & Martinez-Sussmann, 2002; Pearson, Fernández, & Oller, 1993). As a result, bilinguals' vocabularies in the individual languages may appear reduced in comparison to children who only speak one language. Indeed, research on Spanish–English preschoolers from low-income backgrounds has demonstrated that bilinguals score below monolingual norms in both languages. Our study, along with others, found that bilingual preschoolers scored one to two standard deviations below the mean of Spanish and English vocabulary tests standardized on monolingual populations (Hammer, Lawrence, & Miccio, 2008b; Páez, Tabors, & López, 2007; U.S. Department of Health and Human Services, 2003). Even though children made gains, they exited preschool with vocabulary abilities that were significantly lower than the test mean.

Differences occurred in bilingual children's development depending on the timing of English language exposure in relation to school entry (Hammer et al., 2008b; see Figure 8.1). In the fall of the children's first year in Head Start, SEC children had higher Spanish receptive vocabularies, as measured by the *Test de Vocabulario en Imágenes—Peabody* (TVIP; Dunn, Padilla, Lugo, & Dunn, 1986), than HEC children. Growth curve modeling revealed that over the 2 years in Head Start, SEC children's Spanish vocabulary scores increased, which means that children were making gains when compared to the monolingual normative sample. By the end of their second Head Start year, children's standard scores were within one-half of a standard deviation of the monolingual norm. HEC children demonstrated no change in their standard scores in Spanish over the 2-year period. This, however, did not indicate that their Spanish vocabularies were not increasing. Children passed more items over time but did not pass a sufficient number of items to make gains in their standardized test scores. HEC children began and ended Head Start with Spanish receptive vocabularies that were 1.5 standard deviations below the test mean.

In terms of children's English vocabulary development, HEC children began Head Start with higher receptive vocabularies than did SEC children. Both groups' standard scores on the Peabody Picture Vocabulary Test–III (PPVT-III; Dunn & Dunn, 1997) grew over their 2 years in Head Start. SEC children, however, demonstrated a faster rate of growth than HEC children. This may be because they had more vocabulary knowledge to acquire than the HEC children.

Despite the observed growth, HEC children ended preschool with scores that were slightly less than one standard deviation below the mean, and SEC children left pre-

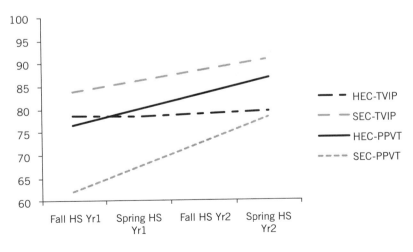

FIGURE 8.1. Growth trajectories of children's Spanish and English vocabulary development during Head Start (standard scores). TVIP, Test de Vocabulario Imágenes—Peabody; PPVT, Peabody Picture Vocabulary Test–III.

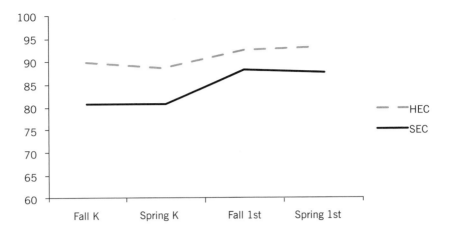

FIGURE 8.2. Children's average standard scores on the Peabody Picture Vocabulary Test–III in kindergarten and first grade.

school with an average score that fell 1.5 standard deviations below the mean (Hammer et al., 2008b). During kindergarten and first grade, the receptive vocabulary scores of children in both groups continued to gain on the English monolingual mean, and children ended first grade with scores within the typical range for monolingual children. HEC children had scores of 94, whereas SEC children had scores of 88 on the PPVT-III (see Figure 8.2).

ORAL COMPREHENSION

Similar to the findings on children's vocabulary development, both groups of bilingual preschoolers scored one standard deviation or more below monolingual norms in their oral comprehension in both languages at the beginning of the study. Additionally, SEC children had higher Spanish comprehension scores than HEC children, and HEC children performed better in English comprehension than SEC children (see Figure 8.3).

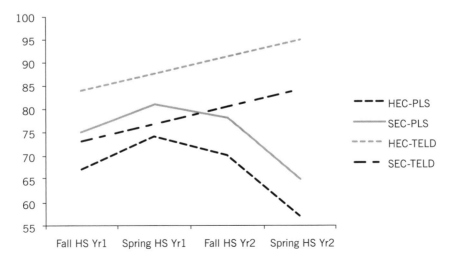

FIGURE 8.3. Growth trajectories of children's Spanish and English Oral Comprehension Development during Head Start (standard scores). PLS, Preschool Language Scale–3, Spanish Version; TELD, Test of Early Language Development.

During their time in Head Start, both groups' Spanish comprehension abilities, as measured by the Spanish version of the Auditory Comprehension subtest of the Preschool Language Scale–3 (PLS-3; Zimmerman, Steiner, & Pond, 1992), grew during their first year of Head Start, then decreased significantly in their second year. Although they passed more items over this 2-year period, neither group made gains on the monolingual norms.

In contrast, both groups' English comprehension grew over the 2-year period based on their performance on the Receptive Language subtest of the Test of Early Language Development–3 (TELD-3; Hresko, Reid, & Hammill, 1999). By the end of Head Start, HEC children's scores approached the test mean, and SEC children's scores increased to one standard deviation below the mean. By the end of kindergarten, both groups' scores met the expectations for monolingual English-speaking children. Both groups scored very near to or above 100. Once again, this shows that bilingual preschoolers do make gains in their English abilities, but that it may take several years for them to catch up to their monolingual peers (Cummins, 1979; Hammer et al., 2008b).

Individual differences were observed in both groups. In particular, a subset of children in both the HEC and SEC groups experienced increases in their English comprehension during the first Head Start year, and another subset experienced decreases in comprehension. However, over the summer, when the children were at home, children who displayed increases during the school year demonstrated decreases in their English comprehension. In contrast, children who experienced decreases during the school year showed increases over the summer months. Then, in the second year of Head Start, children who showed gains during the first year also showed gains in their second year. Children with decreases their first year had decreases in scores again in their second year.

These findings are difficult to explain. It may be that the language input received by children who experienced gains was of sufficient complexity to foster growth in their comprehension during the school year. On the other hand, the language input received by children whose scores decreased may

have been too advanced. This assertion is supported by the fact that the group whose scores decreased had lower English comprehension scores than children whose scores increased when they entered Head Start. These findings imply that all children may not benefit equally from the language input they receive in preschool (Hammer, Lawrence, & Miccio, 2008a).

GRAMMATICAL DEVELOPMENT

Few studies have investigated Latino preschoolers' grammatical development. Research conducted on bilinguals has shown that differences occur in the order of acquisition of morphological (i.e., grammatical) forms in the children's two languages. The salience of the forms and the frequency of occurrence may explain this. Grammatical forms that are similar between bilinguals' two languages are likely to be acquired earlier because their presence in both languages makes them more salient and children encounter them more frequently (Bedore & Peña, 2008).

Additionally, our work has shown that the order in which bilingual children acquire the 14 early-developing morphemes of English differs from the order documented in the research on English monolinguals. This was determined through analyses of conversational samples collected in the fall and spring of the children's 2 years in Head Start. We also found differences between HEC and SEC children in the order the morphemes were acquired. Additionally, the number of morphemes mastered differed between the two groups. At the beginning of Head Start, HEC children had mastered more morphemes than SEC children. By the end of Head Start, both groups had mastered a similar number of morphemes, although some of the morphemes mastered differed between the two groups (Davison, 2008).

In addition, changes in children's English morphosyntactic complexity were analyzed by examination of growth in children's mean length of utterance (MLU) based on the longest three utterances. Overall, children's morphosyntactic complexity grew at an accelerated rate during Head Start. Although HEC children had consistently higher syntactic complexity, SEC children increased their level of complexity faster. Thus, bilingual preschoolers made rapid changes in their morphosyntactic abilities; however, the order they acquired specific morphemes differed from monolinguals (Davison, 2008).

With regard to Spanish, research suggests that Spanish-speaking children living in the United States are at risk of losing or not fully developing their Spanish expressive language abilities (cf. Anderson, 2004). Our research supports this conclusion. Over time, the number of children who produced language samples in Spanish decreased. Not surprisingly, more SEC children than HEC children maintained their Spanish expressive language abilities.

We examined changes in the grammatical abilities of six HEC and six SEC children who maintained their Spanish-speaking abilities during Head Start. Children were matched on their initial Spanish receptive language scores. SEC children had a higher MLU than HEC children during their Head Start years; however, both groups' MLUs increased over time. Additionally, children made relatively few grammatical errors. Thus, some Spanish-speaking children made advances in their expressive language, whereas others appeared to lose their productive abilities (Rodríguez, Winslow, Hammer, & Miccio, 2008).

PHONOLOGY

Our work and that of other researchers shows that bilingual children's phonological systems develop at the same rate in Spanish and English as the phonological systems of monolingual children (Goldstein, Fabiano, & Washington, 2005; Goldstein & Washington, 2001; Guildersleeve-Neumann, Kester, Davis, & Peña, 2008; Miccio, Hammer, López, Rodríguez, & Scarpino, 2009). Additionally, bilingual preschoolers had complex speech sound inventories by 3½ years of age; that is, children produced sounds from all major sound classes (stops, nasals, fricatives, etc.) at the same age as monolinguals, regardless of when they were exposed to English.

Differences, however, noted in the accuracy with which they produced consonants depending on when children were exposed to English. Specifically, overall accuracy was quite high for both groups, but HEC children demonstrated a higher percentage of correct consonants in English and SEC children demonstrated a higher percentage of consonants correct in Spanish (Miccio & Hammer, 2006). A detailed examination of children's consonant productions revealed that many errors made by children during their preschool years often reflected a mixing of Spanish and English sounds. These cross-linguistic effects disappeared as children grew older.

SUMMARY

The findings from our study revealed differences in bilingual children's development depending on the timing of exposure to English. In general, differences were found between the HEC and SEC groups, with HEC children having stronger abilities in English and SEC children having stronger abilities in Spanish. More specifically, the groups differed in terms of their consonant production accuracy, the order of acquisition and mastery of English morphological forms, as well as the rate of morphosyntactic and vocabulary development. They did not differ in terms of their rate of growth in oral comprehension in either language.

The HEC and SEC groups were similar in that both approached monolingual expectations in English. Over the 2-year period in Head Start, children made great advances in their English abilities. And once in elementary school, they caught up to their monolingual peers. They simply needed time to catch up. Research has shown that bilingual children need 2–3 years to reach monolinguals' conversational abilities, and 5–7 years to perform similarly to their monolingual peers academically (Cummins, 1979). Unfortunately, children's Spanish language development did not fare as well. The increases in language abilities observed in English did not occur in Spanish. Also, some children lost their Spanish expressive abilities. This was not surprising, however, given that the children received instruction in English, and that support for their Spanish language abilities came only from the home.

Emergent Literacy and Early Reading Development

PHONOLOGICAL AWARENESS

In general, school-age bilingual children have superior metalinguistic skills (e.g., ability to recognize and manipulate components of words, such as onsets, rimes, and sounds) in comparison to monolinguals (Bialystok, 1986, 1991; Bialystok, Majumder, & Martin, 2003; López & Greenfield, 2004). Less work has focused on the preschool period. The work has demonstrated that Spanish–English bilingual preschoolers' phonological abilities in Spanish are related to their phonological abilities in English (Dickinson, McCabe, Clark-Chiarelli, & Wolf, 2004; López & Greenfield, 2004; Tabors, Páez, & López, 2003). In fact, the greatest predictor of children's phonological awareness in one language is their phonological awareness competence in the other.

We also investigated bilingual preschoolers' phonological awareness during their Head Start years and beyond. A forced-choice picture task based on the work of Bird, Bishop, and Freeman (1995) was used to examine children's rime matching, onset matching, and onset segmentation and matching in Spanish and English. The Spanish version also included a first syllable matching task. During their time in Head Start, children demonstrated difficulty completing the phonological awareness tasks. They performed at levels below chance in both languages early in Head Start, and although their scores increased slightly over time, they performed at only slightly better than chance levels by the time they left Head Start. These results are consistent with those of Tabors and her colleagues, who found that the bilingual preschoolers in their study scored low in phonological awareness (Páez et al., 2007; Tabors et al., 2003).

The children in our study demonstrated significant improvement in their phonological awareness in both languages in the fall of their kindergarten year, when they received more explicit literacy instruction. In fact, both groups scored at the test mean of the Comprehensive Test of Phonological Processing (CTOPP; Wagner, Torgesen, & Rashotte, 1999) in kindergarten and first grade (Hammer & Miccio, 2006).

Differences in the structure of Spanish and English should be considered when studying bilinguals' phonological awareness. In particular, Spanish contains clear syllabic boundaries in comparison to English. Research has shown that the processing unit most important for reading words in Spanish is the syllable (Carreiras, Alva-

rez, & deVega, 1993; Jiménez & Garcia, 1995). In contrast, monolingual English-speaking children are most sensitive to onset–rime units. Therefore, awareness of onset–rime is less important in learning to read in Spanish than in learning to read in English (González, González, Monzo, & Hernandez-Valle, 2000). As a result of this difference, sensitivity to onset and rime may not be as well developed in Spanish–English bilingual children compared to English-speaking children. Although it is evident that phonological awareness skills transfer across languages, further research is needed to investigate which particular phonological awareness skills transfer and which skills best predict cross-linguistic competence in phonological awareness.

EMERGENT LITERACY

We also assessed the emergent literacy abilities of the children in our study, using the Test of Early Reading Abilities–2 (*TERA-2*; Reid, Hresko, & Hammill, 1991), which targets understanding of early print conventions; knowledge of the alphabet, letters, letter–sound correspondences; and concepts of print in English. No differences were observed between the two groups. At the end of their first Head Start year, children scored two-thirds of a standard deviation below the test mean. In the fall of their second year, children's standard scores decreased, with children averaging more than one standard deviation below the test mean (Hammer, Miccio, & Wagstaff, 2003). Children experienced a significant increase in their scores in kindergarten and scored close to the monolingual norm by the end of kindergarten (see Figure 8.4). HEC children had average standard scores that were near the test mean (standard score = 98), and SEC children's average scores were less than one-half of a standard deviation below the mean (standard score = 94), with no statistical differences between the two groups. (Note that children's emergent literacy abilities were not tested in Spanish because instruments did not exist in Spanish at the time of the study.)

LETTER–WORD KNOWLEDGE

Bilingual preschoolers' letter knowledge has also received relatively little attention in the

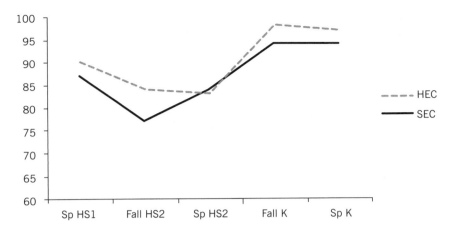

FIGURE 8.4. Children's average standard scores on the Test of Early Reading Abilities–2.

literature. We used an informal measure to assess bilingual preschoolers' ability to identify English and Spanish lower- and uppercase letters and letter–sound correspondences. Similar to their phonological awareness abilities, when in Head Start, the children were able to identify relatively few letters or letter sounds, and their scores increased slightly over time. These findings complement the work of Tabors and colleagues (2003; Páez et al., 2007) and the results of the Family and Child Experiences Survey (FACES; U.S. Department of Health and Human Services, 2001), which found that Latino children enter and leave Head Start with abilities that are below the norms for monolingual English speakers.

However, in the fall of kindergarten, the children in our study dramatically increased their abilities in both languages and passed nearly all of the items on the English instrument on average. Children's knowledge of English letters and letter–sound correspondences were stronger than their Spanish knowledge, and no differences were observed between the two groups. The gains that children made after leaving Head Start were also observed in their English letter–word identification abilities as measured by the Woodcock Language Proficiency Battery—Revised (WLPB-R; Woodcock & Muñoz-Sandoval, 1995). The children performed at the standardized test mean at the end of kindergarten. By the end of first grade, children in both groups had an average standard score of 109, which was two-

thirds of a standard deviation *above* the test mean at the end of first grade.

Children's Spanish reading abilities were less developed. This was expected because the children were not instructed in Spanish. In kindergarten and first grade, the two groups' Spanish letter–word identification abilities were at least one standard deviation below the test mean.

READING COMPREHENSION

Children's reading comprehension was assessed in first grade using the Passage Comprehension subtest of the WLPB-R. By the end of first grade, bilingual children had strong English reading comprehension. Both groups had an average standard score of 110, which was two-thirds of a standard deviation *above* the mean. Children's abilities in Spanish were not as strong. Both groups' scores were two-thirds of a standard deviation below the test mean.

SUMMARY

The bilingual children in our study began Head Start with low phonological awareness, letter identification, and emergent literacy abilities, and they made minimal gains over their 2 years in the program. This outcome was not unexpected because Head Start classrooms the children attended did not focus on children's emergent literacy abilities. However, the children made great progress in all areas of emergent and early reading when they entered elementary school, where emphasis was placed on building children's skills in these areas. Greater gains were made in English compared to Spanish. By the end of first grade, children's English reading abilities were at or above expectations for their age.

Predictors of Early Reading Development

Relationships between Preschool Language and Later Reading Outcomes

Studies have shown that monolingual preschoolers' oral vocabulary and overall language abilities positively impact their later reading comprehension, letter knowledge, and decoding (Dickinson & McCabe, 2001; Lonigan, Burgess, & Anthony, 2000; NICHD [National Institute of Child Health and Human Development] Early Child Care Research Network, 2005). Some research shows, however, that the strength of the relationships changes over time. In particular, studies have revealed that the relationship between kindergarten oral language and first-grade reading abilities weakens, when emphasis is placed on decoding in this grade. The relationship strengthens in later grades, when reading comprehension becomes the focus (Evans, Shaw, & Bell, 2000; Sénéchal & LeFevre, 2002; Storch & Whitehurst, 2002).

Less attention has been paid to the relationship between bilinguals' language abilities and their later reading outcomes, which is more complicated because children are learning two languages. Two models address this issue: the *separate underlying proficiency model* and the *common underlying proficiency model* discussed earlier in the chapter. Consistent with the common underlying proficiency model, we hypothesized that preschoolers' receptive language abilities (i.e., receptive vocabulary and oral comprehension combined) in Spanish and English would support their later reading abilities in both languages. We found that children's English language abilities at the end of Head Start negatively predicted their Spanish letter–word identification abilities at the end of kindergarten (see Table 8.1). Similarly, children's Spanish language abilities at the end of Head Start negatively pre-

dicted their kindergarten English emergent literacy and letter–word abilities, as well as their Spanish letter–word abilities.

Our results also revealed that *growth* (or the rate of change) of children's oral language abilities in English during their 2 years in Head Start positively predicted their kindergarten emergent literacy outcomes and their letter–word identification abilities in both Spanish and English. Similarly, *growth* of children's Spanish oral language abilities over the 2-year period positively predicted their reading outcomes in both languages. When explaining our results, we concluded that language scores at the end of Head Start reflected children's abilities at a discrete point in time and did not capture the changes in language development children were experiencing. Instead, the findings related to growth provided us with a stronger understanding of bilingual children's development (Hammer, Lawrence, & Miccio, 2007).

We also investigated the relationships between growth in children's receptive vocabulary and oral comprehension in Spanish and English during Head Start, and their English phonological awareness at the end of kindergarten, as measured by the CTOPP. Similar to previous results, growth in Spanish and English vocabulary and oral comprehension positively predicted children's kindergarten phonological awareness (Davison, Scarpino, & Hammer, 2009).

Because relationships between children's language abilities and their reading abilities may change over time, we studied the contributions of language development during preschool to first-grade reading outcomes. Specifically, we examined contributions of children's receptive vocabulary and oral comprehension growth during preschool to their reading outcomes in first grade. The results showed that children's growth in their English receptive vocabulary and oral comprehension positively predicted their letter–word identification abilities and reading comprehension in both Spanish and English at the end of first grade. Additionally, growth in children's Spanish vocabulary and oral comprehension during Head Start positively impacted their first-grade letter–word identification and reading comprehension abilities in both languages (Davison, Hammer, & Lawrence, 2010).

TABLE 8.1. Parameter Estimates for Receptive Language Growth Parameters Predicting Kindergarten Reading Outcomes

Parameter	Estimate	Standard error	*t*-value	$Pr(> |t|)$
English receptive language				
English letter–word identification standard scores				
End of Head Start	−0.77	0.29	−2.67	.012
Rate of growth	13.92	1.61	8.67	.000*
Spanish letter–word identification standard scores				
End of Head Start	−1.12	0.34	−3.31	.002*
Rate of growth	14.53	1.88	7.73	.000*
TERA-2 standard scores				
End of Head Start	−0.91	0.36	−2.51	.017
Rate of growth	14.42	2.02	7.16	.00*
Spanish receptive language				
English letter–word identification standard scores				
End of Head Start	−5.60	0.76	−7.90	.000*
Rate of growth	74.11	6.35	11.67	.000*
Spanish letter–word identification standard scores				
End of Head Start	−5.45	1.06	−5.14	.000*
Rate of growth	66.34	8.89	7.47	.000*
TERA-2 standard scores				
End of Head Start	−6.21	0.95	−6.55	.000*
Rate of growth	75.24	7.95	9.47	.000*

Note. TERA-2, Test of Early Reading Ability–2.
*$p \leq .008$, the adjusted type I error rate.

SUMMARY

Language *growth* is a key factor that predicts bilingual children's later reading abilities. In particular, growth of both Spanish and English receptive abilities during Head Start positively predicted children's later English phonological awareness, English emergent literacy, English and Spanish letter–word identification abilities, and English and Spanish reading comprehension. These results support the common underlying proficiency model as children's development of their two languages contributed to their reading outcomes in both languages.

Relationship between the Environment and Later Reading Outcomes

MATERNAL LANGUAGE USAGE

Many educators and policymakers believe that parents should speak English to their bilingual children, so they can become fluent in English. Others assert that parents should use their native language because this will enable children to build a strong foundation in their home language, on which they can capitalize as they learn English.

Evidence suggests that home language usage promotes language and literacy abilities in that language. However, the relationships between home language usage and outcomes in the majority language are less well understood because the findings are mixed. Differences in the populations studied, educational environments, and measures used may explain the differences in the results (Hammer, Davison, Lawrence, & Miccio, 2009).

Given lack of understanding of the impact of Spanish on the development of children living in the United States who attend English immersion Head Start programs, we investigated the effect of maternal language usage on children's outcomes. The results revealed that, as a group, mothers used more English with their children over the 3 years. This change in language usage, however, did not impact their children's growth in English. Specifically, changes in maternal language usage to equal amounts of Spanish and English or to predominantly English had no effect of children's English vocabulary growth or emergent literacy. Similarly, maternal usage of Spanish did not impact English outcomes. We hypothesized that children received sufficient exposure to English in their Head Start programs and the community, so that the mothers' language choice at home did not impact their children's English development.

Differing results were found for children's Spanish vocabulary development. Increased usage of English had a negative impact on children's Spanish vocabulary development. Children whose mothers increased their usage of English over time had slower rates of Spanish vocabulary growth. On the other hand, maternal usage of Spanish promoted children's Spanish vocabulary development. Children whose mothers used more Spanish or all Spanish experienced faster vocabulary growth. These results are explained by the fact that the home environment is the place where children's Spanish language development was supported. The results are consistent with the work of Gutiérrez-Clellen and Kreiter (2003) and Duursma and colleagues (2007), who concluded that Spanish is needed in children's homes to promote their abilities in that language (Hammer et al., 2009).

HOME LITERACY ENVIRONMENT

Building on Hess and Holloway's (1984) work, Snow and colleagues (1998) proposed a framework of the home literacy environment that comprises four factors: value placed on literacy, press for achievement, availability and use of reading materials, and parent–child book reading. We applied this model when investigating the role of home literacy practices in bilingual children's emergent literacy (Hammer et al., 2003).

This study involved 43 children and mothers from the larger investigation. Bilingual home visitors completed a home literacy questionnaire with the mothers in the language of the mothers' choice. From the questionnaire,

three scales were formed: (1) value placed on literacy, which included items about the frequency of maternal literacy activities (e.g., "How often do you look at books a week? A newspaper? Sale ads? The Bible?"); (2) press for achievement, which contained items about mother and child literacy activities (e.g., "How often do you teach the alphabet to your child? Teach letter names? Take your child to the library?"); (3) availability of reading materials (e.g., number of children's books and number of adult books). Additionally, mothers were asked how frequently they read books to their children.

No differences were found between the HEC and SEC groups in the frequency of maternal literacy activities and availability of books in the home. Mothers engaged in adult literacy activities once a month, on average, and homes averaged less than 10 books. Mothers of HEC children read books to their children 2–4 days per week, whereas mothers of SEC children read to their children once a week. This difference approached the level of significance. When comparisons were made in a subsequent investigation involving the entire sample, the difference between the groups was significant (Hammer, Rodríguez, Lawrence, & Miccio, 2007).

A significant difference was found between the two groups in the frequency of mother–child literacy-related activities. Mothers of HEC children engaged their children in literacy-related activities weekly, whereas mothers of SEC children engaged in these activities two to three times per month. This difference was also observed in the entire sample (Hammer, Rodríguez, et al., 2007).

Relationships among the four factors of the home literacy environment and children's emergent literacy outcomes, as measured by the TERA-2, were not found. We concluded that a critical level of literacy events is needed for the home environment to have an effect on outcomes. Given that the frequency of literacy events and the availability of literacy materials were low, the home literacy environment did not contribute to children's emerging literacy skills.

Summary

Mothers' use of Spanish helped to support children's Spanish vocabulary development, and use of English slowed Spanish vocabulary growth. Neither Spanish nor English language usage affected children's English vocabulary or emergent literacy development, most likely because children were immersed in English at school. This finding should relieve the fears of those who believe that using Spanish will impede bilingual children's English development.

Mothers of HEC children engaged their children in literacy-related activities and read to their children more frequently than did mothers of SEC children. However, the frequency of literacy activities was low in both groups. No relationship was found between the home literacy environment and emergent literacy during Head Start.

Educational Interventions

Our investigation has implications for educational interventions. Before discussing these implications, it is important to review existing research that has examined the effects of bilingual preschools, dual-language preschools, and specific curricula on children's outcomes.

Effects of Preschool on Language Learning of Bilingual Children

BILINGUAL PRESCHOOLS

Rodríquez, Díaz, Duran, and Espinosa (1995) examined the effect of bilingual preschools (i.e., preschools that instruct in Spanish and English) on bilingual children's development of Spanish and English. Language development of children who did not attend preschool was compared to that of children who attended a bilingual preschool. The bilingual preschools varied in the amount of instruction provided in Spanish and English, from 30% Spanish instruction and 70% English instruction to 30% Spanish instruction and 70% English instruction. Children who attended bilingual preschools made similar gains in their Spanish language abilities to the gains of children who did not attend preschool. Children who attended a bilingual preschool, however, made greater gains in their English language development.

DUAL-LANGUAGE VERSUS ENGLISH IMMERSION PRESCHOOLS

Barnett, Yarosz, Thomas, Jung, and Blanco (2007) compared the effect of dual-language and English immersion preschools on children's development through a randomized control trial. Children assigned to the dual-language preschools rotated weekly between two teams that comprised a teacher and an assistant. One team taught the children in English, and other instructed the children in Spanish. Teachers in the English immersion program taught in English. All classrooms used the High/Scope curriculum.

The results revealed no group differences in children's English vocabulary, early reading, and math scores at the end of preschool. However, children in both programs performed one standard deviation below the monolingual test mean in these areas of language development. Children in the dual-language program made greater gains in their Spanish receptive vocabulary, but not their Spanish expressive vocabulary, early reading, or math scores. Thus, both programs supported children's English development; however, the dual-language program better supported one aspect of children's Spanish language development.

EFFICACY OF SPECIFIC CURRICULA

Two investigations studied the impact of particular curricula on bilingual children's outcomes. Barnett and colleagues (2008) studied the effect of Tools of the Mind on preschool children's language, literacy, and self-regulation. Tools of the Mind, a curriculum based on Vygotskian theory of child development, is designed to promote development of self-regulation and language, which in turn support children's reading, math, and socioemotional development.

Participating children were randomly assigned to a Tools of the Mind classroom ($n = 7$) or a control classroom ($n = 11$), where they received balanced literacy instruction. Nearly all children were Hispanic (93%) and 69% were from Spanish-speaking homes. Children in the Tools of the Mind classrooms made similar gains in their English vocabulary and Spanish receptive–expressive language development to children in the control classrooms. (*Note.* Only children whose home language was Spanish were assessed in Spanish.) Additionally, children in the Tools of the Mind classrooms had better self-regulation than children in the control classrooms.

The second study was conducted by Farver, Lonigan, and Eppe (2009), who investigated the efficacy of Literacy Express on bilingual children's language and literacy outcomes. Literacy Express focuses on promoting children's language, emergent literacy, early math, science, and socioemotional development. As in the previous study, children were randomly assigned to intervention ($n = 32$) or to control classrooms ($n = 31$). High/Scope was employed in the control classrooms. In both conditions, instruction was provided in either English (English immersion) or in Spanish at the beginning of the year, transitioning to English (transitional program).

Regardless of the language of instruction, children in the Literacy Express classrooms made greater gains in their Spanish and English literacy, which included print knowledge and phonological awareness. With regard to language outcomes, children in the transitional and English immersion classrooms made significant increases in their English vocabulary, with no differences between the two groups. Children in the transitional program, however, had better English definitional vocabularies than children in the English immersion program. Additionally, only children in the transitional classrooms made significant gains in their Spanish vocabularies.

Continued Research Needs

Additional research is needed on educational practices and curricula used in classrooms that serve bilingual preschoolers. First, research is needed that tests the efficacy and effectiveness of specific curricula designed for use with bilingual children. One can anticipate that more than one curriculum will be effective. Second, longitudinal studies are needed that follow children who receive preschool interventions into elementary school to determine whether curricular interventions have long-term effects. Third, it is imperative that researchers identify key teaching and language facilitation techniques

that promote bilingual children's outcomes. Regardless of the curriculum used, effective strategies are needed that promote children's language and literacy outcomes.

Finally, it is critical that researchers examine the efficacy and effectiveness of various bilingual education models (e.g., English immersion, dual language). Currently, programs in the United States are moving to English-only instruction, without a research base to support its effectiveness (Barker et al., 2001). A panel commissioned by the American Psychological Association concluded that "there is no support for the English-only initiatives, and that the English-only movement can have negative consequences on psychological development, intergroup relations, academic achievement, and psychometric and health-service delivery systems" (Padilla et al., 1991, p. 120). As reviewed in this chapter, evidence suggests that bilingual preschoolers achieve similar English abilities when attending English immersion and dual-language programs, but that bilingual children lose their home language if it is not supported in school. As a result, children who speak two languages early in life are at risk of not becoming bilingual. This is unfortunate given the benefits of bilingualism. Development and maintenance of Spanish assist individuals to identify with members of their communities, and they support psychological well-being (Padilla et al., 1991; Zentella, 2002). Bilingualism also promotes many cognitive skills, including heightened awareness of semantic relationships, better phonological awareness abilities (Bialystok, 1986, 1988, 1992, 1997), increased awareness of grammatical rules and structures, enhanced creativity, and better academic outcomes (Hakuta & Diaz, 1985). In addition, there are economic benefits to being bilingual. In this global economy, the demand for bilingual workers and professionals is growing. English-only educational policies do not afford Spanish-speaking children the opportunity to become bilingual. As stated by Cummins (2005), "We are faced with the bizarre scenario of schools successfully transforming fluent speakers of foreign languages into monolingual English speakers, at the same time they struggle, largely unsuccessfully, to transform English monolingual students into foreign language speakers" (p. 586). Educational models that promote children's development in both languages may promote academic outcomes, as well as children's overall well-being across the lifespan.

Implications

The research we have reviewed in this chapter has several implications for educators and professionals who work with young bilingual children. First, bilingual children cannot be viewed as a homogeneous group; therefore, it is important for educators to learn about children's exposure to their home language and English at the beginning of the school year. For example, our work has shown that bilingual children's language development differs depending on when they are exposed to English. Differences in children's initial language abilities and developmental trajectories were found in several areas of language depending on whether they were exposed to English or Spanish prior to school entry.

Second, bilingual preschoolers should not be expected to have language abilities in their two languages that equal the abilities of their monolingual peers. Many bilingual preschoolers enter preschools with English and Spanish language abilities that are below the abilities of typical monolingual child. This does not mean, however, that they have deficient language abilities. Consistent with studies of older children, our children made advances in their English abilities and caught up to their monolingual peers over time. They needed time to learn English and to catch up to monolingual English speakers. By the early elementary grades, they had English reading abilities that equaled or exceeded the monolingual norm.

Third, it cannot be assumed that all children will make language gains during the preschool year. Although, as a group, our children's English language abilities improved, some children's language scores decreased during the school year. Therefore, ongoing, regular monitoring of children's language abilities is needed to ensure that all children's abilities are increasing. If children's abilities are not developing, efforts are needed to modify the language-learning experiences so that children make progress.

Fourth, our findings demonstrated that Spanish does not harm children's English development. Indeed, we found that preschoolers' Spanish language development positively contributed to their English reading abilities in early elementary grades.

Finally, maternal usage of Spanish did not have a negative effect on children's developing English vocabulary and emergent literacy skills. Use of English had no effect, suggesting that the often-made recommendation that Spanish-speaking parents should speak only English to their children is unwarranted. Our findings demonstrate that usage of Spanish promotes Spanish vocabulary development, while having no effect on children's English growth. Additionally, use of the home language fosters relationships between parents and their children, and allows parents the opportunity to provide well-formed language models to their children. If parents are not proficient in English, their ability to provide their children with quality English language models will be limited. However, usage of Spanish allows parents to provide their children with quality language models, and provides them the opportunity to share their culture and language with their children.

Acknowledgments

We wish to recognize the valuable contributions of Dr. Adele W. Miccio to our work. Adele, who passed away in 2009, was the Co-Principal Investigator of Bilingual Preschoolers: Precursors to Literacy and, more importantly, was a dear friend and colleague. Bilingual Preschoolers: Precursors to Literacy was supported by a grant from the National Institutes of Health–National Institute of Child Health and Human Development and the United States Department of Education–Institute of Education Sciences (No. 5-R01-HD-39496-05).

References

Anderson, R. (2004). First language loss in Spanish-speaking children: Patterns of loss and implications for clinical practice. In B. Goldstein (Ed.), *Bilingual language development and disorders in Spanish-English speakers* (pp. 163–186). Baltimore: Brookes.

August, D., & Hakuta, K. (Eds.). (1997). *Improving schooling for language-minority children: A research agenda*. Washington, DC: National Academy Press.

Barker, V., Giles, H., Noels, K., Duck, J., Hecht, M., & Clement, R. (2001). The English-only movement: A communication analysis of changing perceptions of language validity. *Journal of Communication, 51,* 3–37.

Barnett, S. W., Jung, K., Yarosz, D., Thomas, J., Hornbeck, A., Stechuk, R., et al. (2008). Educational effects of the Tools of the Mind curriculum: A randomized trial. *Early Childhood Research Quarterly, 23,* 299–313.

Barnett, W. S., Yarosz, D., Thomas, J., Jung, K., & Blanco, D. (2007). Two-way and monolingual English immersion in preschool education: An experimental comparison. *Early Childhood Research Quarterly, 22,* 277–293.

Beals, D. E., De Temple, J. M., & Dickinson, D. K. (Eds.). (1994). *Talking and listening that support early literacy development of children from low-income families.* Malden, MA: Blackwell.

Bedore, L. M., & Peña, E. D. (2008). Assessment of bilingual children for identification of language impairment: Current findings and implications for practice. *International Journal of Bilingual Education and Bilingualism, 11*(1), 1–29.

Bialystok, E. (1986). Factors in the growth of linguistic awareness. *Child Development, 57*(1), 498–510.

Bialystok, E. (1988). Levels of bilingualism and levels of linguistic awareness. *Developmental Psychology, 24*(4), 560–567.

Bialystok, E. (1991). Letters, sounds, and symbols: Changes in children's understanding of written language. *Applied Psycholinguistics, 12,* 75–89.

Bialystok, E. (1992). Attentional control in children's metalinguistic performance and measures of field independence. *Developmental Psychology, 28,* 654–664.

Bialystok, E. (1997). Effects of bilingualism and biliteracy on children's emerging concept of print. *Developmental Psychology, 33,* 429–440.

Bialystok, E., Majumder, S., & Martin, M. M. (2003). Developing phonological awareness: Is there a bilingual advantage? *Applied Psycholinguistics, 24,* 27–44.

Bird, J., Bishop, D. V. M., & Freeman, N. H. (1995). Phonological awareness and literacy development in children with expressive phonological impairments. *Journal of Speech and Hearing Research, 38,* 446–562.

Britto, P., & Brooks-Gunn, J. (2001). Beyond shared book-reading: Dimensions of home literacy and low-income African American preschoolers' skills. *New Directions for Child and Adolescent Development, 92,* 73–88.

Bronfenbrenner, U. (1979). *The ecology of human development: Experiments by nature and design.* Cambridge, MA: Harvard University Press.

Burgess, S., Hecht, S., & Lonigan, C. (2002). Relations of the home literacy environment (HLE) to the development of reading-related abilities: A one-year longitudinal study. *Reading Research Quarterly, 37,* 408–426.

Butler, Y., & Hakuta, K. (2004). Bilingual and second language acquisition. *The handbook of bilingualism* (pp. 114–144). Malden, MA: Blackwell.

Carreiras, M., Alvarez, C., & deVega, M. (1993). Syllable frequency and visual word recognition in Spanish. *Journal of Memory and Language, 32,* 766–780.

Catts, H., Fey, M., Tomblin, B., & Zhang, X. (2002). A longitudinal investigation of reading outcomes of children with language impairments. *Journal of Speech, Language, and Hearing Research, 45,* 1142–1157.

Catts, H., Fey, M., Zhang, X., & Tomblin, J. B. (1999). Language basis of reading and reading disabilities: Evidence from a longitudinal investigation. *Scientific Studies of Reading, 3,* 331–361.

Conboy, B., & Thal, D. (2006). Ties between the lexicon and grammar: Cross-sectional and longitudinal studies of bilingual toddlers. *Child Development, 77,* 712–735.

Cummins, J. (1979). Linguistic interdependence and the educational development of bilingual children. *Review of Educational Research, 49,* 222–251.

Cummins, J. (1981). The role of primary language development in promoting educational success for language minority students. In Office of Bilingual Bicultural Education (Ed.), *Schooling and language minority students: A theoretical framework* (pp. 3–49). Sacramento: California State Department of Education.

Cummins, J. (1986). Empowering minority students: A framework for intervention. *Harvard Educational Review, 56,* 18–36.

Cummins, J. (2005). A proposal for action: Strategies for recognizing heritage language competence as a learning resource within the mainstream classroom. *Modern Language Journal, 89,* 585–592.

Davison, M. D. (2008). *Spanish–English bilingual preschoolers' English grammatical development.* Unpublished doctoral dissertation, Penn State University.

Davison, M. D., Hammer, C. S., & Lawrence, F. (2010). *Associations of language and reading outcomes of bilingual preschool children.* Manuscript submitted for publication.

Davison, M. D., Scarpino, S., & Hammer, C. S. (2009, November). *Early language and phonological awareness in bilingual children.* Presented at the American Speech–Language–Hearing Association Convention, New Orleans, LA.

DeNavas-Walt, C., Proctor, D., & Lee, C. (2005). *Income, poverty, and health insurance coverage in the United States: 2004.* Washington, DC: U.S. Government Printing Office.

Dickinson, D., & McCabe, A. (2001). Bringing it all together: The multiple origins, skills, and environmental supports of early literacy. *Learning Disabilities Research and Practice, 16,* 186–202.

Dickinson, D. K., McCabe, A., Clark-Chiarelli, N., & Wolf, A. (2004). Cross-language transfer of phonological awareness in low-income Spanish and English bilingual preschool children. *Applied Linguistics, 25,* 323–347.

Dunn, L. W., & Dunn, L. M. (1997). *Peabody Picture Vocabulary Test–III*. Circle Pines, MN: American Guidance.

Dunn, L. W., Padilla, E., Lugo, D., & Dunn, L. M. (1986). *Test de vocabulario en imágenes Peabody*. Circle Pines, MN: American Guidance Service.

Duursma, E., Romero-Contreras, S., Szuber, A., Proctor, P., Snow, C., August, D., et al. (2007). The role of home literacy and language environment on bilinguals' English and Spanish vocabulary development. *Applied Psycholinguistics, 28*, 171–190.

Evans, M., Shaw, D., & Bell, M. (2000). Home literacy activities and their influences on early literacy skills. *Canadian Journal of Experimental Psychology, 2*, 65–75.

Farver, J. A., Lonigan, C. J., & Eppe, S. (2009). Effective early literacy skill development for young Spanish-speaking English language learners: An experimental study of two methods. *Child Development, 80*, 703–719.

Federal Interagency Forum on Child and Family Statistics (2007). *America's children: Key national indicators of well-being*. Washington, DC: U.S. Government Printing Office.

Genesee, F. (2004). What do we know about bilingual education for majority-language students? In P. Fletcher & B. MacWhinney (Eds.), *The handbook of bilingualism* (pp. 547–576). Malden, MA: Blackwell.

Goldstein, B., & Washington, P. (2001). An initial investigation of phonological patterns in typically developing 4-year-old Spanish–English bilingual children. *Language, Speech, and Hearing Services in Schools, 32*, 153–164.

Goldstein, B. A., Fabiano, L., & Washington, P. S. (2005). Phonological skills in predominantly English-speaking, predominantly Spanish-speaking, and Spanish-English bilingual children. *Language, Speech, and Hearing Services in Schools, 36*, 201–208.

González, J. E., González, C. J., Monzo, A. E., & Hernandez-Valle, I. (2000). Onset–rime units in visual word recognition in Spanish normal readers and children with reading disabilities. *Learning Disabilities, 15*, 135–148.

Guildersleeve-Neumann, C. E., Kester, E. S., Davis, B. L., & Peña, E. D. (2008). English speech sound development in preschool-aged children from bilingual English–Spanish environments. *Language, Speech, and Hearing Services in Schools, 39*, 314–328.

Gutiérrez-Clellen, C., & Kreiter, J. (2003). Understanding child bilingual acquisition using parent and teachers reports. *Applied Psycholinguistics, 24*, 267–288.

Hakuta, K., & Diaz, R. (1985). The relationship between degree of bilingualism and cognitive ability: A critical discussion and some new longitudinal data. In K. E. Nelson (Ed.), *Children's language* (Vol. 5, pp. 319–344). Hillsdale, NJ: Erlbaum.

Hammer, C. S., Davison, M. D., Lawrence, F. R., & Miccio, A. W. (2009). The effect of home language on bilingual children's vocabulary and emergent literacy development during Head Start and kindergarten. *Scientific Studies of Reading, 13*(2), 99–121.

Hammer, C. S., Lawrence, F. R., & Miccio, A. W. (2007). Bilingual children's language abilities and reading outcomes in Head Start and kindergarten. *Language, Speech, and Hearing Services in Schools, 38*, 237–248.

Hammer, C. S., Lawrence, F. R., & Miccio, A. W. (2008a). The effect of summer vacation on bilingual preschoolers' language development. *Clinical Linguistics and Phonetics, 22*(9), 686–902.

Hammer, C. S., Lawrence, F. R., & Miccio, A. W. (2008b). Exposure to English before and after entry into Head Start: Bilingual children's receptive language growth in Spanish and English. *International Journal of Bilingual Education and Bilingualism, 11*(1), 30–56.

Hammer, C. S., & Miccio, A. W. (2000). *Bilingual preschoolers: Precursors to literacy* (Grant funded by the National Institutes of Health). Rockville, MD: National Institute of Child Health and Human Development.

Hammer, C. S., & Miccio, A. W. (2006). Early language and reading development of bilingual preschoolers from low-income families. *Topics in Language Disorders, 26*(4), 302–317.

Hammer, C. S., Miccio, A. W., & Wagstaff, D. (2003). Home literacy experiences and their relationship to bilingual preschoolers' developing English literacy abilities. *Language, Speech, and Hearing Services in Schools, 34*, 20–30.

Hammer, C. S., Rodríguez, B. L., Lawrence, F. R., & Miccio, A. W. (2007). Puerto Rican mothers' beliefs and home literacy practices. *Language, Speech, and Hearing Services in Schools, 38*, 216–224.

Hess, R. D., & Holloway, S. (1984). Family and school as educational institutions. In R. D. Parke (Ed.), *Review of child development research: Vol. 7. The family* (pp. 179–222). Chicago: University of Chicago Press.

Hresko, W., Reid, D. K., & Hammill, D. (1999). *Test of Early Language Development–3*. Austin, TX: Pro-Ed.

Jiménez, J. E., & Garcia, D. R. H. (1995). Effects of word linguistic properties on phonological awareness in Spanish children. *Journal of Educational Psychology, 87*, 193–201.

Lonigan, C., Burgess, S., & Anthony, J. (2000). Development of emergent literacy and early reading skills in preschool children: Evidence from a latent-variable longitudinal study. *Developmental Psychology, 26*, 596–613.

López, L. M., & Greenfield, D. B. (2004). The cross-language transfer of phonological skills of Hispanic Head Start Children. *Bilingual Research Journal, 28*, 1–18.

Marchman, V. A., & Martinez-Sussmann, C. (2002). Concurrent validity of caregiver/parent report measures of language for children who are learning both English and Spanish. *Journal of Speech, Language, and Hearing Research, 45*, 983–997.

McCardle, P., Scarborough, H., & Catts, H. (2001). Predicting, explaining, and preventing children's reading difficulties. *Learning Disabilities Research and Practice, 16*, 230–239.

McSwan, J., & Rolstad, K. (2005). Modularity and the Facilitation Effect: Psychological Mechanisms of Transfer in Bilingual Students. *Hispanic Journal of Behavioral Sciences, 27*, 224–243.

Miccio, A. W., & Hammer, C. S. (2006, November). *Bilingual Spanish–English phonological acquisition: The longitudinal course of change.* Paper presented at the American Speech–Language Hearing Association Convention, Miami, FL.

Miccio, A. W., Hammer, C. S., López, L. M., Rodríguez, B. L., & Scarpino, S. E. (2009, April). *Bilingual Spanish–English phonological assessment for young children.* Paper presented at the biennial meeting of the Society for Research in Child Development, Denver, CO.

National Center for Education Statistics. (2009). *The condition of education.* Washington, DC: U.S. Government Printing Office.

NICHD Early Child Care Research Network. (2005). Pathways to reading: The role of oral language in the transition to reading. *Developmental Psychology, 41*, 428–442.

Oller, D. K., & Eilers, R. E. (2002). *Language and literacy in bilingual children.* Tonawanda, NY: Multilingual Matters.

Padilla, A., Lindholm, K., Chen, A., Duran, R., Hakuta, R., Lambert, W., et al. (1991). The English-only movement: Myths, reality, implications for psychology. *American Psychologist, 46*, 120–130.

Páez, M. M., Tabors, P. O., & López, L. M. (2007). Dual language and literacy development of Spanish-speaking preschool children. *Journal of Applied Developmental Psychology, 28*(2), 85–102.

Pearson, B. Z., Fernandez, S., & Oller, D. K. (1993). Lexical development in bilingual infants and toddlers: Comparison to monolingual norms. *Language Learning, 43*, 93–120.

Reid, D. K., Hresko, W., & Hammill, D. (1991). *Test of Early Reading Ability–2.* Austin, TX: Pro-Ed.

Rodríguez, B. L., Winslow, A., Hammer, C. S., & Miccio, A. (2008). *Bilingual children's English and Spanish expressive language skills: A focus on individual differences in syntactic complexity, lexical diversity and verb morphology.* Paper presented at 9th Head Start Research Conference, Washington, DC.

Rodríquez, J., Díaz, R., Duran, D., & Espinosa, L. (1995). The impact of bilingual preschool education on the language development of Spanish-speaking children. *Early Childhood Research Quarterly, 10*, 475–490.

Scarborough, H. (2001). Connecting early language and literacy to later reading (dis)abilities: Evidence, theory and practice. In S. B. Neumann & D. K.

Dickinson (Eds.), *Handbook of early literacy* (Vol. 1, pp. 97–110). New York: Guilford Press.

Schatschneider, C., Fletcher, J., Francis, D., Carlson, C., & Foorman, B. (2004). Kindergarten prediction of reading skills: A longitudinal comparative analysis. *Journal of Educational Psychology, 96*, 265–282.

Sénéchal, M., & LeFevre, J. (2002). Parental involvement in the development of children's reading skill: A five-year longitudinal study. *Child Development, 73*, 445–460.

Snow, C. E., Burns, M. S., & Griffin, P. (1998). *Preventing reading difficulties in young children.* Washington, DC: National Academy Press.

Speece, D. L., Ritchey, K. D., Cooper, D. H., Roth, F. P., & Schatschneider, C. (2004). Growth in early reading skills from kindergarten to third grade. *Contemporary Educational Psychology, 29*, 312–322.

Storch, S., & Whitehurst, R. (2002). Oral language and code-related precursors to reading: Evidence from a longitudinal structural model. *Developmental Psychology, 38*, 934–947.

Tabors, P. O., Páez, M. M., & López, L. M. (2003). Dual language abilities of Spanish–English bilingual four-year-olds: Initial findings from the early childhood study of language and literacy development of Spanish-speaking children. *NABE Journal of Research and Practice, 1*, 70–91.

U.S. Department of Health and Human Services. (2001). *Head Start FACES: Longitudinal findings on program performance.* Retrieved February 17, 2008, from *www.acf.hhs.gov/programs/opre/hs/faces/reports/perform_3rd_rpt/meas_99_title.html.*

U.S. Department of Health and Human Services. (2003). *Head Start FACES 2000: A whole-child perspective on program performance.* Washington, DC: Author. Retrieved March 6, 2008, from *acf.hhs.gov/programs/opre/hs/faces/reports/faces00_4thprogress/faces00_title.html.*

Wagner, R., Torgesen, J., & Rashotte, C. (1999). *Comprehensive Test of Phonological Processing.* Austin, TX: Pro-Ed.

Whitehurst, G., & Lonigan, C. (1998). Child development and emergent literacy. *Child Development, 69*, 848–872.

Woodcock, R. W., & Muñoz-Sandoval, A. F. (1995). *Woodcock Language Proficiency Battery—Revised.* Itasca, IL: Riverside.

Zentella, A. C. (2002). Latina languages and identities. In M. Suarez-Orozco & Páez, M. A. (Eds.), *Latinos: Remaking America* (pp. 321–338). Berkeley: University of California Press.

Zimmerman, I., Steiner, V., & Pond, R. (1992). *Preschool Language Scale–3, Spanish Edition.* San Antonio, TX: Psychological Corporation.

9

Supporting the Language and Early Literacy Skills of English Language Learners: Effective Practices and Future Directions

MARIELA M. PÁEZ
KRISTEN PARATORE BOCK
LIANNA PIZZO

Educational and language researchers have emphasized the urgency of addressing the needs of young bilingual learners, particularly those from Spanish-speaking backgrounds, who make up a high percentage of the English language learners (ELLs) entering American schools (Suárez-Orozco & Páez, 2008). In 2007, an estimated 10.9 million school-age children (children ages 5–17) speaking a language other than English at home were enrolled in public schools, representing approximately 20.4% of the total population (National Center for Education Statistics, 2007). The higher risk of reading problems associated with lack of proficiency in English on school entry is widely documented (National Assessment of Educational Progress, 2003). This risk is compounded when literacy instruction is in the child's second language and poverty and low levels of parental education are also present (Snow, Burns, & Griffin, 1998). In response to these concerns, current research with ELLs has been growing, and efforts are being made to understand better and improve the language and literacy skills of these students.

Research has shown that language experiences and early exposure to literacy are important precursors for children's language development and reading success (Snow et al., 1998). In particular, several language skills

have been identified as important during the early childhood years, including a strong vocabulary, phonological awareness, letter knowledge, background knowledge, and understanding of print concepts (Dickinson & Snow, 1987; Dickinson & Tabors, 2001; Snow & Tabors, 1993; Whitehurst & Lonigan, 1998). Research with bilingual populations supports the importance of these critical dimensions of language and literacy for ELL students. The National Literacy Panel on Language-Minority Children and Youth (August & Shanahan, 2006) concluded that instruction in the key components of reading, as identified by the National Reading Panel (2000), including phonological and phonemic awareness, phonics, fluency, vocabulary, and text comprehension, has clear benefits for students learning English as a second language. However, the reviewers added that "instruction in the key components of reading is necessary—but not sufficient—for teaching language-minority children to read and write proficiently in English. Oral proficiency in English is critical as well—but student performance suggests that it is often overlooked in instruction" (August & Shanahan, 2006, p. 4).

In light of these findings, oral language skills, including vocabulary and listening comprehension, have recently received particular attention from educators and researchers trying to meet the learning needs of bilingual students. Research with monolingual and bilingual populations reveals that vocabulary is one of the best predictors of reading comprehension, is a complex construct that has many components, and is learned in multiple contexts both at home and in school (August, Carlo, Dressler, & Snow, 2005). Furthermore, ELLs' level of vocabulary knowledge has been shown to be an important predictor of reading ability, comprehension, and achievement on reading assessments (August & Shanahan, 2006). Research with ELL students has also identified vocabulary skills as a domain of particular weakness for this population (Carlo et al., 2004).

Our purpose in this chapter is to provide an overview of research on the development of oral language skills for ELL students, with special attention to Spanish-speaking children. We summarize some of the developmental and intervention research conducted by Páez and her colleagues to highlight some of the trends in the bilingual development of young children. In addition, we discuss the research on effective practices and interventions for building oral language skills in this group of students as it relates to classroom approaches, family literacy approaches, and future directions for connecting learning across these two contexts.

We begin by presenting an overview of research on the development of oral language skills for ELLs, with special attention to Spanish-speaking children. Next, we describe the design, implementation, and preliminary findings of the Kindergarten Language Study (KLS), a research study aimed at improving the language and literacy skills of Spanish-speaking, bilingual kindergarten students. In particular, we explain how research on oral language development and family literacy guides and informs our current research. We conclude by identifying promising directions for future research in this area.

Oral Language Skills and ELLs

Vocabulary knowledge is a key aspect of oral language development because it is tied to early reading development and predicts reading comprehension (Biemiller, 2006). Yet only recently has the relationship between vocabulary and early reading skills among bilingual students received attention commensurate with the needs of this growing population (Proctor, August, Carlo, & Snow, 2005). The vocabulary challenge facing young bilingual students can be described as a knowledge gap that students encounter when they start school in a new language and try to keep pace with native English speakers. This challenge extends to different aspects of word learning, including knowledge of word meanings, word associations, and morphological knowledge (Carlo et al., 2004). A research review of vocabulary and second language acquisition found that Spanish–English bilingual learners lag behind their monolingual English-speaking peers in both depth and breadth of vocabulary knowledge (August et al., 2005). This means that ELLs know fewer English vocabulary words than monolingual English speakers. Furthermore, ELLs know less about the meaning of those words. Recent comparative research with various bilingual populations has also found this gap in vocabulary with Hebrew–English, Spanish–English, and Chinese–English bilingual students in first grade (Bialystok, Luk, & Kwan, 2005).

The language gap experienced by young bilingual learners could be explained by multiple factors including demographic factors such as living in poverty and parents' level of education (Hart & Risley, 1995). The limited research with dual language learners from high socio-economic backgrounds indicates that bilingual children catch up to monolingual norms during the elementary grades and some even exceed their monolingual peers' achievement in English (Umbel, Pearson, Fernandez, & Oller, 1992).

Research on Young ELLs

Much of the research on language acquisition in bilingual students has focused on children in kindergarten or early elementary school. However, a few studies have examined questions relating to language development among preschool-age children. Most of these studies have been conducted with children who are Latino Spanish-speakers from low-income families and attend English preschool programs. These studies are important because they shed light on the importance of early language influences and the role of home literacy practices.

Carol Hammer's research (see Hammer, Scarpino, & Davison, Chapter 8, this volume) with preschoolers from low socioeconomic status backgrounds examines the differences in language development of bilingual students as they relate to exposure to English before and after school entry (Hammer, Lawrence, & Miccio, 2008). In a longitudinal study of Head Start children from Spanish-speaking homes, researchers compared the language development of preschoolers who communicated in English at home prior to beginning Head Start and those who did not communicate in English until they entered Head Start. The study investigated English and Spanish receptive vocabulary and language comprehension abilities of bilingual preschoolers attending English immersion Head Start programs for 2 years. Results revealed that the two groups' language abilities in Spanish and English differed when children were 3 years, 8 months of age, and that these differences were maintained over 2 years. Exceptions to this were found in the children's vocabulary abilities, with the difference between the two groups' English standard scores narrowing over time and the difference between their Spanish standard scores increasing during the 2-year period (Hammer et al., 2008). Hammer and her colleagues discuss the importance of studying growth of language abilities for this group of students and their research notes the limitations of considering only one point in time when predicting the contributions of first language skills to English early reading abilities (Hammer, Lawrence, & Miccio, 2007; see Hammer et al., Chapter 8, this volume).

The ECS Study

Another line of research that has included preschoolers and examined their longitudinal growth and trajectories is the Early Childhood Study of Language and Literacy Development of Spanish-Speaking Children (ECS) by Patton Tabors and Mariela Páez. The ECS longitudinal study was designed to answer three interrelated research questions:

1. What are the Spanish and English language and early literacy skills of young Spanish-speaking children as they enter and as they leave PreK?
2. How do these children's language and early literacy skills in Spanish and English change over time from PreK to second grade?
3. What precursor factors, from their home and school contexts, predict Spanish-speaking children's Spanish and English literacy abilities in second grade?

The basic sample for this research consisted of 350 children from Spanish-speaking homes in Massachusetts and Maryland (ECS sample) and a comparative sample of 152 children in Puerto Rico (Puerto Rican Comparative [PRC] sample). Results from language and literacy assessments from two data-collection periods during the children's PreK and kindergarten years, as well as home demographic and classroom observational data, have been published in several articles (see Páez & Rinaldi, 2006; Páez, Tabors, & López, 2007; Tabors, Páez, & López, 2003; Uccelli & Páez, 2007). In this chapter, we discuss five sets of findings that relate to oral language skills and are directly connected to our current intervention work with this population.

First, we found that young Spanish–English bilingual students have limited oral language skills in English and Spanish, especially in the area of vocabulary. Language and literacy assessments were administered in the fall and spring of the PreK year and in the spring of the kindergarten year.

Results from the Woodcock Language Proficiency Battery—Revised (WLPB-R) subtests show that children in the ECS sample performed better in the early literacy tests (Letter–Word Identification and Dictation) than in the oral language tasks (Picture Vocabulary and Memory for Sentences) in both English and Spanish. Given that these children are young ELLs, it is not surprising that they scored, on average, close to two standard deviations below the norm in the oral language subtests in English when compared to monolingual English children. However, they also scored, on average, close to two standard deviations below the monolingual norm in the oral language subtests in Spanish. Furthermore, the PRC sample, which was matched for socioeconomic status, scored on average only one standard deviation below the monolingual norm.

Second, we found that young bilingual children display a considerable range of proficiency in both Spanish and English language skills (Páez & Suarez-Munist, 2010). Children in the ECS sample could be grouped into one of four categories based on their fall PreK language scores: (1) high English and high Spanish, above the sample mean in both languages; (2) high English and low Spanish, above the sample mean in English and below the sample mean in Spanish; (3) low English and high Spanish, below the sample mean in English and above the sample mean in Spanish; and (4) low English and low Spanish, below the sample mean in both languages. Of particular relevance to our current work is that 14% of the children in the ECS sample could be categorized as having low proficiency skills in English and Spanish.

Third, the ECS study showed significant relationships between children's Spanish and English skills. Positive transfer from Spanish to English (e.g., as revealed by positive cross-language correlations) occurs in letter and word recognition, writing and spelling, and general language ability. We found positive, significant correlations between English and Spanish for all the assessments except vocabulary. The within-assessment, across-language correlations for Phonological Awareness are $r = .34$ at Time 1 and $r = .53$ at Time 2. The stronger correlation at Time 2 for this task indicates more transfer between English and Spanish phonological skills at the end of preschool. The correlations for Letter–Word Identification (Time 1, $r = .52$; Time 2, $r = .57$), Dictation (Time 1, $r = .49$; Time 2, $r = .52$), and Memory for Sentences (Time 1, $r = .27$; Time 2, $r = .32$) were similar across time. The correlations across language for the Picture Vocabulary subtests show a different pattern (Time 1, $r = -.27$; Time 2, $r = -.12$). The cross-language relationship for vocabulary does not support transfer of skills between Spanish and English for this group of children. However, the relationship between English and Spanish vocabulary, and the possibility of transfer for these skills might differ if there were more direct links between the languages, such as the same topics or books being discussed in both languages.

Fourth, the ECS study revealed great variability in the language and literacy support available in the children's home environments. Furthermore, the ECS study has identified variables in the home (relating to families' sociodemographic background, and language and literacy support in the home) that have an impact on students' language and literacy skills.

Regression analyses used to predict language proficiency, as indexed by the children's Picture Vocabulary scores in each language, indicate that 32.7% of the variation in Spanish vocabulary can be explained by three factors: The child was born outside the United States; the child was read to in Spanish at home; and the child was exposed to and used Spanish at home, with home exposure in Spanish relating to stronger Spanish abilities. Thirty-three percent of the variation in English vocabulary can be explained by the following four factors: number of people in the family (negative), household income, preschool attendance at age 3, and exposure to and use of English at home.

Fifth, the ECS study found diversity of quality and language use in the classrooms of bilingual children. Classroom observation data are currently being analyzed to provide descriptions of what language(s) were used in the classrooms and how different classrooms supported the language and literacy development of bilingual children. Classroom observations and teacher questionnaires were collected in the 75 classrooms of the ECS children and the 16 classrooms of the PRC sample children in PreK. During the kindergarten year, we collected data for 170 classrooms and teachers in the ECS sample and 34 classrooms and teachers in the PRC sample. We continued to collect classroom information in first and second grade through teacher questionnaires, and these data are currently under analysis. In general, results indicate that the type of language used in the classrooms and teachers' language use are an important predictor of children's language skills and growth. For example, in classrooms where English was used most of the time and teachers reported an emphasis on teaching English language skills to ELL students, students demonstrated large gains in English vocabulary.

In summary, findings from the ECS study of young Spanish-speaking children from low socioeconomic status backgrounds revealed that these children might be at risk for delays in their early literacy development due to their low levels of vocabulary in both languages—English and Spanish (Páez et al., 2007; Páez & Rinaldi, 2006; Tabors et al., 2003). Of particular importance to our current research is that results from the ECS study showed limited English vocabulary skills when children in the sample were first assessed as 4-year-olds, with the gap between monolingual norms and the sample persisting through first grade. These findings are similar to Hammer's work on preschool-age ELLs and are corroborated by other research on young Spanish-speaking children (e.g., Lindsey, Manis, & Bailey, 2003; Manis, Lindsey, & Bailey, 2004; Umbel et al., 1992).

Taken together the findings highlight the variability of students' skills and family background, while establishing oral language skills and vocabulary as a critical area in need of intervention. Furthermore, findings from this study support the use of interventions that combine the use of Spanish at home and English in the classroom. Finally, it is important to note the lack of data disaggregated by socioeconomic status because the majority of studies have focused on bilingual children from low-status socioeconomic backgrounds.

In the next section, we highlight some of the most prominent literature on combining home and school interventions to improve early language and literacy skills among ELLs.

Home–School Connections: Promising Approaches to Building Language and Early Literacy Skills for ELLs

In light of findings from previous research on the language acquisition of young bilingual students, it is clear that oral language development and vocabulary skills are challenging areas of language and early literacy development. Therefore, it is essential to understand effective instructional approaches that focus on developing these skills across multiple contexts, including the language and early literacy environments of classrooms and homes.

As such, another line of intervention research has focused on the combination of classroom and home factors. These studies confirm causal relationships between parental behaviors and child outcomes, and confirm as well the malleability of adult interactive behavior. For example, Whitehurst and Lonigan (1998) conducted an intervention study designed to increase the vocabulary skills of 3- and 4-year-old children. Teachers and parents were trained in *dialogic reading*, a method of posing open-ended questions and encouraging child conversation during book reading. Whitehurst and Lonigan found that the intervention was most effective when both parents and teachers were trained (see also Whitehurst et al., 1994). Simply increasing the frequency of home reading by providing books or encouraging parents and children to read together has also been shown to be effective (Feitelson & Goldstein, 1986; McCormick & Mason, 1986; Sénéchal, Lefevre, Thomas, & Daley, 1998).

Another intervention program, Early Access to Success in Education (Project EASE; Jordan, Snow, & Porche, 2000), also used parent–child book reading to promote language development with English-speaking kindergarten students attending elementary schools with a high incidence of poverty. This model improved on previous intervention designs, which focused on either frequency of interactions during storybook reading (e.g., Feitelson & Goldstein, 1986) or quality of talk during the interactions (e.g., Whitehurst et al., 1988) by introducing procedures to increase both quality and quantity. Project EASE modeled effective language interactions through "systematic parent coaching, and then increased the frequency of higher quality interactions by linking them to homework assigned by the kindergarten teacher" (Jordan et al., 2000, p. 527). In a yearlong intervention study using the Project EASE model with a sample of 248 kindergarten students (71 students in a control group and 177 students in the experimental group), researchers found that children whose families engaged in the at-home activities made significantly greater gains in language scores than control children. These research studies demonstrate both the potential for schools to engage parents in a meaningful way to support their children's language development and the sensitivity of children's oral language skills to the impact of structured enrichment of the oral language environment. However, these approaches, including the Project EASE model, have not been tested with bilingual children.

The few studies that do directly address young bilingual populations indicate that providing family literacy programs and interventions in combination with classroom approaches is a promising way to improve the language and early literacy skills of ELL children. In a recent example, Roberts (2008) conducted a study aimed at explaining how primary language and second language home storybook reading influenced second language (English) vocabulary development when combined with English language storybook reading in classroom settings. Overall, this study found that primary language storybook reading in the home was as effective as home storybook reading in English for promoting English vocabulary acquisition in preschool ELLs from two different language groups.

This line of research presents a new direction for intervention models because previous studies have not focused on exploiting the capacities of ELL families to enhance their children's oral language skills in their first language as a possible contribution to their performance in English literacy. Family-based interventions may be particularly powerful for young children, who spend more time with their parents and are more susceptible to incidental learning. Furthermore, linking the family support for oral language development in a content-specific way to classroom activities in English has the potential to speed acquisition of English oral skills, yet such an approach has never been developed systematically.

In the remainder of this chapter, we describe our current research on Spanish-speaking bilingual families. In particular, we focus on the design and implementation of the KLS and outline some preliminary findings. We begin with an overview of the study, then separately describe the classroom and home components in detail.

The Kindergarten Language Study

The KLS is a 5-year longitudinal research project that comprises the design, implementation, and assessment of an intervention program to improve the language skills of Spanish–English bilingual kindergarten students. The intervention program focuses on improving vocabulary and extending discourse skills, aspects of children's oral language that research has identified as related to literacy outcomes and as areas of weakness for young bilingual students. Using a quasi-experimental design, including a control group, three types of intervention models have been developed: a Spanish home intervention, an English classroom intervention, and a Spanish home intervention linked with an English classroom intervention. The hypothesis for KLS is that the intervention model linking Spanish language enrichment in the home to English development in the classroom will be the most effective to develop and sustain English reading skills for K–2 students. Participants include schools and classrooms with a high density of Spanish–English bilingual children attending public schools in Massachusetts.

The KLS has five specific aims:

1. To develop and implement an intervention program designed to improve Spanish-speaking children's oral language skills.
2. To compare the impact of delivering the program in the native language at home with the impact of delivering it in English in the kindergarten classroom, and the impact of delivering it in both languages and venues simultaneously.
3. To explore the nature of transfer from Spanish to English by explicitly comparing outcomes for the Spanish-only to the Spanish-plus-English versions of the program.
4. To compare the impact of the program on children with varying degrees of skill in Spanish and English.
5. To examine the relationships between the short-term effects of the intervention on oral English skills and their long-term effects on English literacy through second grade.

This study differs from previous work focusing on vocabulary for ELLs in that it matches English language development in classrooms with Spanish language development in the home. Conceptually, the classroom and home interventions are linked by targeting similar language and literacy skills in the home and school environments. Practically, these components are linked by use of the same books in the classroom and in the home. This approach is designed to provide maximum vocabulary exposure in both Spanish and English, while testing theories of language transfer.

The intervention lasts for 16 weeks and is organized into four thematic units. For each week, four classroom lessons are implemented, each lasting 15–20 minutes. Additionally, parents attend a monthly workshop during which they are taught various strategies and activities they can do with their children using Spanish versions of the same books (one parent training session per unit). Prior to formal implementation of the intervention, initial demographic questionnaires are given, and classroom observations are conducted. Data collection for the implementation includes pre- and postintervention assessments in English and Spanish, fidelity of implementation observations, and teacher and parent questionnaires. Students are assessed pre- and postintervention with standardized measures and with research-developed vocabulary assessments that target the words taught during the intervention.

The first 2 years of the study focused on designing, developing, and piloting the intervention program. The design of the intervention studies is quasi-experimental, with assignment at the classroom level. The target population is Spanish-speaking kindergarten children and their families, defined as children who are exposed to Spanish at home and have some knowledge of this language. In Year 2, the intervention program was piloted in two school sites with high numbers of Spanish-speaking kindergarten children for a total of eight classrooms participating in the study (four intervention and four control classrooms). The goals of Year 2 included the development and refinement of intervention materials and assessment instruments. In Year 3, the study is being expanded to include a larger sample of Spanish-speaking kindergarten children to test three conditions: English classroom intervention, Spanish home intervention linked to English classroom intervention, or no intervention (control group). In Years 4 and 5, follow-up standardized assessments will be conducted for students in the spring of their first- and second-grade years.

The KLS takes into account the gaps and limitations of previous research by addressing the specific vocabulary needs of the ELL population. As such, the intervention aims at improving children's oral language skills, with a particular focus on vocabulary development. In the next sections, we separately describe the classroom and family components of the intervention.

Classroom Approaches to Building Oral Language Skills

The classroom intervention consists of four thematic units organized around a 4-week structure for reading books aloud. Within each unit, a new book is introduced in each of the first 3 weeks, then concludes with a review week. Each week consists of four 15- to 20-minute lessons based on read-alouds with book prompts, preteaching activities for academic vocabulary, structured vocabulary activities for basic words, and visual and kinesthetic review of words and story content. The structure and activities incorporate knowledge regarding effective instructional approaches with bilingual students. In particular, the methodology employed in KLS is informed by research on specific vocabulary teaching methods shown to be effective with ELL students, as conducted by Diane August, Margarita Calderón, and their colleagues at the Center for Applied Linguistics (Calderón et al., 2005). Additionally, design of the KLS interventions has been framed using the vocabulary program proposed by Michael Graves (2006, 2009). Through a four-tier approach, Graves advocates employing teaching strategies that engage diverse learners in linguistically rich educational experiences. This program has the following four components (Graves, 2006, 2009): (1) providing frequent, varied, and extensive language experiences; (2) teaching individual words; (3) teaching word-learning strategies; and (4) fostering word consciousness. He proposes that teachers should integrate these instructional strategies in their classroom vocabulary program "to create effective, engaging, and efficient vocabulary instruction" (Graves, 2009, p. 9). KLS includes aspects of these four components to build rich language experiences and increase vocabulary skills.

Providing Frequent, Varied, and Extensive Language Experiences

For monolingual and bilingual learners alike, rich and diverse instructional approaches include the use of meaningful contexts for learning new words (Calderón et al., 2005; Nagy & Herman, 1985). One widely recognized avenue for providing such contexts is through the use of read-alouds (Cunningham, 2005). Reading aloud to children is believed to promote the learning of new words in an enjoyable and natural way (Graves, 2009). Repeated reading of stories aloud supported by provision of word meanings builds upon the context provided in the narrative to assist in the acquisition of novel words (Biemiller & Boote, 2006). By adding prereading, during-reading, and postreading activities to the reading aloud of instructionally appropriate texts, teachers are further able to scaffold students' learning of vocabulary words (Fitzgerald & Graves, 2004). The KLS intervention is based on read-aloud experiences, including activities to reinforce selected vocabulary words. Furthermore, the discourse elicited through the read-aloud experience is a particularly powerful tool for embedding vocabulary learning for ELLs by providing engagement with new words through varied and distinct approaches designed to meet students' instructional needs for each particular target word encountered (Calderón et al., 2005).

Teaching Individual Words

In addition to Graves's (2006) program, a robust vocabulary framework that contributes to KLS, is the work of Isabel Beck and her colleagues (Beck, McKeown, & Kucan, 2002), who present a three-tiered approach to the word selection process that ranges from the most straightforward to the most sophisticated vocabulary. Tier 1 consists of basic, everyday, familiar words. Tier 2 includes high-frequency words appearing across contexts (importance and utility), words that have instructional potential to create profound understandings and representations of words, and words that create nuance and precision in language (conceptual understanding). Tier 3 words are domain-specific and are encountered much more infrequently in reading.

For monolingual learners, Tier 2 words have received the most attention for early instruction because monolingual students have already acquired many Tier 1 words prior to entering formal reading instruction (Biemiller & Slonim, 2001). As mentioned earlier, there is a the gap in second language vocabulary for ELLs because they often do not possess basic words in their second language and require explicit instruction of both Tier 1 and Tier 2 words to promote vocabulary development (August et al., 2005; Carlo et al., 2004). Therefore, a necessary layer of instruction in any viable vocabulary program for ELLs should consist of basic vocabulary learning. Relying on incidental instruction of Tier 2 and Tier 3 vocabulary is not recommended for any student (Carlo et al., 2004). It is also important to recognize that while Tiers 1 and 2 are both considered important for instruction, treatment of the Tier 1 words should be quantitatively and qualitatively different than that of Tier 2 words because they may require less time and effort to learn.

We have selected both Tier 1 and Tier 2 vocabulary words for each monthly unit. Tier 1 words are thematically linked and presented with visual scaffolds. We select more sophisticated Tier 2 key words that are presented throughout the lessons, reviewed, and reinforced, so that students are exposed to each word 10–12 times during the monthly unit. In selecting these words, we have consulted the work of Andrew Biemiller and his colleagues to identify words that are commonly known by monolingual students, as well as a means to determine word difficulty (Biemiller & Boote, 2006; Biemiller & Slonim, 2001). In addition, we selected words because of their high importance and utility, while we considered their instructional potential and saliency within the context of the books.

Teaching Word-Learning Strategies

Strong instruction for ELLs includes individual word learning that is supplemented by multimodal engagement with the definitions for review and reinforcement. Beyond the explicit instruction of basic vocabulary (Tier 1 words), August and colleagues (2005) identified two more key instructional strategies for unlocking word meanings for ELLs: (1) capitalizing on a student's first language abilities, and (2) providing sufficient review and reinforcement of newly learned words.

By capitalizing on first language knowledge, ELLs are able to maximize their learning by utilizing the full range of their linguistic experiences. In particular, the use of cognate instruction to transfer existing linguistic knowledge from the first to second language (Cummins, 1979, 1991) has been shown to promote English vocabulary acquisition for ELLs (Carlo et al., 2004). The KLS intervention words were selected with particular attention to cognates, and 35% of the vocabulary words taught in the program are cognates.

The review and reinforcement of recently learned words should be developmentally appropriate and occur through instructional approaches that engage students in various aspects of words through different avenues to develop depth of understanding. Review activities of particular utility include providing visuals depicting the words, providing multiple exposures to meaningful information about each word, engaging in visualization and kinesthetic activities surrounding the word meaning, and allowing ELLs to experience quality interactions with word meanings in multiple contexts (August et al., 2005; Carlo et al., 2004; Graves, 2006, 2009). The KLS intervention activities incorporate many of these strategies for review and reinforcement of vocabulary learning. For example, students are presented with pictures that depict the different vocabulary words and are at the same time provided with child-friendly definitions of the words. Postreading activities include visualization and kinesthetic prompts for reviewing the meaning of the words taught during the lessons.

Fostering Word Consciousness

Although individual word learning is paramount to a strong vocabulary program, it is impossible for children to learn all the words of the English language through individual word instruction. It is therefore important to incorporate word-learning strategies, including those that relate to *word consciousness* (Graves, 2006, 2009; Nagy, 2005; Nagy & Scott, 2000), which refers to addressing students' awareness of and interest in learning new words. Our KLS intervention program incorporates a focus on word consciousness by adding activities in which students are able to develop an appreciation for words, understand the nuances of word meanings, and recognize when they are encountering a word for the first time (Graves, 2006). Because word consciousness instruction is embedded in the development of metacognitive skills, a strength that ELLs bring to the learning of second language vocabulary (Bialystock, 2001), it may be an underutilized tool for ELLs in the classroom.

Family Literacy Approaches to Building Oral Language Skills

The parent component of KLS parallels the classroom component in that it is broken into four units. Parents at each school site attend a total of four workshops (one per month), in which they are exposed to between three and six concepts pertaining to language learning. The four overarching themes are vocabulary, phonological awareness and decoding, extended discourse, and narrative retelling. During each workshop, participating parents receive five picture books. Three of these books are Spanish versions of the books children read in English in the classroom. The additional books provide diversity in terms of content, length, and difficulty. Additionally, parents receive a packet at each workshop that includes a list of the vocabulary words in Spanish, corresponding with the English vocabulary words taught in school; suggested prompts related to the stories they have been provided; suggested materials and activities for parents to do with their children; and additional resources, such as a list of where parents can acquire books in Spanish or places that offer adult education courses.

Although it is evident that involving families in children's education has social and academic benefits, implementing an intervention linking home and school activities necessitates consideration of several challenges. First, intervention activities must be aligned with families' lives. In particular, successful interventions must offer activities at times when parents are able to attend, must be held at a location to which parents have access and feel comfortable, and must provide child care and refreshments and the resources necessary for participation in intervention activities.

Additional challenges to garnering parent participation include uncertainty about the extent to which literacy is valued in the home (Purcell-Gates, 1996), variability in home practices among different families (Auerbach, 1989; Teale, 1986), differences in parents' beliefs about their role in educating their children (Gillanders & Jiménez, 2004; Vasquez, Pease-Alvarez, & Shannon, 1994), a mismatch between school activities and families' cultural models (Janes & Kermani, 2001), parents' lack of confidence in their ability to help their children (Krol-Sinclair, 1996), and limitations in access to literacy-related materials (Purcell-Gates, 1996).

In the design and implementation of KLS we take into account the challenges discussed in previous research and efforts at helping parents support their children's language and literacy development. In particular, we seek to improve the language skills of Spanish–English bilingual kindergarten students by conceptually and practically linking home and classroom activities. The family component of KLS is informed by research on family literacy.

Overall, this research supports five claims. First, different types of parent–child activities are associated with different types of results. Second, families practice literacy in different ways. Third, families often have their own cultural models of literacy activities and development. Fourth, families are often willing to adapt these cultural models to meet the needs of their children. Fifth, several existing family literacy programs and interventions reflect current research on effective strategies for supporting children's language and literacy development.

Different Literacy Events Are Associated with Different Learning Outcomes

Several researchers have found that training parents to use specific strategies when interacting with their children in literacy-related actives is effective in supporting children's language and literacy development (Goldenberg, Reese, & Gallimore, 1992; Krol-Sinclair, 1996; Sénéchal & Young, 2008; Whitehurst & Lonigan, 1998). In a recent review, Sénéchal and Young (2008) present a meta-analysis of the scientific literature on the role parents play in children's acquisition of literacy from kindergarten to grade 3. In particular, the authors focus on

parent–child activities aimed at improving early reading acquisition. They reviewed 16 intervention studies that were divided into three types of interventions: parents reading books with their children ($n = 3$); parents listening to children read books ($n = 6$); and parents tutoring their children, with a focus on specific skills ($n = 7$). All of these studies used experimental and quasi-experimental designs. The most significant effect was for parents trained to do literacy activities ($d = 1.15$). In some of these studies, parents were trained to do specific exercises with their children, such as learning the alphabet, using flashcards to help children learn and read new words and sentences, and selecting appropriate reading environments. In other studies, parents used a structured program that included exercises and books or texts. The studies in which parents listened to their children read also produced a significant effect ($d = 0.52$). There was no effect for parents reading to their children ($d = 0.18$).

This finding conflicts with earlier research (e.g., Bus, van IJzendoorn, & Pelligrini, 1995; Scarborough & Dobrich, 1994), and the authors suggest that an indirect relationship may exist. In particular, (1) training parents to read to their children enhances oral language, which may result in better reading comprehension; (2) book reading increases children's knowledge of the literate discourses, which might facilitate reading later; and (3) book reading in kindergarten might increase children's motivation to read, which will in time result in more frequent reading for pleasure (Sénéchal & Young, 2008). As supported by the research, KLS focuses on teaching parents several specific strategies for supporting their children's language and literacy acquisition. As described earlier, at each parent training session, researchers describe between one and three concepts, model strategies for teaching these concepts, and provide parents with an opportunity to practice these strategies with each other.

Different Families Use Literacy in Different Ways and for Different Purposes

The theoretical perspective framing much of the research on family literacy reflects a sociocultural lens. From this perspective, literacy is defined as more than the ability to read and write. Rather, *literacy* is "a set of social practices associated with different domains of life that are purposeful and embedded in broader social goals and practices" (Purcell-Gates, Degener, Jacobson, & Soler, 2002, p. 73). Moreover, "a view of literacy from a sociocultural theory of learning considers and seeks to understand the cultural context within which children have grown and developed. It seeks to understand how children interpret who they are in relation to others, and how children have learned to process, interpret, and encode their world" (Pérez, 1998, p. 4).

Consistent with this theory, several studies describe variability in the home literacy practices of different families (Auerbach, 1989; Purcell-Gates, 1996; Teale, 1986) and variability within families. For example, in a study documenting the range and frequency of literacy practices in 20 low socioeconomic status homes, Purcell-Gates (1996) found that the families she observed all used print for various purposes as they went about their daily activities. These purposes ranged from using text at the phrasal/clausal level (reading food containers, flyers, coupons, etc.) or reading more abstract types of text, though the former was most common. More specifically, according to Pérez (1998), "as the specific purposes and contexts for literacy use change . . . a person's ability to perform literacy tasks or to learn at optimum levels also changes" (p. 24). Additionally, Pérez posits that "multiple literacies develop to meet the broad spectrum of functions required within diverse social contexts, and they begin in the home and community, before children enter school" (p. 24).

To make KLS accessible to individual families, and to address some of the challenges to participation described earlier, we offer morning and afternoon workshops, provide a range of activities, and include books that are diverse in content and difficulty so that families can tailor the intervention to fit their lifestyles.

Cultural Models and the Need for Authentic Activities

Some researchers have suggested that variation among and within families is at least in part associated with differences in parents' cultural models of literacy development, including their beliefs about their own roles in educating their children and the literacy experiences they had growing up (Heath, 1983; Reese & Gallimore, 2000). In particular, cultural models of literacy development might include the bedtime story, reading for meaning, decoding words, memorizing vocabulary, or retelling familiar narratives (Reese & Gallimore, 2000).

An example of the tension associated with variations in cultural models of language and literacy development is the idea that there is a disconnect between home and school ideologies. For example, multiple studies found that parents do participate in their children's academic life in ways that are not consistent with the school's ideas about what is most effective (e.g., Gillanders & Jiménez, 2004; Goldenberg et al., 1992). In one such study, which aimed at determining the school's effects on children's home literacy experiences, researchers found that "repetition and lack of attention to print-meaning characterized children's [home] literacy experiences with school materials" (Goldenberg et al., 1992, p. 514). The authors posited that the reason for this behavior is that many Latino parents' knowledge of how children learn to read, often based on their own school experiences, suggests that repetition of sounds is most effective. Therefore, in this study, if parents perceived activities as being school-related, they focused on copying and repetition. But if they perceived activities as fun for kids, they focused more on content and meaning making.

As one way to address the gap between cultural models, several programs build on what families are already doing at home—consciously or subconsciously—that may help prepare children to succeed in schools in the United States (Auerbach, 1989, 1995; Morrow, 2008; Paratore, 2001; Pérez, 1998; Purcell-Gates, 2000; Rodríguez-Brown, 2003; Roser, 2008). Authentic activities may include direct child–parent interactions around literacy tasks; reading with or listening to children; or talking about other literacy activities, such as cooking or shopping. Additional activities may include parents working independently on reading and writing; using literacy to address family and community problems; addressing childrearing concerns through family literacy class; supporting the development of the home language and culture; and interacting with the school system (Paratore, 2001; Purcell-Gates, 2000; Rodríguez-Brown, 2003).

Such programs are designed to increase children's exposure to school-like language and literacy at home by "grounding the 'new' literacy practices within parents' knowledge, beliefs, and cultural models" (Paratore, Krol-Sinclair, Páez, & Paratore-Bock, 2010, p. 304). Furthermore, these programs are designed around the belief that "rather than being literacy impoverished, the home environments of poor, undereducated and language minority children often are rich with literacy practices and artifacts" (Auerbach, 1997, p. 154).

In light of this research, KLS offers engaging and authentic activities to complement storybook reading. Activities include doing crafts related to stories or exploring a part of the city referenced in a book. Furthermore, these activities are linked to what teachers are doing in the classroom, which increases children's investment and helps parents connect to their children's school lives.

Many Families Adapt Home Practices to Support Their Children's School Success

Despite variations in families' cultural models of literacy development, recent research documents families' willingness to adapt their models to meet the needs of their children. Gillanders and Jimenéz (2004) explain:

> Some families do not react passively to the differences between home and school but rather are willing to adapt to the new circumstances of their children's schooling and add new practices to their repertoire if this means helping their children succeed in school. However, these new adaptations occur within the parents' original cultural model. (p. 262)

For example, although reading aloud may not be a common activity in immigrant families, once students begin school, families might increase the amount they read together and improve the quality of the interactions, particularly if the stories chosen are culturally meaningful (Goldenberg et al., 1992; Krol-Sinclair, 1996).

KLS supports families by linking school and classroom activities and by educating parents about schools' expectations and ac-

tivities. Furthermore, holding the workshops at the school site provides an opportunity for parents to feel more connected and comfortable at the school and to build common experiences with their children.

Helping Families Support the Children's School Success

That we know there is variability among home literacy practices and that some strategies are more effective than others in promoting children's language and literacy development points to a need to disseminate this knowledge through family literacy programs and interventions. Programs that connect home and school activities are particularly effective (Gillanders & Jiménez, 2004; Roberts, 2008).

Furthermore, research demonstrates the positive effects of several family literacy programs that aim at influencing immigrant families and targeting ELL students. For example, in the Intergenerational Literacy Program (ILP) (Paratore, 2001; Paratore et al., 2010), parents are taught and provided time to rehearse specific strategies for engaging in joint storybook reading and are encouraged to use daily routines as opportunities for literacy events (e.g., preparing grocery shopping lists, writing notes and letters to family members, reading maps). Program outcomes include parents communicating more effectively with teachers; reading more with their children at home; learning strategies for supporting their children; becoming more confident in using English in their daily lives; and feeling secure in their ability to maintain their rich home languages and cultures while building customs that reflect their new lives (Paratore et al., 2010).

Like the ILP, Project FLAME (Family Literacy: Aprediendo, Mejorando, Educando) provides English as a second language instruction to parents; increases the availability of literacy materials in the homes by teaching parents to select appropriate books and magazines for their children and to use the library; improves parents' Spanish and English literacy skills; shows parents how to teach language to their children using games, songs, and language experience; and increases contact between parents and school personnel (Shanahan, Mulhern, & Rodríguez-Brown, 1995).

One of the common themes in these programs is that they "offer simultaneous and connected education for adults and children" (Shanahan, Mulhern, & Rodríguez-Brown, 1995, p. 587). Consistent with the multiple-literacies theory, these programs are "informed by participants' beliefs and practices, [and] they [sic] incorporate *culturally familiar and relevant content.*" Moreover, the emphasis of these programs "is on *cultural maintenance and negotiation rather than cultural assimilation*" (Auerbach, 1995, p. 653, original emphasis). Similarly to these programs, KLS makes use of native language and culturally relevant learning materials and activities. We take into account the sociocultural background of our Latino families; and since it is a longitudinal study, we have been able to incorporate feedback from administrators, teachers, and families in our design and implementation. Finally, inherent in the design of our program is an awareness of local realities, such as time, child care, and transportation constraints.

It is evident from the research on children's language and literacy development that the way in which children are exposed to and learn language at home is related to their success in school. According to Pérez (1998),

> Children born into a rich and varied literate world where important others in their lives use print regularly do acquire reading and writing with relative ease. They understand reading and writing as part of the cultural and social practices needed to live. They acquire literacy implicitly as they develop knowledge about the "ways of meaning" and "ways of saying" of print, texts, and written language in general. (p. 22)

Therefore, knowledge about literacy activities that occur in the home, particularly as they relate to classroom activities, is essential for the design of interventions aimed at improving the language and literacy development of ELLs.

Although there is a considerable amount of research on family literacy, a paucity of research specifically addresses immigrant families or families that do not speak English as a first language. For example, of the 16 studies in Sénéchal and Young's (2008) review, only two were conducted in languages other than English. Moreover, these studies did not specifically address immigrants. Rather, they focused on people doing literacy activities in their native languages. Thus, our study adds to the limited body of research by addressing the needs of diverse families and combining family and classroom approaches to improve the language and early literacy skills of young bilingual children.

Preliminary Findings

Our current research work focuses on linking classroom and home activities, with the aim of designing and implementing an intervention program to improve the language skills of Spanish–English bilingual kindergarten students, and assessing the impact of the intervention on their early literacy skills (Páez, Pizzo, & Bock, 2009). We have now completed the first phase of this 5-year initiative, which included development, piloting, and refinement of the intervention program. The pilot implementation included two school sites for a total of eight kindergarten classrooms participating in the study (four intervention and four control classrooms). Classrooms were randomly assigned to intervention and control conditions, and pre- and postintervention data were collected for 48 Spanish-speaking students (27 in the intervention group and 21 in the control group) and 12 parents participating in the family component. Our observations allow us to draw four preliminary conclusions about this work and the likelihood that it will make a difference in the literacy learning of the children in these families.

First, parents eagerly seek support to use Spanish at home. Providing parents with first-language resources, in this case Spanish, allows them to draw on their rich language knowledge to continue to introduce complex and sophisticated language structures that are likely to transfer to and support their children's English language learning. Additionally, by deliberately connecting home texts and activities to classroom learning, we introduce or expand parents' knowledge of "classroom literacy" (Corno, 1989), making it more likely that parents will initiate related and supportive activities on their own. Moreover because parents may bring a different store of knowledge to the focal topic, children have the potential to learn more about the topic than they may have learned from the teacher and classroom resources alone.

Second, preliminary evidence indicates that parents have increased the frequency of parent–child shared reading. Preintervention questionnaires indicate that 75% of all participating parents read to their children at least once a week in English, and 45% read to their children at least once a week in Spanish. Data from weekly evaluations show that 100% of participants read in Spanish with their children at least once a week. Additionally, these evaluations indicate that all parents who participated in the workshops read the same books multiple times (number of readings ranges from one to seven). As noted previously, rereading the same book increases the likelihood that children's vocabulary and language knowledge will improve.

Third, although there were no significant differences between the control and the intervention students at pre- or postassessment on the standardized measures, on average, students could identify more basic and key words as part of the intervention at postassessment compared with performance at preassessment. Almost every student in the intervention classrooms showed gains in word recognition from pre- to postassessment, while only half of the students in the control classrooms demonstrated an increase in the same measure. Another promising finding is that students in the intervention classrooms showed large gains in *word depth* (i.e., ability to define key vocabulary words). Thus, the intervention has the potential to increase both word recognition and depth of the target vocabulary words.

Fourth, the school appreciates and supports the intervention. The principals and teachers demonstrate enthusiasm about the collaboration by encouraging children to share and talk about home reading and writing, and to display the products of literacy activities done at home. Additionally, at one site, the principal attends the workshops.

In summary, preliminary data indicate that supporting parents and children in the use of Spanish at home is an effective strategy for encouraging home literacy practice. Data gained from current intervention activities will enable us to assess the effect of enhanced parent–child interaction designed to produce richer home language environments in children's oral Spanish and English literacy performance, and to explore the mechanism for any impact on English literacy by varying the classroom component of the intervention. We are completing the first years of development for the intervention program and look forward to testing its effectiveness in upcoming research activities.

Conclusions

Additional research is needed to understand better the potential of capitalizing on home and school connections for improving the oral language skills and vocabulary development of young bilingual learners. Our focus in this chapter has been discussion of promising new directions for combining the knowledge of effective instructional approaches in the classroom with family literacy interventions. It would be interesting to determine whether programs that combine these approaches are effective means for building language and early literacy skills in diverse populations.

Future research on intervention programs that combine home and school might address the effectiveness of different models for improving the language and early literacy skills of diverse ELL students. For example, research should investigate the impact of particular approaches on students with varying skills in their first and second language. Also, it is important to examine ELL populations from different language backgrounds, since the majority of the research has been conducted with Spanish-speaking populations. In addition, there are still many unanswered questions about transfer from first- to second-language skills, especially when it comes to the vocabulary skills of young bilingual learners. Thus, testing for cross-language effects of different intervention models would advance of our understanding of transfer of vocabulary skills, and the mechanisms and factors that play a role in this process.

We need to conduct research that informs teachers and professionals working with young bilingual learners how best to develop the necessary oral language and early literacy skills for reading success. New models for comprehensive programs are needed to capitalize in all possible sources of instruction, including students' first language skills, language and literacy practices at home, and classroom teaching approaches that are good for all students but particularly useful for building the vocabulary skills of ELLs.

Acknowledgments

The writing of this chapter was supported by a grant from the Eunice Kennedy Shriver National Institute of Child Health and Human Development (Grant No. P01HD03950, Vocabulary Instruction and Assessment for Spanish Speakers). The content is solely the responsibility of the authors and does not necessarily represent the official views of the National Institute of Child Health and Human Development or the National Institutes of Health.

References

Auerbach, E. R. (1989). Toward a socio-cultural approach to family literacy. *Harvard Educational Review, 59,* 165–181.

Auerbach, E. R. (1995). Deconstructing the discourse of strengths in family literacy. *Journal of Reading Behavior, 27,* 643–661.

Auerbach, E. R. (1997). Family literacy. In V. Edwards & P. Corson (Eds.), *Encyclopedia of language and education* (Vol. II, pp. 153–162). Norwell, MA: Kluwer Academic.

August, D., Carlo, M., Dressler, C., & Snow, C. (2005). The critical role of vocabulary development for English language learners. *Learning Disabilities Research and Practice, 20,* 50–57.

August, D., & Shanahan, T. (2006). Developing literacy in second-language learners. *Report of the National Literacy Panel on Language-Minority Children and Youth.* Mahwah, NJ: Erlbaum.

Beck, I. L., McKeown, M. G., & Kucan, L. (2002) *Bringing words to life: Robust vocabulary instruction.* New York: Guilford Press.

Bialystok, E. (2001). *Bilingualism in development: Language, literacy and cognition.* Cambridge, UK: Cambridge University Press.

Bialystok, E., Luk, G., & Kwan, E. (2005). Bilingualism, biliteracy, and learning to read: Interactions among languages and writing systems. *Scientific Studies of Reading, 9*(1), 43–61.

Biemiller, A. (2006). Vocabulary development and instruction: A prerequisite for school learning. In D. K. Dickinson & S. B. Neuman (Eds.), *Handbook of early literacy research* (Vol. 2, pp. 41–51). New York: Guilford Press.

Biemiller, A., & Boote, C. (2006). An effective method for building meaning vocabulary in primary grades. *Journal of Educational Psychology, 98*(1), 44–62.

Biemiller A., & Slonim, N. (2001). Estimating root word vocabulary growth in normative and advantaged populations: Evidence for a common sequence of vocabulary acquisition. *Journal of Educational Psychology, 93*(3), 498–520.

Bus, A., van IJzendoorn, M. H., & Pelligrini, A. (1995). Joint book reading makes for success in learning to read: A meta-analysis in intergenerational transmission of literacy. *Review of Educational Research, 65*(1), 1–21.

Calderón, M., August, D., Slavin, R., Duran, D., Madden, N., & Cheung, A. (2005). Bringing words to life in classrooms with English-language learners. In E. Hiebert & M. Kamil (Eds.), *Teaching and learning vocabulary: Bringing research to practice* (pp. 115–136). Mahwah, NJ: Erlbaum.

Carlo, M. S., August, D., Mclaughlin, B., Snow, C. E., Dressler, C., Lippman, D. N., et al. (2004). Closing the gap: Addressing the vocabulary needs of English-language learners in bilingual and mainstream classrooms. *Reading Research Quarterly, 39,* 188–215.

Corno, L. (1989). What it means to be literate about classrooms. In D. Bloome (Ed.), *Classrooms and literacy* (pp. 29–52). Norwood, NJ: Ablex.

Cummins, J. (1979). Linguistic interdependence and the educational development of bilingual children. *Review of Educational Research, 49,* 222–251.

Cummins, J. (1991). Interdependence of first and second-language proficiency in bilingual children. In E. Bialystok (Eds.), *Language processing in bilingual children* (pp. 70–88). New York: Press Syndicate of the University of Cambridge.

Cunningham, A. E. (2005). Vocabulary growth through independent reading and reading aloud to children. In E. Hiebert & M. Kamil (Eds.), *Teaching and learning vocabulary: Bringing research to practice* (pp. 45–68). Mahwah, NJ: Erlbaum.

Dickinson, D., & Tabors, P. (Eds.). (2001). *Beginning literacy with language: Young children learning at home and school.* Baltimore: Brookes.

Dickinson, D. K., & Snow, C. E. (1987). Interrelationships among prereading and oral language skills in kindergartners from two social classes. *Early Childhood Research Quarterly, 2,* 1–25.

Feitelson, D., & Goldstein, Z. (1986). Patterns of book ownership and reading to young children in Israeli school-oriented and nonschool-oriented families. *Reading Teacher, 39,* 924–930.

Fitzgerald, J., & Graves, M. F. (2004). *Scaffolding experiences for English language learners.* Norwood, MA: Christopher-Gordon.

Gillanders, C., & Jiménez, R. T. (2004). Reaching for success: A close-up of Mexican immigrant parents in the USA who foster literacy success for their kindergarten children. *Journal of Early Childhood Literacy, 4,* 243–267.

Goldenberg, C., Reese, L., & Gallimore, R. (1992). Effects of literacy materials from school on Latino children's home experiences and early reading achievement. *American Journal of Education, 100,* 497–536.

Graves, M. F. (2006). *The vocabulary book: Learning and instruction.* New York: Teachers College Press.

Graves, M. F. (2009). *Teaching individual words: One size does not fit all.* New York: Teachers College Press.

Hammer, C. S., Lawrence, F. R., & Miccio, A. W. (2007). Bilingual children's language abilities and reading outcomes in Head Start and kindergarten. *Language, Speech, and Hearing Services in Schools, 38,* 237–248.

Hammer, C. S., Lawrence, F. R., & Miccio, A. W. (2008). Exposure to English before and after entry into Head Start: Bilingual children's receptive language growth in Spanish and English. *International Journal of Bilingual Education and Bilingualism, 11*(1), 30–56.

Hart, B., & Risley, T. R. (1995). *Meaningful differences in the everyday experience of young American children.* Baltimore: Brookes.

Heath, S. B. (1983). *Ways with words: Language, life, and work in communities and classrooms.* Cambridge, UK: Cambridge University Press.

Janes, H., & Kermani, H. (2001). Caregivers' story reading to young children in family literacy programs: Pleasure or punishment? *Journal of Adolescent and Adult Literacy, 44*(5), 458–466.

Jordan, G. E., Snow, C. E., & Porche, M. V. (2000). Project EASE: The effect of a family literacy project on kindergarten students' early literacy skills. *Reading Research Quarterly, 35*(4), 524–546.

Krol-Sinclair, B. D. (1996). *Immigrant parents with limited formal education as classroom storybook readers.* Boston: Boston University.

Lindsey, K. A., Manis, F. R., & Bailey, C. E. (2003). Prediction of first-grade reading in Spanish-speaking English language learners. *Journal of Educational Psychology, 95*(3), 482–494.

Manis, F. R., Lindsey, K. A., & Bailey, C. E. (2004). Development of reading in grades K–2 in Spanish-speaking English language learners. *Learning Disabilities Research and Practice, 19*(4), 214–224.

McCormick, C. E., & Mason, J. M. (1986). Intervention procedures for increasing preschool children's interest in and knowledge about reading. In W. H. Teale & E. Sulzby (Eds.), *Emergent literacy: Writing and reading* (pp. 90–115). Norwood, NJ: Ablex.

Morrow, L. (2008, October). *Characteristics of three family literacy programs that worked.* Paper presented at the Ball Foundation Family Literacy Symposium, Chicago.

Nagy, W. E. (2005). Why vocabulary instruction needs to be long-term and comprehensive. In E. Hiebert & M. Kamil (Eds.), *Bringing scientific research to practice: Vocabulary* (pp. 27–44). Mahwah, NJ: Erlbaum.

Nagy, W. E., & Herman, P. A. (1985). Incidental vs. instructional approached to increasing vocabulary. *Educational Perspective, 23,* 16–21.

Nagy, W. E., & Scott, J. A. (2000). Vocabulary processes. In M. Kamil, P. Mosenthal, P. D. Pearson, & R. Barr (Eds.), *Handbook of reading research* (Vol. 3, pp. 269–284). New York: Longman.

National Assessment of Educational Progress. (2003). *The NAEP 2003 technical report.* Princeton, NJ: Educational Testing Service.

National Center for Education Statistics. (2007) *Participation in education.* Retrieved November 4, 2009, from *nces.ed.gov/programs/coe/2009/section1/indicator08.asp.*

National Reading Panel. (2000). *Teaching children to read: An evidence-based assessment of the scientific research literature on reading and its implications for reading instruction.* Washington, DC: National Institute for Literacy.

Páez, M., Pizzo, L., & Bock, K. P. (2009, June). *Vocabulary instruction through home–school connections: Findings from an intervention program for Spanish–English bilingual students.* Presentation at the annual meeting of the Society for the Scientific Study of Reading, Boston.

Páez, M., & Rinaldi, C. (2006). Predicting English word reading skills for Spanish-speaking students in first grade. *Topics in Language Disorders, 26*(4), 338–350.

Páez, M., & Suarez-Munist, O. (2010). *Bilingual students' patterns of vocabulary growth from pre-K through first grade: Home and school factors that impact oral language development.* Manuscript submitted for publication.

Páez, M., Tabors, P. O., & López, L. M. (2007). Dual language and literacy development of Spanish-speaking preschool children. *Journal of Applied Developmental Psychology, 28*(2), 85–102.

Paratore, J. (2001). *Opening doors, opening opportunities: Family literacy in an urban community.* Needham Heights, MA: Allyn & Bacon.

Paratore, J. R., Krol-Sinclair, B., Páez, M., & Paratore-Bock, K. (2010). Supporting literacy learning in families for whom English is an additional language. In G. Li & P. Edwards (Eds.), *Best practices in ELL instruction* (pp. 299–327). New York: Guilford Press.

Pérez, B. (1998). *Sociocultural contexts of language and literacy.* Mahwah, NJ: Erlbaum.

Proctor, P., August, D., Carlo, M., & Snow, C. (2005). Native Spanish-speaking children reading in English: Toward a model of comprehension. *Journal of Educational Psychology, 97*(1), 159–169.

Purcell-Gates, V. (1996). Stories, coupons, and the *TV Guide*: Relationships between home literacy experiences and emergent literacy knowledge. *Reading Research Quarterly, 31*(4), 406–428.

Purcell-Gates, V. (2000). Family literacy. In M. L. Kamil, P. B. Mosenthal, P. D. Pearson, & R. Barr (Eds.), *Handbook of family literacy* (Vol. III, pp. 853–870). Mahwah: Erlbaum.

Purcell-Gates, V., Degener, S. C., Jacobson, E., & Soler, M. (2002). Impact of authentic adult literacy instruction on adult literacy practices. *Research Reading Quarterly, 37*(1), 70–92.

Reese, L., & Gallimore, R. (2000). Immigrant Latinos' cultural model of literacy development: An evolving perspective on home–school discontinuities. *American Journal of Education, 108,* 103–134.

Roberts, T. A. (2008). Home storybook reading in primary or second language with preschool children: Evidence of equal effectiveness for second-language vocabulary acquisition. *Reading Research Quarterly, 43*(2), 103–130.

Rodríguez-Brown, F. V. (2003). Family literacy in English language learning communities: Issues related to program development, implementation, and practice. In A. Debruin-Parecki & B. Krol-Sinclair (Eds.), *Family literacy: From theory to practice* (pp. 126–146). Washington, DC: International Reading Association.

Roser, N. (2008, October 2). *Talking over books at home and in schools*. Paper presented at the Ball Foundation Family Literacy Symposium, Chicago.

Scarborough, H. S., & Dobrich, W. (1994). On the efficacy of reading to preschoolers. *Developmental Review, 14*, 245–302.

Sénéchal, M., Lefevre, J., Thomas, E., & Daley, K. (1998). Differential effects of home literacy experiences on the development of oral and written language. *Reading Research Quarterly, 33*, 96–116.

Sénéchal, M., & Young, L. (2008). The effect of family literacy interventions on children's acquisition of reading from kindergarten to grade 3: A meta-analytic review. *Review of Educational Research, 78*(4), 880–907.

Shanahan, T., Mulhern, M., & Rodríguez-Brown, F. V. (1995). Project FLAME: Lessons learned from a family literacy program for linguistic minority families. *Reading Teacher, 48*(7), 586–593.

Snow, C. E., Burns, M. S., & Griffin, P. (1998). *Preventing reading difficulties in young children*. Washington, DC: National Academy Press.

Snow, C. E., & Tabors, P. O. (1993). Language skills that relate to literacy development. In B. Spodek & O. Saracho (Eds.), *Language and literacy in early childhood education* (Yearbook in Early Childhood Education) (Vol. 4, pp. 1–20). New York: Teachers College Press.

Suárez-Orozco, M. M., & Páez, M. M. (2008). *Latinos: Rethinking America* (2nd ed.). Berkeley and Los Angeles: University of California Press.

Tabors, P. O., Páez, M., & López, L. M. (2003). Dual language abilities of Spanish–English bilingual four-year olds: Initial finding from the Early Childhood Study of Language and Literacy Development of Spanish-Speaking Children. *NABE Journal of Research and Practice, 1*, 70–91.

Teale, W. H. (1986). Home background and young children's literacy development. In W. H. Teale & E. Sulzby (Eds.), *Emergent literacy: Writing and reading* (pp. 173–207). Norwood, NJ: Ablex.

Uccelli, P., & Páez, M. (2007). Narrative and vocabulary development of bilingual children from kindergarten to first grade: Developmental changes and associations among English and Spanish skills. *Language, Speech, and Hearing Services in Schools, 38*(3), 225–236.

Umbel, V. M., Pearson, B. Z., Fernandez, M. C., & Oller, D. K. (1992). Measuring bilingual childrens' receptive vocabularies. *Child Development, 63*(4), 1012–1020.

Vasquez, O. A., Pease-Alvarez, L., & Shannon, S. M. (1994). *Pushing boundaries: Language and culture in a Mexicano community*. Cambridge, UK: Cambridge University Press.

Whitehurst, G. J., Arnold, D. S., Epsiten, J. N., Angell, A. L., Smith, M., & Fischel, J. E. (1994). A picture book reading intervention in day care and home for children from low-income families. *Developmental Psychology, 30*(5), 679–689.

Whitehurst, G. J., Falco, F. L., Lonigan, C. J., Fischel, J. E., De Baryshe, B. D., Valdez-Menchaca, M. C., et al. (1988). Accelerating language development through picture book reading. *Developmental Psychology, 24*(4), 552–559.

Whitehurst, G. J., & Lonigan, C. J. (1998). Child development and emergent literacy. *Child Development, 69*(3), 848–872.

10

Young Children with Language Impairments: Challenges in Transition to Reading

ANN P. KAISER
MEGAN Y. ROBERTS
RAGAN H. McLEOD

Both learning to talk and learning to read are normative processes in typical children. For most children, language develops in an orderly progression, without systematic intervention to support the acquisition of the phonological, lexical, and morphosyntactic skills that are foundational to becoming a fluent communicator. Parents do play an important role in their children's language development by providing models of language and participating in interactions that scaffold acquisition of the forms and functions of language; however, very few parents systematically and intentionally instruct their children in the fundamentals of language.

Typically, children acquire sufficient oral language skills before the age of 5 to enter into the process of learning to read. The transition to reading is supported by both oral language skills and emergent phonological processing abilities (Poe, Burchinal, & Roberts, 2004). *Oral language skills* include mastery of core vocabulary, strategies for efficiently learning new words from linguistic and environmental contexts, and language comprehension strategies at word and sentence levels (Mervis & Bertrand, 1994). In addition to specific verbal learning skills, children's general cognitive abilities provide a foundation for both language and reading.

When children do not have a strong foundation of early language skills, they are at greatly increased risk of not learning to read (Bishop & Snowling, 2004; Catts & Kamhi, 2005). Catts (1997) identified six language-related indicators that may signal children at risk for later problems in learning to read: (1) limited speech-sound awareness, (2) problems in word retrieval, (3) limited verbal memory, (4) limitations in speech production and/or perception, (5) difficulties with oral language comprehension, and (6) limited oral language production (related to difficulties with syntax, productivity, narration, and complex vocabulary). In general, these six indicators correspond to the two broad predictors of reading outcomes: general language abilities, including vocabulary knowledge, and phonological awareness (Dickinson & Tabors, 1991). There is also considerable evidence that later difficulties in reading comprehension are likely to be accompanied by earlier deficiencies in oral language (Nation & Snowling, 1998; Stothard & Hulme, 1992). While early deficits in oral language are associated with later reading skills (Spear-Swerling & Sternberg, 2001; Strucker, 1995), persistent oral language deficits are even more strongly associate with reading skills (Catts, Fey, & Proctor-Williams, 2008).

Our goal in this chapter is to describe young children who are at high risk for learning to read due to early language deficits. In particular, we focus on contributions of early language to later reading abilities, and on strategies for early identification and intervention for children who evidence early language delays. We discuss phonological development, vocabulary development, and early syntactic skill in relation to risk for reading disabilities in children with developmental delays and children with specific language delays and typical cognitive abilities. We also discuss the risks for reading associated with co-occurring language delays and behavior problems, and consider the difficulties of identifying and intervening with children from poverty backgrounds who may also have language impairments. We propose principles for early identification of language delays and suggest language teaching approaches that might moderate language-based risks for reading problems in these populations of young children.

Language as a Basis for Learning to Read

Before discussing specific populations of children at risk, we briefly consider three aspects of early language development as they relate to children's ability to begin reading: mastery of basic phonological processes related to rule-based sound production, development of vocabulary, and mastery of the rules underlying production and comprehension of syntax.

Acquisition of Basic Phonological Principles in Language Lays the Foundation for Phonological Processes in Reading

Learning the implicit rule-based sound system of spoken language (*phonology*) occurs concurrently with the development of speech sounds in young children. Speech is an extremely complex system, and the perceptual processes that allow children to perceive fluent connected speech are equally complex. Speech-sound perception begins to emerge in typical children between ages 3 and 4. While children are able to produce nearly the full array of sounds in English before this,

they do not demonstrate awareness of the phonetic structure or individual phonemes of language until the late preschool period. Not surprisingly, it is near the age when clear discrimination of phonemes emerges that children begin to evidence the phonological processes that are linked to reading, such as rhyming, word segmentation into individual sounds, deletion of sounds, and recombination of sounds. Acquisition of phonology requires both specific perceptual skills and memory for phonologic sequences.

Early Vocabulary Development Provides an Important Basis for Reading

Acquisition of vocabulary is the foundation of early language development. By age 5, when most children begin to read, typical children's vocabularies include 4,000–6,000 words. *Words* are unique, consistent phonological and orthographic forms that refer to objects, actions, qualities of objects, and relations among objects and events. Most core vocabulary words represent concepts that can be indexed as specific combinations of unique features that differentiate objects, actions, and events. Thus, the acquisition of vocabulary and the building of an early lexicon is also the process of developing and indexing concepts, a skill requiring general cognitive skill and the development of specific phonological and lexical–semantic memory.

Rapid vocabulary learning across word types co-occurs with the extension of meanings expressed by the relations among words (*semantics*) and by the emergence of *morphology* (rules for marking modifications of the meanings of words; e.g., plurality, tense, and manner) and *syntax* (rules for ordering words to convey meaning in sentences). The modifiability of word meaning based on the linguistic context (semantic, morphological, and syntactic) increases the dimensions of word meaning and introduces new complexity to the task of vocabulary acquisition. Rapid expansion of vocabulary and syntax learning appear to facilitate one another; that is, typical children "bootstrap" between vocabulary growth and syntactic development, with growth in one area facilitating growth in the other (Moyle, Weismer, Evans, & Lindstrom, 2007). When either vocabulary learning or syntactic development are delayed or disrupted, both processes are slowed.

Both the number of words in children's vocabularies and the depth and precision of meaning are important as a basis for learning to read. As suggested by Henriksen (1999), children may (1) exhibit partial to precise knowledge of word meanings, (2) vary in depth of knowledge about word meaning, and (3) vary in their ability to produce and use words that are known receptively in productive language. Meaning construction is a process that is significantly influenced by the richness of the learner's preexisting lexical knowledge (Nassaji, 2004). In addition, the organization of words into categories is essential for language-learning processes, such as fast mapping new word meanings and essential for oral comprehension and rapid access to words in production (Mervis & Bertrand, 1994).

Acquisition of Semantic Relations and Early Syntax Are Fundamental to Comprehension in Reading

The foundations for reading comprehension emerge in oral language first. *Semantics*, or the understanding of meaning of words individually and in relation to other words, appears to be the key linkage in the development of reading, as illustrated by Snowling (2005). When children have difficulty learning vocabulary and constructing meaning from syntactic structures, they are likely to have both persistent language deficits and reading problems. Children acquire word meaning from the linguistic context of sentences and comprehend the meanings of sentences in part through their knowledge of the meaning of individual words. Accurate comprehension of meaning requires both sufficient working vocabulary and an understanding of how syntax as a rule-based system functions to convey meaning. For example, English yields predictable meanings based on word order (e.g., subject–verb–object is the most basic word order). Before age 3, children are comprehending meaning of language spoken to them based on word order and knowledge of individual word meanings (Mervis & Bertrand, 1994). By age 4, most children comprehend and produce

sentence structures that include negation, inversion of sentence forms in question asking, concurrent use of direct and indirect objects, as well as conjoining and embedding of relative clauses. Concurrently, children demonstrate mastery of morphological markings for plurality and tense, as indicated by their understanding of the modifications in word meaning that correspond to these markings. Thus, by the time typical children come to the task of learning to read, they have a well-developed ability to use sentence structure to decode meaning. They have learned to pay attention to key morphemes that mark important changes in meaning and have some understanding of the rules that govern changes in word form associated with important changes in meaning.

In summary, children who have developed typical language skills by age 5 arrive at the task of learning to read with a basis in phonology, vocabulary, and syntax. They have already developed strategies for understanding and producing oral language consistent with their knowledge of these rule-based systems. In order to have accomplished these language development milestones, they have relied on perceptual processes, short-term memory specific to phonological and linguistic units of meaning, and sufficient environmental input and experience with English language.

The Impact of Language Delay

Delays or deficits in any of the three key systems of oral language (phonological, lexical, morphosyntactic) are likely to impact the process of learning to read. Because language is such a complex system that depends on so many different developmental processes (e.g., general cognitive processes such as short term memory, language-related cognitive abilities, perceptual and auditory processes, and motor abilities for production of speech), any biological or environmental disruption of development is likely to impact the oral language. As a general principle, the type, timing, and extent of developmental disruptions that affect primary acquisition of oral language will be reflected in difficulties in learning to read as well. Mild disruptions in language development (e.g., productive language delays in typical late talkers) may have modest effects on reading. Major disruptions in the development of language, such as those associated with primary genetic syndrome and intellectual disabilities, will constrain the potential for learning to read.

Table 10.1 summarizes the specific characteristics of children with language impairments in relation to key processes that affect reading.

Young Children with Language Delays

Children who experience early language delay represent an extremely heterogeneous population. Here we include three broadly defined groups: (1) children with global developmental delays, (2) children with language delays only, and (3) children from poverty or other high-risk backgrounds who are at risk primarily due to differences in early language experience (see Table 10.2 for an overview of the general characteristics of these populations). It is not possible to characterize the language development of the many subgroups of children with language impairments specifically within the framework of the current chapter; we give selected examples of frequently occurring populations. Our discussion of children is poverty is necessarily limited. We do not address children who are second language learners and may be delayed in their acquisition of English. We do note that children

who are English language learners (ELLs) may have language-learning difficulties associated with language impairment, in addition to the expected challenges of learning English as a second language.

Estimates of the incidence of early language delays vary based on the age of the population and criteria used in making the estimate. Approximately 16% of children between 24 and 36 months of age are considered "late talkers" who exhibit delays in productive vocabulary (Horwitz et al., 2003; Law, Boyle, Harris, Harkness, & Nye, 2000). This estimate includes late talkers, children with language disorders, and those with more severe developmental disabilities. At age 5, about 10% of children qualify for language-related school interventions; about 7% of children demonstrate specific language impairments and no other identified disabilities (Tomblin et al., 1997).

Children with Developmental Disabilities

Nearly all young children with significant developmental disabilities demonstrate delays in the acquisition of language during the preschool years. *Developmental disabilities* frequently are defined by a delay of at least 40% in one domain of development or delays of greater than 20% in two or more domains of development (Rosenberg, Zhang, & Robinson, 2008). Use of the term *developmental delay* allows provision of early in-

TABLE 10.1 Characteristics of Children with Language Impairment Reflect Specific Limitations in Abilities That Will Affect Reading

	Phonological processing	Vocabulary learning and comprehension	Comprehension of meaning	Cognitive abilities
Limited speech sound awareness	×	+	+	
Problems in word retrieval		+	+	×
Limited verbal memory		+	+	×
Limitations in speech production and/or perception	×	+	+	
Difficulties in oral language comprehension		×	×	+
Limited oral language production (syntax, complex vocabulary)	+	×	×	

Note. Based on Catts (1997). ×, primary impact; +, secondary impact

TABLE 10.2. Populations of Children with Language Impairments Vary in Deficits Linking Language and Reading

Population	Phonological processing	Vocabulary learning and comprehension	Comprehension of meaning at sentence level	General cognitive abilities	Verbal memory and cognition
Children with developmental delays	Yes	Yes	Yes	Yes	Yes
Children with productive language delays	No	Yes, learning	No	No	?
Children with productive and receptive language delay	Varies	Yes, learning and comprehension	Yes	?	Yes

tervention and preschool services to children with or without a specific diagnosis (e.g., Down syndrome, cerebral palsy, hearing impairment) without specification of the child's intellectual abilities. Given the broad criteria for developmental delay, as well as individual differences in development, language and communication skills in this population of children vary widely.

Language development is a complex process that requires concomitant development of cognitive, motor, and social skills. Thus, any disruption of the biological system during prenatal and early development is likely to result in delays in developing language. When intellectual disabilities are present, children typically show delays in language similar to or greater than their deficits in cognitive development. For children with IQs below 70 (2 *SD* below the expected norm), both receptive and productive language development typically are impaired significantly. Wide variations in language development are observed among children with development disabilities. These variations are related to the specific source of the developmental delay (e.g., a genetic cause such as Down syndrome vs. a later acquired disability such as traumatic brain injury), the relative impact or severity of the disability (e.g., mild vs. moderate intellectual impairment), the co-occurrence of other disabilities (e.g., motor disabilities, sensory impairments), as well as the timing and extent of early communication intervention (Guralnick, 2005).

Patterns of receptive and productive language delays vary among children with developmental disabilities. For some children

with motor impairments (e.g., cerebral palsy, paralysis associated with stroke, severe oral apraxia), productive language may be relatively more delayed than their receptive language. Children with Down syndrome may demonstrate early patterns of acquisition of receptive and productive skills similar to typical children until around 24 months of age, with relatively milder delays in receptive language compared to production. Later development in children with Down syndrome typically follows a pattern of significant receptive and productive delays, with relatively greater delays in complex syntax than in vocabulary development (Abbeduto, Warren, & Conners, 2007). In rare instances (e.g., children with Williams syndrome; Mervis & Klein-Tasman, 2000), language production may appear to be relatively more advanced than receptive skills, but the reverse is true for most children with intellectual disabilities. Children with autism spectrum disorders (ASDs) appear to have relatively greater difficulty with the social use of language than with acquisition of the rule-based systems that form the linguistic basis of communication. However, the disruption in social processes that support language development (e.g., emergence of joint attention) and everyday social interaction are often sufficiently severe to limit children's opportunities to learn language (Tager-Flusberg & Caronna, 2007). Furthermore, it is difficult to assess these children's language comprehension accurately or to assess fully their abilities to produce spoken language because of their behavioral characteristics (Tager-Flusberg et al., 2009).

Children with hearing and no other cognitive impairments still evidence delays in early language development (Briscoe, Bishop, & Norbury, 2001). The extent of these delays is strongly associated with age of identification of hearing loss and adequacy of early intervention to improve hearing and ensure access to speech and language input. Both degree of hearing loss and adequacy of early intervention impact language outcomes. When adequate auditory speech and linguistic input can be provided early in development (e.g., via cochlear implants, adequate aided hearing), children with hearing impairments learn language in stages similar to those of typical children. Limited access to the phonological system has specific implications for speech perception and fluency, and for the phonological processes involved in learning to read and the relationship between hearing abilities, access to oral input, and reading outcomes are complex (Moeller, Tomblin, Yoshinaga-Itano, Connor, & Jerger, 2007). Children with relatively mild hearing losses may be undetected in the general population, even with the advent of universal screenings at birth, and such losses have effects on early speech and language development and later reading.

IMPLICATIONS FOR LEARNING TO READ

Many children with intellectual and other developmental disabilities can learn to read (Allor, Mathes, Champlin, & Cheatham, 2009; Browder et al., 2009; Koppenhaver & Yoder, 1992); however, their existing phonological, vocabulary, and syntax deficits, as well as their general cognitive skills and specific reading-related cognitive skills, affect the extent to which they are likely to become fluent readers. Processes related to phonological awareness as well as those related to word learning, syntactic production, and comprehension, are likely to be affected in children with moderate to severe cognitive impairments. Children with language delays and mild nonverbal cognitive deficits (i.e., IQ between 70 and 85) are at high risk for persistent language impairment (Bishop & Edmundson, 1987) and, thus, later reading difficulties (Catts, Fey, Tomblin, & Zhang, 2002). Children with ASDs are expected to have difficulty learning to read given their characteristic limitations in oral communication (Tager-Flusberg & Joseph, 2003); however, several studies have indicated better than expected reading skills in this population. For example, Nation, Clarke, Wright, and Williams (2006) reported highly variable profiles of reading-related skills (word and nonword reading, comprehension) in children with autism. As a whole, the group showed normal-range levels of reading accuracy, but reading comprehension was lower than expected. Nearly two-thirds of children showed impaired reading comprehension.

As in the case of language acquisition, specific and intensive language and literacy instruction are needed for most children with developmental disabilities to acquire entry-level reading skills. Language intervention in general, and in support of reading, includes strengthening phonological processes, extending productive and receptive vocabulary, and supporting emergent use and understanding of syntax and morphology. Intensive instruction to support the range of phonological skills, as well as early literacy skills, may be required for children to begin reading. Because general intellectual abilities and specific verbal learning skills impact both language learning and reading, children's intellectual functioning determines the scope and probable outcomes of intervention. For children with mild to moderate intellectual disabilities, it is reasonable to expect that functional language and reading skills can be mastered; however, the trajectories of both language and reading development are likely to differ from typical development. Systematic instruction across the areas of potential language and related reading skills deficits may be needed. Even with specific instruction, differences in reading comprehension and fluency may persist. There is extensive literature to support a range of instructional strategies to teach reading to children with mild intellectual and learning disabilities (see Allor et al., 2009, for a review). Although children with ASD present a special case in that their pathways to reading may be different, there is also evidence that systematic reading interventions produce positive outcomes for this population (Whalon, Otaiba, & Delano, 2009).

In summary, in the very diverse population of children with developmental disabilities, there is consistent evidence of early speech and language delays. In most instances, specific early intervention is needed to support both speech and language development. Even with effective and intensive intervention, their progress in acquisition of speech, vocabulary, and syntax may continue to be slower and/or different in comparison to typically developing children. Given persistent language impairments, it is likely that these children with also have persistent difficulty with specific reading processes. Children with developmental disabilities that include intellectual disabilities are likely to need systematic reading instruction through each stage of learning to read and to use reading as basis for learning in the curriculum. Early systematic language and preliteracy interventions should be individualized for these children to ensure access to language as a communication system and entry into reading.

Children with Language Delays and Typical Cognition

While language delays are expected in children who have general developmental or cognitive delays (e.g., children with genetic syndromes, ASDs, and significant motor impairments), the majority of children with early language delays have cognitive skills near the normal range (Tomblin, Zhang, Buckwalter, & Catts, 2000). And, while it is generally assumed that cognition is the pace setter in language development, a large number of children exhibit specific difficulty in acquiring language without general cognitive delays.

CHILDREN WITH EXPRESSIVE LANGUAGE DEFICITS

Early acquisition of vocabulary follows a predictable pattern. Thus, the first indication of expressive language deficit is slower than expected acquisition of the first 10–50 words. About 13% of 24-month-olds have "late language emergence" based on parent reports (Zubrick, Taylor, Rice, & Slegers, 2007). The majority of these late-talking children are reported to recover (i.e., score within the normal range at age 5) without significant intervention (Weismer, 2007). However, about 7.5% of late talkers show persistent language delays at age 5. Recent studies have suggested that early expressive

delays may not be fully resolved and reappear in the early elementary years, impacting reading progress (Catts, Bridges, Little, & Tomblin, 2008).

CHILDREN WITH CO-OCCURRING RECEPTIVE AND EXPRESSIVE LANGUAGE DEFICITS

When preschool children evidence concurrent delays in both receptive and productive language, the impact on both language development and later reading is more significant. Law and colleagues (2000) estimated that 3% of 3-year-olds show both receptive and expressive language delays, and 75% of these children (approximately 2.25% of the population) show persistent patterns of language impairment. Tomblin and colleagues (1997) reported that 7% of 5-year-olds present with features of speech–language impairment (SLI): delays in receptive and productive language equivalent to 1 *SD* below the expected norms with IQ in the normal range. In general, the literature suggests that preschool children with delays only in expressive language have a much higher recovery rate than children with co-occurring receptive and expressive deficits. Children with co-occurring receptive and productive language deficits and mild cognitive impairment (IQ between 70 and 85) are at much higher risk for persistent language deficits and reading problems as they enter school than typical children or those with cognitive skills in the near normal range.

Young children with expressive and receptive language delays produce fewer words and combine words later than typically do developing children. In addition, they use fewer different verbs and use verbs less frequently than do typical children (Moyle et al., 2007). Their syntactic development is typically delayed, with two–and three-word utterances emerging later than normally expected. Typically, their syntax shows some of the same indicators that are evident in older children diagnosed with SLI. They omit morphological markers for plurals, third-person singular, past tense, and present progressive (-*ing*). In addition, their comprehension of syntax is often impaired (Leonard, 2000). Children in this population may be relatively less delayed in comprehension as compared to production, but any delay in comprehension (beyond 1 *SD*) increases the likelihood of persistent production delay (Thal, Reilly, Seibert, Jeffries, & Fenson, 2004).

IMPLICATIONS FOR LEARNING TO READ

Reading consists of two broad categories of skills: *decoding* (recognizing printed words) and *comprehension* (understanding the meaning of the printed words). Language-related reading difficulties occur in relation to both these categories. Reading difficulties include problems decoding individual words (*dyslexia*) and/or problems in comprehending or understanding the meaning of text at the phrase or sentence level. Impairment in several language domains (e.g., phonology, semantics, syntax) may be present in children with reading comprehension difficulties. For example, Nation, Clarke, Marshall, and Durand (2004) found that children with poor reading comprehension exhibited semantic weaknesses and poor performance on morphosyntactic tasks (e.g., syntactic comprehension, past tense inflection in oral language). Children with poor reading comprehension skills also had difficulty with tasks requiring broad language use (e.g., understanding figurative language). Oral language production (Catts et al., 2002) and comprehension (Wise, Sevcik, Morris, Lovett, & Wolf, 2007) are among the key factors that predict long-term reading and other language-based problems.

The presence of an early language delay, even in children with typical cognition, is most likely to impact reading if that delay persists over time or is not successfully remediated prior to attempting to learn to read (Beitchan, Wilson, Brownlie, Walters, & Lance, 1996). When children have limited vocabulary and/or difficulty with comprehension of word and sentence meanings, and these limitations are not successfully addressed, they are at greater risk for difficulties in reading throughout the elementary school years. Bishop and Adams (1990) found that children with resolved language impairments at 5½ did not have reading difficulties at age 8½. However, children with persistent language difficulties at age 5½ had poor reading comprehension at age 8½, and pervasive problems with word-level and reading comprehension and weak spelling at age 15 (Stothard, Snowling, Bishop, Chipchase, & Kaplan, 1998). Catts and col-

leagues (2002) replicated these findings with children identified as language impaired in kindergarten. Those children with persistent language delays in second and fourth grade performed significantly more poorly on reading outcome measures than did their counterparts no longer identified with language impairments. For children with language impairments in kindergarten, approximately 50% met requirements for a reading disability in second and fourth grades (Catts et al., 2002).

Children with persistent language impairments also have difficulty with written language tasks such as narrative composition (Fey, Catts, Proctor-Williams, Tomblin, & Zhang, 2004; Mackie & Dockrell, 2004). Last, children with persistent language impairment perform below typical peers in basic number skills and working memory. These factors, coupled with the linguistic demands of many mathematical tasks, increase the risk for mathematics difficulties in children with persistent language impairment (Cowan, Donlan, Newton, & Lloyd, 2005). Thus, it appears that early language competence, and the lack thereof, is associated with a range of achievement skills, including most directly, reading ability.

Children with Language Delay and Behavior Problems

Many children referred for speech and language problems are subsequently identified as having significant behavior problems. Estimates of the associations between language and behavior vary widely. Parents of young children with language delays are four times more likely to report externalizing behaviors than parents of children with typical language development (Horwitz et al., 2003). Among children with identified language impairments, rates of prevalence for behavior problems have been reported to range from 29% (Tomblin et al., 2000) to nearly 60% (Stevenson & Richman, 1978). Evidence of increased problem behavior and lower social skills in preschoolers with identified language delays is relatively consistent (Carson, Klee, Lee, Williams, & Perry, 1998; Whitehurst, Fischel, Caulifield, DeBaryshe, & Valdez-Menchaca, 1989). Baker and Cantwell's (1982) landmark study of the prevalence of psychiatric impairments in children with speech and language disorders found that 95% of the children who presented with a language disorder met DSM-III criteria for psychiatric illness. The overall prevalence rate for psychiatric problems in their total sample (n = 291) of children referred for both speech and language problems was 42%. In a study involving 1,655 Canadian kindergartners, Beitchman, Nair, Clegg, Ferguson, and Patel (1986) found 47% of the children met the criteria for co-occurrence of psychiatric problems and language disorders. An important caveat in interpreting findings from these earlier studies of language and behavior is that children with ASDs were not excluded from studies prior to the last 10 years. However, recent studies of school-age children suggest that about 30% of children with expressive and receptive language delays evidence clinical-level behavior problems (Hart, Fujiki, Brinton, & Hart, 2004).

The linkages between language deficits and the development of behavior problems in children are not well understood. Possibly, both arise from a common set of underlying variables, including poor parent–child interactions, lower IQ, significant stress during early childhood, or unspecified neural developmental dysfunctions (Beitchman, Peterson, & Clegg, 1988; Prizant & Meyer, 1993). In some young children with language delays, behavior problems derive from a lack of social competence. For example, Horwitz and colleagues (2003) reported that when social competence was adjusted in the multivariable model, behavior problems were no longer associated with language delay, suggesting that poor social competence rather than behavior problems may be the critical early correlate of low expressive language development. In a meta-analysis of 24 studies measuring language delays, behavior problems and social skills, researchers found significant associations between expressive language and behavior (d = 0.40), receptive language and behavior (d = 0.39) and language and social skills (d = 0.83) (Kaiser, Roberts, Feeney-Kettler, Frey, & Hemmeter, 2009). These findings confirm not only a strong association between social skills and behavior problems but also point to robust associations between behavior and receptive and expressive language in preschool children.

IMPLICATIONS FOR READING

For those children with language delays who develop behavior problems, the risk for reading problems and other academic difficulties is greatly increased. Two large-scale studies suggest that early co-occurring language and behavior problems predict relatively poor school-age outcomes. In a birth cohort of approximately 6,000 children, Carter, Briggs-Gowan, Jones, and Little (2003) reported that children at 24 months who were rated as having problems in both language and behavior had significantly poorer reading at grade 2. These children performed worse than children with only language or behavior problems at age 2. Longitudinal data on more than 3,200 children in Head Start indicated that high problem behavior predicted low reading scores at grades 2 and 3 (Zill & Sorongon, 2004). There is considerable evidence from school-age populations that language deficits, reading, and behavior continue to be strongly associated (Nelson, Benner, & Cheney, 2005). For example, Benner, Nelson, and Epstein (2002) reported that 71% of elementary school–age children identified with behavior disorders across 26 studies had clinical-level language disabilities. Finally, children with language and behavior problems are less responsive to early intervention for reading than children with either of these problems alone (Kamps et al., 2003).

In summary, children who evidence both delayed language development and early emergent behavior problems are at high risk for continuing problems in both areas, and for developing persistent reading and academic deficits. Early screening and early intervention in all three domains (language, reading, and behavior) may be essential for this population. There are surprisingly few large-scale interventions targeting both language and problem behavior in preschool children (Qi & Kaiser, 2003), although small-scale interventions targeting both domains report positive results (Hancock, Kaiser, & Delaney; 2002; Stanton-Chapman, Kaiser, & Wolery, 2006).

Children from Impoverished Backgrounds

It is well established that growing up in poverty increases the risk for early delays in the acquisition of vocabulary and may impact general language skills as well (Hart & Risley, 1995; Hoff, 2006). Poverty also increases the risk for reading problems and later difficulties in academic learning that depend on reading (Kaiser & Delaney, 1996; Whitehurst & Fischel, 2000). Increased risk for language delays in this population is related to a range of factors, including limited language experiences associated with differences in parent education, family structure, and increased family stressors (Stanton-Chapman, Chapman, Kaiser, & Hancock, 2004; Vernon-Feagans, Hammer, Miccio, & Manlove, 2001). Children born in poverty are more likely to have limited prenatal care and relatively more health problems during the preschool years. Early reading skills are affected by the same set of experiences that promote language development, and by family (Hoff, 2003; Landry, Smith, & Swank, 2002) and contextual support available specifically for reading. The amount of book reading, exposure to text, and informal teaching about sounds and words differs between children in poverty and children growing up in more advantaged social economic backgrounds (Neuman, 1999; Neuman & Celano, 2001; Snow et al., 1998).

The most extensive data available on the language abilities of children growing up in poverty come from the national evaluation studies of Head Start and its extensive reporting system. For example, at entry to Head Start, about 50% of 4-year-old children are a year or more behind in vocabulary development, and 75% of these children recognize fewer than 10 letters (U.S. Department of Health and Human Services [USDHHS], Administration for Children and Families [ACF], 2004). High-quality preschool experiences can improve the language and literacy development of these children at risk for later academic failure (Barnett, 2001; Dickinson & Tabors, 2001; Peisner-Feinberg et al., 2001; Schweinhart & Weikart, 1999). Nonetheless, 35% of children participating in Head Start still had vocabulary deficits greater than 1 year during the spring assessment (USDHHS, ACF, 2004). In addition, among children in poverty, more children are subsequently identified for special education, suggesting a pattern of both early risk and pervasive language delays. Between 14 and 19% of Head Start children are identified for special education by third grade, compared to 11% of the general population.

CHILDREN WITH SIGNIFICANT LANGUAGE DELAYS AND OTHER DISABILITIES WHO GROW UP IN POVERTY

Within the population of children growing up in poverty, there are also children with a range of significant language disabilities that may be independent of their poverty status or may be exacerbated by the supports for language learning that are available to them. The effects of Head Start and other early intervention programs on language and emergent reading skills of children with identified disabilities and those with the lowest language abilities at entry to the program have not been studied extensively. Both the Family and Child Experiences Survey (FACES; USDHHS, ACF, 2004) and the National Impact Study (USDHHS, ACF, 2004) indicate that Head Start children who have identified disabilities and Individualized Education Plans (IEPs) do make gains in vocabulary and complex language skills; however, these gains are less than those made by children without IEPs. Approximately 13% of 4-year-old children in Head Start have IEPs. In addition, as many as 20% of Head Start children who do not have IEPs may have language deficits that place them at least 1.5 standard deviations below expected performance for their age (Kaiser, Hester, & McDuffie, 2001). Parents of children enrolled in Head Start report that 19% of their children have language, behavior, or cognitive disabilities at entry to the program (USDHHS, ACF, 2004).

The evaluations of impact of Head Start, as well as the modest findings from recent research curriculum interventions to improve vocabulary outcomes (McLeod & Kaiser, 2009), have a number of important implications for children with language delays. First, although general curriculum-level instruction may be sufficient to improve language and literacy outcomes for some children from poverty backgrounds, these interventions are not sufficient for all children in this population. Second, relatively little is known about child and environmental factors that contribute to differential outcomes within this population during curriculum interventions. For example, it is important to identify children who are likely to have persistent language delays within the large population of children who begin early intervention with poor language skills. Third, the population of children from poverty backgrounds is diverse. Within this population, it is expected that the rate of children with developmental disabilities and specific language delays not directly associated with poverty is similar or somewhat higher than that in the general population. Distinguishing between children whose language is delayed due primarily to impoverished environments and children with delayed or disordered language arising from other primary causes is difficult, particularly when children are from culturally and linguistically diverse backgrounds.

Among children from low-income backgrounds, children with poor language skills and emergent behavior problems are of special concern. Children with poor language skills are less likely to engage in learning activities and positive peer interactions than children with better language skills (Qi & Kaiser, 2004). These children are also more likely to be disruptive and inattentive during structured learning activities in the classroom (Qi, Kaiser, & Milan, in press). Children who enter Head Start with low language skills and high levels of problem behavior show less growth in language skills from ages 3 to 5 than children with low language skills only or children with higher language skills. Results from the Kamps and colleagues (2003) early intervention study for children with language and behavior problems also demonstrated less growth during intervention for children of low socioeconomic status (SES) with co-occurring problems. Table 10.3 provides a summary of early indicators of language delays in the populations of children discussed here.

Recommendations for Practice

From this discussion, it is evident that early identification and intervention to resolve language delays in young children is a necessary first step in preventing problems in learning to read. Table 10.4 provides an overview of recommended practices for screening and intervention.

Identification of Children with Language Impairments

Early identification of children with language delays or impairments is essential. For most children, difficulties related to learning language are likely to be persistent and to have both short–and long-term effects on reading. Because of the diversity of the population of children with early language delays that affect their ability to learn to read, there is a need for systematic early screening that includes cognitive, behavioral, and language-specific assessments. In addition to typical well-child and school entry screening for hearing, language, and motor delays, three additional early identification strategies are recommended: (1) comprehensive and continuing early screenings of language development and preliteracy skills for children with indicated developmental risks; (2) screening for the full range of expressive and receptive language development and for problem behavior in children entering preschool, particularly children from low-SES or high-risk backgrounds; (3) monitoring of response to preschool instructional experiences, with specific measures of progress in vocabulary learning, phonological, and social skills and behavior. Several studies have reported the underidentification of children with significant language delays in the preschool years (Law et al., 2000; Tomblin et al., 2000), suggesting that more systematic early screening is needed. Attention to secondary risk indicators among populations of children at elevated risk for language delay is particularly important. For example, family history of speech, language, or reading problems among children from poverty background and elevated cumulative family risk (Stanton-Chapman et al., 2004) may distinguish children in Head Start who are most likely to have significant early language delays. Similarly, children who present with significant behavior problems should be screened for delays in language development.

Early identification is important, but not sufficient, for preventing persistent language delays. Among children participating in early intervention, the most important method for determining persistent language problems and early reading difficulties is to monitor their response to available treatments

TABLE 10.3. Indicators of Early Language Delay

Population	Individual variability	Birth–12 months	12–24 months	24–36 months	36–60 months
Children with developmental delays • Genetic • Unspecified, global	Depends on specific cause, degree of cognitive impairment, and level of motor involvement Early intervention moderates extent of language delays	Risk evident at birth Delayed in meeting multiple developmental milestones Speech perception, and production	Social communication Speech perception and production Expressive and receptive vocabulary Receptive syntax	Social communication Speech perception and production Expressive and receptive vocabulary Expressive and receptive syntax	Social communication Speech perception and production Expressive and receptive vocabulary Expressive and receptive syntax
Children with autism spectrum disorders	Wide variation, may include cognitive impairment; 25%+ may be nonspeaking Early and intensive intervention positively affects developmental trajectory	Early indicators vary Social engagement, joint attention	Social communication and joint attention Expressive and receptive vocabulary	Social communication Expressive and receptive vocabulary Expressive and receptive syntax	Social communication Expressive and receptive vocabulary Expressive and receptive syntax
Children with hearing impairments	Variation in development associated with degree of loss and extent of resolution via hearing aids or implants Early intervention positively affects developmental trajectory	Speech perception and production	Speech perception and production Expressive vocabulary	Speech perception and production Expressive vocabulary Expressive syntax	Speech perception and production

	Description				
Children with productive language delays only	Delayed language resolves without intervention for majority of late talkers	No indicators	Expressive vocabulary	Expressive vocabulary	Few indicators
Children with productive and receptive delays without cognitive delay	Heterogeneous population and associated indicators vary (motor, speech, degree of receptive language delay, behavior) Early intervention may resolve or moderate language delays	No indicators	Expressive and receptive vocabulary Speech production	Expressive and receptive vocabulary Expressive and receptive syntax Speech production	Vocabulary deficits may persist Specific aspects of expressive and receptive syntax
Children from low-socioeconomic backgrounds	Variability similar to general population with larger proportion of children at risk for delays		Expressive and receptive vocabulary	Expressive and receptive vocabulary	Expressive and receptive vocabulary Use of complex syntax may differ
Children with behavior problems	Severe behavior problems, cognitive impairments and co-occurring mental health diagnosis associated with increased language delay Some children may not have language impairments Population overlaps with others	Few indicators, may be temperament differences	Expressive and receptive vocabulary	Expressive and receptive vocabulary Expressive and receptive syntax	Social communication especially with peers Expressive and receptive vocabulary Expressive and receptive syntax

TABLE 10.4. Preventing Problems in Reading: Screening and Intervention for Populations at Risk for Reading Problems

Population	Universal screening	Language evaluation	Language intervention	Early reading intervention
Children with developmental delays • Genetic • Unspecified, global	Yes	Yes, every 6 months from birth	Yes, continuous from identification, Tier 3	Yes, Tier 3
Children with autism spectrum disorders	Yes	Yes, every 6 months from identification	Yes, continuous from identification, Tier 3	Yes, Tier 3
Children with hearing impairments	Yes	Yes, every 6 months from birth	Yes, continuous, Tier 3	Yes, especially phonological awareness, Tier 2 and 3
Children with productive language delays only	Yes	Yes, beginning at 18 months; monitor through age 5	As needed, if delay persists	Not usually needed
Children with productive and receptive delays without cognitive delay	Yes	Yes, beginning at 18 months	Yes, intensity depends on severity, persistence	Yes, Tier 1 and Tier 2 recommended
Children from low-socioeconomic backgrounds	Yes	Yes, beginning at preschool entry	Yes, Tier 1 plus Tier 2 and Tier 3 as needed	Yes, Tier 1, plus early identification for Tier 2 and Tier 3
Children with behavior problems	Yes	Yes, concurrent with problem behavior diagnosis	Yes, intensity depends on severity, persistence; address behavior problems concurrently	Yes, Tier 1, plus early identification for Tier 2 and Tier 3

Note = Tier 1, high-quality universal intervention typically in classrooms; Tier 2, specified intervention within classroom or small group; Tier 3, individualized, intensive intervention.

(Justice, 2006; VanDerHeyden, Snyder, Broussard, & Ramsdell, 2008). General indicators of progress in vocabulary and morphosyntactic development provide an index of children's relative skills, but most general assessments neither identify the underlying sources of children's difficulties in learning these aspects of the language system nor are they sufficiently sensitive to detect important variations in child progress. When children are participating in early intervention, two additional types of assessment may be required: (1) additional in-depth assessment of underlying processes (e.g., phonological discrimination, auditory processing, verbal learning abilities) to focus intervention on teaching specific skills that will help chil-

dren learn language, and (2) examination of children's response to the language learning opportunities already available.

Language development reflects both children's abilities and the environmental conditions supporting language. When children are not learning language, it is possible that they have not had sufficient opportunities to learn these skills due to environmental input or individual access to environmental input (e.g., hearing impairment). Examining environmental contributions to children's language is an essential aspect of screening for language delays. Limited input may be a primary cause for language delay, but child characteristics or specific language-learning abilities frequently interact with environment to result in delays. Second, when children have been identified early, their subsequent language outcomes reflect the adequacy of early intervention. When children do not show progress in language learning after intervention, it may be that either the instruction does not provide sufficient dosage or it does not precisely target the underlying skills needed to support language development, or that the impairment is more significant and pervasive that expected. Examining children's response to treatment in the context of the type, fidelity, dosage, and specificity of the intervention is essential to determine the extent of the language impairment. Children who do not respond to moderately intense, individualized interventions delivered with reasonable fidelity are likely to have pervasive developmental deficits that impact multiple aspects of the language system and make learning to read difficult.

In addition, a comprehensive assessment should examine children's behavior that may inhibit or disrupt the language-learning process. Among children with significant language delays are those with internalizing (withdrawn, anxious) behavior and externalizing behavior (aggressive, acting out behavior) (Qi & Kaiser, 2004). Children who are withdrawn may exhibit low levels of engagement in classroom activities and with peers and teachers, and, as result may have fewer opportunities to learn and use language. Children who display aggressive or acting out behavior may also have fewer opportunities to learn due to adult and peer responses to their behavior. In children with either behavior profile, even modest delays in receptive language may make language learning in the classroom more difficult.

Early Language Intervention

Early intervention for children with or at risk for language impairments should follow a contemporary, three-tiered prevention-to-intervention approach that includes Tier 1 universal intervention, Tier 2 targeted interventions, and Tier 3 individualized interventions. Because early language development is closely linked to early literacy and emergent reading, there may be advantages to overlapping language and literacy interventions, especially at Tier 1. For preschoolers, universal interventions to promote language and literacy involve the provision of language-rich curriculum, as well as teacher–child and parent–child interactions that model vocabulary, complex syntax, and sociopragmatic use of language. For children who enter preschool with early indicators of language delay, increased risks for delay, and/or cognitive impairments, ensuring child contact with the language curriculum may require (1) modifications in teacher interactional style (e.g., more responsive to child communication), (2) use of specific instructional strategies in a group context (language modeling, prompting child responses, using expansions and other contingent feedback strategies), and (3) arrangement of the environment to support child engagement and learning from the curriculum. Such modifications are within the range of adaptations effective teachers can make to ensure access to the curriculum that will benefit all children with language learning needs, as well as typical language learners. Tier 2 interventions are also delivered within the context of the preschool classroom and take advantage of opportunities to provide instruction that is more specific to the children's learning needs and level of skills but still referenced to the general curriculum. Tier 2 interventions may be delivered in small groups or embedded within daily activities, such as center work or snack time. It is the *content* (specified to the child's learning needs and current skills) rather than the context that defines a Tier 2 intervention. Additional instructional planning that references the child's assessment profile, providing additional input related to target skills and ensuring opportunities to respond and receive feedback for targeted skills is included in Tier 2 interventions. Small groups, if they are used, can include typical children as models for language and literacy skills. Embedding instruction in natural environments and monitoring delivery of instruction and children's responses to instruction are essential for effective Tier 2 instruction. Use of individual growth and develop indicators (IGDIs; Carta et al., 2002) for language or criterion-based measures that track children's progress in learning targeted skills (McCauley, 1996) are helpful in determining the effectiveness of the intervention at this level. Consultation from a communication specialist or speech–language pathologist may be needed to design effective Tier 2 interventions. Tier 3 interventions are intensive, targeted, and individualized to address specific skills and learning deficits in children who are not responding quickly to Tier 1 and Tier 2 interventions. Children with developmental disabilities almost always require Tier 3 interventions, but other children may benefit from them as well. It is important to note that children may participate in all three tiers of intervention simultaneously. The combined support offered by a classroom language curriculum delivered by a responsive teacher (Tier 1), targeted instruction embedded across the day or in small groups (Tier 2), and individualized one-on-one instruction with a specialist (Tier 3) can provide a scaffold for language learning that supports the transition into literacy. As noted earlier, both language and entry-level reading skills can be taught in this tiered instruction model.

Although there is a rich history of early language intervention that suggests promising outcomes for children with language delays and developmental disabilities (Kaiser & Trent, 2007), there are not yet many examples of research examining the effects of a tiered intervention model for children with language delays (Justice, 2006). Little research has examined the contributions of early language intervention for children with identified language delays to concurrent and later literacy outcomes. Research on tiered interventions for reading in kindergarten and early elementary school does support use of this intervention approach to address difficulties in learning to read (Denton, Fletcher, Anthony, & Francis, 2006; O'Connor, Harty, & Fulmer, 2005).

Conclusion

The linkages between early language impairment and problems in learning to read are complex and robust. Acquisition of both oral language and reading is affected by children's global development of specific skills for learning the phonological, lexical, and morphosyntactic systems. Children with language delays vary widely in the source of their impairments, and these variations have implications for the nature and severity of subsequent difficulties in learning to read. Early identification, early language interven-

tion, and assessment of children's response to language intervention are essential to preventing persistent language delays that may affect reading. Although a relatively large database supports the linkages between oral language impairment and later problems in learning to read, research on preventing reading deficits through early and effective language intervention for children with significant language impairments is needed.

Acknowledgment

Preparation of this chapter was supported in part by Institute of Education Sciences Grant No. R324E060088.

References

Abbeduto, L., Warren, S. F., & Conners, F. A. (2007). Languages development in Down syndrome: From the prelinguistic period to the acquisition of literacy. *Mental Retardation and Developmental Disabilities Research Reviews, 13,* 247–261.

Allor, J. H., Mathes, P. G., Champlin, T., & Cheatham, J. P. (2009). Research-based techniques for teaching early reading skills to students with intellectual disabilities. *Education and Training in Developmental Disabilities, 44,* 356–366.

Baker, L., & Cantwell, D. P. (1982). Developmental, social and behavioral characteristics of speech and language disordered children. *Child Psychiatry and Human Development, 12,* 195–207.

Barnett, W. S. (2001). Preschool education for economically disadvantaged children: Effects on reading achievement and related outcomes. In S. B. Neuman & D. K. Dickinson (Eds.), *Handbook of early literacy research* (Vol. 1, pp. 421–443). New York: Guilford Press.

Beitchman, J. H., Nair, R., Clegg, M., Ferguson, B., & Patel, P. G. (1986). The prevalence of psychiatric disorders in children with speech and language disorder. *Journal of the American Academy of Child Psychiatry, 25,* 528–535.

Beitchman, J. H., Peterson, M., & Clegg, M. (1988). Speech and language impairment and psychiatric disorder: The relevance of family demographic variables. *Child Psychiatry and Human Development, 18*(4), 191–207.

Beitchman, J. H., Wilson, B., Brownlie, E., Walters, H., & Lance, W. (1996). Long-term consistency in speech/language profiles: Developmental and academic outcomes. *Journal of the American Academy of Child and Adolescent Psychiatry, 35,* 804–814.

Benner, G. J., Nelson, J. R., & Epstein, M. H. (2002). Language skills of children with EBD. *Journal of Emotional and Behavioral Disorders, 10*(1), 43–59.

Bishop, D., & Adams, C. (1990). A prospective study of the relationship between specific language impairment, phonological disorders and reading retardation. *Journal of Child Psychology and Psychiatry and Allied Disciplines, 31,* 1027–1050.

Bishop, D., & Edmundson, A. (1987). Language-impaired 4-year-olds: Distinguishing transient from persistent impairment. *Journal of Speech and Hearing Disorders, 52,* 156–173.

Bishop, D. V. M., & Snowling, M. J. (2004). Developmental dyslexia and specific language impairment: Same or different? *Psychological Bulletin, 130,* 858–888.

Briscoe, J., Bishop, D., & Norbury, C. F. (2001). Phonological processing, language, and literacy: A comparison of children with mild-to-moderate sensorineural hearing loss and those with specific language impairment. *Journal of Child Psychology and Psychiatry and Allied Disciplines, 42,* 329–340.

Browder, D. M., Gibbs, S. L., Ahlgrim-Delzell, L., Courtade, G., Mraz, M., & Flowers, C. (2009). Literacy for students with severe developmental disabilities: What should we teach and what should we hope to achieve? *Remedial and Special Education, 30*(5), 269–282.

Carson, D. K., Klee, T., Lee, S., Williams, K. C., & Perry, C. K. (1998). Children's language proficiency at ages 2 and 3 as predictors of behavior problems, social and cognitive development at age 3. *Children's Communication Development, 19*(2), 21–30.

Carta, J. J., Greenwood, C. R., Walker, D., Kaminski, R., Good, R., McConnell, S., et al. (2002). Individual growth and development indicators (IGDIs): Assessment that guides intervention for young children. *Young Exceptional Children Monograph Series, 4,* 15–28.

Carter, A. S., Briggs-Gowan, M. J., Jones, S. M., & Little, T. D. (2003). The infant–toddler social and emotional assessment: Factor structure, reliability, and validity. *Journal of Abnormal Child Psychology, 31,* 495–514.

Catts, H. W. (1997). The early identification of language-based reading disabilities. *Language, Speech, and Hearing Services in Schools, 28,* 86–89.

Catts, H. W., Bridges, M. S., Little, T. D., & Tomblin, J. B. (2008). Reading achievement growth in children with language impairments. *Journal of Speech, Language, and Hearing Research, 51*(6), 1569–1579.

Catts, H. W., Fey, E., & Proctor-Williams, K. (2008). The relationship between language and reading: Preliminary results from a longitudinal investigation. *Journal of Speech, Language, and Hearing Research, 51,* 1569–1579.

Catts, H., Fey, M., Tomblin, J. B., & Zhang, X. (2002). A longitudinal investigation of reading outcomes in children with language impairments. *Journal of Speech, Language, and Hearing Research, 45,* 1142–1157.

Catts, H. W., & Kamhi, A. G. (2005). *The connections between language and reading disabilities.* Mahwah, NJ: Erlbaum.

Cowan, R., Donlan, C., Newton, E. J., & Lloyd, D. (2005). Number skills and knowledge in children with specific language impairment. *Journal of Educational Psychology, 97,* 732–744.

Denton, C. A., Fletcher, J., Anthony, J. L., & Francis, D. (2006). An evaluation of intensive intervention for students with persistent reading difficulties. *Journal of Learning Disabilities, 39,* 447–466.

Dickinson, D. K., & Tabors, P. O. (1991). Early literacy: Linkages between home, school, and literacy achievement at age five. *Journal of Research in Childhood Education, 6,* 30–46.

Dickinson, D. K., & Tabors, P. O. (2001). *Beginning literacy with language: Young children learning at home and school.* Baltimore: Brookes.

Fey, M., Catts, H., Proctor-Williams, K., Tomblin, J. B., & Zhang, X. (2004). Oral and written story composition skills of children with language impairment. *Journal of Speech, Language, and Hearing Research, 47,* 1301–1318.

Hancock, T. B., Kaiser, A. P., & Delaney, E. M. (2002). Teaching parents of preschoolers at high-risk: Strategies to support language and positive behavior. *Topics in Early Childhood Special Education, 22*(4), 191–212.

Hart, B., & Risley, T. R. (1995). *Meaningful differences in the everyday experience of young American children.* Baltimore: Brookes.

Hart, K. I., Fujiki, M., Brinton, B., & Hart, C. H. (2004). The relationship between social behavior and severity of language impairment. *Journal of Speech, Language, and Hearing Research, 47,* 647–662.

Henricksen, B. (1999). Three dimensions of vocabulary development. *Studies in Second Language Acquisition, 21,* 303–317.

Hoff, E. (2003). The specificity of environmental influence: Socioeconomic status affects early vocabulary development via maternal speech. *Child Development, 74,* 1368–1378.

Hoff, E. (2006). Environmental supports for language acquisition. In D. K. Dickinson & S. B. Neuman (Eds.), *Handbook of early literacy research* (Vol. 2, pp. 163–172). New York: Guilford Press.

Horwitz, S., Irwin, J., Briggs-Gowan, M., Heenan, J., Mendoza, J., & Carter, A. (2003). Language delay in a community cohort of young children. *Journal of the American Academy of Child and Adolescent Psychiatry, 42,* 932–940.

Justice, L. M. (2006). Evidence-based practice, response to intervention, and the prevention of reading difficulties. *Language, Speech, and Hearing Services in Schools, 37,* 284–297.

Kaiser, A. P., & Delaney, E. M. (1996). The effects of poverty on parenting young children. *Peabody Journal of Education, 71*(4), 66–85.

Kaiser, A. P., Roberts, M. Y., Feeney-Kettler, K., Frey, J., & Hemmeter, M. L. (2009, October). *The relationship between language and behavior in preschool children: Evidence from a meta-analysis.* Albuquerque, NM: Division on Early Childhood.

Kaiser, A. P., & Trent, J. A. (2007). Communication intervention for young children with disabilities: Naturalistic approaches to promoting development. In S. L. Odom, R. H. Horner, M. E. Snell, & J. Blacher (Eds.), *Handbook of development disabilities* (pp. 224–246). New York: Guilford Press.

Kamps, D. M., Wills, H. P., Greenwood, C. R., Thorne, S., Lazo, J. F., Crockett, J. L., et al. (2003). Curriculum influences on growth in early reading fluency for students with academic and behavioral risks. *Journal of Emotional and Behavioral Disorders, 11*(4), 211–224.

Koppenhaver, D. A., & Yoder, D. E. (1992). Literacy issues in persons with severe physical disabilities. In R. Gaylord-Ross (Ed.), *Issues and research in special education* (Vol. 2, pp. 156–201). New York: Teachers College Press.

Landry, S. H., Smith, K. E., & Swank, P. R. (2002). Environmental effects on language development in normal and high-risk child populations. *Seminars in Pediatric Neurology, 9*, 192–200.

Law, J., Boyle, J., Harris, F., Harkness, A., & Nye, C. (2000). Prevalence and natural history of primary speech and language delay: Findings from a systematic review of the literature. *International Journal of Communication Disorders, 35*, 165–188.

Leonard, L. (2000). *Children with specific language impairment.* Cambridge, MA: MIT Press.

Mackie, C., & Dockrell, J. (2004). The written language of children with specific language impairment. *Journal of Speech, Language, and Hearing Research, 47*, 1469–1483.

McCauley, R. J. (1996). Criterion-referenced measures in communication disorders. *Language, Speech, and Hearing Services in Schools, 27*, 122–131.

McLeod, R. H., & Kaiser, A. P. (2009, November). *Curriculum effects on vocabulary outcomes.* Presented at the annual meeting of the American Speech, Language and Hearing Association, New Orleans, LA.

Mervis, C. B., & Bertrand, J. (1994). Acquisition of the novel name–nameless category (N3C) principle. *Child Development, 65*(6), 1646–1662.

Mervis, C. B., & Klein-Tasman, B. P. (2000). Williams syndrome: Cognition, personality, and adaptive behavior. *Mental Retardation and Developmental Disabilities Research Reviews, 6*, 148–158.

Moeller, M. P., Tomblin, J. B., Yoshinaga-Itano, C., Connor, C. M., & Jerger, S. (2007). Current state of knowledge: Language and literacy of children with hearing impairment. *Ear and Hearing, 28*(6), 740–753.

Moyle, M. J., Weismer, S. E., Evans, J. L., & Lindstrom, M. J. (2007). Longitudinal relationships between lexical and grammatical development in typical and late-talking children. *Journal of Speech, Language, and Hearing Research, 50*, 508–528.

Nassaji, H. (2004). The relationship between depth of vocabulary knowledge and learners' lexical inferencing strategy use and success. *Canadian Modern Language Review, 61*(1), 107–135.

Nation, K., Clarke, P., Marshall, C. M., & Durand, M. (2004). Hidden language impairments in children. *Journal of Speech, Language, and Hearing Research, 47*, 199–211.

Nation, K., Clarke, P., Wright, B., & Williams, C. (2006). Patterns of reading ability in children with autism spectrum disorder. *Journal of Autism and Developmental Disorders, 36*(7), 911–919.

Nation, K., & Snowling, M. (1998). Semantic processing and the development of work-recognition skills: Evidence from children with reading comprehension difficulties. *Journal of Memory and Language, 30*(1), 85–101.

Nelson, J. R., Benner, G. J., & Cheney, D. (2005). An investigation of the language skills of students with emotional disturbance served in public school settings. *Journal of Special Education, 39*, 97–105.

Neuman, S. B. (1999). Books make a difference: A study of access to literacy. *Reading Research Quarterly, 34*(3), 286–311.

Neuman, S. B., & Celano, D. (2001). Access to print in low-income and middle-income communities: An ecological study of four neighborhoods. *Reading Research Quarterly, 36*(1), 8–26.

O'Connor, R. E., Harty, K. R., & Fulmer, D. (2005). Tiers of intervention in kindergarten through third grade. *Journal of Learning Disabilities, 38*, 532–538.

Peisner-Feinberg, E. S., Burchinal, M. R., Clifford, R. M., Culkin, M. L., Howes, C., Kagan, S. L., et al. (2001). The relation of preschool child-care quality to children's cognitive and social developmental trajectories through second grade. *Child Development, 72*, 1534–1553.

Poe, M. D., Burchinal, M. R., & Roberts, J. E. (2004). Early language and the development of children's reading skills. *Journal of School Psychology, 42*(4), 315–332.

Prizant, B. M., & Meyer, E. C. (1993). Socioemotional aspects of communication disorders in young children and their families. *American Journal of Speech–Language Pathology, 2*, 56–71.

Qi, C., & Kaiser, A. P. (2003). Behavior problems of preschool children from low-income families: Review of the literature. *Topics in Early Childhood Special Education, 23*(4), 188–216.

Qi, C. H., & Kaiser, A. P. (2004, June). *Maternal education and language measures in Head Start children.* Poster presented at the Symposium on Research in Child Language Disorders, Madison, WI.

Qi, C. H., Kaiser, A. P., & Milan, S. (in press). Identifying language delays in African American preschool children from low-income families using language sampling measures. *Journal of Speech, Language, and Hearing Research.*

Rosenberg, S. A., Zhang, D., & Robinson, C. C. (2008). Prevalence of developmental delays and participation in early intervention services for young children. *Pediatrics, 121*(6), 1503–1509.

Schweinhart, L. J., & Weikart, D. P. (1999). The advantages of High/Scope: Helping children lead successful lives. *Educational Leadership, 57*, 76–77.

Snow, C. E., Dickinson, D. K., Tabors, P. O., Smith, M. W., Porche, M. V., & Jordan, G. E. (1998, November). *How parents and teachers can support children's emergent literacy development.* Paper presented at the annual meeting of the National Association for Educators of Young Children, Toronto.

Snowling, M. (2005). Literacy outcomes for children with oral language impairments: Developmental interactions between language skills and learning to read. In H. Catts & A. Kahmi (Eds.), *The connections between language and reading disabilities* (pp. 55–76). Mahwah, NJ: Erlbaum.

Spear-Swerling, L., & Sternberg, R. J. (2001). What science offers teachers of reading. *Learning Disabilities Research and Practice, 16*, 51–57.

Stanton-Chapman, T. L., Chapman, D. A., Kaiser, A. P., & Hancock, T. B. (2004). Cumulative risk and low income children's language development. *Topics in Early Childhood Special Education, 24*(4), 227–237.

Stanton-Chapman, T. L., Kaiser, A. P., & Wolery, M. (2006). Building social communication skills in Head Start children using storybooks: The effects of prompting on social interactions. *Journal of Early Intervention, 2*(3), 197–212.

Stevenson, J., & Richman, N. (1978). Behavior, language, and development in three year old children. *Journal of Autism and Childhood Schizophrenia, 8*, 299–314.

Stothard, S. E., & Hulme, C. (1992). Reading comprehension difficulties in children: The role of language comprehension and working memory skills. *Reading and Writing, 4*, 245–256.

Stothard, S., Snowling, M., Bishop, D., Chipchase, B., & Kaplan, C. (1998). Language impaired preschoolers: A follow-up into adolescence. *Journal of Speech, Language, and Hearing Research, 41*, 407–418.

Strucker, J. (1995). *Patterns of reading in adult basic education.* Unpublished doctoral dissertation, Harvard University Graduate School of Education.

Tager-Flusberg, H., & Caronna, E. (2007). Social communication and language deficits in children who have autistic spectrum disorder. *Pediatric Clinics of North America, 54*, 469–481.

Tager-Flusberg, H., & Joseph, R. M. (2003). Identifying neurocognitive phenotypes in autism. *Philosophical Transactions of the Royal Society of London, B, 358*, 303–314.

Tager-Flusberg, H., Rogers, S., Cooper, J., Landa, R., Lord, C., Paul, R., et al. (2009). Defining spoken language benchmarks and selecting measures of expressive language development for young children with autism spectrum disorders. *Journal of Speech, Language, and Hearing Research, 52*, 643–652.

Thal, D., Reilly, J., Seibert, L., Jeffries, R., & Fenson, J. (2004). Language development in children at risk for language impairment: Cross-population comparisons. *Brain and Language, 88*, 167–179.

Tomblin, J. B., Records, N. L., Buckwalter, P., Zhang, X., Smith, E., & O'Brien, M. (1997). Prevalence of specific language impairment in kindergarten children. *Journal of Speech and Hearing Research, 40*(6), 1245–1260.

Tomblin, J. B., Zhang, X., Buckwalter, P., & Catts, H. (2000). The association of reading disability, behavioral disorders, and language impairment among second-grade children. *Journal of Child Psychology and Psychiatry and Allied Disciplines, 41*, 473–482.

U.S. Department of Health and Human Services (US-DHHS), Administration for Children and Families (ACF). (2004). *Family and Child Experiences Survey (FACES).* Retrieved September 26, 2005, from *www.acf.hhs.gov/programs/core/ongoing research/faces/faces instrument.*

VanDerHeyden, A. M., Snyder, P. A., Broussard, C., & Ramsdell, K. (2008). Measuring response to early intervention with preschoolers at risk. *Topics in Early Childhood Special Education, 27*, 232–249.

Vernon-Feagans, L., Hammer, C. S., Miccio, A., & Manlove, E. (2001). Early language and literacy skills in low-income African American and Hispanic children. In S. B. Neuman & D. K. Dickinson (Eds.), *Handbook of early literacy research* (Vol. 1, pp. 192–210). New York: Guilford Press.

Weismer, S. E. (2007). Typical talkers, late talkers, and children with specific language impairment: A language endowment spectrum? In R. Paul (Ed.), *The influence of developmental perspectives on research and practice in communication disorders: A festschrift for Robin S. Chapman* (pp. 83–101). Mahwah, NJ: Erlbaum.

Whalon, K. J., Otaiba, S. A., & Delano, M. E. (2009). Evidence based reading instruction for individuals with autism spectrum disorders. *Focus on Autism and Other Developmental Disabilities, 24*(1), 3–16.

Whitehurst, G. J., & Fischel, J. E. (2000). Reading and language impairment in conditions of poverty. In D. M. Bishop & L. Leonard (Eds.), *Speech and language impairments in children: Causes, characteristics intervention and outcomes* (pp. 53–72). Sussex, UK: Psychology Press.

Whitehurst, G. J., Fischel, J. E., Caulifield, M., DeBaryshe, B. D., & Valdez-Menchaca, M. C. (1989). Assessment and treatment of early expressive language delay. In P. R. Zelazo & R. G. Barr (Eds.), *Challenges to developmental paradigms: Implications for theory, assessment, and treatment* (pp. 113–135). Hillsdale, NJ: Erlbaum.

Wise, J., Sevcik, R., Morris, R., Lovett, M., & Wolf, M. (2007). The relationship among receptive and expressive vocabulary, listening comprehension, pre-reading skills, word identification skills, and reading comprehension by children with reading disabilities. *Journal of Speech, Language, and Hearing Research, 50*, 1093–1109.

Zill, N., & Sorongon, A. (2004). *Children's cognitive gains during Head Start and kindergarten.* Presentation at the National Head Start Research Conference, Washington, DC.

Zubrick, S., Taylor, C., Rice, M., & Slegers, D. (2007). Late language emergence at 24 months: An epidemiological study of prevalence, predictors, and covariates. *Journal of Speech, Language, and Hearing Research, 50*, 1562–1592.

III
SUPPORTING CODE-RELATED ABILITIES

11

A Model of the Concurrent and Longitudinal Relations between Home Literacy and Child Outcomes

MONIQUE SÉNÉCHAL

Young children enter school with knowledge, experiences, and predispositions that can facilitate or hinder their entry into literacy. Moreover, differences in children's reading skills are established early and remain fairly stable over time (e.g., Butler, Marsh, Sheppard, & Sheppard, 1985). Strikingly, children who have language difficulties at age 3 are nearly five times more likely to experience literacy problems than control children at age 8 and to continue having difficulties at age 13 (Muter & Snowling, 2009). Moreover, children who have difficulty in grade 1 are more likely to have more difficulty in other school domains later on, are more likely to not complete high school or pursue their education beyond high school (Alexander, Entwisle, & Horsey, 1997; Entwisle, Alexander, & Olson, 2005). Dire probabilistic statistics like these comprise one of the most important motivating forces in trying to understand better how to optimize reading skills early in a child's life because the preschool and early school periods seem particularly sensitive to environmental influences (Hart & Petrill, 2009; Landry, Smith, Swank, & Guttentag, 2008).

Over the past two decades, my colleagues, students, and myself have investigated how young children's experiences with print are associated with the development of language and the acquisition of early literacy. This chapter provided the opportunity to reflect on what we have learned so far. To start the reflection, consider a mother reading a storybook to her 4-year-old son. As the mother reads the story, emphasizing certain aspects of the plot, defining unfamiliar words, or relating aspects of the story to her child's life, their joint attention is on meaning. In contrast, if the attention shifts such that both mother and child look at the printed words, with the mother pointing and naming letters, and asking the child to identify other identical letters, then their joint attention is on the form of the printed word. In our work, we examined whether the focus of the joint attention, be it the meaning conveyed by words or the form of those words, would be related systematically to children outcomes. We elaborated and tested a model of the relations between parent–child literacy-rich activities and child outcomes in a series of longitudinal studies. The key feature of our home literacy model is that it distinguishes between home activities that focus on the meaning of the printed word— labeled *informal literacy activities*—and activities that focus on the form of the printed word—labeled *formal literacy activities* (see also van Kleeck & Norlander, 2008).

The Home Literacy Model

Young children can discover and learn about literacy through their own attempts at reading and writing (e.g., Ferriero, 1986) or through observations of role models (Teale & Sulzby, 1986). As such, children are active participants in their learning, as is suggested by a Piagetian view of literacy learning. Moreover, a Piagetian view suggests that children's understanding of literacy might differ from that of adults. For example, young children often hypothesize that the length of a word is related to the size of the object it represents (Levin & Korat, 1993). In addition, young children learn about literacy from their interactions with learned others, as is suggested by a Vygotskian approach (Rogoff, 1990). Therefore, describing the literacy interactions of children with their parents is essential to understanding the impact of the home literacy environment of children.

In our research, we adopt the view that parent–child interactions can foster language and literacy. As such, our research remains close to activities happening in the home and their association to child outcomes. Sénéchal and LeFevre (2002) presented a summary of their findings on home literacy experiences that served as the framework for subsequent research and was extended by Sénéchal (2006). According to the home literacy model, informal and formal literacy activities are distinct types of activities in most homes. Therefore, one should not expect an association between storybook exposure, an informal activity, and parent tutoring about literacy, a formal literacy activity. The lack of relation suggests that some parents who read also tutor their children to learn early literacy skills, but other parents do not. Moreover, some parents who tutor do not read to their children as frequently. Given that parents differ in the types of literacy activities they include at home, it follows that these differences in home literacy experiences may result in different outcomes for children.

The home literacy model does specify that the two types of literacy experiences are differentially related to language, early lit-

eracy, and phoneme awareness. According to the home literacy model, informal literacy activities promote the development of language skills, whereas formal literacy activities promote the acquisition of early literacy skills. Home literacy activities, however, are not directly related to phoneme awareness. Specifically, the association between home literacy activities and phoneme awareness is mediated by children's language and early literacy skills. Sénéchal and LeFevre (2002) demonstrated that it is necessary to consider language, early literacy, and phoneme awareness separately to disentangle the pattern of relations with home literacy (also see Sénéchal, LeFevre, Smith-Chant, & Colton, 2001). Failure to consider the entire pattern of relations may lead to the conclusion that storybook exposure and/or teaching about literacy have a wider range of associations to reading rather than a more focused impact (Burgess, Hecht, & Lonigan, 2002; de Jong & Leseman, 2001; Mol, Bus, de Jong, & Smeets, 2008).

The home literacy model also includes longitudinal relations between the home literacy activities measured prior to grade 1 and eventual reading outcomes, as represented in Figure 11.1. The home literacy model indicates no direct or indirect link between informal literacy and reading in grade 1 (cf. de Jong & Leseman, 2001). It is not until more advanced reading skills are achieved in grades 3 and 4 that informal literacy experiences become indirectly associated with reading through their relation to early language skills. Interestingly, parent reports of shared reading measured in kindergarten predict the frequency with which children report reading for pleasure in grade 4. The pattern of findings is different for formal literacy activities. The model shows a series of indirect pathways: Parent teaching is related to early literacy, which, in turn, is associated with grade 1 reading, and grade 1 reading predicts more advanced reading skills. There is one exception to the pattern: Parent reports of tutoring measured in kindergarten predict the children's reading fluency in grade 4. The home literacy model has been replicated in English (Bingham, 2009; Hood, Conlon, & Andrews, 2008), as well as extended to French-speaking families (Sénéchal, 2006), Korean families (Lee, Sung, & Chang, 2009), and Spanish families (Farver & Lonigan, 2009). Specific compo-

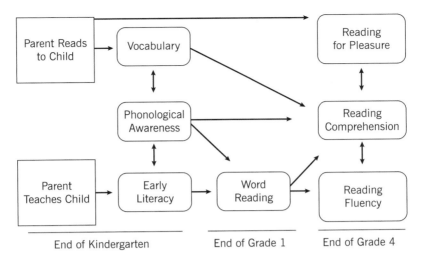

FIGURE 11.1. Reliable relations among home literacy and child outcomes in the home literacy model. Arrows represent statistically significant predictors after controlling for potential confounds.

nents of the model have also been replicated (Evans, Shaw, & Bell, 2000; Frijters, Barron, & Brunello, 2000; Stephenson, Parrila, Georgiou, & Kirby, 2008). Each aspect of the home literacy model is described in more detail in the remainder of the chapter.

Informal Literacy Activities: Shared Reading

Shared reading is first and foremost an activity that parents and children do for pleasure. During shared reading, parent and child can enjoy the language and content of stories, as well as the accompanying illustrations. At the same time, children can learn from shared book reading. Sénéchal, LeFevre, Hudson, and Lawson (1996) described three characteristics of shared book reading that can foster learning about the world and about language. First, the language used in books is more complex than that typically used during conversation. In fact, Hayes and Ahrens (1988) showed that children's books contain 50% more rare words than prime-time television or college students' conversations. Similarly, the language used by mothers is more complex during shared reading than other mother–child conversations during free play or remembering events (Crain-Thoreson, Dhalin, & Powell, 2001). As such, children may be exposed to new syntactic and grammatical forms when listening to shared reading. The second feature of shared reading is that a child has the undivided attention of an adult who can define, explain, and question to facilitate the child's understanding or reinforce new knowledge. Certainly, the abundant literature on dialogic reading has shown the value of shared reading to vocabulary acquisition (for a meta-analysis, see Mol et al., 2008). A third characteristic of shared reading is that books can be read on repeated occasions, thus providing repeated exposure to new knowledge. Some of our work on shared reading has certainly shown the advantage of repeated exposure for comprehending new words (e.g., Sénéchal, 1997; Sénéchal, Thomas, & Monker, 1995). Because of these features, shared book reading is the single most studied aspect of children's home literacy environment.

Recently, Mol, Bus, and de Jong (2009) conducted a meta-analysis on the effects of shared reading and reported moderately strong effect sizes between dialogic reading and children's early literacy in classrooms settings. In contrast, Sénéchal and Young (2008) reported a different pattern in their meta-analysis examining the role of parent support for child literacy. They searched and reviewed literature on interventions with children in kindergarten up to grade 3, in which parents engaged their children in activities intended to promote early literacy or reading. In each study, children in the intervention group were compared to children in a control or alternative treatment group. The search yielded 214 studies, and the application of their selection criteria resulted in 16 studies retained for further analysis. Of these studies, only three included shared reading as the primary means for learning about literacy. It is important to note that Sénéchal and Young used a narrow definition of literacy whereby oral language measures were excluded from the analyses. The advantage of meta-analyses is that they allow one to group effect sizes. In the case of the three studies on shared reading, however, the combination of the three studies yielded a small effect size that was not statistically different from zero, nor were the effect sizes for each individual study statistically and significantly different from zero. The findings are in accord with those of Evans and Saint-Aubin (2005), who showed that young children look at the illustrations, not the written words, during shared reading. At some level, the null effects are in accord with the home literacy model whereby informal literacy activities do not support the acquisition of early literacy per se.

Formal Literacy Activities: Parent Teaching

Researchers have used many different terms—*parent coaching* (Edwards, 1991), *parent mediation* (Aram & Levin, 2004), or *parent scaffolding* (Evans, Moretti, Shaw, & Fox, 2003)—to indicate the support parents provide for learning about literacy. In our research, the terms *parent teaching* and *parent tutoring* refer to parents' attempts to impart knowledge about reading and writing because they were more comprehensive than the others. In our research, we found that the frequency with which parents provide direct support for learning about literacy is an important home literacy experience that is a robust predictor of early literacy. The finding that parent teaching predicts concurrent and subsequent emergent literacy skills contributes to a growing body of evidence on experiential factors, other than book exposure, that explain the development of early individual differences in literacy skills (e.g., Dale, Crain-Thoreson, & Robinson, 1995; Evans et al., 2000; Stephenson et al., 2008).

Parent teaching seems to occur more frequently than once thought. Martini and Sénéchal (2010) found that most parents in their sample (*n* = 108) indicated they often or very often taught their 5-year-old child the names and sound of alphabet letters, and how to print letters and words. In addition, the majority of parents reported teaching their children to read words. According to participating parents, teaching early literacy skills is prevalent in middle-class homes. Interestingly, further statistical analyses of the parent teaching variables revealed that teaching behaviors included two distinct factors: teaching basic literacy skills, such as letter names and sounds, as well as printing one's name, and teaching more advanced skills, such as reading words. This distinction might be important depending on the population studied. For instance, Sénéchal and LeFevre (2002) examined more advanced teaching behaviors in their middle-class sample (*n* = 168), whereas Sénéchal (2006) found that more basic literacy teaching was a unique predictor of children's early literacy in a more socioeconomically varied sample (*n* = 90).

In addition to teaching frequency, Martini and Sénéchal (2010) documented the contexts that parents used to help their child learn about literacy. They found that parents generally reported using a wide variety of learning contexts: Of the 18 contexts presented, parents used on average 14 different contexts at least some of the time. Moreover, parents reported using frequently many of these contexts, such as reading storybooks, and using familiar household items and street signs. They also found that parents who report teaching more frequently tend to use a greater number of learning contexts. Interestingly, the reported frequency of using workbooks was not related to the reported frequency of teaching. Martini and Sénéchal concluded that parents focus on naturally occurring activities to impart knowledge about the alphabet, printing, and reading words.

The finding that parents report using storybooks to help their child learn literacy skills may appear to contradict the finding that shared reading per se is not a robust direct predictor of early literacy skills. Indeed, many researchers have found a zero-order correlation between shared reading and early literacy (see the meta-analysis by Bus, van IJzendoorn, & Pellegrini, 1995). A contribution of the home literacy model, however, was to show that the association was due to a third variable, be it child oral language skills or parent teaching. As the Martini and Sénéchal (2010) findings suggest, it may be the degree to which parents introduce alphabetic and reading information during shared reading that accounts for the known association between shared reading and early literacy (Evans, Fox, Cresmaso, & McKinnon, 2004; Reese & Cox, 1999). For instance, children may learn from *print referencing* during shared reading (see Justice & Ezell, 2004; Justice, Weber, Ezell, & Bakeman, 2002). The key feature to retain, however, is that parents report teaching in a great variety of naturally occurring contexts, not a single activity.

The results discussed so far are correlational in nature, and even though we conduct stringent tests of the obtained relations by controlling for potential confounds, the results cannot be used to address the causal relations between variables. It is therefore important to examine the intervention research to assess whether parent teaching has a positive effect on children's learning. In their meta-analysis, Sénéchal and Young (2008) found seven studies in which parents were trained to tutor their kindergarten or grade 1 children on early literacy or reading. Specifically, parents tutored their children to learn the alphabet in two studies, and parents tutored their children in word reading in others. The meta-analytic results showed that training parents to tutor their children using specific reading activities produced large positive effects on children's early literacy and reading. The large effect size obtained (Cohen's *d* = 1.15) would correspond to a 17-point increase on a standardized measure for the children in the intervention group compared to the children in the control group. Therefore, parents can play a significant role in their young children's reading acquisition.

Child Outcomes Linked to Home Literacy

A comprehensive model of the effect of home literacy on reading should encompass a wide variety of child literacy outcomes. In time, a precise understanding of the role of home literacy on a variety of skills provides valuable information necessary to the elaboration of evidence-based interventions. In our work, we examined a variety of outcomes, including vocabulary; early literacy; phoneme awareness; word recognition; reading comprehension and fluency; spelling, and reading for pleasure. Some measures were included in kindergarten, while others were assessed in grades 1 or 4. Each outcome is discussed in turn.

Vocabulary

In our research, we consistently found that parent reports on shared reading were a robust predictor of children's receptive and expressive vocabulary. We found this to be the case for English-speaking children in kindergarten and grade 1 (LeFevre & Sénéchal, 2002; Sénéchal et al., 1996; Sénéchal & LeFevre, 2002; Sénéchal, LeFevre, Thomas, & Daley, 1998; Sénéchal, Pagan, Lever, & Ouellette, 2008), as well as for French-speaking children (Sénéchal, 2000, 2006). In this research, we typically use multiple indices of shared reading, including parent reports (the frequency of reading, the number of books in the home) and checklists used as proxy measures of book exposure (Sénéchal et al., 1996). The assumption underlying the checklists is that parents who read more to their children should be more knowledgeable about children's literature than parents who read less. The findings consistently show that shared reading accounted for 8–10% of unique variance in children's vocabulary after researchers control statistically for children's intelligence, parent print exposure, and maternal education (when correlated with outcomes) or parent literacy. This finding is consistent with the approximately 8% variance typically found between shared reading and children's vocabulary skills (Frijters et al., 2000; Mol et al., 2008; but see Roberts, Jurgens, & Burchinal, 2005; Weigel, Martin, & Bennett, 2006). In their synthesis of shared reading intervention studies, the National Early Literacy Panel (2008) found that shared reading enhanced vocabulary acquisition (effect size (ES) = 0.60), as well as general aspects of oral language (ES = 0.35).

Other Oral Language Skills

Exposure to the complex language, as well as the variety of narrative forms, found in children's books may have a beneficial effect on a number of child language outcomes. Sénéchal and colleagues (2008) examined this question in a sample (*n* = 106) of English-speaking 4-year-olds. Included were comprehension measures of syntactically complex sentences and morphologically complex words. As expected, Sénéchal et al. found a reliable relation between shared reading and children's comprehension of morphologically complex words after controlling for child intelligence, parent literacy, and education. Interestingly, the relation between shared reading and the comprehension of syntactically complex sentences was entirely mediated by parent literacy. Studies by Stanovich and his colleagues (e.g., Stanovich & West, 1989) certainly show a strong association between print exposure and language in adults. It may be the case that parents who read more for pleasure speak to their children in a more syntactically complex manner than do parents who read less, and, consequently, parents who read more expose their children to more syntactically complex language than what is afforded by shared reading alone.

Sénéchal and colleagues (2008) also examined the relation between narrative knowledge and shared reading. They hypothesized that frequent shared reading introduces children to characters, events, and situations across a variety of books, and that such exposure would help a child produce a cohesive narrative. Surprisingly, they found no relation between narrative knowledge and the frequency of shared reading (zero-order correlations of less than .11). This finding might suggest that the variety of exposure to the stories in children's literature is not sufficient to promote changes in 4-year-old children's production of narratives. It might be the case that parental support is necessary, such that the quality of parent–child interactions during shared reading might influence narrative production more so than simple exposure (Reese & Cox, 1999). For instance, intervention studies using picture books have shown positive effects in preschool children's narrative production (e.g., Zevenbergen, Whitehurst, & Zevenbergen,

2003). It is also possible that frequency of occurrence interacts with the quality of adult reading—a possibility that is never tested in the correlational research on shared reading.

Lever and Sénéchal (in press) tested whether repeated exposure to books within a dialogic reading context would enhance children's storytelling. *Dialogic reading* is a form of shared reading that involves elaborative questioning techniques that increase child participation (for a meta-analytic review, see Mol et al., 2008). After the intervention, children engaged in dialogic reading produced stories that were more structured, that included more descriptions of mental states, and that typically named characters rather than relying on pronouns, compared to children who received an alternative treatment. These children also showed expressive vocabulary gains. The findings clearly showed that repeated, highly interactive shared readings could promote narrative knowledge. As such, the findings do show that it is necessary to consider both frequency and quality in our assessment of shared reading. It also raises the possibility that other outcomes could be affected by the quality of shared reading (as described below).

Early Literacy

In our work, we typically assess three early literacy skills, namely, alphabetic knowledge, early reading, and invented spelling. These skills were selected because of their stable predictive role in children's success in reading once in grade school (Ouellette & Sénéchal, 2008; Sénéchal et al., 2001). Both knowledge of letter names and sounds is assessed. Early reading is a task for which the tester helps children to sound out and blend the letters of familiar simple words (e.g., *cat*). The invented spelling measure is a task in which children are asked to spell words as best they can, then their spelling attempts are scored for the degree to which they capture the phonological structure of the words. We found positive correlations between the frequency of parent teaching and the three early literacy measures (Sénéchal & LeFevre, 2002). Most important, parent teaching accounts for 4–19% of unique variance in children's early literacy after researchers control for child vocabulary and phoneme awareness, child analytic intelligence, parent education, and/or income or parent literacy (LeFevre & Sénéchal, 2002; Martini & Sénéchal, 2010; Sénéchal, 2006; Sénéchal et al., 1998). The findings hold for both concurrent and longitudinal relations between parent reports of teaching frequency and child early literacy.

Phoneme Awareness

Phoneme awareness measured in kindergarten is one of the most important predictors of word reading in grade 1. Although there are still differing positions, most researchers agree that it is awareness of the phonemic structure of spoken language that facilitates children's entry into reading. Moreover, children's alphabetic knowledge is linked to growth in phoneme awareness. Finally, there is some evidence that children's vocabulary knowledge is also linked to growth in phoneme awareness. These relations were nicely illustrated by Sénéchal and colleagues (2001), who tested the longitudinal relations among these three variables from the fall of kindergarten to the fall of grade 1 in a sample of nonreaders (*n* = 84). Figure 11.2 depicts the statistically significant relations found when

researchers included all variables at the same time in regression equations. Of particular interest are the crossover relations over time. As indicated in Figure 11.2, both alphabetic knowledge and children's receptive vocabulary hold bidirectional relations with phoneme awareness from kindergarten to grade 1. Alphabetic knowledge and vocabulary, however, are not related to each other. These results highlight the importance of considering phoneme awareness separately from early literacy, as well as from oral language (cf. Storch & Whitehurst, 2002). Also, the finding that vocabulary and alphabetic knowledge have distinct bidirectional relations with phonological awareness is consistent with existing knowledge (e.g., Lonigan, Burgess, Anthony, & Barker, 1998). Presumably, alphabetic knowledge skills help children understand that words are formed of individual phonemes. This increased phonological awareness subsequently may facilitate further learning about literacy, such as how to spell words phonetically (e.g., Burgess & Lonigan, 1998). Moreover, Metsala and Walley (1998) argued that the relation between vocabulary and phonological awareness can be understood by considering the representation in memory of the phonological structure of words. Presumably, children's growing vocabulary during the preschool years plays a role in the development of accurate representations of the phonological structure of words. In turn, accurate phonological representations are necessary to the development of efficient phonological awareness, as well as continued vocabulary growth (also see Thomas & Sénéchal, 2004).

The importance of considering phoneme awareness separately from other variables is also evident when comparing the results of Sénéchal and colleagues (1998) with those of Sénéchal and LeFevre (2002). Sénéchal and colleagues (1998) had included phonological awareness along with vocabulary and listening comprehension in an oral language factor. In doing so, they found that shared reading predicted this general oral language factor. The analyses in Sénéchal and LeFevre, however, revealed that when phonological awareness was analyzed separately, there was no direct association between home literacy experiences, be it shared reading or parent teaching, and phonological

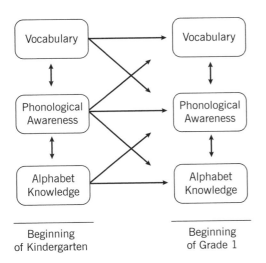

FIGURE 11.2. Reliable concurrent and longitudinal relations among children's vocabulary, phonological awareness, and alphabet knowledge. Arrows represent statistically significant relations after controlling for the other variable(s).

awareness. Fritjers and colleagues (2000) also found that the relation between storybook exposure and early literacy skills was indirect and mediated through phonological awareness and vocabulary.

It is interesting to ponder whether there are any home experiences that are related to the development of phonological awareness. Some researchers have suggested that exposure to rhymes through poems and stories may relate to the development of phonological awareness (Baker, Fernandez-Fein, Scher, & Williams, 1998; Bryant, MacLean, Bradley, & Crossland, 1990). Our research on the home literacy model, however, indicates that some of the more obvious home experiences do not appear to predict phonological awareness directly.

Longitudinal Links to Literacy in Grade School

As described previously and illustrated in Figure 11.1, our research has found indirect and direct links between home literacy and children's eventual success in reading. An *indirect relation* refers to the finding that even though there were significant correlations between home literacy and child outcomes, more strict analyses that allowed us to control for possible confounds reduced the relation with child outcomes to a level that was not statistically significant; that is, an indirect relation signifies that an association between two variables is due to their joint association with a third variable. For instance, we found that shared reading is linked to child vocabulary in kindergarten, which, in turn, is a predictor of reading comprehension in grades 3 (Sénéchal & LeFevre, 2002) and 4 (Sénéchal, 2006). Parent reports of teaching early literacy are linked to child early literacy, which, in turn, predicts word reading in grade 1. Word reading in grade 1 is then predictive of reading comprehension in grades 3 and 4. Noteworthy is the Sénéchal (2006) finding that parent reports of teaching, but not storybook exposure, were directly linked to child reading fluency in grade 4, after controlling for all the appropriate variables. What is it about these early experiences that have such a pervasive impact? It may be that they are markers of different types of orientations toward reading acquisition (Anderson, 1995; Evans et al., 2004; Lynch, Anderson, Anderson, & Shapiro, 2006). It may be that parents who taught frequently in kindergarten continue to provide more support for learning in the form of listening to their child read out loud, and that these continued experiences are the building blocks for reading fluency.

Child Interest

In most studies describing young children's interest in literacy, it is parents who report on their child's interest. For instance, Sénéchal and colleagues (1996) found that parent reports on children's interest in storybook reading was associated with the reported frequency of shared reading, as well as children's vocabulary. Interestingly, parent reports on the frequency with which their 4-year-old children asked them to read was a unique predictor of child vocabulary after we controlled for parent education and literacy, as well as storybook exposure in Study 1 (*n* = 119). This latter pattern, however, was not replicated in Study 2 (*n* = 50).

A study by Frijters and colleagues (2000) stands out in this area because these researchers developed a child measure of interest in literacy. Children were to indicate for each of a series of print-related activities (e.g., reading by self) whether they liked or did not like the activity by pointing to a happy or a sad face, and their degree of interest by pointing to a small or a large circle. Frijters and colleagues showed that interest in literacy activities accounted for a significant proportion of variance in kindergarten children's letter-name and letter-sound knowledge. In a follow-up study, Frijters. Barron, Algire, Humphries, and Vander Zwaag (2001) expanded the child interest measure to include additional questions about interest in learning letters. They found that child interest predicted alphabetic knowledge even after they controlled for the frequency of parent teaching. Similarly, Martini and Sénéchal (2010) found that child interest in learning about letters and reading was a unique predictor of early literacy skills after they controlled for parent teaching and expectations, socioeconomic status (SES), and analytic intelligence (*n* = 108). It seems that children who report being more interested in learning print skills tend to perform better on early literacy tasks than children who report lower levels of interest. These findings lead to the questions of whether home literacy factors account for the child's interest itself. For example, Zhou and Salili (2008) reported that adult readers' role-modeling was the most important factor related to intrinsic motivation in a large sample of 177 preschool Mandarin-speaking children. Certainly the interplay among home literacy, child interest, and child early literacy warrants further attention.

Reading for Pleasure

In her review, Baker (2003) argued that children whose early encounters with literacy are enjoyable are more likely to develop a predisposition to read frequently and broadly in subsequent years. The findings of Sénéchal and colleagues (1998) and the longitudinal follow-up results in Sénéchal and LeFevre (2002) addressed the issue of whether reading that children do themselves enhances eventual success in reading. At the end of grade 1, children were administered a measure of storybook knowledge previously developed in Sénéchal and colleagues (1996). They assumed that children's knowledge of book titles reflected their accumulated exposure to books read to them at home, school, and elsewhere (e.g., the library), as well as the exposure they received from reading books themselves during their first year of school. The results were remarkable. Children's book exposure measured in grade 1 accounted for 7% of unique variance in children's reading skills in grade 3 after researchers controlled for children's age, parent print exposure, end of grade 1 reading, as well as language and emergent literacy measured at the beginning of grade 1. The findings suggest that children's continued exposure to books in situations beyond shared parent–child reading seems to have a role in the development of fluent reading. The finding that experiences with books in grade 1 make a unique contribution to reading in grade 3, after researchers controlled statistically for grade 1 reading skills and language, extends previous concurrent reports on the role of print exposure in grade 1 (Cunningham & Stanovich, 1993, 1998) and grade 3 (Baker et al., 1998). Book exposure, then, can be thought of as an enduring aspect of home experience that is likely to contribute to children's reading performance.

In the same vein, Sénéchal (2006) found a robust long-term relation between parent reports of storybook exposure in kindergarten and the frequency with which children in grade 4 reported reading for pleasure, after she controlled statistically for parent education, child vocabulary and grade 1 reading, as well as grade 4 reading comprehension. This prospective demonstration that shared reading before the onset of formal schooling has a long-lasting association with reading motivation will be of interest to educators and parents. Interestingly, the frequency of reading for pleasure proved to be a good concurrent predictor of grade 4 reading comprehension after controlling for grade 4 reading fluency and parent education. This finding is consistent with those of Allen, Cipielewski, and Stanovich (1992), who showed that reading frequency outside school predicts reading comprehension in grade 5 students. These results, however, are correlational in nature, and, therefore, do not tell us about the direction of the relation between reading for pleasure and reading comprehension. It may be the case that strong reading comprehension skills are necessary if children are to engage more in reading for pleasure, or, more likely, that the two interact.

Other Aspects of the Home Literacy Environment

The home literacy model has been limited, purposefully, to home literacy activities. A more complete model, however, would also consider other aspects of the home literacy environment that could also be linked to child outcomes. Martini and Sénéchal (2010) considered two aspects, namely, parental expectations about child literacy knowledge and parental beliefs about literacy.

Parental Expectations

When asked to rate the relative importance of a number of skills they expect their child to acquire, parents ranked literacy near the top of the list, along with character/moral development, and above all other items, including verbal communication, mathematics, physical fitness, and world knowledge (Evans et al., 2004). Parents clearly value literacy. In addition, Storch and Whitehurst

(2002) demonstrated that parents' expectations for their children's success in reading and spelling were directly related to children's reading and spelling in grade 1. These latter studies, however, did not consider the relation between parent expectations and parent teaching. It may be the case that parental expectations still hold a direct relation to child outcomes once parent teaching is considered. Evidence by LeFevre, Clarke, and Stringer (2002) on numeracy suggests that parental expectations may be linked to teaching behaviors, which in turn are related to child outcomes. To extend these findings to literacy, Martini and Sénéchal (2010) tested the relations among parental teaching, parental expectations, and child early literacy ($n = 108$).

Martini and Sénéchal (2010) found that parents had high expectations about their children's early literacy skills before entering grade 1: More than 80% of parents responded that it was very important for their children to know the names of letters and to print their names; 68% of parents thought that knowing letter sounds was very important; and 50% of parents thought that knowing how to read or to print words was very important. Very few parents indicated that achieving these five literacy skills were not important. Parents' expectations were positively and directly associated with child literacy after researchers considered parental teaching, SES level, and analytic intelligence. This finding is consistent with past research demonstrating that parents' expectations regarding their children's academic success in school is related to their children's letter recognition skills (Hess, Holloway, Price, & Dickson, 1982), the grade the child receives in reading and spelling (Storch & Whitehurst, 2002), and later reading ability (Whitehurst & Lonigan, 1998). Findings from Martini and Sénéchal showed that while the predictive power of parents' expectations for child literacy was reduced when parent teaching was entered into the regression, a direct relation remained. In contrast, LeFevre and colleagues (2002) reported that parent teaching mediated the relation between parent expectations and child early numeracy. It may be that the influence of parents' expectations may be different for literacy skills than for numeracy skills. The Martini and Sénéchal results are also

different from those of Stephenson and colleagues (2008) and may reflect differences in measures used. Martini and Sénéchal used focused measures of teaching and expectations, whereas Stephenson and colleagues used more general measures. Finally, Martini and Sénéchal proposed that the direct relation between early literacy and parental expectations may be because parents with higher expectations teach their children in a manner that is different than that of parents with different levels of expectations. Observational studies are certainly needed to capture how parents teach their young children about literacy.

Parental Beliefs

Of special interest were parents' beliefs pertaining to the home as a literacy-learning environment (Korat & Levin, 2001). It appears that parents, in general, believe it is important to engage their children in literacy learning at home (Evans et al., 2004; Fitzgerald, Spiegel, & Cunningham, 1991). Moreover, low-income mothers who reported believing it was important for their children to participate in reading activities in the home provided their children with literacy learning activities, despite their challenging and precarious living environment (Nespeca, 1995). Similarly, DeBaryshe, Binder, and Buell (2000) showed that mothers' beliefs concerning their children's literacy learning at home were related to the frequency with which they reported engaging their children in writing activities. In addition, Serpell, Baker, and Sonnenschein (2005) reported that parents' perspectives on how to teach their children about letters and words were related to their children's eventual success in mastering early reading skills in first grade. DeBaryshe (1995), however, found that mothers' beliefs were indirectly related to children's ability through parent–child literacy interactions. These findings suggest that parents' perception of literacy learning at home should be related to both the frequency of occurrence of literacy activities at home and child outcomes. More importantly, the Debaryshe findings suggest an indirect relation between parent beliefs about learning literacy at home and child outcomes, via the occurrence of literacy activities. Interestingly, Martini and

Sénéchal (2010) found that parental beliefs about learning literacy at home were related to parental teaching frequency, but that parental beliefs were not related to children's early literacy in their study. Certainly, previous work on parental beliefs suggests that it might be parents' orientation toward literacy activities rather than beliefs about learning that might be linked to children's early literacy (Anderson, 1995; Evans et al., 2004; Serpell et al., 2005).

Limitations

Our research on home literacy has been conducted mostly with middle-class families, and most of it is correlational in nature. Each of these limitations is discussed in turn. In our research on the home literacy model, parental education level was included as a control variable in the studies where a significant relation between education and child outcomes was found. One could argue, however, that the present results are not representative of the entire population because most of the parents in the sample were highly educated. This important criticism was tackled by Sénéchal (2006), who argued that issues of social class differences and generalization are best discussed in terms of proximal versus more distal causes. The view adopted in our research is that home literacy experiences are proximal variables that can affect child outcomes directly, whereas SES (i.e., parent education and income) is a distal cause that can moderate the impact of home literacy experiences. Indeed, there is some evidence to suggest that distal variables, such as SES, play a moderating role for more proximal variables, such as home literacy activities (Marjoribanks, 1979); that is, it appears that the strength of the relations among home literacy experiences and child outcomes varies as a function of different SES levels. Tests of the moderating effect of SES on home literacy activities, however, require representative samples of the different SES levels. Unfortunately, sample sizes rarely reach the appropriate level to provide adequate tests of the moderating role of SES. As a consequence of small sample sizes, SES levels may appear to play a mediating role in the link between home literacy and child outcomes. In studies for which it is not feasible to test representative samples for different SES levels, it is best to limit the sample to one SES level to gain a better understanding of the role of proximal variables. In addition, a focus on proximal variables should provide more explanatory power than a focus on more distal variables (Hess et al., 1982). That being said, in most research on home literacy, parental education and/or income is treated as a mediating variable rather than a moderating variable (e.g., Forget-Dubois et al., 2009; Park, 2008).

Most of our research on home literacy is correlational; therefore, statements about causation should not be made. Our research, however, included strict controls to test the predicted direct and indirect relations among early experiences and children's eventual literacy performance in grade school. The relations existed after we controlled statistically for parent education (or parent literacy), as well as longitudinal relations among literacy behaviors. Most important, many aspects of the obtained pattern of findings in Figure 11.1 have been replicated, as indicated previously. Moreover, the findings of intervention research conducted with families are consistent with the home literacy model (Sénéchal & Young, 2008).

Conclusion

The contribution of the home literacy model is to allow one to understand better the pattern of association between parent–child home literacy activities and child outcomes. The findings for shared reading support the abundant literature on the value of reading books to young children for the pleasure it provides. Shared reading also has wonderful characteristics that provide opportunities for learning about oral language. The robust longitudinal association between parental reports of shared reading when their children are in kindergarten and children's reports of reading for pleasure in grade 4 is a beautiful illustration of the reason we should value reading books to young children. The home literacy model highlights the importance of looking beyond shared reading when examining children's early literacy, that is, children's alphabetic knowledge, early reading, and invented spelling. The descriptive findings show that parents focus on naturally occurring activities to teach about the alphabet, printing, and reading words. Moreover, parental teaching has a robust, positive predictive association with child early literacy. Early literacy, in turn, predicts reading success in grade 1. The meta-analytic review of intervention research by Sénéchal and Young (2008) suggest that parents of children in kindergarten and grade 1 can be effective tutors for literacy when given specific materials and guidelines. Kindergarten teachers who encourage parents' involvement in helping children acquire strong language skills and early literacy might be tapping a highly valuable resource.

References

Alexander, K. L., Entwisle, D. R., & Horsey, C. (1997). From first grade forward: Early foundation of high school dropout. *Sociology of Education, 70,* 87–107.

Allen, L., Cipielewski, J., & Stanovich, K. E. (1992). Multiple indicators of children's reading habits and attitudes: Construct validity and cognitive correlates. *Journal of Educational Psychology, 84,* 489–503.

Anderson, J. (1995). How parents' perceptions of literacy acquisition relate to their children's emergent literacy knowledge. *Reading Horizons, 35,* 209–228.

Aram, D., & Levin, I. (2004). The role of maternal mediation of writing to kindergartners in promoting literacy achievements in school: A longitudinal perspective. *Reading and Writing: An Interdisciplinary Journal, 17,* 387–409.

Baker, L. (2003). The role of parents in motivating struggling readers. *Reading and Writing Quarterly, 19,* 87–106.

Baker, L., Fernandez-Fein, S., Scher, D., & Williams, H. (1998). Home experiences related to the development of word recognition. In J. L. Metsala & L. C. Ehri (Eds.), *Word recognition in beginning literacy* (pp. 263–287). Mahwah, NJ: Erlbaum.

Bingham, G. (2009, April). *Maternal literacy beliefs, joint book reading, home literacy environment, and children's early literacy development.* Poster presented at the biennial meeting of the Society for Research in Child Development, Denver, CO.

Bryant, P. E., Bradley, L. L., MacLean, M., & Crossland, J. (1990). Rhyme and alliteration, phoneme detection, and learning to read. *Developmental Psychology, 26,* 429–438.

Burgess, S. R., Hecht, S. A., & Lonigan, C. J. (2002). Relations of the home literacy environment (HLE) to the development of reading-related abilities: A one-year longitudinal study. *Reading Research Quarterly, 37,* 408–426.

Burgess, S. R., & Lonigan, C. J. (1998). Bidirectional relations of phonological sensitivity and prereading abilities: Evidence from a preschool sample. *Journal of Experimental Child Psychology, 70,* 117–141.

Bus, A. G., van IJzendoorn, M. H., & Pellegrini, A. D. (1995). Joint book reading makes for success in learning to read: A meta-analysis on intergenerational transmission of literacy. *Review of Educational Research, 65,* 1–21.

Butler, S. R., Marsh, H. W., Sheppard, M. J., & Sheppard, J. L. (1985). Seven-year longitudinal study of the early prediction of reading achievement. *Journal of Educational Psychology, 77,* 349–361.

Crain-Thoreson, C., Dhalin, M. P., & Powell, T. A. (2001). Parent–child interaction in three conversational contexts: Variations in style and strategy. In J. Brooks-Gunn & P. Rebello (Eds.) *Sourcebook on emergent literacy* (pp. 23–37). San Francisco: Jossey-Bass.

Cunningham, A. E., & Stanovich, K. E. (1993). Children's literacy environments and early word recognition subskills. *Reading and Writing: An Interdisciplinary Journal, 5,* 193–204.

Cunningham, A. E., & Stanovich, K. E. (1998). The impact of print exposure on word recognition. In J. L. Metsala & L. C. Ehri (Eds.), *Word recognition in beginning literacy* (pp. 235–261). Mahwah, NJ: Erlbaum.

Dale, P. S., Crain-Thoreson, C., & Robinson, N. M. (1995). Linguistic precocity and the development of reading: The role of extralinguistic factors. *Applied Psycholinguistics, 16,* 173–187.

DeBaryshe, B. D. (1995). Maternal belief systems: Linchpin in the home reading process. *Journal of Applied Developmental Psychology, 16,* 1–20.

DeBaryshe, B. D., Binder, J. C., & Buell, M. J. (2000). Mothers' implicit theories of early literacy instruction: Implications for children's reading and writing. *Early Child Development and Care, 160,* 119–131.

de Jong, P. F., & Leseman, P. P. M. (2001). Lasting effects of home literacy on reading achievement in school. *Journal of School Psychology, 39,* 389–414.

Edwards, P. A. (1991). Fostering early literacy through parent coaching. In E. H. Hiebert (Ed.), *Literacy for a diverse society perspectives, practices, and policies* (pp. 199–213). New York: Teachers College Press.

Entwisle, D. R., Alexander, K. L., & Olson, L. S. (2005). First grade and educational attainment by age 22: A new story. *American Journal of Sociology, 110,* 1458–1502.

Evans, M. A., Fox, M., Cresmaso, L., & McKinnon, L. (2004). Beginning reading: The views of parents and teachers of young children. *Journal of Educational Psychology, 96,* 130–141.

Evans, M. A., Moretti, S., Shaw, D., & Fox, M. (2003). Parent scaffolding in children's oral reading. *Early Education and Development, 14,* 363–388.

Evans, M. A., & Saint-Aubin, J. (2005). What children are looking at during shared storybook reading: Evidence from eye movements. *Psychological Science, 16,* 913–920.

Evans, M. A., Shaw, D., & Bell, M. (2000). Home literacy activities and their influence on early literacy skills. *Canadian Journal of Experimental Psychology, 54*(2), 65–75.

Farver, J. M., & Lonigan, C. J. (2009, April). *The development of ELL children's early reading skills in*

Spanish and English: What can immigrant families do? Poster presented at the biennial meeting of the Society for Research in Child Development, Denver, CO.

Ferriero, E. (1986). The interplay between information and assimilation in beginning literacy. In W. H. Teale & E. Sulzby (Eds.), *Emergent literacy: Writing and reading* (pp. 15–49). Norwood, NJ: Ablex.

Fitzgerald, J., Spiegel, D. L., & Cunningham, J. W. (1991). The relationship between parental literacy level and perceptions of emergent literacy. *Journal of Reading Behavior, 23(2), 191–213.*

Forget-Dubois, N., Dionne, G., Lemelin, J., Pérusse, D., Tremblay, R., & Boivin, M. (2009). Early child language mediates the relation between home environment and school readiness. *Child Development, 80,* 736–749.

Frijters, J. C., Barron, R. W., Algire, L., Humphries, N., & Vander Zwaag, K. (2001, June). *Pre-readers' self-reported interest in literacy and math: Associations with early academic skills and parent teaching.* Symposium presented at the annual meeting of the Canadian Psychological Association, Laval, Quebec.

Frijters, J. C., Barron, R. W., & Brunello, M. (2000). Direct and mediated influences of home literacy and literacy interest on prereaders' oral vocabulary and early written language skill. *Journal of Educational Psychology, 92(3),* 466–477.

Hart, S. A., & Petrill, S. A. (2009). The genetics and environments of reading: A behavioral genetic perspective. In Y. Kim (Ed.), *Handbook of behavior genetics: Part II* (pp. 113–123). New York: Springer.

Hayes, D. P., & Ahrens, M. (1988). Vocabulary simplification for children: A special case of "motherese"? *Journal of Child Language, 15,* 395–410.

Hess, R. D., Holloway, S. D., Price, G. C., & Dickson, W. P. (1982). Family environments and the acquisition of reading skills: Toward a more precise analysis. In L. M. Laosa & I. E. Sigel (Eds.), *Families as learning environments for children* (pp. 87–113). New York: Plenum Press.

Hood, M., Conlon, E., & Andrews, G. (2008). Preschool home literacy practices and children's literacy development: A longitudinal analysis. *Journal of Educational Psychology, 100,* 252–271.

Justice, L. M., & Ezell, H. K. (2004). Print referencing: An emergent literacy enhancement strategy and its clinical applications. *Language, Speech, and Hearing Services in Schools, 35,* 185–193.

Justice, L. M., Weber, S., Ezell, H. K., & Bakeman, R. (2002). A sequential analysis of children's responsiveness to parental references to print during shared storybook reading. *American Journal of Speech–Language Pathology, 11,* 30–40

Korat, O., & Levin, I. (2001). Maternal beliefs and child development: Comparisons of text writing between two social groups. *Applied Developmental Psychology, 22,* 397–420.

Landry, S. H., Smith, K. E., Swank, P. R., & Guttentag, C. (2008). A responsive parenting intervention: The optimal timing across early childhood for impacting maternal behaviors and child outcomes. *Developmental Psychology, 44,* 1335–1353.

Lee, K., Sung, M., & Chang, Y. E. (2009, April). *Relations of home literacy environments to preschoolers' vocabulary and reading.* Poster presented at the biennial meeting of the Society for Research in Child Development, Denver, CO.

LeFevre, J., Clarke, T., & Stringer, A. (2002). Influences of language and parental involvement on the development of counting skills: Comparisons of French- and English-speaking Canadian children. *Early Childhood Development and Care, 172,* 283–300.

LeFevre, J., & Sénéchal, M. (2002, August). *Learning to read in a second language: Parent involvement still count.* Paper presented as part of the symposium Literacy Learning to Read: Cognitive, Motivational and Contextual, held during the biennial meeting of the International Society for the Study of Behavioral Development, Ottawa, Canada.

Lever, R., & Sénéchal, M. (in press). Discussing stories: On how a dialogic reading intervention improves kindergartners' oral narrative construction. *Journal of Experimental Psychology.*

Levin, I., & Korat, O. (1993). Sensitivity to phonological, morphological, and semantic cues in early reading and writing in Hebrew. *Merrill–Palmer Quarterly, 39,* 213–232.

Lonigan, C. J., Burgess, S. R., Anthony, J. L., & Barker, T. A. (1998). Development of phonological sensitivity in two- to five-year-old children. *Journal of Educational Psychology, 90,* 294–311.

Lynch, J., Anderson, J., Anderson, A., & Shapiro, J. (2006). Parents' beliefs about young children's literacy development and parents' literacy behaviors. *Reading Psychology, 27,* 1–20.

Marjoribanks, K. (1979). *Families and their learning environments: An empirical analysis.* London: Routledge & Kegan Paul.

Martini, F., & Sénéchal, M. (2010). *Learning literacy skills at home: Parent teaching, expectations, and child interest.* Manuscript submitted for publication.

Metsala, J. L., & Walley, A. C. (1998). Spoken vocabulary growth and the segmental restructuring of lexical representations: Precursors to phonemic awareness and early reading ability. In J. L. Metsala & L. C. Ehri (Eds.), *Word recognition in beginning literacy* (pp. 89–120). Mahwah, NJ: Erlbaum.

Mol, S. E., Bus, A. G., & de Jong, M. T. (2009). Interactive book reading in early education: A tool to stimulate print knowledge as well as oral language. *Review of Educational Research, 79,* 979–1007.

Mol, S. E., Bus, A. G., de Jong, M. T., & Smeets, D. J. H. (2008). Added value of dialogic parent–child book readings: A meta-analysis. *Early Education and Development, 19,* 7–26.

Muter, V., & Snowling, M. J. (2009). Children at familial risk of dyslexia: Practical implications from an at-risk study. *Child and Adolescent Mental Health, 14,* 37–41.

National Early Literacy Panel. (2008). *Developing early literacy: Report of the National Early Literacy Panel.* Washington, DC: National Institute for Literacy.

Nespeca, S. M. (1995). Parental involvement in emergent literacy skills of urban head start children. *Early Child Development and Care, 111,* 153–180.

Ouellette, G., & Sénéchal, M. (2008). Pathways to literacy: A study of invented spelling and its role in learning to read. *Child Development, 79,* 899–913.

Park, H. (2008). Home literacy environments and children's reading performance: A comparative study of 25 countries. *Educational Research and Evaluation, 14,* 489–505.

Reese, E., & Cox, A. (1999). Quality of adult book reading affects children's emergent literacy. *Developmental Psychology, 35,* 20–28.

Roberts, J., Jurgens, J., & Burchinal, M. (2005). The role of home literacy practices in preschool children's language and emergent literacy skills. *Journal of Speech Language and Hearing Research, 48,* 345–359.

Rogoff, B. (1990). *Apprenticeship in thinking: Cognitive development in social context.* New York: Oxford University Press.

Sénéchal, M. (1997). The differential effect of storybook reading on preschooler's expressive and receptive vocabulary acquisition. *Journal of Child Language, 24,* 123–138.

Sénéchal, M. (2000). Examen du lien entre la lecture de livres et le développement du vocabulaire chez l'enfant préscolaire [Examining the link between shared book reading and preschoolers vocabulary development]. *Enfance, 52,* 169–186.

Sénéchal, M. (2006). Testing the home literacy model: Parent involvement in kindergarten is differentially related to grade 4 reading comprehension, fluency, spelling, and reading for pleasure. *Journal for the Scientific Study of Reading, 10,* 59–87.

Sénéchal, M., & LeFevre, J. (2002). Parental involvement in the development of children's reading skill: A 5-year longitudinal study. *Child Development, 73,* 445–460.

Sénéchal, M., LeFevre, J., Smith-Chant, B. L., & Colton, K. (2001). On refining theoretical models of emergent literacy: The role of empirical evidence. *Journal of School Psychology, 39,* 439–460.

Sénéchal, M., LeFevre, J.-A., Thomas, E., & Daley, K. (1998). Differential effects of home literacy experiences on the development of oral and written language. *Reading Research Quarterly, 32,* 96–116.

Sénéchal, M., LeFevre, J.-A., Hudson, E., & Lawson, P. (1996). Knowledge of picture-books as a predictor of young children's vocabulary development. *Journal of Educational Psychology, 88,* 520–536.

Sénéchal, M., Pagan, S., Lever, R., & Ouellette, G. (2008). Relations among the frequency of shared reading and 4-year-old children's vocabulary, morphological and syntax comprehension, and narrative skills. *Early Education and Development, 19,* 28–45.

Sénéchal, M., Thomas, E., & Monker, J.-A. (1995). Individual differences in 4-year-olds' ability to learn new vocabulary. *Journal of Educational Psychology, 87,* 218–229.

Sénéchal, M., & Young, L. (2008). The effect of family literacy interventions on children's acquisition of reading from kindergarten to grade 3: A meta-analytic review. *Review of Educational Research, 78,* 880–907.

Serpell, R., Baker, L., & Sonnenschein, S. (2005). *Becoming literate in the city: The Baltimore Early Childhood Project.* New York: Cambridge University Press.

Stanovich, K. E., & West, R. F. (1989). Exposure to print and orthographic processing. *Reading Research Quarterly, 24,* 402–433.

Stephenson, K. A., Parrila, R. K., Georgiou, G. K., & Kirby, J. R. (2008). Effects of home literacy, parents' beliefs, and children's task-focused behavior on emergent literacy and word reading skills. *Scientific Studies of Reading, 12,* 24–50.

Storch, S. A., & Whitehurst, G. J. (2002). Oral language and code-related precursors to reading: Evidence from a longitudinal structural model. *Developmental Psychology, 38,* 934–947

Teale, W. H., & Sulzby, E. (1986). Emergent literacy as a perspective for examining how young children become writers and readers. In W. H. Teale & E. Sulzby (Eds.), *Emergent literacy: Writing and reading* (pp. vii–xxv). Norwood, NJ: Ablex.

Thomas, E. M., & Sénéchal, M. (2004). Long-term effects of articulation on speech perception, phoneme sensitivity, and decoding: A study from age 3 to age 8. *Applied Psycholinguistics, 25,* 513–541.

van Kleeck, A., & Norlander, E. (2008). Fostering form and meaning in emerging literacy using evidence-based practice. In M. Mody & E. R. Silliman (Eds.), *Brain, behavior, and learning in language and reading disorders* (pp. 275–314). New York: Guilford Press.

Weigel, D. J., Martin, S. S., & Bennett, K. K. (2006). Mothers' literacy beliefs: Connections with the home literacy environment and pre-school children's literacy development. *Journal of Early Childhood Literacy, 6,* 191–211.

Whitehurst, G. J., & Lonigan, C. J. (1998). Child development and emergent literacy. *Child Development, 69,* 848–872.

Zevenbergen, A., Whitehurst, G., & Zevenbergen, J. (2003). Effects of a shared-reading intervention on the inclusion of evaluative devices in narratives of children from low-income families. *Applied Development Psychology, 24,* 1–15.

Zhou, H., & Salili, F. (2008). Intrinsic reading motivation of Chinese preschoolers and its relationships with home literacy. *International Journal of Psychology, 43,* 912–916.

12

Home Support of Children in the Writing Process: Contributions to Early Literacy

DORIT ARAM
IRIS LEVIN

The rising significance attributed to reading and spelling acquisition as a foundation for learning and scholastic success (Echols, West, Stanovich, & Zehr, 1996), has motivated numerous societies to devote considerable resources to the support of this domain. The recognition that reading and spelling do not emerge in children simply through growing up among and interacting with literate people (Ehri, Nunes, Stahl, & Willows, 2001), a belief once quite popular (Goodman, 1967) and still preached today (Edelsky, 2006), led to a search for planned procedures best suited to the promotion of reading and spelling. In many countries, the attempt to enhance reading–spelling acquisition has included supporting competencies from an early age that build the foundations for reading and spelling acquisition later on (Eufimia, 2008; Neuman & Roskos, 2005; Perlman & Fletcher, 2008). Promotion attempts mainly targeted two contexts—school and home. Many educational systems developed curricula to teach early literacy very early, even in pre-preschool. Concomitantly, attempts were made to enhance the home literacy environment.

School and home are different environments with different agendas. While school is more focused on teaching–learning, home provides, first and foremost, parenting and emotional care. Consequently, while literacy should be taught in school through a well-planned curriculum, at home it may be integrated with everyday communication, daily games, and chores that promote a close caregiver–child relationship and provide entertainment. This chapter deals with promoting literacy at home.

Home Literacy Environment

The term *home literacy environment* (HLE) captures family activities and devices that contribute to early literacy. These activities include caregivers' joint book reading with children, teaching children the alphabet, familiarizing them with environmental print, guiding them in spelling their names and words, enriching their vocabulary through verbal communication, supporting their phonological awareness, graphophonemic mappings, and more. The devices counted as HLE signs include storybooks, papers, pencils, markers, blackboards, alphabet cards, commercial literacy-based games, computer games, and educational television programs.

HLE has been mostly measured by (1) interrogation of caregivers on the frequency with which various literate activities are carried out in the family, (2) interrogation about the presence of literate devices at home, (3) observation of such devices in the home, and (4) at times, testing parents' familiarity with children's storybooks (Stanovich & West, 1989). While studies have included some overlapping activities and devices in their measurement of HLE, the measures have often differed greatly, making cross-study comparisons questionable (see Boudreau, 2005; Foy & Mann, 2003; Hood, Conlon, & Andrews, 2008). Researchers have preferred to develop their own measures because of their differential theoretical approaches regarding what constitutes significant aspects of HLE, as well as the differential utility of various criteria as prominent markers of HLE in different cultures and social strata.

Some researchers took a narrower but more focused approach to study home literacy by looking at the impact of a well-defined single activity considered central in its contribution to early literacy. The activity most often studied was storybook reading—its frequency (Bus, van IJzendoorn, & Pellegrini, 1995), its quality assessed by dialogic or interactive reading (Mol, Bus, de Jong, & Smeets, 2008), or its format (e.g., printed books vs. video books) (Korat & Shamir, 2007; Verhallen, Bus, & de Jong, 2006). Studies on storybook reading have mostly shown its impact on expressive and receptive vocabulary and story comprehension (Bus et al., 1995; Mol et al., 2008).

This chapter focuses on a different joint activity, writing mediation. The term *mediation* was adapted from Feuerstein, who used it to refer to guidance given by an expert to a novice, thereby promoting the novice's independent functioning (Feuerstein & Feuerstein, 1991). According to Feuerstein's model, the world of children is mediated through the process of caregivers' matching of what they intend to mediate with children's developmental abilities. The novice's world is transformed through mediation into one in which things have meaning, importance, and relevance. Note that the term *mediation* shares meaning with scaffolding within the *zone of proximal development* (ZPD) presented by the Vygotskian school (Tudge & Winterhoff, 1993; Vygotsky, 1978). In this chapter, *writing mediation* refers to different levels of guidance that caregivers provide to children in writing words, thereby teaching them about the written system.

The Development of Writing: The Shift from a Constructivist to a Sociocultural Approach

Children's interest in writing and their attempts to write, starting even before they can print letters or understand the alphabetic principle, have been documented for over a century (e.g., Hildreth, 1936; Iredell, 1898). This topic has continued to interest researchers from many countries (e.g., Ferreiro & Teberosky, 1982; Levin & Bus, 2003; Sulzby, 1989; Tolchinsky-Landsmann, 1986). However, throughout the years, a shift has occurred in how researchers have conceptualized the factors underlying children's development of writing. This shift has not been unique to the domain of writing but has coincided with a common shift in the view of cognitive development, from Piaget's constructivist model to Vygotsky's sociocultural model.

In a series of seminal studies that analyzed how children's writing underwent gradual changes with age (Bissex, 1980; Clay, 1975; Ferreiro & Teberosky, 1982; Tolchinsky-Landsmann & Levin, 1987), children's development of writing was attributed to their endogenous motivation to experiment with writing. Children were described as constructing their own knowledge about writing through developing and testing hypotheses about writing by exploring ways of writing, as well as comparing their writing with adults' writing, using their age-appropriate general cognitive schemes. Within this framework, the role of the caregiver's input, feedback, or guidance was viewed as minor.

According to children's frequently cited hypothesis concerning the written system, the words for bigger objects are written with more letters (Ferreiro & Teberosky, 1982; Tolchinsky-Landsmann, 2003). For instance, in writing *bear* and *baby bear*, they tend to write *bear* longer, despite its being a shorter word. Ferreiro argued that children are puzzled to find out that words are written with a different number of letters, and that words/names standing for single objects are written with a few letters. Being ignorant about the role of letters, children derive the hypothesis that bigger objects are denoted by longer words.

Children's invented hypotheses, proposed by the constructivist approach, was supported by Levin and Korat (1993), who analyzed how 4- to 6-year-olds use different cues to determine the number of letters they employ for writing words. Children were asked to write pairs of words differing in phonological length, in size of objects they denote, and in number of morphemes. Children considered both phonological length and semantic size, writing the longer-sounding word and the word for the bigger object with more letters or marks. With age, consideration of phonology increased and that of semantics decreased, indicating growth in comprehension of the written code, which is phonologically based.

The constructivist approach was also evident in an early quantitative, quasi-experiment study that examined parental scaffolding of writing. Burns and Casbergue (1992) studied 5- to 6-year-old children writing a letter with their parents. When parents took a leading role in the joint writing activity, their children followed their guidance and produced longer and more conventional texts in terms of spelling, punctuation, and so forth. Children whose parents allowed them to lead took more initiative verbally during the writing session and dealt more with the letter's message. The researchers concluded that joint writing led by children is more motivating and productive in terms of promoting understanding of the written system. This conclusion is based on the constructivist view rather than on their findings.

The shift toward recognizing the significant role of parental mediation in enhancing writing has been taken by DeBaryshe, Buell, and Binder (1996) working within Vygotsky's sociocultural model. They asked 5- to 6-year-old children to write a letter on their own and to write one jointly with their mothers. Whereas the letters written by the children alone included drawings, scribblings, inventing spellings, or conventional spellings, the letters produced jointly included only words spelled correctly. Moreover, jointly written letters were longer and more conventional in terms of letter shapes, letter–word size and position, punctuation, and so forth. Still, mothers did take into account children's estimated level of writing, leading children whose independent written text were longer and more conventional jointly to produce longer and more conventional letters. Thus,

mothers appeared in some respects to be sensitive to their children's level, adapting their writing mediation to children's competence, without giving up the major requirement of conventional writing—printing words in correct spelling.

The major role of parents in enhancing early literacy has recently been illustrated in a case study following a child's literate development between ages 2 and 6 (Neumann, Hood, & Neumann, 2008). From the start, the mother used environmental print to familiarize her son with letter shapes and to encourage him to print letters. Letters were introduced in a multisensory approach to enhance learning. Later, the mother added letter sounds, and finally she guided him in spelling words and phrases. It should be noticed that her parental leading role did not suppress the child's motivation to explore the written system. On the contrary, the child was active in finding ways to master the system in a game-like manner:

> He self-initiated many letter forming activities himself by using food when eating or playing with household materials. For example, Harry made the letter E out of fish fingers, he broke a donut in half and exclaimed that he had made a "C for cat," he made a V from fallen tree branches in the garden, and was excited when he made a round "O for octopus" out of some old string he had found. (p. 315)

This child's acquisition of letter knowledge and writing was relatively fast but normal. What was outstanding was his print motivation and the pleasure he derived from mastering this domain both alone and jointly with his parent.

Interestingly, this case study did not mention any of the self-initiated hypotheses proposed by the constructivist school. The use of these hypotheses in children's writing was frequently observed and documented in the previous era. Perhaps children who become interested in the print around them but get no mediation of the letters and the written code look for underlying rules governing print and find it in developing such hypotheses. In contrast, 4- to 6-year-olds who experience this guidance do not invent the major hypotheses proposed by the constructivist school (e.g., names of bigger objects are denoted by longer written words) because they have learned more from experts on the rules governing print. If this is correct, then caregivers' writing mediation affects not only the pace but also the developmental route through which children reach an understanding of the written system.

Writing Mediation: Assessment of Literate and Emotional Aspects

In the early 21st century, a line of studies appeared that used a new methodology to assess parental level of guided writing. The parents were asked to guide their children, preschoolers or kindergartners, to write words in whatever way they found suitable, with no suggestions on how that could or should be done. The words to be written were mundane and included in children's spoken vocabulary. Parents and children received cards, each of which displayed drawings of two objects depicting the two words to be written. Each pair of words differed in distinct characteristics, allowing examination of whether and how parents utilized these characteristics in their writing mediation. For instance, a pair included a masculine and feminine term with different gender morphemes. Another pair of words rhymed, beginning with different letters and ending with the same letters.

Parental writing mediation was videotaped at the family's home and used to measure parental writing mediation. Analysis referred to two aspects of the interaction: the cognitive–literate and the socioemotional. The *literate* scales assessed the ways parents helped their children cope with the writing task, and the *emotional* scales assessed parental behavior toward their children in the joint endeavor.

The *literate* mediation measures reflect parents' graphophonemic mapping and printing mediation, their demand for precision, as well as their reference to orthography. *Graphophonemic* mediation assesses the degree to which the parents guide their children through the process of segmenting each word into its sounds and retrieving the required letter for each sound when attempting to represent an oral word in writing. The scale begins with a low level at which a parent refers to the word as a whole or as a sequence of sounds, uttering the sequence

as a unit without clarifying that sounds are represented by letters. At the middle level, the parent dictates a letter name. At the high level, the parent encourages the child to retrieve a phonological unit included in the word (mainly subsyllable or phoneme) and to map it onto a letter name. Higher scores indicate that the parent supports the child's writing through a more complete encoding process across letters.

Printing mediation reflects the autonomy allowed or encouraged by the parent in printing each letter. The scale ranges from the low level, at which the parent writes the letter by him- or herself or guides the child's hand, through the middle level, at which the parent writes and the child copies the letter, to the high level, at which the parent encourages the child to discover the letter's shape independently.

Demand for precision assesses the amount of precision the parent demands from the child in shaping the letters, spacing between them, and so forth. It ranges from low demand, in which the parent accepts the print even if unconventional, through a midlevel demand, in which the parent just draws the child's attention to the need to write more accurately, to a high-level demand, in which the parent requires some corrections if the product is unsatisfactory.

Reference to orthography estimates parental reference to aspects of orthography, ranging from no reference through mentioning the orthographic rule, to referencing the rule with its meaning.

The *socioemotional* scales estimate parental behavior toward the child in the writing interaction. They reflect the warmth of the *atmosphere* and parental ability to maintain the child's *cooperation*, ability to stay on-task, and willingness to accept suggestions and directions. The *emotional* scales also include *reinforcements* (e.g., "You wrote it beautifully"), *criticisms* (e.g., "Not good"), *comments on discipline* (e.g., "Sit still"), *urging* comments (e.g., "Move on"), and the number of *physical contacts* between the parent and child (e.g., holding the child's hand).

The emotional nature of parent–child interactions largely predicts the security and confidence of ongoing interactions in general and of teaching interactions in particular (Shonkoff & Phillips, 2002). There is strong evidence that mothers who provide a supportive environment, in which the child feels safe and free to explore, promote their children's adjustment (e.g., Biringen & Robinson, 1991). Similarly, it has been found that the level of mother-to-child warmth, proactive teaching, inductive discipline, and positive involvement predicts the child's social skills and academic performance in kindergarten and in grade 6 (Pettit, Bates, & Dodge, 1997).

To guide a child efficiently on a goal-oriented activity such as word writing, a parent has to perform at a high level in the literate and the emotional spheres. He or she has to have a positive attitude toward the interaction and needs to know both how the writing task can be accomplished and how to help the child approach it in an emotionally positive way.

Typical Parental Writing Mediation and Child Literacy

In a pioneering study on writing mediation (Aram & Levin, 2001), mothers of kindergartners recruited from low socioeconomic status (SES) neighborhoods were asked to guide their children in writing dictated words and a list of names (of invitees to their upcoming birthday party). The videotapes were analyzed in terms of maternal mediation on the literate scales, examined letter by letter (Aram & Levin, 2001), and were later reanalyzed on the emotional scales, examined word by word (Aram, 2002). Practically all mothers used more than a single level on each scale across letters and words. Still, the outstanding finding was that each mother had a typical central level of mediation, and that this level appeared on the two tasks of writing words and names.

The mother's typical level of literate mediation was strongly connected with the child's literacy level, measured by word writing and recognition, phonological awareness, and orthographic awareness, after researchers controlled for sociocultural measures of the family (Aram & Levin, 2001). These findings reflect not only maternal adjustment to the child's literacy level but also, and maybe more so, the phenomenon of children of mothers who guided on a higher level on cognitive tasks surpassing their peers in cognitive or

literate achievements (e.g., Stright & Herr, 2009). In a follow-up study, maternal literate writing mediation in kindergarten was found to predict children's spelling, reading comprehension, and oral literacy (i.e., defining words) in grade 2, beyond variations on SES and literacy assessed in the kindergarten (Aram & Levin, 2004). These findings taken together suggest that joint writing at home at a young age contributes to the child's literacy growth.

The two conclusions—that mothers possess individual typical mediation levels, and that mothers are sensitive to their children's literacy level—were reanalyzed in a twins study (Aram, 2007). Mothers of fraternal twins in kindergarten were videotaped guiding each twin in writing words. On each of the literate and emotional guiding scales, maternal consistent guiding level was reflected in the substantial significant correlations of guiding scores between twins. Pairs of children of different mothers matched on literacy levels to pairs of twins were created, and the correlations between their mothers' guiding scores were calculated. On all literate and emotional guiding scales (except on one scale out of eight), no significant correlation emerged between guiding scores of pairs of mothers. The conclusion drawn is that the correlations between guiding scores of twins reflect maternal consistency rather than similarity in literacy between twins.

Over and above maternal typical mediation level across children, mothers guided the more advanced twin on literacy (measured by word writing, letter naming, and phonological awareness), on a higher literate mediation, demanding more from that twin on graphophonemic mapping, printing, and precision. The correlations between maternal literate mediation and children's level of literacy suggest that mothers either learn about their children's literate abilities while jointly writing with them, and/or they know their children's literate abilities a priori.

Concerning the emotional nature of joint writing, it has been found that mothers who created a positive atmosphere with one twin behaved similarly with their other twin (Aram, 2007). In the same vein, mothers who tended to reinforce or criticize one twin were inclined to do so with their other twin. It has been claimed that emotional aspects of interaction are determined by parents and their history, as well as by cultural beliefs and norms of behavior related to parenting (Korat & Levin, 2001; Lightfoot & Valsiner, 1992).

The emotional scales, unlike the literate scales, are not connected across the board to the child's literacy. However, some of these scales emerged as connected to literacy in each study. Moreover, the scale of atmosphere (i.e., maternal acceptance and warmth toward her child) often appeared to be related to literacy. Notably, in the literature, different emotional scales assess distinctive parental behaviors that are differentially associated with children's outcomes (Grolnick & Slowiaczek, 1994).

Writing Mediation of Mothers versus Fathers

Since the 20th century, major structural changes that have occurred in the division of labor within the family increase fathers' involvement in raising their children (Bond, Galinsky, & Swanberg, 1998; Cinamon, Weisel, & Tzuk, 2007). Accordingly, to reach a current understanding of children's literacy, we must extend the analysis of writing mediation to include the father, comparing his mediation to maternal mediation. Aram (2010) separately videotaped mothers and fathers writing words with their kindergartners at home. Mothers scored higher on both the literate and the emotional mediation scales. In other words, mothers coached their children on a more advanced level in the writing process and maintained a more cooperative atmosphere.

The differences between mothers' and fathers' writing mediation may stem from the differences in their roles in the family, as well as different perceptions of the guiding process. Apparently, mothers are still perceived by themselves, their partners, and society as more responsible for their children's development. They spend more time with their children (Moon & Hoffman, 2008), gain more experience in interacting with them, and are more familiar with activities that take place in their kindergartens. Furthermore, there are some indications that the two parents differ in their perception of a guiding task, with mothers more oriented

to the process and fathers, to task completion (Conner, Knight, & Cross, 1997).

Over and above the differences between fathers' and mothers' writing mediation, parents within a family exhibited similar levels of literate and emotional mediation. This resemblance probably stemmed from their working with the same child, parental mutual influence, and shared pedagogical beliefs.

Writing Mediation in Different Tasks

It has been found in the literature that different tasks affect the nature of parent–child interactions (Kermani & Brenner, 2000). When the tasks are more constructed and require specific outcomes, parents tend to be more directive. Similar trends have appeared in studies in which parents wrote with their children. Aram and Levin (2001) and Aram (2002) employed writing in two tasks: writing words and writing names. Besser-Biron (2010) extended the variation to include writing of words, an invitation to a birthday party, and a story. Task variations had some effects on writing mediation. Aram found that mothers were more directive in guiding writing of words than of names, and were warmer and more cooperative in writing names. These differences probably relate to the dyad's confidence. Notice that writing names is probably more prevalent in the home than writing new words (Levin & Aram, 2004; Treiman, Cohen, Mulqueeny, Kessler, & Schechtman, 2007). Furthermore, children's writing of names is on a more advanced level than their writing of new words, and many mothers may be aware of this phenomenon. Besser-Biron found that parents were least directive and created the warmest atmosphere when writing an invitation to a birthday party, probably because of the message of the text. They were most directive when guiding their children in writing a story, possibly because of task complexity.

Writing Mediation of Children with Special Needs

Children with special needs pose particular difficulties during parent–child teaching interactions (Kelly & Barnard, 2000). Studying the context of parent–child collaborative writing can shed light on the guiding methods of parents of children with special needs. Parental writing mediation was studied in two groups of kindergartners: children with hearing impairment (HI) and children with attention-deficit/hyperactivity disorder (ADHD).

Literacy acquisition is a difficult endeavor for many children with HI (Musselman, 2000). Such children lack access to the phonemes of the spoken language; hence, they have less opportunity to master the alphabetic principle in the way that children with normal hearing do. Still, given a supportive literacy environment, the literacy development of children with HI parallels that of hearing children (Williams, 2004). However, young children with HI experience fewer parent–child literacy-related interactions relative to hearing children (Marschark, 1993). It seems that parents of children with HI attribute high significance to oral linguistic interactions and are less aware of the benefits of literacy interactions with their children.

A comparison was drawn between mothers of HI kindergartners and mothers of normally hearing kindergartners on maternal literate and emotional mediation in a joint writing task. In addition, children's literacy was assessed on word writing, word recognition, letter naming, and so forth (Aram & Most, 2007; Aram, Most, & Ben Simon, 2008; Most, Aram, & Andorn, 2006). Children with HI showed lower literacy skills compared to their normally hearing counterparts, and their mothers used significantly lower levels of literate mediation. Mothers of children with HI were more directive and intrusive, using significantly more reinforcements, criticisms, and physical contacts than did mothers of hearing children. Nevertheless, mothers of children with HI were as warm and cooperative as mothers of hearing children. The success of these mothers in maintaining a harmonious atmosphere in a teaching context may have stemmed from these mothers being highly involved in teaching their children, and their children being accustomed to experiencing frequent maternal teaching from the cradle. Both literate and emotional mediation predicted several literate skills, even beyond children's

level of hearing loss and age, though prediction was higher in literate mediation. These findings suggest that writing mediation possibly contributes to these children's literacy as it does for hearing children, and that writing mediation of children with HI might be improved by decreasing its intrusiveness and increasing its literate mediation level.

Children with ADHD are also at academic risk. There is evidence that their scholastic achievements are often lower than those of their peers (e.g., Merrell & Tymms, 2001). Some studies report that links between symptoms of ADHD and lower literacy already exist in kindergarten (Willicutt et al., 2007). Literate and emotional writing mediation of parents was examined among kindergartners with ADHD and their regular counterparts. Children's literacy was assessed by phonological awareness, word writing, and letter naming (Aram, Bazelet, & Goldman, in press).

Parents in the two groups did not differ on the level of their literate mediation, despite the fact that children with ADHD scored lower on literacy skills. Still, in both groups, children's literacy correlated significantly and substantially with the level of parental literate mediation. Most importantly, parents of children with ADHD differed greatly from their counterparts on the level of emotional mediation. They succeeded less in gaining children's cooperation and in creating a warm atmosphere, and used more reinforcements, criticisms, urging, and physical contacts relative to parents of children without ADHD.

Moreover, among children with ADHD, positive atmosphere and cooperation levels correlated significantly with children's literacy. This finding suggests that parents who succeeded in creating emotionally positive teaching interactions and in gaining their children's cooperation promoted children's literacy. Among children without ADHD, significant negative correlations emerged among criticisms, urging, and physical contacts on the one hand, and children's literacy on the other: The more intrusive the parents, the lower their children scored on literacy. Interestingly, these negative correlations were not found in the group of children with ADHD. It is possible that in children with ADHD, these behaviors (e.g., criticisms, touching) help parents manage their children's behavior, thereby assisting them in learning.

Intervention Promoting Writing Mediation

Intervention studies targeting parents with the aim of improving children's language and literacy were carried out with respect to storybook reading. A recent meta-analysis provided evidence that interventions enhancing interactive reading promoted not only expressive but also receptive vocabulary relative to regular reading (Mol et al., 2008). The question has been raised whether and how to enhance the level of writing mediation of low SES mothers through intervention, thereby increasing their children's alphabetic skills (Levin & Aram, in press).

Mothers of kindergartners were invited to take part in a program to enhance their children's school readiness. They were divided into three groups, with each group learning how to guide children in a different domain: writing, storybook reading, and visual–motor skills. A fourth no-intervention control group was also included. In the writing group, mothers were taught to guide children in writing words on a high level: segmenting words into sounds, searching letters to represent these sounds, and printing letters. In the storybook reading group, mothers were coached in reading books interactively. In the visual–motor skills group, they were taught to guide children in cutting, gluing, coloring, and so forth.

Each group underwent a program that included a 3-hour workshop in which mothers were coached on how to improve their children's competencies in the group's specific domain. Three times a week for 7 weeks the mothers and their children participated in half-hour structured dyadic interactions, and weekly tutorial home visits followed. Maternal *literate* mediation was assessed in all groups by videotaping joint writing of words three times: at pretest, at the immediate posttest, and at the delayed posttest 2½ months later.

The intervention program improved maternal literate writing mediation only in the writing mediation group, with most mothers approaching the highest possible guid-

ance level. These findings suggest that writing mediation can be enhanced uniquely by coaching mothers in guiding children in the process of writing, and that such guidance is highly productive. Coaching mothers on how to guide children's learning in other domains does not affect writing mediation because performing this joint activity on a high level demands understanding and teaching of the principles underlying the written system.

Children's alphabetic skills were assessed three times in kindergarten: at pretest, at the immediate posttest, and at the delayed posttest. Children were tested on naming and sounding letters, isolating initial sounds of spoken words, reporting initial letters of spoken words, recognizing printed words, and spelling words. Children of mothers who were coached on guided writing overall improved more on alphabetic skills than their counterparts in all other groups. This relative improvement was maintained in the delayed posttest. These findings suggest that guiding mothers on the writing task has a substantial and direct effect on children's alphabetic skills, whereas other joint activities related to school readiness have only some effects on these skills. These conclusions indicate the importance of literate interactions within the family in general, and of joint writing in particular, for children's growth in the alphabetic skills that contribute to reading/spelling acquisition in school. Whereas storybook reading has become a normative parent–child activity recommended to parents from the nursery, parents and educators are less aware of the importance and the potential of joint writing activities.

The studies described in this chapter on videotaped parent–child interactions were carried out in Israel among Hebrew-speaking families. However, this approach to measuring parental support of writing has recently been elaborated for other cultures and languages, English and Cantonese, and utilized in original studies (Lin et al., 2009; Worzalla, Pess, Taub, & Skibbe, 2009).

In summary, multiple studies using the new methodology developed by Aram and Levin to assess writing mediation have found that parents have different, typical, central levels of writing mediation that they frequently employ across children and tasks, on the literate and the emotional scales. Parental level of mediation, mostly literate mediation, is connected to children's concurrent alphabetic skills and predicts acquisition of reading and spelling skills in school. Concomitantly, parents adapt their level of writing mediation on the literate scales to their children's literacy, increasing the level for more advanced children. Comparisons between mothers and fathers have shown that mothers exhibit higher literate mediation and maintain a more positive emotional interaction. Yet mothers and fathers of the same family show similar guiding behaviors, reflecting a "family culture." Parental mediation is also adapted to the characteristics of children who have special needs, and to parents' conceptions of their children's difficulties. Mothers of children with special needs (children with HI or ADHD) more frequently use intrusive behaviors, such as criticizing and touching their children. However, mothers of children with HI succeed in maintaining a warm and cooperative atmosphere, whereas mothers of children with ADHD frequently do not. Finally, parental writing mediation can be improved to a high level by an intervention coaching parents to understand the written code and to deliver it to children by guiding them in writing. However, coaching mothers on interactive storybook reading or on training children on visual–motor skills, both of which may be considered relevant to children's writing, has not proved useful in enhancing maternal writing mediation. The work described in this chapter has shed light on the productivity of parent–child writing interaction in early literacy development among children from different backgrounds and with specific needs. It also has demonstrated the ability to improve parent–child writing interactions. All of these findings hold important promise for children's learning and scholastic success.

References

Aram, D. (2002). Joint writing of dictated words versus proper names: Analysis of low SES mother–kindergartner dyads. *Journal of Research in Childhood Education, 17*(1), 47–61.

Aram, D. (2007). Sensitivity and consistency of maternal writing mediation to twin kindergartners. *Early Education and Development, 18,* 71–92.

Aram, D. (2010). Writing with young children: A comparison of paternal and maternal guidance. *Journal of Research in Reading, 33*(1), 4–19.

Aram, D., Bazelet, I., & Goldman, H. (in press). Early

literacy and parental writing mediation in young children with and without ADHD. *European Journal of Special Needs Education.*

Aram, D., & Levin, I. (2001). Mother–child joint writing in low SES: Sociocultural factors, maternal mediation, and emergent literacy. *Cognitive Development, 16,* 831–852.

Aram, D., & Levin, I. (2004). The role of maternal mediation of writing to kindergartners in promoting literacy achievements in second grade: A longitudinal perspective. *Reading and Writing: An Interdisciplinary Journal, 17,* 387–409.

Aram, D., & Most, T. (2007, December). *Parent–child literacy interactions with deaf or hard of hearing (D/HH) kindergartners.* Paper presented at the Conference of the Israeli Society for Language and Literacy, Tel Aviv University, Israel.

Aram, D., Most, T., & Ben Simon, A. (2008). Early literacy of kindergartners with hearing impairment: The role of mother–child collaborative writing. *Topics of Early Childhood Special Education, 28,* 31–42.

Besser-Biron, S. (2010). *Parental mediation in writing assignments and early literacy of precocious readers: A comparison with children of the same age and with children of the same reading level.* Unpublished doctoral dissertation, Tel-Aviv University, Tel-Aviv, Israel.

Biringen, Z., & Robinson, J. (1991). Emotional availability in mother–child interactions: A reconceptualization for research. *American Journal of Orthopsychiatry, 61,* 258–271.

Bissex, G. L. (1980). *GNYS AT WRK: A child learns to read and write.* Cambridge, MA: Harvard University Press.

Bond, J. T., Galinsky, E., & Swanberg, J. E. (1998). *The 1997 National Study of the Changing Workplace.* New York: Family and Work Institute.

Boudreau, D. (2005). Use of a parent questionnaire in emergent and early literacy assessment of preschool children. *Language, Speech, and Hearing Services in Schools, 36,* 33–47.

Burns, M. S., & Casbergue, R. (1992). Parent–child interaction in a letter-writing context. *Journal of Reading Behavior, 24,* 289–231.

Bus, A. G., van IJzendoorn, M. H., & Pellegrini, A. D. (1995). Storybook reading makes for success in learning to read: A meta analysis on intergenerational transmission of literacy. *Review of Educational Research, 65,* 1–21.

Cinamon, R. G., Weisel, A., & Tzuk, K. (2007). Work–family conflict within the family: Crossover effects, perceived parent–child interaction quality, parental self-efficacy, and life role attributions. *Journal of Career Development, 34,* 79–100.

Clay, M. M. (1975). *What did I write?* Portsmouth, NH: Heinemann.

Conner, D. R., Knight, D. K., & Cross, D. R. (1997). Mothers' and fathers' scaffolding of their 2-year-olds during problem-solving and literacy interactions. *British Journal of Developmental Psychology, 15,* 323–338.

DeBaryshe, B. D., Buell, M. J., & Binder, J. C. (1996).

What a parent brings to the table: Young children writing with and without parental assistance. *Journal of Literacy Research, 28*, 71–90.

Echols, L. D., West, R. F., Stanovich, K. E., & Zehr, K. S. (1996). Using children's literacy activities to predict growth in verbal cognitive skills: A longitudinal investigation. *Journal of Educational Psychology, 88*, 296–304.

Edelsky, C. (2006). *With literacy and justice for all: Rethinking the social in language and education* (3rd ed.). Mahwah, NJ: Erlbaum.

Ehri, L. C., Nunes, S. R., Stahl, S. A., & Willows, D. M. (2001). Systematic phonics instruction helps students learn to read: Evidence from the National Reading Panel's meta-analysis. *Review of Educational Research, 71*, 393–447.

Eufimia, T. (2008). Kindergarten reading and writing curricula in the European Union. *Literacy, 42*, 162–170.

Ferreiro, E., & Teberosky, A. (1982). *Literacy before schooling.* Heinemann, Portsmouth, NH: Heinemann.

Feuerstein, R., & Feuerstein, S. (1991). Mediated learning experience: A theoretical review. In R. Feuerstein, P. Klein, & A. J. Tannenbaum (Eds.), *Mediated learning experience (MLE): Theoretical, psychosocial, and learning implications* (pp. 3–51). London: Freund Publishing House.

Foy, J. G., & Mann, V. (2003). Home literacy environment and phonological awareness in preschool children: Differential effects for rhyme and phoneme awareness. *Applied Psycholinguistics, 24*, 59–88.

Goodman, K. (1967). Reading: A psycholinguistic guessing game. *Journal of the Reading Specialist, 6*, 126–135.

Grolnick, W. S., & Slowiaczek, M. L. (1994). Parents' involvement in children's schooling: A multidimensional conceptualization and motivational model. *Child Development, 65*, 237–252.

Hildreth, G. (1936). Developmental sequence in name writing. *Child Development, 7*, 291–303.

Hood, M., Conlon, E., & Andrews, G. (2008). Preschool home literacy practices and children's literacy development: A longitudinal analysis. *Journal of Educational Psychology, 100*, 252–271.

Iredell, H. (1898). Eleanor learns to read. *Education, 19*, 233–238.

Kelly, J. F., & Barnard, K. E. (2000). Assessment of parent–child interaction: Implications for early intervention. In J. P. Shonkoff & S. J. Meisels (Eds.), *Handbook of early childhood intervention* (pp. 258–289). New York: Cambridge University Press.

Korat, O., & Levin, I. (2001). Maternal beliefs, mother–child interaction, and child's literacy: Comparison of independent and collaborative text writing between two social groups. *Applied Developmental Psychology, 22*, 397–420.

Korat, O., & Shamir, A. (2007). Electronic books versus adult readers: Effects on children's emergent literacy as a function of social class. *Journal of Computer Assisted Learning, 23*, 248–259.

Kermani, H., & Brenner, M. E. (2000). Maternal scaf-

folding in the child's zone of proximal development across tasks: Cross-cultural perspectives. *Journal of Research in Childhood Education, 15*, 30–52.

Levin, I., & Aram, D. (2004). Children's names contribute to early literacy: A linguistic and social perspective In D. Ravid & H. Bat-Zeev Shyldkrot (Eds.), *Perspectives on language and language development* (pp. 219–241). Dordrecht: Kluwer.

Levin, I., & Aram, D. (in press). Mother–child joint writing and storybook reading and their effects on kindergartners' literacy: An intervention study. *Reading and Writing: An Interdisciplinary Journal.*

Levin, I., & Bus, A. G. (2003). How is emergent writing based on drawing?: Analyses of children's products and their sorting by children and mothers. *Developmental Psychology, 39*, 891–905.

Levin, I., & Korat, O. (1993). Sensitivity to phonological, morphological and semantic cues in early reading and writing in Hebrew. *Merrill–Palmer Quarterly, 39*, 213–232.

Lightfoot, C., & Valsiner, J. (1992). Parental beliefs systems under the influence: Social guidance in construction of personal cultures. In I. E. Sigel, A. V. McGillicudy-DeLisi, & J. Goodnow (Eds.), *Parental beliefs systems* (pp. 393–414). Hillsdale, NJ: Erlbaum.

Lin, D., McBride-Chang, C., Aram, D., Levin, I., Cheung, Y. M., Chow, Y. Y., et al. (2009). Maternal mediation of writing in Chinese children. *Language and Cognitive Processes, 24*, 1286–1311.

Marschark, M. (1993). *Psychological development of deaf children.* New York: Oxford University Press.

Merrell, C., & Tymms, P. B. (2001). Inattention, hyperactivity, and impulsiveness: Their impact on academic achievement and progress. *British Journal of Educational Psychology, 71*, 43–56.

Mol, S. E., Bus, A. G., de Jong, M. T., & Smeets, D. J. H. (2008). Added value of dialogic parent–child book reading: A meta-analysis. *Early Education and Development, 19*, 7–26.

Moon, M., & Hoffman, C. D. (2008). Mothers' and fathers' differential expectancies and behaviors: Parent × child gender effects. *Journal of Genetic Psychology, 169*, 261–279.

Most, T., Aram, D., & Andorn, T. (2006). The early literacy skills of young hearing impaired children: A comparison between two educational systems. *Volta Review, 106*, 5–28.

Musselman, C. (2000). How do children who can't hear learn to read an alphabetic script?: A review of the literature on reading and deafness. *Journal of Deaf Studies and Deaf Education, 5*, 9–31.

Neuman, S. B., & Roskos, K. (2005). The state of state pre-kindergartners' standards. *Early Childhood Research Quarterly, 20*, 125–145.

Neumann, M. M., Hood, M., & Neumann, D. (2008). The scaffolding of emergent literacy skills in the home environment: A case study. *Early Childhood Educational Journal, 36*, 313–319.

Perlman, M., & Fletcher, B., A. (2008). Literacy instruction in Canadian child care centers. *Journal of Research in Childhood Education, 23*, 139–155.

Pettit, G. S., Bates, J. E., & Dodge, K. A. (1997). Supportive parenting, ecological context, and children's adjustment: A seven-year longitudinal study. *Child Development, 68*, 908–923.

Shonkoff, J. P., & Phillips, D. A. (2002). *From neurons to neighborhoods: The science of early childhood development.* Washington, DC: National Academy Press.

Stanovich, K. E., & West, R. F. (1989). Exposure to print and orthographic processing. *Reading Research Quarterly, 24*, 402–433.

Stright, A. D., & Herr, M. Y. (2009). Maternal scaffolding of children's problem solving and children's adjustment in kindergarten: Hmong families in the United States. *Journal of Educational Psychology, 101*, 207–218.

Sulzby, E. (1989). Forms of writing and rereading from writing: A preliminary report. In J. Mason (Ed.), *Reading and writing connections* (pp. 51–63). Boston: Allyn & Bacon.

Tolchinsky-Landsmann, L. (1986). Literacy development and pedagogical implications: Evidence from the Hebrew system of writing. In Y. M. Goodman (Ed.), *How children construct literacy* (pp. 26–44). Newark, DE: International Reading Association.

Tolchinsky-Landsmann, L. (2003). *The cradle of culture and what children know about writing and numbers before being taught.* Mahwah, NJ: Erlbaum.

Tolchinsky-Landsmann, L., & Levin, I. (1987). Writing in four to six years olds: Representation of semantic and phonetic similarities and differences. *Journal of Child Language, 14*, 127–144.

Treiman, R., Cohen, J., Mulqueeny, K., Kessler, B., & Schechtman, S. (2007). Young children's knowledge about printed names. *Child Development, 78*, 1458–1471.

Tudge, J. R., & Winterhoff, P. A. (1993). Vygotsky, Piaget and Bandura: Perspectives on the relations between the social world and cognitive development. *Human Development, 36*, 61–81.

Verhallen, M. J., Bus, A. G., & de Jong, M. T. (2006). The promise of multimedia stories for kindergarten children at-risk. *Journal of Educational Psychology, 98*, 410–419.

Vygotsky, L. (1978). *Mind in society.* Cambridge, MA: Harvard University Press.

Williams, C. L. (2004). Emergent literacy of deaf children. *Journal of Deaf Studies and Deaf Education, 9*, 352–365.

Willicutt, E. G., Betjemann, R. S., Wadsworth, S. J., Samuelsson, S., Corley, R., Defrie, J. C., et al. (2007). Preschool twin study of the relation between attention-deficit/hyperactivity disorder and prereading skills. *Reading and Writing, 20*, 103–125.

Worzalla, S., Pess, R., Taub, A., & Skibbe, L. (2009, June). *Parent writing instruction and preschoolers' writing outcomes.* Paper presented at the Society for Scientific Studies of Reading Conference, Boston.

13

Developing Children's Print Knowledge through Adult–Child Storybook Reading Interactions: Print Referencing as an Instructional Practice

LAURA M. JUSTICE
SHAYNE PIASTA

A variety of data sources make it clear that the number of children who do not meet their full potential in reading achievement is disproportionate to the number of children who do (e.g., National Assessment of Education Progress [NAEP], 2006; Organisation for Economic Cooperation and Development, 2001). In other words, if we calculate the average level of reading achievement among children in the primary grades, a given child is probabilistically more likely to exhibit reading skills that are *below* the mean for his or her grade (or age) than *above* it. What is particularly perplexing about this issue is that our theoretical understanding of how reading develops over time as a set of intertwined cognitive processes and our applied knowledge of the conditions that can best support children's reading achievement are quite developed as substantive bodies of knowledge. The number of research studies included in recent meta-analyses on the former (Fox, 2009; Hammill, 2004; Swanson, Trainin, Necoechea, & Hammill, 2003) and the latter (e.g., Bus & van IJzendoorn, 1999; Mol, Bus, & de Jong, 2009; National Early Literacy Panel [NELP], 2008; Ritter, Barnett, Denny, & Albin, 2009) helps us to

appreciate the sheer volume of work conducted on these issues. That this volume of empirical work exists simultaneously with data showing that children today, particularly those nested within certain subgroups (e.g., Latino and African American pupils) (NAEP, 2006), starkly underachieve in reading development makes it clear that reading-related research is not being adequately and/ or efficiently translated into effective instructional practices.

In this chapter, we discuss a specific instructional practice—*print referencing*—that can be used to increase children's early literacy development in the preschool years, particularly a specific set of skills we refer to as *print knowledge*. We have drafted this chapter with the explicit goal of translating accumulated research findings on the efficacy and effectiveness of print referencing into meaningful suggestions regarding how one might use this practice within routine educational settings, including both the classroom and the home. Our particular concern is children who may be at risk of not achieving their full potential in reading because of environmental or developmental disadvantages, and readers will note that much of our research on print referencing has involved these populations.

We have organized this chapter to provide first a brief overview of the set of early literacy skills targeted by this instructional practice (print knowledge), as well as the theoretical framework that helps to understand why this instructional practice brings about short-term change in children's early literacy development and longer-term improvements in children's reading achievement. We then discuss specific instructional considerations for using this instructional approach, including issues related to techniques, materials, scope, and sequence. Finally, we close this chapter with a brief summary of research findings on the impact of this instructional approach to support readers' understanding of how findings from research studies can be translated into instructional practices.

Overview and Theoretical Framework

Print Knowledge as a Precursor to Skilled Reading

Theoretical models of skilled reading make it clear that numerous early skills and abilities represent important precursors to being able to read fluently and meaningfully (e.g., Scarborough, 2001). Likewise, empirical reports also show that a variety of early skills and abilities hold significant and reliable relations to future reading outcomes (e.g., NELP, 2008). One particular set of skills that is consistently represented in both theoretical models and empirical reports as an important precursor of skillful reading is that of print knowledge. As we use the term in this chapter, *print knowledge* is a multidimensional construct that describes children's emerging knowledge of the forms and functions of written language (Justice & Ezell, 2002; Storch & Whitehurst, 2002). It describes a constellation of skills to represent children's knowledge of *book and print organization* (the ways print is organized in various texts), *print meaning* (functions of print as a communication device), *letters* (distinctive features and names of individual letters), and *words* (combinatorial units of written language that map onto spoken language). Such skills lay an important foundation for later achievement in reading, particularly word recogni-

tion; numerous studies and several recent meta-analyses have shown that children's knowledge about print, particularly their knowledge of letters, is one of the more reliable and robust indicators of the ease with which they will progress as readers (Hammill, 2004; Morris, Bloodgood, Lomax, & Perney, 2003; Muter, Hulme, Snowling, & Stevenson, 2004; NELP, 2008). The implication of such findings is that intervention practices that increase children's knowledge about print during the years of early childhood may not only have short-term impacts on print knowledge (e.g., knowledge of how books are organized, knowledge of letter names) but also may benefit children's reading trajectory longitudinally.

Within the preschool years, young children show significant individual differences in their knowledge about the forms and functions of print. For instance, it would not be unusual for a preschool teacher with a class of 16 4-year-olds to find that some children can name all of the letters of the alphabet, whereas others can name none or very few. Likewise, some children may even know how to identify some familiar and functional words in their environment, including their own names, whereas others show little awareness of the role or forms of print in their surroundings. What has become increasingly clear in the last decade of research on the nature of these individual differences is that such early differences (1) can be meaningful in the long term for estimating and understanding children's future risks for reading achievement (e.g., Catts, Fey, Tomblin, & Zhang, 2002; Chaney, 1998) and (2) are reliably associated with certain child- and family-level characteristics (e.g., Justice, Bowles, & Skibbe, 2006; Sénéchal & LeFevre, 2002). For instance, children with a specific language impairment (SLI) perform about one standard deviation lower on a variety of measures of print knowledge compared to age-matched children whose language skills are typical (e.g., Cabell, Justice, Zucker, & McGinty, 2009; Justice et al., 2006). These early differences in print knowledge seem to have long-term implications for reading achievement in children with SLI; by some estimates, this one standard deviation difference in early literacy skill perpetuates over time, such that slightly more than 4 out of 10 children with SLI

(42%) exhibit a reading disability in second grade (Catts et al., 2002). When predicting a given kindergartner's risks for being among those who will exhibit a reading disability in second grade, print knowledge (specifically, a measure of alphabetic knowledge) as assessed at age 5 is the single best unique predictor (Catts et al., 2002).

Whether one's concern is children with SLI or the much broader population of children who appear to be disproportionately at risk for future reading problems, such as children reared in homes with limited physical or psychological resources (Roberts, Jurgens, & Burchinal, 2005), the content of this chapter is designed to help educators and other child caregivers actively and explicitly support children's development of print knowledge in the earliest years of literacy development. In so doing, both theory and research point to the likelihood that early boosts in children's print knowledge will have long-term positive impacts on their reading outcomes, while simultaneously reducing risk for future reading problems (Catts et al., 2002).

Theoretical Framework

Development of print knowledge begins to emerge early in life for many children (Rowe, 2008) and largely seems to develop in relation to the frequency and quality of children's experiences with print within those activity contexts in which print is a salient characteristic (Sénéchal, 2006). These diverse activity contexts within our very print-rich culture might include, for instance, children's dramatic play, if that play involves some sort of print (e.g., price tags on items being bartered). Long viewed as a particularly important stimulant to children's development of print knowledge, and the specific context in which we are interested, is adult–child shared book reading; this activity context, by its nature, provides children with direct exposure to print. Indeed, children's participation in adult–child shared book reading interactions has long been viewed principally as an important means for helping young children to learn about print forms and functions, and some children's books— such as alphabet books and others texts that feature highly "salient" print features (e.g., characters with speech bubbles, words em-

bedded within the illustrations; see Zucker, Justice, & Piasta, 2009)—appear specifically designed to support this learning. (It is important to recognize that the shared reading context, and the interactions embedded within, also offers direct support to numerous other areas of development, including language skills.)

Nonetheless, an unexpected finding of an accruing body of research is that most young children appear to have very little contact with print when they participate in adult–child reading interactions (e.g., Evans & Saint-Aubin, 2005; Ezell & Justice, 2000; Hammett Price, van Kleeck, & Huberty, 2009; Justice, Pullen, & Pence, 2008; Phillips & McNaughton, 1990; Yaden, Smolkin, & Conlon, 1989). Developmental research has shown that when children look at storybooks, they direct about 98% of their visual attention to illustrations within the text (Justice et al., 2008); in other words, children show a strong predisposition to look at pictures within storybooks instead of print. While this is perhaps not particularly surprising, at least from a developmental perspective, it does raise questions about a perspective advanced in a number of seminal papers from the 1980s strongly suggesting that young children actively engage with print during adult–child reading interactions and that, in turn, this likely serves as a key mechanism through which most children develop their knowledge about print (e.g., Goodman, 1986; Snow, 1983; Sulzby, 1985). Goodman (1986), for instance, theorized that young children develop knowledge of print within such environmental contexts through the process of "continuously interacting with, organizing, and analyzing the meanings of the visible language" (p. 7); in turn, through this active engagement with print (or "visible language"), children develop a schema or model that represents the "rules about the features of written language in situational contexts" (p. 7). Such perspectives seem to situate the child as an active learner whose attention is directed toward the print within storybooks or other environmental contexts so as to permit analysis and internalization of the rules and features of written language.

This body of work is situated within a larger set of studies from the late 1970s and 1980s that was significant for drawing attention to the relatively sophisticated knowledge about print that young children do indeed possess (e.g., Hiebert, 1978, 1981). Nonetheless, with respect to the actual mechanisms through which children develop their knowledge of print, early theories proposing that children actively engage with print in environmental contexts and, in turn, develop schemas to represent the rules and features of written language, have not resulted in unifying and generalizable theories that represent the diverse circumstances through which children develop print knowledge. In fact, while such observations may well represent valid and highly local interpretations of data drawn from the single cases and small groups of children represented in early study reports, subsequent studies that involve far greater numbers of children and use a more varied set of study methodologies generally fail to find much evidence that young children continuously interact with, organize, and analyze the forms and functions of print when they participate in storybook-reading interactions with adults. This has implications for developing *generalizable* theories of print knowledge development (and the role that storybook-reading interactions can and do play in this developmental area) and for using these theories to derive meaningful educational practices that can help a majority of children.

If we develop instructional practices based on these early theories of print knowledge development, we might presume that the simple practice of reading storybooks often to young children would, in and of itself, provide a healthy boost to this area of development. However, because young children have such a strong predisposition to look at anything but the print within storybooks, it is simply not the case that reading often to young children will substantially stimulate their print knowledge (see Justice & Ezell, 2002). In fact, left to their own accord, preschoolers' fixations on print within storybooks represent less than 5% of their visual attention to the pages of a children's storybook (e.g., Evans & Saint-Aubin, 2005; Evans, Williamson, & Pursoo, 2008; Justice et al., 2008). Similarly, discourse analyses and observational work have shown that even with repeated exposure to books with interesting print features, children's comments and questions focus predominantly on illustrations (< 10% of verbalizations) and seldom on print (Yaden, Smolkin, & MacGillivray, 1993). More recently, Hammett Price and colleagues (2009), in a study of child and parent talk when reading storybooks in the home environment, also found that about 4% of 3- and 4-year-old children's talk focused on print within the books.

Adults, too, show a strong predisposition to talk about the storybook and pictures in books rather than the print within. Study findings show that adults seldom makes any explicit references to the print using verbal (e.g., commenting on print within the text) or nonverbal means (e.g., tracking the print while reading) (Ezell & Justice, 2000; Hammett Price et al., 2009; Phillips & McNaughton, 1990; Zucker et al., 2009; Yaden et al., 1993). Although some types of texts, such as alphabet books and expository texts, do stimulate more attention to print on the part of adults reading with children (Hammett Price et al., 2009; Zucker et al., 2009), the content of adult talk during storybook-reading interactions typically involves very few explicit references to print. Hammett Price and colleagues' (2009) recent study of home-based storybook reading for a predominantly middle- to upper-class sample of parent–child dyads found that about 6% of parents' talk focused on print within storybooks. Their coding system captured not only any talk about letters or words but also general print concepts such as the role of the author and placement of the title.

We certainly recognize *why* adults and children would show a preference for talking about and looking at the illustrations in storybooks; however, it is somewhat perplexing that young children seem to have very little contact with print even within the very print-rich activity of adult–child shared reading. As was recently asserted by Evans and Saint-Aubin (2005), "It is difficult to see how shared reading, without additional explicit references to the print within the books, can be a major vehicle for developing children's understanding of orthography or print-specific skills" (p. 918). Indeed, it is tricky to reconcile these statements (and the convergent findings on which they are based) with earlier accounts asserting that adult–child shared storybook reading and the interactions embedded within this context serve as a critical mechanism for advancing young children's print knowledge.

On the contrary, the assertion of Evans and Saint-Aubin (2005) as well as others earlier (in particular, see Yaden et al., 1989), converge with a body of recent study findings that the frequency of children's storybook-reading interactions with their parents does not appear to be critically linked to or predictive of children's development of print knowledge (see Sénéchal, 2006) or, if it is, only modestly (see Mol et al., 2009). By consequence, the frequency with which young children are read to by their parents or others does not, in and of itself, appear to be a key mechanism through which children learn about print forms and functions, largely because children have virtually no contact with print during adult–child storybook reading interactions. Rather, the *critical mechanism* that has explanatory power based on a variety of research methodologies is that of direct and explicit referencing of or teaching about print by parents (or other adults) that serves to promote children's active engagement with and learning about print embedded within adult–child reading interactions or any other literacy context (e.g., Gong & Levy, 2009; Justice & Ezell, 2000, 2002; Sénéchal, 2006). Explicit referencing of print directs children's visual attention (and related cognitive resources) toward print and provides them with information about print forms and functions, thereby mediating not only children's interactions with print but also their developing knowledge about print. As importantly, we also believe that explicit referencing of print can help children to view print as an interesting and worthwhile focus of attention.

From Theory to Practice

As we look to developing educational practices that are effective in providing explicit support for children's development of print knowledge, particularly for youngsters who may need assistance in this area, there are two key points we may draw from the literature. First, a critical mechanism through which young children develop print knowledge is explicit referencing of print by parents and other caregivers (e.g., teachers), rather than sheer exposure to print within such literacy activities. Second, the prototypical adult–child shared storybook-reading interaction features very little explicit referencing of print by parents or other caregivers, and very little contact with print by the children to whom they read. With these two points in mind, it seems plausible to theorize that we might modify the prototypical adult–child shared storybook-reading interaction so that it features at least modest amounts of explicit referencing of print by caregivers so as to heighten children's contact with print; in turn, we might hypothesize that this would advance children's growth in print knowledge.

Our work and that of others has experimentally tested this hypothesis, showing that, indeed, young children's print knowledge can be significantly advanced through simple modifications to the nature of the adult–child shared storybook-reading interaction, so that children have more contact with print and increased opportunities to learn about the forms and functions of print (Gong & Levy, 2009; Justice & Ezell, 2000, 2002; Justice, Kaderavek, Fan, Sofka, & Hunt, 2009; Lovelace & Stewart, 2007; for nonexperimental treatments of this hypothesis, see also Ezell, Justice, & Parsons, 2000; van Bysterveldt, Gillon, & Moran, 2006). This modification involves adult use of print references comprising both verbal and nonverbal techniques that systematically and explicitly direct children's attention to the print in the book and teach them about specific aspects of print forms and functions, as we discuss next. Before doing so, however, a few points are warranted.

First, while we endorse the developmental importance of drawing children's attention to print within reading interactions, we also wholly recognize that adults read with children for multiple purposes. At times one reads to children to expose them to compelling narrative structures or interesting words, whereas at other times one reads to children to lull them into sleep. By no means are we suggesting that every time one reads to children, one ought to make print the predominant focus. In fact, discussions about print can always be secondary (or even tertiary) to other goals and foci of reading. Second, we also recognize that when one shifts the balance of shared reading interactions to include a heightened focus on print, it could have the unintended consequence of decreasing the adult's or the child's focus on other important features of the text, such as key language structures or words. Consequently, our perspective is that references to print—or any feature of a storybook—should not detract from the adult's or the child's broader experience with the text, including experiencing the story or content embedded within.

Instructional Considerations

Here, we provide a practical overview of how adults—including teachers, parents, and other caregivers of young children—can integrate explicit references to print within their storybook-reading interactions with young children. We base our suggestions on more than a decade of research exploring how adults can best leverage the storybook-reading context as a means to increase significantly what young children know about print across all four areas discussed previously: print and book organization, print meaning, letters, and words. Many of the considerations we present here represent our most recent and thoroughly developed instantiation of this instructional practice, designed to follow a systematic scope and sequence of instruction that spans a 30-week period of implementation by teachers within their classrooms and/or parents within their homes (see Justice et al., 2009; Justice & Sofka, 2010). This noted, the use of print referencing as an early literacy instructional practice is a highly flexible approach: It can be used within one-on-one storybook-reading interactions or during reading sessions with small or large groups; it can be used by teachers, parents, specialists, and others; it can be used once or twice per week, or be part of a daily reading routine; and, it can be used for only brief durations of time (e.g., 4–8 weeks) or longer (e.g., an entire academic year).

Techniques

Integrating explicit references to print into adult–child shared storybook-reading interactions involves use of simple nonverbal and verbal techniques that serve to (1) draw children's attention toward the print within the text and (2) provide children with informa-

tion about specific aspects of print forms and functions. Generally, we differentiate verbal and nonverbal references, with the former referring to questions and comments about print, and the latter referring to tracking the print when reading and pointing to print. Comparisons of children's visual attention to print within a storybook in the context of adult verbal or nonverbal print references have shown that both are equally evocative in recruiting children's visual attention to print (Justice et al., 2009). Table 13.1 provides a transcript of a teacher reading to her pupils while incorporating nonverbal and verbal print references. For purposes of space, we do not include a full-length transcript; however, we do note that discussion centered on print is only a modest aspect of this reading session, and does not predominate the experience. Rather, this transcript shows a brief interaction embedded within a broader reading experience that involves explicit discussion about certain print-related concepts.

Materials

Not all children's texts are equal in the opportunities they provide to encourage both adult and child talk about print. Some texts incorporate specific design features that appear naturally to evoke more talk about or visual attention to print (Justice et al., 2008; Zucker et al., 2009), particularly those texts with the following print-salient features:

- Visible sound: Character or object has a sound written nearby (e.g., *hiss* printed near a snake).
- Visible speech: Character has words nearby denoting spoken language (e.g., speech bubbles).
- Environmental print: Objects within illustrations are labeled (e.g., the word *school bus* is printed on the side of a bus).
- Change of font: Font changes in color or size for accent purposes.

Texts containing such salient print features, by virtue of their design, appear naturally to increase not only adults' and children's attention to and talk about print within texts (e.g., Zucker et al., 2009) but also to provide opportunities for adults to evoke children's

TABLE 13.1. Transcript of Whole-Class Read-Aloud in Which Teacher Uses Verbal and Nonverbal References to Print

Teacher		Reads text ("They liked the . . . freezing arctic winds").
	"It's interesting to me how the words move up the page like this. I wonder why the illustrator had the words move up the page like this?"	Tracks print within the illustration; comments on print; questions about print.
Child	"It's 'cuz it's like the wind. See . . ."	Holds hand up and sweeps pointer finger in a right motion.
Teacher	"Right, the words are moving like the wind. That makes sense to me because one of the words here is *winds*, actually, *arctic winds*."	Points to print; comments on print.
Child	"And it also says *snow* and there's snow in the picture too."	
Teacher	"Right, it says the words *snow, ice*, and *winds*. And you can see each of these things here in the picture; there's the snow, here's the ice, and here's the wind. I wonder what is going to happen next? Does anyone want to guess?"	Points to print (points to each word while reading them).
Child	"It's going to get colder 'cuz it's snowing."	
Child	"It's going to get cold."	
Teacher	"Let's turn the page and find out . . . "	

Note. Teacher and class are reading *Hot Hot Hot* (Layton, 2003).

interest in naturally occurring features of the text and engage them in conversations about these features. Elsewhere we have provided lists of children's texts that feature print-salient characteristics (see Justice et al., 2009).

Scope and Sequence

Print referencing as an instructional practice is designed to increase what young children know about print. As we discussed early in this chapter, print knowledge is a multidimensional construct that comprises, from our perspective, knowledge of print and book organization, print meaning, letters, and words. Children's knowledge in each of these areas is important to establishing a firm foundation of knowledge about print; consequently, the use of print referencing as an instructional approach involves carefully considering how each of these areas of print knowledge can be systematically supported over time. The notion of systematicity is an important one with respect to early

literacy instruction: Systematic instruction adheres to a specific scope and sequence of instruction to ensure that children have reasonable and repeated opportunities to learn crucial instructional targets (Justice, Mashburn, Hamre, & Pianta, 2008). To develop an instructional practice that systematically provides equal weight to the fourfold scope of print knowledge instruction in our most recent and fully manualized instantiation (Justice et al., 2009; Justice & Sofka, 2010) of this instructional approach, teachers and parents follow a prescribed sequence of 15 instructional targets cycled over a 30-week period. Within a given week, two objectives are addressed, typically in two to four reading sessions with a single storybook. For instance, in Week 1, teachers and parents read the storybook *My First Day of School* (Hallinan, 1987) and, within the context of this reading session, explicitly reference the print knowledge targets of environmental print and the concept of reading. These 15 targets are cycled repeatedly over time, meaning that the targets are not linearly or hierarchically ordered over a period of instruction but are revisited repeatedly (see Table 13.2 for a 20-week cycle). We cycle print knowledge targets because this provides repeated learning opportunities distributed over time, fostering not only breadth but also the depth of learning of different targets. Research on language intervention using cycles or alternating approaches to ordering instructional targets has shown superior learning gains relative to more vertically oriented approaches (see Tyler, Lewis, Haskill, & Tolbert, 2003).

Given our view on the importance of systematically organizing instruction over a period of time, we have developed a variety of approaches for supporting adherence to the prescribed instructional sequence. Currently, we couple simple 8½″ by 11″ text inserts that provide guidance on specific print knowledge areas and instructional targets to be addressed during a storybook-reading interaction using that text. The insert presents the two print targets, along with examples of how references to print can address each of the targets. Inserts also provide guidance on how one can scaffold children's participation in conversations about these targets using different strategies (e.g., open-ended questions). These inserts, coupled with professional development (PD) workshops and other materials (e.g., an implementation manual), are highly effective for increasing adults' explicit referencing of print when reading with children. Importantly, as we discuss next, when teachers and parents who read to young children systematically increase the attention they direct toward print, children experience substantial increases in what they know about print.

TABLE 13.2. Cycles Approach to Systematically Addressing Print Knowledge Objectives during a 20-Week Period of Instruction (Two to Four Storybook Reading Sessions per Week)

Week	Objectives
1	Environmental print, concept of reading
2	Print direction, concept of word in print
3	Author of book, function of print
4	Upper- and lowercase letters, page organization
5	Title of book, word identification
6	Concept of letter, page organization
7	Page order, letter names
8	Word identification, concept of letter
9	Author of book, letters and words
10	Short words and long words, function of print
11	Concept of letter, environmental print
12	Upper- and lowercase letters, page order
13	Title of book, function of print
14	Page organization, short words and long words
15	Letter names, concept of reading
16	Concept of letter, page order
17	Letters and words, letter names
18	Upper- and lowercase letters, concept of word in print
19	Short words and long words, print direction
20	Page organization, concept of reading

Note From Justice and Sofka (2010). Copyright 2010 by The Guilford Press. Reprinted by permission.

Research Support

Here, we provide a brief review of some of the available research supporting print referencing as an early childhood instructional practice, particularly evidence supporting the implementation of print referencing by both parents and teachers.

Parent[1] Implementation

Support for parent implementation of print referencing and its effects on children's print knowledge development is derived mainly from two experimental studies by Justice and colleagues (Justice & Ezell, 2000; Justice, Skibbe, McGinty, Piasta, & Petrill, in press), although nonexperimental treatments of this topic are also available (Ezell et al., 2000; van Bysterveldt et al., 2006). Both experimental studies involved 4-year-old children and parental implementation of a home-based book reading program in which some parents were randomly assigned to use embedded print references. Importantly, both studies found reliable effects of parental use of print references on children's print knowledge.

Justice and Ezell (2000) involved 28 parents and their typically developing preschool-age children in the first experimental test of a print-referencing intervention. All dyads completed a 4-week book reading program in their homes; they read two books twice a week, for 16 total reading sessions using eight different books. Dyads were randomly assigned to one of two reading conditions: 14 parents were assigned to embed verbal and nonverbal print references into their reading sessions, and 14 parents in a control condition were asked to read the storybooks to their children as they would normally. (Details on the methods used to instruct parents in use of print referencing are detailed in the original research report.) All dyads participated in an initial shared storybook reading with their children to capture their typical reading practices, and children in both conditions participated in pretest and posttest print knowledge assessments. Results of the study showed important changes in both parents' shared reading behaviors and children's print knowledge gains. Parents assigned to the print-referencing condition significantly increased their rates of verbal and nonverbal print referencing compared to parents in the control condition. Moreover, children who experienced print referencing also demonstrated significantly greater gains in recognizing words in print, segmenting and counting words, and demonstrating knowledge of basic print concepts, but not in naming or recognizing letters, or in recognizing print in context. All effects were moderate to large in size.

In a second study, Justice, Skibbe, and colleagues (in press) recruited 40 parent–child dyads to complete a 12-week home reading program; the primary focus of this study was assessing impacts of print referencing on children with SLI, a condition exhibited by all of the child participants. The dyads read one storybook four times per week for 12 weeks (or the equivalent of 48 reading sessions) using 12 different books. Parents randomly assigned to the print-referencing condition embedded nine print-related questions into each reading (e.g., "Where is the first letter on this page?"), whereas parents in a control condition (i.e., treated comparison) embedded nine picture-related questions into each reading (e.g., "How does the farmer feel now?"). Analysis of the print knowledge gains of children who completed the full 12-week intervention ($n = 29$) revealed results similar to those described earlier. Children who experienced print referencing made significantly greater gains in knowledge of print concepts than those in the comparison condition ($d = 1.13$). Effects did not extend to children's knowledge of letter names.

The latter study contributes to our understanding of the extent to which the impact of print referencing may generalize to children with disabilities (see also van Bysterveldt et al., 2006, for a study involving children with Down syndrome). Given the comparability of findings for both typically developing children and those with disabilities, we can surmise that parental use of print referencing during storybook reading is a relatively robust instructional practice that may benefit the print knowledge of young children of various developmental and skills levels. Moreover, the latter study also provides important information about the ecological and social validity of home-based early literacy intervention, as a large number of parents (28%) were unable to complete the study due to illness, time constraints, or adult reading difficulties (but note that attrition was not nearly as high [6%] in Justice & Ezell, 2000). (Attrition was not differential, however, between parents in the print referencing versus comparison conditions.) Although relatively few studies of book-reading interventions have addressed issues of fidelity and compliance (but see Lonigan & Whitehurst, 1998), these results showed that some parents face difficulties in providing home-based book reading interventions and may require a significant amount of support for successful implementation.

Teacher Implementation

Given the sheer number of children who participate in out-of-home caregiving arrangements during the preschool years, it is important to assess whether print referencing is a viable intervention approach when applied within child-care and preschool programs. Work by Girolametto and colleagues (Flowers, Girolametto, Weitzman, & Greenberg, 2007; Girolametto, Weitzman, Lefebvre, & Greenberg, 2007) represents the first published studies examining the efficacy of early childhood teachers' use of print referencing during shared adult–child storybook reading. Teacher participants in the study by Flowers and colleagues (2007; *n* = 16 at four early childhood centers) were part of a larger evaluation of an early language and literacy curriculum developed by the Hanen Centre of Canada. In the larger study, teachers were randomly assigned to receive PD and materials related to the language and literacy curriculum (i.e., intervention condition) or to a business-as-usual control. Teachers in the intervention condition received eight 2½-hour PD workshops across a 14-week period, one of which was devoted to shared adult–child storybook reading. During this particular inservice, teachers were taught three sets of strategies: (1) strategies for building story comprehension; (2) strategies for increasing print and sound references, including verbal and nonverbal print referencing; and (3) strategies for promoting narrative structure awareness. Teachers were videotaped conducting a small-group shared-reading activity with a group of four children enrolled in their classrooms prior to provision of PD, immediately following the conclusion of PD, and 9-months after the conclusion

of PD. Coding of the frequency with which teachers referenced print showed no reliable differences between those in the intervention versus control conditions. Findings suggested, therefore, that more intensive and/or focused supports may be necessary to influence teacher use of print referencing.

In a follow-up study, Girolametto and colleagues (2007) focused exclusively on teachers' shared storybook reading. Relevant content was excerpted from the original early language and literacy curriculum described earlier, and expanded to create a 2-day, stand-alone PD inservice for early childhood teachers. Sixteen teachers participated in the evaluation of the PD and were randomly assigned to intervention or control conditions. Teachers in both conditions received 12 hours of professional development workshops over a 2-week period. The first 6 hours of content were the same across conditions and targeted teachers' general pedagogical knowledge for fostering children's early language development. The second 6 hours of content differed by condition. Teachers in the intervention condition received PD on using shared adult–child storybook reading as a means of fostering language development and print knowledge, and emphasized use of print referencing. Teachers in the control condition received PD on fostering peer interactions. Teachers were videotaped conducting small-group shared reading and postreading activities with a group of four children enrolled in their classrooms prior to provision of professional development and again 2 weeks after the conclusion of PD. The frequency of teachers' verbal print references and children's responses to such print-related talk was coded for both videos. Results showed that teachers in the intervention condition used twice as many print references compared to teachers in the control condition, representing a significant difference. Children in the intervention condition were also significantly more likely to respond to these print references (rate of one response per minute) than those in the control condition (rate of one response per 3 minutes).

The promising results of Girolametto and colleagues (2007) have recently been scaled up by Justice and colleagues in a large, multistate effectiveness trial, with a particular focus on assessing impacts of teacher use of print referencing on children's short- and long-term development of print knowledge. Justice and colleagues (e.g., Justice et al., 2009; Piasta, Justice, McGinty, & Kaderavek, 2010) have assessed the impact of print referencing in a sample of 85 early childhood teachers and a random selection of 550 children enrolled in their classrooms. All teachers and children were drawn from preschool programs prioritizing enrollment of children considered at-risk for reading difficulties (e.g., Head Start, Title I, state-subsidized PreK). All teachers implemented a 30-week whole-class shared adult–child storybook-reading program involving the same set of 30 titles, and a subset of teachers was randomly assigned to embed print references within either two or four reading sessions per week to represent a planned contrast of dosage (e.g., some children participated in 60 reading sessions over 30 weeks, whereas other children participated in 120). A comprehensive description of the PD program used to support teacher implementation of this reading program is available in Justice and colleagues (2009).

Data collection for this study included twice-monthly videotapes of teachers' in-class shared storybook reading sessions, as well as child pretest (fall of preschool), posttest (spring of preschool), and follow-up (spring of kindergarten and first grade) assessments on a number of literacy-related measures. Videos of teachers' shared storybook reading session were coded with respect to (1) frequency of print referencing, (2) target of print referencing (e.g., letters, words, book and print organization, print meaning), and (3) procedural fidelity to the intervention's specified scope and sequence.

A number of important results concerning teacher implementation of print referencing have been generated from this large-scale study. First, results indicate that teachers who received PD related to print referencing reliably increased their frequencies of print referencing to three or four times as many print references per reading session as teachers in the comparison condition. The extent of print referencing per session did not differ for teachers assigned to the high-dose versus low-dose print referencing conditions. Importantly, the quantitative change in teachers' print referencing was maintained across the full academic year. In addition,

a qualitative shift in the targets of teachers' print references was also demonstrated. Whereas teachers in the comparison condition focused their (infrequent) print references on early developing print targets such as book and print organization (Justice & Ezell, 2002; Zucker et al., 2009), teachers in the print referencing conditions tended to focus their print references on later developing targets such as letters and words. Additional analyses of teachers' shared storybook-reading sessions indicate that all teachers demonstrated high procedural fidelity in implementing the whole-class shared storybook readings as part of their weekly routines, and that teachers in the print referencing conditions followed the intended scope and sequence for instruction.

A second important finding concerns the impact of the print referencing intervention on children's early literacy skills. Children who experienced high-dose print referencing made significantly greater preschool gains in print knowledge than children who participated in the comparison reading program, which featured the same titles and schedule of reading (Justice et al., 2009). This improvement corresponded to an effect size of 0.21 and did not appear to depend on children's age, initial literacy or language skills, classroom quality, program type, or teacher credentials. Rather, the extent of children's print knowledge gains appeared to depend on the frequency with which teachers referenced print during each reading session (Breit-Smith, McGinty, Justice, Kaderavek, & Fan, 2010). Children who experienced higher rates of print referencing, regardless of whether they experienced four or two shared storybook-reading sessions per week, tended to make greater print knowledge gains over the academic year.

Finally, findings from the kindergarten and first-grade follow-up assessments show that teacher-implemented print referencing has long-term effects on children's early literacy skills (Piasta et al., 2010). When children who experienced the 30-week shared storybook intervention featuring teacher use of print referencing during preschool were followed and reassessed in the spring of kindergarten and first grade on the literacy-related subtests of the Woodcock–Johnson Tests of Achievement–III (Woodcock, McGrew, & Mather, 2001), significant differences were apparent between children who experienced high-dose print referencing and those who experienced the regular reading comparison condition (no or minimal print referencing by teachers). Specifically, children who experienced high-dose print referencing had significantly higher letter–word identification, spelling, and passage comprehension scores than those in the comparison condition through the end of first grade. Children who experienced the low-dose print referencing showed similarly higher letter–word identification and spelling scores compared to those in the comparison condition, although these trends fell just short of traditional significance levels. Interestingly, no reliable differences in kindergarten literacy skills were apparent in comparisons of children who experienced high-dose versus low-dose print referencing.

Conclusion

Taken together, both theory and practice support the use of print referencing as an instructional practice that can decisively support children's print knowledge through adult–child shared storybook-reading interactions. Print referencing, a simple instructional practice with great potential for scalability, involves systematically guiding children to engage with print during shared reading interactions to help them learn more about its forms and functions. Although early reports on children's development of print knowledge suggested that children of their own accord will actively engage with print within storybook-reading interactions (and similar literacy-related events) and, as a result, learn a great deal about print on their own, more recent reports have provided a clear assurance that adults have a decisive role to play in mediating children's exposure to, interactions with, and learning about print within storybooks.

These enhanced theoretical insights, while apparently simple in nature, are anything but trivial given that many children today enter formal reading instruction with relatively limited knowledge about print, and that this in turn appears to hinder children's abilities to progress seamlessly and necessarily, over only a few short years, from learning to read to reading to learn. We contend that helping children to engage with print and to learn as much as possible about its forms and functions in the years prior to formal schooling will ease children's transition from early to formal literacy. Indeed, the implications of this chapter with respect to both theory and practice is that we must continue to refine our theories of how children develop their knowledge about print (and other key areas of literacy development, including vocabulary), and we must test these theories explicitly and directly using convergent research paradigms. When theory and research decisively coalesce, as we would assert they do with respect to print referencing as a viable instructional practice, it is important that practitioners, policymakers, and researchers work together to determine how theory and research can be effectively and efficiently translated into effective instructional practices that support young children who are perhaps at the most critical point on the pathway to literacy.

Note

1. For ease of understanding, we use the term *parents* to refer generally to children's primary caretakers and/or legal guardians. This term thus also encompasses the occasional grandparent or other family member who participated as a member of the parent–child dyad in the research described.

References

Breit-Smith, A., McGinty, A., Justice, L. M., Kaderavek, J. N., & Fan, X. (2010). *Does dosage matter?: Preschoolers' emergent literacy growth in high- and low-dosage classroom-based intervention.* Manuscript in review.

Bus, A. G., & Van IJzendoorn, M. H. (1999). Phonological awareness and early reading: A meta-analysis of experimental training studies. *Journal of Educational Psychology, 91,* 403–414.

Cabell, S. Q., Justice, L. M., Zucker, T. A., & McGinty, A. S. (2009). Emergent name-writing abilities of preschool-age children with language impairment. *Language, Speech, and Hearing Services in Schools, 40,* 53–66.

Catts, H. W., Fey, M. E., Tomblin, J. B., & Zhang, X. (2002). A longitudinal investigation of reading outcomes in children with language impairments. *Journal of Speech, Language, and Hearing Research, 45*(6), 1142–1157.

Chaney, C. (1998). Preschool language and metalinguistic skills are links to reading success. *Applied Psycholinguistics, 19,* 433–446.

Evans, M. A., & Saint-Aubin, J. (2005). What children are looking at during shared storybook reading: Evidence from eye movement monitoring. *Psychological Science, 16*, 913–920.

Evans, M. A., Williamson, K., & Pursoo, T. (2008). Preschoolers' attention to print during shared book reading. *Scientific Studies of Reading, 12*, 106–129.

Ezell, H. K., & Justice, L. M. (2000). Increasing the print focus of adult–child shared book reading through observational learning. *American Journal of Speech–Language Pathology, 9*, 36–47.

Ezell, H. K., Justice, L. M., & Parsons, D. (2000). Enhancing the emergent literacy skills of preschoolers with communication disorders: A pilot investigation. *Child Language Teaching and Therapy, 16*(2), 121–140.

Flowers, H., Girolametto, L., Weitzman, E., & Greenberg, J. (2007). Promoting early literacy skills: Effects of in-service education for early childhood educators. *Canadian Journal of Speech–Language Pathology and Audiology, 31*, 6–18.

Fox, E. (2009). The role of reader characteristics in processing and learning from informational text. *Review of Educational Research, 79*, 197–261.

Girolametto, L., Weitzman, E., Lefebvre, P., & Greenberg, J. (2007). The effects of in-service education to promote emergent literacy in child care centers: A feasibility study. *Language, Speech, and Hearing Services in Schools, 38*, 72–83.

Gong, Z., & Levy, B. (2009). Four year old children's acquisition of print knowledge during electronic storybook reading. *Reading and Writing, 22*, 889–905.

Goodman, Y. M. (1986). Children coming to know literacy. In W. H. Teale & E. Sulzby (Eds.), *Emergent literacy: Writing and reading* (pp. 1–14). Norwood, NJ: Ablex.

Hallinan, P. K. (1987). *My first day of school*. Nashville, TN: Ideals Children's Books.

Hammett Price, L., van Kleeck, A., & Huberty, C. (2009). Talk during book sharing between parents and preschool children: A comparison between storybook and expository book conditions. *Reading Research Quarterly, 44*, 171–194.

Hammill, D. D. (2004). What we know about correlates of reading. *Exceptional Children, 70*, 453–468.

Hiebert, F. (1978). Preschool children's understanding of written language. *Child Development, 49*, 1232–1234.

Hiebert, F. (1981). Developmental patterns and interrelationships of preschool children's print awareness. *Reading Research Quarterly, 16*, 236–260.

Justice, L. M., Bowles, R. P., & Skibbe, L. E. (2006). Measuring preschool attainment of print-concept knowledge: A study of typical and at-risk 3 to 5 year old children using item response theory. *Language, Speech, and Hearing Services in the Schools, 37*, 224–235.

Justice, L., & Ezell, H. (2002). Use of storybook reading to increase print awareness in at-risk children. *American Journal of Speech–Language Pathology, 11*, 17–29.

Justice, L. M., & Ezell, H. K. (2000). Enhancing children's print and word awareness through home-based parent intervention. *American Journal of Speech–Language Pathology, 9*, 257–269.

Justice, L. M., Kaderavek, J. N., Fan, X., Sofka, A., & Hunt, A. (2009). Accelerating preschoolers' early literacy development through classroom-based teacher–child storybook reading and explicit print referencing. *Language, Speech, and Hearing Services in Schools, 40*, 67–85.

Justice, L., Mashburn, A. J., Hamre, B. K., & Pianta, R. C. (2008). Quality of language and literacy instruction in preschool classrooms serving at-risk pupils. *Early Childhood Research Quarterly, 23*, 51–68.

Justice, L. M., McGinty, A., Piasta, S. B., Kaderavek, J. N., & Fan, X. (in press). Print-focused read-alouds in preschool classrooms: Intervention effectiveness and moderators of child outcomes. *Language, Speech, and Hearing Services in Schools.*

Justice, L. M., Pullen, P. C., & Pence, K. (2008). Influence of verbal and nonverbal references to print on preschoolers' visual attention to print during storybook reading. *Developmental Psychology, 44*, 855–866.

Justice, L. M., Skibbe, L. E., McGinty, A., Piasta, S. B., & Petrill, S. A. (in press). Increasing the print knowledge of preschoolers with language impairment through parent–child storybook reading. *Journal of Speech, Language, and Hearing Research.*

Justice, L. M., & Sofka, A. E. (2010). *Engaging children with print: Building early literacy skills through quality read-alouds*. New York: Guilford Press.

Layton, N. (2003). *Hot, hot, hot!*. Cambridge, MA: Candlewick Press.

Lonigan, C. J., & Whitehurst, G. J. (1998). Relative efficacy of parent and teacher involvement in a shared-reading intervention for preschool children from low-income backgrounds. *Early Childhood Research Quarterly, 13*, 263–290.

Lovelace, S., & Stewart, S. R. (2007). Increasing print awareness in preschoolers with language impairment using non-evocative print referencing. *Language, Speech, and Hearing Services in Schools, 38*(1), 16–30.

Mol, S. E., Bus, A. G., & de Jong, M. T. (2009). Interactive book reading in early education: A tool to stimulate print knowledge as well as oral language. *Review of Educational Research, 79*(2), 979–1007.

Morris, D., Bloodgood, J., Lomax, R. G., & Perney, J. (2003). Developmental steps in learning to read: A longitudinal study in kindergarten and first grade. *Reading Research Quarterly, 38*, 302–328.

Muter, V., Hulme, C., Snowling, M. J., & Stevenson, J. (2004). Phonemes, rimes, vocabulary and grammatical skills as foundations of early reading development: Evidence from a longitudinal study. *Developmental Psychology, 40*, 665–681.

National Assessment of Education Progress. (2006). *The nation's report card*. Washington, DC: U.S. Department of Education.

National Early Literacy Panel. (2008). *Developing early literacy: Report of the National Early Literacy Panel.* Jessup, MD: National Center for Family Literacy, National Institute for Literacy. Available at *www.nifl.gov/nifl/publications/pdf/nelpreport09.pdf.*

Organisation for Economic Cooperation and Development. (2001). Knowledge and skills for life: First results from the OECD Programme for International Student Assessment (PISA) 2000. Paris: Author. Retrieved October 1, 2009, from *www1.oecd.org/publications/ebook/9601141e.pdf.*

Phillips, G., & McNaughton, S. (1990). The practice of storybook reading to preschoolers in mainstream New Zealand families. *Reading Research Quarterly, 25*(3), 196–212.

Piasta, S. B., Justice, L. M., McGinty, A., & Kaderavek, J. (2010). *Sit together and read: Effects through kindergarten.* Manuscript in review.

Ritter, G. W., Barnett, J. H., Denny, G. S., & Albin, G. R. (2009). The effectiveness of volunteer tutoring programs for elementary and middle school students: A meta-analysis. *Review of Educational Research, 79*, 3–38.

Roberts, J., Jurgens, J., & Burchinal, M. (2005). The role of home literacy practices in preschool children's language and emergent literacy skills. *Journal of Speech, Language, and Hearing Research, 48*, 345–359.

Rowe, D. W. (2008). Social contracts for writing: Negotiating shared understandings about text in the preschool years. *Reading Research Quarterly, 43*(1), 66–95.

Scarborough, H. S. (2001). Connecting early language and literacy to later reading (dis)abilities: Evidence, theory, and practice. In S. B. Neuman & D. K. Dickinson (Eds.), *Handbook of early literacy research* (Vol. 1, pp. 97–110). New York: Guilford Press.

Sénéchal, M. (2006). Testing the home literacy model: Parent involvement in kindergarten is differentially related to grade 4 reading comprehension, fluency, spelling, and reading for pleasure. *Scientific Studies of Reading, 10*(1), 59–87.

Sénéchal, M., & LeFevre, J. (2002). Parental involvement in the development of children's reading skill: A 5-year longitudinal study. *Child Development, 73*, 445–460.

Snow, C. (1983). Literacy and language: Relationships during the preschool years. *Harvard Educational Review, 55*, 165–189.

Storch, S. A., & Whitehurst, G. J. (2002). Oral language and code-related precursors to reading: Evidence from a longitudinal structural model. *Developmental Psychology, 38*(6), 934–947.

Sulzby, E. (1985). Children's emergent reading of favorite storybooks: A developmental study. *Reading Research Quarterly, 20*, 458–481.

Swanson, H. L., Trainin, G., Necoechea, D. M., & Hammill, D. D. (2003). Rapid naming, phonological awareness, and reading: A meta-analysis of the correlation evidence. *Review of Educational Research, 73*, 407–440.

Tyler, A., Lewis, K., Haskill, A., & Tolbert, L. (2003). Outcomes of different speech and language goal attack strategies. *Journal of Speech, Language, and Hearing Research, 46*, 1077–1094.

van Bysterveldt, A. K., Gillon, G. T., & Moran, C. (2006). Enhancing phonological awareness and letter knowledge in preschool children with Down syndrome. *International Journal of Disability, Development and Education, 53*, 301–329.

Woodcock, R., McGrew, K. S., & Mather, N. (2001). *Woodcock–Johnson Tests of Achievement* (3rd ed.). Itasca, IL: Riverside.

Yaden, D. B., Smolkin, L. B., & Conlon, A. (1989). Preschoolers' questions about pictures, print conventions, and story text during home read-alouds. *Reading Research Quarterly, 24*, 188–214.

Yaden, D. B., Smolkin, L. B., & MacGillivray, L. (1993). A psychogenetic perspective on children's understanding about letter associations during alphabet book readings. *Journal of Reading Behavior, 25*, 43–43.

Zucker, T. A., Justice, L. M., & Piasta, S. B. (2009). Pre-kindergarten teachers' verbal references to print during classroom-based large-group shared reading. *Journal of Language, Speech, and Hearing Services in the Schools, 40*, 376–392.

14

Evidence-Based Computer Interventions Targeting Phonological Awareness to Prevent Reading Problems in At-Risk Young Students

VERNA VAN DER KOOY-HOFLAND
CORNELIA A. T. KEGEL
ADRIANA BUS

There are various ways for young children to come into touch with written language in their home environment. Book sharing is often considered one of the most important activities parents can do to promote young children's early literacy skills. However, literacy experiences in literate homes may also include reading and writing of words, whereby children initially demonstrate an emotional bond with names: the proper names Mama and Papa, and the name of a friend or pet. Almost three decennia ago, the Argentinean researchers Emilia Ferreiro and Ana Teberosky (1982) reported research that underscores the importance of the early years for developing the foundation for future literacy. This report had a strong impact on the research community and since then a spate of articles has appeared to explain early learning processes. As research in the field of early literacy underscores the importance of the early years for developing the foundation for future literacy, interest in early interventions has strongly increased as well.

We explore new roles that computers can play to assist and support teachers who practice good literacy teaching for emerging readers and writers. Since it is easier to tailor the format and content of Web-based programs to individual differences than to ensure that classroom instruction meets the needs of all pupils, computer programs may be an attractive tool for providing additional home-like experiences with literacy to advance early literacy skills of young children at risk. However, although there is a dearth of evidence regarding computer programs as tools to provide young children with relevant practice, there is increasing interest in computer programs in support of instruction in early stages of becoming literate. In the Netherlands, the number of computers in kindergarten classrooms has grown from one computer per 17 pupils in 1999, to one computer for five pupils in 2008 in the last decennium. Moreover, 90% of the computers have Internet connections nowadays (Kennisnet, 2008).

Below we present first experiences with one of the Web-based programs created to compensate for homes in which early literacy experiences are sparse. The target program aims at familiarizing children with the *alphabetic principle* (i.e., understanding that letters represent sounds in spoken words and can be used to create an infinite number of words). As a result of this basic understanding, children may benefit more from experiences with letters and words at home and in school. Understanding the alphabetic principle is not obvious, as is clearly demonstrated by a 3-year-old boy's reaction to a picture storybook entitled *O van Opa* [G of Granddad]. A recurring theme in the booklet is the first letter /o/ of *opa*. For instance, the main character in the booklet notices that when Granddad smokes his cigar, he produces circles like his letter O. After having heard the storybook several times, the 3-year-old boy wondered what the letter of his own *opa* [Granddad] would be now that O had been taken by the granddad of the boy in the booklet.

Summarizing, our aims are fivefold:

1. To discuss research that shows how young children familiarize themselves with the alphabetic principle in literate homes.
2. To present a Web-based program that simulates the content of early literacy training in literate homes to boost young children's understanding of the alphabetic principle.
3. To evaluate the efficacy of a Web-based program to promote early literacy skills that underlie reading development, directly after working with the program as well as on the long run in the first years of formal reading instruction.
4. To test whether exposure to an individual training program on the computer might make too strong an appeal to independent learning for some young children, especially when they are easily distracted and often respond impulsively.
5. To discuss opportunities and challenges that must be considered when Web-based computer programs are implemented.

Early Literacy Training in Literate Homes

Numerous reviews have supported alphabetic knowledge as one of the early-developing pillars of learning to read (Byrne, Fielding-Barnsley, & Ashley, 2000; Snider, 1995). Understanding the alphabetic principle enables children to gain access to decoding procedures that form part of the reading activity (Silva & Alves-Martins, 2002). To advance children from homes in which early literacy skills are sparse, we took into account how learning about the alphabetic principle starts in literate homes and designed a Web-based computer program that boosts similar learning processes.

The Proper Name as Starting Point

In literate homes children develop an interest in writing the proper name. Children are exposed to the written form of their name on such personal possessions as their bedroom door, their drinking glass, or their artwork. As a result, children start to copy their names and to write them on their own. Given these experiences and children's interest in their own names, it is not surprising that children's knowledge of their names develops before knowledge of any other word. Children's writing of their own names is identifiable as writing prior to other words (Levin, Both-de Vries, Aram, & Bus, 2005). From studies in which words were dictated to young children, it appears that name writing is the first stable written form with meaning that children can write conventionally (Levin & Bus, 2003).

Because the name is the first stable written form with meaning, it may fulfill a very special function in the psychogenesis of alphabetic skills and represent a singularly important benchmark in early literacy development (Ferreiro & Teberosky, 1982; Welsch, Sullivan, & Justice, 2003). Even though writing the proper name may not automatically imply understanding of the alphabetic principle that the letters of printed language stand for sounds in spoken words, the proper name may be a pathway through which children develop alphabetic knowledge, thereby influencing reading and spelling of other words (Byrne, 1998). This reasoning is in line with Badian's finding (1982) that name writing is one of the top three predictors of both first- and second-grade reading achievement, using the Stanford Achievement Test Total Reading Score as an outcome measure.

Early Invented Spellings

It seems a plausible assumption that familiarity with the written form of the name may affect young children's letter knowledge and invented spellings of unpracticed words (Both-de Vries & Bus, 2008). In a first attempt to test effects of the name, we reanalyzed the writings of young children, all at the age of 4, who mostly produced strings of conventional letters when asked to write words (Levin & Bus, 2003). We separated the least advanced children not yet writing phonetically from more advanced children who had just started to produce some phonetic spelling. The two groups differed in name writing. Of the more advanced group, 65% wrote almost all letters of their name correctly, whereas 76% of the less advanced children wrote only one or two letters correctly.

Consistent with Bloodgood's (1999) finding, about half of the letters used to write dictated words were letters from the children's proper names. The least advanced children had a strong preference for the first letter of the name, whereas the advanced group used other letters from the name as often as the first letter. More importantly, the first letter of the name was the one to be written phonetically by the more advanced group. They used the first letter of the name significantly more often in words that actually included the letter than in words without the letter, indicating that it is not merely chance that children use the first letter of the name phonetically. Other letters were rarely used phonetically. The group that mainly produced random letter strings often used the first letter of the name in their writings, but just as often in words that included the letter as in words that did not. So their use of the letter was not phonetic but random. In other words, it seems that the first letter of the child's name is the one and only letter that is written phonetically at the very start of phonetic writing.

In a follow-up study (Both-de Vries & Bus, 2009), we dictated the same number of words including the first letter of the child's name as words not including this letter. Dictations thus differed to some extent for the participants in this study. In this sample, the majority (65%) of the 4- to 5½-year-olds wrote their name readably (i.e., they produced at least an invented spelling; e.g., Slva instead of Silva). The rest (35%) wrote the first letter and one or more other letters (e.g., jT instead of Juliet) or made strings composed of pseudoletters or pseudocursive writing. This study demonstrated again that, if children were able to write their name, they selected

the first letter of the name more often for words that actually included this letter (in five out of eight words) than for words without this letter (in three out of eight words). In the group yet unable to write the name, the first letter occurred in two out of eight words, whether word included the name letter or not.

Mediators between Name Writing and Phonetic Spelling

To explain the effects of name writing on the earliest invented spellings we hypothesized that adult feedback to children's attempts to write the proper name explains learning (Levin & Aram, 2004). The name may elicit teaching of the first letter's sound and phonetic sensitivity for the first letter of the name, and due to this knowledge, phonetic writing arises (Ehri & Wilce, 1985; Frost, 2001). By focusing children's attention on letter units and how they sound in the name (e.g., adults may say: "It's /pi/ of Peter"), adults provide children with fairly substantial amounts of direct instruction about letters as symbols for sounds (Molfese, Beswick, Molnar, & Jacobi-Vessels, 2006). They thus stimulate children's *phonetic sensitivity*, the ability to identify the sound of the first letter of their name in a spoken word, and alphabetic–phonetic writing that goes beyond imitation of the form. According to this line of reasoning, we expected that invented spelling with the first letter of the name would be mediated by familiarity with the letter name and how it sounds in words.

Of those who wrote their names readably, most children (80%) were able to name the first letter of the proper name. A small minority (19%) of the children who could not write their names readably was able to name or sound out the first letter of the name. When testing ability to identify the sound of the first letter and other letters in spoken words, we found that children identified the sound of the first letter of their names correctly more often than other sounds (Both-de Vries & Bus, 2009). The contrast between the name and non-name sound was significant when children wrote their names readably but not when they were unable to write their names.

Further analyses were commensurate with the hypothesis that name writing affects phonetic spelling through knowing the first letter's name and phonemic sensitivity to this letter. This appeared from a hierarchical multiple regression analysis on the ability to use the first letter of the name phonetically. Ability to write the proper name was a strong predictor (ß = 0.41). Yet after familiarity with the first letter of the name and the ability to identify this letter in spoken words were entered, effects of the proper name were no longer significant. The finding that phonemic sensitivity explains variance beyond the variance explained by familiarity with the letter name, and vice versa, means that learning is not modulated by either prior phonemic sensitivity or letter knowledge (Castles, Coltheart, Wilson, Valpied, & Wedgwood, 2009).

A Web-Based Intervention Program

Researchers, including Labbo and Reinking (1999), hold the opinion that well-founded computer programs that, in contrast to many commercial programs, balance "edutainment" with instruction and practice could make a substantial contribution to the learning environment of young learners at home and in classrooms. In particular programs that are modeled on the early literacy training in literate homes, and that take account of which activities boost young children's learning may compensate for homes in which early literacy experiences are sparse. In this section we present an example of an attractive Web-based, computer program that simulates the previously described "real-world" activities around name writing in literate homes. The computer program uses young children's emotional bond with the proper name and the pleasure they have in recognizing their own names to draw attention to the first letter of the name and how this letter sounds in the name and other words.

A Web-Based Program for Young Children

The Internet program Living Letters was developed and installed by a private company in schools across the Netherlands. Unlike popular educational computer programs like Daisy Quest and Daisy's Castle (Foster, Erickson, Forster, Brinkman, & Torgeson, 1994), Living Letters is tailored to a child's

knowledge by using the name of the child to draw attention to phonemes in spoken words (Bus & van IJzendoorn, 1999; Ehri et al., 2001).

The program, developed in close collaboration with computer experts, designers, and experts in the field of education, encompasses three different layers. After a series of games in which children identify their proper names among other words, the program instructs children in naming the first letter and how the name's first letter sounds in other words. Figure 14.1 presents screenshots that illustrate each layer:

- All children start with games in which they are asked to recognize the proper name or *Mama* among other words (e.g., "Find your name"; Figure 14.1a–d).
- These games are followed by games with the first letter of the name. The program uses the child's proper name unless the spelling is inconsistent with Dutch orthography (e.g., Chris or Joey). The program then switches to *Mama*, another high-frequency name known by young children. Figure 14.1e illustrates a game in which children have to find the first letter of *Mama* ("Which one is the /m/ of *Mama*?").
- Games to identify pictures that start with the same sound as the child's name or *Mama*, or with this sound in the middle. In Figure 14.1f, Tom should click on *tent* and ignore *vlieger* [kite] or *boom* [tree].

In all, the program is composed of seven sets that each include five or six different games. Each set starts with an attractive animation using the two main characters to explain the upcoming games; for instance, the two main characters, a boy and a girl named Sim and Sanne, discover that their names start with the same sound.

Feedback Loops in the Web-Based Program

Apart from games, the program has built-in feedback loops that imitate the adult responses. Where feedback encourages children to try again, it facilitates repetition. However, the program also provides children with strategies to solve the tasks, thus enabling engagement in similar tasks independently. The oral feedback promotes

FIGURE 14.1. The screenshots have been derived from six different games: selecting the proper name (a and c), selecting *mama* (b and d), selecting the first letter of *mama* (e), and selecting the painting that starts with the letter of the child's own first name (e.g., *Tom–tent*) (f). When the mouse skims a picture, the computer names the words. Reprinted with permission from Bereslim BV.

letter-sound knowledge, as well as phonemic sensitivity to the sound of the letter. For instance, where children have to click on the picture that starts with the same sound as the proper name, they receive as feedback: "The /p/ of Peter sounds just like /p/ in *pear.*" To summarize, errors are followed by increasingly supportive feedback:

- The task is repeated when children do not solve the task the first time.
- After two errors in a task, clues are given: For instance, when a child does not succeed in finding the words that start with the sound of his or her name, the child receives a clue tailored to the child's name (e.g., "In which word do you hear /k/ of Koen?").
- The correct solution is demonstrated and confirmed by adding a verbal explanation tailored to the child's name ("The /t/ of Tom is also the /t/ of *tent*").

The program facilitates routines in which children operate through repetition of tasks and introduces variations on those tasks, so that children internalize not only the task but also the ability to engage in similar tasks independently. Computer pals personalize the interaction between child and computer by looking the child in the eyes while asking a question, as illustrated in Figure 14.1e. To make the feedback less intimidating to the child, corrective feedback is not given by agemates Sim or Sanne, but by Sim's stuffed bear, as illustrated in Figure 14.1f.

Effects of a Web-Based Computer Intervention

Our aims in testing the effects of Web-based computer programs on literacy development were twofold:

1. Testing whether computer-assisted instruction of foundational alphabetic understanding in support of teacher-delivered literacy training in kindergarten narrows the early gaps in early literacy skills.
2. And, most importantly, testing effects of the computer treatment on the long run, assuming that successful programs enable children at risk to benefit from reading instruction in the first years of formal instruction.

Effects in Support of the Kindergarten Curriculum

The program is only meaningful for children who do not yet understand the alphabetic principle. Therefore, senior kindergarten children were screened upon entry with a test battery that consisted of assessments of writing (the proper name Mama, and four other words), rhyming, and letter knowledge (Van der Kooy-Hofland & Bus, 2009). The experiment was carried out in 15 primary schools in a western province of the Netherlands (South Holland). Of a total of 404 pupils in the senior kindergarten year, 135 were eligible for the computer treatment. However, the percentage of eligible children per classroom varied from 19.1% to 54.8%, with the highest percentages in classrooms in rural areas with mainly low educated parents.

With a randomized pretest–posttest experiment we tested whether alphabetic skills catch up as a result of exposure to the computer intervention. All eligible children played computer games "teacher-free" (i.e., without support from a teacher, peer, or other adult). Given that the program could be completed in 2½ to 3 hours, computer activities did not interfere with participation in the regular curriculum, which in the Netherlands mainly includes teacher-guided instruction in rhyming, and identifying sounds in names and other words during circle time for about 15 minutes per day. To prevent research from falling prey to the difficulty of valid comparison groups, the same number of eligible children was assigned per classroom to the control and experimental groups. We compared children from the Living Letters group with a group from the same classrooms exposed to another computer program that stimulates other literacy-related skills. The program in the comparison group incorporated as key elements vocabulary learning and story comprehension. Because the latter program, Living Books, does not include written words or letters, the groups exposed to Living Letters, or to both Living Letters and Living Books, were expected to show advantages in early literacy skills over the group merely exposed to Living Books. Children were compared on skills such as identifying sounds in spoken words, creating invented spellings, and susceptibility for training in decoding. The two programs shared the same structure and were designed to run over a 15-week period, once a week for 10–15 minutes.

This intervention is unique because young children were exposed to treatment without any direct adult support. Children sat alone at the computer screen in their classroom or the computer room, with a headset on. Researchers logged children in on the website and made sure they completed all sessions, thus guaranteeing that the program was used with high fidelity across all classrooms, and that there was no variation among students in amount of time spent using the target software. When the system had identified the child, the correct game appeared and the system discontinued the session automatically after four games. We tested whether children make progress in skills that actually go beyond what is practiced by Living Letters (recognition of the proper name, naming the first letter of the proper name, or identifying the sound of the first letter in spoken words). The expectation was that children can benefit more from their literate environment and teacher-delivered training in kindergarten when they have practiced with Living Letters and have developed a basic alphabetic understanding.

A relatively short, computer-assisted intervention can boost the ability to identify sounds in words (phonological skills), produce invented spellings, and make children more susceptible to instruction in decoding. Controlling for parent education, gender, age, and prior scores, the Living Letters group outperformed children from the same classrooms with equally low scores on the screening tests who were exposed to Living Books. A mean gain of 0.5 standard deviation on the early literacy skills means that the group that at the start of the intervention scored among the 30% lowest scoring children would score on literacy skills just below the mean of a large sample from the same classes after being exposed to Living Letters. Though children have practiced their names, the first letter of their names, and phonemic sensitivity to the first letter of the names, benefits accrued in a broader set of sounds.

Compared to the Living Books group, the Living Letters group started to understand more about how reading works, more about how letters and words work, and to make better early attempts at reading real words. To explain this effect we assume that the proper name stirs up a basic understanding that letters relate to sounds, which may encourage children to continue practicing in daily situations or to benefit more from instruction during circle time in kindergarten. Other researchers have also reported significant and comparable gains on phonological processing tasks as a result of a computer program standing in for teacher-delivered instruction (e.g., Segers & Verhoeven, 2005; van Daal & Reitsma, 2000), but rarely as a remedial program in a group of children who lag far behind (Macuruso & Walker, 2008).

Differential Effects

Unlike classroom instruction or stand-alone computer programs, Web-based computer programs are equipped to register child responses while playing the games to enable adaptive feedback. From the registrations we can determine how successful children were at solving the tasks. If children are less successful, we may not expect them to benefit from the program to the same extent as children who are rather successful. Our findings are in support of the hypothesis that benefits only accrue to students who often succeed in completing computer tasks at the first attempt. When children make many errors, their literacy skills do not benefit from the program. Correlations between number of errors in the computer tasks on the one hand and letter knowledge, phonological skills, and susceptibility to training in decoding on the other are as high as −.52, −.47, and −.57, respectively.

The Capacity to Benefit from Formal Reading Instruction

A main ground for early interventions is that as children's academic ability lags behind early in life, their capacity to benefit from reading instruction in later years falls short of the average group, and the lags increase rather than decrease (Raudenbush, 2009). Hence, it is most important to test whether a computer intervention in support of the regular kindergarten curriculum plays a role in later reading achievements. At best, intervention children run less risk to finding themselves in a downward spiral of failing to comprehend instruction and complete assignments in school, leading to weaker achievements and increased problems in completing assignments. There is, for instance, research demonstrating that children who can identify letter sounds or phonemes in spoken words (Byrne et al., 2000), have a better starting position for learning to decode in first and second grade (Bus & van IJzendoorn, 1999). According to this model, early interventions in preschool-age children should still be manifest in reading achievement at the end of grade two, when the stage of beginning reading instruction is almost complete and average Dutch pupils are assumed to read simple words fairly fluently.

Alternatively, a compensatory trajectory of development predicts that for several reasons gaps may narrow even without early interventions (Leppänen, Niemi, Aunola, & Nurmi, 2004). Teachers of slow starters use pedagogical practices that decrease rather than increase individual differences across the early grades of primary school. Furthermore, the development of initially precocious children may level off. Learning processes beyond basic reading skills require substantially more practice than is needed for the acquisition of basic skills, leading to the narrowing of individual differences in reading trajectories. After all, gaining reading fluency is a very time-consuming process.

Effects in the Long Run

Halfway through grade 2, we retested the reading and spelling of all children from 15 schools that completed the screening in kindergarten (Van der Kooy-Hofland & Bus, 2009). Because outcomes for a battery of tests (reading nonsense words, reading real words, spelling, and reading comprehension) were similar, the discussion hereafter is limited to one of the tests—proficiency in reading nonsense words after 18 months of instruction. The expectation is that knowledge delays, if not addressed in the early years, may lead to an ongoing knowledge gap. If the early intervention yields benefits, we may expect scores of children in the intervention group to match those of their classmates, and scores of initially poor achievers to show a pattern similar to that of the complete group. The contrast group exposed to Living Books, a language program, on the other hand, may improve to some extent due to regression to the mean but continue to perform more weakly than the intervention group.

The bell curves in Figure 14.2 represent the total sample of about 400 children on screening and somewhat fewer children (about 350) due to attrition in grade 2. Figure 14.2 (top) presents scores of the contrast group on screening (left) and after about 18 months of formal reading instruction (right). In comparison with the screening, more children in the contrast group scored at or above the median after 18 months, implying that children who initially lagged far behind catch up without any specific intervention as the compensatory trajectory predicts. The number scoring at or above the median increased from 0% in kindergarten to 28.9% after 18 months of reading instruction. Figure 14.2 (bottom) demonstrates that scores of the Living Letters group have risen more in second grade. The distribution of scores in this group is similar to the distribution in the complete sample despite the poor start in kindergarten. The number of children in this group scoring at or above the median increased from 0% at pretest to 45.7% at posttest.

Even though both groups show gains in achievement in grade 2, the contrast group performed unfavorably in comparison with the treatment group with an equally weak start in kindergarten. The number of children in the contrast group scoring at or above the median of the complete sample was significantly lower than the number scoring at or above the median in the intervention group ($p < .05$). Because children in both groups were from the same classrooms and were, without doubt, receiving similar instruction in reading, exposure to Living Letters was the only stable difference. Taken together, these outcomes strongly indicate that an early computer intervention simulating elements of early literacy training in literate homes reduces the risk of students entering

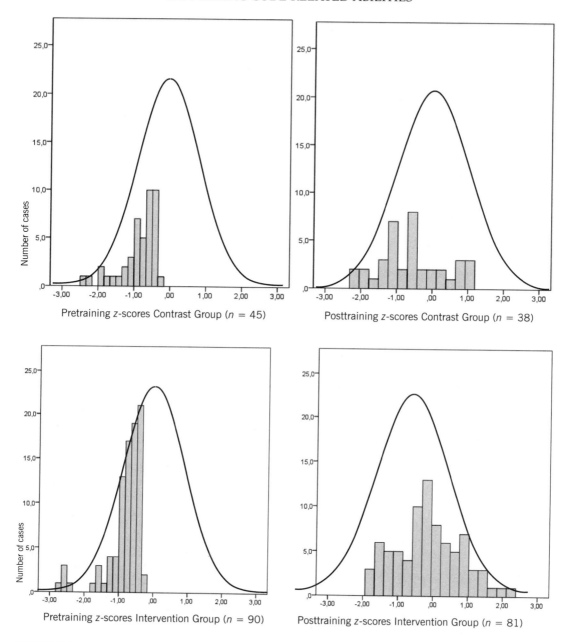

FIGURE 14.2. Distribution of scores of contrast and intervention groups on the normal distribution of the complete groups at the pretest ($n = 404$) and posttest ($n = 355$). Note that the control group included fewer children than the treatment group.

kindergarten with poor literacy skills developing reading problems. Target children were better prepared to benefit from formal reading instruction when they were exposed to the computer treatment in kindergarten.

Matthew Effects

The differences between the treatment and contrast group harmonize best with the so-called *cumulative model* (Leppänen et al., 2004). The contrast children encounter problems with learning to read as a result of less well-developed early literacy skills, read less, and without practice are more at risk of developing reading problems, as is demonstrated here by the difference between treatment and contrast groups. In his classic article, Stanovich (1986) referred to this phenomenon as the *Matthew effect*, which posits that early developmental differences in literacy ability are often maintained and may even be magnified over time as development proceeds and no interventions are carried out to compensate for achievements gaps. The reading development of some children with low foundational knowledge accelerates as formal instruction starts, and they catch up with those who began at a higher level, but without early intervention, a substantially larger proportion of the low achievers do not catch up.

Differential Effects of Computer Programs

Children with poor regulatory skills are less proficient in planning, organizing, and applying rules (Meltzer, 2007); are easily distracted and impulsive (Hughes, 2002); and have problems dealing with changing tasks (Moffitt, 1993). Whatever the causes— immaturity, neurological deficits, or child-rearing practices (Oh & Lewis, 2008; Ponitz et al., 2008)—poor regulatory skills may interfere with learning behavior (Blair, Protzko, & Ursache, Chapter 2, this volume; Blair & Razza, 2007; Dally, 2006), and regulatory skills may be better predictors of literacy skills than verbal or nonverbal intelligence (Diamond, Barnett, Thomas, & Munro, 2007; Spira, Bracken, & Fischel, 2005). Even more than regular instruction in class-

rooms, learning through computer tasks may be susceptible to children's independent regulatory skills. Except for feedback by the computer program, the children's behavior is not corrected.

Inability to Learn through Computer Tasks

For young children who are unable to stay attentive and focused without an adult to correct distraction and poor problem-solving behavior, exposure to an individual training program on the computer might place too high a demand on their learning skills. Especially when the computer tasks are rather complex, children may demonstrate uncontrolled behavior resulting in many mistakes in the computer tasks. We therefore hypothesized that not all pupils at risk may benefit from exposure to a computer program. Young children with poor regulatory skills may profit less from the interventions compared to same-age children with intermediate regulatory skills, especially when targeted activities require children to listen and to retain information to complete the tasks.

Differential Outcomes of a Computer Intervention

As expected, there were differential effects of regulatory skills assessed with Stroop-like tasks (e.g., saying "blue" upon seeing a red dog and "red" upon seeing a blue dog) (Beveridge, Jarrold, & Pettit, 2002) or saying "fat" in response to seeing someone who is thin, and vice versa (Berlin & Bohlin, 2002). Children scoring in the normal range on regulatory skills did benefit from Living Letters. After treatment, this subgroup scored on average more than half a standard deviation (0.70 SD) beyond the grand mean on skills assessed at posttest (Kegel, Van der Kooy-Hofland, & Bus, 2009). Children with equally poor literacy skills who scored among the lowest 25% on regulatory skills were less likely to benefit from the computer treatment, probably because the regulatory demands of the program may have outstripped these children's regulatory skills. Likewise, the computer treatment was no incentive for literacy skills of children with high regulatory skills. Given the fact that these children scored in the lowest 30% despite relatively strong regulatory skills, we suppose that this group included relatively more children at risk for a phonological deficit and thereby benefited less from phonological skills training (Snowling, 2000).

Computer Behavior as Correlate of Regulatory Skills

Because the Web-based format enables the recording and storage all children's mouse behavior, clicks, movements, and response rate during the computer sessions, we have unique and objective information at our disposal that enables us to test how children approach the tasks and determine to what extent their computer behavior may be disruptive for learning (Kegel et al., 2009). By registering during sessions the position of the mouse onscreen every one-tenth of a second and where it was clicked or hovered, we could derive information about various aspects of children's computer behavior: how much time it took the children to solve the problems, whether random clicking and unnecessary mouse movements occurred, and how often children made appeals to feedback functions of the computer program (Bippes et al., 2003; Kegel et al., 2009). In particular children with poor regulatory skills may try to solve tasks randomly. They may often be distracted and not succeed in staying attentive without support.

Our results seem to corroborate this hypothesis because lower scores on regulatory skills typically coincide with problematic computer behavior. The group scoring lowest on regulatory skills needed more time to respond, clicked more often, spent more time manipulating the mouse, and made more errors (Kegel et al., 2009). The alternative to this explanation would be that poor literacy skills create a need for more feedback, and therefore more time and mouse clicks to complete the games. However, our findings refute this hypothesis because after we controlled for pretested literacy skills, the relation between computer behavior and regulatory skills still existed. Because computer behavior was quite stable over the course of the games, we can only conclude that the feedback loops built into Living Letters (e.g., repetition or providing cues to find the correct answer) were insufficient to counterbalance problems in planning and choosing the right steps.

Computer Behavior as Predictor of Progress over a 2-Year Period

The relationship between computer behavior and reading and spelling in the long run was surprisingly strong (Van der Kooy-Hofland & Bus, 2009). For instance, the correlation between the number of errors in the computer tasks in kindergarten and reading fluency after 18 months was moderately strong ($r = .38$). One explanation for this may be that the regulatory skills that lay the foundation for errors while children solve computer tasks also result in less benefit from classroom instruction. An alternative explanation may be that a phonological deficit is manifest in solving the computer tasks and in children's ability to benefit from reading instruction in the first grades. Whatever the best interpretation may be, it has been firmly established that computer behavior while playing educational games predicts learning in the years to come.

Future Directions and Limitations

Value of Early Interventions

The studies support the need for interventions that simulate the content of early literacy training in literate homes, and demonstrate that without early intervention, more children from at-risk groups lack the capacity to benefit from beginning reading instruction in the early grades (Raudenbush, 2009). The step into conventional reading appears to be seriously impeded when children are not exposed to the kinds of early educational experiences found in literate homes. In the long run, preemptive measures in kindergarten may prove more effective and less expensive than remediation in the future (Stanovich, 1986). From an economic point of view, Heckman (2006) has argued that later compensation for deficient early family environments is more costly.

Promise of Web-Based Interventions

Our speculations about Web-based interventions in support of classroom instruction are constrained by the limitations of our data. However, several features of Living Letters are common to other Web-based computer treatments; thus, we cautiously speculate on what our findings might have to say about using this kind of program for literacy instruction of young children who start school with less well-developed literacy skills. There is evidence that Web-based programs support the development of early literacy skills even though no evidence supports the claim that such programs are superior to teachers' using what have been deemed best practices in literacy instruction. In addition to Living Letters, discussed in this chapter, Living Books, a Web-based intervention to stimulate skills such as vocabulary, grammatical knowledge, and reading comprehension, appears to be another valuable intervention for children during the early school years (Bus, Verhallen, & Van der Kooy-Hofland, 2009; Silverman & Hines, 2009; Verhallen & Bus, 2009; Verhallen, Bus, & de Jong, 2006). Tailoring the activities to children's interests and knowledge may be one of the crucial ingredients of Web-based programs, thus raising the effects of computer interventions above those of regular classroom instruction or stand-alone computer programs. By using the children's names and the first letter of the names, Living Letters creates optimal opportunities to draw attention to letter–sound relations in spoken words. Further research (Kegel, unpublished data) is in progress to test which elements of Web-based educational programs are most needed to advance learning.

In the Netherlands, and probably also in the rest of the world, there is a lack of promising Web-based programs that can help to compensate children from homes with sparse early literacy experiences. Dutch publishers are not keen on investing in platforms with evidence-based Internet programs for the children; they know that maintenance and overhauling are expensive. Having a sufficient number of schools subscribe to Internet sites with educational programs such as Living Letters and Living Books might cover the costs, but as long as computer programs are not part of daily routines in classrooms, schools adopt a reserved attitude, and earnings and costs are unbalanced.

Computer Behavior as Predictor of Learning

Our findings also suggest that Web-based programs can be used as diagnostic tools to detect poor problem-solving skills that are barriers to learning about literacy; computer programs are also a valuable teaching aid. Registration of computer behavior, such as the time it takes children to solve the problems, random clicking and unnecessary mouse movements, and number of errors, seems to provide a valid tool for identifying children at risk for long-term reading difficulties (Vellutino, Scanlon, Zhang, & Schatschneider, 2008). Considering that computer behavior relates not only to academic skills but also to tests of regulatory skills, we hypothesize that academic skills may not provide a complete picture of children's preparedness to meet the demands of the classroom. Computer behavior may predict later achievements because school success also depends on regulatory skills. Research in progress further explores this theory, as well as feedback loops that can be added to Web-based programs to improve young children's learning competence.

Design and Implementation of Web Portals in Classrooms

We should mention that availability of programs in classrooms does not guarantee that they are beneficial to pupils who need help. During the past year, we analyzed how often teachers logged in on the Web portal when their schools had a subscription to Living Letters and Living Books. Teachers in only a small proportion of the approximately 150 schools used the program weekly. In a study in progress, we asked the teachers of 15 schools to put particular pupils in their classrooms to work with Living Letters once a week (Kegel, unpublished data). The program was rarely used the way it was meant to be used. Automatic registrations of log-in data revealed that pupils in some classrooms did not access the program for weeks, while on rare days it was continuously in use. Such observations indicate that we cannot take for granted that teachers are successful in integrating Living Letters into a broader curriculum of literacy instruction. As the availability of computer programs improves and the number of optional activities further increases, teachers may not realize which children in particular can benefit from regular access to a Web portal.

It may be helpful to incorporate algorithms in the Web portal to guide teacher decisions about children who need the programs (McDonald, Morrison, Fishman, Schatschneider, & Underwood, 2007). The program may provide recommendations, updated monthly, regarding the pupils for whom the programs should be invoked. Standardized test scores may be used to determine which pupils are most eligible for exposure to the program. Conditional upon the number of errors children make while playing the games, tasks can be skipped or repeated. With the help of built-in algorithms, fine-tuning of feedback to children may make the program even more effective. For instance, more reflective children may need different feedback than do children who mostly respond immediately, without taking any time for reflection between tasks.

References

Badian, N. A. (1982). The prediction of good and poor reading before kindergarten entry: A 4-year follow-up. *Journal of Special Education, 16,* 309–318.

Berlin, L., & Bohlin, G. (2002). Response inhibition, hyperactivity, and conduct problems among preschool children. *Journal of Clinical Child Psychology, 31,* 242–251.

Beveridge, M., Jarrold, C., & Pettit, E. (2002). An experimental approach to executive fingerprinting in young children. *Infant and Child Development, 11,* 107–123.

Bippes, H., Lohuis, R. O., Meurs, J., Smit, M., Wetterauw, M., Dekker, K., et al. (2003). *Pilot Pientere Peuter, Deel II, Inhoudelijk Spelontwerp [Pilot study Clever Toddler, Part II, Intrinsic Game Design].* Groningen: Stichting Edict, Molendrift B.V. & Vertis B.V.

Blair, C., & Razza, R. P. (2007). Relating effortful control, executive function, and false belief understanding to emerging math and literacy ability in kindergarten. *Child Development, 78,* 647–663.

Bloodgood, J. W. (1999). What's in a name?: Children's name writing and literacy acquisition. *Reading Research Quarterly, 34,* 342–367.

Both-de Vries, A., & Bus, A. G. (2008). Name writing: A first step to phonetic writing? Does the name have a special role in understanding the symbolic function of writing? *Literacy Teaching and Learning, 12,* 37–55.

Both-de Vries, A., & Bus, A. G. (2009). The proper name as starting point for basic reading skills. *Reading and Writing, 23*(2), 173–187.

Bus, A. G., & Van IJzendoorn, M. H. (1999). Phonological awareness and early reading: A meta-analysis of experimental training studies. *Journal of Educational Psychology, 91,* 403–414.

Bus, A. G., Verhallen, M. J. A. J., & Van der Kooy-Hofland, V. A. C. (2009). Digital picture storybooks. *Better: Evidence-Based Education, 1,* 16–17. betterevidence.files.wordpress.com/2009/06/94006_saf_final.pdf.

Byrne, B. (1998). *The foundation of literacy: The child's acquisition of the alphabetic principle.* East Sussex, UK: Psychology Press.

Byrne, B., Fielding-Barnsley, R., & Ashley, L. (2000). Effects of preschool phoneme identity training after six years: Outcome level distinguished from rate response. *Journal of Educational Psychology, 92,* 659–667.

Castles, A., Coltheart, M., Wilson, K., Valpied, J., & Wedgwood, J. (2009). The genesis of reading ability: What helps children learn letter–sound correspondences? *Journal of Experimental Child Psychology, 104,* 68–88.

Dally, K. (2006). The influence of phonological processing and inattentive behavior on reading acquisition. *Journal of Educational Psychology, 98,* 420–437.

Diamond, A., Barnett, W. S., Thomas, J., & Munro, S. (2007). Preschool program improves cognitive control. *Science, 318,* 1387–1388.

Ehri, L. C., Nunes, S. R., Willows, D. M., Schuster, B., Yaghoub-Zadeh, Z., & Shanahan, T. (2001). Phonemic awareness instruction helps children learn to read: Evidence from the National Reading Panel's meta-analysis. *Reading Research Quarterly, 36,* 250–287.

Ehri, L. C., & Wilce, L. S. (1985). Movement into reading: Is the first stage of printed word learning visual or phonetic? *Reading Research Quarterly, 20,* 163–179.

Ferreiro, E., & Teberosky, A. (1982). *Literacy before schooling.* Exeter, NH: Heinemann.

Foster, K., Erickson, G., Foster, D., Brinkman, D., & Torgeson, J. (1994). Computer administered instruction in phonological awareness evaluation of Daisyquest program. *Journal of Research and Development in Education, 27,* 126–137.

Frost, J. (2001). Phonetic awareness, spontaneous writing, and reading and spelling development from a preventive perspective. *Reading and Writing, 14,* 487–513.

Heckman, J. J. (2006). Skill formation and the economics of investing in disadvantaged children. *Science, 312,* 1900–1902.

Hughes, C. (2002). Executive functions and development: Emerging themes. *Infant and Child Development, 11,* 201–209.

Kegel, C. A. T., Van der Kooy-Hofland, V. A. C., & Bus, A. G. (2009). Improving early phoneme skills with a computer program: Differential effects of regulatory skills. *Learning and Individual Differences, 19*(4), 549–554.

Kennisnet. (2008). *Stand van zaken over ict in het*

onderwijs [State of ICT in education]. Zoetermeer: Stichting Kennisnet.

Labbo, L. D., & Reinking, D. (1999). Negotiating the multiple realities of technology in literacy research and instruction. *Reading Research Quarterly, 34,* 478–492.

Leppänen, U., Niemi, P., Aunola, K., & Nurmi, J.-E. (2004). Development of reading skills among preschool and primary school pupils. *Reading Research Quarterly, 39,* 72–93.

Levin, I., & Aram, D. (2004). Children's names contribute to early literacy: A linguistic and social perspective. In D. Ravid & H. Bat-Zeev Shyldkrot (Eds.), *Perspectives on language and language development* (pp. 219–241). Dordrecht: Kluwer.

Levin, I., Both-de Vries, A. C., Aram, D., & Bus, A. G. (2005). Writing starts with own name writing: From scribbling to conventional spelling in Israeli and Dutch children. *Applied Psycholinguistics, 26,* 463–477.

Levin, I., & Bus, A. G. (2003). How is emergent writing based on drawing?: Analyses of children's products and their sorting by children and mothers. *Developmental Psychology, 39,* 891–905.

Macuruso, P., & Walker, A. (2008). The efficacy of computer-assisted instruction for advancing literacy skills in kindergarten children. *Reading Psychology, 29,* 266–287.

McDonald, C., Morrison, F. J., Fishman, B. J., Schatschneider, C., & Underwood, P. (2007). Algorithm-guided individualized reading instruction. *Science, 26,* 464–465.

Meltzer, L. (2007). *Executive functions in education: From theory to practice.* New York: Guilford Press.

Moffitt, T. E. (1993). Adolescence-limited and life-course persistent antisocial behaviour: A developmental taxonomy. *Psychological Review, 100,* 674–701.

Oh, S., & Lewis, C. (2008). Korean preschoolers' advanced inhibitory control and its relation to other executive skills and mental state understanding. *Child Development, 79,* 80–99.

Ponitz, C. C., McClelland, M. M., Jewkes, A. M., Connor, M. C., Farris, C. L., & Morrison, F. J. (2008). Touch your toes!: Developing a direct measure of behavioral regulation in early childhood. *Early Childhood Research Quarterly, 23,* 141–158.

Raudenbush, S. W. (2009). The Brown legacy and the O'Connor challenge: Transforming schools in the images of children's potential. *Educational Researcher, 38,* 169–180.

Segers, E., & Verhoeven, L. (2005). Long-term effects of computer training of phonological awareness in kindergarten. *Journal of Computer Assisted Learning, 21,* 17–27.

Silva, C., & Alves-Martins, M. (2002). Relationships between phonological skills and levels of development in the writing of pre-syllabic children. *Reading Research Quarterly, 37,* 466–483.

Silverman, R., & Hines, S. (2009). The effects of multimedia-enhanced instruction on the vocabulary of English-language learners and non-English-language learners in pre-kindergarten through second grade. *Journal of Educational Psychology, 101,* 305–314.

Snider, V. E. (1995). A primer on phonemic awareness, what it is, why it's important, and how to teach it. *School Psychology Review, 24,* 443–455.

Snowling, M. J. (2000). *Dyslexia* (2nd ed.). Oxford, UK: Blackwell.

Spira, E. G., Bracken, S. S., & Fischel, J. E. (2005). Predicting improvement after first-grade reading difficulties: The effects of oral language, emergent literacy, and behavior skills. *Developmental Psychology, 41,* 225–234.

Stanovich, K. E. (1986). Matthew effects in reading: Some consequences of individual differences in the acquisition of reading. *Reading Research Quarterly, 21,* 360–407.

Van Daal, V. H. P., & Reitsma, P. (2000). Computer-assisted learning to read and spell: Results from two pilot studies. *Journal of Research in Reading, 23,* 181–193.

Van der Kooy-Hofland, V. A. C., & Bus, A. G. (2009, August). *Efficacy of a web-based intervention for kindergarten children with poor early reading skills.* Poster presented at the EARLI conference, Amsterdam.

Vellutino, F. R., Scanlon, D. M., Zhang, H., & Schatschneider, C. (2008). Using response to kindergarten and first grade intervention to identify children at-risk for long-term reading difficulties. *Reading and Writing, 21,* 437–480.

Verhallen, M. J. A. J., & Bus, A. G. (2009). Low-income immigrant pupils learning vocabulary through digital picture storybooks. *Journal of Educational Psychology, 102*(1), 54–61.

Verhallen, M. J. A. J., Bus, A. G., & de Jong, M. T. (2006). The promise of multimedia stories for kindergarten children at risk. *Journal of Educational Psychology, 98,* 410–419.

Welsch, J. G., Sullivan, A., & Justice, L. M. (2003). That's my letter!: What preschoolers' name writing representations tell us about emergent literacy knowledge. *Journal of Literacy Research, 2,* 757–776.

15

Developmental Differences in Early Reading Skills

SCOTT G. PARIS

There is an unprecedented level of global attention to reading research among a variety of stakeholders, including teachers, parents, publishers, and policymakers because reading is such an important foundation for education. As a consequence, policymakers have scrutinized research studies on reading development and reading education for evidence about effective educational practices. For example, national reports from the United States, *Developing Early Literacy* (National Early Literacy Panel, 2008); the United Kingdom, *Independent Review of the Teaching of Early Reading: Final Report* (Rose, 2006); and New Zealand, *Literacy Learning Progressions: Meeting the Reading and Writing Demands of the Curriculum* (New Zealand Ministry of Education, 2009) seek to identify how children learn to read and what educators can do to foster better learning.

In the United States, the need to distill the scientific evidence from a potpourri of studies and theoretical stances motivated the establishment of panels of experts to review reading research, for example, *Preventing Reading Difficulties* (Snow, Burns, & Griffin, 1998), the Report of the National Reading Panel (2000), and *Developing Early Literacy* (National Early Literacy Panel, 2008). Among many important findings, the re-

views identified five essential components of reading development—the alphabetic principle, phonemic awareness, oral reading fluency, vocabulary, and comprehension—that became the cornerstone of Reading First legislation, part of No Child Left Behind (NCLB; 2002). These components, although not a theory of reading development, have been used to make decisions about what skills to assess and teach young children. In particular, research that has shown strong correlations (i.e., predictive validity) between skills related to the first three components and subsequent reading achievement has been used to justify primary emphases on these skills for instruction and assessment in grades K–3. Although the practical and political exigencies of reading education may be served by identification of the five essential components, there is still a need to integrate these components (and others) in a developmental framework. There is a corresponding need to examine the developmental claims about the components.

This chapter clarifies distinctions among early reading skills and suggests ways that readings skills may be related longitudinally. The main focus is three specific developmental constraints on reading skills and their implications for statistical analyses and interpretations of reading skills. The constraints help to explain the different developmental trajectories of reading components and why some components should not be treated as normally distributed variables. The constraints illustrate differences between (1) temporary developmental delays and enduring developmental differences, and (2) necessary and sufficient conditions for learning to read.

Developmental Differences among Reading Skills

Nearly all theories about reading development portray the acquisition of multiple skills in a series of steps that focus on (1) acquisition and initial use followed by a period of (2) practice and automatic use that permits (3) amalgamation and coordination among skills. The general approach can be regarded as an assembly and cumulative integration of components. The progression to expertise through accumulated skills is evident in information-processing theories proposed by Adams (1990), LaBerge and Samuels (1974), Rumelhart (1994), and Stanovich (2000). The themes of increasing fluency, interaction, automaticity, consolidation, and flexibility of various skills have been used to describe the sequence of reading development in discrete domains such as alphabetic knowledge, phonological awareness, spelling, word recognition, and comprehension. However, the various skills are undifferentiated components in the conceptual models and the research designs. By *undifferentiated*, I mean that differences among the skill trajectories are not specified in the theories or treated differently in statistical analyses.

Three consequences of the assembly model are important. First, the approach yields descriptions of developmental milestones, such as the list of K–3 accomplishments identified by Snow and colleagues (1998, pp. 80–83). Descriptions of developmental benchmarks in reading skills development provide targets for instruction and assessment, as well as grade-level standards or expectations. However, milestones do not imply causal or sequential orders for development or instruction. A second consequence is the assumption that all skills in the theoretical models are normally distributed and dis-

play linear growth. Thus, researchers routinely use parametric statistics that compare various skills without regard for potential differences in developmental trajectories. Third, researchers use multivariate research methods with nonexperimental data to infer causal relations among variables in cross-sectional and longitudinal designs. Many studies collect data on multiple skills and knowledge from children at several time points, then analyze the developmental relations with multiple regression, path analyses, factor analyses, and structural equation models (SEMs). The general goal is to identify early predictors of later reading achievement that then become good candidates for early assessment and instruction. The undifferentiated skills assembly model and the corresponding multivariate analyses of correlated data underlie most research on reading development during the past 30 years.

Some theories of specific reading skills have made developmental distinctions. For example, researchers have analyzed detailed skills that contribute to phonological processing, spelling, and word recognition (e.g., Ehri, 1995; Gillon, 2004; Stahl & Murray, 1994; Torgesen, Wagner, & Rashotte, 1994). More general theories of reading development distinguish word recognition from comprehension skills. Gough and Tunmer (1986) proposed a "simple view" of reading that posits that reading is composed of two main factors: the ability to decode words efficiently, and the ability to comprehend language. Stahl, Kuhn, and Pickle (2006) proposed a model for clinical assessment of reading development that included three strands of skills. Skills in the first strand include print concepts, awareness, purpose, and strategic knowledge. Skills in the second strand include phonemic awareness, decoding knowledge, sight word knowledge, fluency, and word recognition. Skills in the third strand include background knowledge, vocabulary, language knowledge, and comprehension, and that reflect language and experience that develop across the lifespan in contrast to the first two strands that are learned by school-age children.

Chall's (1996) six-stage model that emphasizes progressive knowledge about (1) print and books, (2) phonics, (3) fluency, (4) reading to learn, (5) comprehension with analysis, and (6) comprehension with synthesis can be condensed to the development of two basic tasks: learning to read (Stages 1–3) and reading to learn (Stages 4–6).

> Learning to read takes place normally in the primary grades and involves two major tasks: acquiring the concept of reading, its purpose and uses; and learning the code. Learning the code involves (1) word identification processes, (2) use of language and cognitive resources in response to text characteristics, and (3) integration of (1) and (2). . . . Children begin to achieve this integration by the end of first grade and many tend to complete the acquisition process by the end of third grade when they achieve automaticity of decoding and word identification skills. By contrast, the second phase of reading (learning from text) is open-ended and infinite. (Athey & Singer, 1987, p. 86)

Collectively, these researchers suggested that both knowledge and skills in the first stage are mastered in grades 1–3, whereas development of skills in the second stage (and Strand 3) is open-ended. I want to use those developmental distinctions as springboards for closer examination of differences among developing reading skills and knowledge. The terms *skills* and *knowledge* are used together and interchangeably in the following discussion for convenience because the distinction, for example, among "knowing the alphabet," "saying the alphabet," and "identifying names and sounds of letters" do not alter the conceptual claims.

Trajectories of Skills Development

Traditional models of skills development can examine the time of onset, period of growth, and asymptote of performance. Growth is considered to be monotonic and continuous until some level (i.e., the y intercept on a scale of measurement) is attained. Data derived from these parameters can yield information about differences among individuals in terms of when a skill emerges, rate of growth, duration of growth, and so forth, but the most common outcome variable is the intercept. For example, one could measure, at many ages, how fast children can tie their shoelaces, name an array of letters, or

read 100 words in text. The outcomes, or *intercepts*, from a large sample at any given age yield normally distributed data, and the outcomes across ages can be compared to identify cross-sectional developmental changes. Most reading research conforms to this model of continuous growth whereby the main data are the skills intercepts (i.e., what children know or do), and the approach is similar to analyses of physical growth (e.g., height and weight) in which early values (and a variety of independent variables) can be used to predict later values.

There are good reasons to question the accuracy and usefulness of this conventional growth model for reading development (Paris, 2005). First, some reading skills do not develop continuously. Stage theories and information-processing theories alike suggest that skills such as naming the letters of the alphabet and learning elementary concepts of print, Stage 1 or Strand 1 skills, are learned early and entirely. In contrast, vocabulary knowledge and comprehension skills develop continuously throughout life. Second, the period of growth is briefer for Stage 1 skills compared to vocabulary and comprehension. Third, the reason for discontinuous and brief growth periods for some skills is due in part to the small set of knowledge or the discrete and less complex nature of the skills. Fourth, group data may indicate that some reading skills develop in a linear or monotonic fashion, but individual data suggest that growth occurs irregularly, with spurts and stops, that is modeled better by a logistic function than by a straight line (Fischer & Bidell, 1998).

In general, the component skills related to the alphabetic principle, concepts of print, phonemic awareness, and oral reading fluency develop in a nonlinear and discontinuous fashion compared to the component skills related to vocabulary and comprehension, a distinction similar to Athey and Singer's (1987) claim about Stage 1 versus Stage 2 skills. The constraints are stated as conceptual claims, but they have statistical ramifications that challenge traditional research designs and analyses. I suggest that new theories of reading development should incorporate the constraints, and that reanalyses of data derived from constrained skills are warranted.

Claim 1: Some Skills Are Mastered Universally to the Same Intercept

The Alphabetic Principle

Learning the names and sounds of the letters in the alphabet are constrained skills. Children who know the alphabet before age 4 years are as unusual as children who do not know the alphabet by age 7. It is a discrete set of knowledge that can be taught directly within a brief period, and growth is discontinuous and nonlinear. Most importantly, all children master the entire alphabet and attain the identical intercepts. They all have the same knowledge about the names and sounds of letters. (It is acknowledged that not all children hear/say the identical sounds and that some exceptional children do not learn the alphabetic principle as quickly as most, but exceptions based on dialect or dyslexia do not invalidate the general developmental claim.) Universal mastery of the alphabetic principle stands in contrast to learning vocabulary because vocabulary assessments yield intercepts that are normally distributed data at all ages (i.e., people know different words and different numbers of words when compared at any age). Knowledge of letter names and sounds is not normally distributed among adults, proficient readers, or children before age 4 or after age 7 years. The only time that data on the alphabetic principle approach a normal distribution is when the data are gathered from a sample of children who have partial knowledge of the alphabet.

The claim about identical intercepts for novices and experts is more than a claim about floor and ceiling effects in data. It is a claim about the construct validity of the alphabetic principle, namely, that knowledge (and the associated skills intercept measures) of letter names and sounds is identical (or at least functionally isomorphic) among the general population of readers. The construct is conceptually different from other knowledge and skills that vary in intercepts among people. A universally mastered skill, such as alphabetic knowledge, is by definition discontinuous and normally distributed only in special times of partial mastery. Thus, variations in the intercepts (i.e., how many letter names or sounds a child can identify) depend entirely on the specific sample

tested. Any inferences from the data must be restricted to similar samples that exhibit partial mastery. It is also clear that samples including many novices have a positive skew, whereas data that include many experts exhibit negative skew. Both cases attenuate the variances and alter the strength of relations with other variables. That is why differences in alphabetic knowledge among children are temporary delays in mastery, not enduring individual differences, and data derived from samples with partial mastery exhibit transient relations to other variables. I suggest that traditional approaches to research on alphabetic knowledge, both conceptual and statistical, may not meet standards of scientific construct and criterion-related validity (Messick, 1995).

There is abundant empirical evidence to support Claim 1 about the alphabetic principle. Most children begin kindergarten knowing some letter names and learn them all quickly (e.g., Treiman & Bourassa, 2000). For example, Morris, Bloodgood, Lomax, and Perney (2003) used a task of identifying 15 letters in upper and lower cases and reported that children knew about half of them in September of kindergarten and all of them by the end of kindergarten. The letter names that are easiest to learn occur early in the alphabet and may occur in the child's name. Letter sounds are easiest to learn when the sound of the letter is in the letter name and when letters usually occur in the initial position of words rather than in the final position (McBride-Chang, 1999). Thus, there are fixed and nonrandom effects in learning letter names and sounds.

However, a meta-analysis of instructional effects on alphabetic knowledge used a random effects model and ignored the developmentally constrained aspects of the construct (Piasta & Wagner, 2010). The meta-analysis updated the NELP Report (2008) by including more studies (37) in a greater variety of publication sources. The results revealed smaller effect size for alphabetic training (0.14–0.65) than the NELP and no evidence of transfer. The authors concluded:

> Results were generally inconclusive with respect to the causal relations between alphabet learning and development of other early literacy skills. Small effects on reading skills

were found when assessed immediately following instruction, but effects were no longer apparent 2 to 12 months later. No effects were found for phonological awareness or spelling outcomes at either immediate or follow-up assessment, nor did initial effects on alphabet outcomes persist. (p. 24)

These findings are consistent with the constrained skills view of alphabetic knowledge because the differences between training conditions, like all differences between samples of children learning the alphabet, are temporary. The alphabet is learned entirely in a relatively short time; explicit training is only one source of learning, so the effects are modest, temporary, and show little transfer to other skills because it is a universal and necessary condition for other reading skills but not sufficient by itself.

Concepts of Print

Claim 1 extends to other kinds of reading knowledge. Concepts of print include children's understanding of letters, words, sentences, punctuation, and directionality of reading (Chall, 1996; Clay, 1979). The set of knowledge is constrained in size, period of acquisition, and intercepts. The core knowledge is identical for everyone who reads text in the same language. The particular concepts about print may be specific to languages such as English, Chinese, or Arabic, but the scope and target of the concepts are similar across languages. For example, all English readers know to read from left to right and top to bottom of the page, and they understand word and sentence boundaries in the same ways. They also attain the identical knowledge about word boundaries, upper and lower case, commas, question marks, and other punctuation conventions. Although concepts about print and text (in any language) can be extended to a huge number of nuanced meanings and become quite sophisticated, such as the structure of iambic pentameter in poetry, the core concepts that children are expected to master in K–3 grades are similar and small in number. Almost all early reading assessments of concepts of print (e.g., Clay, 1979) examine the same prototypical concepts, and children are expected to master all of them as beginning readers. Thus, conceptually as well as

empirically, children's early print concepts is a construct defined by mastery and not a normal distribution around some mean of concepts.

Evidence about the development of children's central concepts of print supports this claim. Clay (1979) presented a little book to 5-year-olds and asked them to indicate the front of the book, the direction of reading, errors in inverted text, and the function of punctuation marks. The 24 items included a variety of concepts about both functions and conventions of print. Clay presents normalized scores in stanine groups that show how many concepts are mastered by samples of children. Although there is value in providing norm-referenced rates of acquisition, it is important to note that nearly all children master all the concepts about print by 7 to 8 years of age, so the critical difference among children is in their rate of mastery, not their final knowledge.

Rathvon's review (2004) indicates that assessments of children's print awareness may be correlated with other measures of early reading, but they have little predictive power when measures of letter naming and phonemic awareness are included in the regressions. One reason may be due to the multicolinearity of the variables. Letter naming and phonemic awareness usually are taught about the same age as print awareness skills, and they emerge from the same kinds of shared reading experiences, so the intercorrelations of the three variables remove their unique variance. Lonigan, Burgess, and Anthony (2000) suggested that print awareness serves as a proxy measure for print exposure and literacy experiences. This means that children who score high on assessments of concepts about print are ahead of their agemates, but their superior print awareness is temporary and only an indicator of different previous literacy experiences.

Phonological Awareness

Phonological awareness (PA) refers to the understanding of the sound structure of spoken language, and it includes awareness of syllables, onset–rime patterns, and phonemes (Gillon, 2004). It is important for reading because readers must learn the correspondence between graphemes and phonemes (i.e., phonics) and use both visual and auditory information to recognize words (Ehri, 1995). Gillon (2004) suggests that PA should be separated from storing and retrieving phonological information during information processing because differences in working memory can influence phonological processing. She also suggests that PA is one part of metalinguistic awareness. Others (e.g., Stanovich, 1992) have suggested that the term *phonological sensitivity* is more accurate than PA because conscious awareness is not necessarily involved in applying the knowledge to decoding text. Anthony and Lonigan (2004) suggest that there are four distinct conceptualizations of PA, with the critical differences in claims about whether PA is one general construct or several separate abilities. I use the term PA because it is conventional and includes both knowledge and skills involved in understanding the distinct sounds associated with letters and letter combinations in words.

PA includes many different subskills that begin to develop with oral language in early childhood, but some fundamental features are mastered by the primary grades. In general, children learn distinctions among larger phonological units before smaller units (Anthony & Lonigan, 2004). For example, children can detect syllables in words before they can detect phonemes, and they can blend and delete units at the word level before the syllable level before the subsyllabic level (Lonigan, Burgess, Anthony, & Barker, 1998; Stanovich, Cunningham, & Cramer, 1984). Evidence also suggests that children can identify consonant before vowel sounds and initial consonant sounds before medial and final consonants, and they can identify rhyming words before they can segment and blend syllables or phonemes within words (Rathvon, 2004). Gillon (2004) notes that PA is nonexistent or limited in 2- to 3-year-olds, quite variable during rapid learning by 3- to 5-year-olds, and more "stable" after 5 to 6 years of age. A review of studies in the United States, United Kingdom, Australia, and New Zealand "suggest general, universal trends in phonological awareness development for the English language" (Gillon, 2004, p. 39).

I suggest that some skills involved in PA are discrete and universally mastered in a relatively brief period of growth. For example, by age 6 years, nearly all English-speaking children can identify familiar onset–rime patterns in oral language, they can identify rhyming words such as *cat–hat*, and they can blend initial consonants with different rimes to create words such as *s-at, s-it*, and *s-et*. Identifying initial consonant sounds in print may be done informally during adult–child reading or may be the target of instruction, but phoneme identification while reading usually begins by age 4 and is often highly skilled by age 8 (Adams, 1990). Identification of final consonants occurs later and recognition of vowel sounds is more complex (Snow et al., 1998; Stahl & Murray, 1994). Segmenting phonemes in words and blending phonemes to create words are more difficult skills, but they are usually acquired as children are asked to decode and spell words in early instruction (Ehri, 1995). PA, especially about central and prototypical phonemes, develops rapidly during primary grades and formal reading instruction. Claim 1 asserts that some skills and knowledge included in PA are universally mastered.

Certainly, many struggling readers do not exhibit adequate PA by 9 years of age so it may be incorrect to claim universal mastery. I agree that some children have lower intercepts (i.e., less PA) and less dramatic slopes (i.e., slower rates of learning and mastery), but even struggling readers master many of the identical aspects of PA that proficient readers acquire when adequate opportunities for learning and instruction are provided. Most children who by 9 years of age do not know the 41 phonemes of English or have difficulty representing, storing, and retrieving phonological information are diagnosed with some type of dyslexia or language impairment (Gillon, 2004). Distinguishing which features of PA are learned readily from those that are not can be diagnostically useful (Stanovich, 2000). The small percentage of struggling readers who do not master some aspects of PA by 9–11 years of age does not invalidate Claim 1 as a general developmental accomplishment. Indeed, cross-linguistic data suggest that mastery of PA may be more evident in alphabetic languages other than English that have more regular phoneme–grapheme correspondences (Gillon, 2004; Katz & Frost, 1992).

Claims about universally mastered identical knowledge and skills are most evident for discrete, small sets of knowledge characteristic of Stage 1 skills. The alphabetic principle and concepts of print are the clearest examples. Skills involved in word recognition and decoding become more numerous, more complex, and more interrelated with expertise. Claim 1 may extend to some of these skills, such as identifying initial consonant sounds more readily than others (e.g., phoneme elision) because of frequency, practice, and instruction. However, mastery of essential and prototypical knowledge about phoneme–grapheme correspondence occurs in a relatively brief period for most individuals learning to read. It is acknowledged that speed, automaticity, and flexible use of decoding skills vary among beginning readers, but those differences diminish with increasing skill (Snow et al., 1998; Stanovich, 2000). I suggest that Stage 1 knowledge and skills involved in decoding text, the hallmark of initial reading in all theories of reading development, are constrained because nearly all individuals acquire the same set of knowledge and apply similar skills to say the words in text. They may differ in speed, automaticity, and efficiency of processing, but those are differences in performance not competence.

Alphabetic knowledge, print knowledge, and PA are different from vocabulary and comprehension in at least three fundamental ways. First, constrained knowledge and skills are relatively small and discrete sets; second, they can be taught directly; and third, they are mastered nearly entirely by 9 years of age by most children learning to read. Some might argue that the domains of print knowledge and PA are larger than I portray them so their acquisition curves are longer over time and never mastered completely. That may be true for some concepts and skills, but the essential, central, and prototypical knowledge and skills, which are exactly the kinds of knowledge and skills assessed by early reading tests, develop from nonexistent or modest at age 3–4 years to asymptotic levels by 9 years. Different rates of acquisition, for most children, signal developmental delays in learning rather than individual differences in abilities that are maintained, even though initial delays may be exacerbated by other conditions to produce slower and lower developmental trajectories for other reading skills (i.e., Matthew effects) (Stanovich, 1986).

Although space does not permit extended discussion here, several corollaries of Claim 1 are possible. For example, Claim 1A is that alphabetic languages with more letters or sounds take longer to master than alphabetic systems with fewer letters or sounds. This claim simply asserts that the size of the knowledge set, whether specified in letters, graphemes, or phonemes, influences the ease and rate of learning, but people learning to read in any alphabetic language reach the same knowledge asymptotes. Claim 1B is that languages with more transparent orthographies (i.e., more regular and consistent grapheme–phoneme correspondence) are mastered more quickly than less transparent languages. For example, children learning transparent orthographies, such as Spanish, Italian, or Turkish, perform at asymptotic levels on syllable and phoneme awareness tasks by first grade, much earlier than children learning English, a more opaque orthography (Katz & Frost, 1992).

Claim 2: Some Skills Exhibit Discontinuous and Nonlinear Growth

Universally mastered skills are discontinuous because growth is complete when the intercept is attained. There is also a period before learning begins when knowledge is nil or nearly so. Thus, for most of a person's life, universally mastered knowledge and skills have no variability; they are either at floor or ceiling levels. Nonlinear growth is also evident in phonemic awareness and oral reading fluency because they exhibit floor and ceiling effects in developmental data with similar asymptotes (at least for some components). Development from novice to expert for any of these skills follows a sigmoid-shaped curve that can be described by a logistic function. Because reading skills are usually measured after acquisition has started, growth could also resemble a power curve that reaches asymptote (Logan, Taylor, & Etherton, 1999; Stahl & Hiebert, 2005). The shape of the growth trajectory depends in part on the choice of beginning and end points, and that is often empirically defined by the timing of assessments. If growth is only measured during the period of rapid learning, the curve could be monotonic, but partial growth analyses do not accurately represent the underlying construct or adequately measure nonlinear components of development.

In addition to the nonlinear portions of developmental trajectories of constrained skills and knowledge, it is important to note that variances are not equal across the periods of acquisition, growth, and automatic use (Pennington & Lefly, 2001). More specifically, variances are greatest during the periods of rapid growth and attenuated at initial and expert parts of the trajectories. This creates a large, and hitherto unacknowledged, statistical problem when skills are measured from very different points along their developmental trajectories. For example, if skill *A* has a large variance at partial mastery and skill *B* has a smaller variance because it is near asymptote, then the relation between *A* and *B* may be less than when *B* is measured during its period of rapid learning. Measurements of skills *A* and *B* a year earlier or later with the same sample can yield a very different pattern of results because the variances of constrained skills change longitudinally. Thus, during the period of rapid learning, the variances of emerging skills will be greatest, so correlations with other variables are stronger during this period (Pennington & Lefly, 2001).

Phonological Awareness

Some researchers suggest that the development of PA is nonlinear, perhaps because PA includes a variety of skills and knowledge. Some subskills of PA display logistic growth and asymptotic levels in early childhood, and many do so by middle childhood. Rhyme detection is above chance for a few 2- to 3-year-olds and is very good for 5- to 6-year-olds (Bradley & Bryant, 1983; Lonigan, Burgess, Anthony, & Barker, 1998). Segmenting words into syllables approaches asymptote by 6 years of age, and segmenting words into phonemes by 7 years of age (Liberman, Schankweiler, Fischer, & Carter, 1974). Lonigan and colleagues (1998) examined all three levels of PA—phoneme, syllable, and onset–rime awareness—among 2- to 5-year-olds. There were floor effects in the data for 2- to 3-year-olds, and the researchers applied mathematical transformations to the data and nonparameteric analyses, but the primary analyses were analyses of variance

(ANOVAs) and correlations. They found accelerated growth between ages 3 and 4 years for children from middle-income families but not for children from low-income families. This illustrates how different samples of children can exhibit nonlinear growth patterns at different ages. Performance generally was low and unstable for 2- to 3-year-olds but highly stable by age 5. Presumably, if the study had included older children, the measures would have maintained stability and approached ceiling levels. Lonigan and colleagues said:

> The pattern of results indicates that the development of phonological sensitivity is not a continuous function represented as a steady increase in ability with increasing age. Although trend analyses indicate that there were linear effects of age on tasks, significant higher order trends suggest that growth in phonological sensitivity was accelerated in the older groups. (p. 305)

Nonlinear growth is evident in the Comprehensive Test of Phonological Processing (CTOPP; Wagner, Torgeson, & Rashotte, 1999). The CTOPP includes 13 subtests, seven for children ages 5–6 years and 10 for people ages 7–24. The older subjects actually receive all of the same subtests as the younger sample except Sound Matching, presumably because it is mastered by age 7 years, then four more difficult subtests, blending and segmenting nonwords, and rapid naming of colors and objects. Examination of Table C.1 in the CTOPP manual reveals wide variation in the developmental growth rates of the performance on the subtests between ages 5 and 15. For example, Sound Matching is at 100% by 8 years, 3 months; Blending Words is at 87% mastery by age 8 years, 9 months; Blending Nonwords is at 80% mastery by the same age; and Phoneme Reversal is at 70% mastery by age 9 years. Floor effects are evident for Segmenting Words because all children who segment fewer than nine words receive the same low score. Growth from ages 5 to 7 years, 9 months ranges from 0 to 9 on that scale; increases in scores for segmenting words only advance from 9 to 12 between ages 7 years, 9 months and 14 years, 9 months. Likewise, the Memory for Digits scale of raw scores is from 0 to 14 between ages 5 and 14 years, 9 months, but the conversions to age equivalents show that 0 to 10 scores are all expected before age 6 with growth during the next 9 years limited to increases of four items. Clearly, growth and variances on the subtests are not linear or uniform.

Oral Reading Fluency

The second type of evidence for Claim 2 is derived from data on oral reading fluency (ORF). Fluent oral reading is the coordination of automated decoding skills through practice. Fluency includes reading text quickly, accurately, and with intonation (Kuhn & Stahl, 2002). Research suggests that accuracy and rate begin to reach asymptotic levels by 10–12 years of age for most children (Fuchs & Fuchs, 1999). This means that a group of second-grade children may exhibit widely different reading rates and levels of accurate decoding among them, but the variability in rate and accuracy will decrease with age, practice, and mastery as children reach their asymptotic levels. Indeed, the differences between children in fluency scores are greatest during initial learning in grades 1–3.

Reading rate scores calculated as words read correctly per minute yield ORF scores that follow a power curve from grades 1–8 in published norms by Hasbrouck and Tindal (1992, 2006). The norms include data from 5,000 to 20,000 students at each grade level (fewer at upper grades) assessed in fall (except first graders), winter, and spring. The mean spring scores reveal a power curve reaching asymptote by grade 6. Inspection of the data tables by grade level reveals that ORF scores display greater growth during the school year in early grades, about 30–40 wcpm compared to 18–23 in grades 6–8. They may not be normally distributed either, even with the huge sample sizes because the mean scores at grades 1–4 are always higher than the scores at the 50th percentile, indicating a negative skew. There are also large standard deviations at each grade level, above 40 for all grades except 1 and 2, where floor effects restricted the SDs to a range of 32–42. Thus, reading rates do not follow linear trajectories, and the rate of growth varies within and between grades. ORF scores also display large variances at all ages, with a skew toward slow reading,

so struggling readers may influence ORF scores disproportionately. With smaller sample sizes that are characteristic of most reading studies, nonlinear growth and unequal variances in ORF scores are likely to be greater and more idiosyncratic.

Analyses of fluency data are also confounded because accuracy and prosody are not normally distributed variables. Oral reading accuracy is skewed by definition, so the construct is not normally distributed. It makes little sense to think of oral reading accuracy as normally distributed between 0 and 100% because the mean expected value is not 50% mastery, but closer to 100%. In fact, the clinically accepted definitions of ORF are *independent* (95–100%), *instructional* (90–94%), and *frustration* (85–89%), so whenever accuracy is below 90%, readers are expected to be frustrated and comprehension is expected to suffer (Lipson & Wixson, 2003). Stahl and Hiebert (2005) suggest that oral reading accuracy below 95% may interfere with the construction of an adequate text-based representation. Because understanding text requires a very high level of accuracy, comprehension can only be assessed when accuracy is near ceiling levels. This codependency constraint (elaborated in Claim 3) is conceptual as well as analytical, but it has been neglected in reading assessments, especially when establishing validity and reliability of the assessment tools.

Prosody is a feature of oral reading that is not evident in beginning readers, but it is evident to a high degree of proficiency among skilled readers. Granted that prosody can be developed into theatrical proportions, it is usually assessed with a 4-point rubric with students in grades 1–8. Thus, it has a small range and a potentially skewed distribution if the sample includes mostly novice or expert readers. The National Assessment of Educational Progress (NAEP) study of fluency (Pinnell et al., 1995), conducted with 1,136 fourth graders, is one of the most thorough and frequently cited sources of evidence about prosody, so it serves as an example of the problems. The research team followed conventional practice of assessing prosody with a 4-point rubric that created categorical data by assigning numerical values. However, the interrater reliability was $r = .70$, and there was only 58% agreement on assigning scores to exact categories. In fact, 80% of the subjects were classified into the two middle categories. The NAEP report provides a series of tables that claim to show that prosody is related modestly to reading accuracy, rate, and proficiency. However, the data derived from accuracy, rate, and prosody measures were assumed to be continuous and normally distributed and were analyzed with parametric statistics that treated the data as ordinal and interval. These assumptions are not warranted, and the analyses are not appropriate so the conclusions of the report are suspect. The fundamental problem is not just erroneous statistics; it is a failure to identify the nonlinear developmental trajectories of fluency scores based on oral reading accuracy, rate, and prosody.

Claim 3: Some Skills Are Temporarily Codependent on Other Skills

Traditional models of skills assembly and integration typically employ correlational and multivariate analyses to determine when different skills are related to each other during development. The result has been a confusing array of (1) correlations that differ widely in strength and (2) controversy about causal relations among various skills. However, the discrepant findings may be reconciled with a reconceptualization of different developmental trajectories of constrained and unconstrained skills according to Claims 1 and 2. Claim 3 posits that developing relations among skills can be temporarily codependent. One implication of this view is that skill *A* must meet some minimum threshold value to enable skill *B* to develop. Another implication is that beyond the threshold, variations in skill *A* do not influence skill *B*. Both implications would be evident in strong correlations between skills *A* and *B* early in acquisition but not later. Examples from the alphabetic principle, phonemic awareness, and ORF illustrate these relations.

Alphabetic Principle

Letter-name knowledge is essential for reciting the alphabet in order, and it precedes and supports letter–sound correspondence (Stahl & Murray, 1994). Thus, letter-name knowledge is correlated with letter–sound knowledge but not subsequent word-reading skills (Rathvon, 2004). This may explain why teaching children to name letters does not improve other reading skills (Fugate, 1997). Similarly, the speed of saying individual letter names and sounds is not correlated with reading ability (Stanovich, Cunningham, & West, 1981). Sequential dependencies may exist among different components of the alphabetic principle and other reading skills, but the relations are complicated by reciprocal benefits. For example, learning the name of a letter can facilitate learning its sound, and that may increase the automatic recognition of the correspondence between the grapheme and phoneme over repeated occurrences. It appears that letter-name knowledge precedes and facilitates letter-sound knowledge, and letter-sound knowledge in turn directly promotes phonemic awareness, decoding, and word recognition (Treiman & Bourassa, 2000).

Morris and colleagues (2003) report a longitudinal study of the relations among reading skills in children during kindergarten and first grade. They used a LISREL model to test the relations among emerging skills, but they failed to consider the conceptual and methodological constraints in their data. For example, children's alphabetic knowledge and beginning consonant awareness were at ceiling levels at Times 2, 3, and 4 in their study, while measures of children's word recognition and phoneme segmentation were at floor levels for Times 1, 2, and 3. They concluded that the developmental sequence of acquisition for seven reading skills is alphabetic knowledge, beginning consonant awareness, concept of word in text, spelling with beginning and ending consonants, phoneme segmentation, word recognition, and contextual reading ability. This is a plausible order that implies sequential dependencies even though the parametric statistics seem inappropriate.

Phonemic Awareness

Phonemic awareness, the part of PA that is directly related to print, is important because vast research shows that children who are poor readers generally have poor phonemic awareness. Researchers have debated whether (1) phonemic awareness directly or indirectly influences other reading skills, and whether (2) phonemic awareness develops before, after, or concomitantly with other reading skills. Many studies have shown that phoneme identification and manipulation (e.g., segmenting and blending) in kindergarten children are significant predictors of reading and spelling achievement in grades 1 and 2 (e.g., Lundberg, Olofsson, & Wall, 1980; Share, Jorm, Maclean, & Matthews, 1984; Torgeson et al., 1994; Torneus, 1984). However, phonemic awareness at older ages approaches asymptote and is less correlated with achievement (Adams, 1990). For example, Willson and Rupley (1997) showed that phonemic awareness was related strongly to comprehension in grades 2 and 3, but the relation diminished in upper grades. Thus, phonemic awareness may be correlated most strongly with reading and spelling during initial acquisition, when it signals multiple advances in language and literacy development. In contrast, PA reflects broader phonological knowledge and may be related to phonological processing over a longer age range (i.e., PA is less constrained than phonemic awareness).

Some researchers suggest that the developing relations between phonemic awareness (or PA) and reading achievement are bidirectional (Torneus, 1984). In particular, children's emerging awareness of phonemes within words may support their phonetic spelling, which in turn facilitates word recognition (Ehri, 1995; Ellis, 1994). It is possible that the relation is more subtle than bidirectional correlation; perhaps phonemic awareness, spelling, and word recognition help to bootstrap one another through a series of codependencies during acquisition that decrease as spelling and word recognition become automatic. Metsala (1999) made a similar proposal about the relation between PA and vocabulary in the lexical restructuring model (Metsala & Walley, 1998). This model suggests that vocabulary growth helps children restructure words into segments, and this knowledge is necessary for phonemic awareness. They suggest that vocabulary size may influence phonemic awareness most during preschool years, when both develop rapidly, another developing relation that is codependent during initial acquisition. Given the high correlations among developing reading skills and knowledge in Stage 1, it seems reasonable that (1)

some relations are sequential, (2) other relations bootstrap others, and (3) still other relations are codependent only early in development.

Oral Reading Fluency

In a similar vein, ORF may exhibit stronger relations with comprehension in beginning or struggling readers than in skilled readers (Kendall & Hood, 1979). LaBerge and Samuels (1974) proposed a model in which comprehension is the consequence of automatic decoding. However, research has shown that some readers can decode all the words and still have poor comprehension. It is possible that ORF may display a threshold relation with comprehension, in which a certain level of reading accuracy and speed are necessary to enable comprehension. Evidence for a threshold effect can be seen in the correlations between fluency and comprehension across age and proficiency. For example, within-subject correlations between ORF (both accuracy and rate) and comprehension are positive for first and second graders. Pearson correlations range from $r = .2$ to .4, but the correlations decline to near zero by grade 4 (Paris, Carpenter, Paris, & Hamilton, 2005). The same pattern is evident when fluency–comprehension scores are correlated by grade level or passage difficulty, and it led researchers to hypothesize that fluency and comprehension become disjunctive with increasing oral reading fluency.

Stahl and Hiebert (2005) suggest that reading accuracy and prosody are most strongly related to word recognition for beginning readers. They said:

> The relation between comprehension and fluency appears to be developmental. There seems to be a stronger relation between word recognition, accuracy, rate, and prosody and comprehension in the first and second grades. This relation appears to diminish in the third and fourth grades. (p. 176)

Inspection of the data tables in the NAEP report on fluency reveals the source of the modest relations among fluency and comprehension is the most struggling readers (Pinnell et al., 1995). Of the students who received a Level 1 (lowest score on the 4-point rubric) for prosody, 76% were reading less than 80 words per minute. Of those who were classified in Level 2, 76% were reading less than 105 words per minute, below the median of the sample. Likewise, the nonfluent readers had the most deviations (i.e., mistakes) in their oral reading, and they had more meaning-changing miscues than fluent readers. My interpretation of the data is that nonfluent readers, those fourth graders who struggled the most reading the 300-word passage, could not easily read many words so they read more slowly and with less expression than the majority of children who were more fluent readers. The fluent readers, conversely, were not necessarily always fast or accurate. Thus, there is an asymmetrical relation showing that lack of prosody is related to lack of accuracy and slow reading, but high levels of fluency do not entail accurate and speedy reading. This is consistent with the "necessary but not sufficient" interpretation offered by the NAEP report authors.

Implications and Conclusions

The claims about constrained skills imply that traditional analyses need to be reconsidered and reevaluated with other statistical methods and interpretations (see Paris & Paris, 2006). Claims that young children's alphabetic knowledge, print knowledge, phonemic awareness, and fluency predict future reading achievement must be more guarded and acknowledged as limited to times of partial mastery. The implications for instruction are that constrained skills are necessary for reading development so they should be taught thoroughly and early, but not exclusively. The potential liability in early reading instruction that emphasizes only constrained skills is that children may miss out on important experiences with oral language, writing, speaking, vocabulary, and comprehension that can all be nurtured when constrained skills are still developing.

The implications for policymakers are numerous, but the main suggestion is to keep the development of skills related to decoding in perspective so that they do not become the sole focus of instruction or assessment for beginning readers (Paris, 2009). Psychological studies of component skills have yielded a great deal of detailed and quantitative in-

formation about early reading, but the preference among policymakers for quantitative information should not limit educational practices to easily measured skills. Children and teachers deserve rich interactions with literacy through reading assessments and curricula that are engaging and thoughtful. Understanding differences in developmental trajectories among skills and the broader goals of motivated reading for learning in multiple media for multiple purposes should reinforce the importance of early instruction on a broad set of language and literacy experiences for children.

References

Adams, M. J. (1990). *Beginning to read: Thinking and learning about print.* Cambridge, MA: MIT Press.

Anthony, J. L., & Lonigan, C. J. (2004). The nature of phonological awareness: Converging evidence from four studies of preschool and early grade school children. *Journal of Educational Psychology, 96*(1), 43–55.

Athey, I., & Singer, H. (1987). Developing the nation's reading potential for a technological era. *Harvard Educational Review, 57*(1), 84–93.

Bradley, L., & Bryant, P. E. (1983). Categorizing sounds and learning to read—a causal connection. *Nature, 301,* 419–421.

Chall, J. S. (1996). *Stages of reading development* (2nd ed.). Orlando, FL: Harcourt Brace.

Clay, M. M. (1979). *Reading: The patterning of complex behavior* (2nd ed.). Auckland: Heinemann.

Ehri, L. C. (1995). Development of the ability to read words. In R. Barr, M. Kamil, P. Mosenthal, & P. Pearson (Eds.), *Handbook of reading research* (Vol. 2, pp. 383–417). Hillsdale, NJ: Erlbaum.

Ellis, N. (1994). Longitudinal studies of spelling development. In G. Brown & N. Ellis (Eds.), *Handbook of spelling* (pp. 155–178). West Sussex, UK: Wiley.

Fischer, K. W., & Bidell, T. R. (1998). Dynamic development of psychological structures in action and thought. In R. Lerner & W. Damon (Eds.), *Handbook of child psychology: Vol. 1. Theoretical models of human development* (pp. 467–561). New York: Wiley.

Fuchs, L. S., & Fuchs, D. (1999). Monitoring student progress toward the development of reading competence: A review of three forms of classroom-based assessment. *School Psychology Review, 28,* 659–671.

Fugate, M. H. (1997). Letter training and its effect on the development of beginning reading skills. *School Psychology Quarterly, 12*(2), 170–192.

Gillon, G. T. (2004). *Phonological awareness: From research to practice.* New York: Guilford Press.

Gough, P. B., & Tunmer, W. E. (1986). Decoding, reading, and reading disability. *Remedial and Special Education, 7,* 6–10.

Hasbrouck, J. E., & Tindal, G. (1992). Curriculum-based oral reading fluency norms for students in grades 2 through 5. *Teaching Exceptional Children, 24*(3), 41–44.

Hasbrouck, J. E., & Tindal, G. (2006). Oral reading fluency norms: A valuable assessment tool for reading teachers. *The Reading Teacher, 59*(7), 636–644.

Katz, L., & Frost, R. (1992). The reading process is different for different orthographies: The orthographic depth hypothesis. In L. Katz & R. Frost (Eds.), *Orthography, phonology, morphology, and meaning* (pp. 67–84). Amsterdam: North Holland.

Kendall, J. R., & Hood, J. (1979). Investigating the relationship between comprehension and word recognition: Oral reading analysis of children with comprehension or word recognition disabilities. *Journal of Reading Behavior, 11*(1), 41–48.

Kuhn, M. R., & Stahl, S. A. (2003). Fluency: A review of developmental and remedial practices. *Journal of Educational Psychology, 95*(1), 3–21.

LaBerge, D., & Samuels, S. J. (1974). Toward a theory of automatic information processing in reading. *Cognitive Psychology, 6*, 293–323.

Liberman, I. Y., Schankweiler, D., Fischer, F., & Carter, B. (1974). Explicit syllable and phoneme segmentation in the young child. *Journal of Experimental Child Psychology, 18*(2), 201–212.

Lipson, M. Y., & Wixson, K. K. (2003). *Assessment and instruction of reading and writing difficulty.* Boston: Allyn & Bacon.

Logan, G. D., Taylor, S. E., & Etherton, J. L. (1999). Attention and automaticity: Toward a theoretical integration. *Psychological Research, 62*, 165–181.

Lonigan, C. J., Burgess, S. R., & Anthony, J. L. (2000). Development of emergent literacy and early reading skills in preschool children: Evidence from a latent-variable longitudinal study. *Developmental Psychology, 36*(5), 596–613.

Lonigan, C. J., Burgess, S. R., Anthony, J. L., & Barker, T. (1998). Development of phonological sensitivity in 2- to 5-year-old children. *Journal of Educational Psychology, 90*(2), 294–311.

Lundberg, I., Olofsson, A., & Wall, S. (1980). Reading and spelling skills in the first years predicted from phonemic awareness skills in kindergarten. *Scandinavian Journal of Psychology, 21*, 159–173.

McBride-Chang, C. (1999). The ABCs of the ABCs: The development of letter-name and letter-sound knowledge. *Merrill–Palmer Quarterly, 45*(2), 285–308.

Messick, S. (1995). Validity of psychological assessment: Validation of inferences from persons' responses and performances as scientific inquiry into score meaning. *American Psychologist, 50*, 741–749.

Metsala, J. L. (1999). Young children's phonological awareness and nonword repetition as a function of vocabulary development. *Journal of Educational Psychology, 91*(1), 3–19.

Metsala, J. L., & Walley, A. C. (1998). Spoken vocabulary growth and the segmental restructuring of lexical representations: Precursors to phoneme awareness and early reading ability. In J. L. Metsala

& L. C. Ehri (Eds.), *Word recognition in beginning literacy* (pp. 89–120). Mahwah, NJ: Erlbaum.

Morris, D., Bloodgood, J. W., Lomax, R. G., & Perney, J. (2003). Developmental steps in learning to read: A longitudinal study in kindergarten and first grade. *Reading Research Quarterly, 38*(3), 302–328.

National Early Literacy Panel [NELP]. (2008). *Developing early literacy: Report of the National Early Literacy Panel.* Washington, DC: National Institute for Literacy.

New Zealand Ministry of Education. (2009). *Literacy learning progressions: Meeting the reading and writing demands of the curriculum.* Auckland: Author.

No Child Left Behind Act of 2001. (2002). Public Law No. 107–110, paragraph 115 Stat. 1425.

Paris, S. G. (2005). Re-interpreting the development of reading skills. *Reading Research Quarterly, 40*(2), 184–202.

Paris, S. G. (2009). Constrained skills—so what? In K. M. Leander, D. W. Rowe, D. K. Dickinson, M. K. Hundley, R. T. Jimenez, & V. J. Risko (Eds.), *59th yearbook of the National Reading Conference* (pp. 34–44). Oak Creek, WI: National Reading Conference.

Paris, S. G., Carpenter, R. D., Paris, A. H., & Hamilton, E. E. (2005). Spurious and genuine correlates of children's reading comprehension. In S. G. Paris & S. A. Stahl (Eds.), *Children's reading comprehension and assessment* (pp. 131–160). Mahwah, NJ: Erlbaum.

Paris, S. G., & Paris, A. H. (2006). The influence of developmental skill trajectories on assessments of children's early reading. In W. Damon, R. Lerner, K. A. Renninger, & I. E. Siegel (Eds.), *Handbook of child psychology: Vol. 4. Child psychology in practice* (6th ed., pp. 48–74). Hoboken, NJ: Wiley.

Pennington, B. F., & Lefly, D. L. (2001). Early reading development in children at family risk for dyslexia. *Child Development, 72*(3), 816–833.

Piasta, S. B., & Wagner, R. K. (2010). Developing early literacy skills: A meta-analysis of alphabet learning and instruction. *Reading Research Quarterly, 45*(1), 8–38.

Pinnell, G. S., Pikulski, J. J., Wixson, K. K., Campbell, J. R., Gough, P. B., & Beatty, A. S. (1995). *Listening to children read aloud: Data from NAEP's Integrated Reading Performance Record (IRPR) at grade 4.* Washington, DC: National Center for Education Statistics.

Rathvon, N. (2004). *Early reading assessment: A practitioner's handbook.* New York: Guilford Press.

Report of the National Reading Panel. (2000). *Teaching children to read: An evidence-based assessment of the scientific research literature on reading and its implications for reading instruction.* Washington, DC: National Institute of Child Health and Human Development, U.S. Department of Education.

Rose, J. (2006). *Independent review of the teaching of early reading: Final report.* London: Department for Education and Skills.

Rumelhart, D. E. (1994). Toward an interactive model of reading. In R. B. Ruddell, M. Rapp-Ruddell, & H. Singer (Eds.), *Theoretical models and processes of reading* (4th ed., pp. 864–894). Newark, DE: International Reading Association.

Share, D. L., Jorm, A. F., Maclean, R., & Matthews, R. (1984). Sources of individual differences in reading acquisition. *Journal of Educational Psychology,* 76(6), 1309–1324.

Snow, C. E., Burns, M. S., & Griffin, P. (1998). *Preventing reading difficulties in young children.* Washington, DC: National Academy Press.

Stahl, S. A., & Hiebert, E. H. (2005). The "word factors": A problem for reading comprehension assessments. In S. G. Paris & S. A. Stahl (Eds.), *Current issues in reading comprehension and assessment* (pp. 161–186). Mahwah, NJ: Erlbaum.

Stahl, S. A., Kuhn, M. R., & Pickle, J. M. (2006). An educational model of assessment and targeted instruction for children with reading problems. In S. A. Stahl, A. Dougherty, & M. C. McKenna (Eds.), *Reading research at work: Foundations of effective practice* (pp. 373–393). New York: Guilford Press.

Stahl, S. A., & Murray, B. A. (1994). Defining phonological awareness and its relationship to early reading. *Journal of Educational Psychology,* 86, 221–234.

Stanovich, K. E. (1986). Matthew effects in reading: Some consequences of individual differences in the acquisition of literacy. *Reading Research Quarterly,* 21, 360–407.

Stanovich, K. E. (1992). Speculations on the causes and consequences of individual differences in early reading acquisition. In P. Gough, L. Ehri, & R. Treiman (Eds.), *Reading acquisition* (pp. 307–342). Hillsdale, NJ: Erlbaum.

Stanovich, K. E. (2000). *Progress in understanding reading: Scientific foundations and new frontiers.* New York: Guilford Press.

Stanovich, K. E., Cunningham A. E., & Cramer, B. (1984). Assessing phonological awareness in kindergarten children: Issues of task comparability. *Journal of Experimental Child Psychology,* 38, 175–190.

Stanovich, K. E., Cunningham, A. E., & West, R. F. (1981). A longitudinal study of the development of automatic recognition skills in first graders. *Journal of Reading Behavior,* 13, 57–74.

Torgesen, J. K., Wagner, R. K., & Rashotte, C. A. (1994). Longitudinal studies of phonological processing and reading. *Journal of Learning Disabilities,* 27(5), 276–286.

Torneus, M. (1984). Phonological awareness and reading: A chicken and egg problem? *Journal of Educational Psychology,* 76, 1346–1358.

Treiman, R., & Bourassa, D. C. (2000). The development of spelling skill. *Topics in Language Disorders,* 20(3), 1–18.

Wagner, R. K., Torgeson, J. K., & Rashotte, C. A. (1999). *Comprehensive test of phonological processing.* Austin, TX: Pro-Ed.

Willson, V. L., & Rupley, W. H. (1997). A structural equation model for reading comprehension based on background, phonemic, and strategy knowledge. *Scientific Studies in Reading,* 1(1), 45–63.

16

Studying and Modifying Young Children's Visual Attention during Book Reading

MARY ANN EVANS
JEAN SAINT-AUBIN

Background

In the mid-1960s, when *Sesame Street*—perhaps the most successful educational television series for young children—was launched, considerable research (e.g., Fisch & Truglio, 2001; Flagg, 1982) examined children's attention to different program formats and content. These studies showed that children were more likely to look at letters that moved, that appeared in the middle of the screen, and that were themselves the focus of the characters so many children have come to know in Big Bird's neighborhood.

To our knowledge, until recently, the same scrutiny has not been applied to storybooks for young children. This neglect may stem from a variety of reasons. First, storybooks are relatively low-cost compared to educational television series, and the stakes for success and expectations for benefits are concomitantly more modest. Second, storybooks are highly valued in mainstream North American culture and are increasingly accessible to children of diverse backgrounds and locales, with the help of book sharing programs, such as Dolly Parton's Imagination Library, that provide children's books to low-income families in the United States, and Lt. Governor James Bartleman's annual children's book appeal to do the same for First Nations communities in the far north of Ontario. In keeping with the "Have you read to your child today?" bumper sticker, providing almost any reasonable children's book is better than no book at all. Third, books for young children are often used in conjunction with an adult reading the text to the child or helping the beginning reader to take on the reader role, thereby orchestrating the child's experience with the book. Finally it seems logical that when adults hold books directly in front of children, they look at the print and gain knowledge of written language.

Ample research has shown that book-reading experiences benefit young children's knowledge of vocabulary (Evans, Shaw, & Bell, 2000; Frijters, Barron, & Brunello, 2000; Raikes et al., 2006; Sénéchal, 2006; Sénéchal, Pagan, Lever, & Oulette, 2008; see reviews by Bus, van IJzendoorn, & Pellegrini, 1995, Scarborough & Dobrich, 1994). There is also research supporting its facilitating role in the development of young children's sentence structure and morphology (Crain-Thoreson & Dale, 1992; Sénéchal et al., 2008) and narrative schemas (Harkins, Koch, & Michel, 2001; Neuman, 1999; Zevenbergen, Whitehurst, & Zevenbergen, 2003). The benefit of reading books to children is often assumed to extend to the development of print knowledge. However, this assumption requires more specification. It appears that there is a relation between the amount of shared book reading and the development of basic book/print concepts such as direction of reading, position of the book's title and the front of the book, and the spacing of words (Brachen & Fischel, 2008; Sonnenschein & Munsterman, 2002; Weigel, Martin, & Bennett, 2006), although the relation can disappear when parental education is first taken into account (Skibbe, Justice, Zucker, & McGinty, 2008). In contrast, the benefit for children's alphabetic knowledge and word reading appears to be more modest, if not negligible (Brachen & Fischel, 2008; Evans et al., 2000; Levy, Gong, Hessels, Evans, & Jared, 2006; Sénéchal, LeFevre, Thomas, & Daly, 1998). For example Levy and colleagues (2006) found that the extent to which 4-year-olds were read storybooks at home predicted their rejection of upside-down words, words with backwards letters, and strings of letter–number combinations as readable, but did not predict their performance on the early items of the Wide Range Achievement Test requiring the identification of letters. In contrast, Neuman (1999) found that flooding child-care centers with high-quality children's books did result in gains in letter knowledge, although these gains may have been boosted by accompanying classroom activities.

Our purpose in this chapter is threefold. First we briefly review what has been learned about children's attention to print when looking at books, with and without parent reading partners, as a means of explaining the lack of a relation between young children's experiences with books and the acquisition of alphabetic knowledge and word identification skills. Second, we present what is known about the features of books themselves that may affect children's learning about print, and aid in the selection and design of books to facilitate the development of children's print knowledge. Third, we review research on parental behaviors that may modify children's attention to print when interacting with books, and affect their progress in learning to read. In keeping with the goals of this volume, our emphasis is on the studies in our research programs, particularly studies that have monitored children's visual attention with eye-tracking technology and those that have observed parents'

behavior during shared book reading. From both sets of studies, we highlight major lessons learned as the studies are presented.

Studying Children's Attention to Print via Eye Movements

Although eye movement research as a window on cognitive processes has been conducted since the beginning of the 20th century (e.g., see overviews by Findlay, Walker, & Kentridge, 1995; Rayner, 1978, 1998), technological improvements within the last 20 years have allowed for substantial advances in our understanding. This includes the development of hardware and software that can map eye fixations (the points on which the eyes are relatively still) onto the visual display at which a person is looking and handle large amounts of data to calculate the number of fixations, the latency of fixations, and the length of fixations on visual zones specified by the researcher. It also includes the development of video-based systems that have made eye-tracking systems more child-friendly than older method that required some sort of apparatus to minimize head movement.

The SR Research EyeLink II system used in our research program is a video-based pupil-tracking apparatus (see Figure 16.1). Developed by Eyal Reingold (University of Toronto); it consists of a lightweight adjustable headband on which two cameras are mounted. When the headband is worn, the two cameras are located underneath the participant's eyes. After being calibrated, these cameras follow the movements of the pupils. An infrared transmitter is located approximately at the middle of the participant's forehead. In conjunction with sensors located on each of the corners of the computer monitor on which the stimulus material (in our case, pages of a book) are displayed, this transmitter allows for compensation of head movements. Through dedicated software, eye movements are analyzed after the reading session. This software superimposes locations of all fixations of the child on each presented screen (or page from the book). The software also provides precise measurement of the moment when the child began looking at this location and how long he or she looked there.

FIGURE 16.1. A preschool child with his mother in our laboratory. The child is wearing the Eye-Link II helmet during the familiarization phase before the presentation of the book on the computer screen.

Because accuracy of vision is very high in the central 2° of vision, one makes a series of rapid eye movements called *saccades*, so that the part of a visual display one wants to see clearly is directly in line with the fovea. The calibration procedure sets the EyeLink system to correspond to specific points of the computer monitor display at which participants are asked to look. During this calibration procedure, participants must keep their heads relatively still while fixating twice on at least three specified points. This procedure is relatively demanding for young children, and some 4-year-olds are not able to fixate long enough on a specific point. However, the benefit is that once calibrated, the Eye-Link II system allows for very high temporal and spatial resolution eye data. Thus, we can aggregate fixations on areas of a book's pages, such as a whole word or an illustrated object, to arrive at more coarse-grained findings and also detail finer grained fixations on, for example, the first letter of a word. In addition we can calculate associated onset times following a saccade, latencies to a fixation's onset, length of fixations, and total fixation duration on particular parts of a display. Across the studies we have completed, these displays have included storybooks and alphabet books with varying print and picture components to determine the effect of the characteristics of print and pictures on children's attention. The studies have also included children ranging from junior kindergarten through grade 4. These studies and those of other researchers addressing these same topics are summarized below according to the main lessons derived from the research findings.

Lesson 1. When Read Storybooks,
Children Largely Look at the Pictures

In 2005, the first two studies investigating eye movements of preschoolers were independently published (Evans & Saint-Aubin, 2005; Justice, Skibbe, Canning, & Lankford, 2005). In our study, 4-year-old children were read five storybooks by one of their parents. In one book, the text was at the bottom and the top of each illustration. In another, the illustration was on the right page and the text was on the left-facing page, with a small line drawing at the bottom. As well, the first letter of each text page was in a large decorative font. In the third book, the text was in speech bubbles embedded in the illustrations. These books all had colored illustrations. Another two had monochromatic, simple line drawings. The results were clear: Preschoolers' attention was uniformly low across the five books. On average, children spent less than a second on all text elements on a page, that is, less than 6% of their total viewing time. Even when speech bubbles were in the illustrations, the children were extremely skilled in bypassing this text. Similar results were obtained by Justice and colleagues (2005). In their study, 4- and 5-year-olds were read two storybooks: a "print-salient" book, with few words per page, large letters, and print embedded within the picture, and a "picture-salient" book, with more words per page, smaller letters, and text in a distinct area. As in our study, children rarely looked at print, and book design had very little effect. For the print-salient book, an average of 6% of children's viewing time was on the text versus an average of 2% for the picture-salient book. Similar results were obtained by Guo and Feng (2007) with Chinese children and books with Chinese characters.

Evans, Williamson, and Pursoo (2008) also examined children's visual attention in a larger sample of children. They were able to include 3-year-old children, for whom calibration with the EyeLink II would not be possible, by videotaping the direction of eye gaze. Children were read two storybooks modified to a large format, with illustrations and print on right or left facing pages. On half of the text pages, one word was visually salient and distinctive from the rest of the text by being printed in an unusual font or surrounded by a colorful border. By holding the book at the child's midline while reading it and videotaping eye gaze toward right- or left-facing pages, Evans and colleagues showed that children turned their eyes toward the pages with text less than 4% of the time. This equaled roughly 6 seconds of print-looking time over a 2½-minute reading session. Thus, despite the different methodology, it replicated the eye-tracking findings and extended them downward to 3-year-olds.

Establishing that young children rarely look at print elements raised the question of how they inspect pictures during shared book reading. Do children inspect the illustration in conjunction with the narration by the adult, or do they process the narration and the visual display in parallel but independently of each other? Evans and Saint-Aubin (2005) also tested these possibilities by reading to children two versions of the same book. The illustrations and the main storyline were the same in both cases. However, on each page, the text of each version highlighted a different element in the picture. Results revealed that children spent more time looking at the illustration element when it was highlighted by the storyline.

These laboratory findings support previous observations of shared book reading that indicate children's comments rarely concern the print (e.g., Shapiro, Anderson, & Anderson, 1997; van Kleeck, 2003; Yaden, Smolkin, & Conlon, 1993). For example, in a small descriptive study in which 4-year-old children's shared storybook sessions were recorded weekly for a 1-year period, Yaden and colleagues (1993) found that spontaneous questions asked by children were least likely to be about the graphic form of text (e.g., letters, punctuation, printed word arrays) and instead favored questions about the pictures, story meaning, and word meaning. Thus, it seems clear that while adults focus on the printed text during shared book reading, children do not.

Lesson 2. Children's Literacy Skills Affect Their Attention to Print

As most parents have experienced, shared book reading is often pursued during the early school years (van Kleeck, Stahl, & Bauer, 2003). This situation raises the question of whether children's visual attention when read a book remains similar as their reading skills develop. We tested this by sampling children from senior kindergarten to grade 4 inclusively (Roy-Charland, Saint-Aubin, & Evans, 2007). Children were read three storybooks of different difficulty levels. We also assessed children's ability to read these books by themselves. Results revealed that if the children could read the book by themselves, they spent about half of their time looking at print while the adult was reading. However, if they were unable to read the book by themselves, even older children spent less than 10% of their time on print elements. Thus, reading skill appears to affect children's attention to print in shared book reading.

The videotape study by Evans and colleagues (2008) introduced earlier also examined the extent to which child characteristics would predict children's attention to print, as well as their ability to recall print and pictures items that appeared in the book. Prior to being read the two storybooks, children's receptive vocabulary and visual memory were assessed. As well, their literacy skills were tested with the Letter–Word Identification subtest of the Woodcock Reading Mastery Test (Woodcock, McGrew, & Mather, 2001) and a measure of emergent orthography knowledge developed by Levy and colleagues (2006) to assess children's understanding of English print and spelling conventions. After accounting for 10% of the variance predicted by receptive vocabulary and visual memory, children's emergent orthography and letter–word identification scores significantly predicted an additional 10% variance in even the small extent (just 6 seconds on average) to which children looked toward pages having printed text. This study also included a recognition component, in that after the books had been read, children were asked to pick out from a set of foils which picture items and visually enhanced words had appeared in the books. All children displayed well above chance accuracy in recognizing items from the pictures, but only the 4- and 5-year-olds scored above chance accuracy in recognizing the visually enhanced words. Receptive vocabulary and visual memory predicted variance (16%) in recognizing the print items, with literacy skills adding a further 8%. As a last step, the amount of time looking at the print predicted an additional 16% of the variance, reminding us of the importance of visual attention for children's learning. As reviewed by Shiffrin (1997), orientation and attention to an external stimulus is the first and an essential step in processing it.

Together these studies suggest that children require a base of emergent literacy skills to attend to printed text, and to develop their print-specific knowledge from exposure to storybooks without adult tuition in this activity. The importance of letter knowledge in prereading has been demonstrated by others. Ehri and Sweet (1991) and Uhry (1999) showed that children need some knowledge of letters and sounds, and some phonological sensitivity to the initial and final phonemes in words to finger point accurately to text that they have frequently been read. Similarly, de Jong and Bus (2002) and Yaden and colleagues (1993) noted that children ask more questions about text during shared book reading once they have developed a base of knowledge about letters and print concepts. Lomax and McGee (1987) suggested that it is the child's interest at play here—that when children have developed some emergent literacy skills, such as phonemic awareness and letter-name knowledge, they become more interested in interpreting printed words in their environment. While interest may well be a factor, it is also likely that children's sense of self-efficacy and ability (see discussion by Zimmermann, 2000) to make at least rudimentary sense of the letters on the page contributes to their visual attention to print and possibility of learning from it. Self-efficacy may also account for why older children look more at the print in storybooks when it falls at their reading level.

Modifying Children's Attention to Print

Lesson 3. For Emergent Readers, Less Print May Make for More Attention to It

A natural outcome of the shared book-reading studies reviewed earlier is that use of alphabet books may be a better way to foster emergent readers' overt attention to print elements by offering a reachable challenge. In fact, alphabet books are often the first type of book purchased by parents, and the vast majority of preschoolers have at least one of them at home (Levy et al., 2006; Mason, 1980).

In a recent study, Evans, Saint-Aubin, and Landry (2009) monitored eye movements of 20 senior kindergarteners as they explored an alphabet book with a limited number of elements on each page, namely, a large uppercase letter, a single word, an illustration of the word, and a small panda bear. On average, children fixated the letter and the word for about 1 second each. Thus, they spent more time looking at the print elements in this book of a single letter and a single word than at one or more lines of text in storybooks. Children's knowledge of the particular letter on a page did not influence their inspection of that page. However there was a strong relation between children's overall letter knowledge and their pattern of eye movements. More specifically, the number of letters children knew on a test of letter names predicted the amount of time they spent on the word on each page and on its first letter, even if they were unable to read those words. In addition, children with greater alphabetic knowledge directed their eyes more rapidly to the uppercase letter after the onset of the page than did those knowing fewer letters. Again, both child interest and self-efficacy may explain these findings.

Lesson 4. Particular Book Features Might Make for More Attention to Print

The characteristics of the books themselves may also play a role in the development of children's knowledge. Davis, Evans, and Reynolds (2010) showed that the salience of pictured objects on a page contributes to the accuracy with which kindergarten children complete the common alphabet book phrase "Letter is for object." For example, they frequently read the N page of an ABC book as "N is for eggs," attending to the visually salient blue eggs rather than the nest in which the eggs were cradled. Similarly, it may be that the particular visual layout or design of books affects the likelihood that children will attend to the print.

For young children, print with iconic features may be especially attention getting and memorable. Evans and colleagues (2008) noted that children most accurately recognized print targets contained within shapes that had meaningful iconic properties. For example, the highest accuracy rate (75%) for the print targets was a sign shaped like an arrow that read "detour." Past research has also suggested that children may be drawn to icons and stylized elements of print (de Jong & Bus, 2002; Yaden et al., 1993). Embedding print very closely within illustrations has also been used to positive effect by De Graff, Verhoeven, Bosman, and Hasselman (2007) and Ehri, Deffner, and Wilce (1984) in teaching letter sounds. Here, lowercase letters were embedded within pictures of objects that follow the letters' contours (e.g., *f* in a wilted flower or *s* in a snake). The picture acted as a mnemonic for the sound in that the object's name began with it. In both studies, children learned letters sounds better when letters were embedded within pictures that mirrored their shape than when they were not. Thus, it seems likely that isolated letters and words can be made more eye catching and memorable.

With respect to the overall design of storybooks in shared book reading, however, we have little to go on from the research to date. In the study by Evans and Saint-Aubin (2005), the children did not look more at print when it was embedded in speech bubbles than when it was on the opposing page. The number of words per page also had no effect on attention to print. Specifically, while the number of words per page correlated ($r = .88$) with the time spent on the illustration, there was no correlation ($r = .10$) with the time spent on the text. In contrast, Justice and colleagues (2005) found a slightly different pattern of results, in that 2% of children's time was spent on the text with their picture-salient book and 6% with their print-salient book. In both studies the books contained an average of just seven words per page. Thus, the amount of text could not have been the relevant factor. Print size might have played a role because it was larger in the print-salient books in the Justice and colleagues study. However, the different findings are more likely due to differences in participants' letter knowledge—an average of 13 letters named correctly in the study by Evans and Saint-Aubin versus more than 20 in the study by Justice and colleagues. Thus, particular features of book design in interaction with children's reading skills may affect their attention to print.

If children's knowledge moderates the effect of book design on attention to print, then it might be hypothesized that a simpler design is better for less skilled children. As we suggested here and in Evans, Saint-Aubin, and Landry (2009), a simply designed alphabet book with only one word per page presents a reachable challenge for children with some alphabetic skill to read on their own. In a recent study (Saint-Aubin & Evans, 2009), we pursued this notion by asking young children to read two contrasting versions of an alphabet book. In the simpler experimenter-created version, one word per page (e.g., *bath*) named an item in the illustration. In the published version, a sentence named three items appearing in this same illustration (e.g., "The boa bathes in bubbles"). In both versions the featured letter was in the same visually distinct zone. Results revealed that children spent more time on the featured letter when there was only one word per page than when there was a sentence. In addition, children spent more time on the single word than on all three content words in the sentence condition. It may be that a single word and letter are visually more distinct and salient.

In summary, a key in understanding the effect of design features appears to be the intersection of these features with children's skills and understanding. Arousal models of learning and attention, such as those of Berlyne (1960) and Speilberger and Starr (1994), postulate that individuals are motivated to approach stimuli that are novel and complex, but not too complex, so as to maintain an optimal level of stimulation. Accordingly, the greater attention to print shown with an alphabet book and shown with one word per page versus three per page likely may not generalize to younger children for whom even one printed word will be too complex, nor to older children for whom one and three words may be equally easy.

Lesson 5. What Parents Do
in Shared Book Reading Likely Matters
for Emergent Readers

What might be expected to most modify children's attention are the scaffolding behaviors of their adult reading partner. Reading books with an adult is a common activity in North American homes. In a study of over 2,500 households in the United States, Bradley, Corwyn, McAdoo, and Garcia Coll (2001) found that 67% of families reported reading at least three times a week to their children from birth to 3 years of age, and Britto, Fuligni, and Brooks-Gunn (2002) found that 45% of parents of toddlers reported reading daily to their children. Similarly, in Canada, with a sample of over 500 families of children ages 4–7 years in southwestern Ontario, Mansell, Evans, Levy, and Shankar (2005) found that parents reported reading an average of 5.5 days a week with their children. This practice continues in the early school years, in that teachers frequently request that parents listen to their children read as a means to assist their reading progress (Becker & Epstein, 1982/2001; Tracey, 1995).

When reading storybooks to young children, parents almost inevitably change and elaborate on the material by adding comments on the story and pointing to pictures on the pages. Among preschool and kindergarten children, researchers such as Sonnenschein and Munsterman (2002), Hammett, van Kleeck, and Huberty (2003), and Haden, Reese, and Fivush (1996) have observed that parents frequently elaborate on the ideas and content of the text. Maternal elaborations during book reading have been observed in other cultures, such as Japan (Murase, Dale, Ogura, Yamashita, & Mahieu, 2005), New Zealand (McNaughton, 1995), the Netherlands (Leseman & de Jong, 1998) and Israel (Korat, Klein, & Segal-Drori, 2007). However, mothers rarely comment on or reference the print, as shown by several studies (Audet, Evans, Mitchell, & Reynolds, 2008; Baker, Mackler, Sonnenschein, & Serpell, 2001; Ezell & Justice, 1998, 2000; Phillips & McNaughton, 1990; Shapiro et al., 1997; Sonnenschein & Munsterman, 2002; van Kleeck, Gillam, Hamilton, & McGrath, 1997). For example, Sonnenschein and Munsterman (2002) found an average frequency of just 1.63 print referencing comments by mothers within a total average of 23.22 maternal comments when they read to 5-year-olds. Similarly Audet and colleagues (2008) observed an average of just 2.57 comments among a total average of 19.21 comments when parents read a print-enhanced storybook to children (average age 4 years, 8 months). Finally Phillips and McNaughton (1990) observed just 21 print-related comments in a total of 647 comments across 10 preschool dyads.

Several studies have shown that comments and questions about print, from both parent and child, are more frequent during shared reading of alphabet books than storybooks (Smolkin, Yaden, Brown, & Hofus, 1992; Stadler & McEvoy, 2003; van Kleeck, 1998) and, as noted earlier, our research has shown that children fixate the print more often and longer in an alphabet book having a simple design. Thus, an easy way to alter the frequency of print-referencing comments and attention to print may be to include such alphabet books in home–school reading activities.

As well, studies by Ezell and Justice (2000) and Justice and Ezell (2000) have shown that parents can be trained to increase their print-referencing behavior by making more comments and asking questions about book concepts (e.g., direction of reading, book components), individual letters (e.g., visual features, names and sounds), words (e.g., rhymes, word shapes), pointing to print, and tracking print with their finger while reading it to their children. Four-year-old children of parents who received this training obtained higher scores on tests assessing concept of a word and concepts about print (Justice & Ezell, 2000). Similarly, effects were also observed in a 30-week preschool intervention project. Children whose teachers had been trained in these print-referencing behaviors and received sample scripts of how to include them when reading books obtained higher scores in print knowledge, alphabetic knowledge, and name-writing than children in control classrooms (Justice, Kaderavek, Fan, Sofka, & Hunt, 2009).

However because these strategies were employed together in these interventions, it is unknown which of these behaviors carried the most weight in facilitating gains in the children's understanding. A subsequent eye-tracking study by Justice, Pullen, and Pence (2008) provides some insight into this. They trained graduate students to read four books to children ages 48 to 61 months according to four different scripted conditions: a verbatim condition, with general comments; a verbal picture condition, with comments and questions about the illustrations; a verbal print condition, with questions and comments about print and features or functions of print; and a nonverbal condition, in which the adults pointed to each word as they read the text. Both the nonverbal condition and the verbal print condition increased the number of fixations on print over that of the other two conditions, and the nonverbal condition increased the proportion of time looking at print over these conditions. Simply pointing to the text doubled the proportion of fixations on words, from roughly 2–5%, but did not affect fixations on words embedded in the illustrations. Justice and colleagues did not examine whether these effects changed in the interval from the first to the fourth book.

Evans and colleagues (2008) also examined the effect of pointing to the text. In this study, half the children were read two storybooks in a standard fashion. For the other half of the children, adults pointed to each word as they read it. As noted earlier, on half of the pages with text, one word was visually salient and distinctive from the rest of the text. Children in all three age groups (3, 4, and 5 years) in the pointing condition spent a significantly greater percentage of time looking at the print than those in the standard condition, echoing the results of Justice and colleagues (2008). Findings by Apel, Wolter, and Masterson (2006) also support the practice of pointing to individual words. They found that when words reappear four times in a book and are printed in distinctive 32-point font, pointing to these words resulted in 5-year-olds' learning of orthographic information about them. Given that attention to print predicts memory for print, and that pointing to print increases attention to print, pointing to print may indeed be an effective strategy to facilitate children's acquisition of letter and word forms.

Despite these findings, we voice only cautious enthusiasm for pointing to print during shared book reading as a means to enhance attention to and knowledge of print at this time. First, Evans and colleagues (2008) found that pointing to the words did not improve the recognition of print targets by 3-year-olds who remained at chance accuracy but did enhance 4-year-olds' memory for these print elements. Thus, pointing to the print during shared book reading may be an effective strategy for increasing the amount of attention paid to print only if there is an optimal match between the child's knowledge and the print. In this case, children appear to have needed a preliminary awareness of phonemes and to have known some of the letters that represent them to benefit from an adult pointing to the words. Second, research on the effects of pointing to text (Apel et al., 2006; Evans et al., 2008; Justice et al., 2008) has been conducted in a single experimental session, and it is not known whether the effect would remain over time. Within the single experimental session of Evans and colleagues, the effect of pointing was less in the second book read than in the first, suggesting that the initial novelty of an adult pointing to each word increased children's attention to print, but that this effect might not be maintained if pointing to text were repeatedly used. Clearly there is much to learn about the conditions under which only pointing to text may be effective.

Lesson 6. What Parents Do in Shared
Book Reading Likely Matters
for Beginning Readers

A recent meta-analysis of parents listening to children read by Sénéchal and Young (2008), one of the few experimental studies having a control group, revealed a significant and moderate effect size of 0.52 when parents were trained to listen to their children read, versus a nonsignificant effect size of 0.18 when parents read to their children. Similarly Toomey (1993) concluded from his review of the literature that encouraging parents to listen to their children read can be an effective means of fostering development of children's reading skill.

The effectiveness of listening to children read may be because, in contrast to the scant print referencing that normally occurs when adults read to emergent readers, these behaviors constitute a high proportion of parental comments once children begin to take on the reading role. In fact, print referencing in the form of responding to children's reading errors constitutes the vast majority of parental comments when parents listen to their children read (Bergin, Lancy, & Draper, 1994). Various studies from different research laboratories (Evans, Barraball, & Eberle, 1998; Evans, Moretti, Shaw, & Fox, 2003; Hannon, Jackson, & Weinberger, 1986; Lancy, Draper, & Boyce, 1989; Mansell, Evans, & Hamilton-Hulak, 2005; Stoltz & Fischel, 2003; Tracey & Young, 2002) have shown that parents ignore very few reading errors when listening to children read, offering instead some type of corrective comment to help them with difficult words. This entails explicit coaching on how to decode the words using a variety of graphophonemic strategies (e.g., letter sounds, root words, rime, and syllabification), contextual strategies (pictures, meaning and extratextual clues), and encouragements to try the word again. These behaviors continue from kindergarten through at least grade 2 as their children's reading skills develop (Mansell et al., 2005).

In addition, researchers have noted that parents manifest different styles when listening to their children read. In their longitudinal study, Mansell and colleagues (2005) found two main styles in the way parents respond to their children's reading errors, and that parents tend to maintain their style from kindergarten through grade 2. One group of parents, characterized as "code coaxers," similar to a group labeled "learner-centered parents" by Stoltz and Fischel (2003), focused on helping their children to sound out unknown words. In contrast, a second group, characterized as "word suppliers," similar to a group labeled "direct parents" by Stoltz and Fischel, primarily told the child the misread words. These different styles may partly reflect parents' goals, expectations, and beliefs relative to shared reading. For example, some parents highly value it as much as a means to foster their children's reading development as a time for enjoyment (Audet et al., 2008; Meagher, Arnold, Doctoroff, & Baker, 2008; Sonnenchein et al., 1997), and some parents view reading as a more bottom-up decoding process than as a top-down inferencing process (DeBaryshe, 1995; Evans, Fox, Scott, & McKinnon, 2000).

A critical question is whether how parents respond in listening to children read affects development of their children's reading skill. Across all socioeconomic and educational strata, parents are highly interested in helping with their children's education (Epstein, 2001; Hoover-Dempsey et al., 2005; Jeynes, 2003). Regrettably, however, there is little experimental research with parents to determine the best advice to help them in listening to their children read (Fan & Chen, 2001; Fishel & Ramirez, 2005; Sénéchal & Young, 2008) While there is agreement that some kind of feedback is better than none at all (Kuhn & Stahl, 2003; Pany & McCoy, 1988), Sénéchal and Young (2008) concluded that it is unclear whether it is more effective for parents to provide children with corrective feedback to build accurate and efficient word reading skills (e.g., Leach & Siddall, 1990; Miller, Robson, & Bushell, 1986), to encourage children to use context clues to aid comprehension (e.g., Wilks & Clarke, 1988), or to praise and read along with children to promote self-confidence and motivation (e.g., Leach & Siddall, 1990). A recent study by Goudey (2009) with second-through fourth-grade children adds to the evidence in favor of the first approach. Teaching parents to implement word recognition strategies used in the remedial Phonological and Strategy Training (PHAST) program

(Lovett et al., 2000) after a miscue during paired reading resulted in greater gains over a 16-week period in children's scores on tests of word attack, sound–symbol knowledge, word identification, and passage comprehension than traditional paired reading in which words are supplied when miscued.

The answer is also not completely clear from naturalistic studies. Among kindergartners and first graders, greater use of picture clues has been found to be negatively related to word recognition (Evans et al., 1998), and graphophonemic clues and encouragements to try the word again were found to be positively related to children's word recognition (Evans et al., 1998; Stoltz & Fischel, 2003). In contrast, Bergin and colleagues (1994) found that early fluent readers tended to have parents who used relatively few decoding-oriented strategies compared to late nonfluent readers whose parents used relatively few context-oriented strategies. However, the contemporaneous data collection in all of these studies does not allow us to determine whether the observed correlations result from parents altering their behavior in response to their children's skills or children's skills level changing as a result of parental behavior.

In a longitudinal study from kindergarten through grade 2 of 64 children showing average reading development in kindergarten, Evans, Mansell, and Shaw (2006) compared their subsequent reading skills according to whether their parents had adopted a code-coaxing versus a word supply style of miscue feedback. After the researchers controlled for kindergarten reading scores on the Test of Early Reading Achievement and phonological awareness scores on the Test of Phonological Awareness, children of code-coaxing parents obtained higher word attack scores in grade 1 than children of parents who primarily supplied the misread word, but they did not differ in word identification. In grade 2, after the researchers controlled for grade 1 word identification scores, code-coaxed children obtained higher word identification scores in grade 2, but a parallel advantage was not observed for word attack. No advantages on any measure were found for the children of parents whose response style was to supply the word. These findings are consistent with those of Moseley and Poole (2001) and Hoffman and colleagues (1984),

who found that supplying the word was associated with less gain in reading skill. It appears then, that directing beginning reader's attention to the print in listening to them read facilitates reading skills development.

Concluding Comments

The National Reading Panel (2000), Adams (1990), and Snow, Burns, and Griffin (1998) have discussed the importance of explicitly teaching children the sound–symbol code of written English and the application of related strategies for identifying words. Facility with the forms and names of the letters of the alphabet provides the basis and vocabulary for this teaching to occur, whether it be when children are age 5 or, as is the case in some countries, age 7. From the research, we know that preschool children rarely look at the print when being read books, and that the same is true for older children when the text exceeds their reading level. Even when these older children can read the text, they do not follow along with all of it as the adult reads. A good thing—shared book reading—may be made even better by including books that match a child's literacy level to foster attention to print.

Parents who read to their preschoolers continue to read with their children in the early grades of school. It may be that some of the presumed benefit of reading to children for the development of reading skills is a function of how parents negotiate shared book reading in kindergarten and grade 1, and coach reading within it. However, research is sparse in this area and more research, especially experimental studies, is needed on the effect of different coaching styles when adults listen to children read.

Similarly, we are only beginning to examine how the design characteristics of books affect children's attention to print, one component of the rich interaction of children looking at/reading books on their own and in shared reading with an adult. Although the simple alphabet books used in our studies appear to facilitate attention to print, books of this type are a small minority of an enormous range of quite visually complex alphabet books on the market. This is not to suggest that the latter are of lesser value, for they may benefit other aspects of a child's development. Rather it is to suggest that adults should not assume that children will look at the alphabetic parts of such complex visual arrays, and that they should be cognizant of this in selecting books for young children.

Finally, given the little attention to print displayed by young children during shared book reading, it seems wise for parents to include explicit questions and comments to teach their children about print in this activity from the preschool years through the primary grades, without interfering with the enjoyment and comprehension of the story. In group situations in the classroom, teacher questions and prompts directed to a group may elicit answers from some children as a means to instruct others. Both home and school shared reading call for adult wisdom in encouraging children's attention to the code of written language, fostering children's interest and sense of competence to sustain the effort required to master the code of written language, and supporting the development of semantic knowledge and reasoning skills to facilitate children's comprehension of what they listen to and/or read.

Acknowledgments

Research reported in this chapter coauthored by Mary Ann Evans and/or Jean Saint-Aubin was supported by grants from the Social Sciences and Humanities Research Council of Canada and the Canadian Language and Literacy Research Network, to which we express grateful appreciation.

References

Adams, M. (1990). *Beginning to read: Thinking and learning about print*. Cambridge, MA: MIT Press.

Apel, K., Wolter, J. A., & Masterson, J. J. (2006). Effects of phonotactic and orthotactic probabilities during fast mapping on 5-year-olds' learning to spell. *Developmental Neuropsychology, 29*, 21–42.

Audet, D., Evans, M. A., Mitchell, K., & Reynolds, K. (2008). Shared book reading: Parental goals across the primary grades and goal-behavior relationships in junior kindergarten. *Early Education and Development, 19*, 113–138.

Baker, L., Mackler, K., Sonnenschein, S., & Serpell, R. (2001). Parents' interactions with their first-grade children during storybook reading and relations with subsequent home reading activity and reading achievement. *Journal of School Psychology, 39*, 415–438.

Becker, H. J., & Epstein, J. L. (2001). Parent involvement: A survey of teacher practices. In J. L. Epstein (Ed.), *School, family and communities: Preparing educators and improving schools* (pp. 101–119). Boulder, CO: Westview Press. (Original work published 1982)

Bergin, C., Lancy, D., & Draper, K. D. (1994). Parents interactions with beginning readers. In D. F. Lancy (Ed.), *Children's emergent literacy: From research to practice* (pp. 53–73). Westport, CT: Greenwood Press.

Berlyne, D. E. (1960). *Conflict, arousal and curiosity*. New York: McGraw-Hill.

Brachen, S. S., & Fischel, J. E. (2008). Family reading behavior and early literacy skills in preschool children from low-income backgrounds. *Early Education and Development, 19*, 45–67.

Bradley, R. H., Corwyn, R. F., McAdoo, H. P., & Garcia Coll, C. (2001). The home environments of children in the United States: Part 1, Variations by age, ethnicity and poverty status. *Child Development, 6*, 1844–1867.

Britto, P. R., Fuligni, A., & Brooks-Gunn, J. (2002). Reading, rhymes and routines: American parents and their young children. In N. Halfon, K. T. McLearn, & M. A. Schuster (Eds.), *Childrearing in America: Challenges facing parent with young children* (pp. 117–145). New York: Cambridge University Press.

Bus, A., van IJzendoorn, M., & Pellegrini, A. (1995). Joint book reading makes for success in learning to read: A meta-analysis of intergenerational transmission of literacy. *Review of Educational Research, 65* 1–21.

Crain-Thoreson, C., & Dale, P. (1992). Do early talkers become early readers?: Linguistic precocity, preschool language, and emergent literacy. *Developmental Psychology, 27*, 412–429.

Davis, B., Evans, M. A., & Reynolds, K. (2010). Child miscues and parental feedback during shared book reading and relations with child literacy skills. *Scientific Studies of Reading, 14*(4), 341–364.

DeBaryshe, B. (1995). Maternal belief systems: Linchpin in the home reading process. *Journal of Applied Developmental Psychology, 16*, 1–20.

De Graff, S., Verhoeven, L., Bosman, A., & Hasselman, F. (2007). Integrated picture mnemonics and stimulus fading: Teaching kindergarteners letter sounds. *British Journal of Educational Psychology, 77*, 519–539.

de Jong, M. T., & Bus, A. G. (2002). Quality of book-reading matters for emergent readers: An experiment with the same book in a regular or electronic format. *Journal of Educational Psychology, 94*, 145–155.

Ehri, L. C., Deffner, N. D., & Wilce, L. S. (1984). Pictorial mnemonics. *Journal of Educational Psychology, 76*, 890–893.

Ehri, L. C., & Sweet, J. (1991). Fingerpoint-reading of memorized text: What enables beginners to process the print. *Reading Research Quarterly, 26*, 442–462.

Epstein, J. L. (2001). *School, family and community partnerships: Preparing educators and improving schools*. Boulder, CO: Westview Press.

Evans, M. A., Barraball, L., & Eberle, T. (1998). Parental responses to miscues during child-to-parent book reading. *Journal of Applied Developmental Psychology, 19*, 67–84.

Evans, M. A., Fox, M., Scott, L., & McKinnon, L. (2004). Beginning reading: The views of parents and teachers of young children. *Journal of Educational Psychology, 96*(1), 130–141.

Evans, M. A., Mansell, J., & Shaw, D. (2006). *Parental coaching of normally and slowly progressing young readers.* Paper presented at the Parenting and Early Literacy Symposium at the Society for the Scientific Study of Reading, Vancouver, BC, Canada.

Evans, M. A., Moretti, S., Shaw, D., & Fox, M. (2003). Parent scaffolding in children's oral reading. *Early Education and Development, 14*, 363–388.

Evans, M. A., & Saint-Aubin, J. (2005). What children are looking at during shared storybook reading. *Psychological Science, 16*, 913–920.

Evans, M. A., Saint-Aubin, J., & Landry, N. (2009). Letter names and alphabet book reading by senior kindergarteners: An eye-movement study. *Child Development, 80*, 1824–1841.

Evans, M. A., Shaw, D., & Bell, M. (2000). Home literacy activities and their influence on early literacy skills. *Canadian Journal of Experimental Psychology, 54*, 65–75.

Evans, M. A., Williamson, K., & Pursoo, T. (2008). Preschoolers' attention to print during shared book reading. *Scientific Studies of Reading, 12*, 106–129.

Ezell, H. K., & Justice, L. M. (1998). A pilot investigation of parents' questions about print and pictures to preschoolers with language delay. *Child Language Teaching and Therapy, 14*, 273–278.

Ezell, H. K., & Justice, L. M. (2000). Encouraging the print focus of shared reading session through observational learning. *American Journal of Speech Language Pathology, 9*, 36–47.

Fan, X., & Chen, M. (2001). Parental involvement and students' academic achievement: A meta-analysis. *Educational Psychology Review, 13*, 1–22.

Findlay, J. M., Walker, R., & Kentridge, R. W. (Eds.). (1995). *Eye movement research: Mechanisms, processes and applications.* Amsterdam: North Holland.

Fisch, S., & Truglio, R. (2001). *"G" is for growing": 30 years of research on Sesame Street.* Mahwah, NJ: Erlbaum.

Fishel, M., & Ramirez, L. (2005). Evidence-based parent involvement interventions with school-aged children. *School Psychology Quarterly, 20*, 371–402.

Flagg, B. N. (1982). Formative evaluation of *Sesame Street* using eye movement photography. In J. Baggaley (Ed.), *Proceedings of the International Conference on Experimental Research in Televised Instruction* (5th ed., pp. 17–27). Montreal: Concordia Research.

Frijters, J., Barron, R., & Brunello, M. (2000). Direct and mediated influences of home literacy and literacy interest on preschoolers' oral vocabulary and early written language skill. *Journal of Educational Psychology, 92*, 466–477.

Goudey, J. (2009). *A parent involvement intervention with elementary school students: The effectiveness of parent tutoring on reading achievement.* Unpublished doctoral dissertation, University of Alberta, Alberta, Canada.

Guo, J., & Feng, G. (2007, April). *Eye movements during shared storybook reading: Do children look at the text?* Poster session presented at the biennial meeting of the Society for Research in Child Development, Boston.

Haden, C. A., Reese, E., & Fivush, R. (1996). Mothers' extratextual comments during storybook reading: Stylistic differences over time and across texts. *Discourse Processes, 21*, 135–169.

Hammett, L. A., van Kleeck, A., & Huberty, C. J. (2003). Patterns of parents' extratextual interactions during book sharing with preschooler children: A cluster analysis study. *Reading Research Quarterly, 38*, 442–468.

Hannon, P., Jackson, A., & Weinberger, J. (1986). Parents' and teachers' strategies in hearing young children read. *Research Papers in Education, 1*, 6–25.

Harkins, D., Koch, P., & Michel, G. H. (2001). Listening to maternal storytelling affects narrative skill of 5-year-old children. *Journal of Genetic Psychology, 155*, 247–257.

Hoffman, J., O'Neal, S., Kastler, L., Clements, R., Segal, K., & Nash, M. (1984). Guided oral reading and miscue focused verbal feedback in second grade classrooms. *Reading Research Quarterly, 19*, 367–384.

Hoover-Dempsey, K. V., Walker, J. M., Sandler, H. M., Whetsel, D., Green, C. L., Wilkins, A. S., et al. (2005). Why do parents become involved?: Research findings and implications. *Elementary School Journal, 106*, 106–130.

Jeynes, W. H. (2003). A meta-analysis: The effects of parental involvement on minority children's academic achievement. *Education and Urban Society, 35*, 202–218.

Justice, L. M., & Ezell, H. K. (2000). Enhancing children's print and word awareness through home-based parent intervention. *American Journal of Speech–Language Pathology, 9*, 257–269.

Justice, L. M., Kaderavek, J. N., Fan, X., Sofka, A., & Hunt, A. (2009). Accelerating preschoolers' early literacy development through classroom-based teacher–child storybook reading and explicit print referencing. *Language, Speech, and Hearing Services in the Schools, 40*, 67–85.

Justice, L. M., Pullen, P. C., & Pence, K. (2008). Influence of verbal and nonverbal references to print on preschoolers' visual attention to print during storybook reading. *Developmental Psychology, 44*, 855–866.

Justice, L. M., Skibbe, L., Canning, A., & Lankford, C. (2005). Preschoolers, print and storybooks: An observational study using eye movement analysis. *Journal of Research in Reading, 28*, 229–243.

Korat, O., Klein, P., & Segal-Drori, O. (2007). Maternal mediation in book reading, home literacy environment, and children's emergent literacy: A comparison between two social groups. *Reading and Writing, 20*, 361–398.

Kuhn, M. R., & Stahl, S. A. (2003). Fluency: A review of developmental and remedial practices. *Journal of Educational Psychology, 1*, 3–21.

Lancy, D. F., Draper, K., & Boyce, G. (1989). Parental influence on children's acquisition of reading. *Contemporary Issues in Reading, 4*, 83–93.

Leach, D. J., & Siddall, S. W. (1990). Parental involvement in the teaching of reading: A comparison of paired reading, paired reading, pause, prompt, praise, and direct instruction methods. *British Journal of Educational Psychology, 60*, 349–355.

Leseman, P. P. M., & de Jong, P. F. (1998). Home literacy: Opportunity, instruction, cooperation and social-emotional quality predicting early reading achievement. *Reading Research Quarterly, 33*, 294–318.

Levy, B. A., Gong, Z., Hessels, S., Evans, M. A., & Jared, D. (2006). Understanding print: Early reading development and the contributions of home literacy experiences. *Journal of Experimental Child Psychology, 93*, 63–93.

Lomax, R. G., & McGee, L. M. (1987). Young children's concepts about print and reading: Toward a model of word reading acquisition. *Reading Research Quarterly, 22*, 237–256.

Lovett, M. W., Lacerenza, L., Borden, S. L., Frijters, J. C., Steinbach, K. A., & de Palma, M. (2000). Components of effective remediation for developmental reading disabilities: Combining phonological and strategy-based instruction to improve outcomes. *Journal of Educational Psychology, 92*, 263–283.

Mansell, J., Evans, M. A., & Hamilton-Hulak, L. (2005). Developmental changes in parents' use of miscue feedback during shared book reading. *Reading Research Quarterly, 40*, 294–317.

Mansell, J., Evans, M. A., Levy, B. A., & Shankar, S. (2005, June). *Demographic associations with shared book reading.* Presented at the Perspectives on Shared Book Reading and its Contribution to Children's Development I Symposium at the Canadian Psychological Association, Montreal, Canada.

Mason, J. M. (1980). When do children begin to learn to read: An exploration of four-year-olds children's letter and word reading competencies. *Reading Research Quarterly, 15*, 203–227.

McNaughton, S. (1995). *Patterns of emergent literacy.* New York: Oxford University Press.

Meagher, S. M., Arnold, D. H., Doctoroff, G. L., & Baker, C. N. (2008). The relationship between maternal beliefs and behavior during shared book reading. *Early Education and Development, 19*, 138–160.

Miller, A., Robson, D., & Bushell, R. (1986). Parental participation in paired reading: A controlled study. *Educational Psychology, 6*, 277–284.

Moseley, D., & Poole, S. (2001). The advantages of rime-prompting: A comparative study of prompting methods when hearing children read. *Journal of Research in Reading, 241*, 163–172.

Murase, T., Dale, P. S., Ogura, T., Yamashita, Y., & Mahieu, A. (2005). Mother–child conversation during joint picture book reading in Japan and the USA. *First Language, 25*, 197–218.

National Reading Panel. (2000). *Teaching children to read: An evidence based assessment of the scientific literature and its implications for reading instruction: Reports from the subgroups.* Bethesda, MD: National Institute of Child Health and Development.

Neuman, S. (1999). Books make a difference: A study of access to literacy. *Reading Research Quarterly, 34*, 286–311.

Pany, D., & McCoy, K. (1988). Effects of corrective feedback on word accuracy and reading comprehension of readers with learning disabilities. *Journal of Learning Disabilities, 21*, 546–550.

Phillips, G., & McNaughton, S. (1990). The practice of storybook reading to preschool children in mainstream New Zealand families. *Reading Research Quarterly, 25*, 196–212.

Raikes, H., Luze, G., Brooks-Gunn, J., Raikes, A., Pan, B. A., Tanis-LeMonda, C., et al. (2006). Mother–child book reading in low-income families: Correlate and outcomes during the first three years of life. *Child Development, 77*, 924–953.

Rayner, K. (1978). Eye movements in reading and information processing. *Psychological Bulletin, 85*, 618–660.

Rayner, K. (1998). Eye movements in reading and information processing: 20 years of research. *Psychological Bulletin, 124*, 372–422.

Roy-Charland, A., Saint-Aubin, J., & Evans, M. A. (2007). Eye movements in shared book reading with children from kindergarten to grade 4. *Reading and Writing: An Interdisciplinary Journal, 20*, 909–931.

Saint-Aubin, J., & Evans, M. A. (2009, June). *When more is less: The effect of alphabet book text length on pre-readers' eye movements.* Poster presented at the 16th annual meeting of the Society for Scientific Study of Reading, Boston.

Scarborough, H., & Dobrich, W. (1994). On the efficacy of reading to preschoolers. *Developmental Review, 14*, 245–302.

Sénéchal, M. (2006). Testing the home literacy model: Parent involvement in kindergarten is differentially related to grade 4 reading comprehension, fluency, spelling and reading for pleasure. *Scientific Studies of Reading, 10*, 59–87.

Sénéchal, M., LeFevre, J., Thomas, E., & Daly, K. (1998). Differential effects of home literacy experiences on the development of oral and written language. *Reading Research Quarterly, 33*, 96–116.

Sénéchal, M., Pagan, S., Lever, R., & Oulette, G. P. (2008). Relations among the frequency of shared reading and 4-year-old children's vocabulary, morphological and syntax comprehension, and narrative skills. *Early Education and Development, 19*, 27–44.

Sénéchal, M., & Young, L. (2008). The effect of family literacy interventions on children's acquisition of reading from kindergarten to grade 3: A meta-analytic review. *Review of Educational Research, 78*, 880–907.

Shapiro, J., Anderson, J., & Anderson, A. (1997). Diversity in parental storybook reading. *Early Child Development and Care, 127–128*, 47–59.

Shiffrin, R. (1997). Attention, automatism, and consciousness. In R. T. Shiffrin, J. D. Cohen, & J. W.

Schooler (Eds.), *Scientific approaches to consciousness: Carnegie Mellon Symposia on Cognition.* Hillsdale, NJ: Erlbaum.

Skibbe, L. E., Justice, L. M., Zucker, T. A., & McGinty, A. S. (2008). Relations among maternal literacy beliefs, home literacy practices, and the emergent literacy skills of preschoolers with specific language impairment. *Early Education and Development, 19,* 68–88.

Smolkin, L. B., Yaden, D. B., Brown, L., & Hofus, B. (1992). The effects of genre, visual design choices, and discourse structure on preschoolers responses to picture books during parent–child read-alouds. In C. K. Kinzer & D. J. Leu (Eds.), *Literacy research, theory, and practice: Forty-first yearbook of the National Reading Conference* (pp. 291–301). Chicago: National Reading Conference.

Snow, C. E., Burns, M. A., & Griffin, P. (Eds.). (1998). *Preventing reading difficulties in young children.* Washington, DC: National Academy Press.

Sonnenschein, S., Baker, L., Serpell, R., Scher, D., Goddard-Truitt, V., & Munsterman, K. (1997). Parental beliefs about ways to help children learn to read: The impact of an entertainment or a skills perspective. *Early Child Development and Care, 127–128,* 111–118.

Sonnenschein, S., & Munsterman, K. (2002). The influence of home-based reading interactions on 5-year-olds reading motivations and early literacy development. *Early Education Research Quarterly, 17,* 318–337.

Speilberger, C. D., & Starr, L. M. (1994). Curiosity and exploratory behavior. In H. F. O'Neil, Jr. & M. Drillings (Eds.), *Motivation: Theory and research* (pp. 221–243). Hillsdale, NJ: Erlbaum.

Stadler, M. A., & McEvoy, M. A. (2003). The effect of text genre on parent use of joint book reading strategies to promote phonological awareness. *Early Childhood Research Quarterly, 28,* 502–512.

Stoltz, B. M., & Fischel, J. E. (2003). Evidence for different parent–child strategies while reading. *Journal of Research in Reading, 26,* 287–294.

Toomey, D. (1993). Parents hearing children read: A review: Rethinking the lessons of the Haringey Project. *Educational Research, 35,* 223–236.

Tracey, D. H. (1995). Children practicing reading at home: What we know about how parents help. In L. Mandel-Morrow (Ed.), *Family literacy: Connections in schools and communities* (pp. 253–268). New Brunswick, NJ: Rutgers University.

Tracey, D. H., & Young, J. W. (2002). Mothers' helping behaviors during children's at-home oral-reading practice: Effect of children's reading ability, children's gender, and mothers' educational level. *Journal of Educational Psychology, 94,* 729–737.

Uhry, J. K. (1999). Invented spelling in kindergarten: The relationship with finger-pointing. *Reading and Writing: An Interdisciplinary Journal, 11,* 441–464.

van Kleeck, A. (1998). Preliteracy domains and stages: Laying the foundations for beginning reading. *Journal of Children's Communication Development, 20,* 33–51.

van Kleeck, A. (2003). Research on book sharing: Another critical look. In A. van Kleeck, S. Stahl, & E. B. Bauer (Eds.), *On reading books to children: Parents and teachers* (pp. 271–320). Mahwah, NJ: Erlbaum.

van Kleeck, A., Gillam, R. B., Hamilton, L., & McGrath, C. (1997). The relationship between middle class parents' books sharing discussions and their preschoolers abstract language development. *Journal of Speech and Hearing Research, 40,* 261–127.

van Kleeck, A., Stahl, S. A., & Bauer, E. B. (2003). *On reading books to children.* Mahwah, NJ: Erlbaum.

Weigel, D. J., Martin, S. S., & Bennett, K. K. (2006). Contributions of the home literacy environment to preschool-aged children's emerging literacy and language skills. *Early Child Development and Care, 176,* 357–378.

Wilks, R., & Clarke, V. (1988). Training versus non-training of mothers as home reading tutors. *Perceptual and Motor Skills, 67,* 135–142.

Woodcock, R. W., McGrew, K. S., & Mather, N. (2001). *The Woodcock–Johnson III.* Itasca, IL: Riverside.

Yaden, D. B., Jr., Smolkin, L. B., & Conlon, A. (1993). Preschooler's questions about pictures, print convention, and story text during reading aloud at home. *Reading Research Quarterly, 24,* 189–214.

Zevenbergen, A., Whitehurst, G., & Zevenbergen, J. (2003). Effects of a shared-reading intervention on the inclusion of evaluative devices in the narratives of children from low-income families. *Applied Developmental Psychology, 24,* 1–15.

Zimmerman, B. J. (2000). Self-efficacy: An essential motive to learn. *Contemporary Educational Psychology, 25,* 82–91.

17

Child Characteristics–Instruction Interactions: Implications for Students' Literacy Skills Development in the Early Grades

CAROL McDONALD CONNOR

The idea that the impact of literacy instruction might depend on children's aptitudes, characteristics, and skills is not new. Indeed, the idea of aptitude–treatment interactions (ATIs) was first suggested by Cronbach, noted scholar and statistician, in 1957. The theory was generally appealing because it helped to explain why some students seemed to learn to read well but some did not, even when provided the same amount and type of literacy instruction. Ten years later, in 1967, Bond and Dykstra identified five factors (intelligence, perceptual speed, spatial perception, listening skills, and learning rate) for which there was some evidence of interaction effects. At the same time, other researchers found little sound evidence of ATIs, leading Cronbach and Snow to conclude in 1977 that there was no rigorous evidence of ATIs. They wrote, "Well-substantiated findings are scarce. Few investigations have been replicated. Many reports (of both positive and negative results) must be discounted because of poor procedure" (p. 6). The concept of ATIs remained highly appealing and was never been fully abandoned, even in the face of equivocal evidence. As late as 1984, in her *Handbook of Reading Research* chapter on primary reading, Barr described ATIs and cited supporting evidence.

Reliably predicting which children (with which characteristics) should respond to specific reading instruction strategies, and which might not, would help us design effective instructional strategies matched to students' learning needs (Torgesen, 2000; Vellutino et al., 1996). It might also improve "response-to-intervention" (RTI) models (Gersten et al., 2008) and help close the well-documented achievement gap between children living in poverty or from underrepresented minorities and their more affluent or majority peers.

Why Are We Now Finding ATIs?

Since the late 1990s, evidence has been accumulating that the effect of literacy instruction strategies does indeed appear to depend on student characteristics. There is accumulating longitudinal and correlational evidence of ATIs, which more recently are called child characteristic–by-instruction (C-I) interactions (Connor, Morrison, & Katch, 2004). C-I interactions have been found from preschool through third grade (Connor, Morrison, & Katch, 2004; Connor, Morrison, & Petrella, 2004; Connor, Morrison, & Slominski, 2006; Connor, Morrison, &

Underwood, 2007), across samples (Connor, Jakobsons, Crowe, & Meadows, 2009), and by different research teams (Al Otaiba et al., 2008; Foorman et al., 2006; Mathes et al., 2005). Over the past two decades, three advances in our understanding likely contributed to the reliable identification of C-I interactions. First, our understanding of the linguistic, cognitive, and social processes that contribute to proficient reading has vastly increased (Rayner, Foorman, Perfetti, Pesetsky, & Seidenberg, 2001; Snow, Burns, & Griffin, 1998). By focusing on individual differences among students' skills that are relevant to reading (word reading, phonological awareness, vocabulary, etc.), rather than other less predictive skills (e.g., spatial perception) researchers have identified reliable C-I interactions. Among early studies finding C-I interactions, Juel and Minden-Cupp (2000) found that students who started first grade with weaker word-reading skills made more progress in classrooms where there was greater emphasis on word recognition, whereas students with stronger reading skills showed greater reading gains in the classroom where the teacher focused on providing a literature-rich environment, with less emphasis on code-based instruction.

Second, with improved computer processing speed, more sophisticated analytic strategies, such as hierarchical linear modeling (Raudenbush & Bryk, 2002), are available. These models take into account that children who share a classroom are more likely to have similar learning environments than are children who do not. Such strategies have allowed more precise investigation of students (with certain characteristics) in classrooms where they participate in specific types of reading instruction, the effects of this instruction on their literacy gains, as well as cross-level student–classroom instruction–environment interactions.

Third, with the waning of the reading wars, it has become increasingly clear that more effective teachers use a variety of reading strategies (Taylor, Pearson, Clark, & Walpole, 2000; Wharton-McDonald, Pressley, & Hampston, 1998) and may use activities that are not necessarily part of their principal literacy approach. For example, we observed during the late 1990s that some first-grade teachers in a school district that promoted a whole-language meaning-focused approach would still use phonic charts and teach the alphabetic principle (i.e., code-focused activities) (Connor, Morrison, & Katch, 2004). By moving beyond a one-dimensional curricular view of teaching, individual teacher differences in the amounts and types of instruction they provided could be assessed. This allowed more defined investigation of C-I interactions and is a critical part of the research described in this chapter. Our multidimensional view of the classroom environment (Connor, Morrison, Fishman, Ponitz, et al., 2009; Morrison, Bachman, & Connor, 2005) attends to salient dimensions of teaching and provides support for the application of developmental dynamic systems theories (Yoshikawa & Hsueh, 2001) such as ecological theory (Bronfenbrenner, 1986), as well as sociocultural theories (Gee, 2001), to elucidate individual student differences and students' learning in the classroom. Among other crucial sources of influence (parenting and home environment, socioeconomic status [SES], preschool) (Morrison, Connor, & Bachman, 2005), the classroom learning environment is an ongoing and accessible proximal source of influence on students' learning and development.

Multiple Dimensions of Teaching

If one imagines a three-dimensional crystal, with each facet representing a dimension of teaching, such a model begins to describe the complex and interconnected influences that affect the classroom learning environment (Connor, Morrison, Fishman, Ponitz, et al., 2009; Gee, 2000). *Foundational dimensions* include how teachers interact with students, including their warmth and responsiveness to students and regard for students' cultural heritage (Gee, 2001; Rimm-Kaufman, Paro, Downer, & Pianta, 2005); classroom management (e.g., organization, time spent in transitions, discipline) (Brophy, 1985; Cameron, Connor, & Morrison, 2005; Wharton-McDonald et al., 1998); specialized knowledge about literacy (e.g., phonological awareness, linguistic processes) (Piasta, Connor, Fishman, & Morrison, 2009); understanding of students' instructional needs, including the savvy use of assessment results to inform instruction; and ability to support students' social interactions (Rimm-Kaufman et al., 2005). What characterizes these foundational dimensions is that they are necessary but not sufficient to ensure student learning. First-grade teachers may be highly knowledgeable, but if they never provide explicit reading instruction, students are less likely to show reading gains. At the same time, as teachers with low levels of specialized knowledge spend more time in explicit reading instruction, their students generally show *weaker* reading gains (Piasta et al., 2009).

The *dimensions of instruction* capture the learning environment and the content of the instruction provided. In our model, we identify four dimensions: content, management, context or grouping, and timing/duration—although there are certainly others (Connor, Morrison, Fishman, Ponitz, et al., 2009). For example, there is emerging evidence that the characteristics of classmates affect individual students' learning in the classroom. In a recent study that examined the impact of students' self-regulation using a direct measure that tapped working memory, attention, task inhibition, and task switching (Skibbe, Glasney, Connor, & Brophy-Herb, 2010), first graders with weaker self-regulation demonstrated weaker reading and language skill growth compared to students with stronger self-regulation. The greater the proportion of students in the classroom with weaker self-regulation (below the 25th percentile on the assessment), the weaker was the reading growth for all of the students, regardless of individual students' initial literacy and self-regulation skills.

Content of Instruction

Content of instruction can be conceptualized in several ways. For example, we have described first-grade literacy instruction as being explicitly versus implicitly focused on code-based instruction (Connor, Morrison, & Katch, 2004), and third-grade instruction as being explicitly or implicitly focused on comprehension (Connor, Morrison, & Petrella, 2004). Most recently in our work with teachers, we have described reading instruction as comprising code-focused and meaning-focused activities (Connor, Morrison, Fishman, Schatschneider, & Underwood, 2007). In this conceptualiza-

tion, code-focused instruction is explicitly targeting skills that research indicates will support development of phonological awareness, phonics, letter and word fluency, and so on—any activity design to support children's mastery of the alphabetic principle (Adams, 2001). *Meaning-focused activities* are those designed to support students' active extraction and construction of meaning from text (Snow, 2001), for example, vocabulary, comprehension strategies, discussion, reading books, and so forth. The key is that the focus is on the intent of the activity (improving listening comprehension) and not the method (teachers reading to students).

Teacher–Child- and Child-Managed Instruction

Among the more important dimensions is whether the teacher is interacting directly with students and focusing their attention on the learning activity, or whether students are working independently or with peers. The former we call *teacher–child-managed instruction* because the teacher and students are interacting around a learning activity; the teacher is either explicitly teaching the activity or scaffolding the students' learning. When students are working independently or with peers, this is considered *child- or peer-managed instruction*. These dimensions differ substantially from instruction described in the early literacy literature as teacher-directed and child-centered (Bowman, Galvez-Martin, & Morrison, 2005). Teacher–child managed activities may, in fact, be child-centered. For example, if a student selects a book from the library and the teacher and student read it together, that would be considered a teacher–child-managed activity that is also child-centered. If the teacher assigns a book chapter to be read alone silently that is a child-managed activity that is actually teacher-directed because the teacher selected the activity.

It turns out that whether an instructional activity is teacher–child- or child–peer-managed is important regardless of the content of that instruction. In general, children with weaker skills (e.g., comprehension) make greater progress when they receive teacher–child-managed instruction specifically focused on the particular skill, but do not tend to show gains when provided similar content that is child–peer managed (Connor, Morrison, & Petrella, 2004). In contrast, for children with stronger skills, child–peer-managed instructional activities are generally (but not always) associated with stronger skills growth (Connor, Morrison, & Katch, 2004).

Context

The context of the instruction considers the setting in which the instruction is provided. For example, the teacher reading to a small group of students might have a substantially more powerful impact on students' reading than a teacher reading to the entire class. In the same way, a phonics worksheet completed by an individual student at his or her desk might be less effective than a similar activity completed with peers. When considering C-I interactions, the context becomes increasingly important. Whole-class instruction will likely be less effective for students who are least proficient *and* who are most proficient because teachers frequently calibrate their instruction to the middle of the class. For example, when we examined preschoolers' whole-class and small-group/individual emergent literacy instruction, there were C-I interactions when teacher–child-managed code-focused instruction was provided in a whole-class setting (less effective for children with weaker letter skills) but main effects (positive regardless of initial skills) when similar activities were provided in small groups and individually (Connor, Morrison, & Slominski, 2006).

Duration and Timing

This dimension focuses on the idea that time is spent in particular activities with particular content, and these activities can affect student literacy development. Obviously, the content and types of activities should differ for first graders and third graders as students' literacy skills improve. At the same time, there is evidence that timing of instructional content and activities *within* grades is vital. For example, in first grade, students with stronger reading and vocabulary skills in the fall tended to show greater gains by spring when provided greater amounts of time in child–peer-managed meaning-focused activities all year long (30 minutes per day of, for

example, sustained independent reading). However, students with weaker skills in the fall demonstrated weaker gains by spring in the same classrooms. For students with weaker skills, smaller amounts of child–peer-managed meaning-focused reading activities in the fall but with increasing amounts each month (10 minutes in September, 15 minutes in October, 20 minutes in November, etc.) were associated with greater reading skills gains (Connor, Morrison, & Katch, 2004; Connor, Piasta, et al., 2009).

All of these dimensions operate simultaneously to describe any literacy activity and the classroom learning environment overall (see Table 17.1). For example, a teacher working with a small group of third graders on inferring meanings of words using root words, prefixes, and suffixes (e.g., *natural, unnatural, naturally*) would be a teacher–child-managed, meaning-focused (TCM-MF), small-group activity that would be provided for a certain length of time at a particular time of year. First graders completing a phonics worksheet on word families (e.g., *bat, cat, sat*) would be a child-managed code-focused (CM-CF) activity. During these activities, teachers might be more or less interactive with students, might vary in their classroom management strategies, and might bring more or less specialized knowledge (e.g., knowledge about morphemes and morphological awareness) to the learning opportunity.

These dimensions inform how we conduct classroom observations. By videotaping classrooms and using video-coding software, we are able to capture these dimensions of teaching and the instruction provided to each student (i.e., at the level of the individual student) within his or her classroom (Connor, Morrison, Fishman, Ponitz, et al., 2009). As described below, this has been critical to our research findings, to translating the correlational findings into practice, and to the development of dynamic forecasting intervention models.

Dynamic Systems Forecasting Intervention Models

Anyone who lives in the tropics quickly becomes an expert at reading maps that indi-

TABLE 17.1. Examples of Literacy Activities That Fall into the Four Types of Instruction Defined by the Dimensions of Content and Management

	Teacher–child-managed (TCM)	Child–peer-managed (CM)
Code focused (CF)	A second-grade teacher is explaining the "silent *e*" phonics rules for whether a vowel will be long (*pine*) or short (*pin*) to an individual student.	First graders are completing a phonics worksheet on word families (e.g., *bat, cat, sat*) at their desks, while the teacher works with another small group of students.
Meaning focused (MF)	The teacher is working with a small group of students on inferring meanings of words using root words, prefixes, and suffixes (e.g., *natural, unnatural, naturally*)	Small groups of third graders are writing books together and discussing titles, characters, and plots as they brainstorm ideas.

cate the projected trajectory of hurricanes and the ever-widening cone that shows where the hurricane is likely to go 1, 2, and even 5 days into the future. Prediction of the widening of the cone into the future indicates the increasing uncertainty regarding the hurricane's path. Nevertheless, it is not assumed that the hurricane can go anywhere (not that hurricanes have not surprised meteorologists); the widening cone of the projected path is still constrained. In forecasting the path of hurricanes, meteorologists use dynamic system forecasting models, which utilize atmospheric information (prevailing winds, location of high and low pressure areas, etc.) and information about where the hurricane was previously to compute (using algorithms) potential trajectories or paths the hurricane is likely to follow (Rhome, 2007).

In a not dissimilar way, the results of longitudinal correlational studies that include fall and spring outcomes for students, combined with classroom observation data, can be used to predict students' outcome as a function of the instruction they receive. Indeed, researchers can predict students' progress in learning to read, taking into account documented sources of influence (e.g., instruction, home support) and constraints (e.g., previous achievement, lack of resources, documented disabilities), and explain much of the between-student variability in literacy outcomes (Catts, Fey, Zhang, & Tomblin, 2001; National Institute of Child Health and Human Development [NICHD] Early Child Care Research Network, 2002, 2005). The difference here is that, unlike meteorologists who are not trying to change

the trajectory of the hurricane but only to predict it, our goal is to move beyond predicting student outcomes and to change their trajectory of achievement. The underlying assumption of dynamic systems forecasting intervention models is that with reliable estimates of students' language and literacy skills (and perhaps other attributes such as social skills, self-regulation, or behavior), we can do a better job of predicting students' reading skills development or their potential trajectories of growth (Raudenbush, 2005). Taking this a step further, we argue that carefully designed reading instruction that is individualized, taking into account children's current reading and language skills, and the ways these skills interact with instruction, can influence the projected path of learning so that children reach the highest levels of reading skill within their projected cone of achievement. Moreover, by monitoring students' reading skills, we can make better predictions regarding their end-of-grade outcomes and can redesign planned instruction so as to influence the achievement trajectory upward.

To create dynamic forecasting intervention models, we reverse-engineered, so to speak, the hierarchical linear models used to predict students' literacy outcomes in correlational and quasi-experimental studies. Instead of creating models that predict students' outcomes as a function of the instruction amounts and types received, we developed models that estimated the amounts and types of instruction required to reach a targeted literacy achievement outcome. We set the target outcome as grade level by the end of the school year or a year's worth of growth (if we use grade equivalent [GE] as the metric, then the target in second grade would be 2.9 or the students' fall GE + 0.9). We assess students' vocabulary and literacy skills, plug the information into the model equations, and solve for the recommended amounts of each type of instruction (TCM-CF, TCM-MF, CM-CF, CM-MF, etc.).

These models (which are then translated into computer algorithms that compute recommend amounts and types of instruction for each student) follow the main principles of dynamic systems forecasting. A set of complex nonlinear equations, the algorithms use information from multiple sources to predict specific amounts and types of reading instruction that should, theoretically, lead to stronger student reading skills. The multiple sources include children's assessed reading and vocabulary skills, target outcomes based on societal norms for acceptable levels of end-of-grade reading, predicted reading skills growth (implicit assumptions about limitations to gains), and the kinds of reading instruction strategies that are empirically recognized to promote stronger student reading outcomes. Moreover, key to these models is the implicit understanding that human interactions are better described within a transactional, bidirectional framework (Bronfenbrenner & Morris, 2006; Connor, Piasta, et al., 2009; Morrison & Connor, 2009; Tudge, Odero, Hogan, & Etz, 2003). Thus, the skills and aptitudes (Kyllonen & Lajoie, 2003) children bring to the classroom (including additional aptitudes not discussed here) and how they interact with the classroom environment more generally are likely crucial information for developing dynamic systems forecasting intervention models and indicating directions for future research. An assumption in our models is that students' initial reading and vocabulary skills reflect the influence of measured and unmeasurable sources of influence. This might include the effect of previous instruction received, the influence of the home and community environments, children's health and well-being, potential and identified disabilities, and genetic influences. Thus, the ending width of the forecast cone might be narrower for a child with a familial history of dyslexia or an identified disability than for a child living in an impoverished neighborhood, even if both

have similar reading and vocabulary scores at the beginning of first grade. The goal is to recommend and implement instruction that will allow each student to achieve at his or her highest potential (Taylor, Roehrig, Connor, & Schatschneider, 2010).

Testing Child–Instruction Interactions from First through Third Grade

Using longitudinal correlational and quasi-experimental evidence, we have developed dynamic systems forecasting intervention models for first through third grade and used them to test our over arching research question: Are C-I interactions causally implicated in students' literacy achievement? We then conducted randomized control efficacy trials to test whether instruction that was individualized using these models and, hence, explicitly taking into account C-I interactions, would be more effective than the literacy instruction students currently received in schools. Randomized controlled trials are among the most efficient methods to begin to establish causal links (Shavelson & Towne, 2002) because they help to eliminate other potential reasons for observed associations. Efficacy trials compare an intervention to what is currently occurring in schools—frequently referred to as a business-as-usual control—under ideal circumstances. Oftentimes researchers rather than classroom teachers implement the intervention, which ensures high and consistent fidelity of the intervention's implementation (Mathes et al., 2005). Efficacy trials ask whether there is an effect of treatment under ideal circumstances. This differs from effectiveness trials, which attempt to assess the impact of an intervention as it might actually be implemented in schools by typical teachers. We consider the studies we have conducted to be efficacy trials. As we designed the intervention to test C-I interactions, however, it became increasingly clear that it would be impractical and very expensive to use researchers to implement the intervention. Thus, we decided to provide intensive support and training for the participating classroom teachers and have them implement the intervention, which is a consideration when thinking about the implications of the findings.

In the two earlier first-grade studies, we matched and randomly assigned schools with a delayed treatment design: Teachers in the control group implemented the intervention the year following the trial. All subsequent studies randomly assigned teachers within schools to an alternative treated control—either vocabulary or mathematics. Our most recent and ongoing studies were longitudinal, in which students were followed from first through third grade, so that accumulation of effects could be tested. For all studies, approximately half of the students qualified for free and reduced-price lunch (FARL), a widely used marker of low SES. About one-half to one-third of the students were African American, small percentages (about 8%) were Hispanic and Asian American, and the remaining students were European American. All teachers were certified and approximately 25% held advanced degrees and certifications. Schools ranged from urban to rural and from high-poverty to low-poverty status; schoolwide percentage of students receiving FARL ranged from 4 to 98%. However, we intentionally oversampled higher poverty schools.

The Individualized Student Instruction Intervention

The *Individualized Student Instruction Intervention for Reading (ISI)* is conducted daily during a 60- to 90-minute literacy block and has three important components: (1) Assessment to instruction (A2i) Web-based software, which computes recommended amounts of each type of instruction using dynamic systems forecasting intervention models, and provides planning tools and online professional development resources; (2) professional development; and (3) implementation of differentiated instruction in the classroom, which incorporates the A2i recommended amounts of each type of instructional activity for each student and considers students' skills levels when selecting the content and delivery of the activities. It is assumed that all three components of the intervention contribute to the results reported below. For example, it is unlikely that teachers would be able to use the A2i software or to implement the recommendations without training and support. Without A2i, it would be difficult to know the actual recommended amounts or to access easily the assessment and planning tools. And even if teachers used A2i consistently but never actually differentiated instruction in their classrooms, it is unlikely that the ISI intervention would be effective.

Assessment to Instruction (A2i) Software

Dynamic systems forecasting intervention models translated into computer algorithms form the heart of A2i software, which is a Web-based teacher professional development support tool. Over the past 5 years, A2i has been developed and improved using teacher feedback. Such systems are gaining wide support as "clinical decision support systems" in the medical field (Kawamoto, Houlihan, Balas, & Lobach, 2005, p. 765; Garg et al., 2005). Kawamoto and colleagues (2005) conducted a meta-analysis of over 70 randomized control trials examining the features of clinical decision support systems associated with stronger practitioner and patient outcomes. Features included (1) provision of a recommendation rather than just assessment results; (2) computer-based generation of decision support; (3) automatic provision of decision support as part of clinician workflow; and (4) provision of support at the time and location of decision making. A2i was designed (with extensive teacher input) to include each of these components. Teachers' use of A2i was automatically recorded and, in general, the more teachers used A2i, the more likely they were to implement ISI in the classroom, and the stronger were their students' reading skill gains (Connor, Morrison, Fishman, & Schatschneider, in press; Connor, Morrison, Fishman, et al., 2007).

The A2i system is password protected, so that teachers are taken directly to their classrooms and no unauthorized staff can view confidential student information. Students have their own password for online assessments, such as the Word Match Game, a semantic matching task that is adaptive, appropriate for students from grades K through 3, and can be used to monitor progress in students' oral language skills development.

A Tour of A2i

Navigating to *isi.fcrr.org*, and after they enter their password (demonstration login: A2idemo, password: isi06!), teachers enter the home screen (see Figure 17.1a) where they can access the components of A2i. The menu along the left side takes the teacher to online professional development resources, including a monthly reading for communities of practice and video of master teachers. The menu along the top navigates to the key components of A2i. Starting with the classroom view (see Figure 17.1b), the teacher views the recommended instruction plan for each student. Each horizontal bar represents the recommended number of minutes (per day in the daily view and number of minutes per week in the weekly view) for each type of instruction (TCM-MF, TCM-CF, CM-MF, and CM-CF). As students' assessed skills change, the recommended numbers of minutes are automatically updated.

Clicking any student's name in the classroom view will take the teacher to the *child information screen*, where the student's test scores and progress monitoring graphs may be viewed (see Figure 17.1c). The preferred A2i metric for students' scores is GE, although raw, standard, and percentile rank scores are provided. Based on teachers' feedback, GE has been found to be a meaningful indicator of students' skills (teachers know what a third grader can read compared to a first or second grader) and is sensitive enough to allow progress monitoring. Moreover, students whose scores rise above benchmarks on, for example, the Dynamic Indicators of Basic Early Literacy Skills (DIBELS; Good & Kaminski, 2002) may actually have stagnating skills. Use of GE limits the obfuscation of progress for students who rise above benchmarks and helps teachers conceptualize literacy as a continuous construct (i.e., children's skills fall on a continuum and are not dichotomous). Easy access to assessment results appears to support teacher efficacy. In a recent study, we found that the amount of time teachers spent viewing students' scores and the progress-monitoring charts in A2i was positively correlated with students' passage comprehension skills growth (Connor, Morrison, Fishman, & Schatschneider, in press).

In the classroom view, students are automatically assigned to flexible homogeneous skills groups based on their most recent word reading GE in kindergarten and first grade, and most recent passage comprehension GE in second and third grade. Computer algorithms essentially rank-order students within a class and assign homogeneous groups by looking for clusters of students with similar GE skills levels. Hence, group sizes vary. Students are reassigned to groups each time their skills are reassessed and GEs change. Teachers may also change students' assigned group using the drop-down menu to the right of the group assignment. Teachers set the number of groups in the classroom setup page, and can add specialists and aides who are assisting them. This is also where teachers select their core curriculum (e.g., Imagine It!) and center activities (e.g., Florida Center for Reading Research [FCRR] activities), which are indexed to the four types of literacy instruction (TCM-MF, etc.).

Teachers schedule their dedicated literacy block in the literacy minutes manager (Figure 17.1d). Here teachers create a master schedule that they follow daily. Teachers click the black bars and are taken to a pop-up window that allows them to schedule the type of minutes (e.g., CM-MF for Group 2). Once minutes are scheduled, the black bar becomes the group color and the time block is indicated in the time line below. The number in square brackets by the group header is the mean GE of the assessment used for grouping for that grade. By clicking the ± by the group name, the teacher can view the students assigned to that group. Again, clicking the child's name shows tests scores and progress-monitoring charts.

The lesson plan view (see Figure 17.1e) shows the recommended daily lesson plan incorporating the core literacy curriculum (e.g., Houghton Mifflin) and center activities the teacher selected in the classroom setup window. This new feature of A2i was tested last year and is designed to encourage teachers to match the content of instruction to students' skills levels. Prepopulated activities are commensurate with the group mean achievement GE level (in square brackets in the group header) and proceed through the curriculum in sequence. In this way, teachers learn to use their existing materials, but

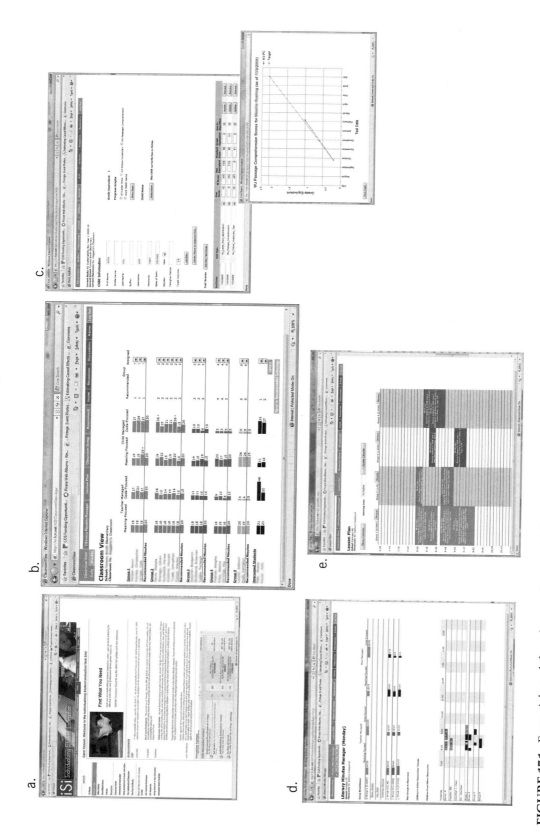

FIGURE 17.1. From right to left and top to bottom: (a) home screen; (b) first-grade classroom view; (c) child information screen accessed by clicking child's name and progress chart; (d) literacy minutes manager; and (e) lesson plan. Reprinted with permission from Florida State University.

differentiated based on students' assessed skills. Teachers may select other activities. In all cases, we rely on teachers' professional judgment, in consultation with the research partner, to make changes to recommended groups and activities.

The assessment view allows teachers to view scores for the entire classroom. This is also where they access online assessments, such as the Word Match Game. Although in our research we conduct and enter all the assessment scores, teachers theoretically would also be able to add new scores using this view.

Professional Development

Based on the extant research on effective professional development, we used a coaching or mentoring model (Gersten, Chard, & Baker, 2000; Showers, Joyce, & Bennett, 1987; U.S. Department of Education, 2004; Vaughn & Coleman, 2004) in which teachers formed a study-level community of learners, guided by a highly trained reading specialist (research-funded and called the *research partner*), who also provided classroom-based support to teachers (Lave & Wenger, 1991; Ramanathan, 2002). The goal was to create genuine partnerships between teachers and research partners, most of whom were also certified teachers, with respect for teachers' expertise and incorporating their ideas, thoughts, and concerns into implementing ISI (DuFour & Eaker, 1998; Freeman & King, 2003; Helterbran & Fennimore, 2004). Although intensive, it is not unreasonable to think that this kind of practice-based professional development can be provided in typical school districts.

The overall focus of ISI professional development was to help teachers use A2i to plan instruction, then implement the management and instruction plans in the classroom. In addition to accessing the A2i online professional development materials, teachers participated in a half-day workshop during the summer that covered (1) the overall aims of the research study, (2) an overview of the ISI intervention, and (3) an introduction to the A2i software. Focus was on the goals of the research and what to expect when participating in the study.

Teachers also participated in monthly community of practice meetings either at their school or at a central location, where they had the opportunity to interact with other teachers at other schools in the study. These meetings followed a scope and sequence using a teacher study group format (Gersten, 2007) that frequently included discussing a research paper (accessed, with study questions, through A2i) relevant to the topic; group strategizing and problem solving; and instruction in using the software, including technical support. Topics included (1) the first 6 weeks, organizing the classroom and getting ready to differentiate instruction; (2) dimensions of instruction; (3) using assessment to guide instruction; (4) the individualized classroom (strategies for differentiating instruction, classroom management, stations/centers); and (5) using research in the classroom.

Additionally, teachers received biweekly classroom-based support in which their research partner worked with them to implement individualized instruction in the classroom. Using a participant observer format, research partners strategized with the teachers on how to provide the recommended amounts and types of instruction for students, classroom management and organization, instructional strategies and activities, interaction with students, and other relevant topics. This part of the professional development was more informal and teacher-centered.

Classroom Implementation

When ISI was fully implemented, teachers used the schools' core reading curriculum, supplemented with other research-supported literacy activities, such as the FCRR activities (*www.fcrr.org*), during the schools' 1- to 2-hour block of time dedicated to literacy instruction (Taylor & Pearson, 2002). Students within the classroom were receiving instruction at varying skills levels matched to their assessed literacy skills, using appropriate lessons within the curriculum or other materials. Flexible homogeneous skills-based groups focused on learning needs were used consistently (Taylor et al., 2000; Wharton-McDonald et al., 1998). A2i-recommended amounts of explicit and systematic teacher–child-managed instruction, both CF and MF, were provided to small groups of students. Group size varied from as many as six children to as few as one or two. Groupings changed with students' changing reading skills. There was a clear plan of instruction (Borko & Niles, 1987; Fuchs, Fuch, & Phillips, 1994), using either the A2i lesson plan or other district-approved lesson plans.

Classroom management was an important and specific focus of professional development (Brophy, 1979; Brophy & Good, 1986). Ideally, transitions were quick and well rehearsed (Wharton-McDonald et al., 1998), with clear indicators (e.g., a bell or a buzzer, "freeze" game), and all of the children were engaged in meaningful literacy activities for virtually the entire literacy block (Pressley et al., 2001; Taylor et al., 2000; Wharton-McDonald et al., 1998). Students followed a daily routine, with a clearly displayed organizational or work chart showing them where to go and what to do, so that they did not have to disturb the teacher as he or she worked with a small group of students at the teacher table. During child-managed activities, students worked individually, in small groups, in pairs, or they accomplished seatwork. These activities were designed to provide practice for skills learned during teacher–child-managed instruction. Many teachers used colored folders and bins at each center or station (e.g., the library center) to make sure students completed work and read books at their skills levels. Although there was frequently quiet chatter, in general the overall classroom environment was conducive to learning.

Results by Grade

First Grade

Overall, results are most consistent for first grade, where we have completed two longitudinal correlational studies (Connor, Jakobsons, et al., 2009; Connor, Morrison, & Katch, 2004) and three randomized control field trials (Connor, Crowe, Morrison, Fishman, & Schatschneider, 2010; Connor, Morrison, Fishman, Schatschneider, Toste, et al., in press; Connor, Morrison, Fishman, et al., 2007; Connor, Piasta, et al., 2009). Figure 17.1b provides a classroom view screenshot from the most recent first-grade study (2008–2009). In the three randomized trials (2005–2006, 2006–2007, 2008–2009), hierarchical linear modeling (HLM)

results revealed significant effects of treatment compared to a business-as-usual control (2005–2006 and 2006–2007) or to a group of teachers receiving the same amount of professional development, but focused on providing a mathematics intervention: Effect sizes (d) were 0.25, 0.24, and 0.36, respectively, for word reading residualized change, with similar results for passage comprehension in Studies 1 and 3.

One dilemma with intent-to-treat findings is that one cannot disentangle the various key or active ingredients: What actually caused the treatment effect? Thus, the treatment effects could be a result of only the professional development provided, better reading instruction provided in general, access to assessment information, the differentiation of instruction generally but not necessarily following the A2i recommended amounts, and so on. In an attempt to identify whether the C-I interactions (represented through the dynamic forecasting systems intervention models) were a key active component of the intervention and specifically related to students' varying achievement, we examined how precisely the treatment and control teachers provided the A2i recommended amounts to each student in their classroom for the four principal types of instruction, TCM-CF and TCM-MF, and CM-CF and CM-MF. We found that the total amounts of TCM-CF CM-CF, and CM-MF each student received did not predict their passage comprehension skills gains. However, the *distance from recommendation* (DFR), which is the absolute value of the difference between the student's A2i recommended amount and the amount he or she was actually observed to receive in the classroom, did significantly predict students' reading gains. In general, students whose teachers were in the ISI group had smaller DFR scores than did students in control classrooms (i.e., ISI teachers tended to provide amounts of TCM-CF and CM-MF instruction closer to the A2i recommended amounts than did control teachers). The effect was large. The effect size (d) for a student with a DFR of 10 minutes (standard score = 112) compared to one with a DFR of 30 minutes (standard score = 90) was 1.4, where a standard score of 100 ($SD = 15$) represents grade level. To date, this is our strongest evidence that C-I interactions are causally implicated in the varying impact of first-grade reading instruction (Connor, Piasta, et al., 2009).

Converging results incorporating classroom observation results reveal that there do appear to be optimal patterns of instruction. For TCM-CF, first graders who struggle with reading (i.e., enter first grade with reading skills below grade expectations) generally make greater gains in word reading and passage comprehension when they spend more time in TCM-CF instruction, whereas children with stronger skills generally show weaker reading gains the more time they spend in TCM-CF activities. The function is nonlinear when recommended amount is plotted against students' assessed reading score. Exponentially more time in TCM-CF small-group activities is recommended as students' skills fall below grade expectations.

In our most recent studies (Connor, Crowe, et al., 2010; Connor, Piasta, et al., 2009), using classroom observation and student assessment data, we found that the more time first graders spent in TCM-MF activities (e.g., reading and discussion of books), the greater their reading comprehension skill gains overall. Also, the effect of TCM-MF activities was a main effect; that is, regardless of students' reading or vocabulary skills levels, more time in TCM-MF small-group instruction was associated with greater reading comprehension skills gains. When developing the dynamic forecasting intervention models for A2i we used a shallow U-shaped function. Students with very strong reading comprehension skills or very weak (well below grade level) would, theoretically, require more time in TCM-MF to achieve either grade-level or a year's worth of growth. We tested these new algorithms in our most recent first-grade study (2008–2009) and found a significant effect of treatment (d = 0.36, 0.39) for both word reading and passage comprehension, respectively, that was larger than the intent-to-treat effect sizes in the previous two studies in which TCM-MF and CM-CF did not have differentiated recommendations for each student (in the first two studies, these types of instruction were set at a constant mean based on classroom observation data).

A consistent finding is that in general, child–peer-managed activities, whether CF or MF, have a smaller overall impact on students' reading skills gains (Connor, Morrison, & Slominski, 2006; Connor, Piasta, et al., 2009), compared to teacher–child-managed activities. We found that CM-MF activities were generally effective for first graders with strong vocabulary and reading skills. For students with weaker skills, the more time they spent in CM-MF activities, the weaker their reading skills growth. If the CM-MF opportunities were limited in the fall but increased over the course of the school year, then children with weaker skills did show reading skills gains (Connor, Morrison, & Katch, 2004; Connor, Piasta, et al., 2009). While observing classrooms in the fall, one potential explanation emerged. Children with fairly strong reading skills actually read during the times allotted for CM-MF activities (e.g., sustained silent reading). However, children with weaker skills held the book upside down, placed their heads on the desks, or got a drink of water. They were not reading or enjoying the activity. Other researchers have also found that peer-group instructional activities may be less beneficial for children with weaker skills overall (Christian & Bloome, 2004; Palincsar, Collins, Marano, & Magnusson, 2000).

Recently we found that CM-CF activities, primarily students completing workbook pages at their desks, interact with students' initial word-reading skills to affect reading gains (Connor, Crowe, et al., 2010). For first graders who were reading at or below grade level, time spent in CM-CF activities (e.g., phonics workbook pages) was generally associated with stronger reading skills growth. In contrast, for children with reading skills even slightly above grade level, more time in CM-CF activities was associated with weaker reading skills growth. The function for this algorithm is provided in Figure 17.2. Again, this new model was tested in our most recent first-grade study that yielded stronger treatment effects (d = 0.36 for word reading; 0.39 for passage comprehension) than the studies without the additional dynamic forecasting intervention models (d = 0.24 and 0.25).

Second Grade

The results for second grade are similar to those for first grade (Connor, Jakobsons, et al., 2009; Connor, Morrison, & Under-

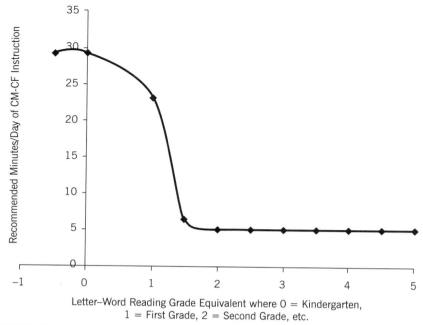

```
COMPUTE

CMCFRec = 2 * LW_GE +.6*TO² - 8*LW_GE³ + 27.

EXECUTE .

RECODE CMCFRec (Lowest thru 5=5) .

EXECUTE .
```

FIGURE 17.2. Recommended of minutes per day of child–peer-managed code-focused (CM-CF) instructional activities for first grade. Dynamic forecasting systems intervention model algorithms are provided to the right of the chart, where CMCFRec is the recommended minutes, LW_GE is the students' word-reading grade equivalent (GE), and TO is the target outcome, which is end of grade (1.9) or fall word reading GE + .9. Data from Connor, Crowe, Morrison, Fishman, and Schatschneider (2010).

wood, 2006). Students who received greater amounts of TCM-CF instruction (about 10 minutes per day in small groups) made greater reading gains than did students who spent less time in TCM-CF. Also, we observed that the amount of TCM-CF generally decreased from first to second grade. Thus, the dynamic forecasting systems intervention models continued to recommend TCM-CF instruction in small groups—about 10–15 minutes per day, with less, about 5 minutes per day, for students reading above grade expectations.

In our first second-grade study (*n* = 569 students, 39 classrooms), we found a trend in which students in the ISI condition dem-

onstrated greater passage comprehension gains than did students in a vocabulary intervention, but it did not meet our test of significance (alpha = .05). When we considered teachers' fidelity, we did find a significant difference in reading skills gains, but this depended on teacher fidelity; greater teacher fidelity was associated with stronger student gains. Thus, there was an ISI treatment effect, but *only* if the treatment group teacher implemented ISI with at least moderate fidelity. We are now conducting a second study with revised dynamic forecasting intervention models, in which we hope to achieve stronger and more consistent teacher fidelity of ISI implementation.

When we followed children from first to second grade (*n* = 235 students), we found that the effect of ISI accumulated (Connor, Morrison, Fishman, Schatschneider, et al., 2009). Thus, students participating in ISI in both first and second grade showed greater gains by the end of second grade compared to children who received only 1 year of ISI in either first or second grade. Still, students who received 1 year of ISI in either first or second grade demonstrated greater reading gains than students who did not receive any individualized reading instruction. Coupled with correlational longitudinal study findings, second grade may provide a second chance for students who struggle with reading (Connor, Morrison, Fishman, Schatschneider, et al., 2009; Connor, Morrison, & Underwood, 2007; Spira, Bracken, & Fischel, 2005).

In second grade, content area instruction may provide an effective context for improving reading comprehension (Connor, Rice, Canto, Underwood, & Morrison, 2010; Guthrie et al., 2004; Williams, Stafford, Lauer, Hall, & Pollini, 2009). Emerging correlational evidence suggests that there may be C-I interactions in content area instruction such as science. For example, we found that CM inquiry-focused science activities (e.g., hands-on science) were associated with greater vocabulary and science learning, as well as reading skills growth, with an important exception: These activities had no significant effect on content area gains for students with weaker vocabulary skills (Connor, Kaya, et al., 2010). Instead, more time in TCM science activities supported their reading and science knowledge growth. We were able to design individualized science instruction, taking into account these C-I and science instruction interactions, that appears generally to support students' science and literacy learning regardless of their initial skills levels (Connor, Kaya, et al., 2010).

Third Grade

We have conducted one randomized alternative treatment control efficacy study and two correlational studies in third grade (Connor, Jakobsons, et al., 2009; Connor, Morrison, & Petrella, 2004). We observed that the focus of instruction was increasingly on comprehension and reading for understanding (Connor, Morrison, & Petrella, 2004). In the 2004 longitudinal correlational study, we found that although third graders who struggle with reading continued to show greater gains when provided with more time in TCM-CF instruction, more important for them (i.e., associated with stronger reading gains) was increasing time in TCM-MF instruction that was explicitly focused on learning about and using comprehension strategies. This included substantial amounts of time in discussion about books, learning about strategies, and actually practicing them. The recently completed randomized control efficacy study grade (*n* = 448 students in 33 classrooms, 2008–2009 school year) (Connor, Morrison, et al., 2010) used dynamic forecasting intervention models based on these correlational results. Findings revealed that third graders in ISI classrooms made greater reading comprehension skill gains (on the Gates–MacGinitie Reading Test) than did students in the vocabulary intervention classrooms with a treatment effect of (*d* = 0.24). Figure 17.3 shows the classroom view for third grade.

Implications

The most straightforward implication of this work is that *one size does not fit all*— that it is highly unlikely that researchers and practitioners will find *the* perfect reading intervention that works for all students. Rather, multicomponent or balanced reading interventions are more likely to be effective for greater numbers of students. Going a step further, these results suggest that we can predict with a fairly high degree of precision exactly what mix of reading instructional activities (using a multidimensional view of instruction) are going to be effective for particular students if we know enough about their profile of language, literacy, and, potentially, other skills and aptitudes. The models used to recommend amounts and types of instruction are analogous to meteorologists' dynamic systems forecasting models used to predict the trajectory of storms, so we have called them dynamic forecasting intervention models. These models allow us to consider the complexities of the classroom instructional environment and the

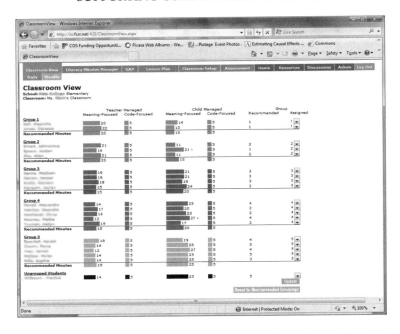

FIGURE 17.3. Third-grade classroom view. Groups increase in reading skills level from Group 1 (weakest) to Group 5 (strongest). Note that the teacher has changed some of the grouping configurations. Reprinted with permission from Florida State University.

dynamic nature of students' literacy development, which affect one another reciprocally: Instruction affects students' literacy development and students' characteristics, including their changing reading skills, impact the effective instructional environment. With enough information and support, teachers can design and implement effective literacy instruction that varies for each student depending on the skills and aptitudes he or she brings to the classroom initially and changing skills as each student receives instruction. So far, we have focused on the strongest predictors of students' literacy development, their language and reading skills. However, emerging evidence suggests that other student characteristics, such as background knowledge, self-regulation, and social skills, may also help to prescribe the types of instruction and overall classroom environment that will be more conducive to their literacy achievement (Connor, Ponitz, et al., 2010; Skibbe et al., 2009).

Developing and refining dynamic forecasting intervention models and implementing the instructional recommendations lead to several other considerations, including

classroom observation as a vital part of school research and assessment, and teachers' training, skills, and effectiveness. Although it is tempting (and easier) to consider more distal school and classroom influences on students development, such as teacher qualification and school resources, these variables typically do not explain substantial amounts of the variability in students' literacy skills (Cohen, Raudenbush, & Ball, 2003; Goldhaber & Brewer, 1999). Classroom observations that provide a reliable metric of the classroom at the level of the individual student are more likely to help us understand why some students develop proficient literacy skills, whereas others struggle (Connor, Morrison, Fishman, Ponitz, et al., 2009). Our classroom observations at the level of the individual student reveal that, intentionally or not, students who share the same classroom receive differing amounts and types of literacy instruction, that some classrooms spend more time in noninstruction (waiting in line, waiting for the teacher, disruptions, etc.) than in meaningful instruction (Connor, Piasta, et al., 2009), and that classroom environment (e.g., disruptions, transitions, chaos) matters when we consider student learning (Connor, Ponitz, et al., 2010). As our newest research is showing, the teacher alone does not affect the classroom: Students also contribute to the classroom environment (Skibbe et al., 2010). Teachers may be highly qualified (e.g., hold advanced degrees) and still not teach reading effectively (Connor, Son, Hindman, & Morrison, 2005). Finally, if dynamic forecasting intervention models continue to be useful in recommending optimal patterns of instruction, they cannot be developed and refined without classroom instruction data. It may be that until greater focus is given to the classroom environment, we will not be able to address the most pressing issue facing education: How do we better support all students' learning?

Our findings also point to the importance of valid and reliable formative assessments. Without good information on students' progress, the dynamic forecasting intervention models are less precise, and teachers may be less effective. Many of the progress-monitoring (also called curriculum-based) assessments currently available focus almost exclusively on basic decoding and fluency skills. More than likely, access to these progress-monitoring results has contributed to the general improvement in students' word-reading skills (Gamse, Jacob, Horst, Boulay, & Unlu, 2008). However, we consistently find that students' reading comprehension skills and language skills, particularly their assessed vocabulary skills, are an important consideration for individualizing literacy instruction, especially after first grade. In our studies, teachers had access to passage comprehension and picture vocabulary scores, as well as word-reading scores, and we found that the more teachers accessed the scores and progress-monitoring graphs in A2i, the stronger were their students' outcomes (Connor, Morrison, Fishman, & Schatschneider, in press).

An encouraging finding across the randomized control trials is that changing teachers' practice in the classroom in ways that improve students' literacy outcomes is possible. Consider this: We found consistent significant effects of treatment on well-regarded standardized tests of word reading and reading comprehension that were achieved by typical classroom teachers who began ISI training and use of A2i software in the fall of the school year. Teachers were able to change their literacy instruction practices and sustain these changes so that, overall, their students made greater gains in word reading and reading comprehension compared to students whose teachers received professional development but were not taught how to individualize student instruction. While fairly intense, the ISI professional development protocol is similar to protocols that are successfully used by school districts to improve practice (May & Supovitz, 2006). One difference is that we provided a technology designed to support teacher decision making, the A2i Web-based software. Emerging evidence indicates that training in and use of A2i may be a key component of our effective professional development protocol in much the way that clinical decision support systems are improving medical practice. Teachers represent a key source of influence on students' literacy development and learning more generally. It is increasingly clear that teachers do matter (Taylor et al., 2010), and that effective teachers can make a difference in children's lives. Taken together, our research reveals that focused professional development and support to teachers can improve students' literacy skills growth. Providing such support may be a more fruitful policy than focusing on performance pay or teacher qualifications. Our experience shows that teachers do care about their students' learning and are more than willing to change their practice if they observe meaningful improvement in their students' learning.

All together, accumulating research indicates that we can systematically predict the amounts and types of early literacy instruction that will support students' reading development, but no single type or philosophy of instruction is likely to be the silver bullet. With a strong understanding of components of the classroom environment, valid and reliable progress-monitoring measures, and true support for teachers, including technology, we can begin to ensure that students receive effective instruction, so that they gain the proficient literacy skills that they need to be successful in our 21st-century information-driven society.

Acknowledgments

Although I wrote this chapter, the work is not solely mine. First and foremost, I acknowledge the key contributions of Frederick J. Morrison, University of Michigan, and thank him for his invaluable insights and support. I also thank my other co-investigators Stephanie Al Otaiba, Barry Fishman, and Christopher Schatschneider, as well as coauthors (cited throughout) Elizabeth Crowe and Phyllis Underwood, project directors, and the doctoral students and research assistants of the ISI project. I also thank the teachers, students, parents, and school administrators without whom this research would not be possible. These studies were funded by Grant Nos. R305H04013 and R305B070074, "Child by Instruction Interactions: Effects of Individualizing Instruction," from the U.S. Department of Education, Institute of Education Sciences, and by Grant No. R01HD48539 from the National Institute of Child Health and Human Development. The opinions expressed are mine and do not represent views of the funding agencies.

References

Adams, M. J. (2001). Alphabetic anxiety and explicit, systematic phonics instruction: A cognitive science perspective. In S. B. Neuman & D. K. Dickinson (Eds.), *Handbook of early literacy research* (Vol. I, pp. 66–80). New York: Guilford Press.

Al Otaiba, S., Connor, C. M., Kosanovich, M., Schatschneider, C., Dyrlund, A. K., & Lane, H. (2008). Reading First kindergarten classroom instruction and students' phonological awareness and decoding fluency growth. *Journal of School Psychology, 48,* 281–314.

Barr, R. (1984). Beginning reading instruction: From debate to reformation. In P. D. Pearson, R. Barr, M. L. Kamil, & P. Mosenthal (Eds.), *Handbook of reading research* (pp. 545–581). New York: Longman.

Bond, G. L., & Dykstra, R. (1967). The cooperative research program in first-grade reading instruction. *Reading Research Quarterly, 2*(4), 5–142.

Borko, H., & Niles, J. (1987). Descriptions of teacher planning: Ideas for teachers and research. In V. Richardson-Koehler (Ed.), *Educators' handbook: A research perspective* (pp. 167–187). New York: Longman.

Bowman, C. L., Galvez-Martin, M., & Morrison, M. (2005). Developing reflection in preservice teachers. In S. E. Israel, K. L. Bauserman, C. C. Block, & K. Kinnucan-Welsch (Ed.), *Metacognition in literacy learning: Theory, assessment, instruction, and professional development* (pp. 335–349). Mahwah, NJ: Erlbaum.

Bronfenbrenner, U. (1986). Ecology of the family as a context for human development: Research perspectives. *Developmental Psychology, 22,* 723–742.

Bronfenbrenner, U., & Morris, P. A. (2006). The bioecological model of human development. In R. M.

Lerner & W. Damon (Eds.), *Handbook of child psychology: Theoretical models of human development* (6th ed., Vol. 1, pp. 793–828). Hoboken, NJ: Wiley.

Brophy, J. E. (1979). Teacher behavior and its effects. *Journal of Educational Psychology, 71*(6), 733–750.

Brophy, J. E. (1985). Classroom management as instruction: Socializing self-guidance in students. *Theory Into Practice, 24*(4), 233–240.

Brophy, J. E., & Good, T. L. (1986). Teacher behavior and student achievement. In M. C. Wittrock (Ed.), *Handbook of research on teaching* (3rd ed., pp. 328–375). New York: Macmillan.

Cameron, C. E., Connor, C. M., & Morrison, F. J. (2005). Effects of variation in teacher organization on classroom functioning. *Journal of School Psychology, 43*(1), 61–85.

Catts, H. W., Fey, M. E., Zhang, X., & Tomblin, J. B. (2001). Estimating the risk of future reading difficulties in kindergarten children: A research-based model and its clinical implementation. *Language, Speech, and Hearing Services in Schools, 32,* 38–50.

Christian, B., & Bloome, D. (2004). Learning to read is who you are. *Reading and Writing Quarterly, 20,* 365–384.

Cohen, D. K., Raudenbush, S. W., & Ball, D. L. (2003). Resources, instruction, and research. *Educational Evaluation and Policy Analysis, 25*(2), 119–142.

Connor, C. M., Crowe, E., Morrison, F. J., Fishman, B., & Schatschneider, C. (2010). *Differentiating first grade literacy instruction: Refining and improving dynamic forecasting intervention models.* Manuscript submitted for publication.

Connor, C. M., Jakobsons, L. J., Crowe, E., & Meadows, J. (2009). Instruction, differentiation, and student engagement in Reading First classrooms. *Elementary School Journal, 109*(3), 221–250.

Connor, C. M., Kaya, S., Luck, M., Toste, J., Canto, A., Rice, D. C., et al. (2010). Content-area literacy: Individualizing student instruction in second grade science. *Reading Teacher, 63*(6), 474–485.

Connor, C. M., Morrison, F. J., Fishman, B., Guiliani, S., Luck, M., Underwood, P., et al. (2010). *Child × instruction interactions and the impact of individualizing student instruction on third graders' reading comprehension.* Manuscript submitted for publication.

Connor, C. M., Morrison, F. J., Fishman, B., Ponitz, C. C., Glasney, S., Underwood, P., et al. (2009). The ISI classroom observation system: Examining the literacy instruction provided to individual students. *Educational Researcher, 38*(2), 85–99.

Connor, C. M., Morrison, F. J., Fishman, B., & Schatschneider, C. (in press). Assessment and instruction connections: The implications of child × instruction interactions effects on student learning. In J. Sabatini & E. Albro (Eds.), *Assessing reading in the 21st century: Aligning and applying advances in the reading and measurement sciences.* Lanham, MD: Rowman & Littlefield Education.

Connor, C. M., Morrison, F. J., Fishman, B., Schatschneider, C., Toste, J., Lundblom, E. G., et al. (in press). Effective first grade classroom instruction depends on student characteristics: Implications of child × instruction interactions on student achievement. *Journal of Education and Effectiveness.*

Connor, C. M., Morrison, F. J., Fishman, B., Schatschneider, C., Underwood, P., & Crowe, E. C. (2009, April). *First and second grade literacy skill growth: Independent and cumulative effects of Individualized Reading Instruction.* Paper presented at the biennial meeting of the Society for Research in Child Development.

Connor, C. M., Morrison, F. J., Fishman, B. J., Schatschneider, C., & Underwood, P. (2007). The early years: Algorithm-guided individualized reading instruction. *Science, 315,* 464–465.

Connor, C. M., Morrison, F. J., & Katch, E. L. (2004). Beyond the reading wars: The effect of classroom instruction by child interactions on early reading. *Scientific Studies of Reading, 8*(4), 305–336.

Connor, C. M., Morrison, F. J., & Petrella, J. N. (2004). Effective reading comprehension instruction: Examining child by instruction interactions. *Journal of Educational Psychology, 96*(4), 682–698.

Connor, C. M., Morrison, F. J., & Slominski, L. (2006). Preschool instruction and children's literacy skill growth. *Journal of Educational Psychology, 98*(4), 665–689.

Connor, C. M., Morrison, F. J., & Underwood, P. (2006, June). *A second chance in second grade: The independent and cumulative impact of first and second grade reading instruction on students' letter–word reading skill growth.* Paper presented at the annual meeting of the Society for the Scientific Study of Reading, Vancouver, BC, Canada.

Connor, C. M., Morrison, F. J., & Underwood, P. (2007). A second chance in second grade?: The independent and cumulative impact of first and second grade reading instruction and students' letter–word reading skill growth. *Scientific Studies of Reading, 11*(3), 199–233.

Connor, C. M., Piasta, S. B., Fishman, B., Glasney, S., Schatschneider, C., Crowe, E., et al. (2009). Individualizing student instruction precisely: Effects of child by instruction interactions on first graders' literacy development. *Child Development, 80*(1), 77–100.

Connor, C. M., Ponitz, C. E. C., Phillips, B., Travis, Q. M., Glasney, S., & Morrison, F. J. (2010). First graders' literacy and self-regulation gains: The effect of individualizing instruction. *Journal of School Psychology, 48,* 433–455.

Connor, C. M., Rice, D. C., Canto, A., Underwood, P., & Morrison, F. J. (2010). *Second-grade science instruction and its relation to students' content-area knowledge, vocabulary, and reading skill gains.* Manuscript submitted for publication.

Connor, C. M., Son, S.-H., Hindman, A. H., & Morrison, F. J. (2005). Teacher qualifications, classroom practices, family characteristics, and preschool experience: Complex effects on first graders' vocabulary and early reading outcomes. *Journal of School Psychology, 43,* 343–375.

Cronbach, L. J. (1957). The two disciplines of scientific psychology. *American Psychologist, 12,* 671–684.

Cronbach, L. J., & Snow, R. E. (1977). *Aptitudes and instructional methods: A handbook for research on interactions.* New York: Irvington.

DuFour, R., & Eaker, R. (1998). *Professional learning communities at work: Best practices for enhancing student achievement.* Alexandria, VA: Association for Supervision and Curriculum Development.

Foorman, B. R., Schatschneider, C., Eakin, M. N., Fletcher, J. M., Moats, L. C., & Francis, D. J. (2006). The impact of instructional practices in grades 1 and 2 on reading and spelling achievement in high poverty schools. *Contemporary Educational Psychology, 31,* 1–29.

Freeman, G. D., & King, J. L. (2003). A partnership for school readiness. *Educational Leadership, 60*(7), 76–79.

Fuchs, L. S., Fuch, D., & Phillips, N. (1994). The relation between teachers' beliefs about the importance of good student work habits, teacher planning, and student achievement. *Elementary School Journal, 94*(3), 331–345.

Gamse, B. C., Jacob, R. T., Horst, M., Boulay, B., & Unlu, F. (2008). *Reading First Impact Study Final Report (NCEE 2009-4038).* Washington, DC: National Center for Education Evaluation and Regional Assistance, Institute of Education Sciences, U.S. Department of Education.

Garg, A. X., Adhikari, N. K. J., McDonald, H., Rosas-Arellano, M. P., Devereaux, P. J., Beyene, J., et al. (2005). Effects of computerized clinical decision support systems on practitioner performance and patient outcomes. *Journal of the American Medical Association, 293*(10), 1233–1237.

Gee, J. P. (2000). Discourse and sociocultural studies in reading. In M. L. Kamil, P. B. Mosenthal, D. P. Pearson, & R. Barr (Eds.), *Handbook of reading research* (Vol. 3, pp. 195–207). Mahwah, NJ: Erlbaum.

Gee, J. P. (2001). A sociocultural perspective on early literacy development. In S. B. Neuman & D. K. Dickinson (Eds.), *Handbook of early literacy research* (Vol. 1, pp. 30–42). New York: Guilford Press.

Gersten, R. (2007, July). *Impact of teacher study groups on observed teaching practice and student vocabulary and comprehension for first grade teachers: Results of a large scale randomized controlled trial.* Paper presented at the SSSR Conference, Prague.

Gersten, R., Chard, D., & Baker, S. (2000). Factors enhancing sustained use of research-based practices. *Journal of Learning Disabilities, 33*(5), 445–457.

Gersten, R., Compton, D., Connor, C. M., Dimino, J., Santoro, L., Linan-Thompson, S., et al. (2008). *Assisting students struggling with reading: Response to intervention and multi-tier intervention for reading in the primary grades: A practice guide.* Washington, DC: National Center for Education Evaluation and Regional Assistance, Institute of Education Sciences, U.S. Department of Education.

Goldhaber, D. D., & Brewer, D. J. (1999). Teacher licensing and student achievement. In M. Kasteroroon & C. E. Finn (Eds.), *Better teachers, better schools* (pp. 83–102). Washington, DC: Thomas B. Fordham Foundation.

Good, R. H., & Kaminski, R. A. (2002). *Dynamic Indicators of Basic Early Literacy Skills (DIBELS)* (6th ed.). Eugene, OR: Institute for Development of Educational Achievement.

Guthrie, J. T., Wigfield, A., Barbosa, P., Perencevich, K. C., Taboada, A., Davis, M. H., et al. (2004). Increasing reading comprehension and engagement through concept-oriented reading instruction. *Journal of Educational Psychology, 94*(3), 403–423.

Helterbran, V. R., & Fennimore, B. S. (2004). Collaborative early childhood professional development: Building from a base of teacher investigation. *Early Childhood Education Journal, 31*(4), 267–271.

Juel, C., & Minden-Cupp, C. (2000). Learning to read words: Linguistic units and instructional strategies. *Reading Research Quarterly, 35*(4), 458–492.

Kawamoto, K., Houlihan, C., Balas, E. A., & Lobach, D. F. (2005). Improving clinical practice using clinical decision support systems: A systematic review of trials to identify features critical to success. *British Journal of Medicine, 330*, 765–733.

Kyllonen, P. C., & Lajoie, S. P. (2003). Reassessing aptitude: Introduction to a special issue in honor of Richard E. Snow. *Educational Psychologist, 38*(2), 79–83.

Lave, J., & Wenger, E. (1991). *Situated learning legitimate peripheral participation.* Cambridge, UK: Cambridge University Press.

Mathes, P. G., Denton, C. A., Fletcher, J. M., Anthony, J. L., Francis, D. J., & Schatschneider, C. (2005). The effects of theoretically different instruction and student characteristics on the skills of struggling readers. *Reading Research Quarterly, 40*(2), 148–182.

May, H., & Supovitz, J. A. (2006). Capturing the cumulative effects of school reform: An 11-year study of the impacts of America's Choice on student achievement. *Education Evaluation and Policy Analysis, 28*(3), 231–257.

Morrison, F. J., Bachman, H. J., & Connor, C. M. (2005). *Improving literacy in America: Guidelines from research.* New Haven, CT: Yale University Press.

Morrison, F. J., & Connor, C. M. (2009). The transition to school: Child-instruction transactions in learning to read. In A. Sameroff (Ed.), *The transactional model of development: How children and contexts shape each other* (pp. 183–201). Washington, DC: American Psychological Association.

Morrison, F. J., Connor, C. M., & Bachman, H. J. (2005). The transition to school. In D. K. Dickinson & S. B. Neuman (Eds.), *Handbook of early literacy* (Vol. 2, pp. 111–135). New York: Guilford Press.

NICHD Early Child Care Research Network. (2002). The relation of global first grade classroom environment to structural classroom features and teacher and student behaviors. *Elementary School Journal, 102*(5), 367–387.

NICHD Early Child Care Research Network. (2005). Pathways to reading: The role of oral language in the transition to reading. *Developmental Psychology, 41*(2), 428–442.

Palincsar, A. S., Collins, K. M., Marano, N. L., & Magnusson, S. J. (2000). Investigating the engagement and learning of students with learning disabilities in guided inquiry science teaching. *Speech, Language, and Hearing Services in Schools, 31*(3), 240–251.

Piasta, S. B., Connor, C. M., Fishman, B., & Morrison, F. J. (2009). Teachers' knowledge of literacy, classroom practices, and student reading growth. *Scientific Studies of Reading, 13*(3), 224–248.

Pressley, M., Wharton-McDonald, R., Allington, R., Block, C. C., Morrow, L., Tracey, D., et al. (2001). A study of effective first-grade literacy instruction. *Scientific Studies of Reading, 5*(1), 35–58.

Ramanathan, V. (2002). Enhancing the critical edge of (L2) teacher-education: Some issues in advanced literacy. In M. J. Schleppegrell & M. C. Colombi (Ed.), *Developing advanced literacy in first and second languages: Meaning with power* (pp. 187–207). Mahwah, NJ: Erlbaum.

Raudenbush, S. W. (2005). How do we study "what happens next"? *Annals of the American Academy of Political and Social Science, 602*(1), 131–144.

Raudenbush, S. W., & Bryk, A. S. (2002). *Hierarchical linear models: Applications and data analysis methods* (2nd ed.). Thousand Oaks, CA: Sage.

Rayner, K., Foorman, B. R., Perfetti, C. A., Pesetsky, D., & Seidenberg, M. S. (2001). How psychological science informs the teaching of reading. *Psychological Science in the Public Interest, 2*(2), 31–74.

Rhome, J. R. (2007). Technical summary of the National Hurricane Center track and intensity models. Retrieved October 12, 2008, from *www.nhc.noaa.gov/modelsummary.shtml.*

Rimm-Kaufman, S. E., Paro, K. M. L., Downer, J. T., & Pianta, R. C. (2005). The contribution of classroom setting and quality of instruction to children's behavior in kindergarten classrooms. *Elementary School Journal, 105*(4), 337–345.

Shavelson, R. J., & Towne, L. (Eds.). (2002). *Scientific research in education.* Washington DC: National Academy Press.

Showers, B., Joyce, B., & Bennett, B. (1987). Synthesis of research on staff development: A framework for future study and a state-of-the-art analysis. *Educational Leadership, 45*(3), 77–87.

Skibbe, L., Glasney, S., Connor, C. M., & Brophy-Herb, H. E. (2010). *Children's early literacy growth in relation to classmates' self-regulation.* Manuscript submitted for publication.

Snow, C. E. (2001). *Reading for understanding.* Santa Monica, CA: RAND Education and the Science and Technology Policy Institute.

Snow, C. E., Burns, M. S., & Griffin, P. (Eds.). (1998). *Preventing reading difficulties in young children.* Washington, DC: National Academy Press.

Spira, E. G., Bracken, S. S., & Fischel, J. E. (2005). Predicting improvement after first-grade reading difficulties: The effects of oral language, emergent literacy, and behavior skills. *Developmental Psychology, 41*(1), 225–234.

Taylor, B. M., & Pearson, D. P. (Eds.). (2002). *Teaching reading: Effective schools, accomplished teachers.* Mahwah, NJ: Erlbaum.

Taylor, B. M., Pearson, D. P., Clark, K., & Walpole, S.

(2000). Effective schools and accomplished teachers: Lessons about primary-grade reading instruction in low-income schools. *Elementary School Journal, 101*(2), 121–165.

Taylor, J. J., Roehrig, A. D., Connor, C. M., & Schatschneider, C. (2010). Teacher quality moderates the genetic effects on early reading. *Science, 328*, 512–514.

Torgesen, J. K. (2000). Individual differences in response to early intervention in reading: The lingering problem of treatment resisters. *Learning Disabilities Research and Practice, 15*, 55–64.

Tudge, J. R. H., Odero, D. A., Hogan, D. M., & Etz, K. E. (2003). Relations between the everyday activities of preschoolers and their teachers' perceptions of their competence in the first years of school. *Early Childhood Research Quarterly, 18*(1), 42–64.

U.S. Department of Education. (2004). *No Child Left Behind: A toolkit for teachers.* Washington, DC: Author.

Vaughn, S., & Coleman, M. (2004). The role of mentoring in promoting use of research-based practices in reading. *Remedial and Special Education, 25*(1), 25–38.

Vellutino, F. R., Scanlon, D. M., Sipay, E. R., Small, S. G., Pratt, A., Chen, R., et al. (1996). Cognitive profiles of difficult to remediate and readily remediated poor readers: Early intervention as a vehicle for distinguishing between cognitive and experiential deficits as basic causes of specific reading disability. *Journal of Educational Psychology, 88*(4), 601–638.

Wharton-McDonald, R., Pressley, M., & Hampston, J. M. (1998). Literacy instruction in nine first-grade classrooms: Teacher characteristics and student achievement. *Elementary School Journal, 99*(2), 101–128.

Williams, J. P., Stafford, K. B., Lauer, K. D., Hall, K. M., & Pollini, S. (2009). Embedding reading comprehension training in content-area instruction. *Journal of Educational Psychology, 101*(1), 1–20.

Yoshikawa, H., & Hsueh, J. (2001). Child development and public policy: Toward a dynamic systems perspective. *Child Development, 72*(6), 1887–1903.

IV

INTERVENTIONS: CURRICULUM AND PROFESSIONAL DEVELOPMENT

18

Fostering Early Development and School Readiness in Pediatric Settings

ALAN L. MENDELSOHN
BENARD P. DREYER
CAROLYN A. BROCKMEYER
SAMANTHA B. BERKULE-SILBERMAN
LESLEY MANDEL MORROW

There is an extensive literature documenting that socioeconomically disadvantaged children are delayed in their language development soon after they utter their first words. These early delays translate into marked limitations in literacy and school readiness upon entrance to kindergarten, as well as lifelong setbacks in achievement (Aber, Jones, & Cohen, 2000; Shonkoff, 2000). While these disparities in school preparedness and education success are partially determined by the scarcity of material resources associated with poverty, they are also a result of poverty-related disparities in the quantity and quality of parent–child interactions. With limited education and literacy, parents often are unaware of the importance of shared reading and play for the development of school readiness. In addition, psychosocial stressors, such as lack of social support and depression, impede parents from engaging in cognitively stimulating activities, such as shared reading and play, with their children (Field, 1998; Osofsky & Thompson, 2000). This is of primary concern because *responsive parenting* in these contexts—defined in this chapter as verbal scaffolding, verbal responsivity, contingent responsivity, and positive regard/warmth—

is vital for helping children to develop the cognitive, language, and literacy skills needed to succeed in school.

This chapter begins with a review of literature that suggests addressing responsive parenting is crucial for promoting school readiness and enhancing the developmental course for children at risk due to poverty. The section that follows includes a review of recent programs that have aimed to enhance language and emergent literacy outcomes of low-income children by targeting responsive parenting in the home. Next, we discuss the rationale for intervening in pediatric primary health care, using Reach Out and Read (ROR) as an example. We then introduce our approach to improving these outcomes by bolstering parent–child interactions through an innovative pediatric program called the Video Interaction Project (VIP), which incorporates evidence-based strategies for promoting early child development and, ultimately, emergent literacy and school readiness. Finally, we present longitudinal findings from two randomized controlled trials indicating that VIP significantly impacts both parenting and child development. Findings yield recommendations for utilizing the pediatric primary care platform to address poverty-related disparities in school readiness on a population level by targeting parenting behaviors, beginning in the first year of a child's life.

Responsive Parenting and School Readiness

It has long been known that the quality of parent–child interactions in the home is a significant determinant of children's language and cognitive development. The richness of parental *verbal input* is one critical aspect of these interactions driving child outcomes, with evidence suggesting that children need to receive rich language input, such as labeling objects and actions, to develop vocabulary knowledge adequately (Weizman & Snow, 2001). A number of studies also find that rich language input is important for later cognitive and memory skills, and positively influences later reading comprehension. Other significant aspects of parent–child interactions related to child language and cognitive outcomes are *verbal scaffolding* (i.e., structuring language interaction to meet the child's abilities) and *verbal responsivity* (i.e., responding to vocalizations with imitations or expansions, engaging in back-and-forth conversation, and asking questions). Snow (1977), in line with Vygotsky's (1978) sociocultural framework, demonstrated that language learning is best supported when parents structure their interactions to adjust to the level of their child by simplifying or repeating utterances, using child-directed speech, and asking questions. Furthermore, it has been shown that both imitating and responding contingently to babies' vocalizations help to foster more advanced communicative abilities in infants (Hardy-Brown & Plomin, 1985).

While the importance of the verbal components of parent–child interactions cannot be overemphasized, their impacts are both contingent on and interwoven with other domains of parenting responsivity that function to support children's attentional and emotional regulatory capacities. For instance, children's language and cognitive outcomes are best fostered in social contexts in which parents follow and maintain their child's focus of interest (e.g., Landry, Miller-Loncar, Smith, & Swank, 2002;

Tomasello & Farrar, 1986). Parents' *contingent responsivity*—that is, the promptness and sensitivity with which parents respond to children's verbal and nonverbal signals—also significantly impacts children's communication, and has implications for language and cognitive development (e.g., Bornstein & Tamis-LeMonda, 1989; Tamis-LeMonda, Bornstein, & Baumwell, 2001). Positive child outcomes are also best generated and sustained through parent–child interactions that contain a high degree of *positive regard and warmth*. Landry and colleagues (Landry, Smith, Swank, Assel, & Vellet, 2001; Landry, Smith, et al., 2002) have found that parents' use of affirmations and praise, coupled with the lack of anger, rejection, or negative tones, is positively associated with a variety of school readiness outcomes.

Given the strong link between responsive parenting and child outcomes, it is critically important for children to be frequently engaged in contexts that generate warm, reciprocal, language-rich parent–child interactions. Shared book reading and play—in addition to affecting the development of imagination, reasoning, and decontextualized oral language skills—are critical for school readiness because they provide the ideal contexts for such interactions (e.g., Bus & van IJzendoorn, 1992; Morrow & Young, 1997; Tabors, Roach, & Snow, 2001; Tamis-LeMonda, Cristofaro, Rodriguez, & Bornstein, 2006). Interactions in these domains allow for extensive back-and-forth verbal exchanges between parent and child, with clear benefits for emergent literacy and language outcomes (e.g., Hoff-Ginsberg, 1991; Morrow & Schikedanz, 2006; Neuman, 1996; Sénéchal & LeFevre, 2002; Whitehurst et al., 1988). These interactions also give rise to conversation related to emotions and experiences, and are therefore important for promoting self-regulation and socioemotional aspects of school readiness (e.g., Nelson, 2007; Riggs, Greenberg, Kusché, & Pentz, 2006).

The identification of responsive parenting as an impetus for school readiness, particularly in the contexts of shared book reading and play, sheds some light on the origin of the disparities in school readiness experienced by low-income children. To begin, there are striking differences in the amount of shared book reading that occurs in the homes of middle- and low-income families, with low-income children entering kindergarten with about 25 hours of book reading compared to the 1,000–1,700 hours experienced by middle-income counterparts (Adams, 1990). Also, when low-income parents do engage in shared book reading with their children, their interactions often do not resemble the language-rich, responsive interactions required for enhancing language and cognitive development. Instead, parent–child interactions in low-income homes frequently contain fewer vocabulary words, fewer complex sentences, less elaborative language, fewer questions directed at children, and fewer attempts to elicit language from children (Hart & Risley, 1995; Ninio, 1980; Peralta de Mendoza, 1995; Reese, Cox, Harte, & McAnally, 2003). Evidence also suggests that these considerably different responses in parenting experienced by low-income children permeate the domain of pretend play, with negative implications for literacy and cognitive development (see Morrow & Shickedanz, 2006, for review). The discovery of such striking differences in the home language environments of low- and middle-income children in past decades has inspired psychologists, educators, and health practitioners alike to create innovative ways to target responsive parenting in these contexts in efforts to reduce disparities in poverty-related school readiness.

Enhancing Responsive Parenting in the Home

Programs aiming to promote parenting responsiveness and child school readiness have met with varying success (see Britto, Fuligni, & Brooks-Gunn, 2006, for review). The most consistent and strong impacts on parenting and school readiness have been found for programs utilizing targeted and focused intervention strategies (Dickinson & Caswell, 2007; Dickinson, McCabe, & Essex, 2006).

One such targeted program that has shown long-term impacts on child outcomes, focusing in particular on home language interactions, is the Parent–Child Home Program (PCHP; Madden, Levenstein, & Levenstein, 1976). In PCHP, home visitors provide toys and books, and model interactive activities

twice a week when children are age 2–4 years. Participation in this program has been shown to result in improved children's school readiness, measured by the Cognitive Skills Assessment Battery (Levenstein, Levenstein, & Oliver, 2002), as well as long-term outcomes, such as reduced high school dropout rates (Levenstein, Levenstein, Shiminski, & Stolzberg, 1998). A more recent program that has also demonstrated success in promoting school readiness through enhanced parenting is Playing and Learning Strategies (PALS; Landry, Smith, & Swank, 2006; Landry, Smith, Swank, & Guttentag, 2008). In PALS, home visitors converse with parents about their interactions with their children, describe responsive parenting behaviors, and show parents a videotape of a mother–child dyad from a similar background modeling target parenting behaviors. The home visitor then creates a videotape of the mother and child interacting together (in a context of their choice) and reviews this videotape with the mother to encourage self-reflection regarding parenting. There are two phases of the PALS program (infancy—10 visits; toddler–preschool—10 visits), each of which has been shown to have both independent and additive impacts on responsive parenting and on child development.

While the documented impact of these targeted home parenting programs supports the need for their expansion and dissemination, the cost associated with home-based programs is a potential barrier to widespread implementation. Pediatric health care represents an innovative alternative route for the implementation of low-cost, preventive interventions to improve school readiness populationwide.

Pediatric Primary Care: A Novel Platform for Promoting Parenting and School Readiness

Rationale for Placing Interventions within Pediatric Primary Health Care

The recognition within the pediatric community that there might be a role for pediatrics in facilitating parenting and child development began approximately 35 years ago, in 1975, when "the new morbidity" in pediatrics was first described as consisting of child developmental and behavioral problems, social issues, and family mental health concerns. A recent commentary in *Academic Pediatrics* (Dreyer, 2009) describes the importance of these issues in primary care pediatrics, from 1975 to the present day, and the continued need for pediatric primary care to address them actively. In addition, the commentary describes the commitment of the American Academy of Pediatrics (AAP) to the prevention, early detection, and management of developmental, behavioral, and social problems as a focus in pediatric practice (which the AAP reaffirmed in 1993 and 2001).

Pediatric primary care represents an important and unique platform for intervention to promote child development and school readiness through enhanced responsive parenting for a number of reasons. First and foremost is the potential it offers to widely disseminate interventions to all children in the United States, in part due to requirements for screening and immunizations prior to school entry (AAP, 2009). Primary care visits to meet these requirements provide the opportunity to intervene with low-income families, who generally are at greatest risk yet may be the most difficult to reach. Frequency and timing of pediatric primary care also play a role. With 13–15 standard pediatric primary care visits from birth to age 5 years (AAP, 2009; Jellinek, Patel, & Froehle, 2002; Sturner, 1998), and additional visits related to medical problems common in low-income populations (e.g., obesity, asthma), visit frequency is sufficient to provide a dose of intervention comparable to that of targeted home visitation programs that have been shown to be effective (e.g., Landry et al., 2008). In addition, with visits beginning shortly after birth, pediatric primary care provides an opportunity to intervene early, with potential for greater impacts, with lower net costs than interventions later in life (Knudsen, Heckman, Cameron, & Shonkoff, 2006; Shonkoff, 2000).

Another unique aspect of intervening in pediatric primary care is the relationship built between the provider and family, which provides a foundation for both standard preventive counseling ("anticipatory guidance") related to parenting (Brazelton, 1976; Dinkevich & Ozuah, 2002) and the parenting interventions described in this chapter. Finally, intervention in the pediatric primary care setting brings the potential for low cost due to the opportunity for leveraging existing health-care infrastructure and travel. Compared to home visitation programs such as PCHP (described earlier), which cost approximately $1,000/child/year (Levenstein et al., 2002) and center-based programs such as Head Start and the Abecedarian Project, which cost at least $7,000/child/year, and potentially much more (Barnett, & Robin, 2006; Masse & Barnett 2002), pediatric primary health-care programs such as ROR (see discussion below) and VIP cost far less (approximately $8/child/year [Zuckerman, 2009] and $270/child/year, respectively).

Evidence of Success with Pediatric Primary Care Interventions

The rationale for placing parenting interventions in the pediatric primary care setting is supported by findings that targeted interventions in this setting have been successful in changing parent behavior and child development outcomes. The most widely studied targeted intervention to date is ROR, developed at Boston City Hospital in 1989 by Barry Zuckerman, Robert Needlman and Kathleen Fitzgerald Rice (Needlman, Klass, & Zuckerman, 2006). ROR is an intervention program that takes place during well-child visits from age 6 months to 5 years, and integrates parent–child reading activities into children's medical care. The program consists of a waiting room component, anticipatory guidance about literacy development given by providers, and distribution of age-appropriate children's books at each visit. The waiting room component typically consists of volunteers who model reading activities. Child health-care providers counsel parents about the importance of and techniques for shared reading; they also distribute new children's books free of charge at each regular health maintenance visit. Thus, between nine and 11 books are distributed over the period spanning infancy through preschool.

Numerous studies of ROR's impact have documented increased parent–child shared reading and enhanced child language (High, LaGasse, Becker, Ahlgren, & Gardner, 2000; Mendelsohn, 2002; Mendelsohn et al., 2001; Needlman, Toker, Klass, Dreyer, & Mendelsohn, 2005; Sharif, Reiber, & Ozuah, 2002). ROR's simplicity and low cost have facilitated successful dissemination to more than 4,500 sites in the United States and internationally (Zuckerman, 2009). These ROR sites are assisted and/or coordinated by the ROR National Center (*www.reachoutandread.org*), directed by Perri Klass. While studies of ROR have shown that impacts can be made through intervention in pediatric primary care, they do not provide information regarding the ultimate potential of such interventions.

VIP 0–3: Pushing the Limits of Pediatric Primary Health Care

VIP 0–3 Program Development

In the late 1990s, following the initial studies of ROR, we convened a research team at the Department of Pediatrics at New York University School of Medicine and Bellevue Hospital Center, with the aim to determine whether increasing intensity of targeted interventions in pediatric care, building on ROR, would further enhance school readiness outcomes. This group and its efforts are now referred to as the BELLE Project (Bellevue Project for Early Language, Literacy and Education Success). The research team initially consisted of developmental–behavioral and academic general pediatricians working together with early childhood development and education specialists. Over the next 10 years, the research team was broadened to include strong representation across disciplines in multiple areas of expertise, such as literacy, developmental psychology, school readiness, and poverty. Initial work was performed to develop VIP from birth to 3 years (VIP 0–3); work in progress focuses on extending VIP into the 3- to 5-year period (VIP 3–5).

In developing VIP 0–3, we considered and reviewed strategies utilized in pediatric primary care and home-based interventions, and shown to be effective in enhancing responsive parenting. Four such identified strategies were ultimately utilized in VIP 0–3:

1. *Maintaining a targeted focus for intervention.* VIP 0–3 expands on ROR as a targeted intervention promoting parental responsivity in play and shared reading. Targeting parent–child interaction also represented a key component of home-based programs sharing goals with VIP, such as PHCP and PALS, as described earlier.

2. *Providing learning materials such as toys and books.* Toys and books have in numerous studies been documented to facilitate interactions between parents and children (Bradley, 1993; Bradley & Caldwell, 1984; Katz, 2001; Tomopoulos et al., 2006). Utilization of toys and books has been shown to potentiate effect sizes in home-based parenting programs (Dickinson & Caswell, 2007). Examples of programs successfully utilizing this strategy include ROR and PCHP.

3. *Encouraging self-reflection through the use of videotaping.* A significant body of research beginning in the 1990s documented the utility of videotaping with self-reflection to enhance parent–child interaction and infant mental health outcomes. Development of VIP built in part on programs utilizing this technique, including Interaction Guidance (McDonough, 1995), Steps toward Effective, Enjoyable Parenting (STEEP; Erickson & Egeland, 1999), and Partners in Parenting Education (PIPE) (1997; Kubicek, 1996). Examples of more recent programs are PALS (discussed earlier), and the Family Check-Up (Dishion et al., 2008). In the latter, home visitors, in the course of three visits per year, assess families and provide guidance based on review of videotaped interactions, with results that include enhanced parenting and child behavior.

4. *Building a relationship with an interventionist.* The VIP curriculum is relationship-based, with a single facilitator building a caring, trusting relationship that becomes a foundation for the intervention (Barnard, 1998; Erickson, Endersbe, & Simon, 1999; Foley & Hochman, 1998). This strategy has been effectively utilized by many parenting programs, including home visitation programs, such as PCHP, PALS, and the Nurse Family Partnership (Olds et al., 2007); pediatric primary care programs, such as Healthy Steps (Minkovitz et al., 2003); and Touchpoints (Brazelton, 1994).

The VIP 0–3 Curriculum

The VIP 0–3 curriculum was developed, refined, and implemented by integrating the principles and strategies described earlier. VIP 0–3 is an individualized, relationship-based intervention situated in the pediatric primary care clinic and takes place on days of routine pediatric appointments. While waiting to see the health-care provider, the family meets with a child development specialist (CDS) in one-on-one sessions. The 15 sessions extend from shortly after birth (approximate age 2 weeks) to 3 years, with each session lasting 30–45 minutes. At each session, the CDS meets with the family, using a curriculum focused on supporting responsive parenting to enhance child development and school readiness. The curriculum targets responsivity (contingent and verbal) and verbal scaffolding, primarily in the contexts of pretend play and shared reading. The curriculum is delivered at each visit through three components.

VIDEOTAPE OF PARENT AND CHILD INTERACTING

This is the core component of VIP 0–3. At each visit, the CDS models ideas and provides suggestions for interacting with the child using developmentally appropriate learning materials and parenting pamphlets (described below), then creates a videotape or DVD of mother and child interacting for 5–7 minutes. Immediately after creating this videotape, the CDS reviews the tape/DVD with the mother. During this review, the CDS comments on the mother's and the child's interactions to promote self-reflection, to reinforce strengths in the interaction, and to highlight missed opportunities for responsive interaction with the child that the mother may utilize in future interactions. For example, the CDS positively reinforces having the mother ask the child questions related to their play ("Do you want to feed the doll?"; "What color is the apple?"). After the CDS and mother have watched the tape/DVD together, with the mother listening to the CDS's comments and suggestions, the CDS and the mother have a discussion in which the mother expresses her feelings and observations about the interaction on the tape/DVD, and asks any questions or expresses any concerns she may have. A copy of the tape/DVD is given to the mother to take home for review to facilitate implementation of strategies and activities at home, as well as to watch together with family members.

PROVISION OF LEARNING MATERIALS

During each visit, prior to videotaping the dyad, the CDS provides the mother with developmentally appropriate, stimulating learning materials (toy and/or book) to take home for use with her child. Learning materials are selected to promote parent–child interactive play, verbal engagement, and emergent literacy. The CDS explains the utility of the materials for fostering parent–child interaction and child development, makes specific suggestions for different ways to play with the materials, and models some of these suggestions for the mother. Although a book is not given at every visit, the CDS regularly speaks to parents about the importance of shared reading, helps the mother to make plans for incorporating shared reading into daily routines, and discusses the use of interactive techniques, such as dialogic reading.

VIP 0–3 learning materials include a lullaby CD (at age 2 weeks); plush shapes with contrasting colors (1 month); a mirror (2 months); a soft book (4 months); a set of parent–child duck puppets that can be used in the bath (6 months); a toy phone (9 months); a doll (12 months); a set of farm animals (15 months); a bus with little figures (18 months); a set of plates, cups, and utensils, and a book (21 months); toy food (24 months); a doctor's kit (27 months); an animal puzzle (30 months); a picture book (33 months); and a toy shopping basket (36 months). Although families receive different learning materials at each visit and are given suggestions for interaction that are specific to each visit's assigned learning material, the overarching goal is to increase verbal interaction, responsiveness, flexibility, and teaching. The possible uses of the learning materials become more sophisticated as children age from 2 weeks to 3 years, and this is reflected in the CDS's suggestions for the interactions. For example, one CDS suggestion for using the plush shapes with contrasting colors at 1 month is to label the pictures and colors on the shapes, while allowing and encouraging the child to feel their texture and to look at their contrasting colors. In contrast, by 27 months, one example of a CDS suggestion is for mother and child to create a story about a visit to the doctor, and have the child play the role of the doctor examining the mother as patient with the toy stethoscope.

Although these suggestions differ in scope and complexity, both target increased verbal interactions, continued learning about the child's environment, and fostering flexibility and exploration.

PAMPHLETS

Messages are reinforced by a written, visit-specific pamphlet addressing development and behavior. Pamphlets are available in English or Spanish, and written at a fourth- to fifth-grade reading level. To ensure that all parents of all literacy levels understand the pamphlet, the CDS reviews it with each mother. Each pamphlet includes suggestions for interacting with the child through play and shared reading. An important component of each pamphlet is space for the parent to write down observations about the child, plans for activities, and questions for the pediatric health-care provider. The CDS encourages the parent to show the pamphlet to the pediatric provider, so that the provider can not only answer any questions that may have arisen, further reinforcing VIP's messages, but also demonstrate the strong partnership between VIP and pediatric clinic care providers.

VIP 0–3 Research

VIP 0–3 has been studied in two randomized controlled trials (RCTs). Both studies took place at Bellevue Hospital Center, an urban public hospital serving low socioeconomic status, primarily immigrant families.

STUDY 1 (VIP 0–3 PILOT STUDY)

Consecutive mother–newborn dyads were enrolled in the postpartum unit at Bellevue and randomized to VIP 0–3 or to a control condition; both groups received routine pediatric services and ROR as standard of care. Inclusion criteria for mothers were as follows: Latina ethnicity, primary language either English or Spanish, age 18 years or over, and low education (not having completed high school, as a marker of risk); inclusion criteria for newborns were full-term, normal birthweight, and no significant medical complications. Assessments were performed by blinded research assistants at

21 months, 33 months, and following school entry (K–1).

Responsive parenting related to cognitive stimulation was assessed using StimQ (Dreyer, Mendelsohn, & Tamis-LeMonda, 1996), a parent report instrument with four subscales developed and validated by our research team that measure reading activities (READ), teaching activities (Parent Involvement in Developmental Advance; PIDA), verbal interactions (Parental Verbal Responsivity; PVR), and provision of stimulating toys (Availability of Learning Materials; ALM). Anxiety and depression related to parenting was assessed using the Parenting Stress Index—Short Form (PSI-SF) Parental Distress subscale.

Child development was assessed in the child's dominant language across multiple domains: cognitive (Bayley Scales of Infant Development, second edition, Mental Development Index [MDI]; Wechsler Intelligence Scale for Children–III [WISC-III]); language (Preschool Language Scale–3 [PLS-3]; observational measure of language and maternal responsivity based on coded, videotaped play); early reading achievement (Woodcock–Johnson/Batería III Woodcock–Muñoz Tests of Achievement, Basic Reading Skills cluster); and behavior (Child Behavior Checklist [CBCL], based on parent report).

Analyses were based on intent to treat. Because this was a randomized study with groups similar across all sociodemographic characteristics (e.g., 88.2% immigrant; 83.6% Spanish-speaking; mean [SD] maternal education 7.3 [2.5] years), statistical analyses were performed without adjustment, including independent samples t-tests for comparisons of means, chi-square analyses for nonordered categorical data, and Spearman's rank correlation for ordered categorical data.

One hundred fifty dyads were enrolled and randomized to VIP or to control groups. As shown in Table 18.1, VIP 0–3 was associated with enhanced responsive parenting (Mendelsohn et al., 2007), with significant differences found for teaching activities, and trends for verbal responsivity, shared reading, and provision of learning materials. VIP was also associated with reduced parenting stress related to depression and anxiety. While developmental impacts were found

TABLE 18.1. Impact of VIP on Parenting Practices and Stress (Pilot Randomized Controlled Trial; 33 Months)

Domain/assessment	VIP (n = 45–46)	Control (n = 51–52)	p
Parenting practices (StimQ)			
ALM subscale	5.7 (1.5)	5.0 (1.8)	.06
READ subscale	7.4 (3.7)	8.4 (3.8)	.15
PIDA subscale	7.5 (1.7)	6.1 (2.8)	.003
PVR subscale	2.6 (1.2)	2.1 (1.3)	.07
Parenting stress (Parenting Stress Index)			
Total score	71.8 (23.8)	80.6 (18.8)	.048
% in clinical range	39.2%	58.7%	.09
Parenting Distress subscale	60.9 (25.1)	68.9 (19.6)	.09
% in clinical range	23.5%	34.8%	.32

Note. Data are presented as mean (*SD*) or %. *p*-values based on *t*-test or chi-square. ALM, Availability of Learning Materials (toys); READ, reading; PIDA, Parent Involvement in Developmental Advance (teaching); PSI, Parenting Stress Index; PVR, Parental Verbal Responsivity (verbal interactions). Lower scores on the PSI are indicative of lower levels of parenting stress; scores at or above the 85th percentile are considered to be within the clinical range for parenting. From Mendelsohn et al. (2007). Copyright 2007 by Wolters Kluwer Health. Adapted by permission.

for the sample as a whole, an interaction was found between level of maternal education and impact, such that impacts were strongest and most consistent for mothers with greater than seventh-grade education. As shown in Table 18.2, 21-month-old children of mothers with seventh-grade or higher education (the median for this high-risk sample) showed impacts related to VIP 0–3 for cognitive development (MDI; effect size [ES] ~ 0.75), expressive language (based on both PLS-3 and a naturalistic measure), and a trend toward a nearly 50% reduction (25.0% for VIP families, compared to 52.9% for controls) in Early Intervention (EI) eligibility (Mendelsohn et al., 2005). In contrast, for mothers with less than seventh-grade education, VIP showed significant impacts only for expressive language based on the observational measure.

As shown in Table 18.3, the interaction between group and education persisted at 33 months, with enhanced cognitive development (considered categorically) for the sample as a whole but strongest findings for mothers with seventh-grade or higher education. A trend was found at 33 months toward reduced behavior problems based on the CBCL, with differences stronger for mothers with seventh-grade or higher education than for the sample as a whole. As at the 21 month assessment, VIP 0–3 was associated

with approximately 50% less EI eligibility at 33 months (15.8% for VIP 0–3 compared to 31.8% for controls), but this was not statistically significant. Finally, as shown in Table 18.4, VIP 0–3 was associated with enhanced full-scale IQ (primarily related to processing speed and working memory; ES ~ 0.3) in first grade, as well as a trend toward enhanced early reading achievement (Forrest et al., 2008). While these findings were very promising, small sample size limited power to show statistical significance for many of the tests. We therefore began a larger, replication study.

STUDY 2 (NATIONAL INSTITUTE OF CHILD HEALTH AND HUMAN DEVELOPMENT [NICHD]–FUNDED, LARGE-SCALE REPLICATION STUDY)

The second, ongoing study is an RCT assessing VIP 0–3 impacts across a broader range of families. As with the pilot study, consecutive mother–newborn dyads were enrolled at Bellevue Hospital Center. Inclusion criteria were mostly similar to the pilot study (English- or Spanish-speaking mother, at least age 18 years; child full-term, normal birthweight without medical complications). However, in contrast to the pilot study, dyads were enrolled regardless of ethnicity and education, resulting in a more heterogeneous sample. Enrolled families were randomized to three

TABLE 18.2. Impact of VIP on Cognitive and Language Development, Stratified by Level of Maternal Education (Pilot Randomized Controlled Trial; 21 Months)

Domain/assessment	Maternal education < 7 years			Maternal education ≥ 7 years		
	VIP (*n* = 35)	Control (*n* = 25)	*p*	VIP (*n* = 16)	Control (*n* = 17)	*p*
Cognitive development (Bayley MDI)						
Mean score	74.2 (11.7)	73.1 (13.4)	.75	81.8 (12.5)	70.3 (11.9)	.01
% Normal	22.9%	16.0%	.58	43.8%	5.9%	.02
% Borderline	48.6%	52.0%		43.8%	64.7%	
% Delayed	28.6%	32.0%		12.5%	29.4%	
Expressive language development (PLS-3)						
Mean Expressive Language score	78.5 (8.0)	80.0 (12.2)	.58	83.3 (8.8)	76.1 (4.1)	.008
% Normal	14.3%	32.0%	.47	43.8%	0.0%	.03
% Borderline	71.4%	48.0%		50.0%	100.0%	
% Delayed	14.3%	20.0%		6.3%	0.0%	
Receptive language development (PLS-3)						
Mean Receptive Language score	80.6 (9.8)	79.7 (8.7)	.72	82.5 (9.8)	78.9 (7.3)	.25
% Normal	25.7%	20.0%	.29	25.0%	20.0%	.56
% Borderline	71.4%	68.0%		69.8%	66.7%	
% Delayed	2.9%	12.0%		6.3%	13.3%	
Language development (observational)						
% Normal	31.4%	16.7%	.04	62.5%	11.8%	.001
% Indeterminate	57.1%	50.0%		31.3%	52.9%	
% Delayed	11.4%	33.3%		6.3%	35.3%	
Early intervention eligibility						
% Eligible	60.0%	52.0%	.55	25.0%	52.9%	.11

Note. Data are presented as mean (*SD*) or %. Independent-samples *t*-tests used to compare means. Spearman rank correlation used to compare ordered categorical data. From Mendelsohn et al. (2005). Copyright 2005 by Wolters Kluwer Health. Adapted by permission.

groups (VIP, control, and an additional program called Building Blocks, all of which received routine pediatric care and ROR); the discussion that follows focuses on differences between VIP and control families. Assessments of parenting responsivity have been completed at 6 months; assessments of both responsivity and child developmental outcomes are in progress at 14, 24, and 36 months. As with the pilot study, responsive parenting at 6 months was assessed by parent report using StimQ; an additional measure of shared reading activities in this study was a 24-hour recall diary based on an interview (adapted from our previous work studying electronic media exposure; see Tomopoulos et al., 2007). Beginning with the 14-month assessment, responsive parenting assessment

was also based on microanalytically coded tapes of parent–child play. Analyses were conducted, as with the pilot study, without adjustment and based on intent to treat.

Two hundred twenty-five dyads were each randomized to VIP 0–3 and control groups. Groups were similar for all sociodemographic characteristics (e.g., 91.7% Latino/Hispanic; 83.7% immigrant; 75.9% Spanish-speaking; mean [*SD*] maternal education 10.1 [3.7] years). Based on independent-sample *t*-tests, analyses at child age 6 months are shown in Table 18.5. VIP 0–3 was associated with consistent impacts on responsive parenting for the sample as a whole, with approximate ESs between 0.3 and 0.5; the greatest differences were found for teaching activities (Mendelsohn, in press). Impacts were even

TABLE 18.3. Impact of VIP on Child Developmental Outcomes (Pilot Randomized Controlled Trial; 33 Months)

Domain/assessment	Overall sample			Maternal education ≥ 7 years		
	VIP (*n* = 52)	Control (*n* = 45–47)	*p*	VIP (*n* = 19)	Control (*n* = 22–23)	*p*
Cognitive development (Bayley MDI)						
Mean score	86.1 (7.5)	83.9 (9.7)	.20	88.0 (5.8)	82.5 (10.8)	.049
% Normal	63.5%	44.4%	.048	73.7%	36.4%	.01
% Borderline	34.6%	48.9%		26.3%	54.5%	
% Delayed	1.9%	6.7%		0.0%	9.1%	
Child Behavior Checklist (CBCL)						
Total mean score	50.2 (10.0)	53.2 (9.7)	.13	49.9 (9.1)	55.6 (9.9)	.07
% in clinical range	7.7%	17.0%	.16	5.3%	21.7%	.14
Early intervention eligibility						
% Eligible	25.0%	28.9%	.67	15.8%	31.8%	.24

Note. Data are presented as mean (*SD*) or %. Independent-samples *t*-tests used to compare means. Spearman rank correlation used to compare ordered categorical data. Lower scores on the Child Behavior Checklist are indicative of less problematic behavior. Clinically significant behavior on the Child Behavior Checklist was defined as a *T*-score of 64 or greater. From Mendelsohn et al. (2007). Copyright 2007 by Wolters Kluwer Health. Adapted by permission.

TABLE 18.4. Impact of VIP on Cognitive Development and Achievement (VIP Pilot Cohort; First Grade)

Domain/assessment	VIP (*n* = 27)	Control (*n* = 26)	*p*
Cognitive (WISC-III)			
Full Scale IQ (FSIQ) mean	93.9 (11.4)	89.0 (9.4)	.09
FSIQ categorical			.04
FSIQ < 85 (1 *SD* below mean)	19.2%	33.3%	
FSIQ 85–99	42.3%	55.6%	
FSIQ 100+	38.5%	11.1%	
Processing speed (PS) mean	101.4 (7.3)	94.7 (12.4)	.02
PS < 85 (1 *SD* below mean)	3.8%	18.5%	.09
Working memory (WM) mean	95.4 (11.5)	92.3 (8.6)	.28
WM < 85 (1 *SD* below mean)	11.5%	25.9%	.16
Reading achievement (Woodcock–Johnson/Woodcock–Muñoz Batería III)			
Basic reading skills	114.2 (17.2)	108.0 (17.2)	.19

Note. Data are shown as mean (*SD*) or %. *p*-value based on independent-samples *t*-test, chi-square, or Spearman rank correlation.

TABLE 18.5. Impact of VIP on Responsive Parenting (Replication Randomized Controlled Trial; 6 Months)

	Overall			Literacy ≥ 9th grade		
	VIP (*n* = 126)	Control (*n* = 134)	*p*	VIP (*n* = 86)	Control (*n* = 95)	*p*
StimQ						
ALM	2.8 (1.1)	2.3 (1.2)	< .001	3.0 (1.1)	2.4 (1.2)	.002
READ	8.0 (4.2)	6.8 (4.4)	.02	8.5 (4.0)	7.0 (4.4)	.02
PIDA	3.3 (1.6)	2.5 (1.5)	< .001	3.7 (1.5)	2.6 (1.6)	< .001
PVR	5.7 (2.6)	4.8 (2.3)	.003	6.4 (2.4)	5.1 (2.2)	< .001
Reading diary						
Time spent reading (minutes/day)	18.3 (25.6)	10.8 (16.3)	.007	20.3 (27.5)	10.4 (13.7)	.003
Reading instances (times/day)	1.1 (1.3)	0.6 (0.7)	.001	1.3 (1.5)	0.6 (0.7)	< .001

Note. Data are shown as mean (*SD*). *p*-values based on independent-samples *t*-test. ALM, Availability of Learning Materials (toys); READ, reading; PIDA, Parent Involvement in Developmental Advance (teaching); PVR, Parental Verbal Responsivity (verbal interactions).

greater for mothers with a ninth-grade or higher reading level (based on Woodcock–Johnson/Batería III Woodcock–Muñoz Tests of Achievement Letter–Word Identification subscale), with approximate ESs between 0.5 and 0.7. Preliminary analyses at 14 months showed VIP to be associated with increased maternal vocalization during play; VIP mothers vocalized during 47.8% of the interaction, compared to 34.6% for controls (ES = 0.75, *p* < .01; Mendelsohn et al., 2009).

Implications

Our results strongly support a role for pediatric primary care parenting intervention programs in reducing poverty-related disparities in early child development and school readiness. The combination of low cost, potential for universal dissemination, and evidence of clinically important impact resulting from the VIP suggests that this approach may be useful in expanding on the ROR model in providing preventive developmental services for at-risk children.

While ESs due to VIP 0–3 have been modest (0.3 to 0.7), they are remarkable considering the low cost of the program (which is about half that of home-based programs, and vastly lower than that of preschool programs). There are several explanations for

findings documenting VIP 0–3 impacts despite low intensity and cost. First, the placement of this program within pediatric health care is potentially an advantage given the opportunity that health care presents, with multiple visits beginning in early infancy, an existing family–provider relationship on which to build, and the potential for building on existing anticipatory guidance strategies, as well as proven programs such as ROR. Second, VIP 0–3 provides targeted strategies to enhance parent–child interactions associated with development and school readiness, resulting in specific impacts in targeted domains. Third, VIP 0–3 was designed to empower parents to play an active role in their children's school readiness through the use of videotaping to promote self-reflection. Carryover of activities is facilitated by provision of tapes and learning materials for use in the home and reinforcement of behaviors across multiple visits. Fourth, VIP 0–3 has been developed as a "translational" project, applying current knowledge in basic and clinical research in developmental psychology and educational science to the preventive care of at-risk young children.

One area of challenge regards families with very low levels of education and literacy in the context of poverty. Our results, showing smaller and less consistent ESs in this subgroup, suggest that additional study is needed to determine whether further refinement of primary care parenting interventions can lead to stronger results.

Future Directions: Extension of VIP into the Preschool Period

The strong impacts of VIP 0–3 on child development, along with empirical evidence documenting the importance of ongoing responsive parenting prior to school entry, suggest that similar intervention during the preschool years may have additional benefit. For instance, it has been shown that responsive parenting during both infant and toddler–preschool periods has an additive impact on development compared to either period alone (Landry et al., 2001, 2006), as well as additive impact above and beyond that of preschool and kindergarten (Bradley et al., 1994; Brooks-Gunn & Markman, 2005; Miedel & Reynolds, 1999; Reynolds, Mavrogenes, Bezruczko, & Hagemann, 1996). The need for intervention during this period is further supported by reports that preschool/prekindergarten is not universal, and quality is variable, particularly in low-income populations (Assel, Landry, Swank, & Gunnewig, 2007; Justice, Mashburn, Hamre, & Pianta, 2008; Magnuson & Waldfogel, 2005; NICHD Early Child Care Network, 1997). Interventions outside the school system are therefore likely to remain important through the preschool period, especially for low-income children.

We have therefore begun to develop and implement VIP 3–5 or children ages 3 to 5 years, which builds upon VIP 0–3 by targeting responsive parenting to impact school readiness. VIP 3–5 aims to enhance academic-cognitive (Duncan et al., 2007; National Early Literacy Panel, 2009; Whitehurst & Lonigan, 1998), socioemotional (Domitrovich, Cortes, & Greenberg, 2007; O'Connor & McCartney, 2007), and self-regulation (Blair & Diamond, 2008; Raver, 2004) outcomes that have been highlighted as most important for successful transition to elementary school. In developing VIP 3–5, we have identified techniques linked to these school readiness outcomes that could be adapted for use by parents from existing curricula and programs, such as Houghton Mifflin Pre-K (Bredekamp, Morrow, & Pikulski, 2006; Morrow, 2007, 2009) Opening

the World of Learning (Ashe, Reed, Dickinson, Morse, & Wilson, 2009; Schickedanz, Dickinson, & the Charlotte-Mecklenburg Schools, 2005), Head Start REDI (Research based, Developmentally Informed)–P (Parent) Home Visiting Program (Bierman, Rhule, & Gest, 2008) and Tools of the Mind (Bodrova & Leong, 2006). There are two key aspects of VIP 3–5 that represent enhancements for the preschool period. First, there is explicit development of stories for use in pretend play, built on integration of themes developed for each visit, with provision of toys and books. Second, specific strategies are built into play and shared reading to target school readiness outcomes, with emphases on integrating written materials into play to enhance academic–cognitive outcomes, such as emergent literacy, relative to talking about emotions within play, shared reading to enhance socioemotional outcomes, and planning and role playing to enhance self-regulation. Research in progress into VIP 3–5 will provide evidence regarding efficacy of VIP for children beyond age 3 years.

Conclusion

In conclusion, we have provided evidence that pediatric primary care–based intervention can enhance early developmental and school readiness outcomes of at-risk young children. Our results suggest that increasing intervention intensity through videotaping, with feedback to promote self-reflection, may result in increased impact, above and beyond that of ROR alone. Additional work is needed to understand better the impact on long-term educational trajectories, generalizability across low socioeconomic status populations, and potential for coordination and integration with preschool educational programs.

Acknowledgments

This work was supported by the National Institutes of Health/National Institute of Child Health and Human Development–funded grant "Promoting Early School Readiness in Primary Health Care" (No. R01 HD047740 01-04), the Tiger Foundation, the Marks Family Foundation, the Rhodebeck Charitable Trust, the New York Community Trust, the New York State Empire Clinical Research Investigator Program, the Academic Pediatric Association Young Investigator Award Program, the Society for Developmental and Behavioral Pediatrics Research Grant, Children of Bellevue, Inc, and KiDS of NYU Foundation, Inc. We would like to thank many colleagues for their guidance and support, including J. Lawrence Aber, Jose Alvir, Clancy Blair, David Dickinson, Arthur Fierman, Virginia Flynn, Gilbert Foley, Emily Forrest, Harris Huberman, Matthew Johnson, Perri Klass, Gloria Mattera, Gigliana Melzi, MaryJo Messito, Erin O'Connor, Cybele Raver, Catherine Tamis-LeMonda, Wendy Tineo, Suzy Tomopoulos, Purnima Valdez, Linda van Schaick and Hiro Yoshikawa. Finally, we gratefully thank many additional individuals who have contributed to this project, including Melissa Acevedo, Jenny Arevalo, Miriam Baigorri, Nina Burtchen, Hannah Goldman, Ruee Huang, Alexandra Pappas, David Rhee, Maria Rodado, Daniela Romero, Jessica Urgelles, Linda Votruba, Margaret Wolff and Brenda Woodford.

References

Aber, J. L., Jones, S. M., & Cohen, J. (2000). The impact of poverty on the mental health and development of very young children. In C. Zeanah, Jr. (Ed.), *Handbook of infant mental health* (2nd ed., pp. 113–128). New York: Guilford Press.

Adams, M. J. (1990). *Beginning to read: Thinking and learning about print.* Cambridge, MA: MIT Press.

American Academy of Pediatrics (AAP) Committee on Psychosocial Aspects of Child and Family Health. (2009). *Guidelines for immunizations/vaccines, revised.* Elk Grove Village, IL: Author.

Ashe, M. K., Reed, S., Dickinson, D. K., Morse, A. B., & Wilson, S. J. (2009). Opening the world of learning: Features, effectiveness and implementation strategies. *Early Childhood Services, 3*(3), 179–191.

Assel, M. A., Landry, S. H. Swank, P. R., & Gunnewig, S. (2007). An evaluation of curriculum, setting, and mentoring on the performance of children enrolled in pre-kindergarten. *Reading and Writing, 20*(5), 463–494.

Barnard, K. E. (1998). Developing, implementing, and documenting interventions with parents and young children. *Zero to Three, 18*(4), 23–29.

Barnett, W. S., & Robin, K. B. (2006). *How much does quality preschool cost?* (Working paper, National Institute for Early Education Research). Available online at *nieer.org/resources/research/costoffectivepreschool.pdf.*

Bierman, K. L., Rhule, G. L., & Gest, J. R. (2008). *Head Start REDI Home Visiting manual.* Unpublished manual, Penn State University.

Blair, C., & Diamond, A. (2008). Biological processes in prevention and intervention: The promotion of self-regulation as a means of preventing school failure. *Development and Psychopathology, 20,* 899–911.

Bodrova, E., & Leong, D. J. (2006). Self-regulation as a key to school readiness: How early childhood teachers can promote this critical competency. In M. Zaslow & I. Martinez-Beck (Eds.), *Critical issues in early childhood professional development*(pp. 203–224). Baltimore: Brookes.

Bornstein, M., & Tamis-LeMonda, C. S. (1989). Maternal responsiveness and cognitive development in children. In M. H. Bornstein (Ed.), *Maternal responsiveness: Characteristics and consequences* (pp. 49–61). San Francisco: Jossey-Bass.

Bradley, R. H. (1993). Children's home environments, health, behavior, and intervention efforts: A review using the HOME inventory as a marker measure. *Genetic, Social, and General Psychological Monographs, 119*(4), 437–490.

Bradley, R. H., & Caldwell, B. M. (1984). 174 children: A study of the relationship between home environment and early cognitive development in the first five years. In A. Gottfried (Ed.), *The home environment and early cognitive development* (pp. 5–56). Orlando, FL: Academic Press.

Bradley, R. H., Whiteside, L., Munfrom, D. J., Casey, P. H., Caldwell, B. M., & Barrett, K. (1994). Impact of the Infant Health and Development Program on the home environment of infants with low birth weight. *Journal of Educational Psychology, 86,* 531–541.

Brazelton, T. B. (1976). Anticipatory guidance. *Pediatric Clinics of North America, 22*(3), 533–544.

Brazelton, T. B. (1994). Touchpoints: Opportunities for preventing problems in the parent–child relationship. *Acta Paediatrica Supplement, 394,* 35–39.

Bredekamp, S., Morrow, L. M., & Pikulski, J. (2006). *Houghton Mifflin Pre-K.* Boston: Houghton Mifflin.

Britto, P. R., Fuligni, A. S., & Brooks-Gunn, J. (2006). Reading ahead: Effective interventions for young children's early literacy development. In D. K. Dickinson & S. B. Neuman (Eds.), *Handbook of early literacy research* (Vol. 2, pp. 311–332). New York: Guilford Press.

Brooks-Gunn, J., & Markman, L. B. (2005). The contribution of parenting to ethnic and racial gaps in school readiness. *The Future of Children, 15*(1), 139–168.

Bus, A. G., & van IJzendoorn, M. H. (1992). Patterns of attachment in frequently and infrequently reading mother–child dyads. *Journal of Genetic Psychology, 153,* 395–403.

Dickinson, D. K., & Caswell, L. C. (2007). Building support for language and early literacy in preschool classrooms through in-service professional development: Effects of the Literacy Environment Enrichment Program (LEEP). *Early Childhood Research Quarterly, 22,* 243–260.

Dickinson, D. K., McCabe, A., & Essex, M. J. (2006). A window of opportunity we must open to all: The case for preschool with high-quality support for language and literacy. In D. K. Dickinson & S. B. Neuman (Eds.), *Handbook of early literacy research* (Vol. 2, pp. 11–28). New York: Guilford Press.

Dinkevich, E., & Ozuah, P. O. (2002). Well-child care:

Effectiveness of current recommendations. *Clinical Pediatrics, 41*(4), 211–217.

Dishion, T. J., Shaw, D., Connell, A., Gardner, F., Weaver, C., & Wilson, M. (2008). The Family Check-Up with high-risk indigent families: Preventing problem behavior by increasing parents' positive behavior support in early childhood. *Child Development, 79*(5), 1395–1414.

Domitrovich, C. E., Cortes, R. C., & Greenberg, M. T. (2007). Improving young children's social and emotional competence: A randomized trial of the Preschool "PATHS" curriculum. *Journal of Primary Prevention, 28*(2), 67–91.

Dreyer, B. P. (2009). Mental health and child developmental problems: The "not-so-new morbidity." *Academic Pediatrics, 9*(4), 206–208.

Dreyer, B. P., Mendelsohn, A. L., & Tamis-LeMonda, C. S. (1996). Assessing the child's cognitive home environment through parental report: Reliability and validity. *Early Development and Parenting, 5*(4), 271–287.

Dreyer, B. P., Mendelsohn, A. L., & Tamis-LeMonda, C. S. (2009). StimQ—The cognitive home environment. Available online at *pediatrics.med.nyu.edu/patient-care/for-healthcare-providers/stimq-cognitive-home-environment*.

Duncan, G. J., Dowsett, C. J., Claessens, A., Magnuson, K., Huston, A. C., Klebanov, P., et al. (2007). School readiness and later achievement. *Developmental Psychology, 43*(6), 1428–1446.

Erickson, M., & Egeland, B. (1999). The STEEP program: Linking theory and research to practice. *Zero to Three, 20*, 11–16.

Erickson, M. F., Endersbe, J., & Simon, J. (1999). *Seeing is believing: Videotaping families and using guided self-observation to build on parenting strengths*. Minneapolis: Regents of the University of Minnesota.

Field, T. (1998). Emotional care of the at-risk infant: Early interventions for infants of depressed mothers. *Pediatrics, 102*(Suppl. 5), 1305–1310.

Foley, G., & Hochman, J. (1998). Programs, parents and practitioners: Perspectives on integrating early intervention and infant mental health. *Zero to Three, 18*(3), 13–18.

Forrest, E. K., Dreyer, B. P., Valdez, P. T., Baigorri, M., Smoller, A. B., & Mendelsohn, A. L. (2008, May). *An RCT of videotaped interactions during pediatric well-child care to promote child development: Early educational outcomes*. Poster presentation at the Pediatric Academic Societies Annual Meeting, Honolulu, HI.

Hardy-Brown, K., & Plomin, R. (1985). Infant communicative development: Evidence from adoptive and biological families with genetic and environmental influence on rate differences. *Developmental Psychology, 21*, 378–385.

Hart, B., & Risley, T. R. (1995). *Meaningful differences in the everyday experience of young American children*. Baltimore: Brookes.

High, P., LaGasse, L., Becker, B. A., Ahlgren, I., & Gardner, A. (2000). Literacy promotion in primary care pediatrics: Can we make a difference? *Pediatrics, 105*(4), 927–934.

Hoff-Ginsberg, E. (1991). Mother–child conversation in different social classes and communicative settings. *Child Development, 62*, 782–796.

Jellinek, M., Patel, B. P., & Froehle, M. C. (2002). *Bright futures in practice: Mental health practice guide* (Vol. 1). Arlington, VA: National Center for Education in Maternal and Child Health.

Justice, L. M., Mashburn, A. J., Hamre, B. K., & Pianta, R. C. (2008). Quality of language and literacy instruction in preschool classrooms serving at-risk pupils. *Early Childhood Research Quarterly, 23*(1), 51–68.

Katz, J. R. (2001). Playing at home: The talk of pretend play. In D. K. Dickinson & P. O. Tabors (Eds.), *Beginning literacy with language* (pp. 353–373). Baltimore: Brookes.

Knudsen, E. I., Heckman, J. J., Cameron, J. L., & Shonkoff, J. P. (2006). Economic, neurobiological, and behavioral perspectives on building America's future workforce. *Proceedings of the National Academy of Sciences USA, 103*(27), 10155–10162.

Kubicek, L. F. (1996). Helping young children become competent communicators: The role of relationships. *Zero to Three, 17*, 25–30.

Landry, S. H., Miller-Loncar, C. L., Smith, K. E., & Swank, P. R. (2002). The role of early parenting in children's developmental and executive processes. *Developmental Neuropsychology, 21*(1), 15–24.

Landry, S. H., Smith, K. E., & Swank, P. R. (2002). Environmental effects of language development in normal and high-risk child populations. *Seminars in Pediatric Neurology, 9*, 192–200.

Landry, S. H., Smith, K. E., & Swank, P. R. (2006). Responsive parenting: Establishing early foundations for social, communication, and independent problem-solving skills. *Developmental Psychology, 42*, 627–642.

Landry, S. H., Smith, K. E., Swank, P. R., Assel, M. A., & Vellet, S. (2001). Does early responsive parenting have a special importance for children's development or is consistency across early childhood necessary? *Developmental Psychology, 37*(4), 387–403.

Landry, S. H., Smith, K. E., Swank, P. R., & Guttentag, C. (2008). A responsive parenting intervention: The optimal timing across early childhood for impacting maternal behaviors and child outcomes. *Developmental Psychology, 44*(5), 1335–1353.

Levenstein, P., Levenstein, S., & Oliver, D. (2002). First grade school readiness of former child participants in a South Carolina replication of the Parent–Child Home Program. *Journal of Applied Developmental Psychology, 23*(3), 331–353.

Levenstein, P., Levenstein, S., Shiminski, J. A., & Stolzberg, J. E. (1998). Long-term impact of a verbal interaction program for at-risk toddlers: An exploratory study of high school outcomes in a replication of the Mother–Child Home Program. *Journal of Applied Developmental Psychology, 19*, 267–285.

Madden, J., Levenstein, P., & Levenstein, S. (1976). Longitudinal IQ outcomes of the Mother–Child Home Program. *Child Development, 47*, 1015–1025.

Magnuson, K. A., & Waldfogel, J. (2005). Early childhood care and education: Effects on ethnic and racial gaps in school readiness. *The Future of Children, 15*, 169–196.

Masse, L. N., & Barnett, W. S. (2002). A benefit–cost analysis of the Abecedarian Early Childhood Intervention. New Brunswick, NJ: National Institute for Early Education Research. Available online at *nieer.org/resources/research/abecedarianstudy*.

McDonough, S. C. (1995). Promoting positive early parent–infant relationships through interaction guidance. *Child and Adolescent Psychiatric Clinics of North America, 4*(3), 661–672.

Mendelsohn, A. L. (2002). Promoting language and literacy through reading aloud: The role of the pediatrician. *Current Problems in Pediatric and Adolescent Health Care, 32*(6), 183–210.

Mendelsohn, A. L., Berkule, S. B., Huberman, H. S., Morrow, L. M., Tamis-LeMonda, C. S., & Dreyer, B. P. (2009, May). *An RCT of the Video Interaction Project (VIP) and Building Blocks (BB): 14 month impacts of primary care based parenting interventions.* Platform presentation at the Pediatric Academic Societies Annual Meeting, American Academy of Pediatrics Presidential Plenary, Baltimore.

Mendelsohn, A. L., Dreyer, B. P., Flynn, V., Tomopoulos, S., Rovira, I., Tineo, W., et al. (2005). Use of videotaped interactions during pediatric well-child care to promote child development: A randomized, controlled trial. *Journal of Developmental and Behavioral Pediatrics, 26*(1), 34–41.

Mendelsohn, A. L., Huberman, H. S., Berkule-Silberman, S. B., Brockmeyer, C. A., Morrow, L. M., & Dreyer, B. P. (in press). Primary care strategies for promoting parent–child interactions and school readiness in at-risk families: Early findings from the Bellevue Project for Early Language, Literacy, and Education Success (BELLE). *Archives of Pediatrics and Adolescent Medicine.*

Mendelsohn, A. L., Mogilner, L. N., Dreyer, B. P., Forman, J. A., Weinstein, S. C., Broderick, M., et al. (2001). The impact of a clinic-based literacy intervention on language development in inner-city preschool children. *Pediatrics, 107*(1), 130–134.

Mendelsohn, A. L., Valdez, P. T., Flynn, V., Foley, G. M., Berkule, S. B., Tomopoulos, S., et al. (2007). Use of videotaped interactions during pediatric well-child care: Impact at 33 months on parenting and on child development. *Journal of Developmental and Behavioral Pediatrics, 28*(3), 206–212.

Miedel, W. T., & Reynolds, A. J. (1999). Parent involvement in early intervention for disadvantaged children: Does it matter? *Journal of School Psychology, 37*(4), 379–402.

Minkovitz, C. S., Hughart, N., Strobino, D., Scharfstein, D., Grason, H., Hou, W., et al. (2003). A practice-based intervention to enhance quality of care in the first 3 years of life: The healthy steps for young children program. *Journal of the American Medical Association, 290*, 3081–3091.

Morrow, L. M. (2007). *Developing literacy in preschool.* New York: Guilford Press.

Morrow, L. M. (2009). *Literacy development in the early years: Helping children read and write* (6th ed.). Boston: Allyn & Bacon.

Morrow, L. M., & Schikedanz, J. A. (2006). The relationships between sociodramatic play and literacy development. In D. K. Dickinson & S. B. Neuman (Eds.), *Handbook of early literacy research* (Vol. 2, pp. 269–280). New York: Guilford Press.

Morrow, L. M., & Young, J. (1997). A family literacy program connecting school and home: Effects on attitude, motivation, and literacy achievement. *Journal of Educational Research Journal, 98*(4), 736–742.

National Early Literacy Panel. (2009). *Developing early literacy: Report of the National Early Literacy Panel.* Available online at *www.nifl.gov/nifl/publications/pdf/nelpreport09.pdf*.

Needlman, R., Klass, P., & Zuckerman, P. (2006). A pediatric approach to early literacy. In D. K. Dickinson & S. B. Neuman (Eds.), *Handbook of early literacy research* (Vol. 2, pp. 333–346). New York: Guilford Press.

Needlman, R., Toker, K. H., Klass, P., Dreyer, B. P., & Mendelsohn, A. L. (2005). Effectiveness of a primary care intervention to support reading aloud: A multi-center evaluation. *Ambulatory Pediatrics, 5*(4), 209–215.

Nelson, K. (2007). *Young minds in social worlds: Experience, meaning, and memory.* Cambridge, MA: Harvard University Press.

Neuman, S. B. (1996). Children engaging in storybook reading: The influence of access to print resources, opportunity and parental interaction. *Early Childhood Research Quarterly, 11*, 495–513.

NICHD Early Child Care Research Network. (1997). Familial factors associated with the characteristics of nonmaternal care for infants. *Journal of Marriage and the Family, 59*, 389–408.

Ninio, A. (1980). Picture-book reading in mother–infant dyads belonging to two subgroups in Israel. *Child Development, 51*, 587–590.

O'Connor, E., & McCartney, K. (2007). Examining teacher–child relationships and achievement as part of an ecological model of development. *American Educational Research Journal, 44*, 340–369.

Olds, D. L., Kitzman, H., Hanks, C., Cole, R., Anson, E., Sidoro-Arcoleo, K., et al. (2007). Effects of nurse home visiting on maternal and child functioning: Age-9 follow-up of a randomized trial. *Official Journal of the American Academy of Pediatrics, 120*, 832–845.

Osofsky, J. D., & Thompson, M. D. (2000). Adaptive and maladaptive parenting: Perspectives on risk and protective factors. In J. P. Shonkoff & S. J. Meisels (Eds.), *Handbook of early childhood intervention* (2nd ed., pp. 54–75). Cambridge, UK: Cambridge University Press.

Partners in Parenting Education. (1997). *How to Read Your Baby: A new instructional model and curriculum for parent educators to use with adolescent and high-risk parents.* Denver, CO: How to Read Your Baby, Inc.

Peralta de Mendoza, O. A. (1995). Developmental changes and socioeconomic differences in mother–infant picture book reading. *European Journal of Psychology of Education, 10*, 261–272.

Raver, C. C. (2004). Placing emotional self-regulation

in sociocultural and socioeconomic contexts. *Child Development, 75*(2), 346–353.

Reese, E., Cox, A., Harte, D., & McAnally, H. (2003). Diversity in adults' styles of reading books to children. In A. van Kleeck, S. A. Stahl, & E. B. Bauer (Eds.), *On reading books to children: Parents and teachers* (pp. 58–94). Mahwah, NJ: Erlbaum.

Reynolds, A. J., Mavrogenes, N. A., Bezruczko, N., & Hagemann, M. (1996). Cognitive and family-support mediators of preschool effectiveness: A confirmatory analysis. *Child Development, 67,* 1119–1140.

Riggs, N. R., Greenberg, M. T., Kusché, C. A., & Pentz, M. A. (2006). The mediational role of neurocognition in the behavioral outcomes of a social-emotional prevention program in elementary school students: Effects of the PATHS curriculum. *Prevention Science, 7*(1), 91–102.

Schickedanz, J. A., Dickinson, D. K., & the Charlotte-Mecklenburg Schools. (2005). *Opening the World of Learning: A comprehensive early literacy program.* Parsippany, NJ: Pearson Early Learning.

Sénéchal, M., & LeFevre, J. (2002). Parental involvement in the development of children's reading skill: A five-year longitudinal study. *Child Development, 73*(2), 445–460.

Sharif, I., Reiber, S., & Ozuah, P. O. (2002). Exposure to Reach Out and Read and vocabulary outcomes in inner city preschoolers. *Journal of the National Medical Association, 94,* 171–177.

Shonkoff, J. P. (2000). *From neurons to neighborhoods: The science of early child development.* Washington, DC: National Academy Press.

Snow, C. E. (1977). The development of conversation between mothers and babies. *Journal of Child Language, 14*(1), 1–22.

Sturner, R. A. (1998). The child health supervision visit as an opportunity to address parenting issues during infancy. *Pediatric Annals, 21*(1), 44–50.

Tabors, P. O., Roach, K. A., & Snow, C. E. (2001). Home language and literacy environment: Final results. In D. K. Dickinson & P. O. Tabors (Eds.), *Beginning literacy with language* (pp. 111–138). Baltimore: Brookes.

Tamis-LeMonda, C. S., Bornstein, M. H., & Baumwell, L. (2001). Maternal responsiveness and children's achievement of language milestones. *Child Development, 72*(3), 748–767.

Tamis-LeMonda, C. S., Cristofaro, T. N., Rodriguez, E. T., & Bornstein, M. H. (2006). Early language development: Social influences in the first years of life. In L. Balter & C. S. Tamis-LeMonda (Eds.), *Child psychology: A handbook of contemporary issues* (2nd ed., pp. 79–108). New York: Psychology Press.

Tomasello, M., & Farrar, M. (1986). Joint attention and early language. *Child Development, 57,* 1454–1463.

Tomopoulos, S., Dreyer, B. P., Flynn, V., Rovira, I., Tineo, W., & Mendelsohn, A. L. (2006). Books, toys, parent–child interaction and development in young Latino children. *Ambulatory Pediatrics, 6*(2), 72–78.

Tomopoulos, S., Dreyer, B. P., Valdez, P., Flynn, V., Foley, G., Berkule, S. B., et al. (2007). Media content and externalizing behaviors in Latino toddlers. *Ambulatory Pediatrics, 7,* 232–238.

Vygotsky, L. (1978). *Mind in society: The development of higher mental processes.* Cambridge, MA: Harvard University Press.

Weizman, Z. O., & Snow, C. E. (2001). Lexical input as related to children's vocabulary acquisition: Effects of sophisticated exposure and support for meaning. *Developmental Psychology, 37,* 265–279.

Whitehurst, G. J., Falco, F. L., Lonigan, C. J., Fischel, J. E., DeBaryshe, B. D., Valdez-Menchaca, M. C., et al. (1988). Accelerating language development through picture book reading. *Developmental Psychology, 24,* 552–559.

Whitehurst, G. J., & Lonigan, C. J. (1998). Child development and emergent literacy. *Child Development, 69,* 848–872.

Zuckerman, B. (2009). Promoting early literacy in pediatric practice: Twenty years of Reach Out and Read. *Pediatrics, 124*(6), 1660–1665.

19

Improving the Outcomes of Coaching-Based Professional Development Interventions

DOUGLAS R. POWELL
KAREN E. DIAMOND

Intensive forms of professional development (PD) with prekindergarten (PreK) teachers are among the most promising strategies for improving the early literacy and language outcomes of young children at risk of reading difficulty. Coaching and similar approaches to providing individualized support to teachers are increasingly viewed as superior to group-based methods, such as workshops and courses, that leave teachers with the intricate task of determining how to implement evidence-based practices effectively in their classrooms (e.g., Neuman & Cunningham, 2009; Wayne, Yoon, Zhu, Cronen, & Garet, 2008).

Research has not kept pace with the current groundswell of interest in coaching teachers as a tool for bolstering children's literacy knowledge and skills. The superordinate question of whether literacy coaching with PreK teachers leads to positive effects on at-risk children's immediate and long-term outcomes has received limited investigation. A related set of emerging questions about how to strengthen the reach and impact of individualized PD with teachers also requires research attention. Studies are especially needed on innovative uses of technologies for extending the potential benefits of literacy coaching with PreK teachers.

This chapter seeks to advance the field's knowledge base regarding methods and outcomes of coaching-based PD with PreK teachers of at-risk children. It addresses unsettled questions about teacher and child outcomes of early literacy PD, as well as the promise of technologically mediated delivery of coaching with teachers. We feature in this chapter the findings of a random assignment study of a PD intervention with Head Start teachers serving diverse communities. We discuss implications of our research results for identifying critical features of effective coaching-based PD.

The Evidence Base for Early Literacy Coaching with Teachers

Recent evaluations of PD programs for teachers have transcended simplistic use of teacher satisfaction surveys and measures of teachers' perceptions of their knowledge gains to include observational measures of change in instruction as indicators of PD outcomes (Desimone, 2009). There also has been progress in conceptualizations of teacher change processes, including growing understanding that brief workshops and inservice training days are unlikely to yield meaningful change in teaching practices (Wayne et al., 2008). An expanding line of research on early literacy PD now sheds light on the outcomes of coaching-based interventions, including individualized work with teachers delivered through innovations in technology.

Design and Outcomes of Literacy Coaching

Research on the process of initiating and sustaining teachers' use of research-based practices reveals a complex enterprise (e.g., Gersten, Morvant, & Brengelman, 1995). To engage teachers fully, PD content must be grounded in situations that reflect their classroom experiences (Dickinson, Watson, & Farran, 2008) and, at the same time, support teachers' use of more effective instruction. Efforts to alter aspects of teachers' instruction may be particularly challenging when there have been recent and substantial changes in a field's understanding of appropriate and effective approaches to teaching. This is the situation that faces early literacy instruction in PreK classrooms. The field is in transition from a readiness (maturational) perspective, in which a teacher's primary role is that of a guide or facilitator (Bredekamp, 1986), to a perspective that includes attention to the importance of explicit teaching and instruction (Copple & Bredekamp, 2009; Dickinson, 2002; Neuman, Copple, & Bredekamp, 2000). Yet many current early childhood teachers received training focused on child readiness and have taught for numerous years in early childhood programs that reflect a readiness perspective.

The essential task of PD is to support teachers in moving their current instructional practices into closer proximity with evidence-based practices (Sigel, 2006). The change process may involve straightforward enhancements, minor modifications, or a significant reworking or replacement of a prevailing practice (Powell, Steed, & Diamond, in press). The greatest benefits for children's outcomes are likely to be achieved when PD interventions close or considerably narrow the wider gaps between actual and evidence-based practices. Wider gaps can pose a major challenge for PD programs in engaging teachers, however, because the PD intervention's recommended practices may not be viewed by teachers as desirable and "within reach" of their existing approach. Dickinson and his colleagues (2008) provide an illustration of this conundrum in their description of teachers' engagement in a PD intervention. For one teacher, the evidence-based practices promoted in the intervention

were quite different from her usual teaching style, and "her responses indicated minimal engagement in an effort to change" (p. 145).

The distance between evidence-based practice and common practice varies across specific aspects of literacy and language instruction. Studies indicate that, in general, classrooms serving at-risk children infrequently provide code-related instruction, including support for children's phonological awareness skills development (e.g., Hawken, Johnston, & McDonnell, 2005). Not surprisingly, recent research suggests that some PreK teachers of at-risk children believe that code-related skills and instruction are not important to pursue in an early childhood classroom.

We conducted semistructured group interviews with Head Start teachers in an effort to understand better their ideas about literacy learning and effective teaching approaches as part of our development of a PD intervention. Details are reported in Powell, Diamond, Bojczyk, and Gerde (2008). We found that while Head Start teachers shared a common view of the importance of early literacy, there were substantial differences among teachers in terms of how to support children's literacy development in early childhood classrooms. Teachers' views varied in terms of (1) timing of literacy instruction and (2) the extent to which explicit instruction was appropriate. For many teachers, mastery of socioemotional skills (e.g., self-regulation) was a prerequisite to literacy learning, with literacy and other academic goals postponed until a child displayed particular socially competent behaviors. Fewer teachers suggested that academic skills, such as literacy, could be taught concurrently with socioemotional competence. A few teachers felt strongly that literacy skills provided a foundation for growth in all other developmental domains, with one teacher remarking that "literacy is kind of the basis for everything" (Powell et al., 2008, p. 442).

Teachers were similarly divided in their ideas about appropriate instructional strategies. The most commonly held set of beliefs was that the teacher's primary role is one in which he or she provides opportunities for children to explore literacy materials when they are ready, and that variations in children's readiness to engage in literacy activities are the source of variations in children's literacy skills. For example, one teacher suggested that before a child can learn, "a light bulb has to go off; we can't make it happen" (Powell et al., 2008, p. 445). This view is consistent with the long-held conception of maturational readiness that has held sway in recommendations for early childhood practice until recent years. A minority of teachers believed that it was important to not leave "literacy skills to chance" (p. 446). These teachers emphasized benefits of effective instruction to promote children's literacy skills and reported using a range of instructional strategies, including direct teaching, to promote children's development of vocabulary and decoding skills. The approaches described by these teachers reflected more proactive instruction of specific literacy content that was quite different from the readiness approach of their colleagues.

Teachers' ideas of children's readiness for learning appeared almost exclusively in discussions of academic content areas such as literacy or mathematics; teachers never discussed a child's readiness to learn in relation to socioemotional development (e.g., self-regulation, making friends). These results are complemented by those of Hindman and Wasik (2008), who found that Head Start teachers' beliefs about what language and literacy skills young children should be developing, and which specific preschool instructional practices should be implemented to promote these skills, generally were not in agreement with commonly accepted best practices in code-related instruction (e.g., "Children should learn to identify the beginning and ending sounds in words," Hindman & Wasik, 2008, p. 484). In contrast, teachers generally were in agreement with best practices regarding oral language and book reading.

By design, coaching is well suited to promote teachers' implementation of evidence-based practices. Particularly promising is the opportunity to individualize the presentation of information on evidence-based practices and feedback on a teacher's efforts to improve literacy and language instruction. Descriptive portrayals of teachers' literacy and language instruction can mask important differences between teachers' instructional views and practices. Variability across teachers is not surprising in light of relatively recent changes in the early childhood field's recommendations for literacy and language instruction. Moreover, individualized work with teachers can address within-teacher differences in approaches to specific literacy areas. Teacher support for literacy development in one area (e.g., language modeling) is not correlated with the quality of instruction in another literacy area (e.g., purposeful integration of literacy instruction; Justice, Mashburn, Hamre, & Pianta, 2008).

Does literacy coaching with PreK teachers realize its promise of improving the quality of instruction and children's outcomes? There is a thin yet growing evidence base to answer this question. Research on coaching-based PD interventions has found positive impacts on classroom environments (Dickinson & Caswell, 2007; Jackson et al., 2006; Neuman & Cunningham, 2009), teaching practices (Domitrovich et al., 2009; Hsieh, Hemmeter, McCollum, & Ostrosky, 2009; Landry, Anthony, Swank, & Monique-Bailey, 2009; Powell, Diamond, Burchinal, & Koehler, 2010; Wasik, Bond, & Hindman, 2006), and children's literacy skills (Bierman et al., 2008; Jackson et al., 2006; Landry, Swank, Smith, Assel, & Cunnewig, 2006; Powell, Diamond, Burchinal, et al., 2010; Wasik et al., 2006).

A closer look at the evidence base for literacy coaching reveals an important difference in coaching in programs aimed at improving children's literacy and language outcomes. Some interventions have employed coaching to help teachers implement scripted curriculum supplements (Bierman et al., 2008; Wasik et al., 2006) and use of tools to monitor children's progress (Landry et al., 2009). In contrast, other interventions have used coaching to help teachers translate research-based knowledge about literacy development and instruction for use in their classrooms (Dickinson & Caswell, 2007; Jackson et al., 2006; Landry et al., 2006; Neuman & Cunningham, 2009; Powell, Diamond, Burchinal, & Koehler, 2010). Presumably, coaching functions differently when the intent is to promote a teacher's effective adoption of a new curriculum or progress-monitoring tool versus actively help a teacher plan and implement changes in teaching practices in the context of information on evidence-based instruction.

A closer look at the literacy coaching research literature also reveals important differences in the rigor of study methods. Only a handful of coaching-based intervention studies have employed random assignment designs (Bierman et al., 2008; Landry et al., 2009; Powell, Diamond, Burchinal, & Koehler, 2010; Wasik et al., 2006). Other investigations have used quasi-experimental designs that yield equivocal results about impact. The random assignment intervention studies have found small effect sizes for child outcomes in most, but not all, literacy and language outcomes, and somewhat larger effects for teacher instructional outcomes targeted by the respective interventions. Child outcomes varied across research sites in one study (Landry et al., 2009).

Innovative Uses of Technologies

Technology holds great potential to extend the reach of PD. Regular visits to classrooms by coaches can pose logistical and financial barriers, particularly when classrooms are located in geographically remote communities with no or few possibilities for securing high-quality coaches. Two core elements of PD are conducive to technologically mediated delivery to teachers: illustrations of evidence-based practices and individualized feedback to teachers on their implementation of evidence-based instruction.

A case-based hypermedia resource is a technologically advanced way to support teachers' understanding of best practices. A case is a well-defined domain of practice that offers both narrative and video illustrations of evidence-based instruction (Koehler, 2002). Video illustrations of instruction are linked with descriptive and explanatory text, and with other video exemplars. The expectation is that case-based video support will help teachers "unpack" multiple dimensions of teaching and learning that they can then apply to their own instruction (Spiro, Collins, Thota, & Feltovich, 2003). Narrative case studies of specific, real-world situations have been used for many years to promote teachers' understanding of effective instruction in both preservice and PD programs (Barnett, 2008). Technological advances now allow the inclusion of video examples plus interlinked material within and across cases. Uses of a case-based hypermedia resource in improving teaching quality have been examined at elementary and secondary school levels (e.g., Hughes, Packard, & Pearson, 2000; Lampert & Ball, 1998).

In addition to using videotaped exemplars of evidence-based practice in PD interventions, videotapes of classroom teachers' instruction can provide individualized feedback to teachers (Pianta, Mashburn, Downer, Hamre, & Justice, 2008). Advantages of using videotape as a basis for feedback to teachers include the opportunity for teachers and coaches to attend to specific teaching strategies that might go unnoticed or not be easily recalled by the end of a live, real-time classroom observation (Sherin, 2004). Videotapes, rather than classroom visits, reduce some of the complexities of onsite coaching and, because coaching visits and consultations are not tied to a classroom schedule, provide both teacher and coach with opportunities to participate in coaching at times that are most convenient.

Technologically mediated PD is not without challenges. Web-based delivery of PD is not an option for teachers without access to high-speed Internet connections that support the playing of streaming video. This is among the most challenging technical aspects of scaling up Web-based PD (Barnett, 2008), and it affects teachers' ability to view video exemplars, as well as upload videos of their own teaching practices for review by a PD expert. Teacher access to a computer with high-speed Internet connection at school (vs. home) exclusively may be problematic. Work-based access to the Internet restricts the practical affordances of technology (i.e., use of the Web at any time) and may not support confidentiality in a teacher's work with a coach (i.e., colleagues or supervisors may have access to teacher-submitted videotapes or to coach feedback). Another challenge of technologically mediated PD is ensuring that videos of evidence-based practice are authentic and credible from the perspective of teachers. Videotaped examples that are grounded in situations similar to those that teachers encounter in their own classrooms enhance the likelihood that teachers will seriously consider different instructional strategies used by others in similar settings (Barnett, 2008). A rationale for onsite coaching is the opportunity for a coach to model specific best practices in the teacher's classroom, presumably demonstrating for a teacher that children in the current classroom will respond positively to a recommended practice. In a technologically mediated PD program, teachers may dismiss video clips of best practices that appear to be too far removed from their existing situation (e.g., "A nice idea but it won't work with the kids I'm teaching").

Research on the Classroom Links to Early Literacy Program

We developed and studied a coaching-based PD program entitled Classroom Links to Early Literacy in an effort to contribute to the field's empirical understanding of unsettled questions about methods and outcomes of PD interventions. Our intervention study was part of an ongoing program of research on early literacy PD interventions with Head Start teachers initiated in 2001.

Intervention Goal and Design

The goal of the one-semester Classroom Links to Early Literacy intervention was to improve Head Start teachers' use of evidence-based literacy instruction, with the expectation that this would lead to improvements in the rate with which children acquired oral language and code-related skills (phonological awareness and letter knowledge). The intervention comprised a 2-day workshop (16 hours total) designed to provide information about evidence-based practices and to initiate relationships between teachers and their assigned coaches. This was followed by coaching that provided teachers with individualized feedback on their implementation of instructional practices emphasized in the intervention, as well as additional information on evidence-based practices. Coaching sessions occurred approximately biweekly over a 15-week semester. A case-based hypermedia resource was offered as a supplement to coaching. Teacher participation was voluntary. Study details are reported in Powell, Diamond, Burchinal, and Koehler (2010).

CONTENT

Substantive and pragmatic considerations led to the focus on oral language and code-related skills. A substantial body of research points to these preschool outcomes as strongly predictive of later reading competence (e.g., National Early Literacy Panel, 2008). Our experiences with a broad-based early literacy PD intervention implemented with Head Start teachers several years prior to developing and examining the PD

program featured in this chapter led us to question whether phonological awareness and other code-related skills can receive sufficient attention in a PD program focused on a wide range of literacy and language skills. For example, in our earlier PD program, we found that the instructional improvement plans developed by teachers and early literacy experts in 280 coaching sessions conducted across 31 classrooms most frequently addressed children's letter–word knowledge and least frequently addressed phonological awareness. Interestingly, this pattern occurred even though we offered a concurrent semester-long course that gave equal attention to four literacy content areas—reading, writing, letter–word knowledge, and phonological awareness—as an integral component of the PD intervention (Powell, Steed, & Diamond, in press).

As we noted earlier, semistructured group discussions with teachers helped us to appreciate the range of teachers' views about language and literacy instructional practices. Because many teachers appeared to adhere to a readiness perspective, in which the teachers' role is to support children's engagement with literacy activities when they are ready, we adopted a PD approach that emphasized the range of ways children learn early literacy skills (e.g., learning letters by writing their own names), promoting alternatives to more narrow views of how to teach literacy content. As well, teachers' orientation to socioemotional competence as a primary learning objective led us to attend to ways we could highlight how to integrate literacy and social goals in planned (e.g., teaching vocabulary words related to feelings when reading the children's book *The Kissing Hand*) and routine (e.g., using vocabulary related to feelings in a mealtime discussion) learning activities.

APPROACHES TO COACHING

We examined in-class (onsite) and technologically mediated (remote) delivery of coaching. The onsite coaching condition followed a common coaching format in which the coach observed classroom activities for approximately 90 minutes, then met with the teacher for about 30 minutes to provide and to discuss feedback. The observation focused on a specific instructional practice that was agreed upon in advance with the teacher. Coaches recorded their feedback in writing on a form that was shared with the teacher and served as a basis for the consultation with the teacher. Feedback focused on appropriately implemented aspects of the targeted instructional practice and recommendations for improving the practice. Coaches also provided demonstrations of recommended action in person or via video exemplars shown to the teacher on a laptop computer the coach brought to each coaching session. The video exemplars were part of the project's hypermedia resource described below. On a separate form, the coach documented the primary focus of the session and the resources provided to the teacher. The primary focus of coaching sessions was oral language skills (36%) or code-focused skills, including letter knowledge (34%) and phonological awareness (25%). A small percentage of coaching sessions focused about equally on more than one of these literacy outcomes. Less than 2% of all onsite coaching sessions included improvement recommendations that were not directly related to the PD content. No information about the content of individual coaching sessions was shared with others, including teachers' supervisors. Coaches were university employees.

We combined the two main uses of video technology—providing individualized feedback to teachers and demonstrating evidence-based practice—in the remote coaching condition. The intent was to provide support to teachers that approximated the information available to teachers in the onsite coaching condition but enabled teachers in the remote condition to review feedback and video exemplars at any time. Teachers submitted videotapes of themselves teaching and received feedback on those tapes from their literacy coach. Because many teachers did not have easy access to high-speed data transmission over the Internet, teachers sent their videotapes to us by mail using postage-paid envelopes provided by the project. As well, we gave each teacher a Macintosh iBook™ computer, a video camera, a tripod, and mini-DVD tapes to use during the intervention semester. Using this equipment, teachers videotaped themselves once every other week as they implemented a targeted instructional practice, then sent the videotape to the coach for review. Videotapes were on average about 15 minutes in length.

A coach viewed each teacher-submitted videotape and selected an average of nearly six short segments for comment. Using specialized computer software, the coach provided written feedback for each selected segment of videotape, with coach comments appearing on the right side of the computer screen, while the selected video segment was displayed on the left. Along with feedback on each teacher's instruction, coach feedback included links to video exemplars of effective instruction located in the intervention's hypermedia resource. Teachers received this coach feedback in the mail on a compact disc that they could view on their laptops. Coach feedback was typically sent within 2 weeks or less of receipt of a teacher's videotape.

We held constant the content of PD to focus our comparison of remote and onsite coaching conditions squarely on differences in the delivery of coaching. There were no significant differences between remote and onsite conditions in the main content focus of coaching sessions/videotapes, for example. Teachers in each condition participated in a similar average number of coaching sessions (seven onsite classroom visits or teacher-submitted videotapes), though there was greater range in the remote condition (two to nine) than in the onsite condition (six to eight). Also, teachers in both conditions viewed a similar average number of demonstrations of evidence-based practice (16.85 onsite, 17.03 in the remote condition); demonstrations in the onsite condition included video exemplars in the hypermedia resource and instances of a coach modeling a practice in the teacher's classroom.

HYPERMEDIA RESOURCE

The case-based hypermedia resource we developed for the Classroom Links to Early Literacy intervention was designed to function as a supplement to the workshop and coaching component. The resource provided 16 cases of evidence-based instruction in early literacy development organized into five modules (reading, writing, conversations with children, phonological awareness, and individualization). Each case included video exemplars of mostly Head Start teachers (from programs not involved in the intervention) using specific, evidence-based instructional practices designed to promote children's development of important early literacy skills. The video exemplars, typically about 2 minutes in length, were paired with bulleted comments that highlighted key features of the instructional practice shown in the video. Each case also included professional articles, written for teachers, which described important components of effective instruction in that domain. Across all 16 cases, there were 97 video exemplars and accompanying bulleted text, six still photographs coupled with text, and 33 articles (Powell, Diamond, & Koehler, 2010).

Research Design

A total of 88 lead teachers in Head Start classrooms participated in the Classroom Links to Early Literacy program. Most of the teachers (60%) worked in an urban area of 1.1 million residents. Others served communities in small cities (22%) or rural areas (18%). Most of the teachers had a bachelor's degree or higher (64%), typically in early childhood education or a closely related area, and on average almost 10 years of teaching experience ($M = 9.8$, $SD = 7.3$). With parent consent, we collected outcome data on an average of eight children in each of the 88 classrooms. This yielded a total sample of 759 children, a majority of whom represented racial/ethnic minority backgrounds (69%). On average, children were 54 months of age by September 15 of their year of study participation. Per Head Start enrollment requirements, children were from predominantly low-income families. Three specialists in early childhood education served as literacy coaches. Each had a master's degree in early education or child development and experience as the lead teacher of a PreK classroom.

Random assignment occurred in two steps. First, teachers were randomly assigned to an intervention semester (fall or spring) and a participation year (first or second) within location (urban or nonurban). Second, teachers within each intervention semester and location were randomly assigned to the onsite coaching or remote coaching conditions, as noted earlier. The waiting-list control group was a business-as-usual condition. Each literacy coach's caseload consisted of approximately equal numbers of teachers in the onsite and remote conditions,

as well as urban and nonurban locations. The full-time equivalent coach caseload was 14 teachers per semester (one coach worked full time, two worked part time).

Trained research assistants conducted structured observations of classrooms and teaching practices, and assessed children individually with standardized measures of literacy and language skills. Classroom measures included standardized (Early Language and Literacy Classroom Observation [ELLCO]; Smith, Dickinson, Sangeorge, & Anasatopoulos, 2002) and project-developed measures of teachers' language and literacy instructional practices. Children's learning was assessed with commonly used measures of vocabulary, letter and sound awareness, and understanding of print conventions. Data were collected at the beginning of fall semester, the middle of the school year, and at the end of spring semester.

Hierarchical linear model analyses were conducted for two sets of comparisons: intervention (onsite and remote combined) versus control group in fall semester, and onsite versus remote coaching condition. Results are summarized below.

Summary of Findings

We asked three questions in our examination of the Classroom Links to Early Literacy intervention: What were the effects of the intervention on teaching practices and children's literacy outcomes? Were onsite (in-classroom) coaching and remote (technologically mediated) coaching differentially effective? In what ways did teachers engage the case-based hypermedia resource in the remote coaching condition?

INTERVENTION EFFECTS

We found that the Classroom Links to Early Literacy intervention had significant positive effects on the language and literacy environment provided by classroom teachers and on children's code-focused skills. Intervention classrooms showed significantly larger gains than control classrooms over the same period of time on the two ELLCO subscales examined in our study, the General Classroom Environment subscale and Language, Literacy and Curriculum subscale. There were no statistically significant gains in intervention teachers' instructional practices focused on children's oral language skills, including vocabulary knowledge. In terms of child outcomes, children in intervention classrooms showed larger gains and higher mean scores over time on four of the six outcome measures of letter-sound and print awareness. There were no PD intervention effects on children's receptive vocabulary; children in both intervention and control classrooms made significant gains on a standardized measure of receptive vocabulary.

The effect sizes for gains over time were large for each of the ELLCO subscales ($d = 0.99$ for General Classroom Environment, $d = 0.92$ for Language, Literacy and Curriculum). Dickinson and Caswell (2007) reported effect sizes of 0.60 and 0.48 for these two subscales, respectively, in a one-semester PD intervention in a Head Start sample. The effect sizes for gains in child outcomes in our study ranged from 0.17 to 0.29 for the four child outcomes for which there were significant positive PD effects. This compares favorably to the range of effect sizes for the three literacy and language child outcomes (0.15 to 0.39) for which there were significant positive effects in the Bierman and colleagues (2008) intervention. The latter intervention took place across a school year and, as noted earlier, involved implementation of new curricula designed to promote academic and social outcomes.

ONSITE VERSUS REMOTE COACHING

Our random assignment comparison of onsite and remote delivery of coaching found no consistent differences in effectiveness of one coaching delivery method over the other. We concluded that technologically mediated delivery of literacy coaching is a promising alternative to the common practice of in-classroom coaching visits. Our research appears to be the first systematically to compare onsite and remote coaching conditions, and replication of our intervention study would be valuable to pursue in future research. Because technologically mediated feedback and the hypermedia resource were coupled in our intervention, we do not know the mechanisms through which coaching or the case-based hypermedia resource contributed uniquely to positive teacher and child outcomes. We note

that Pianta and his colleagues (2008) found positive effects of Web-mediated feedback to teachers on their videotaped interactions with children in comparison to teachers who had access to a website only, suggesting that individualized coaching feedback adds value to that provided by models or exemplars of evidence-based instruction. Teachers' uses of the hypermedia resource in our intervention, summarized below, also provide some clues about the role of the video exemplars in relation to coaching.

USE OF HYPERMEDIA RESOURCE

With their informed consent, we examined teachers' use of the hypermedia resource by analyzing browser actions logged on software installed on each teacher's laptop. Details are reported in Powell, Diamond, and Koehler (2010). We found that teachers were selectively engaged with videos and case text. On average, teachers visited half of the cases, viewing 17 video exemplars and nearly 19 content pages. There was considerable variability in the number of different pages the 29 teachers in the remote coaching intervention visited: Two teachers viewed no video exemplars, while one teacher twice visited 74 of the 97 videos. These results, both in terms of average use and variability across teachers, are similar to those reported by Downer, Kraft-Sayre, and Pianta (2009) during the first year of PreK teachers' participation in a Web-mediated PD intervention.

In our analyses, we found that teachers used the hypermedia resource on an average of 5.9 different days over 3 months, with most visits occurring in late afternoon and evening hours. On average, teachers viewed only about 20% of the videos that the coach recommended. Yet from teachers' perspectives, about half (49.8%) of the videos they viewed were ones suggested by the coach (although we were not able to determine whether teachers viewed the video in response to the coach's suggestion). Teachers also viewed videos they found, independent of the coach's guidance, suggesting that this information-rich hypermedia resource may meet teachers' needs in ways we had not imagined. Particularly given the substantial variability in teachers' use of the hypermedia resource, we suspect that its use was moderated, in part, by available time. Teachers with particularly limited time may have been more likely to pursue only the coach's recommended videos, while other teachers may have had more time to explore other topics that they thought would be relevant to their teaching.

Our review of computer log data revealed that a majority of teachers used the hypermedia resource in the late afternoon or evening. This supports the promise of flexibility in teachers' participation in Web-based PD. When we asked teachers to evaluate this hypermedia resource, we found that they provided favorable assessments of the video exemplars, including their ecological validity and usefulness in helping them learn new instructional strategies. Comments such as these are noteworthy in that they suggest teachers were able to generalize from the videos to their own classrooms.

Implications and Future Directions

What do the findings of research on the Classroom Links to Early Literacy intervention tell us about critical features of effective early literacy PD programs? Below we describe implications of our research for four areas of future PD intervention development and research.

Uses of PD

Our randomized controlled trial of a one-semester, coaching-based PD intervention with PreK teachers of at-risk children demonstrates that individualized support to teachers in determining how to incorporate evidence-based practices effectively into their existing literacy and language instruction leads to positive effects on teaching practices and on children's literacy outcomes. Prior investigations of similar approaches to early literacy coaching have employed quasi-experimental research designs that limit conclusions about intervention efficacy.

Our findings suggest that coaching-based PD can be effective without the use of a supplemental curriculum resource as the primary focus of work with teachers. We offered teachers a range of research-based examples of how to improve oral language and code-related skills, and provided guidance and feedback on efforts to implement evidence-based practices in their classrooms. In addition to our results, we note that a random assignment study of a similar approach to coaching with Head Start teachers, focused on helping teachers use research-based information on behavior management to improve their classroom climate and sensitivity to children, also revealed positive intervention effects on teaching practices (Raver et al., 2008). Random assignment studies of the alternative approach of using PD to promote teachers' effective implementation of new curriculum supplements also yield positive effects on teaching practices and children's outcomes (Bierman et al., 2008; Domitrovich et al., 2009; Wasik et al., 2006).

The uses of PD with and without a focus on implementing a new curriculum entail potentially significant trade-offs that need to be investigated in research that directly compares these contrasting intervention approaches. PD interventions aimed at promoting teacher adoption of scripted curriculum materials presumably provide a "ready to go" plan of activities (Powell, Diamond, Burchinal, & Koehler, 2010) that teachers eventually may generalize to their behaviors in settings that lack specific curriculum materials (e.g., mealtime; Domitrovich et al., 2009). While materials that set forth the scope and sequence of curriculum activities may yield immediate classroom improvements, a key question is whether changes in teaching practices are sustained long term. Teachers promptly stopped using small reading groups, a central element of dialogic reading strategies, at the postintervention point of a dialogic reading intervention study, for example (Whitehurst et al., 1994). We wonder whether ownership of new teaching practices is enhanced when teachers assume an active role in planning instructional improvements in their existing curriculum, are exposed to a range of evidence-based practice examples, and receive individualized guidance and feedback on implementation. Understanding the extent to which PD interventions lead to long-term improvements in instructional practice is an important area for future research.

More generally, the next wave of research on early literacy PD needs to examine the relative contribution of various intervention components. With few exceptions (Landry et al., 2009; Neuman & Cunningham, 2009),

PD intervention studies have not systematically varied teacher exposure to different intervention components, making it impossible to determine the extent to which coaching, curriculum supplements, coursework or workshop, or some other intervention component was an active ingredient leading to positive PD impact. In our study, for example, we do not know the mechanisms through which the coaching, the case-based hypermedia resource, or the workshop contributed uniquely to positive outcomes.

PD Content

Three of the four positive intervention effects on child outcomes achieved in our PD intervention (letter knowledge, blending, writing) are among the early literacy skills found to be moderately to strongly predictive of later conventional literacy in recent National Early Literacy Panel (2008) meta-analyses. Our fourth child outcome (concepts about print) is among a small set of early literacy skills moderately correlated with later conventional literacy in National Early Literacy Panel results.

Our intervention did not help teachers significantly move their practices in promoting children's oral language development into closer proximity with evidence-based practices. Probably as a consequence, we did not find positive intervention effects on children's oral language skills. PreK teachers' approaches to language use in the classroom are challenging adult behaviors to change (e.g., Justice et al., 2008), and most other early literacy and language PD intervention studies have found no significant intervention effects on children's language skills (e.g., Landry et al., 2009). A notable exception is the Wasik and colleagues (2006) intervention, which found positive effects on children's receptive and expressive language skills.

Two possible avenues for improving children's oral language skills via PD interventions deserve attention in future research. One strategy is to limit PD content to oral language. The Wasik and colleagues (2006) intervention focused exclusively on teachers' book reading and conversation strategies for a school year. Although significant improvements were found in children's oral language

skills, tightly bounded work with teachers may come at the expense of reducing teachers' attention to other aspects of literacy development. In the Wasik and colleagues study, for example, children in the control group had higher alphabet knowledge scores than children in the intervention group at the end of the intervention. Another option is to increase the intensity of support for improvements in oral language instruction in the context of PD intervention with broader content boundaries. We wonder, for example, whether teachers in our intervention would have benefited from feedback on repeated implementation of a single instructional practice (e.g., feedback on multiple, consecutive attempts to expand children's utterances during large-group book reading). Each instance of coaching feedback in the Classroom Links to Early Literacy intervention typically addressed a different instructional practice. These observations lead us to speculate about how to achieve an optimal balance between breadth of attention to important teaching strategies (e.g., improving instruction of both vocabulary and phonological awareness) and the depth of attention given to each instructional strategy within an intervention.

Technological Innovations

The technologically mediated delivery of support to teachers in our remote coaching condition is a promising model for extending the reach of individualized PD. The opportunity to work intensively with teachers in rural communities via innovative uses of technology is particularly exciting. Onsite visits to some of the classrooms in our random assignment design required 2 hours of driving one way from our project's campus base. Our research on remote versus onsite coaching with PreK teachers is novel and, as noted earlier, replication of our study is needed. Future research on the role of teacher-submitted videotapes in technologically mediated work with teachers also may be productive. The videotape itself may be a form of intervention independent of coach feedback. Specifically, teachers' plans for and perhaps selection of a videotaped submission to the literacy coach may prompt focused reflection on evidence-based practices.

Anecdotally, we are aware that some teachers selected their submissions from among several videotaped implementations of a specific practice, akin to a teacher trying out a new practice with children prior to a coach's onsite visit. Teachers' experiences in viewing coach-selected segments of their videotaped submissions also need careful investigation. It would be useful to know how often and under what conditions teachers in our intervention viewed the coach-selected segments of their submitted videotapes (our Web log data did not provide this level of detail) and the relative impact of viewing their own videotaped practices.

A case-based hypermedia resource is an especially promising tool for PD. Our computer log data suggest that in the remote coaching condition, the hypermedia resource took on a life of its own among some teachers who viewed material and video exemplars that were not necessarily recommended by a coach. We speculate that time availability was among the factors in teachers' use of the hypermedia resource (i.e., less time, more use of coach suggestions as a guide to viewing), but this topic needs future research attention. Advances in the design of Web-based resources for teachers also would benefit from research on the organization of video exemplars and text. For example, recently we systematically varied the configuration of video exemplar and accompanying text in a counterbalanced presentation to individual teachers as part of a small-scale study aimed at identifying preferences for when text appears on the screen (teachers generally preferred access to the text alongside, rather than before or after, the exemplar).

Relationships with Teachers

Factors that facilitate or impede positive relationships between teachers and coaches need future research attention. There were no indications in our study that teachers in the remote condition felt less supported or less understood by their coaches than teachers in the onsite coaching condition, even though teachers in the remote condition met their coaches only once (at the introductory workshop) during their semester of participation in the intervention. This prompts us to wonder whether a search for key coach contributors to positive coach–teacher relationships might be productively pursued by examining teachers' reactions to a coaches' written words. We are aware that coaches in our study worked carefully to frame their feedback with words and phrases that offered explicit direction with a supportive tone. We do not know the indicators teachers used to determine whether a coach's recommendations were credible and worthy of pursuit in their classroom. Information on this topic seems critical to considering improvements in the quality of coaching.

Research on the organizational context of coaching-based PD may lead to insights on how to improve the outcomes of PD interventions. As university employees, the coaches in our study were at arm's length from the teachers' agency base and shared no specific information about teachers or the coaching work with teachers' supervisors or others in the agency. Coaching may take on a different quality when coaches are also employees of the agency that hires teachers. The distinction between coaching and supervision is especially blurred when teachers' supervisors or their designees function as coaches. Whether teacher participation in PD is voluntary or mandated is another contextual variable in need of research attention. Although 73% of all lead teachers in our collaborating Head Start programs participated in the Classroom Links to Early Literacy intervention, we speculate that the voluntary nature of involvement was a factor in teachers' generally high levels of participation in coaching. Most research on early literacy PD is based on voluntary participation in the intervention, a condition that may not generalize to mandated programs. Last, we wonder how teacher–coach relationships are shaped by the ways in which PD programs initially present themselves to teachers. The group interviews with teachers described earlier in this chapter represented the first substantive exchange between teachers and our PD intervention. Teachers did not necessarily meet their future literacy coaches at the group session, but the PD program may have conveyed a commitment to learning more about, and being responsive to, teachers' daily situations by providing an opportunity for teachers to share their views on early literacy.

Acknowledgments

The study described in this chapter was supported by Grant No. R305M040167 from the Institute of Education Sciences, U.S. Department of Education, to Purdue University in collaboration with Michigan State University. Margaret R. Burchinal served as the study's methodologist, Matthew J. Koehler managed technical aspects of the case-based hypermedia resource and video review tool, and Hope K. Gerde coordinated data collection. We gratefully acknowledge the participation of Head Start teachers, administrators, and children, as well as the numerous contributions of research assistants.

References

Barnett, M. (2008). Using authentic cases through a web-based professional development system to support preservice teachers in examining classroom practice. *Action in Teacher Education, 29,* 3–14.

Bierman, K. L., Domitrovich, C. E., Nix, R. L., Gest, S. D., Welsh, J. A., Greenberg, M. T., et al. (2008). Promoting academic and social–emotional school readiness: The Head Start REDI program. *Child Development, 79,* 1802–1817.

Bredekamp, S. (Ed.). (1986). *Developmentally appropriate practice.* Washington, DC: National Association for the Education of Young Children.

Copple, C., & Bredekamp, S. (Eds.). (2009). *Developmentally appropriate practice in early childhood programs* (3rd ed.). Washington, DC: National Association for the Education of Young Children.

Desimone, L. M. (2009). Improving impact studies of teachers' professional development: Toward better conceptualizations and measures. *Educational Researcher, 38,* 181–199.

Dickinson, D. K. (2002). Shifting images of developmentally appropriate practice as seen through different lenses. *Educational Researcher, 31,* 26–32.

Dickinson, D. K., & Caswell, L. (2007). Building support for language and early literacy in preschool classrooms through in-service professional development: Effects of the Literacy Environment Enrichment Program (LEEP). *Early Childhood Research Quarterly, 22,* 243–260.

Dickinson, D. K., Watson, B. G., & Farran, D. C. (2008). It's in the details: Approaches to describing and improving preschool classrooms. In L. M. Justice & C. Vukelich (Eds.), *Achieving excellence in preschool literacy instruction* (pp. 136–162). New York: Guilford Press.

Domitrovich, C. E., Gest, S. D., Gill, S., Bierman, K. L., Welsh, J. A., & Jones, D. (2009). Fostering high-quality teaching with an enriched curriculum and professional development support: The Head Start REDI program. *American Educational Research Journal, 46,* 567–597.

Downer, J. T., Kraft-Sayre, M. E., & Pianta, R. C. (2009). Ongoing, web-mediated professional development focused on teacher–child interactions: Early

childhood educators' usage rates and self-reported satisfaction. *Early Education and Development, 20,* 321–345.

Gersten, R., Morvant, M., & Brengelman, S. (1995). Close to the classroom is close to the bone: Coaching as a means to translate research into classroom practice. *Exceptional Children, 62,* 52–66.

Hawken, L. S., Johnston, S. S., & McDonnell, A. P. (2005). Emerging literacy views and practices: Results from a national survey of Head Start preschool teachers. *Topics in Early Childhood Special Education, 25,* 232–242.

Hindman, A. H., & Wasik, B. A. (2008). Head Start teachers' beliefs about language and literacy instruction. *Early Childhood Research Quarterly, 23,* 479–492.

Hsieh, W.-Y., Hemmeter, M. L., McCollum, J. A., & Ostrosky, M. M. (2009). Using coaching to increase preschool teachers' use of emergent literacy teaching strategies. *Early Childhood Research Quarterly, 24,* 229–247.

Hughes, J. E., Packard, W. B., & Pearson, P. D. (2000). Preservice teachers' perceptions of using hypermedia and video to examine the nature of literacy instruction. *Journal of Literacy Research, 32,* 599–629.

Jackson, B., Larzelere, R., St. Clair, L., Corr, M., Fichter, C., & Egertson, H. (2006). The impact of *HeadsUp! Reading* on early childhood educators' literacy practices and preschool children's literacy skills. *Early Childhood Research Quarterly, 21,* 213–226.

Justice, L. M., Mashburn, A. J., Hamre, B. K., & Pianta, R. C. (2008). Quality of language and literacy instruction in preschool classrooms serving at-risk pupils. *Early Childhood Research Quarterly, 23,* 51–68.

Koehler, M. J. (2002). Designing case-based hypermedia for developing understanding of children's mathematical reasoning. *Cognition and Instruction, 20,* 151–195.

Lampert, M., & Ball, D. L. (1998). *Teaching, multimedia, and mathematics: Investigations of real practice.* New York: Teachers College Press.

Landry, S. H., Anthony, J. L., Swank, P. R., & Monique-Bailey, P. (2009). Effectiveness of comprehensive professional development for teachers of at-risk preschoolers. *Journal of Educational Psychology, 101,* 448–465.

Landry, S. H., Swank, P. R., Smith, K. E., Assel, M. A., & Cunnewig, S. B. (2006). Enhancing early literacy skills for preschool children: Bringing a PD model to scale. *Journal of Learning Disabilities, 39,* 306–324.

National Early Literacy Panel. (2008). *Developing early literacy: Report of the National Early Literacy Panel.* Washington, DC: National Institute for Literacy.

Neuman, S. B., Copple, C., & Bredekamp, S. (2000). *Learning to read and write: Developmentally appropriate practices for young children.* Washington, DC: National Association for the Education of Young Children.

Neuman, S. B., & Cunningham, L. (2009). The impact

of professional development and coaching on early language and literacy instructional practices. *American Educational Research Journal, 46,* 532–566.

Pianta, R. C., Mashburn, A. J., Downer, J. T., Hamre, B. K., & Justice, L. (2008). Effects of web-mediated PD resources on teacher–child interactions in pre-kindergarten classrooms. *Early Childhood Research Quarterly, 23,* 431–451.

Powell, D. R., Diamond, K. E., Bojczyk, K. E., & Gerde, H. K. (2008). Head Start teachers' perspectives on early literacy. *Journal of Literacy Research, 40,* 422–460.

Powell, D. R., Diamond, K. E., Burchinal, M. R., & Koehler, M. J. (2010). Effects of an early literacy professional development intervention on Head Start teachers and children. *Journal of Educational Psychology, 102,* 299–312.

Powell, D. R., Diamond, K. E., & Koehler, M. J. (2010). Use of a case-based hypermedia resource in an early literacy coaching intervention with pre-kindergarten teachers. *Topics in Early Childhood Special Education, 29,* 239–249.

Powell, D. R., Steed, E. A., & Diamond, K. E. (in press). Dimensions of literacy coaching with Head Start teachers. *Topics in Early Childhood Special Education.*

Raver, C. C., Jones, S. M., Li-Grining, C. P., Metzger, M., Champion, K. M., & Sardin, L. (2008). Improving preschool classroom processes: Preliminary findings from a randomized trial implemented in Head Start settings. *Early Childhood Research Quarterly, 23,* 10–26.

Sherin, M. G. (2004). New perspectives on the role of video in teacher education. In J. Brophy (Ed.), *Advances in research on teaching: Vol. 10: Using video in teacher education* (pp. 1–27). Oxford, UK: Elsevier.

Sigel, I. E. (2006). Research to practice redefined. In W. Damon & R. M. Lerner (Series Eds.) & K. A. Renninger & I. E. Sigel (Vol. Eds.), *Handbook of child psychology: Vol. 4. Child psychology in practice* (6th ed., pp. 1017–1023). Hoboken, NJ: Wiley.

Smith, M. W., Dickinson, D. K., Anasatopoulos, A., & Sangeorge, A. (2002). *Toolkit for assessing early literacy in classrooms.* Baltimore: Brookes.

Spiro, R. J., Collins, B. P., Thota, J. J., & Feltovich, P. J. (2003). Cognitive flexibility theory: Hypermedia for complex learning, adaptive knowledge application and experience acceleration. *Educational Technology, 43,* 5–10.

Wasik, B. A., Bond, M. A., & Hindman, A. (2006). The effects of a language and literacy intervention on Head Start children and teachers. *Journal of Educational Psychology, 98,* 63–74.

Wayne, A. J., Yoon, K. S., Zhu, P., Cronen, S., & Garet, M. S. (2008). Experimenting with teacher professional development: Motives and methods. *Educational Researcher, 37,* 469–479.

Whitehurst, G. J., Arnold, D. S., Epstein, J. N., Angell, A. L., Smith, M., & Fischel, J. E. (1994). A picture book reading intervention in day care and home for children from low-income families. *Developmental Psychology, 30,* 679–689.

20

Effective Teacher–Child Interactions and Children's Literacy: Evidence for Scalable, Aligned Approaches to Professional Development

ANNE E. HENRY
ROBERT C. PIANTA

Children develop early literacy skills through intentional, instructional interactions with adults who explicitly draw attention to print and the purpose it serves (Justice, Chow, Capellini, Flanigan, & Colton, 2003; Justice, Mashburn, Hamre, & Pianta, 2008). Given that more than 1.1 million children attended state-funded prekindergarten (PreK) in 2007–2008, and more than 80% of all 4-year-olds were exposed to some form of early childhood education setting in those years (Barnett, Epstein, Friedman, Boyd, & Hustedt, 2008), teachers in early childhood education settings clearly have opportunities and responsibilities to influence early literacy development in these ways. Recent work indicates that teachers impact children's social and academic outcomes, including language and literacy outcomes, through interactions that provide children with emotional support, instructional support, and an organized classroom environment (Curby et al., 2009; Hamre & Pianta, 2005; Howes et al., 2008; Mashburn et al., 2008). Much is known about the factors that influence children's early literacy skills specifically, as evidenced by the other chapters in this volume. This chapter highlights a body of work

that strives to bridge the gap between what is known about how children develop early literacy skills and what advances teachers' ability to facilitate this development.

Rigorous studies now indicate that teachers' effective implementation of instruction through interactions with children is the mechanism through which the value of enrollment, as well as exposure to well-developed curricula and instructional activities, is transmitted to children (Hamre & Pianta, 2005; Howes et al., 2008; National Council on Teacher Quality, 2004; National Institute of Child Health and Human Development [NICHD] Early Child Care Research Network, 2000). Because standardized observations involving several thousand U.S. early education classrooms clearly demonstrate that, on average, the quality of teacher–child interactions is not high and effective curriculum implementation is inadequate (NICHD Early Child Care Research Network, 2002b; Peisner-Feinberg & Burchinal, 1997; Pianta et al., 2005), it is increasingly recognized that the promise of early childhood education depends in large part on the professional development and training of teachers in instructional/interaction skills (Zaslow & Martinez-Beck, 2006), particularly as they apply to supporting children's early literacy and language competence (Dickinson & Brady, 2006). Yet rapid expansion of early childhood programs (Barnett et al., 2008; U.S. Department of Education, 2000) has placed demands on the supply chain for early childhood educators and for evidence-based inservice training, with estimates of a total of 200,000 teachers needed to staff universal enrollment programs and 50,000 new teachers needed by 2020 (Clifford & Maxwell, 2002). We know too little about how to prepare teachers to be effective, and there is little evidence that current approaches to training produce demonstrable gains for children (National Council on Teacher Quality, 2004).

Leveraging the value of public investments in early childhood education requires that research and development efforts focus on identifying effective and replicable approaches to teacher training that produce positive, and even accelerated, gains in children's academic performance (Brandon & Martinez-Beck, 2006; Ramey & Ramey, 2006). In this chapter we outline our approach over the course of a decade or more of work that aligns children's skill targets in early literacy and language development with evidence-driven supports for improving the effectiveness of teachers' instructional interactions and implementation, within a potentially scalable, Web-based context. The work began with support from the National Center for Early Development and Learning (NCEDL) and the Foundation for Child Development, which focused on observational assessment of teacher–child interactions, continued with support from the NICHD for additional measurement research and development of professional development supports, and is ongoing under the auspices of the National Center for Research on Early Childhood Education (NCRECE), which focuses on scaling-up and development of effective college courses. We start with some background on the early childhood workforce, describe the conceptual and empirical underpinnings of our approach to professional development, and then move to a detailed description of those resources and effects from controlled evaluations. Implications for larger-scale professional development efforts are discussed in the concluding section.

Projected Workforce Needs

This work has been done in the context of a growing demand for early childhood educators and increasing pressure to hold educators responsible for children's learning outcomes. Spending and enrollment in state-funded PreK programs continue to increase, and there is a high demand for teachers who possess degrees and/or certification (Barnett et al., 2008), and pursue ongoing professional development. Of 38 states with state-funded PreK initiatives in 2007–2008, 27 states required lead teachers to possess at least a bachelor's degree, and 37 states required the lead teacher to have specialized training in early childhood education (Barnett et al., 2008). Urgent personnel needs have supported the development of alternative certification programs and fast-paced induction for new teachers, in addition to traditional training pathways already in place (Boyd, Goldhaber, Lankford, & Wyckoff, 2007). The projected demand on these training systems for more teachers is tremendous. Many states rely on teachers with elementary grade certifications and those with 2-year degrees "grandfathered" into certification (Clifford, Early, & Hills, 1999). Many early childhood educators take courses while already employed and use work sites for student teaching (Howes, James, & Ritchie, 2003).

Unfortunately, there is little evidence that current training and professional development mechanisms are consistently related to child outcomes (Early et al., 2007; NICHD Early Child Care Research Network, 2002b; Pianta, La Paro, Payne, Cox, & Bradley, 2002). These efforts to meet the demand for "trained" teachers are moving ahead rapidly without any systematic evaluation of their impact on the nature and quality of instruction in classrooms and on child outcomes (Clifford et al., 1999; Hart, Stroot, Yinger, & Smith, 2005; Ramey & Ramey, 2006). There is little evidence that accumulating course credits, advancing in terms of degree status (e.g., from AA to BA), or attending workshops produces teaching that leads to improved child outcomes (e.g., Early et al., 2007; National Council on Teacher Quality, 2004). The NCEDL's six-state PreK study demonstrated that even in state-sponsored PreK programs with credentialed teachers with bachelor's degrees, variation in curriculum implementation and quality of teaching was enormous (Pianta et al., 2005) and unrelated to teachers' experience or education. Moreover, teachers' education and experience were also unrelated to the children's progress in academic or social skills (Early et al., 2007). Like nearly every other form of teacher training, including that in grades K–12, there is virtually no evidence linking specific teacher credentials and preservice or inservice training experiences to child outcomes or to observed classroom quality (National Council on Teacher Quality, 2004; NICHD Early Child Care Research Network, 2002b, 2005; Pianta et al., 2002). In short, the early childhood education system is expanding rapidly in response to great demand, but without any direction based on scientific evidence—a recipe for continued mediocrity and inequity that ultimately undermines the promise of early education to close the achievement gap.

If early education programs are going to achieve high quality at scale (National Early Childhood Accountability Task Force, 2005), then new mechanisms of training teachers must be developed and tested both in preservice teacher training and in alternative certification and retraining routes used by large school districts or other suppliers (Birman, Desimone, Porter, & Garet, 2000; Borko, 2004; Clifford & Maxwell, 2002; Cochran-Smith & Zeichner, 2005; Hart et al., 2005; Pianta et al., 2005; Whitebook, Bellm, Lee, & Sakai, 2005). Critical to the reinvention of teacher preparation and support, at scale, is the need to establish empirical, causal links from specific experiences in teacher preparation and support (i.e., coursework and inservice consultation) to student achievement and observed teacher effectiveness.

The Importance of Training in Implementation of Instruction and Interactions in Language and Literacy

Our research program focuses on producing effective, high-quality implementation of instruction and interactional support for literacy and language for several reasons. First, many children lack spoken language and literacy competencies at the start of school, particularly English language learners (ELL)

or those in poverty, many of whom actually attended preschool (Snow, Hamphill, & Barnes, 1991; U.S. Department of Education, 2000; Vernon-Feagans, 1996). Identified emergent language and literacy skills contribute causally to later reading achievement (e.g., Anthony, Lonigan, Driscoll, Phillips, & Burgess, 2003; Lonigan et al., 1998; National Early Literacy Panel, 2009; Storch & Whitehurst, 2002) and provide potential targets for early childhood interventions that can prevent/reduce the prevalence of reading difficulties among at-risk elementary students (e.g., Torgesen, 1998). In fact, recent extensive attention has focused on the importance of utilizing proven, effective manualized curricula or instructional approaches as a means of improving program impacts on children's skills (e.g., Preschool Curriculum Evaluation Research Consortium; see *pcer.rti.org*), and many early language and literacy curriculum interventions have been demonstrated to be effective for use in classrooms and teacher preparation programs (e.g., Byrne & Fielding-Barnsley, 1995; Davidson, Fields, & Yang, 2009; Farver, Lonigan, & Eppe, 2009; Girolametto, Pearce, & Weitzman, 1996; Girolametto, Weitzman, & Clements-Baartman, 1998; Justice & Ezell, 2002; Penno, Wilkinson, & Moore, 2002; Wasik & Bond, 2001; Whitehurst et al., 1999).

There are significant challenges, however, to using professional development interventions to improve teacher practices and children's emergent literacy skills at scale. Although researchers have had some success with curricula tested with small samples and highly controlled implementation (e.g., Justice & Ezell, 2002), observational studies show that these language and literacy interventions do not impact child outcomes when the quality of implementation and instructional interactions is low (Davidson et al., 2009; Dickinson & Brady, 2006; Howes et al., 2008). For this reason, teachers' implementation of instruction has been a major focus of our work.

Implementation can be conceptualized in a variety of ways. Measures of procedural fidelity or program adherence are often included in research on curricula to ensure that programming is implemented as intended (e.g., Davidson et al., 2009; Justice & Ezell, 2002; Lonigan, Anthony, Bloomfield, Dyer, & Samwel, 1999; Wasik, Bond, & Hindman, 2006). Such measures are increasingly being used by practitioners as well to determine whether teachers are using adopted programs as intended, particularly those that are considered to be "scientifically based" and for which procedural fidelity might be a key moderator of pupil outcomes (see Glenn, 2006).

Alternatively, the quality of implementation can be interpreted as the quality of teachers' processes of instruction—*how* they implement activities and interact with children in meaningful ways. According to the National Association for the Education of Young Children (2009, p. 8), developmentally appropriate practice involves care in teachers' "moment-to-moment decisions" and interactions with children to guide learning and development. In addition to addressing key instructional targets, teachers must approach instruction and their relationships with children in specific ways to achieve high-quality instruction that is related to children's outcomes (Dickinson & Brady, 2006; Morrison & Connor, 2002; NICHD Early Child Care Research Network, 2002a; Wasik et al., 2006). Here, *quality of implementation* refers to a teacher's ability to work flexibly with children to differentiate instruction and respond sensitively to what children bring to the task, that is, to exhibit skilled performance within dynamic interactions with children in learning activities that unfold over time in a given instructional episode or "teachable moment." Although quality of implementation is more difficult to capture (Sylva et al., 2006), it reflects the real-time dynamic and interactive nature of classroom processes, and must be carefully distinguished from procedural fidelity that instead assesses a teacher's ability to follow instructions.

In a recent study of 154 PreK teachers' implementation of a scripted set of lessons in language and early literacy, we found that teachers' observed procedural fidelity, though high, was not associated with the quality of language or literacy instruction (Hamre, Justice, et al., 2010). Teachers averaged 3.25 points on a 4-point scale of adherence across the year, indicating that they generally used materials and language in accordance with lesson plans following minimal training in their implementation.

Even this high level of procedural fidelity, however, was not associated with implementation of language or literacy instruction in terms of teachers' strategies to facilitate children's language use and focus attention on both code-based and functional aspects of language. Also important, procedural fidelity was unrelated to children's growth in language and literacy skills over the course of the year. In contrast, the study showed that children whose teachers' quality of literacy instruction was high (teachers who explicitly directed children's attention to code-based and functional aspects of print) made greater gains in emergent literacy skills over the PreK year. This was especially the case for children whose literacy skills were weak at the beginning of the year.

These findings on the importance of teachers' implementation of instruction are consistent with research indicating that supportive teacher–child interactions play an important role in children's development, uniquely predicting gains in young children's literacy and language development, and effectively contributing to closing gaps in performance (e.g., Burchinal et al., 2000; Hamre & Pianta, 2005; Howes et al., 2008; Mashburn et al., 2008; NICHD Early Child Care Research Network, 2002a). Effective teachers provide explicit instruction in the context of sensitive interactions, responsive feedback, verbal engagement/stimulation, and a classroom environment that is not overly regimented (Burchinal et al., 2000; Hyson & Biggar, 2006).

Unfortunately, observed quality of language and literacy instruction in PreK classrooms appears to be low (Hamre, Justice, et al., 2010; Justice et al., 2008). Few PreK teachers consistently use evidence-based strategies to accelerate children's language development, or provide literacy instruction that explicitly directs children's attention to the code-based and functional aspects of written and oral language. There are many possible reasons for this to be the case. Preschool teachers have little accurate knowledge about language and literacy development, particularly the high-priority skill targets (Lonigan, 2004) that should be the focus of instruction and interactional supports (Cunningham, Perry, Stanovich, & Stanovich, 2004; Justice & Ezell, 1999; Moats, 1994); they appear drastically undertrained in how to implement instructional activities in early literacy, and engage in interactions and conversations that promote language skills (Justice & Ezell, 1999; Morrison & Connor, 2002; NICHD Early Child Care Research Network, 2002b); they are rarely exposed to multiple field-based examples of objectively defined high-quality practice (Pianta, 2006); and they receive few, if any, opportunities to receive feedback about the extent to which their classroom interactions and instruction promote these skill domains (Pianta, 2006). Controlled experimentation in teacher training related to effective implementation of literacy and language instruction is clearly a key next step in the nation's program of research on early literacy and the means by which this research will realize its promise for the largest number of children in need (Davidson et al., 2009; Lyon, 2002).

Scalable Professional Development

The NCRECE approach to professional development is focused on learning to use instructional interactions skillfully, implement curricula effectively, and provide language stimulation supports in real time, through dynamic interactions that operate at the intersection of children's developing skills and the available instructional materials or activities (e.g., Burchinal et al., 2000; Howes et al., 2008; Hyson & Biggar, 2006; NICHD Early Child Care Research Network, 2002b). Teacher training that focuses on interactions and implementation of instructional activities must be based on a way of defining and observing practice that has shown strong links to growth in child outcomes, in this case, language and literacy. In our program of professional development research, teachers learn to observe their interactions and receive feedback and suggestions related to improving quality and effectiveness based on the Classroom Assessment Scoring System, or CLASS (Pianta, La Paro, & Hamre, 2008).

The CLASS was used in over 700 PreK classrooms across 11 states through the National Center for Early Development and Learning and was one of the indices of observed quality that consistently predicted child outcomes in language and literacy in that study, including growth in receptive vocabulary and alphabetic knowledge, with effect sizes (d) ranging from 0.15 to 0.28 (Howes et al., 2008; Mashburn et al., 2008). The CLASS focuses exclusively on teachers' instructional, language, and social interactions with children (La Paro, Pianta, & Stuhlman, 2004). In studies involving several thousand PreK through grade 3 classes, higher ratings on CLASS dimensions predicted greater gains on standardized assessments of academic achievement and better social adjustment, even when researchers adjusted for teacher, program, and family selection factors (Hamre & Pianta, 2005; Howes et al., 2008; Mashburn et al., 2008; NICHD Early Child Care Research Network, 2002a, 2002b). The CLASS validly measures aspects of teachers' instruction and interaction focused on language and early literacy that predict gains in these areas during the PreK years; for this reason, in the NCRECE system of professional development training, the CLASS serves as one of the central "targets" for teachers' knowledge and skills training.

The CLASS can be used as a common language for professional development that exposes teachers to field-based examples of objectively defined, high-quality practice and to feedback about the extent to which their classroom interactions and instruction promote these skills domains. The CLASS-based system of teacher training described here was first developed through MyTeachingPartner (MTP), a professional study of 182 PreK teachers in one mid-Atlantic state. Further development, scaling up, and effectiveness testing is in progress through NCRECE; more than 300 PreK teachers in 10 sites are currently participating in a randomized control trial of this program of professional development research.

The NCRECE approach *aligns* (conceptually and empirically) the requisite knowledge of desired skills targets and developmental skills progressions in a particular skills domain (e.g., language development or early literacy), with extensive opportunities for (1) *observation* of high-quality instructional interaction through analysis and viewing of multiple video examples; (2) *skills training* in identifying (in)appropriate instructional, linguistic, and social responses to children's cues, and how teacher responses can contribute to student literacy and language skills growth; and (3) repeated *opportunities for individualized feedback* and support for high-quality and effective instruction, implementation, and interaction with children. Conceptually, there is a system of professional development support that allow for a direct tracing of the path (and putative effects) from inputs to teachers to inputs to children, to children's skill gains. We describe this system briefly below, starting with skills targets for children's development.

Alignment with Skills Targets

In designing professional development programming for MTP, we identified language and literacy skills targets by reviewing research literature, including meta-analyses (Hammill, 2004; National Early Literacy Panel, 2004) and longitudinal studies of early language and literacy predicting later reading and language skills (e.g., Bryant, MacLean, & Bradley, 1990; Catts, Fey, Zhang, & Tomblin, 1999; Chaney, 1998; Christensen, 1997; Gallagher, Frith, & Snowling, 2000; Schatschneider, Fletcher, Francis, Carlson, & Foorman, 2004; Storch & Whitehurst, 2002). Selected high-priority targets for preschool literacy instruction met three criteria (Lonigan, 2004): Each target (1) is consistently and at least moderately linked to school-age reading and language achievement; (2) is amenable to change through intervention; and (3) is likely to be underdeveloped among at-risk pupils.

Specifically, the first three targets (phonological awareness, alphabet knowledge, print awareness) are literacy skills that consistently predict school-age decoding (effect sizes approximately 0.40; National Early Literacy Panel, 2004), are amenable to change via interventions (e.g., Justice & Ezell, 2002; Ukrainetz, Cooney, Dyer, Kysar, & Harris, 2000; van Kleeck, Gillam, & McFadden, 1998; Whitehurst et al., 1999), and are underdeveloped in at-risk pupils (e.g., Bowey, 1995; Lonigan, Bloomfield, et al., 1999; Snowling, Gallagher, & Frith, 2003). The other targets—vocabulary–linguistic concepts, narrative, and social communication–pragmatics—are moderately associated with school-age decoding (average $r = .38$; National Early Literacy Panel, 2004) and reading comprehension (average $r = .39$; National Early Literacy Panel, 2004). Vocabulary,

an area of language weakness for children reared in poverty (Justice, Meier, & Walpole, 2005; Whitehurst & Lonigan, 1998), can be accelerated by use of structured interventions that feature ongoing exposure to new words, as occurs through adult–child shared storybook reading (e.g., Hargrave & Sénéchal, 2000; Lonigan, Anthony, et al., 1999; Penno et al., 2002; Reese & Cox, 1999; Whitehurst et al., 1988).

We developed a curriculum based on these skills targets, the MyTeachingPartner—Language and Literacy Curriculum (MTP-LL; Justice, Pullen, Hall, & Pianta, 2003). For each target, MTP-LL includes a 9-month map of between 10 and 20 ordered, instructional objectives and activities (e.g., Bunce, 1995; Lonigan, Anthony, et al., 1999; Lonigan, Bloomfield, et al., 1999; Notari-Syverson, O'Connor, & Vadasy, 1998). We also needed an effective approach to translate these instructional targets into high-quality sustainable classroom instruction. MTP-LL activities include design features that reflect the current literature on how this can best be achieved, including (1) explicitness (Justice & Ezell, 2000, 2002), (2) intensity and repetition (Elley, 1989; Justice, Chow, et al., 2003; Nash & Donaldson, 2005; Penno et al., 2002; Robbins & Ehri, 1994; Sénéchal, 1997), (3) storybooks as a frequent medium of instruction, and (4) "real-time" consultation to teachers that focuses on their implementation of MTP-LL objectives in their classrooms.

The selected language and literacy skills targets, together with CLASS-based targets, are addressed in the NCRECE professional development system through structured observation opportunities, skills training, and individualized feedback, which we further describe next.

Opportunities for Observation

Teachers participating in the NCRECE program of professional development are exposed to Web-based exemplars of objectively defined, high-quality teaching practices. They access the MTP website, which provides specific, behavioral examples of high-quality teacher–child interactions across 10 CLASS dimensions. The CLASS dimensions are theoretically derived (Hamre & Pianta, 2007), empirically validated (Hamre, Pianta, Mashburn, & Downer, 2008), and directly associated with children's language, literacy, and socioemotional development (Howes et al., 2008; Mashburn et al., 2008). A video library is also available on the MTP website; numerous video examples portray real teachers in actual classrooms and are accompanied by specific, objective descriptions of the relevant CLASS dimensions. Video examples of activities from the MTP-LL curriculum are also presented. The videos and text available on the MTP website help teachers become critical observers of classroom behavior, more attuned to the effects of their behavior on children.

Skills Training

NCRECE investigators have developed a three-credit course offered in partnership with university-based or community-college programs. The course is an intensive, skills-focused, didactic experience in which students learn how the development of language and literacy skills is linked to features of interactions (using CLASS as the focus) with adults in family and early education settings, and how high-quality implementation of language and literacy curricula and activities leads to skills growth (again using CLASS as the focus). Teachers learn to identify behavioral indicators of high-quality/effective teaching on CLASS dimensions and to identify such indicators in their own teaching. The course draws from MTP-LL resources, including instructional activities in language and literacy, explicit lesson plans, and linked video examples of actual high-quality implementation. The effects of this course are being evaluated in a randomized controlled trial implemented with more than 300 PreK teachers in 10 sites across the country.

Individualized Feedback

To help teachers apply knowledge of language and literacy skills targets and effective implementation through high-quality teacher–child interactions, consultants support them with individualized feedback. The MTP consultancy provides observationally based, nonevaluative, practice-focused support and feedback for teachers through Web-mediated remote consultation; thus, this support can be provided wherever teachers work, without consultants having to visit classrooms, which is a cost savings.

The consultancy process is a cyclic one. First, the teacher videotapes up to a 60-minute segment of his or her implementation of a language or literacy instructional activity every 2 weeks. The consultant edits that tape into a 3-minute video of three smaller segments that focus on indicators of quality teaching identified by the CLASS, posted with written feedback to a secure website where the teacher may view and respond to it, with his or her comments sent automatically to the consultant. The teacher and consultant then participate in a regularly scheduled video conference using two-way interactive technologies in real time as they discuss teaching practices face-to-face.

Feasibility and Effects of MTP on Teacher and Child Outcomes

Initial testing of this professional development framework occurred through MTP. In this project, 182 PreK teachers, clustered by district, were randomly assigned to one of three study conditions for a 2-year period: (1) "Materials only" teachers had access to MTP-LL activities and materials; (2) "Web-only" teachers had access to the MTP website, including video exemplars, the MTP-LL, and the Preschool PATHS-Promoting Alternative Thinking Strategies (Domitrovich, Greenberg, Kusche, & Cortes, 2004) curriculum; and (3) "Consultancy" teachers were assigned individual consultants and were also given access to the MTP website, MTP-LL and the PATHS curriculum. Results, further described below, show that the framework was effective for improving teachers' implementation of instruction and interactions, and for improving children's academic and social outcomes. Feasibility and use of the various professional development components is discussed.

Effects on Implementation of Instruction and Interactions

Using data from the first year of this randomized controlled trial, we examined the extent to which randomization into the MTP "Web only" or "Consultancy" conditions was differentially associated with changes in the observed quality of teachers' interactions with children (Pianta, Mashburn, Downer, Hamre, & Justice, 2008), with the expectation that the more intensive Consultation model would have greater effects. The third group of teachers, "Materials only," was not included in this test of treatment effects because their interactions with children were not observed as a condition of participation.

In terms of the main effects of intervention condition on improvement in the quality of teacher–child interactions, all associations were in the expected direction. Teachers assigned to the Consultancy condition had more positive growth compared to teachers assigned to the Web-only condition for each of the seven dimensions of teacher–child interactions. For three dimensions of interaction quality—teacher sensitivity, instructional learning formats, and language modeling—teachers assigned to receive the Consultancy supports, in contrast to those who received support only via on-demand access to video resources on the Web, showed greater improvements in aspects of interaction that involved reading and responding to students' cues, using a variety of formats to engage children actively in instruction, and intentionally stimulating language development.

Based on past evidence that the quality of teachers' interactions with children is significantly lower in PreK classrooms serving a high percentage of poor children (Pianta et al., 2005), we also investigated the extent to which the effects of the treatment conditions (Consultancy or Web only) varied in relation to the concentration of poverty in the classroom. Thus, we were interested in whether higher levels of support for teachers (e.g., Consultancy) were necessary to counteract the increased demands of teaching in a high-poverty classroom. Results confirmed this hypothesis. Although the main effect for Consultancy holds across classrooms that vary according to poverty concentration, in classrooms with 100% of the children enrolled from families at or below 150% of the Federal poverty guidelines, there are remarkable differences in the slopes for teachers' interactions. In 100% poor classrooms, Consultancy was associated with positive changes in teacher sensitivity and instruc-

tional learning formats, while teachers assigned to the Web-only condition actually declined over the year in the quality of their interactions on these dimensions. Thus, it appears that the level or intensity of supports a teacher might need to be successful depend in part on the demand characteristics of the classroom itself.

In summary, we examined the effects of these two conditions of teacher support, Consultancy and Web only, on teacher–child interactions during a wide-scale application of the intervention. Within this real-world context, we learned that the combination of watching oneself and others teach, with ongoing feedback and support from an expert consultant, is effective at changing these interactions in 1 year, particularly in classrooms serving large numbers of children at risk for school failure.

Effects on Children's Language, Literacy, and Social Outcomes

Following evidence that the MTP intervention can alter teacher–child interactions, we examined the extent to which the intervention conditions were differentially predictive of growth in children's literacy, language, and social skills. We used two analytic approaches to address this question: experimental intent to treat and quasi-experimental treatment on the treated.

Taking full advantage of the randomized study design and 2 years of intervention implementation, we first evaluated preschoolers' language and literacy outcomes across the three study conditions (Downer, Pianta, & Fan, 2008); these conditions include the Consultancy and Web-only groups described earlier, as well as the Materials-only group, which functioned as a comparison group. Relative to the Materials-only condition, the Consultancy treatment showed a modest positive effect (0.10) on children's literacy outcome measures, after controlling for prior achievement (fall semester measures). On the other hand, the effect of the Web-only condition in contrast to the Materials-only condition was very small (0.04) and statistically nonsignificant. Further analyses are investigating potential moderators of this effect.

Also using this experimental intent-to-treat approach, we examined the impacts of

MTP on children's development of teacher-rated social skills, task-oriented competence, and problem behaviors during PreK (Hamre, Pianta, Mashburn, & Downer, 2010). Results indicated no differences across study conditions related to children's development of problem behaviors during PreK. However, there were significant differences related to children's development of task-oriented competence and one aspect of social skills—assertiveness. Specifically, children whose teachers were assigned to the Web-only and Consultancy conditions demonstrated higher levels of task orientation and assertiveness compared to children whose teachers were assigned to the Materials-only condition.

Finally, in a series of quasi-experimental treatment-on-the-treated analyses, we examined effects on child outcomes exclusively for teachers in the Consultancy and Web-only conditions, in part because there was considerable variation within these two groups in their use of MTP resources for observing and improving teacher–child interaction (Mashburn, Hamre, Downer, & Justice, 2010). During the intervention, the Web-only and Consultancy teachers varied in their use of MTP Web-based resources, including the website that features video exemplars of high-quality classroom interactions and consultation. We therefore examined the associations between teachers' exposure to these resources and children's development of language/literacy skills during PreK. Results indicate larger positive effects for teachers who utilized more consultation and complement the intent-to-treat findings reported earlier showing main effects for the Consultancy condition on child outcomes (Downer, Pianta, et al., 2008) as well as the findings showing the Consultancy condition to be more effective in changing teacher–child interactions presumed to foster school readiness (Pianta, Mashburn, et al., 2008). In summary, using both intent-to-treat and quasi-experimental treatment-on-the-treated analyses, we have demonstrated that children make significantly greater gains in language, literacy, and social skills when their teacher receives MTP consultation support. The Web-mediated nature of this effective form of one-on-one consultation with teachers has the potential for scale-up cost savings related to travel costs and time. Analysis has shown that the MTP approach to consultation is less costly than typical professional development supports on an annualized basis.

Feasibility and Use of MTP Supports

A central feature of MTP professional development that is particularly relevant for scaled-up support to teachers is continuous, on-demand access to the dynamic, interactive website *www.myteachingpartner.net*, which provides two resources available on demand: (1) lesson plans in language and literacy skills, and (2) video clips that exemplify high-quality teacher–child interactions in early childhood classrooms (Kinzie et al., 2006; Pianta, Mashburn, et al., 2008). The second MTP resource, Web-mediated Consultation, involves observation-based analysis and feedback enacted through a regular cycle of interaction between a teacher and consultant. A central concern at the outset of the project was the feasibility of delivering these video-based professional development resources to a large number of teachers statewide using the Web as the medium for access. Features of access, use, and feasibility were tracked through weblogs and questionnaires, and reported in recent papers (Downer, Kraft-Sayre, & Pianta, 2009; Whitaker, Kinzie, Kraft-Sayre, Mashburn, & Pianta, 2007).

Although we found variability in access and use as expected, use of the Web as a delivery mechanism was from a feasibility standpoint very successful. Teachers assigned to Web-mediated consultation engaged in feedback cycles and spent time on the website, as described earlier, and this high level of average engagement was not predicted by distance between consultant (based at the University of Virginia) and teachers (some as much as several hundred miles away) or teacher characteristics (education or experience). Furthermore, teachers were overwhelmingly positive about the helpfulness of the MTP website and consultation process, and the calculated costs of delivering the website and Web-mediated consultation in terms of consultant time, website maintenance, and teacher time fall at the low end of average per-teacher expenditure on professional development (Odden, Archibald, Fermanich, & Gallagher, 2002). In summary, the feasibility of the MTP approach is supported by evidence of consistent teacher engagement with the website and consultation; the finding that engagement in resources was not predicted by teacher, classroom, or district factors; teachers' own reports that MTP was worth the time and added value to their teaching practice; and reasonable cost estimates. Thus, emerging evidence from this initial field trial indicates the potential scalability of this approach.

Ongoing Work through the NCRECE

Experience and data from MTP have informed scaling-up and further testing of professional development mechanisms through the NCRECE. Studies on the effects of MTP provide direction for NCRECE aims to focus on the Consultancy condition as the primary treatment, to improve treatment fidelity/implementation in providing a more consistently high dosage of consultation, and to include a true no-treatment control group. The MTP website and the consultation process have been finetuned, and a coursework component has been added; all are being tested in the ongoing randomized control trial. Several shortcomings to the MTP study design are also addressed in the NCRECE trial.

For example, although teachers generally reported that the website was worth the time they spent on it and added value to their teaching practice (Downer, LoCasale-Crouch, Hamre, & Pianta, 2009), variability in website usage suggested that there was room for improvements to the Web interface. Enhancements included a simpler interface, increased interactivity, and improvements in the way consultants bring teachers' attention to the website through regular embedded hotlinks in the feedback comments they provide.

Improvements were also made to facilitate implementation in the Consultancy condition, including:

1. A standardized manual for MTP consultants now provides explicit directions in how to interact with teachers; how to select, edit, and annotate clips; and how to respond to teacher comments with a "bank" of sample prompts.
2. The consultation process has been standardized in terms of focusing on a sequence of CLASS-related dimensions over the course of the year.
3. Training and supports for consultants have been expanded and standardized as well, with weekly group and individual supervision sessions.

In this way the intervention and enhanced ongoing supports to implementation ensure that participating teachers in the proposed study are consistently exposed to the highest dose of intervention resources possible within an academic year, and we therefore expect larger effect sizes for teacher–child interactions. The systematic, standardized group supervision process reduces between-consultant variability. And finally, we have improved our measures of implementation fidelity, so that both teachers and consultants provide ongoing information about the quality and content of their experiences at each important phase in their biweekly consultation cycles.

Conclusions

Improving teachers' implementation of instructional interactions is a key mechanism in improving children's academic and social outcomes; evidence from MTP indicates that this is certainly true for preschoolers' early literacy outcomes. Achieving high-quality teaching at scale requires alignment of (1) high-value literacy/language skills targets that we recognize from research on development of those skills, (2) curriculum that maps onto those targets, (3) support for procedural fidelity, and (4) support for high quality implementation through effective teacher–child interactions, all transmitted to teachers in ways that can be easily and efficiently distributed, and at the same time individualized or contextualized. The MTP approach has been to rely on the Web as the medium or channel through which supports (interactive or noninteractive, synchronous or asynchronous) are delivered to teachers.

In this chapter we have described a program of research on the feasibility and impact of a Web-mediated system of professional development to improve teacher–child interactions in preschool programs. The results are promising in terms of both impact and scale, and have implications for how states, universities, and private providers design professional development systems, and for the kinds of support and focus that teachers need to be effective in classrooms.

Acknowledgments

The work described here was supported through funding from the National Center for Early Development and Learning, the Foundation for Child Development, the National Institute of Child Health and Human Development, and the Institute of Education Sciences' National Center for Research on Early Childhood Education. We gratefully acknowledge the support of participating teachers and children who opened their classrooms to us for the purpose of this research.

References

Anthony, J., Lonigan, C., Driscoll, K., Phillips, B., & Burgess, S. (2003). Phonological sensitivity: A quasi-parallel progression of word structure units and cognitive operations. *Reading Research Quarterly, 38*(4), 470–487.

Barnett, W. S., Epstein, D. J., Friedman, A. H., Boyd, J. S., & Hustedt, J. T. (2008). *The state of preschool 2008: State preschool yearbook*. New Brunswick, NJ: National Institute for Early Education Research, Rutgers University.

Birman, B. F., Desimone, L., Porter, A. C., & Garet, M. S. (2000). Designing professional development that works. *Educational Leadership, 57*(8), 28–33.

Borko, H. (2004). Professional development and teacher learning: Mapping the terrain. *Educational Researcher, 33*(8), 3–15.

Bowey, J. A. (1995). Socioeconomic status differences in preschool phonological sensitivity and first-grade reading achievement. *Journal of Educational Psychology, 87*(3), 476–487.

Boyd, D., Goldhaber, D., Lankford, H., & Wyckoff, J. (2007). The effect of certification and preparation on teacher quality. *The Future of Children, 17*(1), 45–68.

Brandon, R., & Martinez-Beck, I. (2006). Estimating the size and characteristics of the United States early care and education workforce. In M. Zaslow & I. Martinez-Beck (Eds.), *Critical issues in early childhood professional development* (pp. 49–76). Baltimore: Brookes.

Bryant, P., MacLean, M., & Bradley, L. (1990). Rhyme, language, and children's reading. *Applied Psycholinguistics, 11*(3), 237–252.

Bunce, B. H. (1995). *Building a language-focused curriculum for the preschool classroom* (Vol. II). Baltimore: Brookes.

Burchinal, M. R., Roberts, J. E., Riggins, R., Jr., Zeisel, S. A., Neebe, E., & Bryant, D. (2000). Relating quality of center-based child care to early cognitive and language development longitudinally. *Child Development, 71*(2), 339–357.

Byrne, B., & Fielding-Barnsley, R. (1995). Evaluation of a program to teach phonemic awareness to young children: A 2-and 3-year follow-up and a new preschool trial. *Journal of Educational Psychology, 87*(3), 488–503.

Catts, H. W., Fey, M. E., Zhang, X., & Tomblin, J. B. (1999). Language basis of reading and reading disabilities: Evidence from a longitudinal investigation. *Scientific Studies of Reading, 3*(4), 331–361.

Chaney, C. (1998). Preschool language and metalinguistic skills are links to reading success. *Applied Psycholinguistics, 19*(3), 433–446.

Christensen, C. A. (1997). Onset, rhymes, and phonemes in learning to read. *Scientific Studies of Reading, 1*(4), 341–358.

Clifford, R. M., Early, D. M., & Hills, T. W. (1999). Almost a million children in school before kindergarten: Who is responsible for early childhood services?: Public policy report. *Young Children, 54*(5), 48–51.

Clifford, R. M., & Maxwell, K. L. (2002). *The need for highly qualified prekindergarten teachers*. Chapel Hill: Frank Porter Graham Child Development Institute, University of North Carolina.

Cochran-Smith, M., & Zeichner, K. (Eds.). (2005). *Studying teacher education: The report of the AERA panel on research and teacher education*. Washington, DC: American Educational Research Association.

Cunningham, A. E., Perry, K. E., Stanovich, K. E., & Stanovich, P. J. (2004). Disciplinary knowledge of K–3 teachers and their knowledge calibration in the domain of early literacy. *Annals of Dyslexia, 54*(1), 139–167.

Curby, T. W., LoCasale-Crouch, J., Konold, T. R., Pianta, R. C., Howes, C., Burchinal, M., et al. (2009). The relations of observed Pre-K classroom quality profiles to children's achievement and social competence. *Early Education and Development, 20*(2), 346–372.

Davidson, M. R., Fields, M. K., & Yang, J. (2009). A randomized trial study of a preschool literacy curriculum: The importance of implementation. *Journal of Research on Educational Effectiveness, 2*(3), 177–208.

Dickinson, D. K., & Brady, J. P. (2006). Toward effective support for language and literacy through professional development. In M. Zaslow & I. Martinez-Beck (Eds.), *Critical issues in early childhood professional development* (pp. 141–170). Baltimore: Brookes.

Domitrovich, C. E., Greenberg, M. T., Kusche, C., & Cortes, R. (2004). *The preschool PATHS curriculum*. State College: Pennsylvania State University.

Downer, J. T., Kraft-Sayre, M., & Pianta, R. C. (2009). On-going, web-mediated professional development focused on teacher–child interactions: Feasibility of use with early childhood educators. *Early Education and Development, 20*(2), 321–345.

Downer, J. T., LoCasale-Crouch, J., Hamre, B. K., & Pianta, R. C. (2009). Teacher characteristics associated with responsiveness and exposure to consultation and online professional development. *Early Education and Development, 20*(3), 431–455.

Downer, J. T., Pianta, R. C., & Fan, X. (2008). *Effects of web-mediated teacher professional development on children's language and literacy development.* Manuscript submitted for publication.

Early, D. M., Maxwell, K. L., Burchinal, M., Alva, S., Bender, R. H., Bryant, D., et al. (2007). Teachers' education, classroom quality, and young children's academic skills: Results from seven studies of preschool programs. *Child Development, 78*(2), 558–580.

Elley, W. B. (1989). Vocabulary acquisition from listening to stories. *Reading Research Quarterly, 24*(2), 174–187.

Farver, J. A. M., Lonigan, C. J., & Eppe, S. (2009). Effective early literacy skill development for young Spanish-speaking English language learners: An experimental study of two methods. *Child Development, 80*(3), 703–719.

Gallagher, A., Frith, U., & Snowling, M. J. (2000). Precursors of literacy delay among children at genetic risk of dyslexia. *Journal of Child Psychology and Psychiatry, 41,* 203–213.

Girolametto, L., Pearce, P. S., & Weitzman, E. (1996). Interactive focused stimulation for toddlers with expressive vocabulary delays. *Journal of Speech, Language and Hearing Research, 39*(6), 1274–1283.

Girolametto, L., Weitzman, E., & Clements-Baartman, J. (1998). Vocabulary intervention for children with Down syndrome: Parent training using focused stimulation. *Infant Toddler Intervention: The Transdisciplinary Journal, 8,* 109–126.

Glenn, D. (2006). Weighing the "scale-up" study. *Chronicle of Higher Education, 52*(45), A12.

Hammill, D. D. (2004). What we know about correlates of reading. *Exceptional Children, 70*(4), 453–469.

Hamre, B. K., Justice, L. M., Pianta, R. C., Kilday, C., Sweeney, B., Downer, J. T., et al. (2010). Implementation fidelity of MyTeachingPartner literacy and language activities: Association with preschoolers' language and literacy growth. *Early Childhood Research Quarterly, 25*(3), 329–347.

Hamre, B. K., & Pianta, R. C. (2005). Can instructional and emotional support in the first-grade classroom make a difference for children at risk of school failure? *Child Development, 76*(5), 949–967.

Hamre, B. K., & Pianta, R. C. (2007). Learning opportunities in preschool and early elementary classrooms. In R. C. Pianta, M. J. Cox, & K. L. Snow (Eds.), *School readiness and the transition to kindergarten in the era of accountability* (pp. 49–84). Baltimore: Brookes.

Hamre, B. K., Pianta, R. C., Mashburn, A. J., & Downer, J. T. (2008). Building a science of classrooms: Application of the CLASS framework in over 4,000 US early childhood and elementary classrooms. Retrieved December 1, 2008, from *www.fcd-us.org/resources/resources_show.htm?doc_id=507559.*

Hamre, B. K., Pianta, R. C., Mashburn, A. J., & Downer, J. T. (2010). *Promoting young children's social competence through the Preschool PATHS curriculum and MyTeachingPartner Professional Development Resources.* Manuscript under review.

Hargrave, A. C., & Sénéchal, M. (2000). A book reading intervention with preschool children who have limited vocabularies: The benefits of regular reading and dialogic reading. *Early Childhood Research Quarterly, 15*(1), 75–90.

Hart, P., Stroot, S., Yinger, R., & Smith, S. (2005). *Meeting the teacher education accountability challenge: A focus on novice and experienced teacher studies.* Mount Vernon, OH: Teacher Quality Partnership.

Howes, C., Burchinal, M., Pianta, R., Bryant, D., Early, D., Clifford, R., et al. (2008). Ready to learn?: Children's pre-academic achievement in pre-Kindergarten programs. *Early Childhood Research Quarterly, 23*(1), 27–50.

Howes, C., James, J., & Ritchie, S. (2003). Pathways to effective teaching. *Early Childhood Research Quarterly, 18*(1), 104–120.

Hyson, M., & Biggar, H. (2006). NAEYC's standards for early childhood professional preparation: Getting from here to there. In M. Zaslow & I. Martinez-Beck (Eds.), *Critical issues in early childhood professional development* (pp. 283–308). Baltimore: Brookes.

Justice, L. M., Chow, S. M., Capellini, C., Flanigan, K., & Colton, S. (2003). Emergent literacy intervention for vulnerable preschoolers: Relative effects of two approaches. *American Journal of Speech–Language Pathology, 12*(3), 320–332.

Justice, L. M., & Ezell, H. K. (1999). Knowledge of syntactic structures: A comparison of speech-language pathology graduate students to those in related disciplines. *Contemporary Issues in Communication Science and Disorders, 26,* 119–127.

Justice, L. M., & Ezell, H. K. (2000). Enhancing children's print and word awareness through home-based parent intervention. *American Journal of Speech–Language Pathology, 9,* 257–269.

Justice, L. M., & Ezell, H. K. (2002). Use of storybook reading to increase print awareness in at-risk children. *American Journal of Speech–Language Pathology, 11*(1), 17–29.

Justice, L. M., Mashburn, A. J., Hamre, B. K., & Pianta, R. C. (2008). Quality of language and literacy instruction in preschool classrooms serving at-risk pupils. *Early Childhood Research Quarterly, 23*(1), 51–68.

Justice, L. M., Meier, J., & Walpole, S. (2005). Learning new words from storybooks: An efficacy study with at-risk kindergartners. *Language, Speech, and Hearing Services in Schools, 36*(1), 17–32.

Justice, L. M., Pullen, P. C., Hall, A., & Pianta, R. C. (2003). *MyTeachingPartner language and literacy curriculum.* Charlottesville: University of Virginia Center for Advanced Study of Teaching and Learning.

Kinzie, M. B., Whitaker, S. D., Neesen, K., Kelley, M., Matera, M., & Pianta, R. C. (2006). Innovative web-based professional development for teachers of at-risk preschool children. *Educational Technology and Society, 9*(4), 194–204.

La Paro, K. M., Pianta, R. C., & Stuhlman, M. (2004).

The Classroom Assessment Scoring System: Findings from the prekindergarten year. *Elementary School Journal, 104*(5), 409–426.

Lonigan, C. J. (2004). Emergent literacy skills and family literacy. In B. A. Wasik (Ed.), *Handbook of family literacy* (pp. 57–81). Mahwah, NJ: Erlbaum.

Lonigan, C. J., Anthony, J. L., Bloomfield, B. G., Dyer, S. M., & Samwel, C. S. (1999). Effects of two shared-reading interventions on emergent literacy skills of at-risk preschoolers. *Journal of Early Intervention, 22*(4), 306–322.

Lonigan, C. J., Bloomfield, B. G., Anthony, J. L., Bacon, K. D., Phillips, B. M., & Samwel, C. S. (1999). Relations among emergent literacy skills, behavior problems, and social competence in preschool children from low-and middle-income backgrounds. *Topics for Early Childhood Special Education, 19*(1), 40–53.

Lonigan, C. J., Burgess, S. R., Anthony, J. L., Barker, T. A., Dyer, S., Carr, C., et al. (1998). Development of phonological sensitivity in 2-to 5-year-old children. *Journal of Educational Psychology, 90*(2), 294–311.

Lyon, G. R. (2002). Reading development, reading difficulties, and reading instruction educational and public health issues. *Journal of School Psychology, 40*(1), 3–6.

Mashburn, A. J., Hamre, B. K., Downer, J. T., Justice, L. M., & Pianta, R. C. (2010). *Teachers' use of web-based professional development resources and children's language and literacy development.* Manuscript under review.

Mashburn, A. J., Pianta, R. C., Hamre, B. K., Downer, J. T., Barbarin, O., Bryant, D., et al. (2008). Measures of classroom quality in prekindergarten and children's development of academic, language, and social skills. *Child Development, 79*(3), 732–749.

Moats, L. C. (1994). The missing foundation in teacher education: Knowledge of the structure of spoken and written language. *Annals of Dyslexia, 44*(1), 81–102.

Morrison, F. J., & Connor, C. M. (2002). Understanding schooling effects on early literacy: A working research strategy. *Journal of School Psychology, 40*(6), 493–500.

Nash, M., & Donaldson, M. L. (2005). Word learning in children with vocabulary deficits. *Journal of Speech, Language, and Hearing Research, 48*(2), 439–458.

National Association for the Education of Young Children. (2009). Developmentally appropriate practice in early childhood programs serving children from birth through age 8. Retrieved February 24, 2009, from *www.naeyc.org/about/positions.asp.*

National Council on Teacher Quality. (2004). Increasing the odds: How good policies can yield better teachers. Retrieved September 29, 2009, from *www.nctq.org/p/publications/reports.jsp.*

National Early Childhood Accountability Task Force. (2005). *Taking stock: Assessing and improving early childhood learning and program quality.* Philadelphia: Pew Charitable Trusts, Foundation for Child Development, the Joyce Foundation.

National Early Literacy Panel. (2004, December). The National Early Literacy Panel: Findings from a synthesis of scientific research on early literacy development (Chairs), *The National Early Literacy Panel: Findings from a synthesis of scientific research on early literacy development.* Symposium conducted at the meeting of the National Reading Conference, San Antonio, TX.

National Early Literacy Panel. (2009). *Developing early literacy: Report of the National Early Literacy Panel.* Jessup, MD: National Institute for Literacy.

NICHD Early Child Care Research Network. (2000). The relation of child care to cognitive and language development. *Child Development, 71*(4), 960–980.

NICHD Early Child Care Research Network. (2002a). Child-care structure process outcome: Direct and indirect effects of child-care quality on young children's development. *Psychological Science, 13*(3), 199–206.

NICHD Early Child Care Research Network. (2002b). The relation of global first-grade classroom environment to structural classroom features and teacher and student behaviors. *Elementary School Journal, 102*(5), 367–387.

NICHD Early Child Care Research Network. (2005). A day in third grade: A large-scale study of classroom quality and teacher and student behavior. *Elementary School Journal, 105*(3), 305–323.

Notari-Syverson, A., O'Connor, R. E., & Vadasy, P. F. (1998). *Ladders to literacy: A preschool activity book.* Baltimore: Brookes.

Odden, A., Archibald, S., Fermanich, M., & Gallagher, H. A. (2002). A cost framework for professional development. *Journal of Education Finance, 28*(1), 51–74.

Peisner-Feinberg, E., & Burchinal, M. (1997). Relations between preschool children's child care experiences and concurrent development: The cost, quality, and outcomes study. *Merrill–Palmer Quarterly, 43*, 451–477.

Penno, J. F., Wilkinson, I. A. G., & Moore, D. W. (2002). Vocabulary acquisition from teacher explanation and repeated listening to stories: Do they overcome the Matthew effect? *Journal of Educational Psychology, 94*(1), 23–33.

Pianta, R. C. (2006). Standardized observation and professional development: A focus on individualized implementation and practices. In M. Zaslow & I. Martinez-Beck (Eds.), *Critical issues in early childhood professional development* (pp. 231–254). Baltimore: Brookes.

Pianta, R. C., Howes, C., Burchinal, M., Bryant, D., Clifford, R., Early, D., et al. (2005). Features of pre-kindergarten programs, classrooms, and teachers: Do they predict observed classroom quality and child–teacher interactions? *Applied Developmental Science, 9*(3), 144–159.

Pianta, R. C., La Paro, K. M., & Hamre, B. K. (2008). *Classroom Assessment Scoring System.* Baltimore: Brookes.

Pianta, R. C., La Paro, K. M., Payne, C., Cox, M. J., & Bradley, R. (2002). The relation of kindergarten classroom environment to teacher, family, and school characteristics and child outcomes. *Elementary School Journal, 102*(3), 225–238.

Pianta, R. C., Mashburn, A. J., Downer, J. T., Hamre, B. K., & Justice, L. (2008). Effects of web-mediated professional development resources on teacher–child interactions in pre-kindergarten classrooms. *Early Childhood Research Quarterly, 23*, 431–451.

Ramey, S. L., & Ramey, C. T. (2006). Creating and sustaining a high-quality workforce in child care, early intervention, and school readiness programs. In M. Zaslow & I. Martinez-Beck (Eds.), *Critical issues in early childhood professional development* (pp. 355–368). Baltimore: Brookes.

Reese, E., & Cox, A. (1999). Quality of adult book reading affects children's emergent literacy. *Developmental Psychology, 35*, 20–28.

Robbins, C., & Ehri, L. C. (1994). Reading storybooks to kindergartners helps them learn new vocabulary words. *Journal of Educational Psychology, 86*(1), 54–64.

Schatschneider, C., Fletcher, J. M., Francis, D. J., Carlson, C. D., & Foorman, B. R. (2004). Kindergarten prediction of reading skills: A longitudinal comparative analysis. *Journal of Educational Psychology, 96*(2), 265–282.

Sénéchal, M. (1997). The differential effect of storybook reading on preschoolers' acquisition of expressive and receptive vocabulary. *Journal of Child Language, 24*, 123–138.

Snow, C. E., Hamphill, L., & Barnes, W. S. (Eds.). (1991). *Unfulfilled expectations: Home and school influences on literacy.* Cambridge, MA: Harvard University Press.

Snowling, M. J., Gallagher, A., & Frith, U. (2003). Family risk of dyslexia is continuous: Individual differences in the precursors of reading skill. *Child Development, 74*, 358–373.

Storch, S. A., & Whitehurst, G. J. (2002). Oral language and code-related precursors to reading: Evidence from a longitudinal structural model. *Developmental Psychology, 38*(6), 934–947.

Sylva, K., Siraj-Blatchford, I., Taggart, B., Sammons, P., Melhuish, E., Elliot, K., et al. (2006). Capturing quality in early childhood through environmental rating scales. *Early Childhood Research Quarterly, 21*(1), 76–92.

Torgesen, J. K. (1998, Spring/Summer). Catch them before they fall: Identification and assessment to prevent reading failure in young children. *American Educator*, pp. 1–8.

Ukrainetz, T. A., Cooney, M. H., Dyer, S. K., Kysar, A. J., & Harris, T. J. (2000). An investigation into teaching phonemic awareness through shared reading and writing. *Early Childhood Research Quarterly, 15*(3), 331–355.

U.S. Department of Education. (2000). *America's kindergartens: Findings from the Early Childhood Longitudinal Study, kindergarten class of 1998–99, Fall 1999.* Washington, DC: National Center for Education Statistics.

van Kleeck, A., Gillam, R. B., & McFadden, T. U. (1998). A study of classroom-based phonological awareness training for preschoolers with speech and/or language disorders. *American Journal of Speech–Language Pathology, 7*(3), 65–76.

Vernon-Feagans, L. (1996). *Children's talk in communities and classrooms.* Cambridge, MA: Blackwell.

Wasik, B. A., & Bond, M. A. (2001). Beyond the pages of a book: Interactive book reading and language development in preschool classrooms. *Journal of Educational Psychology, 93*(2), 243–250.

Wasik, B. A., Bond, M. A., & Hindman, A. (2006). The effects of a language and literacy intervention on Head Start children and teachers. *Journal of Educational Psychology, 98*(1), 63.

Whitaker, S., Kinzie, M., Kraft-Sayre, M. E., Mashburn, A., & Pianta, R. C. (2007). Use and evaluation of web-based professional development services across participant levels of support. *Early Childhood Education Journal, 34*(6), 379–386.

Whitebook, M., Bellm, D., Lee, Y., & Sakai, L. (2005). *Time to revamp and expand: Early childhood teacher preparation programs in California's institutions of higher education.* Berkeley: Center for the Study of Child Care Employment, University of California at Berkeley.

Whitehurst, G. J., Falco, F. L., Lonigan, C. J., Fischel, J. E., DeBaryshe, B. D., Valdez-Menchaca, M. C., et al. (1988). Accelerating language development through picture book reading. *Developmental Psychology, 24*(4), 552–559.

Whitehurst, G. J., & Lonigan, C. J. (1998). Child development and emergent literacy. *Child Development, 69*(3), 848–872.

Whitehurst, G. J., Zevenbergen, A. A., Crone, D. A., Schultz, M. D., Velting, O. N., & Fischel, J. E. (1999). Outcomes of an emergent literacy intervention from Head Start through second grade. *Journal of Educational Psychology, 91*, 261–272.

Zaslow, M., & Martinez-Beck, I. (Eds.). (2006). *Critical issues in early childhood professional development.* Baltimore: Brookes.

21

Identifying Critical Components of an Effective Preschool Language and Literacy Coaching Intervention

BARBARA A. WASIK
ANNEMARIE H. HINDMAN

Quality language and literacy preschool experiences are critical for young children, but especially for children in poverty, who are at increased risk for school failure. A highly skilled, knowledgeable teacher is the most effective means of providing these experiences. Unfortunately, although the knowledge base on teaching and learning for young children has grown considerably over the last two decades, far less is known about how best to help teachers effectively implement these instructional practices in their classrooms. This is especially true with regard to the creation of exceptional language and literacy environments, which require pedagogically unique approaches to discourse with young children that can differ dramatically from the patterns of language exchange typically used in classrooms. One promising professional development (PD) practice to help teachers implement language-rich strategies is coaching, or ongoing, job-embedded, expert support and guidance (International Reading Association, 2004), paired with training in specific concepts and techniques. Despite its increasing popularity, however, myriad questions remain about components and characteristics that are critical for effective coaching, and strategies in which teachers must be coached if they are to create language-rich classrooms with measureable, positive impacts on children.

In this chapter, we describe one coaching model of PD for preschool teachers—*Exceptional Coaching for Early Language and Literacy* (ExCELL; previously Early Learning Partnership [ELP])—which has demonstrated positive effects on teachers' language and literacy instruction and children's vocabulary skills. In particular, we focus on isolating aspects of the model that promote teachers' and children's skills, and highlight remaining questions about how and why this program works. Since the focus of ExCELL is on teaching teachers to support children's language and preliteracy skills, we begin by placing the program in the larger context of vocabulary development in young children, the role of the teacher in that process, and the characteristics of current professional development initiatives that have demonstrated positive impacts on teachers' behaviors and children's early language outcomes.

Vocabulary Development and Children in Poverty

Research in language development and early childhood suggests that there is a strong relationship between the number of opportunities young children have to learn new words, and the depth and breadth of the vocabulary that they know. In turn, children with well-developed vocabularies are more successful in learning to read because knowing the meaning of a word facilitates decoding or recognition of that word, as well as comprehension of the text in which that word appears (Gough, Ehri, & Treiman, 1992; Snow, Burns, & Griffin, 1998). Hart and Risley's seminal work (1995) revealed that children in poverty have fewer conversations with linguistically skilled adults, which limits their opportunities to hear and use language to develop their vocabulary. By the start of kindergarten, there are substantial differences in the vocabulary knowledge of low- and middle-income children (Lee & Burkam, 2002). Moreover, these differences are compounded over time (Alexander, Entwisle, & Horsey, 1997; Stanovich, 1986), such that by the beginning of fourth grade, fully one-half of all children in poverty cannot read at even a basic level (Lee, Grigg, & Donahue, 2007).

Although the early childhood period is a time of potentially rapid vocabulary growth, the process of word learning is quite complex and not automatic. In order to acquire new words, children generally need multiple exposures to new vocabulary in varied, meaningful contexts over time. In fact, some research suggests that children need at least 20 exposures to a novel word to incorporate it into their expressive vocabulary (Childers & Tomasello, 2002). One of the most effective mechanisms for providing such experiences is conversations between children and a more expert adult or peer; these language exchanges are particularly beneficial when children have the chance to use new words and receive feedback on their pronunciation and interpretation (Beals, 1997; Bond & Wasik, 2009). Furthermore, shared book reading, in which a linguistically competent adult or older peer reads a book to a child, is a potentially effective way to expose children to new vocabulary words, and particularly to decontextualized or abstract words that children would not typically encounter in everyday experience (Snow, 1991). Book-reading strategies, such as weaving conversation around the book reading (Lonigan & Whitehurst, 1998; Whitehurst et al., 1994); providing clear, child-friendly explanations of novel words in the book (Elley 1989); revisiting books through repeated readings (Karweit, 1994; Morrow, 1985); and extending the book vocabulary into related class activities (Wasik & Bond, 2001) have been shown to enrich children's vocabulary knowledge.

Preschool Effects on Vocabulary

Given the lack of resources in the homes of many children in poverty (Aikens & Barbarin, 2008; Zaslow, Mariner, Moore, & Oldham, 1998), it is imperative that early schooling experiences provide young children with access to effective opportunities to build vocabulary. Although research in early childhood language and literacy has clearly demonstrated the important impact of vocabulary knowledge on children's developing reading skills, and ultimately their success in school (National Early Literary Panel, 2009; Snow et al., 1998), not enough is known about how to transfer this knowledge effectively into teaching practices to make high-quality early childhood education accessible to young children, and particularly to those in poverty. Data from the Harvard Home–School Study of Language and Literacy Development (Dickinson & Tabors, 2001) indicated that during a free-play activity, 4-year-olds spent just 17% of their time engaged in meaningful conversations with their teacher and 18% of the time talking with peers; they were silent fully 59% of the time. Other studies have identified limited frequency and quality of conversations (Gest, Holland-Coviello, Welsh, Eicher-Catt, & Gill, 2006) and book reading (Dickinson, 2001; Dickinson & Tabors, 2001), and limited access to print and books (Neuman & Celano, 2001). Likely, as a consequence, large-scale analyses of preschool programs, such as the Preschool Curriculum Evaluation Research Consortium report (PCER; 2008), show that, while a few programs promote children's literacy or mathematics skills, none has had significant effects on children's vocabulary.

The transfer of evidenced-based strategies into effective classroom practices is challenging because excellent teachers require a wealth of conceptual and procedural knowledge about subject matter and student learning (Bransford, Brown, & Cocking, 2000; Byrnes, 2001). Simply put, in order to advance children's vocabulary development, teachers need to know *how* children learn words, *what* to do in the classroom to support this learning, *why* these practices are likely to be effective, and *how* to implement and adjust them in ways that result in student learning. Teaching teachers about early vocabulary may be particularly challenging given that teachers may have to change the way that they talk to and interact with young children to foster rich oral language experiences. It would follow, then, that changing teachers' linguistic interaction styles and intentions would best be accomplished through PD that is highly individualized and features consistent, iterative assessment of and feedback about teachers' classroom behaviors, particularly questioning and responding to children. Coaching models offer unique opportunities for this individualization.

Coaching as a Tool for Professional Development

In the past decade, coaching has become the most popular method for training teachers in research-based strategies that promote the development of reading readiness skills (Hall, 2004). Emphasis on and interest in coaching in literacy began in earnest with the work of Joyce and Showers (e.g., 1980, 1982; Showers & Joyce, 1996), who reviewed some 200 studies on teacher training and asserted that the primary features of effective PD are (1) providing teachers with a conceptual rationale for a new concept or technique; (2) modeling or demonstrating that technique; (3) allowing teachers the opportunity to practice that technique in an authentic setting, such as their own classrooms; and (4) providing teachers with structured and/or open-ended feedback on that practice. Given the complexity of these tasks and the limitations of training teachers through written materials aligned with their curricula (Neuman & Dwyer, 2009), 1- or 2-day inservice workshops (Boudah, Logan, & Greenwood, 2001; Lieberman, 1995; Phillips, 2003), or professional coursework (Henk, Morrison, Thornburg, & Raya-Carlton, 2007; Jackson et al., 2006), Joyce and Showers (1982) suggested that a dedicated coach might be necessary to coordinate this effort.

In recent years, millions of federal and state dollars have been allocated to pro-

grams funded by Reading First (RF) and Early Reading First (ERF) initiatives that employ coaching for early childhood teachers around language and literacy. In addition, the International Reading Association (2004), which has developed standards, guidelines, and an online clearinghouse for literacy coaches, has defined a *coach* as "a reading specialist who focuses on providing PD for teachers by giving them the additional support needed to implement various instructional programs and practices" (p. 1). This definition, however, represents a broad umbrella beneath which many distinct interpretations fit, and as a result, coaching models vary dramatically in the characteristics of the coach, the intensity of the coaching, and the method of delivery (e.g., face-to-face contact or video observations with feedback by phone and e-mail). More importantly, language and literacy coaching models vary widely in the content upon which they focus and the sequence in which they present that information (Jackson et al., 2007). Given the variations in coaching, this PD technique can—and does—mean very different things across settings (Hall, 2004).

Recent research has begun to examine more closely the variables associated with effective coaching models. One of the best-studied coaching models, the Literacy Environment Enrichment Program (LEEP), developed by Dickinson and colleagues (Adger, Hoyle, & Dickinson, 2004; Dickinson & Brady, 2006; Dickinson & Caswell, 2007), provided teachers with 45 hours of classes focused on best practices from early literacy research, with a particular focus on enhancing children's language development. Between sessions, teachers completed assignments in their own classrooms and were supported by telephone and e-mail correspondence with coaches. Evaluations of the LEEP model (Adger et al., 2004; Dickinson & Brady, 2005; Dickinson & Caswell, 2007) indicated large improvements in teachers' language classroom environments but did not examine the relations between teachers' practices and children's language and literacy outcomes—especially vocabulary skills. Building on this work, Neuman and Cunningham (2009) compared the effects on teachers' practices of 45 hours of coursework relative to onsite expert coaching plus coursework, or a business-as-usual model. Results showed that coursework plus coaching elicited the greatest gains in educators' techniques. The impact of these coaching models on child outcomes was not evaluated.

Using a different delivery model for coaching, the MyTeachingPartner model (Pianta, Mashburn, Downer, Hamre, & Justice, 2008) connected teachers with offsite coaches, who viewed and critiqued videotapes of teachers' classroom practices. Using the Classroom Assessment Scoring System (CLASS; Pianta, La Paro, & Hamre, 2006) as a guide, coaches provided teachers with extensive feedback on their videotapes via the Internet. Evaluations of this program (Pianta et al., 2008) showed that those who received coaching made greater gains in instructional quality (including language use in the classroom), as well as in sensitivity and organization, than did peers who did not receive coaching but did have access to videos of exemplary classroom practices. At present, however, no data from randomized control trials link the MyTeachingPartner coaching intervention to children's literacy learning, although one promising correlational study (Hamre et al., 2010) shows that, among children whose teachers received coaching, literacy growth over the year was greater when teachers provided more of the target instructional practices.

Other PD models have examined the impact of coaching on teachers, as well as children. The ERF initiative, a federally funded grant program, required that grantees implement a coaching model in their interventions, although individual grantees were able to determine the specifics of their coaching model (e.g., amount of time coaches spent with teachers, content of the coaching sessions). Analyses (Jackson et al., 2007) showed that these interventions had positive impacts on teachers' classroom practices, including the language and literacy environments they provided for children, their classroom instructional practices, and their use of assessment. In turn, children whose educators participated in ERF programs had stronger print and letter knowledge than peers whose teachers did not receive this training. However, children in ERF classrooms were no different from peers on vocabulary skills.

Similarly, a valuable recent study by Powell, Diamond, Burchinal, and Koehler

(2010) compared the learning of Head Start preschool teachers and their students from distance-based coaching (as in MyTeachingPartner) relative to in-person coaching or a business-as-usual model. After biweekly coaching sessions focused on oral language and code-focused (letter and sound) skills, teachers who received either Web-mediated or onsite coaching demonstrated stronger language and literacy environments than teachers in a business-as-usual control. Furthermore, children in classrooms that received coaching outperformed peers in the business-as-usual condition on code-related skills; effects were of a large magnitude. Interestingly, however, teachers' use of language in the classroom did not differ across conditions, nor did children's vocabulary skills.

In contrast, different results emerged from an evaluation of the Center for Improving the Readiness of Children for Learning and Education (CIRCLE) training (Landry, Swank, Smith, Assel, & Gunnewig, 2006), which provided teachers with instruction over the course of 1–2 years, as well as training and in-person coaching in their own classrooms, through which they could receive feedback on their implementation of the target practices. Results of an initial study (Landry et al., 2006) showed gains for the majority of children in both expressive and receptive language, particularly after teachers had received 2 years of training rather than only one. In a follow-up study, Landry, Anthony, Swank, and Monseque-Bailey (2009) found that teachers' and children's skills grew most substantially when they received training and coaching, as well as progress-monitoring information about children's skills. Children in this most comprehensive condition demonstrated significant medium-size gains in literacy skills and vocabulary.

In summary, the developing research base on coaching as a tool to build early childhood teachers' instructional competence and preschoolers' vocabulary skills suggests that the variations in coaching differentially impact teachers' practices, particularly language interactions with children, as well as children's acquisition of vocabulary. However, it is not yet clear which features of coaching models actually distinguish methods that produce vocabulary effects from those that do not because programs differ from one another in their content, modes, and intensity of delivery, duration, and outcomes assessed. Ultimately, the field requires an understanding of what features or "active ingredients" of coaching models of PD produce changes in teachers' knowledge and practice, and what aspects of classroom instruction drive gains in children's vocabulary learning that would help us to efficiently allot resources to coaching.

In an effort to illuminate this issue, we describe one intensive, comprehensive coaching model of professional development— ExCELL, which has repeatedly shown significant effects on children's vocabulary skills even after only 1 year of PD for teachers. This model is also distinctive because a central focus has involved "unpacking" the most critical features of this multifaceted intervention by developing and testing a series of measures of teachers' knowledge and practice, and children's outcomes that elucidate processes of change that underlie the effects of this program.

Exceptional Coaching for Early Language and Literacy

The ExCELL program is a PD model that uses one-on-one coaching and group workshops to train teachers serving low-income communities to enhance young children's language and literacy development. The core principles of ExCELL are grounded in Vygotsky's (1978) theory of learning, as well as the Bransford and colleagues (2000) model presented in *How People Learn*. In brief, the program provides teachers with multiple supports to engender and sustain positive changes in their teaching and, as a consequence, in children's learning. The one-on-one coaching assesses what teachers know and can do, identifying their zones of proximal development. Their subsequent learning is iteratively scaffolded and assessed through individualized, ongoing guidance in their own classrooms that helps them to acquire conceptual and procedural understanding of language and literacy instruction, and to create high-quality, linguistically rich classrooms. Teachers also work closely with peers during the training process to build networks of excellent practitioners that can maintain these conceptual and procedural transformations after the intervention ends.

Similar to Landry and colleagues' (2006) CIRCLE training, ExCELL training takes place over 2 years, allowing teachers ample time to learn and assimilate their new knowledge into classroom practices (Clements, 2007). ExCELL has focused on Head Start teachers, whose varying educational backgrounds, credentials, and levels of experience necessitate the opportunities for individualization that coaching provides. ExCELL provides teachers with conceptual and procedural knowledge regarding oral language development, interactive book reading, phonemic awareness, alphabetic knowledge, and writing. However, in light of findings that adult–child dialog can be rare in preschools (Dickinson & Smith, 1991; Gest et al., 2006; Wasik & Bond, 2001), special attention is devoted to language and vocabulary development. Consequently, a common refrain in the training is that teachers must engineer meaningful opportunities for children to hear and use new words.

In addition to (1) coaching and group training, ExCELL includes (2) routine assessments of teachers' conceptual knowledge and beliefs, (3) systematic fidelity checks to ensure that the teachers are implementing the strategies as intended in their own classrooms, (4) global program fidelity and instructional quality measures, (5) suggested lesson plans with books and supporting materials, (6) a curriculum-embedded assessment system to provide feedback to teachers on children's performance, and (7) a family literacy component.

Coaching and Training

All of the coaches in ExCELL had qualifications and experience equivalent to master teachers, including bachelor's degrees in education and master's degrees in early childhood education. In addition, they had at least 5 years of experience in the classroom and 10 additional years working in early childhood education. Each coach worked with approximately five to six teachers. Before coaches worked with teachers, they received extensive training in the goals and methods of ExCELL from the lead coach, who was also an initial developer of the ExCELL model. Coaches were provided reading material, as well as videotapes of effective practices. New coaches, who were beginning to work with teachers, also observed the lead coach working with teachers in the classroom. This training was completed throughout the fall of the first year of the project. Thereafter, coaches met as a team at least once per week, along with the project coordinators and the lead researchers, to discuss issues related to teachers, classrooms, and children. Furthermore, coaches were provided at least one 2-hour PD session each month that included reading and discussing current research articles, examining new programs or techniques in the field, and reviewing supervision strategies that are key to effective coaching.

ExCELL coaches begin working with teachers during the summer prior to the beginning of the Head Start school year. Lead teachers and assistants participate in a 2-day summer literacy institute that outlines the goals, procedures, and expectations of the project. During each month of the 9-month school year, coaches provide a 3-hour group training session for the teachers, focused on one aspect of early language and literacy (e.g., asking questions during book reading, helping children to focus on rimes). During this training, teachers are presented with a conceptual explanation of the topic, along with specific strategies and activities for implementing effective instruction on this language and literacy topic in their classrooms. For example, in the interactive book reading module, Head Start teachers are guided through explanations of how book reading contributes to language development, as well as different kinds of questions to ask during reading. Finally, teachers reflect on their own practices and plan with their classroom teaching teams how to implement these practices in their own classrooms.

In addition to monthly trainings, ExCELL coaches visit each teacher's classroom for an average of 3 hours per week. During these visits, coaches model the target strategies addressed in the most recent workshop; modeling generally requires about 1 hour. Teachers observe the coach's modeling and use a checklist indicating the key behaviors on which the training focused. For example, the checklist for questioning during book reading taps into whether children were (1) asked open-ended questions, (2) prompted to make predictions, and (3) encouraged to explain recently learned vocabulary words. Coaches and teachers then conference together to discuss the modeling experience and help teach-

ers incorporate these new techniques into their own classrooms. Thereafter, teachers practice the strategies for 1 week, and the coach returns to each classroom to observe and videotape the teacher. The coach employs the same checklist that teachers used previously during modeling, then meets with each teacher to review the checklist and the videotape of the day's instruction. Coaches provide feedback on teachers' implementation of these strategies, discuss how teachers made decisions while implementing the strategies, and confer about areas of success and of potential improvement.

Routine Assessments of Teachers' Conceptual Knowledge and Beliefs

An ongoing, important part of ExCELL is its explicit focus on assessment of teacher knowledge and beliefs about target strategies. Teachers' conceptual knowledge impacts their instructional decisions (Ball, 1992; Cunningham, Perry, Stanovich, & Stanovich, 2004), and tracking the development of this knowledge allows coaches to individualize training better. First, at the start of the summer institute, teachers complete a 50-question, multiple-choice assessment, with 10 questions directed toward each of the five modules of the PD sequence. After each group training, teachers respond to the 5–10 questions from this assessment that are relevant to that day's material, so that their knowledge can be compared to their baseline and to a criterion of 80% correct to demonstrate proficiency. Coaches use data to correct misconceptions and provide review. At the end of the year, teachers respond to all 50 questions again, with slight changes in wording, to gauge drift in their recall.

In addition, in the fall and spring of the school year, teachers respond to a Teacher Beliefs Questionnaire (TBQ) about language and literacy. This questionnaire taps teachers' ideas regarding how children develop vocabulary, phonemic awareness, letter knowledge, and writing skills, as well as how various instructional practices (e.g., book reading, nursery rhymes) can be used in the preschool classroom. Each of the 20 items on the questionnaire features a statement such as, "As a teacher, I believe that Head Start children . . . need to hear the same story more than once or twice to learn new words" or " . . . should not waste time scribbling and drawing when they can be learning to write" (reverse-coded); teachers rate their agreement on a 5-point scale.

Assessments of Fidelity of Teachers' Instructional Practices

In addition to being videotaped during weekly observations, each teacher is observed and videotaped at four other times per year as he or she conducts a book reading, a circle time activity, a morning message, and a center activity. The aim of these observations is to shift attention from the narrow focus on particular practices and capture classroom quality more broadly, and these videos are analyzed to determine the nature and quality of teacher–child interactions. The coach first reviews the tape, then prepares feedback for the teacher. In their weekly meeting, the teacher and coach review the tape together and discuss both the successful practices and the areas in need of improvement. In particular, they discuss why the teacher chose specific practices, and the coach helps to guide the teacher toward reasoning that is grounded in best practices.

Global Measures of Fidelity to the Intervention and Classroom Quality

A fidelity measure, aligned with the training, is used to rate the degree to which teachers' classroom practices are consistent with the strategies emphasized in the group training and coaching. The measure incorporates all of the checklists with which teachers are observed for each of the five training modules (oral language and vocabulary development, book reading, phonological sensitivity, alphabetic knowledge, and writing). For example, following the training on oral language development, teachers are observed while they converse with children and are evaluated on the extent to which they ask open-ended questions, explain vocabulary, and probe children's responses; these items appear on the global fidelity measures as well. Independent observers conduct these measures in fall and spring, and are trained to achieve 90% reliability.

More global still, at the conclusion of each year of the intervention, coaches assign each teacher a fidelity score (1 = *low*, 2 = *average*, 3 = *high*) rating his or her performance on each training module. These five values are averaged into a mean fidelity score for each teacher, reflecting his or her overall understanding and implementation of the ExCELL content and practices over the previous year. This information can be used to plan for subsequent years of coaching, as well as to explore how teachers' fidelity moderates ExCELL's effects on children's learning.

In addition, a broader measure of classroom quality is obtained in the fall and spring of each program year, as a trained independent assessor administers the Early Language and Literacy Classroom Observation (ELLCO; Smith, Dickinson, Sangeorge, & Anastasopoulos, 2002) and the CLASS (Pianta et al., 2006) in each classroom. First, the ELLCO gauges the language and literacy opportunities in the classroom, including children's access to books and writing experiences. In addition, the CLASS Instructional Support subtest focuses on concept development, quality of feedback, and language modeling, and provides a snapshot of the quality of the linguistic interactions available to the children. Both measures, then, systematically assess the language and literacy opportunities provided to preschoolers in each classroom, but from different perspectives.

Materials and Lesson Plans

In addition to coaching, ExCELL provides materials that support language and literacy development, particularly through book reading and vocabulary learning. Teachers receive prop boxes that reflect typical classroom themes (e.g., back to school, the season of fall, visiting the farm, community helpers, transportation). In total, more than 20 prop boxes are available, and teachers can choose the boxes that best support themes they are implementing. Each prop box includes a theme guide detailing theme-related activities that serve as implicit PD. Theme guides are designed as daily schedules that can be easily adapted by teachers, and they outline theme-related book reading and phonemic awareness activities, as well as center (e.g., art, science, dramatic play) and family involvement activities. In particular, guides include a list of approximately 25 words, identified by ExCELL teachers and program staff as key to understanding concepts in that theme and likely to be unfamiliar to children. For example, during the fall theme, children might learn words such as *leaves, autumn, rake,* and *jacket*. Teachers receive training on using these words in multiple contexts around the room to make the vocabulary come alive. Materials also include a selection of theme-related books from various genres (e.g., including fictional, informational, and concept books) that highlight these target words. Concrete objects representing the target words are also provided (e.g., leaves, a small plastic rake, a small jacket that would fit a doll), and theme guides lead teachers to use these materials with children before and after book readings to highlight new vocabulary, as well as to place these materials around the room during center time and free play.

Child Progress Monitoring

In addition to coaching and materials, a trained assessor administers a curriculum-based progress-monitoring measure to each child three times per year. The measure consists of three parts: (1) 10 randomly selected vocabulary words from the words that were key to themes about which children have been learning; (2) 26 uppercase letters of the alphabet, similar to the Phonological Awareness Literacy Screening (PALS); and (3) a brief beginning and ending sound awareness measure, modeled on the Get It, Got It, Go! measure (Missall & McConnell, 2004). The assessments require only 10 minutes per child, so teachers can feasibly administer them. Coaches help teachers to interpret and use these data to identify concepts that were not adequately communicated to the whole group, as well as to individual children who would benefit from additional support. In particular, ExCELL coaches help teachers to engineer small-group activities that allow them to work with children who encountered difficulty on the progress-monitoring assessment. For example, children with the lowest letter knowledge might receive additional small-group opportunities to learn about letters through activities, such as constructing letters out of pre-made shapes.

Family Literacy Component

Finally, since families play an important role in children's learning about vocabulary and other skills (Hart & Risley, 1995), as well as being central to the mission of Head Start

to help families support children's learning, ExCELL provides families with information and activities coordinated with the classroom instruction. In particular, at the start of each new theme, families receive a colorful, reader-friendly handout explaining the focus of the current theme (e.g., spring, fall, creatures in the ocean) and the list of about 20 vocabulary words that will be targeted during that theme. The handout also explains an activity (e.g., book reading, conversation, local trip to a free community organization) through which families might promote children's learning of these target words and concepts. In addition, a classroom lending library is made available to parents to encourage home reading. Each book in the lending library includes a family reading guide that highlights target vocabulary and suggests questions for parents to ask while reading with children.

Furthermore, we have developed a brief family literacy survey for Head Start centers to administer to families at the beginning of the year (Wasik & Hindman, 2010). The easy-to-read questionnaire asks families how often (from *never* to *daily*) they engage children in about 10 different language and literacy learning activities, such as reading books, conversing, or singing.

Program Findings

ExCELL, with its explicit supports for teachers' learning, construction of communities of learning among teachers, individualization for learners, and routine use of assessment to support these aims, provides teachers with conceptual and procedural knowledge that fosters vocabulary and preliteracy skills in young children. To determine the impact of ExCELL on both teachers and children, Head Start centers were randomly assigned to either intervention or control groups (Wasik & Bond, 2001; Wasik, Bond, & Hindman, 2006; Wasik & Hindman, 2010a). Teachers in both conditions were assessed in fall and spring on their knowledge and beliefs about early language and literacy, and both the ELLCO and the CLASS were administered in every classroom at both time points. Throughout the intervention, teachers were videotaped during book reading, circle time, center time, and morning message. Finally, all children were assessed on the Peabody

Picture Vocabulary Test–III (PPVT-III), PALS, and a measure of alphabetic knowledge at the start and at the end of the year, and their curriculum-specific progress was gauged at three points over the year.

One of the important results of our recent work is that children in ExCELL classrooms outperformed their peers in vocabulary, a hard-to-change skills area of import for later school success (Wasik et al., 2006; Wasik & Hindman, 2009, 2010a). These effects, observed on standardized measures such as the PPVT-III and the Expressive One-Word Picture Vocabulary Test, are of moderate to large magnitude. Moreover, fully 75% of children whose initial vocabulary scores fell 1.5 standard deviations below the national mean ended the year with scores in excess of that high-risk zone, whereas only 50% of the highest risk children in the comparison group made the same gains. Beyond vocabulary, recent evaluations (Wasik & Hindman, 2010a) show benefits of medium size for phonological awareness as well. No significant effects of ExCELL on children's alphabetic knowledge, which receives heavy focus in most Head Start classrooms, have been observed.

It is significant that ExCELL produces gains in children's vocabulary, particularly because coaching models do not always show effects in this area, and especially because this population of children is arguably in the greatest need of such gains. However, the value of these findings is limited if we do not understand why these gains occurred. In other words, what specific teacher features or behaviors—including teachers' knowledge and beliefs about language and literacy or their conversations with children—resulted in students in ExCELL classrooms learning more vocabulary words? A series of recent analyses shed light on the aspects of teachers' knowledge and instructional practices that contributed to these gains.

Apart from child outcomes, we have also investigated effects of ExCELL on teachers' procedural competence and conceptual understanding. Teachers who participated in ExCELL demonstrated stronger classroom instructional quality relative to nonintervention teachers. Not surprisingly, teachers who participated in the intervention concluded the academic year with significantly higher fidelity scores than peers who did not participate in the intervention; in other words, teachers in the intervention demonstrated more of the target practices upon which they were trained. This finding implies that (1) intervention teachers did learn and implement the strategies that they were taught, and (2) comparison teachers were not implementing the same strategies in the absence of this training.

Even more striking, intervention teachers showed significantly greater gains on global measures of the language and literacy environment (based on the ELLCO) and instructional quality (based on the CLASS). Specifically, when researchers controlled for classroom environments in the fall (before the intervention was underway) and for teacher background factors, teachers who participated in the ExCELL intervention demonstrated greater availability and use of writing materials. No differences between groups were apparent regarding the availability and use of books. Since both conditions received the same supplies of books, these findings would be expected. The difference between conditions in spring language and literacy environments was large, with intervention participation uniquely predicting an advantage of three-fourths of a standard deviation in year-end ELLCO scores. Differences were largely a result of access to writing materials and activities intimately tied to phonological sensitivity and letter knowledge, which was considerably greater in the intervention classrooms.

In addition, teachers in intervention classrooms demonstrated higher scores in spring on the CLASS measure of instructional quality, when researchers controlled for fall scores and background factors (Wasik & Hindman, 2010a). Gains for each of the three CLASS subtests were large in magnitude, with the greatest differences (more than one-half SD) between conditions apparent in the quality of teachers' language modeling for children, including descriptive talk, open-ended questions, expansion/extension, and use of sophisticated or rare language and vocabulary. This finding is important because these language use practices can be difficult to change (Honig & Martin, 2009; Massey, Pence, Justice, & Bowles, 2008), and are closely linked to children's vocabulary learning. In addition, teachers who participated in ExCELL outperformed their peers by one-half of a standard deviation on quality of feedback, which refers to the degree to which teachers' responses to children's remarks or behaviors engender greater understanding rather than simply assessing accuracy. Finally, ExCELL teachers demonstrated stronger concept development, or greater emphasis on higher-order reasoning and creative problem solving rather than rote learning; here, ExCELL teachers scored one-half of a standard deviation higher than the comparison group.

Data also show that children's vocabulary learning varied with teachers' fidelity to the intervention, with children of low-fidelity teachers showing the smallest gains, whereas those with teachers who implemented the strategies with average or high fidelity showed greater gains. Similar patterns emerged for instructional quality. In summary, the intervention promoted both global quality and implementation of the target instructional practices, and both of these factors explained vocabulary learning disparities between children in the intervention and comparison conditions. In other words, it appears that teacher behaviors, specifically, the use of language in the classroom, were significantly changed by the coaching intervention and may in turn have impacted child outcomes.

In order understand the nature of the change in teachers' use of language and vocabulary, and how this potentially affected children's vocabulary, teachers' book reading practices, which show well-established links to children's vocabulary development, were closely examined. Analyses indicated that teachers who participated in ExCELL afforded children significantly more opportunities to talk, both by responding to teachers' remarks and by volunteering their own spontaneous discussion, than did teachers who did not experience the intervention (Wasik & Hindman, 2010b). In turn, this child talk explained much of the vocabulary disparity between the intervention and comparison conditions. This is significant for two reasons. One is that a primary focus of ExCELL's training and coaching was on guiding teachers to understand the importance of talking with children and to employ instructional strategies that promoted children's use of language. These data suggest that teachers benefited from this aspect of coaching and effectively demonstrated these behaviors. Second, changes in teachers' language and communication had an impact on children's opportunities to speak and use language. For children who may have limited opportunities at home to use language, these classroom experiences are important.

Research exploring the predictive power of teachers' book-related talk relative to children's vocabulary skills in ExCELL is ongoing. However, it is interesting to note that in both the comparison and intervention conditions, both teachers' book-related discussion and extension activities were predictive of children's vocabulary learning, representing moderate to large effect sizes. In particular, the more decontextualized, abstract language that teachers used, the more vocabulary children learned over the course of the year. In contrast, contextualized, or more concrete, talk was predictive of word learning only for children who began Head Start with the lowest vocabulary skills. Finally, the more connections teachers engineered between the book being read and the larger curriculum, likely providing children with opportunities to hear and use new words in multiple, coordinated contexts, the more vocabulary growth children experienced. Forthcoming analyses will explore differences in the frequency with which teachers in each condition used contextualized and decontextualized language, and connected books to the curriculum. Moreover, we will examine whether these features of book reading might make greater contributions to the vocabulary learning of children in the intervention because teachers were guided in strategic use of this talk. In summary, these findings suggest that active ingredients of ExCELL classrooms include teachers' language and literacy instructional practices, including book-related discussion and invitations for children to talk.

Beyond teachers' practices, we have also explored teachers' conceptual knowledge about how children learn, and how they should be taught language and literacy. Specifically, analyses (Hindman & Wasik, 2010) of the 50-item teacher knowledge questionnaires administered in the fall and spring of the school year indicated that intervention and comparison teachers were no different in their knowledge in the fall, before the intervention began, and that there was substantial variation in knowledge across both conditions. However, teachers in the intervention showed stronger knowledge growth over the course of the year. Specifically, intervention participation accounted for a change of about one-fourth of standard deviation in the total knowledge score, over and above factors such as teachers' education and experience. Gains were greatest on subscales of the knowledge measure addressing books and book reading (when teachers who participated in the intervention outscored their peers by one-third of a standard deviation) and writing (when ExCELL teachers grew fully one-half of a standard deviation more than peers in the control condition). Given the focus of the ExCELL intervention on these aspects of the language and literacy environment, these gains in teachers' knowledge appear to be related to the coaching.

Regarding teachers' beliefs, all ExCELL teachers differed substantially before the intervention but, on average, beliefs were more consistent with evidence from research where instruction was concerned (Hindman & Wasik, 2008). For example, teachers generally understood that nursery rhymes and word games were a more appropriate and likely more effective strategy than rote memorization, for teaching children about phonemic awareness, and that book reading was a way to teach children new words. Conversely, teachers were more likely to hold misconceptions about how children's development progressed and why particular techniques were likely to be more or less effective. For example, many teachers were uncertain about the trajectory by which children learned to attend to different sounds in words, or the fact that vocabulary knowledge helps children read fluently. Future work on both knowledge and belief will explore how these factors account, directly or indirectly (e.g., through instruction), for changes in children's vocabulary knowledge.

To further understand the role of teachers' language in children's vocabulary development, teacher–child discourse in activities that reach beyond the book reading experience, such as morning message and center time, are also being examined.

Thus, data on the ExCELL intervention are promising, showing that best practices can be translated to teachers with limited education who are serving children with the greatest need. Despite recurrent findings in the literature indicating that language and literacy interventions often do not benefit Head Start children (Jackson et al., 2006; Powell et al., 2010), especially in the area of vocabulary, these data show that Head Start children can learn substantial vocabulary over the course of a single academic year when instruction is carefully designed to develop and reinforce vocabulary through explicit questioning and conversation strategies woven around rich themes. Furthermore, we are beginning to tease apart how, in the context of the ExCELL coaching model of professional development, effects on children's vocabulary are attributable to particular teacher practices shaped by the intervention.

Although the focus of this work has been on conceptual and procedural knowledge of the teachers and the vocabulary skills of the children, we know far less about the other critical piece of the puzzle in this and other coaching-based PD models: how the coach–teacher relationship affects teachers' practices. Other questions remain as well, all of which have the potential to inform our understanding of how coaching operates on teachers and children, and how this resource-intensive intervention can be best evaluated and streamlined.

Understanding the Role of Coaching in Teacher Change

To date, there is evidence that coaching can build teachers' and children's knowledge. However, the utility of coaching, and this method of PD more broadly, is limited by many unanswered questions because mechanisms by which coaching engenders change, and features that distinguish maximally effective coaching, remain something of a black box.

How Should Coaching Be Delivered?

Research on ExCELL and other coaching-based models of PD generally suggests that coaching is effective, although there is considerable room to compare different methods of coaching. For example, how much coaching time does a teacher need to implement language and literacy strategies effectively? Is more always better, or is there a point at which returns begin to diminish? Some models, such as the CIRCLE project, have yielded positive results on teachers' instruction and children's skills, including language, with fewer than the 3 hours per week of coaching found in ExCELL (Landry et al., 2006, 2009).

ExCELL has provided only face-to-face coaching, although there is evidence (Powell et al., 2010) that coaching via the Web, in which videotapes of teachers' practices are observed by experts in place of site visits, may be equally effective for literacy outcomes. As yet, no study has explored whether a face-to-face coaching intervention that promotes teachers' language practices and children's vocabulary skills can be translated into a Web-mediated design, preserving effects on teacher and child outcomes; such research could lay the foundation of optimally time- and cost-efficient coaching. Similarly, technology has been used to provide the training that accompanies coaching. For example, Landry and colleagues (2009) incorporated extensive videotapes of exemplary classroom instruction with commentary into online course work. This approach, as part of a body of other supports, produced positive results. Similarly, HeadsUp! Reading training included workshops provided to Head Start teachers by experts in the field via videoconference, after which education coordinators followed up with teachers individually. Results (Jackson et al., 2006) showed increases in the quality of teachers' practices and in the strength of children's skills at far less cost than a high-intensity coaching model. Variations in how coaching has been delivered highlight several questions that still need to be investigated as our knowledge of coaching unfolds.

Unpacking the Coach–Teacher Relationship

It is thought that the unique value of coaching lies in the inherently individualized relationship between the coach and the teacher (Steckel, 2009). However, if this is the engine that drives the efficacy of coaching, it is important to understand more about what actually occurs during coaching and how the coaching model works to transform teacher practices. At present, our conceptualization of coaching—in other words, what conversa-

tions, modeling, feedback, or other exchanges actually serve as vehicles for information to teachers—is at best an initial framework. In a recent article, Steckel argues that although the literature describes the range of responsibilities for coaches (Dole & Donaldson, 2006; Toll, 2005; Walpole & Blamey, 2008) and the nuances of the social relationships that evolve within the coach–teacher partnership (Rainville & Jones, 2008), the field has not adequately examined what actually goes on in coaching sessions and what it actually takes for coaches to have an impact on teachers, especially within high-poverty schools. Critically, the small extant literature has focused nearly entirely on teachers in grades K–8, leaving many unanswered questions for preschool educators, a unique and important population (Walpole & McKenna, 2004). This information is essential to understanding how programs like ExCELL work and, by extension, could be effectively and efficiently taken to scale. This matter could be effectively examined through close observation of teacher–coach discussions, interviews and surveys of teachers and coaches, and even examinations of coaches' field notes.

Moderation of Effects of Coaching by Factors Related to Coaches

In the studies on coaching, careful descriptions are provided about teachers' education and experience, but remarkably little information is provided about the coaches. When reported, data indicate that coaches typically have advanced degrees in early childhood education and/or literacy, but some have only bachelor's degrees and extensive experience in the field. Just as differences in teachers may play a role in the efficacy of the coach–teacher relationship, it is plausible that characteristics of the coach might as well. To date, no research has assessed coaches' knowledge about language and literacy development and instruction, which could reveal how coaches are screened for their positions. In addition, although fidelity measures are employed to ensure that teachers adhere to target practices, no research has examined the fidelity with which content is communicated across coaching sessions. Although sessions are expected to be individualized to meet teachers' needs, no data yet suggest that core concepts or information are communicated similarly by different coaches across sessions with different teachers. Instead, results do suggest that teachers' fidelity of implementation varies, which may be linked to the issue of coaches' fidelity to the target content of an intervention.

Sustaining Changes in Teachers' Practices and Children's Learning

Finally, the goal of all coaching-based PD interventions is to provide a relatively short-term experience that engenders a fundamental transformation in teachers' practices and in turn positively affects the learning of every child in their classrooms throughout their subsequent careers. However, almost no research has explored the persistence of the effects of coaching on teachers' practices. Although this issue of sustainability is critical to any intervention, we know little about how teachers' changes in their language interactions with children persist if the coaching relationship is not active. Also, we do not know how the dosage of coaching intervention is linked to the sustainability of teacher change over time. As noted earlier, changing how teachers talk to children is challenging. Without the ongoing support of coaching, can teachers sustain this change? Following up on teachers who have participated in studies like those discussed earlier is likely the best technique for collecting and interpreting these data.

Conclusions

At present, coaching models of PD are favored in the field of early childhood education teacher training, despite the limited evidence to support their efficacy for teachers' knowledge and practice, and for children's language and literacy. ExCELL is a model that shows promise in positively impacting teachers' behaviors and children's language and preliteracy outcomes. It appears that changing teachers' interaction styles and creating opportunities for the purposeful use of language foster children's vocabulary development. However, coaching requires an enormous investment of human and financial capital. In order to promote models that work, it is important to understand fully what essential components make ExCELL work under various conditions in a wide range of sites, and with teachers with varying educational backgrounds and expertise. Understanding the components of ExCELL and other successful coaching models will elucidate what it takes to promote children's vocabulary learning and advance the goal of closing the achievement gap between children of poverty and their more advantaged peers.

References

Adger, C. T., Hoyle, S. M., & Dickinson, D. (2004). Locating learning in in-service education for preschool teachers. *American Educational Research Journal, 41*(4), 867–900.

Aikens, N., & Barbarin, O. (2008). Socioeconomic differences in reading trajectories: The contribution of family, neighborhood, and school contexts. *Journal of Educational Psychology, 100*(2), 235–251.

Alexander, K. L., Entwisle, D. R., & Horsey, C. (1997). From first grade forward: Early foundations of high school dropout. *Sociology of Education, 70*(2), 87–107.

Ball, D. L. (1992). Constructing new forms of teaching: Subject matter knowledge in in-service teacher education. *Journal of Teacher Education, 43,* 347–356.

Beals, D. E. (1997). Sources of support for learning words in conversation: Evidence from mealtimes. *Journal of Child Language, 24,* 673–694.

Bond, M. A., & Wasik, B. A. (2009). Conversation stations: Promoting language development in young children. *Early Childhood Education Journal, 36*(6), 467–473.

Boudah, D. J., Logan, K. R., & Greenwood, C. R. (2001). The research to practice projects: Lessons learned about changing teacher practice. *Teacher Education and Special Education, 24,* 290–303.

Bransford, J. D., Brown, A. L., & Cocking, R. R. (2000). *How people learn: Brain, mind, experience, and school.* Washington, DC: National Academy Press.

Byrnes, J. P. (2001). *Cognitive development and learning in instructional contexts* (2nd ed.). Needham Heights, MA: Allyn & Bacon.

Childers, J., & Tomasello, M. (2002). Two-year-olds learn novel nouns, verbs, and conventional actions from massed or distributed exposures. *Developmental Psychology, 38,* 967–978.

Clements, D. H. (2007). Curriculum research: Toward a framework for research-based curricula. *Journal for Research in Mathematics Education, 38*(1), 35–70.

Cunningham, A. E., Perry, K. E., Stanovich, K. E., & Stanovich, P. J. (2004). Disciplinary knowledge of K–3 teachers and their knowledge calibration in the domain of early literacy. *Annals of Dyslexia, 54*(1), 139–167.

Dickinson, D. K. (2001). Book reading in preschool classrooms: Is recommended practice common? In D. K. Dickinson & P. O. Tabors (Eds.), *Beginning literacy with language: Young children learning at home and school* (pp. 175–203). Baltimore: Brookes.

Dickinson, D. K., & Brady, J. P. (2006). Toward effective support for language and literacy through professional development. In M. J. Zaslow & I. Martinez-Beck (Eds.), *Critical issues in early childhood professional development* (pp. 141–170). Baltimore: Brookes.

Dickinson, D. K., & Caswell, L. (2007). Building support for language and early literacy in preschool classrooms through in-service professional development: Effects of the Literacy Environment Enrichment Program (LEEP). *Early Childhood Research Quarterly, 22*(2), 243–260.

Dickinson, D. K., & Smith, M. W. (1991). Preschool talk: Patterns of teacher–child interaction in early childhood classrooms. *Journal of Research in Childhood Education, 6,* 20–29.

Dickinson, D. K., & Tabors, P. O. (Eds.). (2001). *Beginning literacy with language: Young children learning at home and school.* Baltimore: Brookes.

Dole, J., & Donaldson, R. (2006). "What am I supposed to do all day?": Three big ideas for the reading coach. *Reading Teacher, 59*(5), 486–488.

Elley, W. B. (1989). Vocabulary acquisition from stories. *Reading Research Quarterly, 24,* 174–187.

Gest, S. D., Holland-Coviello, R., Welsh, J. A., Eicher-Catt, D. L., & Gill, S. (2006). Language development subcontexts in Head Start classrooms: Distinctive patterns of teacher talk during free play, mealtime, and book reading. *Early Education and Development, 17*(2), 293–315.

Gough, P. B., Ehri, L. C., & Treiman, R. (1992). *Reading acquisition.* Hillsdale, NJ: Erlbaum.

Hall, B. (2004). Literacy coaches: An evolving role. *Carnegie Reporter, 3*(1), 1–12. Retrieved October 1, 2009, from *www.carnegie.org/reporter/09/literacy/index.html.*

Hamre, B. K., Justice, L. M., Pianta, R. C., Kilday, C. R., Sweeney, B., Downer, J. T., et al. (2010). Implementation fidelity of My TeachingPartner language and literacy activities: Association with preschoolers' language and literacy growth. *Early Childhood Research Quarterly, 25*(3), 267–408..

Hart, B., & Risley, T. R. (1995). *Meaningful differences in the everyday experience of young American children.* Baltimore: Brookes.

Henk, J. K., Morrison, J. W., Thornburg, K. R., & Raya-Carlton, P. (2007). The efficacy of HeadsUp! Reading in Missouri on teacher's knowledge of emergent literacy: A satellite-based literacy development training course. *NHSA Dialog, 10*(1), 20–35.

Hindman, A. H., & Wasik, B. A. (2008). Head Start teachers' beliefs about language and literacy instruction. *Early Childhood Research Quarterly, 23,* 479–492.

Hindman, A. H., & Wasik, B. A. (2010). *The nature of Head Start teachers' conceptual knowledge about*

early language and literacy. Manuscript in preparation.

Honig, A. S., & Martin, P. M. (2009). Does brief in-service training help teachers increase turn-taking talk and Socratic questions with low-income preschoolers? *NHSA Dialog, 12*(1), 33–44.

International Reading Association. (2004). *The role and qualifications of the reading coach in the United States.* Newark, DE: Author.

Jackson, B., Larzelere, R., St. Clair, L., Corr, M., Fichter, C., & Egertson, H. (2006). The impact of HeadsUp! Reading on early childhood educators' literacy practices and preschool children's literacy skills. *Early Childhood Research Quarterly, 21,* 213–226.

Jackson, R., McCoy, A., Pistorino, C., Wilkinson, A., Burghardt, J., Clark, M., et al. (2007). *National evaluation of Reading First.* Washington, DC: Institute of Education Sciences.

Joyce, B. R., & Showers, B. (1980). *Power in staff development through research on training.* Alexandria, VA: Association for Supervision and Curriculum Development.

Joyce, B. R., & Showers, B. (1982). Transfer of training: The contribution of "coaching." *Journal of Education, 163*(2).

Karweit, N. (1994). The effect of story reading on the language development of disadvantaged prekindergarten and kindergarten students. In D. K. Dickinson (Ed.), *Bridges to literacy* (pp. 43–65). Malden, MA: Blackwell.

Landry, S. H., Anthony, J. L., Swank, P. R., & Monseque-Bailey, P. (2009). Effectiveness of comprehensive professional development for teachers of at-risk preschoolers. *Journal of Educational Psychology, 101*(2), 448–465.

Landry, S. H., Swank, P. R., Smith, K. E., Assel, M. A., & Gunnewig, S. B. (2006). Enhancing early literacy skills for preschool children: Bringing a professional development model to scale. *Journal of Learning Disabilities, 39*(4), 306–325.

Lee, V. E., & Burkam, D. (2002). *Inequality at the starting gate: Social background differences in achievement as children begin school.* Washington, DC: Economic Policy Institute.

Lee, J., Grigg, W. S., & Donahue, P. L. (2007). *The nation's report card: Reading 2007.* Retrieved September 24, 2009, from *nces.ed.gov/nationsreportcard/pubs/main2007/2007496.asp.*

Lieberman, A. (1995). Practices that support teacher development. *Phi Delta Kappan, 76*(8), 591–596.

Lonigan, C. J., & Whitehurst, G. J. (1998). Relative efficacy of parent and teacher involvement in a shared-reading intervention for preschool children from low-income backgrounds. *Early Childhood Research Quarterly, 13,* 263–290.

Massey, S. L., Pence, K. L., Justice, L. M., & Bowles, R. P. (2008). Educators' use of cognitively challenging questions in economically disadvantaged preschool classroom contexts. *Early Education and Development, 19*(2), 340–360.

Missall, K. N., & McConnell, S. R. (2004). *Psychometric characteristics of individual growth and development indicators: Picture naming, rhyming, and alliteration*. Minneapolis, MN: Center on Early Education an Development, University of Minnesota.

Morrow, L. M. (1985). Retelling stories: A strategy for improving young children's comprehension, concept of story structure, and oral language complexity. *Elementary School Journal, 85*(5), 647–661.

National Early Literacy Panel. (2009). *Developing early literacy: Report of the National Early Literacy Panel, executive summary*. Washington, DC: National Institute for Literacy.

Neuman, S. B., & Celano, D. (2001). Access to print in low-income and middle-income communities. *Reading Research Quarterly, 36*(1), 8–26.

Neuman, S. B., & Cunningham, A. E. (2009). The impact of professional development and coaching on early language and literacy instructional practices. *American Educational Research Journal, 46*(2), 532–566.

Neuman, S. B., & Dwyer, J. (2009). Missing in action: Vocabulary instruction in pre-K. *Reading Teacher, 62*(5), 384–392.

Phillips, J. (2003). Powerful learning: Creating learning communities in urban school reform. *Journal of Curriculum and Supervision, 18*(3), 240–258.

Pianta, R. C., La Paro, K. M., & Hamre, B. K. (2006). *Classroom Assessment Scoring System (CLASS)*. Baltimore: Brookes.

Pianta, R. C., Mashburn, A. J., Downer, J. T., Hamre, B. K., & Justice, L. M. (2008). Effects of web-mediated professional development resources on teacher–child interactions in pre-kindergarten classrooms. *Early Childhood Research Quarterly, 23*, 431–451.

Powell, D. R., Diamond, K. E., Burchinal, M. R., & Koehler, M. J., (2010). Effects of an early literacy professional development intervention on Head Start teachers and children. *Journal of Educational Psychology, 102*, 299–312.

Preschool Curriculum Evaluation Report (PCER). (2008). *Effects of preschool curriculum programs on school readiness (NCER 2008–2009)*. Washington, DC: U.S. Government Printing Office.

Rainville, K. N., & Jones, S. (2008). Situated identities: Power and positioning in the work of a literacy coach. *Reading Teacher, 61*(6), 440–448.

Showers, B., & Joyce, B. (1996). The evolution of peer coaching. *Educational Leadership, 53*(6), 12–16.

Smith, M. W., Dickinson, D. K., Sangeorge, A., & Anastasopoulos, L. (2002). *Early Language and Literacy Classroom Observation (ELLCO) toolkit, research edition*. Baltimore: Brookes.

Snow, C. E. (1991). The theoretical basis for relationships between language and literacy development. *Journal of Research in Childhood Education, 6*, 5–10.

Snow, C. E., Burns, M. S., & Griffin, P. (1998). *Pre-venting reading difficulties in young children*. Washington, DC: National Academy Press.

Stanovich, K. E. (1986). Matthew effects in reading: Some consequences of individual differences in the acquisition of literacy. *Reading Research Quarterly, 21*, 360–407.

Steckel, B. (2009). Fulfilling the promise of literacy coaches in urban schools: What does it mean to make an impact? *Reading Teacher, 63* (1), 14–23.

Toll, C. A. (2005). *The literacy coach survival guide: Essential questions and practical answers*. Newark, DE: International Reading Association.

Vygotsky, L. (1978). *Mind in society: The development of higher mental processes*. Cambridge, MA: Harvard University Press.

Walpole, S., & Blamey, K. L. (2008). Elementary literacy coaches: The reality of dual roles. *Reading Teacher, 62*(3), 222–231.

Walpole, S., & McKenna, M. C. (2004). *The literacy coach's handbook: A guide to research-based practice*. New York: Guilford Press.

Wasik, B. A., & Bond, M. A. (2001). Beyond the pages of a book: Interactive book reading and language development in preschool classrooms. *Journal of Educational Psychology, 93*(2), 243–250.

Wasik, B. A., Bond, M. A., & Hindman, A. H. (2006). The effects of a language and literacy intervention on Head Start children and teachers. *Journal of Educational Psychology, 98*(1), 63–74.

Wasik, B. A., & Hindman, A. H. (2009). The quality of teacher language and its impact on children's vocabulary development. *National Reading Conference Yearbook*, pp. 82–98.

Wasik, B. A., & Hindman, A. H. (2010a). *Low-income children learning early language and literacy skills: The effects of a teacher professional development model on teacher and child outcomes*. Manuscript under review.

Wasik, B. A., & Hindman, A. H. (2010b). Understanding the home literacy environments of Head Start families: Testing the Family Literacy Survey and interpreting its findings. *NHSA Dialog, 13*(2), 71–91.

Whitehurst, G. J., Arnold, D. H., Epstein, J. N., Angell, A. L., Smith, M. W., & Fischel, J. E. (1994). A picture book reading intervention in day care and home for children from low-income families. *Developmental Psychology, 30*(5), 679–689.

Zaslow, M. J., Mariner, C. L., Moore, K. A., & Oldham, E. (1998). *Reliability and predictive validity of two sets of parenting measures within a sample of low-income families: The HOME-SF and exploratory measures of parenting developed for the JOBS Descriptive Study* (Methods Working Paper No. 98.4). Washington, DC: Child Trends.

22

Why Are So Few Interventions Really Effective?: A Call for Fine-Grained Research Methodology

DAVID K. DICKINSON
JILL B. FREIBERG
ERICA M. BARNES

In this chapter we confront an uncomfortable question for those of us who are in the business of providing professional development, training teachers, and writing curricula: Why do our efforts so frequently result in limited success? We answer by acknowledging that although we have learned much about the development of language and literacy, and we know that classrooms can foster growth, we lack the kind of detailed information about classrooms that we need if we are to provide satisfying answers to our question. To illustrate what a fine-grained approach might provide we draw on our current research and use findings from it to identify some of the factors that may give rise to the disappointing results of some interventions.

We begin by discussing the impressive strides we have made in understanding the emergence of literacy—especially the role of language in fostering literacy learning. It is now clear that there are powerful continuities between early language learning and later academic success, and factors such as poverty place children at elevated risk of failing to acquire language skills associated with later reading. Recently it has become increasingly clear that early language learning facilitates later learning, and this realiza-

tion, combined with awareness of the deleterious effects of poverty, has fueled efforts to intervene with high-risk populations. However, the disturbing but incontrovertible fact is that while many interventions have resulted in some growth in literacy abilities, many have not had substantial lasting effects and, in particular, have struggled to bolster language development. Drawing on our current work we discuss our approaches to study in detail the effects of a language-focused curriculum intervention. We consider the light these analyses shed on the challenges associated with efforts to change patterns of language use that are deeply ingrained, and the fact that language use is affected by both contextual factors that interact with teacher-specific ways of using language and curriculum-based factors.

Language and Reading

By the later elementary school years, reading comprehension, the most important reading skill for long-term academic success, is highly dependent on language abilities nourished from shortly after birth through the elementary school years. The long duration of the maturation of these abilities, combined with the multifaceted nature of language, presents major challenges to teachers as they seek to improve substantially children's rate of language acquisition.

Language and Skilled Reading

In the early years, when basic decoding ability is being mastered, phonemic awareness is the language-related competence of major importance because it facilitates the mapping of sound units onto graphemes (Ehri et al., 2001). Two leading theories of reading development, the simple view (Hoover & Gough, 1990) and the convergent skills model of reading (CSMR) (Vellutino, Tunmer, Jaccard, & Chen, 2007), argue that as decoding skills are established, the semantic and syntactic abilities that support language comprehension are of primary importance for predicting reading comprehension. Vellutino and colleagues (2007) make clear their notion regarding the developmental progression from the primacy of code-based skills toward semantic and syntactic ability as they describe the predicted relationship between language and reading according to the CSMR:

> Phonological skills such as phoneme segmentation and phonological (letter-sound) decoding would carry greater weight as determinants of success in beginning reading than would visual skills, but as children acquire a high degree of proficiency in word identification and other word-level skills, language comprehension and the underlying oral language processes would likely become the primary sources of variability in reading because individual differences in word identification and phonological decoding diminish as a source of such variability. In addition, the more diverse and more advanced reading materials to which developing readers are increasingly exposed tend to make greater demands on higher level language skills (e.g., vocabulary and syntactic knowledge). (p. 4)

They evaluated the CSMR by testing a large group of younger (second and third grade) and older (sixth and seventh grade) children with a battery of tests of cognitive processing abilities, language abilities that included language comprehension and semantic knowledge using the Vocabulary and Similarities subtests of the Wechsler Intelligence Scale for Children—Revised (WISC-R; Wechsler, 1974), phonological awareness, decoding, spelling, and reading comprehension. In the younger group the ability to read words out of context helped predict reading comprehension, but it was not a significant predictor among the older children. Language comprehension predicted reading in both groups, but it was a stronger predictor for the older children. Phonological skills made important contributions to prediction of word reading in younger children and continued to be related to reading in older children, but its effects were reduced in older children. A surprising finding is that semantic knowledge was strongly related to comprehension at both ages. Vellutino and colleagues (2007) concluded that semantic knowledge plays an important role in reading comprehension during early stages, as well as in early adolescence, and that skills in understanding extended language— discourse-level skills—become increasingly important with age.

Broader measures of semantic knowledge, such as those used in the test of the CSMR, of syntactic knowledge (Nation, Clarke, Marshall, & Durand, 2004; Share & Leikin, 2004), and of extended discourse skills (e.g., narratives, explanations) not only play an important role predicting later literacy but are also stronger long-term predictors than receptive vocabulary (National Early Literacy Panel [NELP], 2008). These findings are consistent with many prior studies that have supported the long-standing belief that vocabulary is related to reading comprehension (National Reading Panel [NRP], 2000), and the more recent realization that because vocabulary is only one element of the language system (see Harris, Golinkoff, & Hirsh-Pasek, Chapter 4, this volume), assessing only vocabulary provides a partial picture of language ability (Dickinson, McCabe, Anastasopoulos, Peisner-Feinberg, & Poe, 2003). Skilled reading also has been found to be associated with *morphological awareness*, an awareness of the units of meaning within words (Deacon & Kirby, 2004; Nation et al., 2004).

A takeaway message from these findings is that if we hope to have substantial and sustained impact on children's language learning in ways that translate into improved reading comprehension, a broad-based approach may be necessary. However, as we see later, this runs up against the unfortunate reality that it is far easier to implement interventions and demonstrate their effectiveness when they are narrowly targeted than when they are broad-based and comprehensive.

Mechanisms of Language Effects on Reading

Evidence reviewed elsewhere in this volume makes clear the long-term continuity between language ability in the later preschool years, and later language and reading in the primary grades. An additional source of evidence of the importance of the environment is the findings of a study of 7,179 fraternal and identical twins, which revealed that language development and reading ability are largely determined by environmental factors (Harlaar, Hayiou-Thomas, Dale, & Plomin, 2008). Another twin study of early vocabulary and expressive language learning found that environmental factors account for between 54 and 78% of the variation (Van Hulle, Goldsmith, & Lemery, 2004), further highlighting the need to identify environmental factors associated with enhanced language learning.

INDIRECT EFFECTS

For some time it has been recognized that early language skills are correlated with later performance, but only in recent years have researchers begun to investigate carefully the indirect ways language provides a platform for later literacy (Dickinson, Golinkoff, & Hirsch-Pasek, 2010). In the first such effort, Storch and Whitehurst (2002), reported a moderate-size indirect effect (0.43) of language on fourth-grade reading. This effect was a combination of the relationship between oral language and code-related skills, and the association between code-related skills and later reading. Analysis of data from 1,137 children from the National Institute of Child Health and Human Development (NICHD) Child Care Study (NICHD Early Child Care Research Network, 2005) found a small direct effect of age 3 language on decoding in first grade (ß = 0.10) and modest indirect effects on grade 3 decoding (ß = 0.33) and reading (ß = 0.36). Prekindergarten code-related skills also predicted grade 3 reading, and these PreK influences were indirect and continued

through first-grade assessments of *both* decoding and vocabulary. It may be that prior research has underestimated the potency of language because these indirect effects often have not been considered. Finally, determining the effect of book reading, an activity that is known to support language learning, is subject to underestimation (Sénéchal, Ouellette, & Rodney, 2006).

A methodological implication of the importance of considering indirect effects is the need for longitudinal studies. The only way to understand fully the impact of early learning on later reading is through long-term studies that examine the dynamic growth of the cognitive and linguistic systems that undergird reading language.

MECHANISMS BY WHICH CLASSROOMS AFFECT LANGUAGE

While there have been hundreds of intervention studies (NELP, 2008), some of which we review below, we are woefully ignorant of the particular classroom interactions that foster language learning. Careful analysis of classroom interactions, combined with consideration of long-term indirect effects, may lead to better understanding of how classrooms can foster language learning. Support for this assertion comes from findings generated by a recent reanalysis of data from the Home–School Study of Language and Literacy Development that followed children from low-income homes from preschool through the elementary school years (Dickinson & Tabors, 2001), then through high school (Snow, Porche, Tabors, & Harris, 2007). By tracing pathways of effects from early experiences through later competencies we found evidence that that there may be lasting, complex, mutually reinforcing effects that flow from strong support in early childhood classrooms (Dickinson & Porche, in press). Preschool teachers were audiotaped and videotaped. Researchers transcribed, coded, and analyzed their conversations using computer-based methods, and assessed children using standardized measures of language and reading in kindergarten and fourth grade. We found indirect pathways through which preschool experiences affect fourth-grade reading. Fourth-grade vocabulary, word reading, and comprehension competencies were associated with kindergarten vocabulary and reading, and preschool classroom experiences had moderate effects on the kindergarten print and language abilities linked to fourth-grade reading comprehension (R^2 = .22), vocabulary (R^2 = .38), and decoding (R^2 = .27). Examination of indirect effects associated with specific classroom behaviors revealed that teachers' use of sophisticated vocabulary during informal conversations predicted children's kindergarten vocabulary (r = .31, p < .01) and emergent literacy (a composite that included phonological awareness, letter knowledge, print concepts, and early writing) (r = .33, p < .01). Analytic talk about books in group settings also contributed to prediction of kindergarten vocabulary (r = .41, p < .001). Kindergarten vocabulary, in turn, predicted grade 4 word recognition (r = .40 p < .05) and reading comprehension (r = .46, p < .001).

By studying long-term direct and indirect effects of experiences in classrooms that foster learning rather than simply testing children and studying long-term effects of accumulated language abilities on later learning, we may gain far greater understanding of the complex dynamics through which language learning affects not only language acquisition but also associated competencies. For example, the lasting effects we found for individualized teacher–child conversations might have been only partially the by-product of vocabulary learning. It also may be that children who experienced enriched interactions with their teachers form closer relationships and are subsequently more inclined to connect with teachers. Our finding of the effects of book reading included the unexpected correlation between teacher efforts to hold children's attention and later reading. It may be that engaging book reading experiences have not only the obvious and most often studied effect of teaching vocabulary, but they might also teach children to regulate their attention in groups and learn information in group settings. In addition, children may develop better self-regulatory abilities as they gain stronger language skills (Dickinson, McCabe, & Essex, 2006), and group settings that are conducive to language learning—well organized, interesting, and instructionally rich—may help to foster children's self-regulatory abilities.

Starting at the Beginning

It is now widely acknowledged that language abilities in the later preschool years are a key aspect of children's emerging literacy ability. What is less well recognized is the extent to which those abilities are shaped by earlier experiences and the impact of those prior experiences on children's ability to benefit from classroom learning opportunities. For example, as Metsala discusses in depth (see Chapter 5, this volume), phonemic awareness is in part a by-product of early vocabulary development because during the preschool years, the size of a child's vocabulary is associated with improvements in ability to attend to the sounds of language (Munson, Kurtz, & Windsor, 2005; Storkel, 2001, 2003). Given that phonemic awareness is a potent predictor of early reading success, the finding that vocabulary size in preschool fosters its emergence underscores the importance of early language growth to later reading.

Another indication of how very early language bolsters later language and associated emergent literacy is the finding that the rate at which a child learns new words is partially conditioned by how many words a child already knows. Children learn new words faster when words are similar to those already in their lexicon (Storkel, 2003). The practical importance of this finding is seen when intervention studies use book reading to build vocabulary knowledge and find that children with stronger vocabularies are more able to learn words presented as part of these interventions (Penno, Wilkinson, & Moore, 2002). And the rate at which young children acquire vocabulary also is conditioned by children's syntactic knowledge because they use syntactic cues to help determine the meanings of words (see Harris et al., Chapter 4, this volume). The ability to use syntax to determine meaning varies, and children with weaker language skills have more difficulty employing syntactic cues to learn new words (Kemp, Lieven, & Tomasello, 2005). Language experiences in classrooms also can enhance syntactic knowledge, as Vasilyeva and Waterfall describe (see Chapter 3, this volume), further demonstrating the importance of classrooms that nurture the full range of emerging linguistic competencies and the need to recognize that language is an interdependent system in which one domain relates to and supports the emergence of others.

Evidence that language is an evolving, self-reinforcing system extends into the prelinguistic period. The language comprehension ability of 14-month-old toddlers predicts their subsequent expressive and receptive vocabulary (Watt, Wetherby, & Shumway, 2006). This evidence of continuity between prelinguistic communication efforts and later language suggests that early encouragement to communicate may have beneficial effects. Additional evidence of the importance of the earliest phases of language acquisition to later learning comes from the finding that very young children's capacity to interpret language quickly is related to early vocabulary and language acquisition (Fernald, Perfors, & Marchman, 2006; see Fernald & Weisleder, Chapter 1, this volume). Early processing ability and related language have long-term effects because language processing speed and receptive vocabulary size at age 25 months are predictive of vocabulary when children are 8 years old (Marchman & Fernald, 2008). A meta-analysis of preschool predictors of later reading ability also found that speed of processing reliably predicts later reading skills (NELP, 2008).

In summary, evidence increasingly makes it apparent that language is a multifaceted, self-reinforcing system that gains momentum during the preschool years and fosters later reading skills through complex direct and indirect pathways that affect multiple emerging capacities that underpin reading. Children with a strong early language learning trajectory are at an advantage because, unless a child has a specific language deficiency (Gray, 2005; Johnson & De Villiers, 2009; Nash & Donaldson, 2005), multiple emerging language systems work in concert to facilitate rapid vocabulary acquisition. Children with stronger language skills more quickly pick up language in school and thereby enrich their literacy-related competencies. Thus, it is critically important that we create enriched settings that foster language learning. Unfortunately, at present, we have few examples of interventions that foster the full range of related language competencies; we have only limited understanding of possible causal chains of effects that might lead from specific classrooms practices with children with particular language abilities to acquisition of language and print-related knowledge. Equally daunting, we are far from understanding the multiple factors that shape language use in classrooms, and support and sustain use of effective methods.

Language Interventions

Preschool interventions have not had a very good track record at improving children's language. Some interventions aimed at improving language during early childhood have yielded modest effects at best. We now review research from studies of large-scale preschool and curriculum interventions that have struggled to find effects on language, followed by a brief discussion of studies that have shown more benefits. We conclude with consideration of methodological and intervention-related factors that might help explain challenges we face in seeking to develop and study interventions designed to foster growth of language skills related to literacy development.

Large-Scale Studies

For the most part, large, programmatic efforts to improve early childhood education have proven to have little effect on young children's language. Examples of this phenomenon come from large multistate and national studies of Early Reading First (ERF; Early Reading First Evaluation, 2007), Head Start (Administration for Children and Families [ACF], 2010; Zill & Resnick, 2006), Early Head Start (Love et al., 2005), and public prekindergarten (Howes et al., 2008). These studies have found overall that programmatic early childhood initiatives have very small to null effects on various aspects of children's language. For example, the Head Start Impact Study, a national randomized controlled trial, showed that for 4-year-olds, a year in Head Start led to only a 0.09 effect on vocabulary learning compared to children not selected for Head Start (ACF, 2010). Head Start yielded no significant effects on these children's phonological processing or oral comprehension. Three-year-olds benefited more from a year in Head Start in vocabulary (d = 0.18) and phonological processing (d = 0.10). These programs certainly invest many resources in aiding children's educational, cognitive, and social development. So why do these studies show such small effects on children's language?

We must ask the same question of many preschool curriculum interventions. With few exceptions, large-scale efforts to support language growth in preschool programs through curriculum intervention have had difficulty demonstrating effects on language. The NELP (2008) found no significant difference in children's oral language outcomes between programs that implemented a literacy-focused curriculum and those that did not. Another meta-analysis of the effects of preschool curriculum interventions on vocabulary outcomes yielded no significant effect overall (Darrow, 2009). These reviews examine many of the same studies, the most noteworthy of which are studies conducted by the Preschool Curriculum Evaluation Research (PCER) Consortium (2008). The PCER studies included 14 curricula, 11 of which claimed to have an explicit focus on language development. On the two language outcomes measured, receptive vocabulary and grammatical understanding, only one curriculum yielded positive effects at the end of preschool, and one additional curriculum positively improved language outcomes at the end of kindergarten. We are facing the same challenge in our own effort to bring about enhanced learning using a comprehensive curriculum. Analyses of our randomized control trials intervention that included 52 Head Start classrooms have revealed no clear pattern of effects at the end of preschool or kindergarten (Kaiser et al., 2010). We are now seeking to understand in detail what did and did not happen in the classrooms and draw from those current analyses in the following pages. Thus, even when comprehensive curricula designed to enhance children's language abilities have been implemented, they often have not led to significant improvements. This brings to light the problem: Why, despite correlational evidence of the benefits of early childhood classrooms on later outcomes, have interventions designed to foster development had such limited success? Here we explore some possibilities of why language appears so difficult to change through preschool interventions.

Targeted Interventions

Interventions in which children are pulled out of the classroom and work with teachers one-on-one or in a small-group setting have, in general, shown more promising results than large-scale efforts. For example, the most common early childhood interventions targeting language involve interactive shared book reading. These interventions have yielded consistent, positive effects on oral language skills in meta-analyses, with a sizable average effect size of d = 0.73 (NELP, 2008). In comparison to the meta-analysis of whole-class curriculum interventions described previously, meta-analyses of literacy-focused early childhood curricula that include such small-group intervention found slightly larger effects on children's language. These interventions yielded small average effects on receptive vocabulary (d = 0.10) and modest effects on expressive vocabulary (d = 0.21) for at-risk preschool and kindergarten students (Kaiser & McLeod, 2010). Dialogic reading, the most widespread method of shared book reading examined empirically, has shown some success in improving children's language (Whitehurst et al., 1999). This program is typically implemented one-on-one or in a small-group setting, often by parents. In preschools, it has been evaluated primarily as a pull-out intervention leading to a meaningful effect on expressive (d = 0.62) and receptive (d = 0.45) language (Mol, Bus, & de Jong, 2009), especially when used with preschool-age children. Intensive phonological training interventions in early childhood also had significant positive effects on phonological awareness (d = 0.73) and early reading (d = 0.70) across numerous studies (Bus & van IJzendoorn, 1999). These programs were also delivered in small-group or one-on-one settings.

Hence, the focus and intensity of the intervention may be a key element in fostering language growth. Interventions may claim to target language but fail to provide enough systematic support for language development across contexts, as demonstrated by a recent review of the vocabulary instruction included in preschool curricula (Neuman & Dwyer, 2009). Dosage can be also increased in terms of time in an instructional program (U.S. Department of Education, 2003) to increase children's exposure to the program and boost their language skills. Increasing both the amount and intensity of instruction may lead to improved language outcomes for preschool children.

Why Is It So Hard to Foster Language Learning?

There are several reasons so few successes have been seen in efforts to foster language learning. First, large studies may provide insufficiently detailed information to shed much light on what is and what is not working in interventions, due to averaging out of effects across many classrooms, lack of attention to fidelity of implementation, and lack of detailed examination of those programs and methods that are effective in improving children's language. Also, language abilities are particularly difficult skills to change, in terms of both teaching practices and children's learning. Doing so requires intensive, sustained intervention, which likely requires high researcher involvement and professional development for teachers. These possibilities need to be explored to understand how best to design, deliver, and evaluate language-focused interventions.

METHODOLOGICAL CHALLENGES

The large-scale studies of preschool programs such as the Head Start Impact Study (ACF, 2010) and the ERF national evaluation (Early Reading First Evaluation, 2007) must be considered in light of methodology, in that the successes of individual sites or programs may not be evident in the average effects reported. It is possible that these broad studies average out the effects of the best classrooms, teachers, and programs. Additionally, meta-analyses of many varied interventions may both average out the effects of the most promising interventions and, due to selection constraints used when identifying studies for inclusion, exclude successful interventions that have not been evaluated in the required manner. Perhaps we need to look with a closer lens to see how interventions are—and are not—affecting teachers' practices and supporting—or failing to support—children's learning.

Another important challenge in implementing programs on a large scale is maintaining the core elements of the intervention at a high level. Program implementers need to attend to the fidelity of the intervention because programs may become diluted by being scaled up. Big evaluation studies may not carefully describe fidelity, or the interventions themselves may not be specific enough about how they address the complex nature of language development.

Results of a number of studies indicate that fidelity of implementation of an intervention moderates the extent to which the intervention affects child outcomes. Evidence of this phenomenon comes from evaluations of interventions such as MyTeachingPartner (Hamre et al., 2009; Justice, Mashburn, Hamre, & Pianta, 2008) and dialogic reading (Whitehurst et al., 1988, 1994). When these interventions are implemented as designed, they lead to gains for children. Conversely, low quality of implementation is a key cause of limited effects. This may be a result of poor training and support of teachers, or lack of resources or capacity within natural classroom settings to implement the intervention as designed. However, the result is that programs designed to build children's language skills are often poorly implemented; therefore, children show little or no growth in language. There is clear need to monitor and measure fidelity in intervention research, yet compliance information is not reported in many studies.

When programs are implemented well, results are often robust and meaningful. However, such results may be difficult to replicate with most teachers in typical early childhood settings. For example, the significant effects of dialogic reading in school settings (Mol et al., 2009) may partially be attributed to the interventions being delivered by researchers, as well as the increased control and compliance monitoring that may take place when interventions are delivered in schools and centers. An indication of the importance of high-fidelity implementation is that when dialogic reading was delivered by an experimenter, particularly those that work one-on-one with an individual child, the interventions were more effective than when delivered by teachers in a typical classroom setting. In fact, researcher-delivered preschool literacy curriculum interventions yielded a larger effect on children's receptive and expressive vocabulary than those interventions delivered by teachers (Kaiser

& McLeod, 2010). These results highlight the challenges of high-quality delivery of interventions on a large scale in preschool classroom settings.

In many cases, it is difficult to decipher whether the interventions have been implemented with fidelity because implementation is either not measured or not reported. For example, curriculum evaluators of the PCER study (2008) noted they were hampered by the fact that curricula rarely provided useful fidelity of implementation checklists. These researcher teams had limited ability to track the fidelity of program delivery, a fact that may have contributed to their inability to find much evidence of curriculum effectiveness. In these cases, it is difficult to identify whether the interventions themselves were ineffective as designed, or they were not implemented at a sufficient level to produce growth in children's language skills.

This is not only an issue of research methods but it also raises the issue of the feasibility of scaling up such interventions in a range of settings. While we often see significant positive effects from intensive interventions delivered with intense support in a small-group setting, it is much more difficult to make large-scale improvements in young children's language in settings as diverse as public and private preschools, Head Start centers, and home or community day-care centers.

It is also possible that these studies may not be assessing the most important language skills or a broad enough range of skills. The NELP report (2008) suggests that comprehensive measures of complex language may show greater effects of intervention, and these broader measures are better predictors of later success than measures of discrete language skills, such as receptive or expressive vocabulary.

COMPLEXITY OF LANGUAGE

Another reason many preschool interventions may fall short in improving language is that language is simply difficult to change, both in regard to teachers' support for language and children's skills. Language is a complex construct that influences learning in a number of ways; therefore, language interventions in particular need to be intensive. Preschool teachers must support the develop-

ment of a range of interconnected language systems, including phonological awareness, vocabulary knowledge, and syntactic skills. As we previously mentioned, teachers must have a wealth of pedagogical knowledge and flexible skills to support these language abilities throughout the school day.

Not only are teachers' support strategies for language challenging to change, but also children's language skills are difficult to improve. Because language development includes a complex set of skills that develop over the lifespan, bringing about meaningful effects on children's language can be quite difficult. Language development is much more difficult to improve than other types of skills targeted in early childhood programs, such as letter knowledge (Dickinson et al., 2010). There are patterns of greater effects of interventions on discrete, finite skills compared to broader, complex skills that develop over many years, such as vocabulary. Paris (2009; see also Chapter 15, this volume) calls these easier to change abilities *constrained skills*, and notes that they develop over a shorter period of time, can be taught directly, are easy to measure, and may therefore be overly emphasized in research and intervention.

Although evidence demonstrates that interventions can impact finite sets of knowledge, such as letter knowledge or letter–word skills (ACF, 2010; Early Reading First Evaluation, 2007; NELP, 2008), growth in language is often slower or less pronounced. Additionally, as we note earlier because language develops over a lifetime, small incremental boosts in language skills during early childhood, particularly those skills that relate to literacy attainment, may have important long-term effects on children's overall growth trajectory (Dickinson et al., 2010). Longitudinal studies are needed to understand fully the outcomes of language intervention.

Unfortunately, children who are at risk of educational difficulties due to poverty or other risk factors may have even more difficulty increasing their vocabulary through preschool interventions. Biemiller (2006) suggests that children who are at risk in terms of vocabulary development may need more explicit teaching to make necessary gains. Other interventions have demonstrated a *Matthew effect*, in which children with stronger language skills at the start of a study gain more from intervention than children who begin with weaker skills (Collins, 2005; Penno et al., 2002; Robbins & Ehri, 1994; Reese & Cox, 1999). Clearly, the children who most need language interventions during preschool will need very strong interventions to begin to catch up.

THE CHALLENGE OF CHANGING
INSTRUCTIONAL PRACTICES

Given the difficulty of changing language practices, another problem is that large-scale interventions often have a shortage of the resources, both fiscal and human, needed to change deeply ingrained ways of using language. In particular, to change language support effectively in preschool classrooms, teachers may need intensive support, such as training and in-class coaching.

Increasing language support involves changing teacher behavior in a way that permeates the entire preschool day. Direct teaching strategies in group instructional contexts are relatively easy to prescribe through intervention, yet shifts in conversational practices in informal preschool contexts (e.g., free play or centers, and meal- or snack times) are more difficult (Dickinson, Darrow, & Tinubu, 2008; Dickinson, Flushman, & Freiberg, 2009; Dickinson, Watson, & Farran, 2007). This is one of the greatest challenges of broad interventions that aim to change teacher practices across the school day in multiple instructional settings presenting different demands. Teachers must be comfortable to support language flexibly, taking advantage of teachable moments and adjusting to various contexts. Skilled support for language development relies on teachers' skills in facilitating language development and awareness of language. This is why intensive teacher support is critical in preschool interventions, particularly in terms of the amount of context-rich professional development.

Interventions that include intensive professional development for early childhood teachers have often yielded positive results. One such example is Barbara Wasik and colleagues' work with preschool teachers (see Chapter 21, this volume). Wasik and Bond (2001) studied the effectiveness of training teachers to employ interactive book reading techniques with an emphasis on vocabulary. The intervention resulted in significant positive effects on both expressive and receptive vocabulary. In a follow-up study in Head Start, with similar techniques and more intensive professional development, including in-class coaching, effects on expressive (d = 0.44) and receptive vocabulary (d = 0.73) were statistically and practically significant (Wasik, Bond, & Hindman, 2006). Further evidence of the effectiveness of intensive professional development comes from a large-scale intervention in Michigan. Home- and center-based early childhood professionals across Michigan attended workshops in language and literacy, with teachers who also received coaching displaying significantly greater improvement in practices and environmental supports for language and literacy (Neuman & Cunningham, 2009). Geographically dispersed programs and teachers in remote areas can still benefit from intensive support through technological resources. Long-distance coaching provided through technology has improved teachers' skills and children's outcomes (Jackson et al., 2006; Pianta, Mashburn, Downer, Hamre, & Justice, 2008). Intensive professional development, particularly in-class coaching, leads to real improvements in teachers' language practice and children's language learning.

Interventions that are high-quality, with sufficient resources in place, can successfully boost children's language skills. We find examples of this in individual programs that have yielded positive results on children's language. These individual programs are most effective when they are comprehensive and the researcher is actively involved with the classrooms. By *comprehensive curricula*, we mean those that include a full-day effort to improve the language experiences of children in early childhood classrooms. The examples we consider reflect richer supports for learning than many of the curricula examined by the NELP (2008) and similar research syntheses. Also, these curricula have been coupled with professional development support and in-class coaching.

Examples of effective interventions that have coupled sustained professional development resources and coaching with a curriculum that focuses on language and literacy come from successful ERF grantee programs. In particular, promising results emerged when data were compiled from programs that implemented Opening the World of Learning (OWL) (Schickedanz & Dickinson, 2005) curriculum. The study examined results from eight programs across 2–4 years of data collection involving nearly 100 teachers and over 2,000 children (Ashe, Reed, Dickinson, Morse, & Wilson, 2009; Wilson, Morse, & Dickinson, 2008). During Year 1 of implementation, which was a partial year in all cases but one, children's average receptive vocabulary growth was 2.6 points. In Year 2, the first full year of implementation, it was 5.5 points, and in Year 3 it was 6.6 points. This pattern of improvement within programs suggests that the stronger growth was associated with improvements in the programs, a finding indicating that sustaining a comprehensive intervention for multiple years, with strong support for teachers' implementation, may be critical to increasing programs' effectiveness in improving children's language abilities.

Toward a New Approach to Examining Classroom Support for Language

We have found that large-scale preschool programs are having small, if any, effects on children's language development, and we hypothesize that one source of these problems is methodological in nature. It may be that typical studies of classrooms have not examined interactions in a sufficiently fine-grained way to allow identification of effective classrooms or the impact of specific instructional practices (Dickinson, 2006; Dickinson et al., 2007); therefore, we fail to identify critical ingredients that facilitate growth and do not understand in detail impediments to success. Because we lack nuanced descriptions of what is and what is not changing, we are in a weak position to understand the reasons for the lack of impact when interventions fail to have desired effects. Vague speculation about "lack of intensity" or "low levels of fidelity of implementation" must suffice. With such an approach we run the risk of making repeated efforts to create "better" interventions, without any clear understanding of the dynamics of language use and learning. We believe that there is a serious need for a theory of how teaching and learning in classrooms are affected by curriculum

and professional development. At present, interventions draw on theory as researchers decide what abilities to target, but we have no theoretical frameworks to guide us as we consider how different interventions may shape teaching behavior in ways that foster learning.

Using Fine-Grained Analyses to Describe Classroom Language Environments

In this section we report preliminary insights from a study evaluating the effectiveness of an intervention curriculum, OWL (Schickedanz & Dickinson, 2005), which places an emphasis on language, with special attention to vocabulary. We are developing fine-grained descriptions of teachers' conversational patterns and here provide an example of the measures used and patterns of language use they reveal. We will use what we learn from these descriptions to begin identifying issues that must be addressed in a theory of intervention.

Fifty-two teachers divided into six clusters were randomly assigned to one of three conditions: practice as usual using Creative Curriculum, OWL, and OWL plus tutorial support. Children in the control group received instruction from teachers using Creative Curriculum, and those in OWL classrooms augmented Creative Curriculum with OWL. Teachers in roughly half of the classrooms that used OWL also were trained in the use of Enhanced Milieu Teaching (EMT), an intensive language enhancement method devised by Ann Kaiser (see Kaiser, Roberts, & McLeod, Chapter 10, this volume). All teachers who implemented the OWL curriculum, regardless of the addition of EMT, are labeled as OWL. Videotapes of the 52 teachers were collected and transcribed in CHAT format for analysis in the Computerized Language Analysis [CLAN] program from the Child Language Data Exchange System (CHILDES; MacWhinney, 2000). We discuss three of the constructs that we measured: amount of teacher talk, use of sophisticated words, and lexical diversity.

Amount of teacher talk compares the number of words spoken by the teacher to total words, showing the balance of contributions between teacher and student. Prior work has found evidence that the extent to which children contribute to discussions when they converse with teachers relates to language learning (Dickinson & Porche, in press). Given teachers' superior language competence, one would expect that they would use more words than the students, but teachers who are intent on fostering language during individualized conversations, should instead seek to engage children and draw out their language.

Prior research shows that children benefit from exposure to sophisticated vocabulary because it fosters language learning (Dickinson & Porche, in press; Weizman & Snow, 2001). Our measure of sophisticated vocabulary was derived from the number of sophisticated words used within the transcript. *Sophisticated words* were defined as words that did not appear on the Chall and Dale (1995) list of common words. This list was modified for our study to include common plurals, verb endings, and localized speech (e.g., *cubby*), totaling 7,987 words. Proper nouns were not included as sophisticated words. The total number of different sophisticated words was counted, as well as the number of repetitions of each word (total occurrences).

Lexical diversity was gauged by *D*, which measures the rate at which novel words are added to a conversation (Malvern & Richards, 2002). *D* controls for sample length and utilizes all of the words within a transcript, hence providing more stability than a type/token ratio. A typical 5-year-old would

have a *D* of 64, while an average adult author would have a *D* of 90 (Durán, Malvern, Richards, & Chipere, 2004).

We are seeking to understand the interplay among factors that shape language use because they may help to account for why comprehensive, full-day interventions tend to have limited effects on language learning. Our approach focused on the teachers' language use, since the videotapes we analyzed were made to assess the fidelity of implementation of the curriculum and focused on the teacher. Children's comments often were not audible, and their experiences in settings apart from the teacher were invisible to us. Here we discuss emergent findings on the effect of classroom context, curriculum, and teacher-specific patterns. We also are interested in understanding how these variables relate to each other as we seek to understand better the dynamics of discourse in preschool classrooms. Table 22.1 shows averages for each of these measures by curriculum and across four settings: lunch, small group, centers, and storybook reading. Transcripts are presented in CHAT format. Words in bold type are sophisticated words, while those in italics are OWL target words. Highlighted OWL words are those identified by the curriculum for special instruction because they are central to the stories read, they are thought to be reasonably challenging for 4-year-olds, and because they were often related to the theme of the unit.

TABLE 22.1. Teacher Talk Averages

Setting	Percent Teacher Talk	Sophisticated words		*D*	
		Teacher	Text	Teacher	Text
Book read					
OWL	92	9.61	22.26	75.50	73.89
Control	73	6.30	8.06	72.60	26.90
Lunch					
OWL	66	6.82		75.00	
Control	68	7.27		81.15	
Small group					
OWL	84	5.57		63.80	
Control	82	4.15		64.36	
Centers					
OWL	80	8.56		66.32	
Control	79	7.06		69.40	

Setting Effects

In intervention classrooms we anticipated that there would be distinct profiles of language use across settings because of differences in the number of participants, the nature of the activities, and associated variation in interactional strategies. For example, during center time, when teachers are free to move among children engaged in activities linked to the current unit, we expected individually tailored talk in which children would be important contributors. The curriculum sought to instantiate small groups with a more instructional focus, marked by more conceptually oriented teacher talk that includes varied theme-related words. Book reading was expected to include high-density exposure to rich language as books were read, and discussions that centered on vocabulary and encourage analytic thinking. But that is not what we found. There were similar patterns of language use in the OWL and control group classrooms in all settings except storybook time; therefore, we discuss book reading in the follow section about curriculum differences. There was evidence of variability related to setting across all classrooms.

LUNCH

Consistent with long-standing Head Start policy, lunch was a family-style event that took place in the classrooms, with teachers spending a good percentage of the time seated with children. During lunch, teachers talked substantially less than during other contexts, accounting for 66–68% of the talk compared with settings in which teachers talked between 79 and 92% of the time (see Table 22.1). Lexical diversity was high, with average D scores being higher than any other context ($D = 75.0, 81.15$) and substantially higher than small group ($D = 63.8, 64.36$) and centers ($D = 66.32, 69.4$). A related finding was that they contributed fewer words per minute than in other settings (61.0 vs. 83.0–91.4). The rate of use of sophisticated words was modest, only slightly above what was observed in small groups.

Examination of the transcripts reveals the impact of the reduction in teacher talk during meals. In contrast with the other, more teacher-dominated settings, children were more likely to initiate the topic of discussion during lunch.

CHILD 1: I fitting to go back to another school.

TEACHER: You are? Why?

CHILD 1: I go when I turn five. . . . I go to my sister school.

TEACHER: You go to day care after you leave here?

CHILD 1: Ma'm, I'm going to high school.

CHILD 2: I'm gonna be a *cheerleader* in the high school back there.

The children are clearly providing the direction of the conversation, and the teacher's questions are designed to get children to elaborate on the previous utterance. The teacher is genuinely seeking information, and the children are free to initiate topics of interest and play a role in shaping the flow of the conversation. Also, it is interesting that this discourse structure enabled one child to introduce a sophisticated word (i.e., *cheerleader*), creating a language-learning opportunity for the other children.

CENTERS

During center time teachers moved from one setting to the next, typically spending a few minutes in an activity before moving on to the next. Whereas we anticipated that teachers would be less dominant during centers than in group interactions, we found essentially the same amount of teacher talk in both settings, with teachers accounting for roughly 80% of all the talk. Lexical diversity is slightly higher than in small-group instructional times, and sophisticated word use was substantially higher than in small-groups time. These two findings likely reflect the fact that as teachers moved from one setting to the next, the nature of the activity and materials changed, leading to shifts in conversational topic. It is important to note that because of our teacher-focused approach to data collection, this portrait of the lexical environment of the classroom is a weak reflection of children's overall language experiences during centers time.

When we look at the structure of the conversations, we note a sharp contrast between the structure of talk at mealtime and this typical exchange during centers time.

TEACHER: What are you guys doing over here?

CHILDREN: We cooking.

TEACHER: What are you cooking?

CHILD 1: Mashed potatoes and chicken.

The teacher sees the actions performed by the children and initiates this exchange not to discover information but to monitor behavior and engage the children in talk. In contrast to the lunch conversation that continued for several more turns, with multiple children directing the discourse, the centers time conversation evolves into the teacher commenting on the children's actions, with minimal child response. Centers time talk in these classrooms tended to be teacher-directed and -centered as teachers engaged in a repetitive line of questions requesting that children describe their ongoing activities. Teachers talked with three to four children for 2–3 minutes before moving on to several other centers during the period. The average OWL teachers visited 3.5 centers in 10 minutes, thus having few opportunities for extended discourse with individual children.

SMALL GROUPS

Each day teachers were scheduled to work with small groups of between four and eight children. In the control classrooms, teachers provided activities they felt were appropriate, which often resulted in a skills-oriented experience. In OWL classrooms the curriculum directed teachers to engage in a variety of activities related to the theme, with the intention that teachers discuss a concept at length using varied vocabulary while promoting conceptual development. Contrary to curricular guidance, small groups were typically used to focus on skills development with individual children. Talk was centered around the explanation and execution of the target skill, and tended to be based on the rules of the activity. There was considerable repetition and lack of variation in the teacher–child exchanges.

TEACHER: Now count the number.

CHILD: One, two, three, four . . .

TEACHER: Okay, now place four chips on . . .

CHILD: One, two, three (*whispering*) . . .

TEACHER: Four. OK, now pass it over to Lavon.

This type of interaction is similar to that observed in centers due to the request and response structure. The teacher directs the student, observes his or her demonstration, then repeats the interaction with the next child in the group. This repetition is reflected in the lexical diversity ($D = 64$), which is the lowest of the four settings. While providing one-on-one interaction, the focus is on the child demonstrating a skill rather than verbal expression. The skills-building nature of the exchanges is reflected by the fact that teachers directed and dominated the talk, accounting for 84% of all the talk, but did not promote sophisticated vocabulary use. Small groups had the lowest rate of sophisticated word use, an average of 4.8 words. Because of the skills-oriented nature of the interaction, children rarely engaged each other; rather, they remained focused on the teacher while waiting for their turns.

SUMMARY

Lunchtime, the only nonacademic context we analyzed, was distinctive in that teachers were less dominant and lexical diversity was relatively high. Teachers used small groups mostly for direct instruction of skills, which resulted in limited lexical richness compared with patterns of teacher talk during centers times.

Curriculum Differences

The OWL curriculum was designed with the goal of helping teachers engage children in conceptually based and linguistically rich experiences and conversations throughout the day. It seeks to position the teacher to engage in talk that focuses on concepts and associated vocabulary through monthlong thematic units, with books as the starting point for the introduction of new vocabulary and thematic topics. Although the curriculum sought to lead teachers to engage in conceptually guided and language-focused conversations throughout the day, such patterns were most evident during book reading.

STORYBOOK TIME

The most dramatic difference between curricula was in the language of the books read. In control classrooms, teachers tended to read books linked to a theme, but the books often were big books with predictable text. In OWL classrooms, the books were provided by the curriculum, and all books read during story time were fiction, with plots, interesting characters, and rich language. These books were to be read four times, with a different approach each reading. For each story the curriculum highlights about 14 vocabulary words for instruction, with about one-third appearing on our list of sophisticated words. These book readings are scripted, and considerable professional development was focused on helping teachers learn to employ recommended methods. The analyzed transcripts were initial reads of the stories, in which teachers were directed to read through the text with relatively few conversations but with *asides*—comments designed to define words and explain subtle features of the plot as the book is read. Follow-up questions designed to encourage analysis and explication of the story were provided.

The impact of the curriculum on the book language children heard was dramatic. The lexical diversity of the text in OWL books was $D = 73.89$ as opposed to $D = 26.90$ for the books read in control classrooms. The lexical diversity of language in the OWL books was about equal to that found during lunchtime, the next richest setting. Control group classrooms' books had lexical diversity between one-third and one-half that seen in the other contexts. Analysis of sophisticated word use in the books revealed equally dramatic differences (22.96 vs. 8.06). Sophisticated vocabulary use was somewhat higher than that in other settings, reflecting the fact that predictable books use the same words many times, and some of these words are relatively low-frequency words. Despite the dramatic differences in lexical diversity

of the books read, teachers' talk in the two conditions had similar D's, but OWL teachers used about 30% more sophisticated words than teachers in control classrooms (9.61 vs. 6.3), by far the highest such rate in any context. This difference in use of sophisticated words might reflect difference in the content of books and impact of curricular guidance.

These quantitative differences reflect differences in the content of the interactions. The book *Rabbits and Raindrops*, by Jim Arnosky (1997), included in the OWL curriculum, includes complex vocabulary in a unit on weather: "A rabbit's fur is not *waterproof*. Baby rabbits can become *soaked*, and catch cold" (p. 13). As the book was read, there was talk about the target vocabulary (*hedge, lawn, nibble*):

TEACHER: What does it mean to be soaked?

CHILD: We be wet.

TEACHER: Wet, good Jeremy, gimme five.

This teacher also asked questions about the pictures ("What does the rabbit's tail look like?"), noted letter–sound connections, made connections to real-world topics ("The weatherman said it's gonna rain tonight"), and even talked about the state of mind of the animals:

TEACHER: I wonder if that's a thoughtful turtle.

CHILD: We thoughtful.

TEACHER: We're thoughtful turtles.

During the 4 minutes when this book was being read, this teacher packed into it a lot of high-level thinking, while holding the children's attention. She concluded the story with a discussion that had the same elements, as reflected in this exchange:

TEACHER: Did the babies eat big **mouthfuls** of food, or did they *nibble* on grass?

CHILD: *Nibble*, they didn't eat.

TEACHER: They *nibbled* and *nibbled*. What letter does *nibble* begin with?

She contrasts the sophisticated word **mouthfuls** with the OWL focus word *nibble*, to provide a definition of the target word. While the target word *nibble* from the OWL curriculum is not a sophisticated word, it does prompt the teacher to use a sophisticated word for the definition. It also provides a link to conceptual development as the class move on to discuss the diet and housing needs of a rabbit family, using other sophisticated words such as *shelter* and *hedge*.

An example of book reading from a teacher in a control classroom was a reading of *Brown Bear, Brown Bear, What Do You See?* by Bill Martin, Jr. (1992), used during a weeklong unit on woodland animals. The rhyme scheme makes the text highly predictable—"Brown Bear, Brown Bear, What do you see? I see a redbird looking at me"—and it discourages conversation because it would break up the rhyming and rhythmic pattern. During this reading there was no discussion as the book was read, a practice that also was consistent with long-standing patterns of book reading in the program. The follow-up discussions also were limited in depth because teachers tended to focus on factual information, as exemplified in the following discussion after reading this book:

TEACHER: Where does a horse live?

CHILD: In the barn.

TEACHER: In the barn, yeah, the horse lives in the barn. What animal do you remember from the story, Mara?

This conversational pattern continues as the teacher asks children what animals they remember from the story, and where the animals live. Discussion of beginning letter sounds, which concluded the lesson, provided an opportunity to review animal names and letter sounds but did not move beyond factual knowledge.

The two readings discussed earlier were each 15 minutes long, but the richness of conversation and usage of sophisticated vocabulary varied tremendously. The OWL text had 33 different sophisticated words that appeared 75 times, and the teacher used 20 different sophisticated words. *Brown Bear, Brown Bear, What Do You See?* contained two sophisticated words, neither of which was repeated, and the teacher used six sophisticated words. Lexical diversity ratings were also different, with $D = 87$ for the OWL teacher and $D = 77$ for the control teacher. These contrasting classrooms make tangible the way that curricular guidance was able to shift interaction and alter the lexical environment. Interestingly, the OWL teacher we profiled was the *assistant* teacher, reflecting the fact that a strong curriculum may be able to help bright, motivated teachers, even if they lack advanced educational training, engage children in high-level interactions.

Before discussing other sections it is important to acknowledge that the merit in the type of predictable text books read in control classrooms. They exposed children to rhymes and predictable text, experiences that might foster phonological awareness, and the enlarged text may enable texts to teach letter knowledge more effectively. Also, the frequent repetition of fewer sophisticated words may better support vocabulary learning of children with very limited language skills, children less adept at quickly learning new words from simple exposure.

OTHER SETTINGS

There were hints of curriculum-related differences in small-group and centers time, two settings for which OWL provided guidance designed to encourage high-level conversations. Suggestions of a curriculum effect were visible in the amount of sophisticated word usage. OWL teachers used more sophisticated words in the three settings for which curriculum programming was provided (not in lunchtime). While the difference in sophisticated word usage was statistically significant only for book reading, this pattern suggests that a conceptual focus may provide greater opportunities for sophisticated language use that can be seen in the following transcripts, both of which involve a card-matching game. The following conversation occurred in a control classroom.

TEACHER: What do you have?

CHILD: A **sandbox** (*turns over another card*), and a **sandbox**!

TEACHER: Oh (*claps*) all right! That's a match.

CHILD: Yes! I'm winning!

In this exchange the child uses a sophisticated word represented by the picture on the card when attempting to uncover matches in a game of memory. The child says the word, then looks for another card with the same picture. No talk surrounding the sophisticated word occurred, and no link was made to a conceptual framework.

The teacher in an OWL classroom played the match game in a different manner because the matches are based on relationships found in the real world and with stories that had been read.

TEACHER: What do you call that? (*Points to the picture on the card.*)

CHILD: A stamp.

TEACHER: A stamp, very good. You have to put a stamp on the envelope in order to mail the envelope. And then we gonna put it in . . .

CHILD: **Mailbox!** (*Holds up card.*)

TEACHER: So all of these match right there together.

After this exchange, the discussion later moved on to cover storybooks that contain letters and mailboxes.

In both of these examples the child says the sophisticated word based on picture cues, but only in the OWL classroom does talk build meaning, through the conceptual linking of stamps to envelopes that are placed in mailboxes, an activity children had read about in two different books. This type of discussion provides opportunity for discussion, reflected in the length of each game (OWL = 9 minutes, control = 5 minutes).

Thus, curriculum effects were clearly evident in book reading, the setting where interaction was most fully structured by providing books and prompts, and where the most professional development effort was focused. In other settings, change was less evident because the didactic interactional styles of teachers tended to overshadow the impact of the curriculum. That said, some teachers did appear to grasp the importance of teaching vocabulary, and gave some indication of increased vocabulary teaching and additional attention to building conceptual knowledge needed for deep knowledge of words.

Concluding Thoughts

METHODOLOGY

The measures we are using provide a view of language that brings to light aspects of interaction that vary, are hard to capture with precision using more global measures, and have previously been associated with strong language growth. For example, the percentage of talk by teachers provides a clear and objective measure of children's opportunity to talk, an aspect of informal conversations found to be related to enhanced language (Dickinson & Porche, in press). Use of sophisticated words and lexical diversity provides ways of describing conceptually based conversations, since these tend to draw on a broader range of vocabulary than occurs within routine classroom contexts. While our measure of sophisticated vocabulary has previously been predictive of child learning, it may fail to represent curriculum-specific topics and language adequately. Creation of curriculum-specific measures might better capture this dimension of discourse. Lexical diversity, as measured by *D*, has not been used by classroom researchers, but it may hold promise as a means of describing language environments that complement what is learned by analyzing sophisticated word use. Our use of these measures to describe the language of books revealed drastic differences in the texts children were hearing; such analyses of books might provide an important additional window through which we can view language supports in classrooms.

While the fine-grained analyses yield interesting depictions of language use that vary from classroom to classroom and appear to be at least somewhat sensitive to curriculum effects, they cannot stand alone. Qualitative analysis of the discourse patterns in classrooms and examination of the content of the interactions is essential to understanding the nature of interactions that give rise to the numerical data.

THE CHALLENGES OF INTERVENTION

Our analyses make apparent three major issues we confront as we seek to implement a comprehensive intervention: (1) High-fidelity implementation of a curriculum that requires new behaviors throughout the day is very demanding; (2) teachers' beliefs about what constitutes "teaching" may not change, even if they adopt new activities, and (3) explicit guidance may help teachers shift toward new ways of conversing, but this is not possible throughout the day.

Our curriculum required significant changes in the classroom schedules, the activities teachers used, the books they read, and the types of instruction they were expected to deliver. The small-group approach was new for teachers in terms of structure and content. All children were to be in one of three small groups, two teacher-led and one independent, whereas previously teachers in this program had only worked with selected individuals or small groups during centers time. On many days, the OWL curriculum directed the lead teacher to engage children in conceptually oriented activities and to allow children to work, make observations, and ask questions. This content was quite different from the skills-based activities, such as lotto, used during group instructional times in control classrooms. The books read in OWL were far more sophisticated than those typically read in control classrooms; teachers were directed to engage in more explicit teaching of vocabulary and to have more analytic discussions after the books were read. Finally, in centers time, teachers were encouraged to provide constantly changing theme-related activities and to engage individuals in talk that included target vocabulary words as they discussed concepts addressed during the unit. Such major shifts in classroom routines and teaching expectations may or may not be required by other curricula, but it is our assumption that if we are to achieve significantly accelerated growth, such far-reaching changes are necessary.

We tracked fidelity of implementation in settings by coding videotapes of two lessons, fall and spring. We coded fidelity of settings by noting teacher use of specified behaviors. Overall fidelity was only 54%, with a large standard deviation (9.2), and it varied across settings from 34 to 67%. Surprisingly, the lowest fidelity ratings were for book reading, with a mean of 33.9% and a large standard deviation (10.83). This surprising finding may indicate that the fidelity rating for book reading places a premium on instruction re-

lated to specific words. Although teachers may have grasped the need to define words actively, they might have been less likely to attend to the specific words highlighted by the curriculum. The relatively low levels of fidelity of implementation across contexts point to the need for far more intensive and skilled coaching than we were able to supply.

A second sobering realization forced on us by the linguistic profiles of our classrooms is that changes in ways of using language are only clearly apparent in book reading, and that teachers dominated talk in small-group and centers time, used a limited number of sophisticated words, and had lexical diversity ratings indicating only moderate diversity of word use. Initial qualitative examination suggests that some shift toward more conceptually guided talk occurred in some classrooms during other times of the day, but detailed examination of a teacher from an OWL classroom (DeLisle, 2010) revealed that except during book reading and lunchtime, she employed a didactic instructional method that minimized the frequency of extended, conceptually oriented interactions with individuals. For example, using an OWL activity in small groups in which children were reconstituting dried-out Play-Doh as part of an investigation of water and its properties, her comments were entirely procedural as she verbally guided children in a step-by-step manner. Missing were comments, questions, or conversations about the conceptual issues the activity was designed to explore. Thus, it appears that teachers often continued to use the discourse patterns they employed for teaching—a didactic approach that focuses on information and facts, and involves limited extended exchanges.

On the other hand, if we consider lunchtime, we note context-related variation. During the family-style lunch, teachers were far more equal participants, and children played a larger role in the conversations, often initiating topics. As a result, lexical richness was increased as the topics of discussion varied. We also have some indication of a shift in interactional style during centers time, when teachers engaged in dramatic play with children. Previously we analyzed conversations of four teachers in this program, collected at six different times for 10 minutes each

(Dickinson et al., 2008). In this context there was somewhat less of the didactic teacher-dominated talk than we observed during centers time; all teachers engaged children in extended talk (i.e., five or more topically related utterances). The rate of such connected discourse ranged from a respectable rate of one extended sequence every 2 minutes to the meager rate of one every 6 minutes (Dickinson et al., 2008). Ability to engage in rich, extended interactions while playing was observed in another teacher in this program (DeLisle, 2010) and other preschools (Flushman, 2009). Thus, it appears that the teachers with whom we worked, and others with similar backgrounds, can adopt different and less teacher-dominated and didactic interactional styles when they no longer view themselves as "teaching." This finding suggests that the way teachers conceptualize their role, or the "stance" they assume relative to children, significantly affects how they interact with children (Dickinson, 1991). This stance may not change simply because teachers are provided a new curriculum with different activities unless relatively explicit guidance regarding how to engage children is provided. While our professional development work made clear the importance of language to development, it did not directly address teachers' conceptualization of what it means to "teach" and, except during book reading, there appears to have been minimal change in this core belief that may shape how teachers engage with children.

Patterns of talk during book reading were distinct from other settings, suggesting an effect of the curriculum. This interpretation is consistent with findings of a prior study that tracked teachers' talk as they began using the guidance provided by OWL (Dickinson, Darrow, Ngo, & D'Souza, 2009). It seems that teachers can adopt novel and more cognitively enriched ways of interacting with children when provided clear guidance in the context of a familiar classroom activity such as book reading. It may be a far more challenging matter to get such changes to happen across the day, especially in informal settings such as centers time, when teachers must respond in a flexible way to unpredictable events. This is unfortunate given that research in homes and classrooms reveals that such conversations correlate with language growth.

Conclusions

Evidence clearly points to the critical importance of early language experiences to later language learning and successful acquisition of high-level literacy. Unfortunately, many interventions designed to foster learning have fallen short, including ours. If we are to craft effective methods of intervening and supporting teachers we need better insight into exactly what is and what is not happening in classrooms where interventions are being mounted. The methods we used represent a promising but incomplete start in that direction. Initial results of these fine-grained methods, combined with some qualitative examination of patterns, highlight the difficulty of ensuring that teachers adopt a host of new instructional methods. Also, we note that coaching and professional development may need to address teachers' core conceptions of what it means "to teach," the varied kinds of knowledge children require to become skilled readers, and the differing methods teachers should employ to foster children's acquisition of these abilities. Finally, curriculum developers can be heartened by the fact that guidance provided for relatively predictable group instruction may result in improved discourse, but daunted by the realization that some of the most potent language supporting interactions, those that occur during informal conversations, cannot be scripted.

If we are to craft interventions that truly transform the language-learning trajectories of children we need to continue seeking to understand the dynamics in classrooms that resist change and are amendable to change, and to create curricular and coaching supports that foster sustained changes and result in richer lexical environments in classrooms.

References

Administration for Children and Families. (2010). *Head Start Impact Study: Final report.* Washington, DC: U.S. Department of Health and Human Services.

Arnosky, J. (1997). *Rabbits and raindrops.* New York: Puffin Books.

Ashe, M. K., Reed, S., Dickinson, D. K., Morse, A. B., & Wilson, S. J. (2009). Cross-site effectiveness of Opening the World of Learning and site-specific strategies for supporting implementation. *Early Childhood Services, 3,* 179–191.

Biemiller, A. (2006). Vocabulary development and instruction: A prerequisite for school learning. In D. K. Dickinson & S. B. Neuman (Eds.), *Handbook of early literacy research* (Vol. 2, pp. 41–51). New York: Guilford Press.

Bus, A. G., & van IJzendoorn, M. H. (1999). Phonological awareness and early reading: A meta-analysis of experimental training studies. *Journal of Educational Psychology, 91,* 403–414.

Chall, J. S., & Dale, E. (1995). *Readability revisited: The new Dale–Chall readability formula.* Cambridge, MA: Brookline Books.

Collins, M. F. (2005). ESL preschoolers' English vocabulary acquisition from storybook reading. *Reading Research Quarterly, 40,* 406–408.

Darrow, C. L. (2009, March). *Language and literacy effects of curriculum interventions for preschools serving economically disadvantaged children: A meta-analysis.* Paper presented at the annual meeting of the Society for Research on Educational Effectiveness, Arlington, VA.

Deacon, S. H., & Kirby, J. R. (2004). Morphological awareness: Just "more phonological"?: The roles of morphological and phonological awareness in reading development. *Applied Psycholinguistics, 25,* 223–238.

DeLisle, S. S. (2010). *Dimensions of language use in preschool classrooms: A study of two Head Start teachers across the day.* Unpublished master's thesis, Peabody College, Vanderbilt University, Nashville, TN.

Dickinson, D. K. (1991). Teacher stance and setting: Constraints on conversation in preschools. In A. McCabe & C. Peterson (Eds.), *Developing narrative structure* (pp. 255–302). Hillsdale, NJ: Erlbaum.

Dickinson, D. K. (2006). Toward a toolkit approach to describing classroom quality. *Early Education and Development, 17,* 177–202.

Dickinson, D. K., Darrow, C. L., Ngo, S. M., & D'Souza, L. A. (2009). Changing classroom conversations: Narrowing the gap between potential and reality. In O. A. Barbarin & B. H. Wasik (Eds.), *The handbook of child development and early education: Research to practice* (pp. 328–351). New York: Guilford Press.

Dickinson, D. K., Darrow, C. L., & Tinubu, T. A. (2008). Patterns of teacher–child conversations in Head Start classrooms: Implications for an empirically grounded approach to professional development. *Early Education and Development, 19,* 396–429.

Dickinson, D. K., Flushman, T. R., & Freiberg, J. B. (2009). Language, reading and classroom supports: Where we are and where we need to be going. In B. Richards, M. H. Daller, D. D. Malvern, P. Meara, J. Milton, & J. Trefers-Daller (Eds.), *Vocabulary studies in first and second language acquisition: The interface between theory and application* (pp. 23–38). Hampshire, UK: Palgrave-MacMillan.

Dickinson, D. K., Golinkoff, R. M., & Hirsh-Pasek, K. (2010). Speaking out for language: Why language is central to reading development. *Educational Researcher, 10*(4), 305–310.

Dickinson, D. K., McCabe, A., Anastasopoulos, L., Peisner-Feinberg, E., & Poe, M. D. (2003). The comprehensive language approach to early literacy: The interrelationships among vocabulary, phonological sensitivity, and print knowledge among preschool-aged children. *Journal of Educational Psychology, 95,* 465–481.

Dickinson, D. K., McCabe, A., & Essex, M. J. (2006). A window of opportunity we must open to all: The case for preschool with high-quality support for language and literacy. In D. K. Dickinson & S. B. Neuman (Eds.), *Handbook of early literacy research* (Vol. 2, pp. 11–28). New York: Guilford Press.

Dickinson, D. K., & Porche, M. (in press). The relationship between teacher–child conversations with low-income four-year-olds and grade four language and literacy development. *Child Development.*

Dickinson, D. K., & Tabors, P. O. (Eds.). (2001). *Beginning literacy with language: Young children learning at home and school.* Baltimore: Brookes.

Dickinson, D. K., Watson, B. G., & Farran, D.C. (2007). It's in the details: Approaches to describing and improving preschool classrooms. In L. M. Justice & C. Vukelich (Eds.), Achieving excellent in preschool literacy instruction (pp. 136–162). New York: Guilford Press

Durán, P., Malvern, D., Richards, B., & Chipere, N. (2004). Developmental trends in lexical diversity. *Applied Linguistics, 25,* 220–242.

Early Reading First Evaluation. (2007). *National evaluation of Early Reading First.* Washington, DC: U.S. Department of Education.

Ehri, L. C., Nunes, S. R., Willows, D. M., Schuster, B. V., Yaghoub-Zadeh, Z., & Shanahan, T. (2001). Phonemic awareness instruction helps children learn to read: Evidence from the National Reading Panel's meta-analysis. *Reading Research Quarterly, 36,* 250–287.

Fernald, A., Perfors, A., & Marchman, V. A. (2006). Picking up speed in understanding: Speech processing efficiency and vocabulary growth across the second year. *Developmental Psychology, 42,* 98–116.

Flushman, T. R. (2009, November). *Responsive teaching conversations in a preschool classroom.* Paper presented at the Ethnography in Education Forum, Philadelphia.

Gray, S. (2005). Word learning by preschoolers with specific language impairment: Effect of phonological or semantic cues. *Journal of Speech, Language, and Hearing Research, 48,* 1452–1467.

Hamre, B. K., Justice, L. M., Pianta, R. C., Kilday, C., Sweeney, B., Downer, J. T., et al. (2010). Implementation fidelity of My TeachingPartner literacy and language activities: Association with preschoolers' language and literacy growth. *Early Childhood Research Quarterly, 25*(3), 329–347.

Harlaar, N., Hayiou-Thomas, M. E., Dale, P. S., & Plomin, R. (2008). Why do preschool language abilities correlate with later reading?: A twin study. *Journal of Speech, Language, and Hearing Research, 51,* 688–705.

Hoover, W. A., & Gough, P. B. (1990). The simple view of reading. *Reading and Writing, 28,* 127–160.

Howes, C., Burchinal, M., Pianta, R., Bryant, D., Early, D., Clifford, R., et al. (2008). Ready to learn?: Children's pre-academic achievement in pre-kindergarten programs. *Early Childhood Research Quarterly, 23,* 27–50.

Jackson, B., Larzelere, R., Clair, L. S., Corr, M., Fichter, C., & Egertson, H. (2006). The impact of HeadsUp! Reading on early childhood educators' literacy practices and preschool children's literacy skills. *Early Childhood Research Quarterly, 21,* 213–226.

Johnson, V., & De Villiers, J. G. (2009). Syntactic frames in fast mapping verbs: Effect of age, dialect, and clinical status. *Journal of Speech, Language, and Hearing Research, 52,* 610–623.

Justice, L. M., Mashburn, A. J., Hamre, B. K., & Pianta, R. C. (2008). Quality of language and literacy instruction in preschool classrooms serving at-risk pupils. *Early Childhood Research Quarterly, 23,* 51–68.

Kaiser, A., & McLeod, R. (2010, February). *Curriculum effects on vocabulary outcomes.* Paper presented at the annual meeting of the Conference on Research Innovations in Early Intervention, San Diego, CA.

Kaiser, A. P., Dickinson, D. K., Hefer, K. G., Roberts, M., Darrow, C. L., McLeod, et al. (2010). *The effects of two language-focused preschool curriculum on children's achievement in preschool and kindergarten.* Poster presented at the annual conference of the Institute for Educational Sciences, Washington, DC.

Kemp, N., Lieven, E., & Tomasello, M. (2005). Young children's knowledge of the "determiner" and "adjective" categories. *Journal of Speech, Language, and Hearing Research, 48,* 592–609.

Love, J. M., Kisker, E. E., Ross, C., Raikes, H., Constantine, J., Boller, K., et al. (2005). The effectiveness of Early Head Start for 3-year-old children and their parents: Lessons for policy and programs. *Developmental Psychology, 41,* 885–901.

MacWhinney, B. (2000). *The CHILDES project: Tools for analyzing talk* (3rd ed.). Mahwah, NJ: Erlbaum.

Malvern, D., & Richards, B. (2002). Investigating accommodation in language proficiency interviews using a new measure of lexical diversity. *Language Testing, 19,* 85–104.

Marchman, V. A., & Fernald, A. (2008). Speed of word recognition and vocabulary knowledge in infancy predict cognitive and language outcomes in later childhood. *Developmental Science, 11,* F9–F16.

Martin, B., Jr. (1992). *Brown bear, brown bear, what do you see?* New York: Holt.

Mol, S. E., Bus, A. G., & de Jong, M. T. (2009). Interactive book reading in early education: A tool to stimulate print knowledge as well as oral language. *Review of Educational Research, 79,* 979–1007.

Munson, B., Kurtz, B. A., & Windsor, J. (2005). The influence of vocabulary size, phonotactic probability, and wordlikeness on nonword repetitions of children with and without specific language impairment. *Journal of Speech, Language, and Hearing Research, 48,* 1033–1047.

Nash, M., & Donaldson, M. L. (2005). Word learning in children with vocabulary deficits. *Journal of Speech, Language, and Hearing Research, 48,* 439–458.

Nation, K., Clarke, P., Marshall, C. M., & Durand, M. (2004). Hidden language impairments in children: Parallels between poor reading comprehension and specific language impairment? *Journal of Speech, Language, and Hearing Research, 47,* 199–211.

National Early Literacy Panel (NELP). (2008). *Developing early literacy: Report of the National Early Literacy Panel.* Jessup, MD: National Institute for Literacy.

National Reading Panel. (2000). *Teaching children to read: An evidence-based assessment of the scientific research literature on reading and its implications for reading instruction: Reports of the subgroups* (NIH Publication No. 00-4754). Washington, DC: National Institute of Child Health and Human Development.

Neuman, S. B., & Cunningham, L. (2009). The impact of professional development and coaching on early language and literacy instructional practices. *American Educational Research Journal, 46*(2), 532–566.

Neuman, S. B., & Dwyer, J. (2009). Missing in action: Vocabulary instruction in Pre-K. *Reading Teacher, 62,* 384–392.

NICHD Early Child Care Research Network. (2005). Pathways to reading: The role of oral language in the transition to reading. *Developmental Psychology, 41*(2), 428–442.

Paris, S. G. (2009). Constrained skills—So what? (The Oscar Causey Address). In K. M. Leander, D. W. Rowe, D. K. Dickinson, M. K. Handley, R. T. Jimenez, & V. J. Risko (Eds.), *58th Yearbook of the National Reading Conference* (pp. 34–44). Oak Creek, WI: National Reading Conference.

Penno, J. F., Wilkinson, I. A. C., & Moore, D. W. (2002). Vocabulary acquisition from teacher explanation and repeated listening to stories: Do they overcome the Matthew effect? *Journal of Educational Psychology, 94,* 23–33.

Pianta, R. C., Mashburn, A. J., Downer, J. T., Hamre, B. K., & Justice, L. (2008). Effects of web-mediated professional development resources on teacher–child interactions in pre-kindergarten classrooms. *Early Childhood Research Quarterly, 23*(4), 431–451.

Preschool Curriculum Evaluation Research Consortium. (2008). *Effects of preschool curriculum programs on school readiness.* Washington, DC: National Center for Education Research, Institute for Education Sciences, U.S. Department of Education.

Reese, E., & Cox, A. (1999). Quality of adult book reading affects children's emergent literacy. *Developmental Psychology, 35,* 20–28.

Robbins, C., & Ehri, L. C. (1994). Reading storybooks to kindergarteners helps them learn new vocabulary words. *Journal of Educational Psychology, 86,* 54–64.

Schickedanz, J., & Dickinson, D. K. (2005). *Opening the World of Learning: A comprehensive literacy program.* Parsippany, NJ: Pearson Early Learning.

Sénéchal, M., Ouellette, G., & Rodney, D. (2006). The misunderstood giant: On the predictive role of early vocabulary to future reading. In D. K. Dickinson & S. B. Neuman (Eds.), *Handbook of early literacy research* (Vol. 2, pp. 173–182). New York: Guilford Press.

Share, D. L., & Leikin, M. (2004). Language impairment at school entry and later reading disability: Connections at lexical versus supralexical levels of reading. *Scientific Studies of Reading, 8,* 87–110.

Snow, C. E., Porche, M. V., Tabors, P. O., & Harris, S. R. (2007). *Is literacy enough?: Pathways to academic success for adolescents.* Baltimore: Brookes.

Storch, S. A., & Whitehurst, G. J. (2002). Oral language and code-related precursors to reading: Evidence from a longitudinal structural model. *Developmental Psychology, 38,* 934–947.

Storkel, H. L. (2001). Learning new words: Phonotactic probability in language development. *Journal of Speech, Language, and Hearing Research, 44,* 1321–1337.

Storkel, H. L. (2003). Learning new words II: Phonotactic probability in verb learning. *Journal of Speech, Language, and Hearing Research, 46,* 1312–1323.

Van Hulle, C. A., Goldsmith, H. H., & Lemery, K. S. (2004). Genetic, environmental, and gender effects on individual differences in toddler expressive language. *Journal of Speech, Language, and Hearing Research, 47,* 904–912.

Vellutino, F. R., Tunmer, W. E., Jaccard, J. J., & Chen, R. (2007). Components of reading ability: Multivariate evidence for a convergent skills model of reading development. *Scientific Studies of Reading, 11,* 3–32.

Wasik, B. A., & Bond, M. A. (2001). Beyond the pages of a book: Interactive book reading and language development in preschool classrooms. *Journal of Educational Psychology, 93,* 243–250.

Wasik, B. A., Bond, M. A., & Hindman, A. (2006). The effects of a language and literacy intervention on Head Start children and teachers. *Journal of Educational Psychology, 98,* 63–74.

Wechsler, D. (1974). *Wechsler Intelligence Scale for Children—Revised.* New York: Psychological Corporation.

Weizman, Z. O., & Snow, C. E. (2001). Lexical input as related to children's vocabulary acquisition: Effects of sophisticated exposure and support for meaning. *Developmental Psychology, 37,* 265–279.

Whitehurst, G. J., Epstein, J. N., Angell, A. L., Payne, A. C., Crone, D. A., & Fischel, J. E. (1994). Outcomes of an emergent literacy intervention in Head Start. *Journal of Educational Psychology, 86,* 542–555.

Whitehurst, G. J., Falco, F. L., Lonigan, C. J., Fischel, J. E., DeBaryshe, B. D., Valdez-Menchaca, M. C., et al. (1988). Accelerating language development through picture book reading. *Developmental Psychology, 24,* 552–559.

Whitehurst, G. J., Zevenbergen, A. A., Crone, D. A., Schultz, M. D., Velting, O. N., & Fischel, J. E. (1999). Outcomes of an emergent literacy intervention from Head Start through second grade. *Journal of Educational Psychology, 91*(2), 261–272.

Wilson, S. J., Morse, A. B., & Dickinson, D. K. (2008). *Examining the effectiveness of OWL as used in ERF projects: Final report of results for the OWL Consortium.* Nashville, TN: Center for Evaluation Research and Methodology, Vanderbilt University.

U.S. Department of Education. (2003). *Third national Even Start evaluation: Program impacts and implications for improvement* (Planning, and Evaluation Service, Elementary and Secondary Education Division). Washington, DC: Author.

Zill, N., & Resnick, G. (2006). Emergent literacy of low-income children in Head Start: Relationships with child and family characteristics, program factors, and classroom quality. In D. K. Dickinson & S. B. Neuman (Eds.), *Handbook of early literacy research* (Vol. 2, pp. 347–371). New York: Guilford Press.

23

The Challenge of Teaching Vocabulary in Early Education

SUSAN B. NEUMAN

Given that reading print with understanding requires knowledge of words and their meanings, one would reasonably assume that vocabulary training is a primary focus in the early years. Logically, children must know the words that make up written texts to understand them, especially as vocabulary demands of content-related materials increase in the upper grades. After all, numerous studies (Cunningham & Stanovich, 1997; Scarborough, 2001) have shown that the size of a person's vocabulary is strongly related to how well that person understands what he or she reads not only in the primary grades but also in reading comprehension in high school.

One would also think that the resounding alarm of Hart and Risley's 30 million word catastrophe (2003), the striking differentials in vocabulary between low-income children and their middle-income peers, would initiate a call for a renewed emphasis on vocabulary training in the early years. Just consider the following statistics. Results (Farkas & Beron, 2004) suggest that the inequality in oral vocabulary development by race and social class develops prior to 36 months of age. Halle and her colleagues (2009), analyzing the Early Childhood Longitudinal Birth Cohort, show evidence of initial gaps appearing as early as 9 months of age. Hart and Risley (1995) found that by age 18–20 months, high socioeconomic status (SES) children's vocabulary trajectories are accelerating away from those of working-class and welfare children, and by 24 months, the trajectory of working-class children has separated from that of welfare children. By grade 4, children with below-average vocabulary levels, even if they have adequate word identification skills, are likely to "slump" in reading comprehension, unable to profit from independent reading of most grade-level texts (Biemiller & Boote, 2006).

Counterintuitively, despite these statistics, there has been a striking lack of attention to developing meaningful vocabulary in the early years. Moreover, studies (e.g., Biemiller, 2006) that have examined children's vocabulary over several years of schooling indicate that schools are not doing much to increase children's vocabulary, and the mere act of attending school has little effect on vocabulary development.

This chapter argues for placing vocabulary at the forefront of early literacy instruction. It first reviews what we know about quality vocabulary training for children in the early years. It then examines a number of the stumbling blocks, highlighting why vocabulary training has proven to be especially complex in instructional programming. Finally, it examines the potential of quality instruction for children who need to accelerate word learning.

What Is Quality Vocabulary Instruction?

Starting at about 18 months or so, children need to pick up about two new word meanings per day on average to build up a stock of 6,000 root words by age 2 (Bloom, 2000). They acquire much of their vocabulary through what has been known as fast mapping. Coined by Susan Carey and Elsa Bartlett (1978), *fast mapping* refers to learning words based on a single exposure and is thought to explain (at least in part) the prodigious rate at which children gain vocabulary.

But in part the term has taken on an aura of romance—a view that all words can be learned through fast mapping. Contrary to this view, ample evidence suggests that all children do not learn words through fast mapping but rather learn probabilistic, predictive relationships between objects and sounds that develop over time. Evidence (Bornstein, Kessen, & Weiskopf, 1976) for this comes, for example, from children's struggles to understand color words: Although infants can distinguish between basic color categories, many sighted children use color words in the same way that blind children do up until the fourth year. Typically, words such as *blue* and *yellow* appear in their vocabularies, but their application of individual color terms is haphazard and interchangeable. Children's behavior clearly indicates that they have knowledge of these words, but this knowledge is far from complete; rather it appears to be a predictive as opposed to an all-or-none phenomenon. Words are learned incrementally (Nagy & Scott, 2000) over time through repeated and meaningful exposures.

The notion that all words can be learned through fast mapping, however, has fostered several misconceptions for vocabulary instruction. First, it presumes that single exposures to words are sufficient for word learning. For example, although book reading is clearly a fertile ground for vocabulary

development, studies (Biemiller, 2006; Scarborough & Dobrich, 1994) have revealed that the relation between reading aloud and learning vocabulary contained in the books is far less potent than expected. Several teams of researchers (e.g., Beck & McKeown, 2007; National Early Literacy Panel, 2008) examining the effects on vocabulary of reading aloud have reported findings that range from nonexistent to unimpressive. Second, it suggests that quality oral language environments in schools by themselves may be sufficient to improve children's vocabulary. In this respect, vocabulary development is thought to be learned almost as if through osmosis, from interactions with language-rich environments.

Although there is some truth to each of these presumptions, neither is potent enough to come close to narrowing the substantial gap for children who come from economically disadvantage circumstances compared to their middle-income peers. Rather, it will take intensive interventions early on to improve vocabulary and to help children build a rich conceptual base for comprehending materials in subject-matter texts.

This view has been substantiated in a number of meta-analyses (e.g., Mol, Bus, & de Jong, 2009; Mol, Bus, de Jong, & Smeets, 2008) that have examined the effects of vocabulary training on children's oral language development and print comprehension. These meta-analyses examine the specific benefits of shared reading, dialogic reading, and interactive reading on children's early literacy skills. Together, they reveal that shared book reading, considered the most common strategy for vocabulary instruction, has a significant impact on children's learning. However, in each case, effect sizes (ESs) across studies range from modest (0.17) to only moderate (0.57) in all studies combined.

Looking more broadly across interventions, Loren Maulis and I recently conducted the most extensive meta-analysis (Maulis & Neuman, 2009) to date on all extant vocabulary trainings (published and unpublished) and their effects on oral language development. Our analysis not only revealed a larger overall ES (0.87) but also identified a number of important factors that moderate these effects. Together, they highlight several key features of quality vocabulary training.

Identification of Words

Vocabulary instruction refers to the words we must know to communicate effectively; words in speaking (expressive vocabulary), and words in listening (receptive vocabulary). Children use the words they hear to make sense of the words they will eventually see in print. Vocabulary instruction, therefore, must begin by identifying the words that children will need to build meaning, and the ideas that these words represent.

Explicit and Implicit Instruction

Explicit instruction emphasizes strategies for directly teaching vocabulary, which may include detailed definitions and examples given before, during, or after a storybook reading; or a follow-up discussion of the words in a story. One might contrast this approach with *implicit instruction*, which involves teaching words within the context of an activity. For example, implicit instruction might involve reading a storybook without any intentional stopping or deliberate teaching of word meanings.

Our meta-analysis revealed that explicit instruction enhanced vocabulary learning significantly better than implicit instruction. However, even better, a combination of explicit and implicit instruction improved children's achievement. Interventions in which the deliberately explicit instruction of words was followed by implicit uses of the words in contexts enabled children to be more successful than did either approaches by itself. This suggests that children need instruction in the vocabulary words they are learning, and continuing practice in meaningful contexts. Bringing these approaches together will have greater impact on children's word learning.

Depth of Processing

Another feature of word learning is what Stahl and Fairbanks (1986) have described as *depth of processing*, which refers to the types of activities in which children engage in learning new words. Words are not mere labels of things; rather, children's learning of words, even the simplest names for things, requires rich mental capacities—conceptual, social, and linguistic. Learning a word in-

volves mapping a form, such as a dog, onto a meaning or a concept. And it is the rich, interconnected knowledge of concepts that really drives children's understanding and comprehension of text.

Having children repeat, recite, and immediately recall the words they hear merely engages them in shallow processing tasks. It is like memorization of a list, requiring only short-term memory. In contrast, learning activities that involve children in developing greater meaning of words through play, drama, and problem-solving tasks create greater numbers of connections that require more mental effort, and, therefore, are likely to be more memorable.

Monitoring Progress

Effective vocabulary training monitors children's progress, recognizing that ongoing accountability is essential for tailoring instruction to their needs. Our meta-analysis examined two types of measuring instruments: author-created and standardized. *Author-created measures* focus on gains in the vocabulary taught in the training; *standardized measures* typically examine more global receptive or expressive language development.

Author-created measures are designed to take the pulse of children's progress in the curriculum itself. These measures are developed in order to apply what is learned, often giving teachers' specific strategies for reteaching or practicing a word meaning. In this respect, they are more sensitive to the goals of the instructional program. On the other hand, standardized measures are unlikely to contain the words of the program. Get It, Got It, Go! (Early Childhood Research Institute on Measuring Growth and Development, 2000), for example, is a kind of standardized progress-monitoring tool that examines children's expressive vocabulary. Children are given pictures of common words and asked to name the words within a particular time limit. It is not linked to a particular curriculum.

Not surprisingly, our meta-analysis indicated that author-created measures were more proximal indicators of vocabulary improvement, and more targeted to what was to be learned in the interventions. Global measures are less sensitive to gains in vocabulary interventions. They do, however, provide useful information on whether programs are making progress overall in children's language development.

This means that author-created tests may be the most beneficial approach for monitoring children's ongoing progress. Standardized measures, less sensitive to vocabulary gains, are less likely to help teachers tailor their instruction to meet students' needs. Rather, they may serve as a global road map to determine the effectiveness of programs on changes in overall language development.

Do Early Literacy Curriculum Programs Provide Help for Teaching Vocabulary?

Paradoxically, despite its importance, vocabulary instruction has often been ignored in school instruction. Much of the available evidence (see Beck & McKeown, 2007) indicates that there is little emphasis on the acquisition of vocabulary in curriculum. Given the increasing complexity and academic vocabulary requirements in content-specific texts, it might seem odd to find such a paucity of vocabulary instruction. But as Juel, Biancarosa, Coker, and Deffes (2003) have noted, teachers tend to do much mentioning and assigning, and little actual teaching of new vocabulary. Moreover, studies (Biemiller, 2001) that examined children's vocabulary over several years of schooling have indicated that schools are not doing much to increase student vocabulary, and the mere act of attending school has little effect on vocabulary growth.

Recognizing the discontinuity between instruction needed for children to be successful in reading and the instructional emphases most often reported in schools, we analyzed the vocabulary materials used in 10 preschool curricula (Neuman & Dwyer, 2009). Specifically, we were interested in the scope and sequence of vocabulary instructional materials; that is, what they taught and how they taught it. Furthermore, we wanted to examine how closely these materials might align with what we know about quality vocabulary instruction.

Tables 23.1 and 23.2 provide examples of what we found. First, as shown in Table 23.1, there was no evidence of agreement be-

tween programs on the scope and sequence of instruction. One program, for example, provided a very detailed list of instructional objectives, while others were far more general. Second, there was no sequence of skills or any signs of systematic instruction. Turning to the quality features, we found a scattershot approach to instruction. Only 1 program in 10 had elements that resembled a systematic instructional regimen, that is, a deliberate effort in curriculum materials to teach vocabulary to preschoolers. Briefly, our findings indicated (1) a mismatch between explicitly stated goals in the scope and sequence, and the practical manifestation within the curriculum materials themselves; (2) a general pattern of "acknowledging" the importance of vocabulary but sporadic attention to addressing the skill intentionally; (3) pedagogical strategies for teaching words that involved repeating words in choral response, without attention to building sufficient background knowledge; (4) surprisingly little attention given to which words to teach (i.e., capricious selection of words); and (5) limited to no opportunities to practice, review, and monitor children's progress. In short, these findings might examine why Juel and her colleagues (2003) have reported such limited instruction: Current instructional materials appear to offer little guidance to teachers who want to do a better job of teaching vocabulary to young children.

Are Teachers Engaged in Vocabulary Instruction?

Even with limited guidance from instructional materials, it may be that teachers naturally engage in vocabulary instruction. After all, research has shown that some teachers engage in cognitively challenging talk (Dickinson & Smith, 1994), and that this talk is highly predictive of children's language development in classrooms. Therefore, perhaps vocabulary instruction is part of the discourse of teacher interactions with children as they go about their daily routines of whole-group, small-group, and one-to-one activities. To examine vocabulary development in classrooms and potentially gauge the extent of instruction in daily instruction, we observed 55 kindergarten classrooms in 12 different communities, representing a

TABLE 23.1. Examples of the Variety in the Scope and Sequence of Vocabulary Skills in Several PreK Vocabulary Curricula

Curriculum A	Curriculum B	Curriculum C	Curriculum D
Total: 4	Total: 26	Total: 10	Total: 2
• Uses new words as a part of his or her speaking vocabulary in meaningful ways. • Says new words and dialogue from stories. • Shows a steady increase in the number of words in his or her listening vocabulary. • Refines and expands his or her understanding of known words in English and/or home language.	• Antonyms • Comparatives/ superlatives • Compound words • Connecting words (transition words) • Context clues • Contractions • Figurative language • Greek and Latin roots • High-frequency words • Homographs • Homophones/ homonyms • Idioms • Inflectional endings • Irregular plurals • Multiple-meaning words • Multisyllabic words • Position words • Prefixes • Question words • Base or root words • Selection vocabulary • Suffixes • Synonyms • Time and order words (creating sequences) • Utility words (colors, classroom objects, etc.) • Word families	• Uses newly learned vocabulary on multiple occasions and in new contexts. • Identifies a wide variety of objects through receptive language. • Names, describes actual or pictured objects. • Shows a steady increase in listening and speaking vocabulary. • Identifies the meaning of content specific vocabulary. • Uses position words. • Uses sensory words. • Uses temporal words (before, after, first, next, last). • Begins to understand simple multiple meaning words, homonyms, synonyms, antonyms. • Begins to understand naming words, action words, describing words.	• Uses new vocabulary in every day communication. • Refines and extends understanding of known words.

TABLE 23.2. Vocabulary Instructional Elements in 10 Preschool Literacy Curricula

Instructional element	Curriculum									
	A	B	C	D	E	F	G	H	I	J
1. Identifies words to be learned.	+	+	+	+	+	+	+	+	+	+
2. Uses specific teaching techniques to address these words.	–	+	–	–	+	–	–	–	–	+
3. Provides opportunities to use/practice words.	–	+	–	–	+	+	–	–	–	+
4. Provides opportunities to review previously learned words.	–	+	–	–	–	–	–	–	–	+
5. Provides strategies for ongoing progress monitoring of vocabulary development.	–	–	+	+	–	–	–	–	–	+

Note. +, presence; –, absence.

range of socioeconomic neighborhoods, and public and charter schools (Wright & Neuman, 2009). Our goal was to understand the degree to which kindergarten provides explicit vocabulary training and, if so, in what type of instruction it might occur.

We identified a *vocabulary teaching episode* as an interaction where the teacher provides children with the meaning of a target vocabulary word, for example, "A *cave* is a hole in the mountain" or "*Rhyming* means the words have to sound alike. They have the same ending sound." We used this definition to emphasize word meanings and explicit instruction, including partial definitions, synonyms, antonyms, category membership, and examples used to explain meaning. We spent 12 hours in each class, over 4 different days, audiotaping and coding teachers' language for vocabulary instruction.

We found no evidence of *rich instruction*— or any lessons dedicated vocabulary development. During 660 hours of observation, no planned vocabulary lessons took place. Rather, virtually all vocabulary instruction was embedded in other activities. Within these activities, reading aloud, science, and social studies had the greatest density of episodes. However, although reading aloud was ubiquitous in kindergarten, only 24 of the 55 teachers taught any science or social studies. Content was absent in many classrooms.

Taking into account all observations, we reported an average of eight vocabulary episodes per classroom day, or almost two and a half per hour. More than seven of the eight episodes were different, indicating very little repetition of each word. Slightly more than three of these words might be considered *sophisticated*, indicating that they were outside the Dale–Chall list of everyday vocabulary words. Consequently, the rest of the episodes most likely focused on words that children probably already knew. Even within read-alouds, usually considered a rich context for vocabulary development, teachers provided only one new word per day.

What disconcerted us about these observations was that we found almost no repetitions of the same word during the episodes. In other words, students would have to fast map the word's meaning in the context of other activity. Yet, as Beck and McKeown (2007) found, just providing definitions of words—even rich, meaningful explanations and definitions—will likely not result in deep or sustained knowledge of words. Rather, children need multiple encounters if the goal is more than a surface-level understanding, and if new words are to become a permanent part of children's vocabulary repertoires. The most recent evidence on interventions in vocabulary suggests that extended instruction is critical for creating depth of word meaning.

It is clear that present school practices fall far short of what is needed to improve children's vocabulary development, particularly for those who have had limited opportunity to develop these skills. It is not occurring in teachers' natural, day-to-day interactions with children. Clearly, we need a substantially greater teacher-centered effort to promote vocabulary, especially in the critical early years.

What Are the Current Stumbling Blocks in Providing Vocabulary Instruction?

These findings lead to a number of issues that continue to puzzle, plague, and challenge practitioners and vocabulary researchers. They include the following.

The Size of the Challenge before Us

Sometimes it is argued that the sheer number of words children need to learn is too great to teach. For example, Jenkins, Stein, and Wysocki (1984; see also Beck, McKeown, McCaslin, & Burkes, 1979) found that over the course of a year, one major reading program provided no formal vocabulary instruction and another targeted only 300 new words for instruction, many of which average students already knew. Even under the best-case scenario, Beck and her colleagues (1979) found that students were likely to encounter new vocabulary in their texts only three times: once before reading a story, a second time when the word appears in the story, and a third time in independent practice. Notably absent was any intensity of instruction.

As a result, researchers have suggested that word learning happens best not through direct teaching but through incidental exposure through reading widely and listening to stories (Nagy, Anderson, & Herman, 1987). Nevertheless, Jenkins and his colleagues (1984), and Biemiller and Slonim (2001), who reported only modest gains in vocabulary growth, reported that while incidental learning may account for some vocabulary growth, it has only a modest effect.

Biemiller (2001) argues that the complexity of what students need to learn has been somewhat exaggerated. His research suggests that teachers need to focus on root word growth rather than on acquisition of all inflected and derived forms of words. From this perspective, the average number of root word meanings acquired per year might be somewhat smaller, around 600—from infancy to the end of elementary school.

The Selection of Words to Teach

Surprisingly little attention has been paid to the words selected for vocabulary instruction. Studies (e.g., Coyne, Simmons, Kame'enui, & Stoolmiller, 2004) often indicate little about how the researchers selected words in their various interventions. The usual approach appears to be opportunistic: Words are selected from stories or texts that are judged to be unfamiliar. But this strategy does not tend to address the power of the selected words to enhance children's vocabulary use, its difficulty level, or its importance and relation to specific concepts and content knowledge.

At least three approaches to the selection of words have been proposed. Biemiller (2006), for example, advocates focusing on words that are partially learned—those representing between 40 and 70% of a target groups' knowledge. From his perspective, these are the words that children are likely to learn easily, allowing them to increase their vocabulary more rapidly. Given the cumulative nature of vocabulary growth, this practice can essentially accelerate language development.

Contrary to this approach, Beck and McKeown (2007) have argued that words for vocabulary instruction should be selected from the portion of the word stock that comprises sophisticated words of high utility that characterize written language. Using the heuristic of tiers to describe three different levels of words, these sophisticated words would be Tier 2—more refined labels for concepts with which young learners are already familiar. For example, *superb* would be a refinement of the word *great*; *pleasant* would be a more sophisticated word for *nice*. In this respect, Beck and McKeown would focus on words that are less likely to be learned colloquially through regular discourse. Rather, they would represent words that could improve and enhance verbal functioning.

The approach we use in our work (Neuman, Dwyer, Koh, & Wright, 2007) represents still another consideration for selecting words. We advocate focusing on words that help children develop rich content knowledge that enables them to derive meaning from texts in science, math, social studies, and health in particular. These words are both content-rich *and* sophisticated. For example, learning the word *habitat* relates to a topic and a concept that will be learned in greater depth as children go through the elementary grades. It has *word power*—serving as a catalyst for learning many additional words. Furthermore, these are words that will need further elaboration and development, representing important concepts in increasingly difficult learning progressions throughout the grades.

Although the emphases differ in these approaches, all three suggest that word selection needs to be an important consideration in vocabulary training. Too often, words are selected haphazardly; they may be too easy and not require teaching, or they may be far too difficult and neither memorable nor very important. Rather, intentional teaching requires intentional word selection.

The Dominance of Storybook Reading

Recent meta-analyses (Mol et al., 2008, 2009; National Early Literacy Panel, 2008) confirm that storybook reading tends to dominate the field of vocabulary interventions. Whether it is called shared book reading, interactive reading, dialogic reading, or some combination of these terms, more often than not teachers have relied on storybook reading as their prime intervention to teach vocabulary in the early years. However, there are several problems in such reliance. First, as described earlier, words selected for vocabulary instruction tend to be opportunistic, based on the particular book and not on other criteria. Second, words are likely not to be repeated sufficiently to provide the practice necessary to develop an in-depth understanding of words and their meanings in different contexts. Third, words from different storybooks rarely provide a coherent framework for children to understand words well enough to make inductive inferences.

It is not surprising, therefore, that recent meta-analyses have shown only moderate effects of reading aloud on vocabulary development. To augment the read-aloud experience, a number of vocabulary training studies have used strategies that include direct explanation of words, repeated readings, or dialogic techniques to engage children in more actively discussing stories (Biemiller, 2006; Penno et al., 2002). Furthermore, studies have followed up the read-aloud with enrichment activities designed to help children process words at deeper levels (Coyne et al., 2004; Wasik & Bond, 2001). These strategies have added to the amount of vocabulary learned. Nevertheless, average gains in word meanings in these and other studies have been modest, ranging from approximately 12–25% of the words taught, and may not be sufficiently powerful to erase the vast differences in vocabulary evident early in children's lives (Biemiller & Boote, 2006).

These results, now replicated many different times, suggest that additional training is needed for children who lack opportunities to learn words. A number of studies summarized by Biemiller (2006) and Stahl (1999), for example, clearly indicate that children can acquire and retain words through more direct approaches.

The Need for Systematic Teaching

Children who learn more words almost undoubtedly encounter words with greater frequency, receive a greater number of explanations of word meanings, and have more opportunities to practice using these words in meaningful contexts. This suggests that we can do considerably more than we are currently doing through systematic instruction.

We have already noted that basal readers, at least in their most recent editions, fail to create the kind of instructional regimen necessary for children's acquisition of word meaning. However, if vocabulary acquisition is largely sequential in nature, then it is certainly possible to identify that sequence and ensure that children at a given vocabulary level have the opportunity to develop the appropriate word knowledge with greater depth. Of course, several issues would need to be resolved. Most importantly, long-standing word lists (e.g., Dale–Chall Living Word Vocabulary) do not necessarily represent the words that children need in order to meet standards set in today's content areas. In addition, as Biemiller has noted (2001), existing lists do not necessarily correspond to observed sequences of word acquisition.

If such a list were developed, however, it might provide an important resource as teachers go about introducing, practicing, and reviewing words within the context of meaningful activity. It could serve as a guide for more planned and contextualized introduction of vocabulary through meaningful activity and could support more deliberate approach to vocabulary training in the early years.

Differentiating between Oral and Written Vocabulary Development

Broadly speaking, there are two types of vocabulary—oral and print. A reader who is competent in decoding can translate a strange word into speech. For example, most adults are likely to be able to decode the word *grof*. If this word happens to be in the reader's oral vocabulary, the reader will understand it. But if the word is not known (e.g., in this case, it is a pseudoword), despite the person's ability to decode, the word will have no meaning. Understanding printed text is dependent on oral language comprehension and vocabulary.

Nevertheless, much of the research on vocabulary development has focused on print (see Elleman, Lindo, Morphy, & Compton, 2009). For example, exemplary training strategies reported by the National Reading Panel (2000) include text restructuring, repetition, and multiple exposures to words in text, and rereading, assuming that children are already reading at least at a rudimentary level. In fact, there is a curious logic in many of these vocabulary training studies. As noted in both recent and past meta-analyses, much of this research has emphasized building children's skills in vocabulary by increasing the amount of reading. Given that poor readers are likely to select less challenging texts than average or above-average readers, rather than closing the gap, this strategy could have the unfortunate potential of exacerbating vocabulary differentials.

The evidence is clear: We need to build children's oral vocabulary and comprehension of concepts prior to and during their earliest experiences with print. In their initial efforts at reading, as noted by Jeanne Chall (1983) many years ago, children tend to be "glued to print," focusing their attention on decoding simple words. Without oral vocabulary skills, children are likely to hit a firewall of complex concepts and words when they are introduced to content-specific words in third and fourth grade. Therefore, we must do more to promote a more intentional approach early on to foster oral vocabulary and language growth.

Understanding What Counts as Evidence

It is not an uncommon story. A researcher develops an intervention designed to improve vocabulary development. She uses explicit teaching to emphasize certain words in a big book format, followed by practice with partner reading, play through dramatization, and repeated reading, along with a strong parent involvement program. All together, one would argue that her teaching includes all the elements of an intensive, research-based intervention. Nevertheless, when compared with a comparison group that received similar materials but little direct intervention, there are no statistical differences on standardized measures of language or achievement.

Given the difficulty of affecting and measuring language growth, especially when interventions are of limited length, it is clear that we need to develop further and finetune our criteria for determining what counts when judging young children's language growth. Too often, our measures are too distal from the intervention's goals. For example, one might question why we would even expect changes in overall language as a result of learning particular words in stories.

It suggests that we need to find more effective ways than our typical measures of gaining access to children's language development and growth. For example, data sources (e.g., narration, retellings, number of questions raised, ability to sustain a conversation) may represent more proximal and valid approaches for determining what constitutes evidence of change in children's vocabulary development.

Instructional Design Principles to Accelerate Vocabulary Development and Reduce Disparities

Quality vocabulary instruction has many dimensions, but at its core are the teacher's experience and expertise at delivering instruction, and the design of instructional materials. We begin with the assumption that it is the opportunity to learn, not children's natural ability, that has often stymied their progress in early literacy. Therefore, to accelerate instruction we need to provide better instructional tools through tested principles of design that enhance professional development for teachers. A description of these foundational design principles follows, along with illustrations for how they work within the context of a curriculum we developed, the World of Words (WOW; Neuman et al., 2007).

Principle 1: The Notion of Acceleration

The statistics that differentiate poor children from their mainstream peers are dramatic and highly disconcerting. Hart and Risley (2003) probably describe it best. They estimate that the accumulated experiences of words prior to kindergarten constitute a 30 million word catastrophe. Put simply, this gap is not going to close easily, particularly when we consider that children have spent 20,000 hours with their parents prior to school entry, and the number of hours of instruction in a school year may represent as little as 540 hours.

To narrow these statistics, it is not enough merely to improve children's vocabulary. Rather, we have to find ways to accelerate its development—to create self-teaching strategies early on, so that children can learn new words on their own.

Principle 2: The Organization of Word Knowledge

This principle relates to our first, and suggests how we may be able to accelerate word learning. Too often, words are taught in isolation, with little attention to how these words may fit within larger concepts and ideas. Children learn them, then quickly forget because they do not understand their relationships.

An emerging body of evidence indicates that the organization in which children learn words may support word learning (Booth, 2009). Recent research has shown that when children undergo a "vocabulary spurt" (McMurray, 2007), a point in development in which the pace of word learning increases rapidly, they also begin to display the ability to categorize. The co-occurrence of these abilities has led researchers to speculate a synergistic relationship between them. Borovsky and Elman (2006), for example, in three computational simulations, manipulated the amount of language input, sentential complexity, and the frequency distribution of words within categories. In each of these simulations, they found that improvements in category structure were tightly correlated with subsequent improvements in word-learning ability. Their results were consistent with previous research by Gopnik and Meltzoff (1987), who argued for the "bidirectional interaction" of categorization as a tool for learning language.

Richly organized concepts are structured as *taxonomies* (groupings of like things, e.g., pets) (Markman & Callanan, 1984), a hierarchy in which successive levels refer to increasing generalizations. Taxonomies have similar properties (e.g., pets—dogs and cats are animals that live with people), and fall into an intermediate level of abstraction (Smith, 1995). In this respect, they are different than themes or thematic groupings (e.g., things one does in a grocery store—clusters of things that interact), which are based on associations and have a less clear-cut structure (Markman & Hutchinson, 1984). Specifically, it is the structure and the coherence of taxonomic categories that has been associated with improved word learning.

A number of studies (Gelman & Markman, 1986; Murphy & Lassaline, 1997) have shown that categories can have *inductive potential*, helping children to develop generalizations across categories, and inferencing beyond what is specifically taught. Consequently, learning words in categories seem to promote word learning and can lead to potential acceleration of vocabulary growth and concept development. Specifically, here is what we know:

- Children learn new vocabulary in the context of acquiring new knowledge; concepts come in clusters that are systematically interrelated (Anderson & Freebody, 1979).
- Children tend to organize information into meaningful categories consisting of multiple features.
- Children learn words using this classification decision process, assessing how well the basic features of semantic meaning match existing representations.
- Vocabulary knowledge, then, develops from understanding similarities and differences in categories—efficient method for organizing information (Gelman, Coley, Rosengren, Hartman, & Pappas, 1998).

Principle 3: Word Knowledge

Vocabulary is children's entry to knowledge and the world of ideas. In order to have a good conversation or an inquiry lesson in science, for example, children need a threshold of content-specific words to talk about their ideas. Therefore, our work is based on the selection of content-rich words that represent labels of common items that are necessary to build and ultimately activate background knowledge. For example, the words *stems, leaves,* and *bulbs* are foundational words that children need to discuss things in nature. Examples of background knowledge developed in WOW include concepts and words related to the physical and biological sciences, mathematics, and maintaining one's health and well-being.

In addition, we teach words that help children talk about these concepts. We call them *supporting words,* since they serve the central function of helping to examine, contrast and compare, and differentiate phenomena. Morphology, syntax, and pragmatics provide children with many of the "tricks of the trade" for using language to make meaning.

Children who turn out to be successful in reading use the morphological structure in word forms to understand changes in word meanings (e.g., *big, bigger*); to be able to comprehend sentences of greater syntactic complexity, and to identify and use extended discourse such as narratives, explanations, definitions, and other socially defined genres (Carlisle & Stone, 2005; Snow, Burns, & Griffin, 1998).

To develop proficiency in the forms and functions of language, children need to use it, play with it, and get feedback from their teachers to improve their skills. Therefore, we also included the following functional concepts to help children talk about the vocabulary they are learning to follow instructions, to solve logical problems, and to answer questions.

- Pronouns—*I, you, your, my, we, she, her, he, his, they, their, our*
- Identity statements—"What is this? This is a _____."
- Opposites—*wet/not wet, full/not full*; later teach *full/empty, wet/dry*.
- Part/whole—parts of the body, parts of common objects.
- Comparatives—"Which is bigger?" "Which is smaller?"
- Materials—"What is it made of?": cloth, paper, plastic, leather, glass, wood, metal, concrete, rubber, paper, brick (teach that a circle is still a circle, whether it is made out of cloth, paper, or plastic).
- Spatial and temporal relations—*first, next, last, before/after*.
- Prepositions—*on, over, in front of, in, in back of, under, next to, between*.
- Time—days of the week, months, seasons.
- Plurals—*hand/hands, ear/ears*.
- *Same/different*—"I am going to clap my hands. You do the *same* thing. Which of these is *different*? Which are the same?"
- *Some, all, none*—"Am I holding up *all* of my fingers?"
- *Where, who, when, what* statements.

Somewhat different from previous research, we focus on important words that are taxonomically related to topics and can be applied to higher-order concepts. For instance, children learn to classify vocabulary pictures of concepts with similar proper-

ties, and to differentiate words and concepts through challenge questions, such as "Is a snake an insect? Why or why not?" (It is not an insect because an insect has three segments and six legs.)

Principle 4: The Use of Informational Text

Storybook narratives are a wonderful source for learning new words and developing children's imagination. However, information books also provide children with knowledge about their world that can be used to gain greater depth in content knowledge and to facilitate comprehension. In our work, lessons are organized into related topics (e.g., insects, wild animals, and animals that live in water) to prime background knowledge in high-utility content and to integrate concepts strategically with previously learned material. Children listening to books is followed by comprehension activities to develop knowledge of the text structure and comprehension outcomes. The information book is read and reread, as children dig deeper into concepts over an 8-day sequence. Following the topic, children take home a copy of the book to share with their families.

Principle 5: The Case for Embedded Multimedia

Especially for children who have not had extensive experience with content-rich language, sometimes a picture is more than a thousand words. In our case, we use embedded multimedia, strategies in which animations and other videos are woven into teachers' lessons. The use of embedded multimedia is based on two related theoretical models. One is that multimedia can support word learning and concept development through a synergistic relationship (Neuman, 2009). Supporting evidence comes first from Mayer (2001; Mayer & Moreno, 2003), who demonstrated in a series of studies that the addition of moving images, diagrams, and pictures allows for better retention than information held in only one memory system. Second is dual coding theory (Paivio, 2009), in which Paivio posits that visual and verbal sources of information are processed differently, creating separate representations for information processed in each channel. Together, these codes for representing information can be used to organize and create mental models of knowledge that can be stored and retrieved for subsequent use. Chambers and her colleagues (2008; Chambers, Cheung, Madden, Slavin, & Gifford, 2006), for example, showed that the use of embedded multimedia can enhance learning, reporting a moderate effect size when compared with instruction without media.

We begin each lesson with a "tuning-in" video clip—a rhyme, song, or word play shown from a DVD to bring children together to the circle. (All clips have been specially selected from the archives of *Sesame Street* and *Elmo's World*. Clip length varies from 40 seconds to 1½ minutes.) It builds excitement for the lesson and engages children in rhyming, beginning sounds, segmenting, and blending activities. The "tuning-in" is followed by a "content" video, introducing children to the definition of the category. The first video is designed to act as a prototype of the category, a particularly salient exemplar of the topic, for example, insects (i.e., a katydid). After the video, the teacher engages the children, focusing on *wh*-questions. She might ask, "Where does a katydid live? What is an insect?" Words are then reinforced using the information book (i.e., in this case on insects) specially designed to review the words just learned (e.g., *antennae, segments, camouflage, wings, outside*) and to provide redundant information in a different medium.

On subsequent days, the teacher provides increasing supports to develop these words and uses additional videos that focus on new words inside and outside the category, helping to build children's knowledge of the properties (e.g., insects have six legs and three body segments) related to the category. In addition, videos and teacher questions deepen children's knowledge of the concept by providing information about the topic (e.g., insects live in a habitat that has the food, shelter, and the weather they like). Following the video, children are presented with "time for a challenge" items that require them to problem-solve about the category (e.g., Is a bat an insect?). These challenge items are designed to encourage children to apply the concepts they have acquired to think critically about what may or may not constitutes category membership. Last, the children review their learning through journal-writing activities that involve developmental (phonic) writing. Together, the scientific and word concepts are integrated with daily experiences that bring these words to life.

Principle 6: Gradual Release of Control

This principle refers to the guidance, assistance, and support that teachers provide to their learners. Teachers use different degrees of support, or *scaffolding*, to assist their young learners at the initial stage, then systematically and gradually release control, so that children can try their new activities on their own. In the beginning, for example, teachers focus on explicit instruction, helping children to "get set"—providing critical background information, so that the children establish a purpose for learning. Teachers then "give meaning," to deepen children's understanding of the topic. Rather than ask open-ended questions, they provide information, giving more meaning to each word and the concept it represents. In these initial sessions, teachers use the "call and response" interactive strategy. They say something like "An insect lives outside. Where does an insect live?" or "Insects have three body parts. How many parts does an insect have?" "Three," the children answer. The purpose is to engage children in many rapidly paced responses in unison using the teacher's words. As the instructional sequence progresses, the teacher begins to "build bridges" to what children have already learned and what they will learn (establishing intertextual linkages across media). Here, the teacher begins to release more control to children during the teacher–child language interactions. She digs deeper and talks about other insects that are similar and different from what the children see and watch. Finally, the teacher "steps back," giving children more opportunities for open-ended discussion. Since children now have better background and more words to discuss their ideas, these conversations encourage children to elaborate on what they have learned.

Together these principles underlie the WOW intervention and are designed to maximize children's opportunities to learn words and concepts that target science, math, and health-content standards early on in preschool. Throughout the sequence, familiar words are used to help children talk about a topic, and to incorporate the approximately 10–12 content-specific words for each topic into more known contexts. Lessons last 10–12 minutes daily, most often conducted during circle time.

Two studies have now (Neuman & Dwyer, 2008; Neuman, Newman, & Dwyer, 2009) demonstrated the potential of WOW to improve children's word knowledge and concept development. A quasi-experimental study with 322 children in treatment and control groups provided initial evidence that children can learn content-rich words and retain word knowledge over time. Since then we have conducted a randomized controlled trial, examining the curriculum's potential to accelerate word learning beyond what was specifically taught. We found that Head Start children in our treatment group far exceeded those in the control ($d = 1.2$). However, they not only improved conceptually, categorically, and in knowledge of properties compared to their equivalent control group, they essentially closed the gap between those children who were middle class and more advantaged in subsequent units of instruction.

The lesson of our experience with WOW is that vocabulary development is highly malleable and sensitive to instruction. It is a matter of planned, sequenced, and systematic instruction. It is also a matter of selecting words, concepts, and ideas that matter most to children and to what they need to learn as they enter more formal schooling. Many children from high-poverty circumstances have had only limited experience with language, specifically conceptually based vocabulary. Children who enter school in these situations need skillfully developed instruction that not only improves their word knowledge but also accelerates it, maximizing the limited time they have in school.

Vocabulary development is foundational for learning to read. It is the entry to concepts and comprehension. We cannot leave it to chance. Consequently, we must engage in a substantially greater teacher development effort to ensure that children have the opportunity to discuss, describe, and develop word knowledge and concepts they will need for subsequent grades and content areas. Children's future success is dependent on it.

References

Anderson, R. C., & Freebody, P. (1979). *Vocabulary knowledge.* Champaign–Urbana, IL: Center for the Study of Reading.

Beck, I., & McKeown, M. (2007). Increasing young low-income children's oral vocabulary repertoires through rich and focused instruction. *Elementary School Journal, 107,* 251–271.

Beck, I., McKeown, M., McCaslin, E., & Burkes, A. (1979). *Instructional dimensions that may affect reading comprehension: Examples from two commercial programs.* Pittsburgh, PA: Learning Development and Research Center, University of Pittsburgh.

Biemiller, A. (2001). Teaching vocabulary: Early direct, and sequential. *American Educator, 25* (1), 24–28, 47.

Biemiller, A. (2006). Vocabulary development and instruction: A prerequisite for school learning. In D. K. Dickinson & S. B. Neuman (Eds.), *Handbook of early literacy research* (Vol. 2, pp. 41–51). New York: Guilford Press.

Biemiller, A., & Boote, C. (2006). An effective method for building meaning vocabulary in primary grades. *Journal of Educational Psychology, 98,* 44–62.

Biemiller, A., & Slonim, N. (2001). Estimating root word vocabulary growth in normative and advantaged populations: Evidence for a common sequence of vocabulary acquisition. *Journal of Educational Psychology, 93,* 498–520.

Bloom, P. (2000). *How children learn the meanings of words.* Cambridge, MA: MIT Press.

Booth, A. (2009). Causal supports for early word learning. *Child Development, 80*(4), 1243–1250.

Bornstein, M., Kessen, W., & Weiskopf, S. (1976). Color vision and hue categorization in young human infants. *Journal of Experimental Psychology, 2,* 115–129.

Borovsky, A., & Elman, J. (2006). Language input and semantic categories: A relation between cognition and early word learning. *Journal of Child Language, 33,* 759–790.

Carey, S., & Bartlett, E. (1978). *Acquiring a single new word.* Paper & Reports on Child Language Development, Stanford, CA.

Carlisle, J., & Stone, C. A. (2005). Exploring the role of morphemes in word reading. *Reading Research Quarterly, 40,* 428–449.

Chall, J. (1983). *Stages of reading development.* New York: McGraw-Hill.

Chambers, B., Abrami, P., Tucker, B., Slavin, R., Madden, N., Cheung, A., et al. (2008). Computer-assisted tutoring in Success for All: Reading outcomes for first graders. *Journal of Research on Educational Effectiveness, 1,* 120–137.

Chambers, B., Cheung, A., Madden, N., Slavin, R., & Gifford, R. (2006). Achievement effects of embedded multimedia in a Success for All reading program. *Journal of Educational Psychology, 98,* 232–237.

Coyne, M., Simmons, D., Kame'enui, E., & Stoolmiller, M. (2004). Teaching vocabulary during shared storybook readings: An examination of differential effects. *Exceptionality, 12*(3), 145–162.

Cunningham, A. E., & Stanovich, K. (1997). Early reading acquisition and its relation to reading experience and ability 10 years later. *Developmental Psychology, 33*, 934–945.

Dickinson, D., & Smith, M. (1994). Long-term effects of preschool teachers' book readings on low-income children's vocabulary and story comprehension. *Reading Research Quarterly, 29*, 104–122.

Early Childhood Research Institute on Measuring Growth and Development. (2000). *Individual Growth and Development Indictors (IGDI) for preschool children: Picture naming/expressing meaning, rhyming/early literacy, alliteration/early literacy*. Minneapolis: Center for Early Education and Development, University of Minnesota. Available online at *ggg.umn.edu*.

Elleman, A., Lindo, E., Morphy, P., & Compton, D. (2009). The impact of vocabulary instruction on passage-level comprehension of school-age children: A meta-analysis. *Journal of Educational Effectiveness, 2*, 1–44.

Farkas, G., & Beron, K. (2004). The detailed age trajectory of oral vocabulary knowledge: Differences by class and race. *Social Science Research, 33*, 464–497.

Gelman, S., Coley, J., Rosengren, K., Hartman, E., & Pappas, A. (1998). Beyond labeling: The role of maternal input in the acquisition of richly structured categories. *Monographs of the Society for Research in Child Development, 63*.

Gelman, S., & Markman, E. (1986). Categories and induction in young children. *Cognition, 23*, 183–209.

Gopnik, A., & Meltzoff, A. (1987). The development of categorization in the second year and its relation to other cognitive and linguistic developments. *Child Development, 58*, 1523–1531.

Halle, T., Forry, N., Hair, E., Perper, K., Wandner, L., Wessel, J., et al. (2009). *Disparities in early learning and development: Lessons from the Early Childhood Longitudinal Study—Birth Cohort (ECLS-B)*. Washington, DC: Council of Chief State School Officers and Child Trends.

Hart, B., & Risley, T. (1995). *Meaningful differences*. Baltimore: Brookes.

Hart, B., & Risley, T. (2003). The early catastrophe. *American Educator, 27*, 4,6–9.

Jenkins, J., Stein, M., & Wysocki, K. (1984). Learning words through reading. *American Educational Research Journal, 21*, 767–787.

Juel, C., Biancarosa, G., Coker, D., & Deffes, R. (2003). Walking with Rosie: A cautionary tale of early reading instruction. *Educational Leadership*, pp. 12–18.

Markman, E., & Callanan, M. (1984). An analysis of hierarchical classification. In R. J. Sternberg (Ed.), *Advances in the psychology of human intelligence* (pp. 157–177). Hillsdale, NJ: Erlbaum.

Markman, E., & Hutchinson, J. (1984). Children's sensitivity to constraints on word meaning: Taxonomic versus thematic relations. *Cognitive Psychology, 16*, 1–27.

Maulis, L. M., & Neuman, S. B. (2009, December). *The effects of vocabulary intervention on young children's word learning: A meta-analysis*. Paper presented at the Literacy Reading Conference/National Reading Conference, Albuquerque, NM.

Mayer, R., & Moreno, R. (2003). Nine ways to reduce cognitive load in multimedia learning. *Educational Psychologist, 38*, 43–52.

Mayer, R. E. (2001). *Multimedia learning*. New York: Cambridge University Press.

McMurray, B. (2007). Defusing the childhood vocabulary explosion. *Science, 1126*, 121.

Mol, S., Bus, A., & de Jong, M. (2009). Interactive book reading in early education: A tool to stimulate print knowledge as well as oral language. *Review of Educational Research, 79*(2), 979–1007.

Mol, S., Bus, A., de Jong, M., & Smeets, D. (2008). Added value of dialogic parent–child book readings: A meta-analysis. *Early Education and Development, 19*, 7–26.

Murphy, G. L., & Lassaline, M. E. (1997). Hierarchial structure in concepts and the basic level of categorization. In K. Lamberts & D. Shanks (Eds.), *Knowledge, concepts and categories* (pp. 93–131). East Sussex, UK: Psychology Press.

Nagy, W., Anderson, R. C., & Herman, P. (1987). Learning word meanings from context during normal reading. *American Educational Research Journal, 24*, 237–270.

Nagy, W., & Scott, J. (2000). Vocabulary processes. In M. Kamil, P. Mosethal, P. Pearson, & R. Barr (Eds.), *Handbook of reading research* (Vol. III, pp. 146–173). Mahwah, NJ: Erlbaum.

National Early Literacy Panel. (2008). *Developing early literacy*. Washington, DC: National Institute for Literacy.

National Reading Panel Report. (2000). *Teaching children to read*. Washington, DC: National Institute of Child Health and Development.

Neuman, S. B. (2009). The case for multimedia presentations in learning. In A. Bus & S. B. Neuman (Eds.), *Multimedia and literacy development: Improving achievement for young learners* (pp. 44–56). New York: Taylor & Francis.

Neuman, S. B., & Dwyer, J. (2008, December). *Developing vocabulary and conceptual knowledge for low-income preschoolers: A design experiment*. Paper presented at the National Reading Conference, Austin, TX.

Neuman, S. B., & Dwyer, J. (2009). Missing in action: Vocabulary instruction in Pre-K. *Reading Teacher, 62*, 384–392.

Neuman, S. B., Dwyer, J., Koh, S., & Wright, T. (2007). *The World of Words: A vocabulary intervention for preschool children*. Ann Arbor: University of Michigan.

Neuman, S. B., Newman, E., & Dwyer, J. (2009). *Educational effects of an embedded multimedia vocabulary intervention for economically disadvantaged pre-K children: A randomized trial*. Paper presented at the Literacy Reading Conference/National Reading Conference, Albuquerque, NM.

Paivio, A. (2009). The dual coding theory. In S. B. Neuman (Ed.), *Educating the other America* (pp. 230–245). Baltimore: Brookes.

Penno, J., Wilkinson, A., & Moore, D. (2002). Vocabulary acquisition from teacher explanation and repeated listening to stories: Do they outcome the Matthew effect? *Journal of Educational Psychology, 86,* 139–153.

Scarborough, H. (2001). Connecting early language and literacy to later reading (dis)abilities: Evidence, theory, and practice. In S. B. Neuman & D. K. Dickinson (Eds.), *Handbook of early literacy research* (Vol. 1, pp. 97–110). New York: Guilford Press.

Scarborough, H. S., & Dobrich, W. (1994). On the efficacy of reading to preschoolers. *Developmental Review, 14,* 245–302.

Smith, E. E. (1995). Concepts and categorization. In E. Smith & D. Osherson (Eds.), *An invitation to cognitive science* (2nd ed., pp. 3–33). Cambridge, MA: MIT Press.

Snow, C., Burns, M. S., & Griffin, P. (1998). *Preventing reading difficulties in young children.* Washington, DC: National Academy Press.

Stahl, S. (1999). *Vocabulary development.* Cambridge, MA: Brookline Press.

Stahl, S., & Fairbanks, M. (1986). The effects of vocabulary instruction: A model-based meta-analysis. *Review of Educational Research, 56,* 72–110.

Wasik, B., & Bond, M. A. (2001). Beyond the pages of a book: Interactive book reading and language development in preschool classrooms. *Journal of Educational Psychology, 93,* 243–250.

Wright, T., & Neuman, S. B. (2009, December). *What classroom observations reveal about vocabulary instruction: A study of 55 kindergarten classrooms.* Paper presented at the Literacy Reading Conference/National Reading Conference, Albuquerque, NM.

V
SOCIAL POLICY
AND EARLY LITERACY

24

Assessment in Early Literacy Research

CATHERINE E. SNOW
SOOJIN S. OH

Much of what we know about children's language and literacy development derives from efforts to assess those skills. In fact, language and literacy development might be taken as a case study in the history of assessment—a local domain displaying the full range of tensions, challenges, and approaches that have characterized the field of behavioral assessment, and in particular, the assessment of young children. In this chapter, we discuss language and literacy assessment in young children as an illustrative special case of issues that extend far beyond the language/literacy domain. In that larger domain, as in this specific one, three key questions organize the information: For what purposes should we assess young children? What aspects of their functioning should be assessed? And how do we carry out assessments so as to get good, reliable information with only modest burden on the adult assessor or the child?

We focus in this chapter on the language/literacy domain but draw heavily from the report of the National Academy of Sciences Committee on Developmental Assessment and Outcomes for Young Children (Snow & Van Hemel, 2008), which deals with early childhood assessment across domains. The Committee Report titled *Early Childhood Assessment: Why, What and How* fulfilled

a congressional mandate in response to the discord aroused by the National Reporting System (NRS), an effort by the federal government to collect data on all Head Start children. The NRS controversy can itself be seen as a case study in how assessment can go wrong. The NRS was an ambitious and potentially very useful effort plagued by so much controversy that it was ended by congressional action only 4 years after being launched. One challenge the NRS faced was the high level of ambiguity about its *purpose*. It was seen on the negative side as an effort to impose on Head Start accountability standards similar to those prescribed in No Child Left Behind (NCLB) for K–12 schools and/or as an effort to shut down programs. On the positive side, it was seen as an effort to provide to program staff useful information about the children they were serving and to focus Head Start programs on educational outcomes, literacy in particular. Unfortunately, the mismatch of the stated NRS purpose—to demonstrate that Head Start programs were producing educational gains—and the NRS design—testing all children in all programs, rather than sampling across programs—heightened the ambiguity about purpose and thus the controversy. The NRS was also roundly criticized for *what* it chose to assess. Though only vocabulary and emergent print and numeracy skills were evaluated in the first instance, the NRS battery was subsequently expanded to include attention to socioemotional skills in response to extensive critiques (e.g., Meisels, 2004), but the ire aroused by the sole emphasis on academic skills in the initial test design was never fully quelled. Finally, considerable concern emerged about *how* the NRS was implemented—at child, program, and national levels. At the child level, critics suggested that efforts to standardize the administration led to unnatural adult–child interactions that could disturb children and distort estimates of their skills; furthermore, provisions for assessing bilingual children were viewed as inadequate, and only Spanish-speaking English learners were tested in their native language. At the program level, many complained about the time devoted to individual assessment, the absence of provisions for sharing data with program staff, and the burden on program staff. At the national level, many program directors and others within the early childhood education community felt that the NRS was rolled out too quickly, with insufficient time to develop a coherent message about its purpose and its utility or to ensure optimal administration, leading to considerable anxiety about the potentially misguided interpretations and uses to which the outcomes would be put.

The anxiety about the NRS channeled a more general cultural concern about the appropriateness of assessing young children at all. Many early childhood educators and parents contend that young children should not be subjected to formal assessments, arguing that preschoolers are insufficiently familiar with the formats and the rules of the testing game to produce useful responses. One is reminded of the anecdote told by Roger Brown (1973) about his attempt to assess grammatical knowledge in 3-year-old Adam, using techniques borrowed from linguists' studies of adults' grammatical intuitions.

BROWN: Adam, which is better, a sand or some sand?

ADAM: Pop goes the weasel.

How should one "score" Adam's response here? It clearly provides no information about his knowledge of count versus mass nouns, which was the original goal. Does that imply it should be coded as incorrect, or as missing? On the other hand, it does provide at least indirect evidence that Adam was unused to conversations focusing on linguistic forms. In other words, he was not yet skilled in metalinguistic tasks, though he was conversationally adept at deflecting challenging questions.

The widespread concern about assessing young children reflects an array of underlying worries: that the assessment procedures are themselves burdensome and anxiety-provoking for the child, that the instruments currently available are inadequate, that the outcomes may be tainted by extraneous influences (fatigue, illness, distrust of the assessor, shyness), that children from ethnic and language minority groups and children with disabilities are unlikely to receive the accommodations they would need to reveal their skills, and so on. To all of these legitimate concerns, those who use and interpret assessment results from young children might respond that there is always noise in test data, and that consequential decisions should never be based on a single test for test-takers of any age but that tests nonetheless generate information of high value to educators and policymakers (e.g., whether individual children are developing as expected, what group differences exist, what early skills predict academic or social risk, which groups of children and which individual children should receive prevention services, how intervention and educational programs are functioning, and how those programs could be improved). In addition to the crucial role of early childhood assessment in research and policy, efforts to improve assessment procedures and the interpretation of findings contribute directly to early childhood education by informing teachers about children's needs, as well as helping to guide instruction and to design appropriate learning environments. The crucial commitment to minimizing harm to children and families, while maximizing the utility of the information collected, is shared by researchers and practitioners; in the early childhood policy and practice community, that commitment requires acknowledging both that harm can occur and benefits are possible when young children are subjected to assessments.

Turning to Language and Literacy Skills

Our goal in this chapter is to review what we know about assessing early language and literacy skills, considering to what extent our procedures for doing that are research-based and usable in research undertakings. We are not in a position to rate or review individual instruments exhaustively; the National Research Council report (Snow & Van Hemel, 2008) provides appendices that list early childhood assessments in different domains, though also without rating or ranking them. We aim here to provide the language/literacy researcher with a sense of what kinds of considerations should be brought to bear when selecting assessments, or when evaluating the quality of research that relies on assessments. They should be aware of the technical properties of the instruments they choose, of course, and of the procedures used to develop and select items and, if applicable, to norm and standardize the tests. Equally important, they should be clear about how the assessment instruments define the constructs of interest, and how well the test definition matches the researcher definition. Sometimes it is inevitable that standardized tests fail to represent the full breadth of the researcher-defined construct; this does not imply that the test should be avoided, but that users should be mindful of its limitations when interpreting outcomes.

Again, the key dimensions of decisions about assessment emphasized in the National Research Council report (Snow & Van Hemel, 2008) are reflected in the three questions articulated earlier:

1. *Why*: For what purposes should we assess young children?
2. *What*: What aspects of their functioning should be assessed?
3. *How*: How do we carry out assessments so as to get good, reliable information, with only modest burdens on the adult assessor or the child?

To these three, we add a crucial fourth question: *Who* is being assessed? Particularly when assessing young children, thinking about the characteristics of the specific population to be targeted is indispensable because different assessment decisions are required for children age 2 versus 4, for monolinguals versus bilinguals, for children from academically oriented families versus those likely to be unfamiliar with the formats of formal testing, and so on.

Why Assess Literacy? Why in the Early Childhood Period?

It has become banal to point out that literacy is the key skill associated with academic success, that early success in learning to read sets up a positive cycle of success at reading and at learning through reading (Stanovich, 1986). We also have robust evidence that deficits in key literacy precursor skills at age 4 or 5 are associated with retention in grade, with higher likelihood of being identified for special education, and with increased rates of dropout in later years (Snow, Burns, & Griffin, 1998). Thus, researchers interested in charting developmental pathways, in evaluating the effectiveness of social and educational interventions, and in predicting school readiness and later school success consistently include measures designed to tap the earliest literacy skills, as well as skills shown to be correlates and/or precursors of literacy.

Preliteracy assessments have thus reliably been included in longitudinal descriptive studies (e.g., the National Institute of Child Health and Human Development [NICHD] Child Care study described at *secc.rti.org*, the National Center for Education Statistics [NCES] Early Childhood Longitudinal Studies described at *nces.ed.gov/ecls*), in large-scale policy evaluations (e.g., the Early Head Start research studies described at *www.mathematica-mpr.com/earlychildhood/ehstoc.asp*, the Chilean project *Un Buen Comienzo* at *www.ubc.cl*), in studies designed to use longitudinal data to test the power of various predictors of later literacy outcomes (e.g., the Home–School Study of Language and Literacy Development, or HSSLD, and the Development of Academic Language at Home and School, or DASH, both of which are described more fully below), as well as in studies that focus on identifying differences associated with class, ethnicity, home language, familial dyslexia, and other such factors. We discuss the assessment decisions in some of these studies later in this chapter to illustrate how considerations of purpose, construct definition, administrative ease, and target population interacted to influence researcher choices.

Assessments of literacy skills and their precursors are widely used with very young children in an effort to answer research questions of theoretical and social importance. The transition from a "school readiness" to an "emergent literacy" mindset within educational thinking has extended the relevance of (pre)literacy and literacy precursor assessments downward to age 2 or 3. But what skills do those early assessments really tap, and how much can we trust the information being collected with their help?

What We Assess and How

Decisions about what skills to assess in very young children reflect one's theory of literacy. Assessment instruments for letter-name knowledge and phonological awareness are well developed, reflecting a widespread acceptance of the view that those skills are crucial to normal literacy development and are good early predictors of later literacy outcomes. Assessment instruments for story retelling, for knowledge about environmental print, and for emergent book reading have been developed by researchers who are convinced that the skills reflected in such instruments constitute crucial components of emergent literacy skills. Similarly, measures of sophisticated, academic language use have been developed by researchers who focus on the role of such language skills in predicting later reading comprehension. The mix of skills assessed in any study reflects the researcher's beliefs about the relative importance of these various components to the literacy construct. Unfortunately, instruments to assess some of these skills (e.g., emergent book reading or academic language), though developed adequately for research purposes, have not reached the same level of standardization, quantification, or psychometric sophistication as instruments focused on assessing print and phonological awareness skills, and are thus less likely to find their way into large-scale studies.

Our own research is based on the presumption that literacy is in essence a language-based skill, and that some very sophisticated skills relevant to literacy outcomes can develop and be assessed even in the preschool period, long before conventional reading begins. We, of course, also endorse the importance of assessing the skills Whitehurst and Lonigan (1998) dubbed "inside-out" skills, those associated most closely with the technical challenges of beginning to grasp the alphabetic principle (letter recognition, phonemic awareness). The fact that these "inside-out" assessments are relatively brief and reliable makes them highly attractive as evaluation options, particularly in comparison to assessments that rely on rubrics or other forms of coding of child responses that may require transcription, and that are thus both more expensive and less replicable. Letter-name and phonological awareness assessments are typically brief and reliable, in part because the domains they tap are limited in size and complexity, whereas the more "outside-in" skills associated with understanding the concept of literacy and having the language skills needed to access text tap large, messy, and complex domains that are less susceptible to easy assessment. Nonetheless, we insist that oral language skills need to be included in any credible assessment focusing on literacy for young (or older) children, and furthermore, that attention to the difference between "academic" and "everyday" language is crucial in a fully informative early childhood literacy assessment.

A Brief History of Language Assessment

Language development has traditionally been assessed observationally, with procedures that many would argue should apply to all assessments with young children: Provide engaging activities, ensure that the child has a trusted interlocutor and a familiar setting, then record the behavior that occurs naturally. The naturally occurring behavior is adult–child conversation, which then, of course, must be transcribed for analysis. Transcripts are analyzed using measures sensitive to developmental stage that are based on some combination of theory and empiricism. Some, such as mean length of utterance (MLU), have become standard, whereas other traditionally used measures (e.g., type–token ratio) have been supplanted by more tractable indices.

The burden on the researcher associated with transcription and coding has been addressed in a couple of ways. First, in the early 1980s, the Child Language Data Exchange System (CHILDES) was established for sharing transcripts, so that individual researchers could study far more children than any individual could observe and transcribe (MacWhinney & Snow, 1985, 1990; Snow, 2001). CHILDES prescribed certain rules for transcription to promote the ease of exchange and use of transcripts, and to make possible automated analyses. Second, alternative, less labor-intensive approaches to collecting developmental data were devised, most notably the Communicative Development Inventories (CDI; *www.sci.sdsu.edu/cdi*), a parent report instrument that guided parental responses about the complexity of children's gestural and vocal communications, and grammatical structures produced, as well as number of words understood and used. The CDI is now widely used, sometimes in association with direct observation, and has been adapted to dozens of languages.

In addition to observation and parental report, direct testing of very young children is also used to reflect their language skills. For example, the Peabody Picture Vocabulary Test (PPVT) has norms extending down to 18 months. Receptive assessments of grammatical understanding, such as the Test for Reception of Grammar (TROG), can be used with children starting at age 4. Direct testing of children age 3 and younger must involve very simple formats, and is limited in the information it can yield. Therefore, even for children ages 3–5, direct observation of language use in communicative settings is a highly informative supplement to test results.

This brief history of language assessment offers a template and some useful guiding principles for the development of early literacy measures. First, more streamlined and efficient measures can often be built on learning accumulated from direct observation of undisturbed behavior, just as the CDI was built on data from transcript analysis about the most frequently used early words. Second, parent report of child behavior can be relied upon to reflect individual differences and to be sensitive to development, at least during the early stages of development,

when the child's skills are still constrained in breadth. Third, supplementing direct testing with observational and/or parent-report measures can improve the quality of information available. Fourth, the most interesting and informative aspects of child knowledge may be the most difficult to assess formally. Finally, scores derived from direct testing should not be privileged over observational measures, particularly if the child was distressed, shy, tired, ill, or otherwise unlikely to show best performance during the test session.

The Emerging Field of Academic Language Assessment

There is good evidence that vocabulary size correlates with literacy. Vocabulary is the most robust predictor of reading comprehension for children age 8 and older (Snow, Porche, Tabors, & Harris, 2007) and is a strong correlate of word reading for children ages 6–8 (Snow, Tabors, Nicholson, & Kurland, 1995). More surprisingly, the vocabulary skills of children age 5 predict literacy outcomes in the primary grades (e.g., Dickinson & Porche, in press; Tabors, Roach, & Snow, 2001) and beyond (Snow et al., 2007). In addition to sheer vocabulary size, though, it has been suggested that knowledge of certain kinds of words is particularly powerful in predicting literacy. These words include superordinates (*animal, tool, vehicle*), cognitive verbs (*think, wonder, believe, doubt*), epistemic markers (*maybe, certainly, evidently*), and other words used for talking about verbally constructed rather than physically provided topics (e.g., the physics of magnetic attraction rather than the appearance of a particular magnet; the physiology of digestion rather than the obligation to eat these peas). These so-called "academic" words are unlikely to be learned by children with small vocabularies; thus, vocabulary size does matter, but vocabularies can grow without necessarily including these high-power academic words.

There is increasing consensus on the need to measure academic language skills in school-age children because of their relevance to reading comprehension, test-taking abilities, and so on (e.g., Bailey & Butler, 2007; Snow & Uccelli, 2009). Surprisingly, though, there is also a recent resurgence of interest in assessing academic language skills in preschool-age children, for example, in a large interuniversity project studying monolingual Dutch speakers, as well as Turkish and Berber Dutch bilinguals living in the Netherlands. Children growing up in immigrant, bilingual families are almost inevitably less exposed to the societal language than are monolinguals, and evidence suggests that they are also less exposed to language use that would stimulate academic language skills (in either the home or the societal language) (see, e.g., Leseman, Scheele, Mayo, & Messer, 2007; Scheele, Leseman, & Mayo, 2010). Results from the Netherlands suggest not only that immigrant families on average engage in less academic-language-focused talk than monolingual families but also that social class within both native Dutch and immigrant families influences the amount of academic talk in which they engage. Hoff and Elledge (2005) found that environmental bilingualism accounted for 2% of the variance in children's vocabulary scores, an effect equivalent to that of gender, which typically accounts for 1–2% of variance, but smaller than that of socioeconomic status (SES) (Fenson et al., 1994). It has been widely noted that bilinguals typically have a slower rate of vocabulary development than monolingual children in either language (Ben-Zeev, 1977; Doyle, Champagne, & Segalowitz, 1978; Fernández, Person, Umbel, Oller, & Molinet-Molina, 1992; Hoff & Elledge, 2005; Quiroz, Snow, & Zhao, in press; Rosenblum & Pinker, 1983; Umbel, Pearson, Fernández, & Oller, 1992). Though bilingual children's rates of early vocabulary acquisition fall within the range reported for same-age monolingual counterparts when performance in both languages is considered (Pearson, Fernández, & Oller, 1993), their vocabulary deficits in the language of schooling seem to be associated with academic risk. Documentation of language minority children's particular challenges in the domain of academic language offers both insights into the academic hurdles they face and guidance about the focus of early education designed for them.

A number of features of oral language, in addition to academic vocabulary, have been identified as characteristic of academic language skills, including features that emerge when extended discourses (e.g., narratives or explanations) are produced, such as use of connectives (e.g., *but, while*), greater tense variety, higher lexical density, and greater use of subordinate clauses. For example, the Dutch DASH study is exploring a long list of language features observed in elicited language tasks, as well as in semistructured interactions, with parents and preschool teachers as indicators of academic language (see Table 24.1 for a sample of the DASH data collection procedures).

The specific linguistic features that are the focus of the DASH project emerge under certain conditions of task, topic, and interpersonal communicative goals and relationships. Extremely concrete tasks (e.g., directing a child to put dishes away) are unlikely to elicit such features, nor are everyday topics or interpersonal interactions in which young children are not normatively treated as conversational partners, collaborative problem solvers, and worthy sources of opinion and knowledge (DASH, 2006; Henrichs, 2006; Henrichs & Schoonen, 2009; Leseman & de Jong, 1998; Leseman et al., 2007). These larger dimensions were the categories that were the focus in the HSSLD, an earlier longitudinal study that presaged many concerns of the DASH project. Though focusing exclusively on monolingual English speakers from lower-income households, HSSLD researchers (see Dickinson & Tabors, 2001; Snow et al., 2007) collected data in many of the same situations as the DASH researchers: Interactive tasks such as parent–child or teacher–child book reading or crafts projects, family mealtimes, as well as elicited-talk tasks such as picture description and story (re)telling. The HSSLD analyses investigated the predictive power of broader dimensions of the interactive talk (e.g., the percentage of utterances during book reading that were "nonimmediate," the percentage of talk during toy play that was connected to fantasy themes, the percentage of talk during mealtimes that was narrative or explanatory). These three forms of talk all involved extended discourse—sequences of utterances focused on a elaborating a single topic. Such talk forms inevitably display greater lexical variety and density, a higher incidence of connectives and complex grammatical structures, more variety of tenses, and the other features the DASH researchers are analyzing.

TABLE 24.1. Researcher-Developed Measures Used to Reflect Children's Control over Academic Language, Based on Elicited or Naturalistic Language Production in Two Studies

Study	Task	Process	Variable
DASH	Narrative comprehension	Ten questions, open-ended then guiding	Two points for correct answer to open-ended question, 1 point for correct answer to guiding question
	Narrative production	Story retelling using wordless picture book, transcript analysis of child performance	Number of content words in each utterance (all nouns, verbs, adjectives, count words, and a selection of adverbs with a clear, expressible meaning)
			Use of either no, deictic ("here," "this one"), explicit but nonspecific ("somewhere"), or explicit and specific references to time and place ("under the pile of leaves")
			Use of verb predicate tense and aspect (subcategories: no verb, present simple, present perfect, past simple, past perfect, present future, or past future tense)
			Use of verb predicate mood (subcategories: no verb, declarative, persuasive, interrogative, or imperative verb predicate mood)
			Use of connectives (subcategories: additive, temporal, causal, contrastive, and comparative connectives)
			Use of clause combining (subcategories: coordinate, subordinate, including relative and embedded clause combining)
		Story retelling using wordless picture book, global coding	Textual cohesion of the story told by the child using a 7-point rating scale, with scale point 1 meaning *very low cohesion between separate utterances, virtually all utterances are semantically or linguistically unrelated*, and 7 meaning *the discourse is highly coherent, all utterances together forming one complex statement.*
			Degree of abstractness of the story on a 4-point rating scale derived from Blank, Rose, and Berlin (1978), with scale point 1 meaning that the story produced by the child sticks closely to the immediate situation (e.g., merely labeling the pictures), and scale point 4 meaning that the child reasons about not directly observed aspects of the story.
			Narrative competence of the child using Sulzby's (1986) 12-point scale of narrative reading development, with scale point 1 meaning *the child separately labels depicted items without attempt to connect them into a meaningful whole*, and 7, the highest observed score in this study, meaning *the child does not read, but tells the picture book in a way that closely resembles the original.*

(cont.)

TABLE 24.1. *(cont.)*

Study	Task	Process	Variable
HSSLD	Definitions task	Ten familiar words, responses transcribed for analysis	Percentage of responses that are formal; quality of response, taking into account superordinate chosen and informativeness of qualifiers offered, for definitions categorized as formal.
	Superordinates task	Groups of words presented, superordinate requested	Percent correct.
	Narrative comprehension	Picture book read to child, questions embedded	Percentage of literal and inferential questions answered.
	Picture description	Child asked to describe complicated picture to adult who could not see it	Number of elements from the picture explicitly mentioned, specific lexical indicators of features (size, color) and position (in front of the . . . , next to the . . .), incidence of disambiguating relative clauses.

The child outcome measures in the DASH and the HSSLD projects also share some similarities (see Table 24.1). In both studies, a focus on receptive vocabulary was considered crucial to understanding children's academic language skills, and in both cases, a standardized measure was chosen. DASH researchers made the interesting choice to use a test designed for bilingual children even with their monolingual Dutch-speaking sample, in order to protect comparability. Analyses of the child-produced picture descriptions were rather similar, but the HSSLD researchers included elicited definitions and a test of superordinate knowledge. These measures reflect, we argue, the two dimensions of metalinguistic awareness identified by Bialystok and Ryan (1985) in their influential article on the topic, namely, analyzed knowledge and control of processing. Definitions reflect analyzed knowledge because providing a superordinate and selecting an appropriate restrictive clause require figuring out what features differentiate the definiendum from other members of its own class (e.g., "a bicycle is a vehicle with two wheels" rather than "a bicycle is something you can ride") and at the same time, a good definition requires sufficient control to inhibit the natural tendency to narrate or describe in favor of using a conventionalized language form. As such, it is perhaps not surprising that quality of definitions turned out to be a rather strong predictor of later literacy outcomes.

Emergent Literacy

Very often, the exigencies of funding and of the need to show results on externally creditable measures dictate what we assess and how: Even those of us who are convinced of the importance of including academic language measures as indicators of educationally important outcomes often opt for "small-domain measures." Here we offer an example of the decision-making process that let purpose guide the choice of assessments for evaluating *Un Buen Comienzo* (A Good Start; UBC)—an intervention focused on the teachers of 4- and 5-year-olds attending public municipal schools in Santiago, Chile (Yoshikawa, Barata, Rolla, Snow, & Arbour, 2008). The express purpose of UBC is to evaluate the impact of a scalable early childhood intervention—one that can be delivered for a reasonable per-child, per-classroom cost, such that if the impact is indeed large enough to justify it, one could make an argument for wide-ranging policy changes. The study is designed as a cluster randomized experiment, with the intervention implemented in classrooms in 30+ schools and another 30+ schools randomly assigned to a delayed intervention condition. Because the hope was to influence policymakers, we decided it was crucial to include standardized assessments that would provide externally credible data in measurement units (percentiles, age equivalencies) that make sense across a variety of specific constructs.

Furthermore, working with a monolingual Spanish-speaking sample of children constrained our assessment choices; despite the very large number of Spanish speakers in the world, only a few standardized educational assessments for young children are available in Spanish. We ultimately chose to use the subtests of the Woodcock–Muñoz Language Survey—Revised (WMLS-R), which focus on picture vocabulary, letter–word identification, passage comprehension, and dictation, as well as a standardized measure of numeracy and a battery of socioemotional assessments.

But we worry about the limitations of these direct assessments. They sample children's knowledge rather sparsely. They use formats with which Chilean children might be unfamiliar. They were not normed on Chilean children; thus, conclusions about the meaning of the standardized scores could be questioned. Thus, we have also welcomed opportunities to embed observational studies within the larger evaluation. For example, Diana Leyva is conducting observations with a subset of the mother–child dyads, in which she creates an authentic literacy task (making a list of purchases in preparation for a trip to the market) designed to elicit opportunities for children to display, and mothers to support, use of pictures versus written words or invented spelling to represent items on the list, and use of numbers versus other forms to represent quantities to be purchased (for previous uses of this approach, see Leyva & Wiser, 2007; Leyva, Wiser, & Reese, 2008). Results from the authentic grocery list task are valuable in their own right and, furthermore, serve as validation of the findings from the standardized assessments of dictation, letter–word identification, and numeracy.

Questions about Early Language/ Literacy Assessment

Based on what we know about early literacy assessment so far, a number of questions arise for researchers interested in accurately assessing young children's language and literacy skills. As noted earlier, the first challenge is that the easy-to-access skills quickly absorb the limited time available for assessment and can lead to neglect of constructs, such as concepts of print or academic language, that are more complicated to assess yet critical to generating a full picture of children's literacy skills. The question then arises whether, in the broad-range early childhood assessment systems that are increasingly being used to evaluate early childhood programs, high-quality assessment of language and literacy skills is possible. Second, recognizing that measures appropriate for assessing the skills of bilinguals are few, and rarely come equipped with usable norms or age equivalents, the question remains what solutions are available and what innovative approaches are needed in assessing language minority children. We present in this section a brief review of the language/literacy dimensions of several early childhood assessments commonly used in evaluating the quality of early childhood programs, and a review of the issues that arise in the assessment of bilingual children. Then, in the final section of the chapter, we sketch a few of the most pressing research issues for the field.

Incorporating Language and Literacy Skills into Early Childhood Assessment Systems

We undertook a review of nine early childhood assessment systems (see Table 24.2), to determine to what extent they attended to language and literacy skills, what kind of scores they generated for those skills, and whether they were usable with both language minority and English-only children. We found that all these instruments prioritized language as an outcome domain. This was in some of the instrument manuals explicitly justified by the strong empirical support for vocabulary at school entry as a robust predictor for early, as well as later, literacy outcomes (Craig, Connor, & Washington, 2003; Dickinson & Porche, in press; Dickinson & Tabors, 2001; Poe, Burchinal, & Roberts, 2004; Roth, Speece, & Cooper, 2002; Snow, Tabors, & Dickinson, 2001; Snow et al., 1995, 2007). Furthermore, the reliance on vocabulary as the measure of language skills in many of these instruments is justified by the observation that, at least for normally developing children, vocabulary is highly correlated with other developmental indices of language knowledge (Snow & Van Hemel, 2008).

TABLE 24.2. The Representation of Language/Literacy in Comprehensive Early Childhood Assessment Systems

Instrument and age range	Language/literacy domain(s) represented	Primary form of data	Technical qualities reported for assessment (reliability, validity)	Adapted for language-minority children? How?
Child Observation Record (COR) • Infant–Toddler COR: 6 weeks–3 years • Preschool COR: 2½–6	Built based on early literacy skills proposed by National Reading Panel (2000): 1. Comprehension 2. Phonological awareness 3. Alphabetic principle 4. Concepts about print	Parent and teacher observations consisting of daily anecdotes	Small sample limited to Head Start children	Only English version available; parent guides available in English and Spanish
Developmental Assessment of Young Children (DAYC) • Birth–5 years, 11 months	Communication subscale: 1. Receptive and expressive vocabulary 2. Verbal and nonverbal expressions	Direct assessment, caregiver report, professional observation, parent interview, home observation	The norming sample ($n = 1,269$) in 27 states: 80% white, 16% black; Cronbach's alpha coefficients for content sampling: 0.97; time sampling: .99; interrater reliability: .99; test–retest reliability: .86; some evidence of criterion-related validity and construct validity	English only; some examiners modify or opt for translation services that potentially invalidate assessment results
Creative Curriculum Developmental Continuum Assessment Toolkit • Birth–6 years	Head Start outcomes framework	An observation-based assessment instrument to document children's progress	DCA ages 3–5 has some evidence of validity through exploratory factor analysis and internal consistency coefficients	Spanish version; norming sample limited to Head Start children included ethnic minorities and ELLs; 20% of English norming sample were native Spanish speakers
Early Learning Accomplishment Profile (E-LAP) • Birth–36 months	Language/preliteracy	Flexibility in administration: can be either a formal assessment following a strict protocol or administered informally to guide observations of skills level in the classroom	Internal consistency = .96–.98; test–retest reliability with a sample of 2- to 44-month-old children ($n = 92$) ranged between .96 and .99; high levels of interrater reliability with 2- to 43-month-old children ($n = 49$) content validity = .93; construct validity = .87–.97; criterion validity = .90–.97 ($n = 242$)	Spanish version; nationally representative norming sample with represented ethnic groups proportional to 2000 U.S. Census

Tool	Subdomains/content	Method	Psychometric properties	Language availability
ECHOS: Early Childhood Observation System • PreK and K–grade 2	Four subdomains: 1. Letter knowledge/phonics 2. Oral language and vocabulary 3. Comprehension 4. Emergent writing/writing 5. For PreK/K: print awareness/concepts of print; phonological awareness 6. For K–2: fluency	A comprehensive observational tool implemented by a classroom teacher	Content validity through the expert validation procedure only for PreK scale; construct validity established with Stanford Achievement Test Series, Tenth Edition; strong test–retest reliability; high level of internal consistency	English version only, but home reports are available in Spanish; norming sample included some bilingual children who were required to speak English as their first language
Galileo Pre-K • 24 months–5 years	Galileo Language and Literacy Scale: 1. Listening and understanding—receptive vocabulary, stories, songs, poems, and directions 2. Speaking and communicating—self-expression, conversation, expressive vocabulary 3. Phonological awareness—sound recognition 4. Book knowledge and appreciation—story reasoning, storytelling, interest in books 5. Print awareness and concepts 6. Early reading and early writing 7. Alphabetic knowledge	Questionnaires, observations, and formal assessments integrated with instruction	1. The 1998 Preschool Level 1 Scales Language and Literacy ($n = 2{,}149$; ages 24–70 months): intraclass correlation coefficient (ICC) alpha = .92; validity = stable developmental progressions of capabilities 2. The Fall 2001 Preschool Level 2 Literacy Scale ($n = 3{,}092$; ages 3–5): ICC = .97; validation: discrimination and difficulty values reported; factor analysis also available	Spanish version available; norming sample included 20% ELLs
Infant–Preschool Play Assessment Scale (I-PAS) • Birth–5 years	Communication subscale	Direct observations of children's play to assess their level of functioning in different domains	No supportive psychometric evidence; scale has not been normed	English only

(cont.)

TABLE 24.2. (cont.)

Instrument and age range	Language/literacy domain(s) represented	Primary form of data	Technical qualities reported for assessment (reliability, validity)	Adapted for language-minority children? How?
Learning Accomplishment Profile Diagnostic (LAP-D) • 30–72 months	1. Letter Naming subscale: names 18 pictures of common objects; names the cause for a given event 2. Comprehension subscale: Points to six body parts upon request; follows eight simple commands; responds appropriate to two prepositions; follows two two-step commands in exact order; points to five pictured objects by use; selects four pictures related to a sentence read; points to five printed numerals between 1 and 10	1. Traditional method for individual assessment in one-to-one format 2. Alternative method is station-to-station format	1. For both groups, internal consistency = .94 for Naming and .92 for Comprehension (*n* = 1,075 English-speaking, 947 Spanish-speaking) 2. For English speakers, standard error of measurement (SEM) = 1.62 for Naming, 1.41 for Comprehension; for Spanish speakers, SEM = 1.49 for Naming, 1.38 for Comprehension; test–retest reliability = .93, .94 for English speakers; .89, .91 for Spanish-speaking group 3. Interrater reliability = .86, .89 for English speakers; .82, .79 for Spanish speakers 4. Construct validity = high zero-order correlations 5. Criterion validity = .87; English speakers, .81, Spanish speakers with DIAL-3	Spanish version available; LAP-D can also be administered bilingually in English and Spanish; Spanish norms established with 2,099 children; reliability and validity determined with a different sample of Spanish-speaking children

Learning Accomplishment Profile—Third Edition (LAP-3) • 36–72 months	Similar to E-LAP, follows a flexible approach to administration: A formal evaluation following a strict protocol or an informal observation of children in natural setting	1. Internal consistency (alpha = .96–.99; test–retest reliability = .96–99 (n = 40; 37- to 72-month-olds of different ethnic groups); interrater reliability = .84–.98 (n = 33; 33- to 73-month-olds) 2. Content validity examined for third edition by an expert validation procedure; construct validity = .61–.89; criterion validity = .70–.92 with Batelle Developmental Inventory (n = 230)	English only; norms and psychometric parameters established with a nationally representative sample stratified by region, age, gender, race/ethnicity, and program type; 95% of children spoke English as a primary language

(Developmental Indicators of the Assessment of Learning) language; .67 for English speakers; .50 for Spanish speakers with Woodcock–Johnson Tests—Revised; .83 with Peabody Picture Vocabulary Test–III for English speakers, .64 with TVIP (*Test de Vocabulario en Imágenes Peabody*) for Spanish speakers

It is strongly recommended that early childhood assessment systems used for purposes of reflecting program quality or guiding program improvement be tightly aligned with curriculum and with professional development. Thus, pedagogical approaches such as Creative Curriculum (Teaching Strategies, 2006a, 2006b) or High/Scope have developed their own assessments tied to their curricular emphases, allowing much of the assessment to be carried out in the process of natural classroom interaction. Similarly, Galileo Pre-K operates with an assessment technology that integrates multiple methods of assessment—formal assessment, direct observation, and documentation of student work—to provide a more comprehensive picture of the child's development and to identify areas of congruence and dissonance across diverse sources of information. However, the challenge of adequately reflecting the language skills that are most crucial to later literacy outcomes—in particular, academic language skills—in comprehensive early childhood assessments has, in general, not been a central part of the test designers' thinking. Technology-based assessment systems such as Galileo Pre-K's Electronic Management of Learning enable synthesis of multiple sources of assessment data. Linking advanced technology to assessment in early education may speed the usability of more comprehensive assessments of early literacy skills that incorporate appropriate levels of attention to "outside-in" skills such as academic language.

Assessing Language and Literacy Skills in Children Growing Up Bilingual

Why Focus on Bilinguals and Language-Minority Children?

The U.S. early childhood education and care system is serving a child population that is increasingly diverse in cultural background and language. In response to the compelling need to assess this specific population fairly and accurately, we consider in this section the degree to which available assessment tools are appropriate for that purpose.

Approximately 20% of children in the United States speak a language other than English at home (Hernandez, Denton, & Macartney, 2007). This group is growing faster than any other group of children in the country, and almost half the children in immigrant families have yet to enter first grade. Based on recent immigration trends, children with immigrant parents are the most rapidly growing segment of our nation's child population (Fortuny, Capps, Simms, & Chaudry, 2009). In 2007, more than 1 child in 5 in the United States—16.4 million children—had at least one immigrant parent. This rapidly emerging population of immigrant children made up 23% of all children nationwide in 2006, representing just under 50% of children in California, and 31% or more in New York, Nevada, and Texas.

Whom Are We Assessing?

To conduct purposeful assessments aligned with early education programs, language/literacy researchers must begin with a more nuanced and representative picture of who these children are. Most language minority children are exposed to both a home language and English; 58% of these children have a parent who is a fluent English speaker (Hernandez et al., 2007). Though nearly half of the immigrant children are bilingual (49%), a smaller proportion of children in immigrant families (26%) live in linguistically isolated households where no one speaks English well (Hernandez et al., 2007). Due to their varied experiences and exposure to a first language (L1) and a second language (L2) in the home, as well as other environments, these bilingual children possess varying patterns of language dominance. Understanding the child's early language experience, in particular, the total home language environment (family SES, parent educational attainment, exposure, parent language proficiency, learning opportunities in L1 and L2, family culture and practices) is crucial when assessing oral language proficiency.

In 2006, just above 55% of children of immigrants were Latino/a, and 18% were Asian. Within the younger K–6 population of English language learners (ELLs), three out of four children (76%) speak Spanish (Capps, Fixx, Ost, Reardon-Anderson, & Passel, 2004). Most children of immigrants (40%) in the United States have origins in Mexico (Hernandez, 2005), though 17% had parents from Central and South America.

Studies provide further evidence to suggest that young Spanish-speaking bilinguals are most likely to live in poverty, and only 50% of them have parents with a high school diploma (Capps et al., 2004; Espinosa, Laffey, & Whittaker, 2006).

What to Assess and How to Assess It

How then do we develop innovative strategies for accurately and fairly assessing young bilinguals for their language and literacy skills? Espinosa and Lopez (2007) argue that the tremendous growth in numbers of young ELL children has not spurred corresponding development of a range of appropriate measures for them. Many of the currently available instruments for ELL children have been direct translations or adaptations of English language versions of existing measures, "with varying levels of attention given to ensure comparability in the conceptual, linguistic or semantic content and/or level of difficulty of the translated items across languages" (Espinosa & Lopez, 2007, p. 36). To provide some examples from the measures profiled in Table 24.2, Creative Curriculum, Galileo Pre-K, the Early Learning Accomplishment Profile (E-LAP), and Learning Accomplishment Profile—Diagnostic (LAP-D) provide both English and Spanish versions for assessing emergent literacy among young bilinguals. However, the linguistic sensitivity and cultural appropriateness of the content, as well as the guidelines for administration, require further examination. It is also questionable whether the Spanish versions of the test are designed to assess fully children's literacy knowledge and skills in both languages. Though Galileo Pre-K and Creative Curriculum included 20% of native Spanish-speaking children in their norming sample, other assessments are based on a norming sample of bilingual children whose primary language must be English. Of the early childhood assessment systems we have reviewed, Child Observation Record (COR), Early Childhood Observation System (ECHOS; Pearson Education, Inc., 2005, 2007), Developmental Assessment of Young Children (DAYC; Voress & Maddox, 2006), Infant–Preschool Play Assessment Scale (I-PAS; Fiagler, n.d.), and the Learning Accomplishment Profile–3 (LAP-3) only have English versions available.

The National Association for the Education of Young Children (NAEYC) and the National Association of Early Childhood Specialists in State Departments of Education (NAECS/SDE) formulated a 2003 position statement on early childhood assessment that provides helpful guidelines for the use of child-specific assessments. In 2009 NAEYC published a supplementary position statement focused on English language learners, in which they recommended that assessment methods use linguistically responsive and culturally appropriate instruments and procedures to "track, monitor, and support development in all areas, including language development" (p. 1).

It is widely recommended that language minority children be assessed in their home language, as well as English (Snow & Van Hemel, 2008). The major limitation of an assessment approach that evaluates children only in English is that "it ignores children's existing skills and abilities in their home language, as well as their prior experiences and learning that have occurred, and which directly relate to their future learning development" (Abedi, 2004).

Many have emphasized the critical importance of monitoring young bilingual children's literacy development in both languages as their vocabulary grows and as word learning is distributed across the two languages (Bedore, Peña, García, & Cortez, 2005; Mancilla-Martinez, Pan, & Banu Vagh, in press; Pearson, Fernández, & Oller, 1995), responding to calls for the field to shift away from understanding bilinguals as the simple sum of two monolinguals (Baker, 1995; Grosjean, 1982, 1989, 2008). The *complementarity principle* (Grosjean, 1982, 1989, 2008) holds that bilingual children rarely develop or maintain equal fluency in both languages. Rather, bilingualism is a dynamic system in which children employ different aspects of their languages in different contexts as their linguistic configuration and competence vary across subject areas, topics, and language functions. Good assessments must be able to reflect that dynamism.

Allman (2003) provides empirical evidence that measuring vocabulary knowledge in both languages generates a better estimate of the vocabulary size of bilingual preschoolers than limiting assessment to a single language. Additionally, Espinosa and Lopez (2007) urge practitioners working with young children to understand that *"code switching* (switching languages for portions of a sentence) and *language mixing* (inserting single items from one language into another) are normal aspects of second language acquisition" because language minority children may "lack sufficient vocabulary in one or both languages to fully express themselves or prefer particular words/ phrases to express their intents" (p. 11). Furthermore, the more familiar and culturally appropriate the content of the assessment materials, the more likely will children demonstrate behavior that accurately represents their real abilities (Armour-Thomas, 1992).

One of the key considerations in assessing young bilinguals is deciding what language to use. Though most measures are designed to be administered in a single language, administering the assessment bilingually may provide more accurate information on the child's language development and emergent literacy skills. For children who are simultaneously learning two languages, Escamilla (2000) also found that dual-language administration when assessing young bilinguals provided support rather than serving as a source of confusion.

As discussed earlier in this chapter, ensuring trust with the child being assessed in an unnatural testing environment has been one of the major challenges in administering early assessments. Young children's relationship with the person administering the assessment plays a critical role. The presence of a cultural broker or a translator can help. A well-trained assessor who speaks the child's home language is more likely to be well informed about the child's possible responses, and can play a critical role in obtaining interpretable and reliable results. Additionally, it is important for those administering the assessments to understand the child's language dominance: whether the child primarily speaks English, another language, or two languages and naturally switches between the two depending on contexts, interactions, and prompts.

Young bilingual learners may approach teachers and other school personnel differently than do U.S.-born children. Their cultural background, parental expectations, and complex social interactions with adults outside of school contexts shape how these children interact with adults even in assessment settings. In many cultures, children's questioning of adults may be inappropriate, perhaps perceived as undermining parental authority. Therefore, assessments should create a comfortable and safe space for children to ask clarifying questions or request that certain instructions be repeated, if necessary. Instead of implicitly assuming that children will articulate a question if confused or unclear about directions, guidelines to adult test administrators should include explicit instructions for helping children understand the directions. Since many young bilinguals may experience difficulty comprehending oral English, demonstrating the desired performance and providing practice items or activities, so that children need not rely solely on their listening skills to comprehend fully what is being expected of them, can produce more accurate estimates of child skills.

How to Assess Language-Minority Children

Assessments of ELLs must utilize a different set of evaluative criteria than those used for monolingual English speakers (Hamayan & Damico, 1991). For example, assessment for young bilinguals must combine concepts known in the L1 with the concepts being learned in the L2 (Escamilla, 2000; Grosjean, 1989). Accurate assessments must capture overall language competence in L1, as well as L2 (Espinosa, 2008). Pearson and colleagues (1993) demonstrated that the combined number of vocabulary words and concepts the bilingual child knows is comparable to the number and range of vocabulary items monolingual children know only if knowledge in both languages is counted. Moreover, a sample of 282 first-grade emerging bilinguals in English and Spanish regularly used two languages in the following tasks: letter identification, word tests, writing vocabulary, and text reading (Escamilla, Andrade, Basurto, Ruiz, & Clay, 1996).

DYNAMIC ASSESSMENT

Dynamic Assessment (also known as the test–teach–retest approach) serves two purposes: (1) to identify young bilingual children with possible language impairment; (2) to complement standardized normative tests and psychometric measures in providing a more accurate portrayal of children's actual skills and growth over time. One particular example of dynamic assessment worth mentioning is the *conceptual scoring approach*, in which children may respond in either language, so that all lexicalized concepts can be counted rather than only words in L1 or L2 (Peña, Iglesias, & Lidz, 2001); this is the approach used in the latest version of the bilingual Expressive One-Word Picture Vocabulary Test: Spanish–Bilingual Edition (EOWPVT-2000).

CONCEPTUAL SCORING

Conceptual scoring—that is, developing items simultaneously in both English and Spanish—has been an emerging strategy in the field of bilingual measurement. The manual provides prompts in both languages, thereby allowing the child to respond in either language. In addition to documenting the child's response for each item, the administrator also records the language in which the child responds. This approach is more cost-effective and less burdensome than successive monolingual assessments. However, Espinosa and Lopez (2007) warn that such an approach would not accurately assess the child's full range of receptive language abilities in each separate language.

TOTAL CONCEPTUAL VOCABULARY SCORE

One promising approach is exemplified by an integrative analysis of the bilingual child's vocabulary production in both languages using the Bates–MacArthur Communicative Development Inventory. Mothers were asked to report about the home language, and classroom teachers were asked about children's English language skills to index the child's overall vocabulary knowledge more accurately (Mancilla-Martinez, Pan, & Banu Vagh, in press). This method extends the notion of *total conceptual vocabulary* (or total number of different concepts for which the child knows a word, in either or both languages) first introduced by Pearson and colleagues (1993) and based on their work using transcript analysis. Obviously, the same approach could be used by administering a receptive vocabulary test such as the PPVT in both English and the home language, or providing the stimulus word in both languages.

HOW TO MAINTAIN PSYCHOMETRIC STANDARDS WHEN ASSESSING LANGUAGE-MINORITY CHILDREN

The 2008 National Research Council report (Snow & Van Hemel, 2008) explains that monolingual norms are simply inappropriate for accurately assessing the literacy skills and development of bilinguals:

> Tests normed on monolinguals are unlikely to adequately reflect the knowledge of bilinguals growing up in complex sociolinguistic settings. Yet testing children only in English if they are growing up bilingual clearly threatens to vastly underrepresent their language capacities. (p. 105)

Assessment measures should be evaluated according to their validity, reliability, and fairness (American Educational Research Association, American Psychological Association, and National Council on Measurement in Education, 1999). Some measures that demonstrate adequate validity and reliability may fail on the fairness criterion. A very few standardized language assessment tools have been culturally validated and renormed for the new language minority population (Alberts, Davis, & Prentice, 1995). The WMLS-R Normative Update 2010 offers a new norm-referenced measure of reading, writing, listening, and comprehension for Spanish–English bilingual children as young as 2 years of age. Few tests report normative data to establish reliability and validity even for Spanish-speaking bilingual children, let alone those from other language groups. Furthermore, we must consider whether the normative samples were drawn from monolingual Spanish-speaking or bilingual populations, or some combination of the two (Espinosa & Lopez, 2007). Ensuring large-enough samples of non-Spanish-speaking bilingual children in norming studies is even more challenging.

MAKING THE BEST OF IT

Acknowledging that the desirable array of well-normed and psychometrically impeccable assessments for language minority children does not currently exist, we return to the principles articulated earlier for designing good assessments. Start with observations of naturally occurring behavior under normal conditions. Include parent-

and teacher-report instruments (e.g., the one that Mancilla-Martinez et al. [in press] have shown to be useful) as sources of information. Use test scores in conjunction with observational methods and seminatural elicitations (Espinosa, 2008; NAEYC, 2005). Whenever possible, embed assessment procedures into instruction (Espinosa & Lopez, 2007), and focus professional development on providing teachers with the tools to collect, document, and analyze embedded assessments reliably (Wortham, 2001).

Much of the discourse around assessing the young ELL population centers on detecting risks and diagnosing deficiencies. Reframing is desperately needed to minimize pathologizing and to maximize opportunities to reflect the skills of bilinguals. Too often, assessment focuses on bilinguals as a separate group, and on their deficits or special needs, rather than on the cultural and developmental assets that bilingual children possess. Ensuring that bilingual children be assessed in domains (e.g., control of processing) where they excel over monolinguals would inform researchers and educators more richly about their cognitive profiles. Furthermore, the development of assessments that can be used with *both* bilinguals and monolinguals (e.g., those developed in the Netherlands; see Verhoeven, Narain, Extra, Konak, & Zerrouk, 1995; Verhoeven & Vermeer, 2006) would contribute to an approach to assessment that acknowledges the existence of highly talented bilinguals, as well as children still struggling with an L1 and/or L2. Furthermore, while we emphasize that language/literacy assessment are critical components of research with and education for young children, we nonetheless note that profiles of language minority children should not be limited to these domains.

Future Research

It is clear that future work on the topic of early childhood language and literacy assessment, either for research or for purposes of supporting, informing, and improving early childhood educational programs, would benefit from efforts to address the following issues:

• Development of measures that reflect the bilingual skills of language minority children, producing single scores that can be used in growth modeling and other longitudinal research analyses.

• Development of guidelines for how to select language of testing when only monolingual tests are available, and procedures for linking Spanish to English versions of tests, so that continuous developmental trajectories can be estimated for children undergoing shift of language dominance.

• Evaluation of the most effective methods for training administrators of assessments to young children, with serious attention to the positive and negative effects on stability and interpretability of test outcomes of different degrees of flexibility and responsiveness during the testing session. Besides testing the effects of cultural sensitivity and familiarity with the child's out-of-school environment, understanding the value of training that enables assessors to understand the process and stages of acquiring an L2 for young developing children would further contribute to accurate reflection of children's emergent literacy skills.

• Development of guidelines and procedures for involving parents in the assessment process. At the moment, there are urgent calls to include parents' views (e.g., NAEYC, 2005), and some evidence that parents can provide relevant and useful information about the child's language and overall development (Pavri & Fowler, 2005). But these exhortations generate no change in practice without mechanisms to ensure feasibility, reliability, stability, fairness, and validity of parental reports, and to evaluate the degree to which parents of different backgrounds provide comparable information.

• Attention to non-Spanish-speaking language minorities. Though most language minority children in the United States are Spanish–English bilinguals, the language minority population encompasses a wide spectrum of languages, cultures, nationalities, parenting goals, neighborhood characteristics, and family compositions. While some work has been done to create Spanish versions of several assessment tools, comparable measures to assess other bilingual children in their native language are rare and, when they exist, are meant for monolinguals in those languages, rather than bilinguals.

Research on child development relies inexorably on having good assessment procedures and instruments available, yet too rarely do those of us with a substantive knowledge of language and literacy development connect that knowledge to the practical and time-consuming effort to improve the instruments we use—not just their design, but also their implementation and their interpretation. We resemble the farmer too busy chopping down trees to stop and sharpen his axe. Assessment instruments are the tools we need to keep sharpening.

Acknowledgments

We express our appreciation to the members of the National Academy of Sciences Committee on Development Assessment and Outcomes for Young Children, who contributed their impressive expertise across a variety of domains to the formulation of the research reviews, guidelines, and cautions included in the report, and to Susan Van Hemel, the study director who carefully guided the work of the committee. The National Research Council study was funded by the Office of Head Start, Administration for Children and Families, U.S. Department of Health and Human Services.

References

Abedi, J. (2004). The No Child Left Behind Act and English language learners: Assessment and accountability issues. *Educational Researcher, 33*(1), 4–14.

Alberts, F. M., Davis, B. L., & Prentice, L. (1995). Validity of an observation screening instrument in a multicultural population. *Journal of Early Intervention, 19,* 168–177.

Allman, B. (2003, April–May). *Vocabulary size and accuracy of monolingual and bilingual preschool children.* Paper presented at the Fourth International Symposium on Bilingualism, Tempe, AZ.

American Educational Research Association, American Psychological Association, & National Council on Measurement in Education (NCME). (1999). *The standards for educational and psychological testing.* Washington, DC: Author.

Armour-Thomas, E. (1992). Intellectual assessment of children from culturally diverse backgrounds. *School Psychology Review, 21*(4), 552–565.

Assessment Technology Incorporated. (n.d.). *Galileo Pre-K.* Tucson, AZ: Author.

Baker, C. (1995). The assessment of bilingual children. *Assessment in education: Principles, Policy and Practice, 2*(3), 353–357.

Bedore, L. M., Peña, E. D., García, M., & Cortez, C. (2005). Conceptual versus monolingual scoring: When does it make a difference? *Language, Speech, and Hearing Services in Schools, 36,* 188–200.

Ben-Zeev, S. (1977). The influence of bilingualism on cognitive strategy and cognitive development. *Child Development, 48,* 1009–1018.

Bialystok, E., & Ryan, E. (1985). Towards a definition of metalinguistic skill. *Merrill–Palmer Quarterly, 31,* 229–251.

Blank, M., Rose, S., & Berlin, L. (1978). *The language of learning: The preschool years.* Orlando, FL: Grune & Stratton.

Brown, R. (1973). *A first language: The early stages.* Cambridge, MA: Harvard University Press.

Capps, R., Fixx, M., Ost, J., Reardon-Anderson, J., & Passel, J. (2004). *The health and well-being of young children of immigrants.* New York: Urban Institute.

Craig, H. K., Connor, C. M., & Washington, J. A. (2003). Early positive predictors of later reading comprehension for African American students: A preliminary investigation. *Language, Speech, and Hearing Services in Schools, 34,* 31–43.

Development of Academic Language at Home and School [DASH]. (2006). *Coding protocol for functional linguistic analysis.* Amsterdam: Author.

Dickinson, D. K., & Porche, M. (in press). Relationship between language experiences in preschool classrooms and children's kindergarten and fourth grade language and reading abilities. *Child Development.*

Dickinson, D. O., & Tabors, P. O. (Eds.). (2001). *Beginning literacy with language.* Baltimore: Brookes.

Doyle, A., Champagne, M., & Segalowitz, N. (1978). Some issues in the assessment of linguistic consequences of early bilingualism. In M. Paradis (Ed.), *Aspects of bilingualism* (pp. 13–21). Columbia, SC: Horn-Beam Press.

Escamilla, K. (2000). *Bilingual means two: Assessment issues, early literacy and Spanish-speaking children: A proceeding from the research symposium on high standards in reading for students from diverse language groups: Research, practice and policy.* Washington, DC: U.S. Department of Education Office of Bilingual Education and Minority Languages Affairs (OBEMLA). Available online at *epicpolicy.org/files/report.pdf.*

Escamilla, K., Andrade, A. M., Basurto, A. G. M., Ruiz, O. A., & Clay, M. M. (1996). *Instrumento de observación: De los logros de la lecto-escritura inicial* [Observation instrument: Early literacy achievements]. Portsmouth, NH: Heinemann.

Espinosa, L. (2008, April). *Assessing young English learners across purposes and domains: Promises and pitfalls.* Presented at the Child Care and Early Education Research Connections Roundtable "Supporting Positive Language and Literacy Development in Young Language Minority Children: Research, Policy, and Practice," Washington, DC.

Espinosa, L., Laffey, J., & Whittaker, T. (2006). *Language minority children analysis: Focus on technology use.* Washington, DC: National Center for Education Statistics.

Espinosa, L., & Lopez, M. L. (2007). *Assessment considerations for young English language learners across different levels of accountability.* Paper commissioned by First 5 LA and the Pew Charitable Trust's Early Childhood Accountability Project. Retrieved July 14, 2010, from *www.first5la.org/files/Assessment_ConsiderationsEnglishLearners.pdf.*

Fenson, L., Dale, P. S., Reznick, J. S., Bates, E., Thal, D. J., & Pethick, S. J. (1994). Variability in early communicative development. *Monographs of the Society for Research in Child Development, 59*(Serial No. 242).

Fernández, M. C., Pearson, B. Z., Umbel, V. M., Oller, D. K., & Molinet-Molina, M. (1992). Bilingual receptive vocabulary in Hispanic preschool children. *Hispanic Journal of the Behavioral Sciences, 14*, 268–276.

Fiagler, S. (n.d.). *Infant–Preschool Play Assessment Scale (I-PAS).* Chapel Hill, NC: Chapel Hill Training Outreach Project.

Fortuny, K., Capps, R., Simms, M., & Chaudry, A. (2009). *Children of immigrants: National and state characteristics: Perspectives on low-income working families* (The Urban Institute Brief). Retrieved January 10, 2010 from *www.urban.org/uploaded-pdf/411939_childrenofimmigrants.pdf.*

Grosjean, F. (1982). *Life with two languages: An introduction to bilingualism.* Cambridge, MA: Harvard University Press.

Grosjean, F. (1989). Neurolinguists, beware!: The bilingual is not two monolinguals in one person. *Brain and Language, 36*(3), 3–15.

Grosjean, F. (2008). *Studying bilinguals.* Oxford, UK: Oxford University Press.

Hamayan, E., & Damico, S. (1991). *Limiting bias in the assessment of bilingual students.* Austin, TX: Pro-Ed.

Hardin, B. J., & Peisner-Feinberg, E. S. (2001). *The Early Learning Accomplishment Profile (E-LAP).* Lewisville, NC: Kaplan Early Learning Company, Chapel Hill Training Outreach Project.

Henrichs, L. F. (2006). Schooltaalvaardigheid operationaliseren: De ontwikkeling van een coderingsschema binnen het DASH project [Operationalizing school-language skill: The development of a coding scheme for the DASH project]. In T. Koole, J. Nortier, & B. Tahitu (Eds.), *Artikelen van de Vijfde sociolinguïstische conferentie* (pp. 246–256). Delft: Eburon.

Henrichs, L. F., & Schoonen, R. (2009). Lexical features of parental academic language input: The effect on vocabulary growth in monolingual Dutch children. In B. J. Richards, H. M. Daller, D. D. Malvern, P. P. Meara, J. Milton, & J. Treffers-Daller (Eds.), *Vocabulary studies in first and second language acquisition: The interface between theory and application* (pp. 1–22). Houndmills, UK: Palgrave-Macmillan.

Hernandez, D. (2005). *New indicators for children and families.* In Closing the Gaps: KIDS COUNT 2005 Conference, a workshop session "Immigrant Children and Families." Baltimore: Anne E. Casey Foundation.

Hernandez, D. J., Denton, N. A., & Macartney, S. (2007). *Children in immigrant families—the U.S. and 50 states: National origins, language, and early education* (A research brief by Child Trends and the Center for Social and Demographic Analysis) (Publication No. 2007-11). Albany: State University of New York.

High/Scope Educational Research Foundation. (2004). *Preschool Child Observation Record (COR), second edition.* Ypsilanti, MI: High/Scope Educational Research Foundation.

Hoff, E., & Elledge, C. (2005). IRB4. In J. Cohen, K. T. McAlister, K. Rolstad, & J. MacSwan (Eds.), *Proceedings of the Fourth International Symposium on Bilingualism* (pp. 1034–1040). Somerville, MA: Cascadilla Press.

Leseman, P. P. M., & de Jong, P. F. (1998). Home literacy: Opportunity, instruction, cooperation, and social-emotional quality predicting early reading achievement. *Reading Research Quarterly, 33*(3), 294–318.

Leseman, P. P. M., Scheele, A., Mayo, A. Y., & Messer, M. H. (2007). Home literacy as a special language environment to prepare children for school. *Zeitschrift fur Erziehungswissenschaft, 10*(3), 334–355.

Leyva, D., & Wiser, M. (2007, March). *The role of parental talk in preschoolers' symbolic understanding of a grocery list.* Poster presented at the biennial meeting of the Society for Research in Child Development, Boston.

Leyva, D., Wiser, M., & Reese, E. (2008, June). *Parents' verbal and non-verbal support in preschoolers' symbolic understanding of notations.* Paper presented at the annual meeting of the Jean Piaget Society, Quebec City, Canada.

MacWhinney, B., & Snow, C. E. (1985). The child language data exchange system. *Journal of Child Language, 12*, 271–295.

MacWhinney, B., & Snow, C. E. (1990). The child language data exchange system: An update. *Journal of Child Language, 17*, 457–472.

Mancilla-Martinez, J., Pan, B. A., & Banu Vagh, S. (in press). Assessing the productive vocabulary of Spanish–English bilingual toddlers from low-income families. *Applied Psycholinguistics.*

Meisels, S. J. (2004). Should we test 4-year-olds? *Pediatrics, 113*, 1401–1414.

National Association for the Education of Young Children (NAEYC). (2009). *Where we stand on assessing young English language learners.* Washington, DC: Author. Retrieved July 14, 2010, from *www.naeyc.org/files/naeyc/file/positions/WWSEnglishLanguageLearnersWeb.pdf.*

National Association for the Education of Young Children (NAEYC) and the National Association of Early Childhood Specialists in State Departments of Education (NAECS/SDE). (2003). *Early childhood curriculum, assessment, and program evaluation: Building an effective, accountable system in programs for children birth through age 7.* Retrieved July 14, 2010, from *www.naeyc.org/files/naeyc/file/positions/pscape.pdf.*

National Reading Panel. (2000, April). *Teaching children to read: An evidence-based assessment of the scientific literature on reading and its implications for reading instruction* (NIH Publication No. 00-4769). Washington, DC: U.S. Department of Health and Human Services, Public Health Service, National Institute of Child Health and Human Development.

Pavri, S., & Fowler, S. (2005). Child find, screening,

and tracking: Serving culturally and linguistically diverse children and families. In S. Fowler, R. Santos, & R. Corso (Eds.), *Appropriate screening, assessment, and family information gathering* (pp. 3–22). Longmont, CO: Sopris West.

Pearson, B. Z., Fernández, S. C., & Oller, D. K. (1995). Cross-language synonyms in the lexicons of bilingual infants: One language or two? *Journal of Child Language, 22,* 345–368.

Pearson, B. Z., Fernández, S. C., & Oller, D. K. (1993). Lexical development in bilingual infants and toddlers: Comparisons to monolingual norms. *Language Learning, 43,* 93–120.

Pearson Education, Inc. (2005). ECHOS Early Childhood Observation System K–2. San Antonio, TX: Author.

Pearson Education, Inc. (2007). ECHOS Early Childhood Observation System Pre-K. San Antonio, TX: Author.

Peña, E., Iglesias, A., & Lidz, C. S. (2001). Reducing test bias through dynamic assessment of children's word learning ability. *American Journal of Speech–Language Pathology, 10,* 138–154.

Poe, M. D., Burchinal, M., & Roberts, J. (2004). Early language and the development of children's reading skills. *Journal of School Psychology, 42,* 315–332.

Quiroz, B. G., & Snow, C. E. & Zhao, J. (in press). Vocabulary skills of Spanish/English bilinguals: Impact of mother–child language interactions and home language and literacy support. *International Journal of Bilingualism.*

Rosenblum, T., & Pinker, S. A. (1983). Word magic revisited: Monolingual and bilingual children's understanding of the word–object relationship. *Child Development, 54,* 773–780.

Roth, F. P., Speece, D. L., & Cooper, D. H. (2002). A longitudinal analysis of the connection between oral language and early reading. *Journal of Educational Research, 95,* 259–272.

Scheele, A. F., Leseman, P. P. M., & Mayo, A. Y. (2010). The home language environment of mono- and bilingual children and their language proficiency. *Applied Psycholinguistics, 31,* 117–140.

Snow, C. E. (2001). Database, Core: Linguistics CHILDES. In J. Smelser Neil & P. B. Baltes (Eds.), *International encyclopedia of the social and behavioral sciences.* New York: Elsevier Science.

Snow, C. E., Burns, M., & Griffin, P. (Eds.). (1998). *Preventing reading difficulties in young children.* Washington, DC: National Academies Press.

Snow, C. E., Porche, M., Tabors, P., & Harris, S. (2007). *Is literacy enough?: Pathways to academic success for adolescents.* Baltimore: Brookes.

Snow, C. E., Tabors, P. O., & Dickinson, D. K. (2001). Language development in the preschool years. In D. K. Dickinson & P. O. Tabors (Eds.), *Beginning literacy with language* (pp. 1–25). Baltimore: Brookes.

Snow, C. E., Tabors, P. O., Nicholson, P., & Kurland, B. (1995). SHELL: Oral language and early literacy skills in kindergarten and first grade children. *Journal of Research in Childhood Education, 10,* 37–48.

Snow, C. E., & Uccelli, P. (2009). The challenge of academic language. In D. R. Olson & N. Torrance (Eds.), *The Cambridge handbook of literacy* (pp. 112–133). New York: Cambridge University Press.

Snow, C. E., & Van Hemel, S. B. (Eds.). (2008). *Early childhood assessment: Why, what, and how.* Washington, DC: National Academies Press.

Stanovich, K. (1986). Matthew effects in reading: Some consequences of individual differences in the acquisition of literacy. *Reading Research Quarterly, 21*(4), 360–407.

Sulzby, E. (1986). Writing and reading: Signs of oral and written language organization in the young child. In W. H. Teale & E. Sulzby (Eds.), *Emergent literacy: Writing and reading* (pp. 50–89). Norwood, NJ: Ablex.

Tabors, P. O., Roach, K. A., & Snow, C. E. (2001) Home language and literacy environment final results. In D. K. Dickinson & P. O. Tabors (Eds.), *Beginning literacy with language* (pp. 111–138). Baltimore: Brookes.

Teaching Strategies. (2006a). *The Creative Curriculum Developmental Continuum assessment toolkit for ages 3–5.* Washington, DC: Author.

Teaching Strategies. (2006b). *The Creative Curriculum for Infants, Toddlers and Twos Developmental Continuum assessment toolkit.* Washington, DC: Author.

Umbel, V. M., Pearson, B. Z., Fernández, M. C., & Oller, D. K. (1992). Measuring bilingual children's receptive vocabularies. *Child Development, 63,* 1012–1020.

Verhoeven, L., Narain, G., Extra, G., Konak, O. A., & Zerrouk, R. (1995). Diagnostische toets tweetaligheid *[test for bilingual development].* Arnhem, The Netherlands: CITO.

Verhoeven, L., & Vermeer, A. (2006). *Verantwoording taaltoets alle kinderen (TAK) [Accountability Language Test All Children].* Arnhem, The Netherlands: CITO.

Voress, J. K., & Maddox, T. (2006). *Developmental Assessment of Young Children (DAYC).* Los Angeles: Western Psychological Services.

Whitehurst, G. J., & Lonigan, C. J. (1998). Child development and emergent literacy. *Child Development, 69,* 848–872.

Wortham, S. E. F. (2001). *Narratives in action: A strategy for research and analysis.* New York: Teachers College Press.

Yoshikawa, H., Barata, M. C., Rolla, A., Snow, C. E., & Arbour, M. C. (2008). *Un Buen Comienzo, an initiative to improve preschool education in Chile: Data from the initial year of implementation.* Santiago, Chile: UNICEF.

25

Tell Me a Story:
Examining the Benefits of Shared Reading

ANNE E. CUNNINGHAM
JAMIE ZIBULSKY

For many years now, education reform efforts in the United States have focused on reducing the educational achievement gap between privileged and disadvantaged students. Despite a continued focus on educational equality in our schools, various types of intervention aimed at school-age children have had limited success in closing the gap. It is believed that some of the differences between the academic performance of children of privilege and their underprivileged peers are not simply artifacts of the disparities in formal educational opportunities. Instead, research has demonstrated that children enter school with varying levels of preacademic skills and that, in many cases, it is the discrepancy between these skill sets at school entry that lay the foundation for the differences we observe in achievement and academic performance over time (e.g., Magnuson, Meyers, Ruhm, & Waldfogel, 2004). For that reason, educators, health-care professionals, and political leaders alike have increasingly emphasized the importance of acquiring literacy skills in the home, before school entry.

The quest to minimize this discrepancy between children's skills at school entry necessitates that parents, and those involved in the care of children prior to formal schooling, provide more opportunities for positive and effective early literacy experiences. To that end, parents are being urged to read to their infants early and often, and to consider not only the quantity but also the quality of that shared reading time. Unfortunately, some parents lack the financial resources to provide children with a print-rich environment, while others may lack time or an understanding of how to engage in frequent, high-quality shared reading experiences (Korat, Klein, & Segal-Drori, 2007; Neuman, 1996; Neuman & Celano, 2001). In an attempt to address these needs, many nonprofit and research organizations have provided books to parents and have trained them to read with their children in ways known to foster language and literacy growth.

Because the mission of such organizations is to increase both parent awareness and children's access to high-quality reading experiences, Americans have been inundated with messages about the benefits of reading to children. An oft-repeated refrain in parenting books and magazines, and across various online forums, is that it is never too early to start reading to children. The American Academy of Pediatrics (1998) advises parents to begin reading aloud daily once their children are 6 months old. Scholastic, the largest worldwide children's book publisher, asks parents: "What's the best way to help your child succeed in school and in life? Read to him—early and often!" (*www.scholastic.*

com/familymatters/read/all/readalous.htm). Such messages are ubiquitous. The idea that reading aloud to children brings about positive outcomes is also strongly embraced by the educational community. Teachers, classroom assistants, and parent volunteers are urged to read aloud to students, so that children can engage in conversations about texts that may be above their independent reading level, learn how to make predictions about text, and see reading as a shared activity with many connections to the real world (Hall & Moats, 2000; Lane & Wright, 2007; Strickland & Morrow, 1989).

In *Becoming a Nation of Readers: The Report of the Commission on Reading*, a canonical document in the field of reading research, Anderson, Hiebert, Scott, and Wilkinson (1985) state, "The single most important activity for building the knowledge required for eventual success in reading is reading aloud to children" (p. 23). Parents and teachers receive regular and resolute messages about the importance of reading to children, and many resources are dedicated to ensuring that all children have the opportunity to engage in high-quality shared reading time with an adult. However, although reading aloud with children has long been considered an essential activity for the development of language and literacy skills, we do not yet fully understand the strength of this intervention, or the aspects of language and literacy development that it most affects. Although it may seem obvious to assume that reading with a child will correspond to a positive outcome, a better understanding of exactly how, why, and to what extent reading aloud is so important for language and literacy outcomes could help refine the messages and training that parents and early childhood educators receive regarding literacy development.

Defining Reading Aloud

The term *reading aloud with children* is somewhat indeterminate and open to interpretation. Defining the construct is essential for understanding how to foster shared reading experiences that will be most beneficial to children. In this chapter we discuss the interactive and instructive process of reading aloud, as well as its varied benefits.

How Researchers Define Reading Aloud

For the purposes of this chapter, we define *reading aloud with a child* as a reading strategy that includes an adult or skilled reader and a child or group of children reading together. Shared reading may or may not introduce conventions of print, new vocabulary, rhyming, discussion of pictures, or include other interactive experiences. Depending on which of these activities are embedded in the reading experience, terms such as *reading aloud*, (traditional) *shared book reading, parent–child reading, joint book reading,* or *dyadic reading* are used to describe the experience with some degree of specificity. Notable differences in the language and literacy outcomes associated with reading aloud depend on the specific nature of the reading experience, and we define this experience as specifically as possible when describing the relationship between any of the forms it can take and children's skill development. The two variables most often considered in studies of shared reading are the *quantity* (i.e., frequency and duration) and *quality* (e.g., type of discourse, degree of autonomy afforded to child, and nature of the interaction between adult and child) of the reading experience.

Keeping these aspects of the shared reading experience in mind may alter the way that one imagines such an experience. Generally, we picture the activity as one in which a child sits quietly and listens intently while an adult reads the text word-for-word, rarely stopping, or stopping only to ask basic questions (e.g., "Do you see the puppy in the picture?"). In this instance, the adult, who reads *to* the child, directs the reading experience. But as researchers have developed and investigated strategies to ensure that shared reading sessions boost specific skills, it has become apparent that altering the nature of the reading experience can lead to gains in language and literacy skills. These gains have been made by encouraging the child to play a more active role and read *with* the adult by focusing on specific features of the text or by asking specific types of questions (e.g., Justice & Ezell, 2002; Whitehurst et al., 1988). Thus, it is becoming increasingly clear that all adult–child reading experiences are not created equal. As a result, it is even more critical that we begin to understand the various aspects of reading aloud that are most beneficial.

Dialogic Reading

Dialogic reading is a specific kind of shared reading experience. Although it is not the focus of this chapter, it merits attention because it is the most widely known and researched strategy for engaging children in interactive reading experiences. In dialogic reading sessions, the adult reader encourages the child to participate actively in the reading experience by eliciting comments, providing feedback, and adapting to the child's developing linguistic skills (Lonigan & Whitehurst, 1998; Whitehurst et al., 1988; Whitehurst, Arnold, et al., 1994). The techniques used in dialogic reading (e.g., allowing the child to be the primary storyteller, asking *wh-* questions, expanding upon the child's comments) have been found to affect oral language development positively (Chow & McBride-Chang, 2003; Institute of Education Sciences [IES], 2006a; Whitehurst et al., 1988). In general, interventions that encourage a more interactive experience such as dialogic reading have been found to have stronger effects on children's oral language skills than traditional shared reading (National Center for Family Literacy [NCFL], 2009). Although dialogic reading is most frequently associated with oral language growth, studies have also demonstrated that shared reading may be the type of intervention that can promote the development of other critical emergent and conventional literacy skills (Evans & Shaw, 2008).

What Skills Does Reading Aloud Impact?

When considering the effectiveness of reading aloud and seeking to understand how, why, and to what extent reading aloud with children results in positive outcomes, we need to understand that we identify the specific skills and abilities that are critical to future literacy acquisition. In addition to early language and emergent literacy skills, children must also develop advanced skills in phonics, orthographic processes, vocabulary development, and reading comprehension. All of

these component skills are interrelated, and each is essential to reading acquisition (National Early Literacy Panel [NELP], 2008).

Emergent Literacy Skills

Emergent literacy skills that develop before children begin to read and write, and serve as predictors of later literacy can be facilitated through shared reading. Reading with adults helps children familiarize themselves with the correspondences between written and spoken language and the typical structure of stories (Bus, van IJzendoorn, & Pellegrini, 1995). Through scaffolded reading experiences, young children have the opportunity to identify themselves as competent readers, even before they are able to decode text, through learning how to hold a book, turn its pages, and experiment with "reading" the story from memory or adding their own embellishments to a familiar story.

Phonological Processes and Phonics/ Orthographic Skills

The term *phonological processing* refers to a set of skills and abilities related to children's ability to recognize and mentally manipulate the sound-based structure of language and reading. *Phonics skills* refer to knowledge of the specific letter–sound correspondences (e.g., the letter *m* corresponds to the sound /m/, the letters *ph* and *f* correspond to the sound /f/) (NCFL, 2009). Together these skills—which can be developed through shared explorations of print—allow children to decode written language. Through exposure to text, children are then able to gradually move away from the need to identify words letter-by-letter, sound-by-sound. Instead, they begin identifying words based on complete orthographic representations. This opportunity to become familiar with common orthographic patterns through repeated exposure to written language is one of the primary arguments reading researchers have put forth when making the case for reading with and to children.

Vocabulary Development

Children with larger, more developed vocabularies are better equipped to identify words and, subsequently, to understand what they have read. Although vocabulary growth develops through structured language experiences, such as direct vocabulary instruction (Beck & McKeown, 2007; Beck, Perfetti, & McKeown, 1982; Neuman & Dwyer, 2009), the majority of vocabulary growth occurs through exposure to language and vocabulary in context (Hayes, 1988; Hayes & Ahrens, 1988; Krashen, 1989; Nagy & Anderson, 1984; Nagy & Herman, 1985; Stanovich, 1986, 2000). For this reason, shared reading experiences and the conversations they generate provide opportunities for vocabulary development.

Reading Comprehension

Successful reading comprehension is dependent on a child's ability both to identify words rapidly using phonological and orthographic processes, and to define words based on their meanings in the particular context in which they are read. It is also dependent on other background variables, such as general knowledge, working memory, and the ability to make connections and associations between experiences and concepts (Carretti, Borella, Cornoldi, & De Beni, 2009; Catts, 2009; Hirsch, 2003). The ability to connect one's own experiences to a text is facilitated by shared reading experiences, during which an adult can explain unfamiliar words and concepts, as well as guide a child to think critically about the text. Because adult attention can foster language and literacy growth throughout the long and complex process of reading acquisition, knowing how to engage in reading aloud effectively at different stages of the process may be very beneficial to adults guiding emergent and young readers through shared reading experiences.

Finally, although our focus in this chapter is to specify the ways and degree to which shared reading experiences foster the development of specific component skills of reading acquisition, we would be remiss not to highlight the fact that the quality of the attachment relationship between the adult and child interacts with quantitative variables associated with reading development in complex ways (see Bus & van IJzendoorn, 1997; Clingenpeel & Pianta, 2007). For example, studies detailing the quality of such relationships indicate that children who do not have secure attachment relationships with their parents are less likely than peers to stay engaged in shared reading experiences, resulting in shorter, less frequent shared reading sessions during which fewer words are exchanged. As we discuss the skills required for reading acquisition, we should not lose sight of the fact that the shared reading experience is valuable not only for its potential to influence learning but also because it can be a vehicle for developing and sustaining interpersonal relationships, creating opportunities for shared discourse, and helping children see reading as an enjoyable and social process.

Science Investigating Reading Aloud

Before analyzing the specific attributes, methods, and benefits of shared reading, we should note that parental reports of shared reading and the data gathered during experimental studies of shared reading interventions may be associated with outcome measures of reading in different ways. Correlational studies provide us with information regarding the association between the time a parent spends reading with a child and that child's literacy outcomes, whereas experimental studies (in which specific interventions are implemented with one group of children, while another group serves as a baseline control group) allow us to examine causality and efficacy in a range of ways. The majority of early studies in this field rely on correlational data only, providing readers with important information about the strength of the relationship between shared reading experiences and particular outcome variables, but do not typically address the confounding problem of whether a factor other than shared reading caused children to perform as they did on outcome measures.

To date, only one recent meta-analytic study, undertaken by NELP (2008), has examined experimental studies or interventions that primarily focused on the shared reading experiences of preschoolers and kindergarteners at home, as well as in school, and the effects of these experiences on the development of oral language skills, phonological awareness skills, print knowledge skills, and other important aspects of literacy development. Additionally, two other recent meta-analytic studies (Mol, Bus, de Jong, & Smeets, 2008; Sénéchal, & Young, 2008) examined the efficacy of particular home literacy activities and shared reading methods to assess whether these activities foster more language and literacy growth than other common home literacy activities.

The relationships that exist between reported shared reading practices and later literacy outcomes may be partially explained by mediating variables, such as other aspects of the home literacy environment, sociodemographic factors, individual characteristics of the adult or child, or interpersonal relationship factors. Thus, interventions may be more or less effective depending on the extent to which they address these factors. Many of the intervention studies we describe later in this chapter controlled for sociodemographic factors in their analyses. Other studies (e.g., Bus & van IJzendoorn, 1995; Clingenpeel & Pianta, 2007; Huebner, 2000; Meagher, Arnold, Doctoroff, & Baker, 2008; Vernon-Feagans et al., 2008) considered the role that child temperament, parental knowledge, parent–child attachment relationship, or parental stress may play in the quality of the shared reading experience, important issues that cannot be addressed sufficiently within the scope of this chapter. Indeed, the complexity of the shared reading experience makes it extremely difficult for any single study to address all of the factors that may influence the quality and quantity of shared reading any one child may experience—a fact we cannot overlook when considering the results of the studies to date.

Types of Studies Conducted

Over the past several years, researchers have increasingly focused on conducting experimental, rather than correlational, studies of the effects of shared reading to understand better the specifics of exactly why, when, and the degree to which reading aloud is important for language and literacy development. Simultaneously, as this body of literature grows, it has been analyzed in different ways through sophisticated meta-analytic studies, such as the NELP (2008) study, as well as studies by Mol and colleagues (2008) and

Sénéchal and Young (2008). These research efforts have resulted in substantial data underscoring not only the value, but also the nuances, of this literacy activity.

META-ANALYTIC PROCEDURES

Meta-analysis refers to the statistical analysis of a large compilation of results from individual studies in order to integrate findings more rigorously than do traditional narrative review methods (Glass, 1976). To conduct a meta-analysis, the literature base is searched for investigations relevant to a specific research question or hypothesis. Once gathered, these individual studies become the data points for the subsequent analysis. The study statistics are converted into a common metric, known as *effect size*, which is comparable across studies.

Although interpretation of effect size requires a consideration of the context in which the research was conducted, as well as the potential impact that such an effect could have upon the variable of interest, an effect size of 0.3 or less is generally labeled as a small effect, an effect size above 0.3 and less than 0.8 is generally considered a moderate effect, and an effect size of 0.8 or greater is generally thought of as a large effect (Cohen, 1988). It is notable that because of the number of variables that affect development and the difficulty of designing true controlled experiments, large effect sizes are infrequently reported in social science research (Cohen, 1988). For that reason, effects in the small to moderate range can be a cause for celebration and further exploration in the field of reading research because even small effect sizes can have important implications for our understanding of the literature. By gathering results across studies, one is able to gain a more accurate estimate of the relationship than can be understood from individual investigations. As noted, several meta-analytic studies have served to deepen our understanding of the value of reading aloud with young children.

EXPERIMENTAL STUDIES

The utility of meta-analyses is that they allow us to understand the relationship one can expect to find between variables across a broad population and do not over- or underestimate the relationship in the way that one individual study might. By averaging results across many studies, meta-analyses provide fairly conservative estimates of effects. However, in order to continue to explore the potential of varied shared reading interventions for later reading success, it is also important to examine individual studies that produce promising outcomes yet to be replicated. In this chapter, we highlight some of these rigorous studies whose outcomes still must be replicated in future work.

Early Work in the Field of Shared Reading, 1988–2000

LONIGAN, WHITEHURST, AND COLLEAGUES' DIALOGIC READING STUDIES

The research teams of Christopher Lonigan and Grover Whitehurst, who developed the dialogic reading strategy, conducted many of the early experimental studies evaluating the effects of shared reading interventions. More than two decades ago, these researchers realized that it was important to ascertain what types of shared reading affected specific skills associated with the process of reading acquisition. In 1988, Whitehurst, Lonigan, and their colleagues conducted one of the first experimental studies of shared reading in which, for 1 month, parents in the experimental group were provided with instructions in the dialogic reading method, and parents in the control group were instructed to read to their children as usual. They found that children in the experimental group displayed higher compliance with the instructions and also scored higher on tests of expressive language both at the end of the intervention and again 9 months later. This early work provided preliminary evidence that dialogic reading supports language development more than does typical shared reading.

These researchers continued to investigate and to specify what interventions worked favorably at particular times during a child's development. Lonigan, Anthony, Bloomfield, Dyer, and Samwell (1999) found that "both dialogic reading and typical shared-reading can have positive effects on the emergent literacy skills of at-risk preschool children" (p. 317) and that each approach promoted the development of different skills. A study

examining the efficacy of dialogic reading at home and school (Lonigan & Whitehurst, 1998) found that when parents and teachers adhered to implementation standards, children's engagement in reading increased, as did their scores on measures of receptive and expressive language.

The long-term direct effects of dialogic reading on conventional reading success have not yet been substantiated. However, from the body of research on dialogic reading interventions administered by its creators and their colleagues, it seems likely that dialogic reading—when engaged in frequently and in accordance with training guidelines—is an effective way to increase expressive and receptive language skills, as well as knowledge of print conventions, particularly for low-income children (e.g., Lonigan & Whitehurst, 1998; Whitehurst, Arnold, et al., 1994; Whitehurst, Epstein, et al., 1994). Although this approach has utility for early childhood classrooms, as well as home settings, in studies in which some children received the intervention only in a school setting, "classroom-based interactive reading did not, by itself, generate increases in children's language skills" (Whitehurst, Epstein, et al., 1994, p. 552). This apparent need for parent involvement in early reading experiences is a primary motivation for the studies conducted in this field. Given that our nation's achievement gap endures, researchers have continued to study shared reading in order to specify exactly what behaviors parents need to adopt to boost literacy growth.

SCARBOROUGH AND DOBRICH'S REVIEW

By the mid-1990s, several rigorous studies of the effects of shared reading had been published. Around the same time, and because a body of studies that examined such effects finally existed, meta-analyses examining these same issues were conducted. Scarborough and Dobrich (1994) were the first investigators to undertake this type of analysis. In their meta-analytic study they underscored the importance of oral language abilities, emergent literacy skills, socioeconomic background, and early attitude towards literacy as predictors of subsequent literacy achievement, while highlighting parent–preschooler reading experiences as their key variable of study.

Scarborough and Dobrich (1994) included studies that examined the aforementioned variables during early elementary school. Because these studies did not include many tests that could be compared across samples, only tentative conclusions were drawn. These conclusions contradicted the expectation that stronger relationships would be found between shared reading experiences and more proximal literacy outcomes, rather than those literacy outcomes measured later in the process of reading acquisition. Scarborough and Dobrich theorized that both early language and emergent literacy skills "are probably not much more strongly associated with parent–preschooler reading than are later achievement scores" (p. 267), citing median correlation coefficients between .23 and .28.

The authors, however, did not examine whether parent–preschooler reading experiences were indirectly associated with later reading achievement via their influence on earlier milestones in the process of reading development, such as oral language or emergent literacy skills. Lonigan (1994) raised this point in his response to Scarborough and Dobrich's (1994) review. His question of whether "small initial differences between children in their literacy development may become magnified over time" (Lonigan, 1994, p. 304) is still relevant today.

Scarborough and Dobrich (1994) also examined intervention studies in which children were assigned to experimental or control groups, and the reading practices of families assigned to the experimental group were altered for the duration of the intervention. They found that such interventions strengthened oral language skills (median effect size = 0.28) but did not strengthen children's emergent literacy skills. The authors concluded that altering the quantity or quality of shared reading experiences has the potential to facilitate the development of language skills, at least over the short term. Overall, they surmised that the effects of parent–preschooler reading on literacy acquisition tend to be more modest and interactive than conventional wisdom dictates. They also reiterated throughout their review that measures of both socioeconomic background and early attitude toward literacy tend to be more highly correlated with the outcome variables examined than are measures of parent–preschooler reading.

BUS, VAN IJZENDOORN, AND PELLEGRINI

Shortly after Scarborough and Dobrich (1994) conducted their meta-analysis, Bus and colleagues (1995) reviewed a larger number of studies than those reviewed by Scarborough and Dobrich. Like Scarborough and Dobrich, Bus and colleagues focused primarily on correlational studies that examined the frequency of parent–preschooler book reading and the strength of its association to desired outcomes. The authors also considered whether these outcomes were similarly correlated with measures of reading frequency and composite measures of shared reading that included other characteristics of a literate environment, such as parental interest in reading, in order to assess the utility of reading frequency as a proxy for composite measures. Furthermore, they examined whether socioeconomic status mediated the relationship between shared reading and outcome measures.

Bus and colleagues (1995), in accord with researchers who questioned Scarborough and Dobrich's (1994) results, expected "that book reading would have a stronger effect on more proximal measures of language development than on more distal variables such as reading achievement at preschool and school ages" (p. 2). They also anticipated larger effect sizes from studies that examined reading to younger preschoolers rather than to older preschoolers. In fact, these authors discovered that "the highest effect size was derived from studies relating book reading to the proximal variable of language skills" (p. 7), but that differences between effect sizes for language skills ($d = 0.67$), emergent literacy ($d = 0.58$), and conventional literacy ($d = 0.55$) were not significantly different. Thus, they concluded that book reading experiences help children become familiar with orthographic representations, as well as spoken language.

Interestingly, although Bus and colleagues (1995) utilized slightly different statistical methods than Scarborough and Dobrich (1994), and included studies that were not analyzed in the earlier review, they also did not find significant differences in the relative association between shared reading and the three aspects of literacy used as outcome variables. Despite postulating that the effects of shared reading diminish over time as factors such as independent and school-centered reading opportunities begin to compete with the home literacy environment as contributing factors in reading development, their results seem to indicate that the relationship between shared reading and later literacy outcomes is fairly stable across time and development. They, too, reported that book reading explains 8% of the variance in their outcome measures, but rather than framing this finding as relatively insignificant in the greater process of reading development (as Scarborough and Dobrich did), these authors posited that "parent–preschooler reading is a necessary preparation for beginning reading instruction at school" (p. 17), drawing the reader's attention back to the idea that the indirect effects of shared reading may become more significant over time.

It is also notable that in these analyses, socioeconomic status was not significantly associated with the effects of frequency of parent–preschooler book reading. Bus and colleagues (1995) concluded that increased opportunities for book reading affect language and literacy outcomes for students, regardless of socioeconomic status. This finding addresses Scarborough and Dobrich's (1994) concern that, in many studies, variance that is best accounted for by aspects of the early home literacy environment is instead attributed to more distal measures of socioeconomic background. Bus and colleagues' analysis suggests that when socioeconomic status is controlled for carefully, children of privilege and disadvantaged children make comparable gains when engaged in shared reading. They also found that frequency of reading and composite measures of parent–preschool reading are similarly predictive of outcome measures of language and literacy growth, supporting the idea that frequency of book reading implicitly speaks to the quality of such experiences.

Recent Work in the Field of Shared Reading

SÉNÉCHAL'S INVESTIGATIONS OF PARENT INVOLVEMENT IN EARLY LITERACY

The notion that reading frequency and reading quality are interconnected has led some researchers to explore which home literacy behaviors best support literacy development.

In 2008, Sénéchal and Young conducted a meta-analysis examining the role of parent involvement in early reading acquisition. Their review included studies that examined the impact of home-based parent–child reading activities on the literacy development of children in grades K–3. This analysis differed from those of Scarborough and Dobrich (1994) and Bus and colleagues (1995) in several ways. First, only intervention studies that were experimental or quasi-experimental in nature were included. Also notable is the fact that Sénéchal and Young examined a wider range of parent–child literacy activities in their review (i.e., studies documenting experiences of parents reading to children, parents listening to children read, and parents helping with reading/literacy homework were all included). In addition, although the earlier reviews examined the impact of shared literacy activities on outcome variables such as general language development and emergent literacy skills, Sénéchal and Young's analysis focused on only literacy-specific skills such as knowledge of letter names/sounds, phoneme awareness, word recognition, and reading comprehension. Because most studies of dialogic reading investigate the efficacy of the intervention as it relates to oral language outcomes, only one study of interactive or dialogic reading was included in their review.

In general, the results of Sénéchal and Young's (2008) analysis suggest that parent involvement does indeed have a positive impact on children's reading acquisition. The mean effect size across studies was 0.65, which corresponds to a 10-point gain on a standardized literacy test. However, results across studies were quite variable, with effect sizes ranging from 0.007 to 2.02. Therefore, additional analyses were conducted to ascertain which variables might be associated with the relative impact of parental involvement.

Significant differences were observed in outcomes related to the type of intervention utilized. Specifically, studies in which parents were trained to teach their child a specific literacy skill, such as letter recognition, yielded strong, significant effects ($d = 1.15$), and did so with more frequency than studies in the other categories. This strategy was found to be twice as effective as asking parents to listen to their child read ($d = 0.52$), and six times as effective as simply reading aloud to their child ($d = 0.18$). There were no significant differences based on amount or type of parent training, length of intervention, or feedback provided to parents throughout the intervention. The positive effects of parental involvement were observed across demographic variables such as age (i.e., K–3), the child's reading level, and socioeconomic status.

Highlighting some of Sénéchal's other formative studies may help contextualize these findings because they do much to advance the hypothesis that the early home literacy environment and specific shared reading experiences have long-term indirect effects on reading development that may not be observable until years after children begin their formal education. For instance, Sénéchal and LeFevre (2002) found that, although not predictive of emergent literacy skills, storybook reading at home with kindergartners is predictive of receptive language skills in first graders, and that these language skills are predictive of unique variance in third-grade reading ability. This latter finding provides insight into the changing correlations between varied reading skills over time. The authors explain that it is not until older elementary school students acquire the ability to decode text fluently that their receptive language skills can "exert their full influence" (p. 453). Therefore, the value of early storybook reading may not be fully realized until late in the process of reading development, after children are able to identify words easily and have begun to read somewhat fluently.

Additionally, in a later work, Sénéchal, Ouellette, and Rodney (2006) demonstrated that—after controlling for IQ, parent educational and literacy levels, and the other tested variables—early individual differences in oral vocabulary predict variance in phonological awareness growth from kindergarten to first grade, listening comprehension in first grade, and reading comprehension abilities in third and fourth grade but not first grade. Again, these results support the hypothesis that the impact of oral vocabulary and shared reading may vary across a child's scholastic career, increasing in value as a child's reading progresses. This line of research suggests that the impact of

early shared reading interventions, particularly those that focus on language outcomes (e.g., dialogic reading), may not be seen until lower-level reading processes become automatic.

MOL, BUS, DE JONG, AND SMEETS EXPLORATION OF SHARED READING METHODS

To explore further how the nature of shared reading experiences affects the process of language and literacy development, Mol and colleagues (2008) conducted a meta-analysis to examine the added value of dialogic reading, as compared with "business-as-usual" shared reading, on oral language outcomes of children ages 2–6. Thus, these authors focused on many of the studies not included in Sénéchal and Young's (2008) analysis, and chose not to examine how dialogic reading affects the development of literacy-specific skills. Only studies that included quasi-experimental designs, a control group that included parents reading to their children, and dialogic reading programs in which parents were taught to encourage participation from their child and read interactively, were considered. Mol and colleagues sought to "test the tenability of Whitehurst and colleagues' (1998) conclusion that variations in reading to young children can have appreciable effects on language development" (p. 8). In other words, these researchers sought to differentiate between quality and quantity as predictors of successful shared reading experiences. Thus, when reviewing Mol and colleagues' results, it is important to keep in mind that all of the students in the sample were potentially engaging in reading experiences with their parents. The independent variable in this meta-analysis is the nature of the shared reading experience. For that reason, any added effect of dialogic reading must be construed as a benefit, in addition to the experiences provided by a general shared reading experience, rather than compared with the outcome scores of students with no access to shared reading opportunities.

Mol and colleagues (2008) examined the added effect of dialogic reading on overall language development and the differential effect of dialogic reading interventions on expressive versus receptive language skills, both globally and for children of varying ages and levels of risk (based on maternal education and income level). The results of these analyses indicated that dialogic reading did in fact add to the effects of shared reading, explaining approximately 4% of the variance in general outcome measures. However, dialogic reading interventions explained 8% of the variance in expressive language measures. The authors interpreted this finding to mean that the benefits of shared reading are, at least in part, the result of the quality of the shared reading experience. Thus, the comparatively richer quality of shared reading that occurs when children are asked to participate actively results in more substantial gains in language development and, in particular, in the development of expressive language.

Furthermore, preschool children were found to benefit from dialogic reading significantly more than kindergarten children when both receptive and expressive vocabulary measures were included. Mol and colleagues (2008) speculate that, perhaps because kindergarten-age children are more developmentally equipped to attend to, understand, and enjoy the plot of a story independently (or initiate questions when they have not understood), they may be distracted by an adult's questioning and probing. They suggest that dialogic reading strategies may need to be modified and adapted to accommodate the more developed language skills of the school-age child. This notion of developing more fine-grained shared reading interventions, in which an adult's behavior and responses are tailored to the child's developmental level, is worthy of pursuit. It seems particularly relevant to consider in light of Sénéchal and Young's (2008) work, which indicates that children whose parents provided direct instruction in a specific literacy skill, such as blending words, scored more than a full standard deviation higher on outcome measures than peers who did not receive such instruction.

Mol and colleagues (2008) also found that dialogic reading interventions had significantly stronger effects on children of parents with relatively high income and educational levels, with results revealing a moderate effect size (0.53), than on children whose families were determined to be at risk, where effect sizes were found to be weak (0.13). Mol

and colleagues suggest that the limited impact on at-risk families might indicate that the effective use of dialogic reading strategies is at some level dependent on a parent's level of education. Alternatively, they suggest that the level of participation required of the child in dialogic reading (e.g., making inferences, predicting) may be too advanced for the typical at-risk preschooler. If preschoolers from disadvantaged backgrounds lack the prerequisite language skills required to benefit from dialogic reading, the authors hypothesize that, in contrast to the global findings of the current study, older children in at-risk populations may show greater benefit from dialogic book reading than do younger children. The available dataset was not sufficient to test this hypothesis. This set of results speaks to the need to expand upon the type of literacy training that parents, particularly parents of at-risk children, receive prior to their child's formal school entry.

NATIONAL EARLY LITERACY PANEL

The final meta-analytic project that warrants discussion is the study of the NELP. In 2008, the NELP published its comprehensive study that sought to identify early literacy programs and interventions that lead to gains in the specific skills and abilities most linked to positive outcomes in reading, writing, and spelling. Shared reading was one of five categories of intervention investigated by the panel. Similar to the other recent meta-analyses conducted in this field, the NELP study design was subjected to a rigorous set of screening criteria to increase the likelihood that obtained effects represent causally interpretable effects. Given the rigorous nature of the screening process by which studies were included in the NELP analyses and the recency of the project, many consider this report to be among the most valuable in helping us draw conclusions about the complete body of research on shared reading. Most of the studies in this category of interventions examined the impact of shared reading on oral language skills, while a few studies examined variables reflecting phonological awareness, general cognitive ability, alphabetic knowledge, print knowledge, reading readiness, and writing.

The NELP (2008) analysis revealed that shared reading interventions had the largest impact on oral language outcomes, with an average effect size of 0.68. This result means that, on average, children who received a shared reading intervention scored almost 0.7 standard deviation higher on measures of oral language than children who did not receive a shared reading intervention. It is notable that this effect size, which approaches the upper limits of the moderate range, is consistent with the findings of both Bus and colleagues (1995) and Sénéchal and Young (2008). The panel found that these effects were consistent regardless of variations in the type of shared reading intervention, age, and risk status (Lonigan, Shanahan, & Cunningham, 2008).

Given the fact that shared reading is among the most common recommendations and practices for those involved in the education of young children, it is somewhat surprising that more studies have not investigated the impact of this intervention. Although there is ample evidence that shared reading improves oral language skills, and burgeoning evidence of its effect on print knowledge, there is still no conclusive support for the idea that shared reading promotes the development of other emergent literacy skills or any conventional literacy skills.

The NELP report (2008) noted that given the limited number of studies available, it is unlikely that analysis of potential moderators such as age, risk status, and agent of intervention represent independent sets of studies. For instance, most dialogic reading studies with younger children employed parents as the agents of intervention and were conducted with middle- to upper-income families (e.g., Arnold, Lonigan, Whitehurst, & Epstein, 1994; Huebner, 2000; Whitehurst et al., 1988). In addition, most dialogic reading studies with older children employed teachers as the agents of intervention (i.e., in preschool or child-care settings) with children from low-income families (e.g., Lonigan & Whitehurst, 1998; Whitehurst, Arnold, et al., 1994; Whitehurst, Epstein, et al., 1994). Finally, across studies, duration of the intervention is often confounded with age, agent of intervention, and risk status of the children. Therefore, it is not possible to examine combinations of these potential moderators (e.g., the impact of parents using

a shared reading intervention for younger, at-risk children).

Regardless of the limitations concerning the ability to examine results for specific subgroups of children, these studies do indicate that shared reading interventions provide early childhood education teachers and parents with a method for fostering the development of young children's oral language skills. Although it is not possible to draw conclusions at this time, the NELP shared reading analysis (Lonigan et al., 2008) does allow for the possibility that, as Sénéchal and others have suggested, perhaps the impact of shared reading is indirect in nature and may not exert its full impact on reading-related skills until later in a child's education. Additional research is required to specify more clearly the impact of shared reading interventions on different aspects of oral language skills and reading-specific skills.

Work in Progress: New Chapters in the Field of Shared Reading

The NELP report (2008) indicates that shared reading interventions support oral language development, as we already knew from the work of researchers such as Whitehurst, Lonigan, and Mol and colleagues. Additionally, the report states that shared reading supports the development of print knowledge. Although there is not currently a large enough body of research to examine the effects of shared reading on later reading skills at a meta-analytic level, many other individual studies indicate that shared reading experiences may independently contribute to subsequent conventional reading, writing, and spelling development.

For example, Justice and Ezell (2002) found that asking at-risk Head Start students direct questions about the print in a storybook, such as cueing children to examine or identify particular letters or words on a page during small-group book reading sessions, led to greater gains (in terms of identifying number of words in a sentence, letter and word recognition, and phonological awareness) than asking questions about the pictures and characters in the book. Although the print focus, in and of itself, is not a strong enough intervention to support the development of all prerequisite reading skills, it demonstrates the utility of embedding direct instruction into dialogic reading programs.

Other studies provide evidence that early literacy experiences have a lasting and wide-reaching impact on children's overall academic achievement. In one longitudinal study, Dickinson, Tabors, and Roach (Dickinson & McCabe, 2001) found that first-grade decoding and vocabulary skills, and the rate of growth in decoding between first and fourth grade, accounted for 76% of the variance in fourth-grade reading comprehension scores. Their data also suggested that associations between performance in kindergarten and in seventh grade were equally as strong, if not stronger, than associations between performance in kindergarten and fourth grade.

Providing further evidence that early literacy experiences may predict reading success throughout life, Cunningham and Stanovich (1997) found that first-grade reading ability was a strong predictor of 11th-grade reading ability, even when measures of cognitive ability were statistically controlled. In other words, given two children with equal general intellectual abilities and, thus, seemingly equal academic potential, the child with superior reading skill in first grade is likely to outperform an equally capable peer for the duration of their primary and secondary school experience. Thus, regardless of children's general cognitive ability, their reading skill in first grade has a significant impact on their reading comprehension across the span of elementary school, middle school, and high school.

The work of each of the researchers highlighted in this chapter has advanced arguments regarding the developmental trajectory of reading skills, and the still little-known indirect effects that early language and literacy development can have on the acquisition of critical skills years later. In the field of reading science, we currently have a clear understanding of the way early home literacy experiences affect the development of oral language skills, and of the way early elementary reading experiences affect later reading skills. Yet our understanding of what happens in between those points is less established. The field must continue to search for ways to bridge the gap and develop our understanding of the long-term effects of early reading experiences on later reading success.

FROM SHARED TO INDEPENDENT READING

In order to understand better how and why shared reading affects later development, it is useful to turn to a related area of study: reading volume (Cunningham & Stanovich, 1990, 1998; Stanovich, 1993). In contrast to the relatively inconclusive research associated with the cognitive and academic benefits of shared storybook reading, research investigating the value of independent reading quite consistently indicates that reading volume, or print exposure, is associated with literacy-specific skills and broader intellectual skills. In light of substantial evidence to support the hypothesis that children may develop better reading habits as a result of socialization, it is important to consider this field of research in conjunction with the results of shared reading studies. Research suggests that children who have stronger reading support systems are more likely to develop an appreciation for reading and become active, successful readers (Foertsch, 1992). Most researchers and theorists consider literacy to be a sociocultural process involving social and cultural interactions both at home and at school, suggesting that children become literate as a result of experiences in their families, communities, and classrooms (Bodrova & Leong, 2006; Heath, 1983; Moll, 1992; Schmidt, 1995). Thus, environmental and social variables (e.g., access to print) and the number of literacy-related activities engaged in at home have a notable influence on reading volume. The relationship between a child's home literacy environment and his or her independent reading behavior is well supported (Callaway, 1981; Chandler, 1999; Gauvin, Savage, & McCollum, 2000; Greaney, 1980, 1986; Neuman, 1996, 1999; Snow, Burns, & Griffin, 1998; Van Stensel, 2006).

By necessity, the majority of research examining the effects of reading volume has been conducted with independent readers (generally in grade 3 or higher). For example, in a study of fourth-, fifth-, and sixth-grade students, Cunningham and Stanovich (1991) found that print exposure accounted for significant and independent variation in spelling, vocabulary, verbal fluency, word knowledge, and general information. These results were replicated in a subsequent study of third- and fourth-grade students that utilized even more stringent tests of the contribution of reading volume to verbal skills by controlling for the contributions of reading ability, including reading comprehension and general intelligence (Stanovich & Cunningham, 1992).

Stanovich and Cunningham's line of research has also suggested that print exposure is an independent contributor to the acquisition of domain knowledge among older students. In a study involving nearly 300 college students, Stanovich and Cunningham (1993) collected data on the subjects' general cognitive and reading abilities, print exposure, and general knowledge regarding practical and cultural issues. After the variance associated with general cognitive ability and reading comprehension was partialed out, print exposure accounted for a notable portion of the variance in general knowledge. In fact, not only was print exposure a unique predictor of general knowledge, it was also a more robust predictor of general knowledge than was general cognitive ability.

The results of the studies by these two researchers suggest that once basic reading skills are established, independent reading can help children of all ability levels further develop their reading skills and, perhaps more importantly, their critical thinking skills. In other words, the relationship between intelligence and reading success is not unidirectional. Reading more can enhance children's innate intellectual abilities, regardless of their initial ability level. However, within a generally literate society, and even among individuals with similar levels of reading ability and education, there are vast differences in reading volume (Anderson, Wilson, & Fielding, 1988; Cunningham & Stanovich, 2003; Guthrie & Greany, 1991; Stanovich, 2000; Stanovich & West, 1989). One possible explanation for the differences we observe in independent reading behavior is that children who are immersed in a literacy-rich environment (i.e., children who are surrounded by books and engage in shared reading frequently) develop an enjoyment of and interest in reading and are, therefore, more likely to read independently.

Alas, it is possible that one of the most critical benefits of shared storybook reading has been overlooked by much of our research. Maybe the greatest value of shared reading is not in the direct development of specific early academic or literacy-related skills but in the fact that shared reading promotes independent reading, which in turn develops one's ability to read, to think critically, and to process and comprehend text at a deeper level. This hypothesis would help to support and explain the research of Sénéchal and others suggesting that shared reading does not have its greatest impact on reading abilities until later in schooling.

The indirect benefits of shared reading experiences on skills such as reading comprehension may be even more powerful than the direct benefits on oral language, but few researchers have tried to measure such effects. In addition, research has generally failed to look at the longitudinal relationship between shared reading experiences, independent reading volume, and reading ability. Until further research is conducted, it seems prudent to move forward with the research and practice recommendations included in the NELP (2008) report, which states that "it seems reasonable to proceed with the idea that shared reading would help all or most subgroups of children" (p. 164). We have sufficient evidence to demonstrate that shared reading can indeed lead to the growth of language and literacy skills, and put young children on the path to becoming enthusiastic, lifelong readers. Mol and colleagues (2008) framed their work by asking what additional value dialogic reading interventions provide, above and beyond the benefits of the reading practices in which families generally engage, and further research should follow suit by not merely trying to demonstrate that shared reading is good, but by specifying which reading practices are most helpful for children advancing through the steps toward reading acquisition. Because such work necessitates consideration of characteristics of both the parent and child, utilizing mixed methods to examine the quality and quantity of shared reading experiences is essential.

Finally, it is important to note that in addition to engaging in shared reading experiences, more formal instruction in alphabetic knowledge and decoding is necessary to facilitate early reading development. As detailed in the work of researchers such as Mol and colleagues (2008) and Justice and Ezell (2002), interventions in which parents and educators provide children with direct instruction in specific literacy skills lead to gains in component skills that shared reading may not target as often or as well. Together, the findings detailed here demonstrate the need for a balanced approach to early literacy instruction that provides opportunities for both embedded language and literacy development, and more explicit practice in phonemic awareness and decoding. Until early literacy practices in home and school settings address these varied needs, the achievement gap that motivated this work will persist. Children who are read to early and often succeed not because of the simple fact that they are exposed to books but because the opportunity to engage in these shared reading experiences is a function of the quality of their engagement in the experience, the particular strategies utilized by their parent or teacher, and their interpersonal relationships with adults. Although our image of an adult reading to a child often conjures memories of relaxing and uncomplicated times, the work presented in this chapter demonstrates that there is more to shared reading than meets the eye.

Acknowledgments

Special thanks to Colleen Ryan O'Donnell for her careful review, analysis, and background research for the chapter. This project was supported by the U.S. Department of Education, Institute of Education Sciences, under Grant No. R305M05037.

References

American Academy of Pediatrics. (1998). *Read me a story check-up guide*. Retrieved May 19, 2006, from *www.aap.org/healthtopics/stages.cfm*.

Anderson, R. C., Hiebert, E. H., Scott, J. A., & Wilkinson, I. A. (1985). *Becoming a nation of readers: The report of the Commission on Reading*. Washington, DC: U.S. Department of Education.

Anderson, R. C., Wilson, P. T., & Fielding, L. G. (1988). Growth in reading and how children spend their time outside of school. *Reading Research Quarterly, 23*, 285–303.

Arnold, D. H., Lonigan, C. J., Whitehurst, G. J., & Epstein, J. N. (1994). Accelerating language development through picture book reading: Replication and extension to a videotape training format. *Journal of Educational Psychology, 86*, 235–243.

Beck, I. L., & McKeown, M. G. (2007). Increasing young low-income children's oral vocabulary repertoires through rich and focused instruction. *Elementary School Journal, 107*(3), 251–271.

Beck, I. L., Perfetti, C. A., & McKeown, M. G. (1982).

Effects of long-term vocabulary instruction on lexical access and reading comprehension. *Journal of Educational Psychology, 74*, 506–521.

Bodrova, E., & Leong, D. J. (2006). Vygotskian perspectives on teaching and learning early literacy. In D. K. Dickinson & S. B. Neuman (Eds.), *Handbook of early literacy research: Volume 2* (pp. 243–256). New York: Guilford Press.

Bus, A. G., & van IJzendoorn, M. H. (1995). Mothers reading to their three-year-olds: The role of mother–child attachment security in becoming literate. *Reading Research Quarterly, 30*, 998–1015.

Bus, A. G., & van IJzendoorn, M. H. (1997). Affective dimension of mother–infant picturebook reading. *Journal of School Psychology, 35*, 46–61.

Bus, A. G., van IJzendoorn, M. H., & Pellegrini, A. D. (1995). Joint book reading makes for success in learning to read: A meta-analysis on intergenerational transmission of literacy. *Review of Educational Research, 65*, 1–21.

Callaway, B. (1981). What turns children on or off in reading? *Reading Improvement, 18*(3), 214–217.

Carretti, B., Borella, E., Cornoldi, C., & De Beni, R. (2009). Role of working memory in explaining the performance of individuals with specific reading comprehension difficulties: A meta-analysis. *Learning and Individual Differences, 19*, 246–251.

Catts, H. W. (2009). The narrow view of reading promotes a broad view of comprehension. *Language, Speech, and Hearing Services in Schools, 40*, 178–183.

Chandler, K. (1999). Reading relationships: Parents, adolescents, and popular fiction by Stephen King. *Journal of Adolescent and Adult Literacy, 43*(3), 228–239.

Chow, B., & McBride-Chang, C. (2003). Promoting language and literacy development through parent–child reading in Hong Kong preschoolers. *Early Education and Development, 14*, 233–248.

Clingenpeel, B. T., & Pianta, R. C. (2007). Mothers' sensitivity and book-reading interactions with first graders. *Early Education and Development, 18*(1), 1–22.

Cohen, J. (1988). *Statistical power analysis for the behavioral science* (2nd ed.). Hillsdale, NJ: Erlbaum.

Cunningham, A. E., & Stanovich, K. E. (1990). Assessing print exposure and orthographic processing skill in children: A quick measure of reading experience. *Journal of Educational Psychology, 82*(4), 733–740.

Cunningham, A. E., & Stanovich, K. E. (1991). Tracking the unique effects of print exposure in children: Associations with vocabulary, general knowledge, and spelling. *Journal of Educational Psychology, 83*(2), 264–274.

Cunningham, A. E., & Stanovich, K. E. (1997). Early reading acquisition and its relation to reading experience and ability 10 years later. *Developmental Psychology, 33*, 934–945.

Cunningham, A. E., & Stanovich, K. E. (1998). What reading does for the mind. *American Educator, 22*, 8–15.

Cunningham, A. E., & Stanovich, K. E. (2003). Reading matters: How reading engagement influences cognition. In D. Lapp & J. Flood (Eds.), *The handbook of language arts* (pp. 666–675). Mahwah, NJ: Erlbaum.

Dickinson, D. K., & McCabe, A. (2001). Bringing it all together: The multiple origins, skills and environmental supports of early literacy. *Learning Disabilities Research and Practice, 16,* 186–202.

Evans, M. A., & Shaw, D. (2008). Home grown for reading: Parental contributions to young children's emergent literacy and word recognition. *Canadian Psychology, 49,* 89–95.

Foertsch, M. A. (1992). *Reading in and out of school: Factors influencing the literacy achievement of American students in grades 4, 8, and 12, in 1988 and 1990.* Washington, DC: Office of Educational Research and Improvement, U.S. Department of Education.

Gauvin, M., Savage, S., & McCollum, D. (2000). Reading at home and at school in the primary grades: Cultural and social influences. *Early Education and Development, 11*(4), 447–463.

Glass, G. V. (1976). Primary, secondary, and meta-analysis of research. *Educational Researcher, 5,* 3–8.

Greaney, V. (1980). Factors related to amount and type of leisure time reading. *Reading Research Quarterly, 3,* 337–356.

Greaney, V. (1986). Parental influences on reading. *Reading Teacher, 39,* 813–818.

Guthrie, J. T., & Greany, V. (1991). Literacy acts. In R. Barr, M. L. Kamil, P. Mosenthal, & P. D. Pearson (Eds.), *Handbook of reading research* (Vol. 2, pp. 68–96). New York: Longman.

Hall, S. L., & Moats, L. C. (2000). Why reading to children is important. *American Educator, 24,* 26–33.

Hayes, D. P. (1988). Speaking and writing: Distinct patterns of word choice. *Journal of Memory and Language, 27,* 572–585.

Hayes, D. P., & Ahrens, M. (1988). Vocabulary simplification for children: A special case of "motherese." *Journal of Child Language, 15,* 395–410.

Heath, S. B. (1983). *Ways with words: Language, life and work in communities and classrooms.* Cambridge, UK: Cambridge University Press.

Hirsch, E. D. (2003). Reading comprehension requires knowledge of words and the world. *American Educator, 27,* 10–13, 16–22, 28–29, 48.

Huebner, C. E. (2000). Promoting toddlers' language development through community-based intervention. *Journal of Applied Developmental Psychology, 21,* 513–535.

Institute of Education Sciences (IES). (2006). *What Works Clearinghouse (WWC): Dialogic reading* (WWC Intervention Report). Washington, DC: Early Childhood Education, U.S. Department of Education.

Justice, L. M., & Ezell, H. K. (2002). Use of storybook reading to increase print awareness in at-risk children. *American Journal of Speech–Language Pathology, 11,* 17–29.

Korat, O., Klein, P., & Segal-Drori, O. (2007). Maternal mediation in book reading, home literacy environment, and children's emergent literacy: A comparison between two social groups. *Reading and Writing, 20,* 361–398.

Krashen, S. (1989). We acquire vocabulary and spelling by reading: Additional evidence for the input hypothesis. *Modern Language Journal, 73,* 440–464.

Lane, H. B., & Wright, T. L. (2007). Maximizing the effectiveness of reading aloud. *Reading Teacher, 60*(7), 668–675.

Lonigan, C. J. (1994). Reading to preschoolers exposed: Is the emperor really naked? *Developmental Review, 14,* 202–323.

Lonigan, C. J., Anthony, J. L., Bloomfield, B. G., Dyer, S. M., & Samwell, C. (1999). Effects of two shared reading interventions on emergent literacy skills of at-risk preschoolers. *Journal of Early Intervention, 22,* 306–322.

Lonigan, C. J., Shanahan, T., & Cunningham, A. (2008). Impact of shared-reading interventions on young children's early literacy skills. In *Developing early literacy: Report of the National Early Literacy Panel* (pp. 153–171). Washington, DC: National Institute for Literacy.

Lonigan, C. J., & Whitehurst, G. J. (1998). Relative efficacy of parent and teacher involvement in a shared reading intervention for preschool children from low-income backgrounds. *Early Childhood Research Quarterly, 13,* 263–290.

Magnuson, K. A., Meyers, M. K., Ruhm, C. J., & Waldfogel, J. (2004). Inequality in preschool education and school readiness. *American Educational Research Journal, 41,* 115–157.

Meagher, S. M., Arnold, D. H., Doctoroff, G. L., & Baker, C. N. (2008). The relationship between maternal beliefs and behavior during shared reading. *Early Education and Development, 19,* 138–160.

Mol, S. E., Bus, A. G., de Jong, M. T., & Smeets, D. J. (2008). Added value of dialogic parent–child book readings: A meta-analysis. *Early Education and Development, 19,* 7–26.

Moll, L. (1992). Bilingual classroom studies and community analysis: Some recent trends. *Educational Researcher, 21*(2), 20–24.

Nagy, W. E., & Anderson, R. C. (1984). How many words are there in printed school English? *Reading Research Quarterly, 19,* 304–330.

Nagy, W. E., & Herman, P. A. (1985). Incidental vs. instructional approaches to increasing reading vocabulary. *Educational Perspectives, 23,* 16–21.

National Center for Family Literacy (NCFL). (2009). *What works: An introductory teacher guide for language and emergent literacy instruction.* Louisville, KY: Author. Retrieved from *www.famlit.org.*

National Early Literacy Panel (NELP). (2008). *Developing early literacy: Report of the National Early Literacy Panel.* Washington, DC: National Center for Family Literacy. Retrieved from *www.nifl.gov.*

Neuman, S. B. (1996). Children engaging in storybook reading: The influence of access to print resources, opportunity, and parental interaction. *Early Childhood Research Quarterly, 11,* 495–514.

Neuman, S. B. (1999). Books make a difference: A study of access to literacy. *Reading Research Quarterly, 34*(3), 286–311.

Neuman, S. B., & Celano, D. (2001). Access to print in low-income and middle-income communities: An ecological study of four neighborhoods. *Reading Research Quarterly, 36*, 8–26.

Neuman, S. B., & Dwyer, J. (2009). Missing in action: Vocabulary instruction in Pre-K. *Reading Teacher, 62*(5), 384–392.

Scarborough, H. S., & Dobrich, W. (1994). On the efficacy of reading to preschoolers. *Developmental Review, 14*, 245–302.

Schmidt, P. R. (1995). Working and playing with others: Cultural conflict in a kindergarten literacy program. *Reading Teacher, 48*(5), 403–412.

Sénéchal, M., & LeFevre, J. (2002). Parental involvement in the development of children's reading skills: A five-year longitudinal study. *Child Development, 73*, 445–460.

Sénéchal, M., Ouellette, G., & Rodney, D. (2006). The misunderstood giant: On the predictive role of early vocabulary in future reading. In D. K. Dickinson & S. B. Neuman (Eds.), *Handbook of early literacy research, Volume 2* (pp. 173–184). New York: Guilford Press.

Sénéchal, M., & Young, L. (2008). The effect of family literacy interventions on children's acquisition of reading from kindergarten to grade 3: A meta-analytic review. *Review of Educational Research, 78*(4), 880–907.

Snow, C. E., Burns, M. S., & Griffin, P. (1998). *Preventing reading difficulties in young children.* Committee on the Prevention of Reading Difficulties in Young Children. Washington, DC: National Academy Press.

Stanovich, K. E. (1986). Matthew effect in reading: Some consequences of the individual difference in the acquisition of literacy. *Reading Research Quarterly, 24*, 402–433.

Stanovich, K. E. (1993). Does reading make you smarter?: Literacy and the development of verbal intelligence. In H. W. Reese (Ed.), *Advances in child development and behavior* (Vol. 24, pp. 133–180). San Diego, CA: Academic Press.

Stanovich, K. E. (2000). *Progress in understanding reading: Scientific foundations and new frontiers.* New York: Guilford Press.

Stanovich, K. E., & Cunningham, A. E. (1992). Studying the consequences of literacy within a literate society: The cognitive correlates of print exposure. *Memory and Cognition, 20*, 51–68.

Stanovich, K. E., & Cunningham, A. E. (1993). Where does knowledge come from?: Specific associations between print exposure and information acquisition. *Journal of Educational Psychology, 85*(2), 211–229.

Stanovich, K. E., & West, R. F. (1989). Exposure to print and orthographic processing. *Reading Research Quarterly, 24*, 402–433.

Strickland, D. S., & Morrow, M. (1989). Emerging readers and writers: Interactive experiences with storybook reading. *Reading Teacher, 42*, 322–323.

Van Stensel, R. (2006). Relations between sociocultural factors, the home literacy environment and children's literacy development in the first years of primary education. *Journal of Research in Reading, 29*(4), 367–382.

Vernon-Feagans, L., Pancsofar, N., Willoughby, M., Odom, E., Quade, A., & Cox, M. (2008). Predictors of maternal language to infants during a picture book task in the home: Family SES, child characteristics and the parenting environment. *Journal of Applied Developmental Psychology, 29*, 213–226.

Whitehurst, G. J., Arnold, D. S., Epstein, J. N., Angell, A. L., Smith, M., & Fischel, J. E. (1994). A picture book reading intervention in day care and home for children from low-income backgrounds. *Developmental Psychology, 30*, 679–689.

Whitehurst, G. J., Epstein, J. N., Angell, A. L., Payne, A. C., Crone, D. A., & Fischel, J. E. (1994). Outcomes of an emergent literacy intervention in Head Start. *Journal of Educational Psychology, 86*, 542–555.

Whitehurst, G. J., Falco, F. L., Lonigan, C. J., Fischel, J. E., DeBaryshe, B. D., Valdez-Menchaca, M. C., et al. (1988). Accelerating language development through picture book reading. *Developmental Psychology, 24*, 552–559.

26

Language and Literacy Insights
from Research Based on Early Head Start

BARBARA ALEXANDER PAN

Oral language is the foundation for literacy in general, and for reading comprehension specifically (Dickinson & Tabors, 2001; National Institute of Child Health and Human Development [NICHD] National Early Child Care Research Network, 2005). Although much attention and intervention are focused on print skills in kindergarten and first grade (e.g., letter recognition, grapheme–phoneme correspondence), these code-related skills, important as they are, represent a small problem space relative to the vocabulary, world knowledge, and comprehension skills that are ultimately critical for reading and academic success (Snow, Porche, Tabors, & Harris, 2007; Storch & Whitehurst, 2002). For children from low-income and language-minority families, vocabulary and oral language represent a particular challenge. A substantial body of literature demonstrates that these children, on average, fall behind their peers in vocabulary by age 3, and that the gap persists throughout the school years (Alexander, Entwisle, & Horsey, 1997; Farkas & Beron, 2004; Hart & Risley, 1995).

However, the applied developmental literature also demonstrates that developmental trajectories are amenable to change, particularly when intervention occurs *early* in life (Shonkoff, & Phillips, 2000). Furthermore, programs that have shown success in narrowing the gap for at-risk children have

tended to be *comprehensive* (e.g., Ramey & Campbell, 1991) rather than focused specifically on language or cognitive development. Infants and toddlers learn more effectively when they are healthy, in strong relationships with key adults, and in stimulating environments. Particularly for younger children, simply presenting rich input is not sufficient. Uptake happens most efficiently when the children are able to focus their attention on the world, confident that their physical and emotional needs will be consistently met (Spieker, Nelson, Petras, Jolley, & Barnard, 2003). Finally, successful intervention must be *intensive* and *sustained*. Programs such as the Carolina Abecedarian Project (Campbell & Ramey, 1994; Ramey & Campbell, 1991) were full-day programs that ran 5 days a week and included a follow-up program. Scaling up interventions such as the Abecedarian Project to national levels, however, may be unrealistic for multiple reasons, including fiscal, logistical, and cultural considerations. Particularly for families living in isolated, rural settings, transportation to day care may be difficult, if not impossible, at least during some parts of the year. Additionally, not all parents want their infants and toddlers in full-time, out-of-home care. One alternative, then, has been to include parents in the intervention, recognizing that they are children's earliest teachers, and that their relationship with their children usually outlasts every other. Examples of these two-generation interventions include the Infant Health and Development Program and the Comprehensive Child Development Program, both of which showed positive, though quite modest, impacts on children's language development for some subgroups of participants (Brooks-Gunn, Gross, Kraemer, Spiker, & Shapiro, 1992; McCarton et al., 1997). The Early Head Start (EHS) program was designed to profit from all these lessons from earlier interventions. It begins early, is comprehensive and intensive, and offers the possibility of follow-up through the Head Start program.

Research generated by the EHS Research and Evaluation Project (EHSRE) is hardly confined to experimental analyses of the effects of EHS on participant versus comparison children and families. In fact, such analyses represent a rather small portion of a broad and growing body of developmental research that examines the variability of environmental input experienced by low-income children and its relationship to language and literacy outcomes. It is this broader body of research into which this chapter delves.

What Is EHS?

EHS is a comprehensive, two-generational program that begins prenatally or during the child's first year of life. There is no single, prescriptive "model" that EHS programs must follow, although most provide a wide range of services, including child development, parenting education, case management, child care, health care, referrals for other services, and family support. Programs adopt either a home-based, center-based, or mixed model of intervention delivery. Mixed models may provide home-based services in early infancy, and then transition families to center-based, or alternatively, provide home-based services to some families and center-based to others, depending on family circumstances. Intervention is intensive, involving provision of services to children and families on a daily or weekly basis. Finally, and importantly for our purposes here, EHS is not specifically a literacy, or even solely a language intervention. Rather, it is a comprehensive program with positive

child developmental outcomes as its primary goal and secondary goals related to family development, including parent education, employment, and mental health.

EHS and the Research and Evaluation Project

The EHS program grew out of the 1994 reauthorization of Head Start, which for the first time mandated infant–toddler services. The Department of Health and Human Services Advisory Committee for Services for Families with Infants and Toddlers recommended that four domains be targeted: child development, family development, staff development, and community development.

In addition, the Committee also recommended continuous program improvement, to be informed by national and local research. Thus, from the beginning, research has had a central evaluative and formative role in EHS. Broadly speaking, EHS research is meant to answer two questions: Who benefits from EHS and under what circumstances? In reality, the EHSRE has provided the opportunity for researchers to address many basic developmental questions having to do with children from low-income families in the period from birth to age 5 and beyond.

The EHS Consortium, a Model of National– Local Research Collaboration

One unusual feature of the EHSRE is the purposeful combination of national and local research, carried out through the EHS Consortium, which comprises the national contractor, Mathematica Policy Research (MPR), representatives from Columbia University and the Administration for Children and Families (ACF), and university-based research partners at each of the 17 programs selected by the Head Start Bureau to participate in the evaluation. Programs were selected to include diverse regions of the United States, rural as well as urban sites, all three major program models (home-based, center-based, mixed model), and families of diverse backgrounds. The relevance and rigor of research proposed by the program's local research partner was an additional key consideration. Research proposed and subsequently undertaken by local research partners of the

17 sites focused on topics such as children's language, cognitive, and socioemotional development; children with special needs; the complexity of home visiting; the impact of welfare reform on families; child care; and the influence of community context on program efficacy. MPR and Columbia University were responsible for core national data collection and key planned analyses. Local researchers in the consortium provided consultation on study design, in addition to carrying out site-specific data collection and analysis, and secondary analyses of national data. In its second year, the consortium made a successful case for the inclusion of a parallel strand of investigation focusing specifically on the role of fathers in the lives of EHS children, an undertaking that has also yielded a rich body of work.

Design of the EHSRE

The 3,001 families that participated in the EHSRE enrolled during the mother's pregnancy or before the target child's first birthday and were randomly assigned to either the program or a comparison group. Those assigned to the comparison group were free to take advantage of any services other than EHS available in their community. Experimental data were collected at study enrollment and at child ages 14 months, 24 months, and 36 months. After age 3, both program and comparison families that still qualified based on family income were eligible to enroll their child in Head Start (or any other preschool or child-care arrangement of their choice). Follow-up data were collected in the spring before the child was to enter kindergarten and again at grade 5. Data sources for national analyses included parent interviews, direct child assessments, videotaped parent–child interaction in the home, and child-care observations and provider interviews for children in out-of-home care. Interviews and videotaped father–child interaction are available for a large subsample at child ages 24 and 36 months, and at prekindergarten. Detailed descriptions of participating families, research design, and results of the implementation and evaluation studies, as well as synopses of representative local research studies, are provided in publicly available reports (ACF, 2002a, 2003). These reports show an overall, modest posi-

tive impact of EHS on a broad range of child outcomes at age 3, with important subgroup differences related both to program model and degree of implementation, and to family demographic risk characteristics.

Some 12 years after EHS was authorized and the EHS Consortium was formed, a substantial body of literature based on the EHS studies has emerged and continues to grow. Here, we focus particularly on those national and local analyses related to family support for language and literacy, children's language development, and their emergent literacy skills.

Early Experiences and Children's Prekindergarten Skills

Unlike most large-scale, nationally representative studies, such as the Early Childhood Longitudinal Study—Birth Cohort (ECLS-B; NCES, 2009), research emerging from the EHS Consortium focuses exclusively on low-income families, a population at increased risk for reading and academic difficulties during the school years (Lee & Burkam, 2002). Thus, the focus shifts from *group differences* between children from low-income families and their more advantaged peers to *variability within low-income families and their children*. This shift in focus provides an important supplement to findings from large-scale national studies (e.g., ECLS-B) as well as more intensive, small-scale ethnographic studies. For example, Hart and Risley's (1995) elegant documentation of the language and literacy environments of 42 children from the first year of life to age 3 nonetheless included only six welfare-eligible families (all African American), necessarily limiting meaningful insight into variation among low-income families and their children. Similarly, only a small proportion of participants in the important and influential NICHD Study of Early Child Care and Youth Development (NICHD Early Child Care Research Network, 1994) were from low-income families or spoke a language other than English. In contrast, the EHSRE examined the experience of approximately 3,000 children and their families, beginning at birth, continuing through age 5, and then through grade 5. Even studies based on a single EHS site generally involve more than 100 families. All this by no means suggests that families participating in the EHS study are representative of low-income families in the United States. On the contrary because participant families chose to enroll in EHS, they may be more motivated and possibly higher functioning than the population of low-income families at large. Nonetheless, key subgroups differing in background characteristics such as race/ethnicity, home language, maternal age and education, and family structure are represented: Approximately 37% of the mothers were white, 34% were African American, 17% were non-English-speaking Hispanic, 6% were English-speaking Hispanic; 39% were teens when the target child was born; 53% had a high school diploma or graduate equivalency degree (GED); and 26% were living with a husband (Raikes et al., 2006).[1] Thus these studies shed light on key dimensions of variability that may help policymakers, intervention programs, and classroom teachers target their efforts more effectively by answering the following questions: Which children from low-income families are at highest risk, based on family background characteristics? Which children are most vulnerable based on their early literacy-related experiences?

In addition to offering the advantages of a large sample of low-income families, the longitudinal design of the EHSRE allows examination of questions about the timing of experiences from birth to age 5, thus providing an important theoretical and empirical link between research on infancy and toddlerhood (e.g., Hart & Risley, 1995) and the larger body of work on children's home and school experiences during the preschool period (e.g., Dickinson & Tabors, 2001; Payne, Whitehurst, & Angell, 1994). This longitudinal look promises to be further enhanced by follow-up at grade 5 (ACF, 2006).

Other design advantages include the availability of multiple sources of data, including parent report, direct observation of the home and child-care environments, and detailed analysis of videotaped parent–child interaction (Brady-Smith, O'Brien, Berlin, Ware, & Fauth, 2000), as well as the inclusion of fathers at most data points. Many of the instruments used have been employed in other large-scale studies, including the NICHD Study of Early Child Care, the ECLS Birth and Kindergarten Cohort Studies, and Head Start Family and Child Experiences Survey (FACES; ACF, 2003), thereby facilitating cross-study comparison.

To summarize, the body of work growing out of the EHSRE provides a rich and textured look at the intervention program as it is realized in differing contexts, the variability among low-income families seeking such services, and the development of children from low-income families over infancy, toddlerhood, early childhood, and beyond. These studies span multiple domains of child and family development, including children's socioemotional development (e.g., Spieker et al., 2003), parenting (e.g., Berlin et al., 2009; Ispa et al., 2004), maternal mental health (e.g., Chazen-Cohen et al., 2007), developmental disabilities (e.g., Peterson et al., 2004), and the role of fathers in children's lives (e.g., Boller et al., 2006; Cabrera & Bradley, in press). For the remainder of this chapter, we focus on those findings that relate directly to language and early literacy.

Variation in Children's Early Language Skills

As noted earlier, a source of particular richness in the EHS dataset is its potential for allowing researchers to explore variation in development during infancy and toddlerhood among children from low-income families and to identify correlates of the observed variation. Also, as argued earlier, children's language skills are of particular interest because of the strong, documented relationship between language and literacy, especially reading comprehension (Roth, Speece, & Cooper, 2002; Storch & Whitehurst, 2002). Previous evidence based on heterogeneous socioeconomic scale (SES) samples (Fenson et al., 1994; Huttenlocher, Haight, Bryk, Seltzer, & Lyons, 1991) indicates tremendous variability, for example, in the size of children's productive vocabularies by the third year of life. Despite documenting group-level differences in vocabulary size between children from middle-income and low-income families, Hart and Risley's (1995) work also hints at considerable within-group variation and, indeed, some overlap in the distribution of vocabulary size of children from differing SES backgrounds. The questions arise: How much variability is observable between the ages of 1 and 3 in the size and growth rate of productive vocabulary in children from low-income families? What factors are associated with those differences? These questions were addressed in a study by Pan, Rowe, Singer, and Snow (2005), using data from 108 EHS children and their parents from a rural New England site. When children were 14, 24, and 36 months old, mother–child dyads were videotaped as they interacted around a set of researcher-provided materials (a book and age-appropriate toys). Mother and child verbal and gestural communication was transcribed using the conventions of the Child Language Data Exchange System (CHILDES; MacWhinney, 2000) and lists of words produced by each speaker at each time point were generated. Mothers' vocabulary and literacy skills were measured at study entry using the Wechsler Adult Intelligence Scale—Revised (WAIS-R; Wechsler, 1981) and the Letter–Word Identification subscale of the Woodcock–Johnson Tests of Achievement (Woodcock, 1978). Maternal depression was measured using the Center for Epidemiologic Studies—Depression (CES-D; Radloff, 1977) scale, which asks respondents to rate frequency of depressive symptoms recently experienced.

Results showed considerable variability at each age in the number of different words children produced, with variability increasing with age. Individual growth modeling revealed that growth in vocabulary use over the period observed was fairly linear. Next, researchers examined how variation in rate of children's vocabulary growth was related to maternal factors (input, mothers' own language and literacy skills, and depression). Results showed that maternal input, as expected, predicted children's growth in vocabulary use. This finding is in keeping with earlier reports on socioeconomically heterogeneous samples (Hart & Risley, 1995; Huttenlocher et al., 1991). More specifically, the diversity of vocabulary mothers used with children (i.e., the number of *different* words) was a stronger predictor of growth in children's vocabulary use than mothers' sheer *talkativeness* (i.e., total number of words produced). Children's vocabulary growth was also positively predicted by maternal language and literacy skills, and negatively predicted by maternal depression; moreover, the effect of maternal depression grew over time. The findings of this study provide important signposts for practitioners and interventionists who hope to alter the trajectories of vocabulary growth of at-risk children. Parent educators may want to encourage parents not just to talk more to their infants and toddlers but to use more varied vocabulary in conversation with them. In addition, comprehensive intervention with an eye toward laying a strong language foundation for later literacy development must also consider support for parental mental health.

Mother–Child Book Reading in Low-Income Homes during Infancy and Toddlerhood

The frequency of parental book reading with preschoolers is well documented (National Center for Education Statistics, 1999), as are links between joint book reading and later language and literacy outcomes (Bus, van IJzendoorn, & Pellegrini, 1995; Sénéchal & Cornell, 1993). Few studies, however, focus on parent–child book reading during the first 3 years of life, particularly in low-income families (cf. ACF, 2003; NICHD Early Child Care Research Network, 2001). Raikes and colleagues (2006) examined the variation in book reading frequency reported by a sample of 2,581 parents participating in the EHSRE. They also examined stability in book reading frequency over time, and how frequency and stability were related to children's cognitive and language skills. Study sample participants were all mothers whose families had been assigned to either the EHS program (50.9%) or a comparison group, and who identified their primary home language as either English or Spanish. Data sources were parent interviews at study entry and at child ages 14, 24, and 36 months; the Woodcock–Johnson Psychoeducational Battery—Revised, Picture Vocabulary Test (Woodcock & Johnson, 1990) as a measure of maternal expressive verbal ability; the MacArthur Communicative Development Inventories (Fenson et al., 2000), providing parental report of children's vocabulary at 14 and 24 months; the Peabody Picture Vocabulary Test–III (PPVT-III, Dunn & Dunn, 1997), a direct assessment of children's receptive vocabulary administered at age 36 months; and the Bayley Scales of Infant Development (Bayley, 1993) Mental Development Index (MDI), a direct assessment of children's cognitive skills, administered at ages 14, 24, and 36 months.

Results showed that slightly less than half the study sample mothers reported reading to their children daily when children were 14 months old, and slightly more than half did so when children were ages 24 and 36 months. The frequency of reported book reading varied quite widely, however, as a function of maternal and child characteristics. The odds of being read to at ages 24 and 36 months were higher for children whose mothers were more highly educated and had stronger verbal ability, for children who were firstborn, and for those families receiving EHS services. At most ages, the odds of experiencing daily book reading were lower for children of color. At 14 months, boys were less likely than girls to be read to daily, and although gender differences narrowed with age, at 36 months, boys were still less likely than girls to experience regular book reading. Parents who began reading regularly to their children by the time they were 14 months old tended to continue the practice throughout toddlerhood.

Raikes and colleagues (2006) also investigated concurrent and predictive relationships between reported book reading and children's language and cognitive skills. For English-speaking children, reading was concurrently associated with vocabulary at ages 14 and 24 months. Consistent daily reading over time was associated with both language and cognitive skills at 36 months for English-speaking children, whereas daily reading at even one observation predicted Spanish-speaking children's language and cognitive skills at 36 months. Based on path analyses, the researchers propose the metaphor of a snowball to describe the reciprocal and increasingly strong relationship between frequent book reading and child outcomes important for later literacy acquisition. Furthermore, the positive effects of participation in EHS on frequency of parent–child book reading is notable given that EHS is a comprehensive child and family development program rather than one that targets book reading specifically.

Fathers as Partners in Shared Book Reading

Another of the strengths of the EHSRE noted earlier was the inclusion of biological fathers and father figures. Those fathers who were identified by mothers and who agreed to participate were interviewed and observed interacting with their children at child ages 24 months, 36 months, as well as prekindergarten. Sample sizes vary depending on the data point and questions to be addressed. Most relevant for our immediate purpose is information the national study has yielded about father–child book reading and its effects on children's language and emergent literacy skills.

Duursma, Pan, and Raikes (2008) examined predictors and outcomes of fathers' reading with children at 24 months ($n = 803$) and 36 months ($n = 698$). Results showed that fathers on average reported reading less frequently to children than did mothers. Nonetheless, more than half of fathers at each child age reported reading with their children at least weekly. Similar parent and child background characteristics predicted frequency of father and mother book reading. Children whose fathers were more highly educated, who were white, who reported English as the home language, and whose families received EHS services were more likely to be read to frequently (i.e., daily or weekly) by fathers. Girls were also somewhat more likely to be read to regularly by their fathers. Frequency of father book reading at 24 months predicted children's cognitive (i.e., Bayley Scales MDI) and receptive vocabulary (PPVT-III) scores 1 year later.

Next, Duursma (2007) examined book reading within family, asking whether children in two-parent families experienced regular book reading with *each* parent. In a sample of 803 fathers at child age 24 months and 750 fathers at child age 36 months, she found that about one-third of children do read regularly with each parent, where *regularly* is defined as daily reading with the mother and at least weekly reading with the father. Despite the encouraging result that a substantial proportion of children in two-parent low-income families experience regular reading with both their parents, fathers clearly remain an undertapped resource. As might be expected based on this research (Duursma et al., 2008; Raikes et al., 2006), children whose parents both had higher levels of education were more likely to enjoy the benefits of regular book reading with two different adults. Given the likelihood that different adults engage in shared book reading in slightly different ways, it is reasonable to expect that book reading with each parent would provide a broader, richer literacy experience for children, thus facilitating children's language and literacy development.

In a related study, Duursma (2007) examined predictive relationships between fathers' book reading at child ages 24 and 36 months, and children's emergent literacy and oral language skills at prekindergarten. At the latter data point, children were administered the PPVT-III, the Woodcock–Johnson Letter–Word Identification subtest, and the Story and Print Concepts task (ACF, 2002b), which required them to demonstrate print skills and book knowledge (e.g., how to hold the book, location of book title, where to begin reading). Parents were also asked in the prekindergarten interview whether their child ever pretended to read or to write. A composite based on these three measures (letter–word identification, book knowledge, and pretend reading/writing) provided the emergent literacy outcome variable. Results showed that children with fathers who read either *daily* or *weekly* to them at 24 months tended to have better prekindergarten emergent literacy skills and stronger oral language skills than children whose fathers read to them only rarely. At 36 months, only *daily* reading by fathers predicted children's prekindergarten emergent literacy skills, after researchers controlled for the effect of maternal book reading. The finding in this sample of low-income families, that fathers', not mothers', book reading when children were 24 months old predicts children's prekindergarten *oral* language skills, is an intriguing one given previous research showing that fathers' speech with young children tends to include more *wh-* questions and explicit clarification requests (Rowe, Coker, & Pan, 2004).

Home Support for Literacy and Child Outcomes at Age 3

Rodriguez and colleagues (2009) widened the lens beyond shared book reading to examine variation in three aspects of children's home literacy experience: frequency of participation in literacy activities (including, but not limited to, book reading), quality

of mothers' engagement with children, and availability in the home of age-appropriate learning materials. The study sample included participants (*n*= 1,046) from the larger EHSRE with English-speaking children for whom complete data were available at child ages 14, 24, and 36 months. Data sources included parent interviews, direct observation of the home environment, and videotaped mother–child interaction. At each age, mothers were asked how frequently they engaged in *literacy activities* such as shared book reading, storytelling, and singing nursery rhymes with their children. At 36 months, additional questions were asked about other family members reading to the child, taking the child to museums, and teaching the child letters, numbers, shapes, sizes, and colors. Assessment of quality of *maternal engagement* was based on selected items from the Home Observation for Measurement of the Environment (HOME) scale (Caldwell & Bradley, 1984) and coding of mother–child interaction during semistructured play sessions in the home. *Provision of learning materials* (e.g., children's books, toys that facilitate learning) was assessed through parent interview and items from the HOME. Composite scores for each aspect of the literacy environment were categorized as representing *low, moderate,* or *high* levels of experience at each age (see Appendix 26.1 for a more complete listing of items and Rodriguez et al. [2009] for details about measures; coding; and definitions of low, moderate, and high composite scores; and results of confirmatory factor analyses). Child cognitive and language outcomes were based on Bayley MDI scores at each age, parent report of child language at 14 and 24 months (MacArthur CDI; Fenson et al., 2000), and PPVT-III standard scores at age 36 months.

Results for frequency of literacy activities and children's books in the home paralleled and expanded upon results reported by Raikes and colleagues (2006). At each age, most mothers reported reading, telling stories, and singing nursery rhymes with their child at least a few times a week. At 36 months, the majority of mothers reported teaching their child preacademic skills such as letters, numbers, and colors, and about one-fourth reported a family member taking their children to a museum at least a few times a month. A large majority of children had access to at least a small number of children's books in the home at each age and to age-appropriate learning tools.

Analysis of videotaped mother–child interaction showed that mothers on average displayed moderate levels of sensitivity and cognitive stimulation, and that nearly all mothers engaged in spontaneous and responsive verbal interactions with their child at each age. A smaller proportion of mothers spontaneously labeled people or objects in the environment for their child at 14 months (67%).

Composite scores at each age showed that the majority of children were exposed to moderate levels of literacy activities and learning materials at each age. About half of the children were rated as experiencing low quality of maternal engagement, although this proportion decreased slightly over time.

Variation in literacy activities, maternal engagement, and provision of learning materials was related to a number of maternal and child characteristics. In keeping with a large body of related literature (e.g., Brooks-Gunn & Duncan, 1997; Hoff, 2003; Raikes et al., 2006), maternal education was positively related to literacy activities, quality of maternal engagement, and availability of learning materials at all three ages. Maternal employment also was positively associated with quality of engagement and provision of learning materials at each age. Those mothers who were teenagers when their children were born were more likely to demonstrate poor-quality engagement at each child age. Overall literacy environment scores were generally lower for children of color (see Rodriguez et al., 2009, for details). Quality of maternal engagement at 14 and 24 months, and availability of learning materials at 24 and 36 months were higher for children with a resident father or father figure. Weak associations favoring firstborn children and girls were observed at some ages for some aspects of the literacy environment.

Hierarchical multiple regression analyses showed that the three aspects of the literacy environment (activities, quality of maternal engagement, and learning materials) each explained unique variance in children's *concurrent* cognitive and language skills, over and above maternal and child demographic characteristics.[2] Furthermore, when these three aspects were considered jointly, total literacy environment scores *at each age* explained unique variance in children's cognitive and language outcomes at age 36 months. Together, literacy experiences across the three ages explained 27% of the variation in children's Bayley MDI and PPVT scores at 36 months. Exploratory analyses showed that the receptive and productive language scores of children with high-quality literacy environments were twice as large as those of children with low-level literacy environments.

To summarize, this study by Rodriguez and colleagues (2009) demonstrates the enormous variability in home literacy environments, broadly conceived (including activities, quality of maternal engagement, and learning materials), experienced by children from low-income families from birth to age 3. Furthermore, it identifies maternal and child characteristics associated with such variation, as well as their concurrent and predictive significance for children's cognitive and language skills.

Home Literacy Environments over Time and Children's PreK Skills

As noted earlier, the EHSRE has offered the unusual opportunity to follow a large sample of children of low-income families from birth to age 5. Building on the work just described, Rodriguez and Tamis-LeMonda (2009) described trajectories of children's home literacy environments from infancy through the preschool years, and how those trajectories relate to children's PreK language and literacy skills. Data were from 1,852 mothers and their English-speaking children at ages 14, 24, and 36 months, and again at approximately 60 months, in the spring before children were eligible to enter kindergarten. Inclusion criteria were availability of home literacy environment data from at least one of the four ages and at least one language or cognitive outcome measure administered in English at 60 months.[3] Home environment measures and child language and cognitive measures at the first three observations were identical to those described earlier (Rodriguez et al., 2009). PreK outcome measures were standard scores on the PPVT-III and the Letter–Word Identification subscale of the Woodcock–Johnson Tests of

Achievement—Revised (Woodcock & Johnson, 1989).

The researchers' stated goals were to identify different trajectories (i.e., patterns of stability or change over time) in children's home literacy environments experience from birth to 5, and to examine associations between those patterns and children's PreK language and literacy skills. A semiparametric, group-based modeling approach (Nagin & Land, 1993) revealed six patterns of children's home literacy environment: (1) environments that were consistently of *low* quality (approximately 8% of the sample); (2) those that were *low quality but improved steadily over time* (3%); (3) those that were of *moderate quality and stable through 36 months but declined sharply by 60 months* (46%); (4) those that were *moderate and improved steadily over time* (31%); (5) those that were *high quality but declined over time* (3%); and (6) those that were consistently of *high* quality (10%).

It is not terribly surprising that the study showed that more optimal and stable home literacy environments were associated with better vocabulary and emergent literacy skills at PreK, and that poorer literacy environments predicted poorer language and literacy outcomes at age 5. The magnitude of the differences is, however, striking. On average, children in the *low progress* group scored nearly two standard deviations lower on the PPVT at PreK than children in the *high stable* group. Scores on the Woodcock–Johnson Letter–Word Identification and Applied Problems subtests showed a similar pattern. The largest group of children, those in the *moderate decline* group, showed generally better outcomes than either the *low stable* or *low decline* groups, but worse outcomes than either the *high decline* or *high stable* groups. Analyses addressing the question of *timing* of input for particular outcomes showed that the vocabulary and emergent numeracy skills of children with strong, stable home literacy environments and those with strong early environments that declined over time were indistinguishable, suggesting that early environments are a lasting boost for vocabulary. In contrast, early home literacy experiences are less influential than experiences in the preschool period for letter–word identification because children in *high stable* environments outperformed those in *high but declining* environments in this area of emergent literacy ($d = 0.53$). These findings have important implications for the timing and specificity of effects of language and literacy environments from birth to age 5 on children's PreK skills. For example, they suggest that emphasis on letter–word skills in toddlerhood, rather than in the more developmentally appropriate late preschool period, does not result in higher literacy skills as children enter kindergarten.

Moreover, the fact that home literacy environments declined over time for approximately half the sample points to the intervention challenge of educating and supporting parents in their efforts to provide children with the best possible preparation for school. Not only must intervention begin early and be maintained over the preschool years, the form and focus of parent education must be age-appropriate and multifaceted, including literacy activities, maternal engagement, and availability of learning materials.

Narrative Skills of PreK Children and Cultural Considerations

As part of the national PreK protocol, parents and their children were asked jointly to tell about something exciting that had happened recently. Some local sites also collected personal narratives or story retellings at child ages 36 months and/or 78 months. Some of the work just beginning to emerge from these data is briefly described here.

At one local EHSRE site in rural New England, 62 mother–child dyads read *The Very Hungry Caterpillar* (Carle, 1983) during the PreK visit. Later in the same visit, children were asked to retell the story, consulting the book if they liked. Results of the study by Kang, Kim, and Pan (2009) showed that during joint book reading, children on average contributed nearly as much extratextual talk (i.e., talk *about* the book, as opposed to verbatim reading or recitation of the text) as mothers did, suggesting that at least some children see book reading as a meaning-making activity. There was substantial variation across children, with those whose mothers produced greater amounts of extratextual talk tending themselves to produce more such utterances. Children's subsequent retelling of the book was related to the extent to which their mothers encouraged their verbal participation during joint book reading. These results are of interest because once children begin school, they are generally expected to display two different kinds of skills related to book reading: the ability to talk about what they read and to summarize or retell what they have read.

In a related study with the same sample that focused specifically on children's *spontaneous* (rather than responsive) utterances during joint book reading, Kim, Kang, and Pan (in press) found that children who produced more frequent spontaneous utterances during joint book reading tended subsequently to produce higher-quality story retelling. More specifically, children who produced more frequent spontaneous utterances about interpretation of the story and spontaneous repetition of maternal utterances tended to include more story events and to use more sophisticated language in their story retelling. These findings suggest that children's propensity for spontaneous verbal participation during joint book reading may have a direct relationship with their retelling skills. One limitation of this study is that frequency of early joint book reading experience was not included as a control variable.

Connections between book reading and other aspects of the home language and literacy environment and children's narrative skills were also documented by Guerra (2008) for a sample of 65 Mexican-heritage families, all of whom received EHS services up to age 3. Children who were more frequently read to at 36 months, according to parent report, participated more in producing joint narratives with their mothers at the PreK observation. Furthermore, those who enjoyed richer language and literacy environments in general at 36 months, based on the HOME, produced more complex personal narratives in first grade.

Finally, work by Christofaro and Tamis-LeMonda (2008) with 37 mother–child and father–child dyads at the New York EHSRE site provides important information for teachers about narrative topics and themes with which Latino children are likely to be familiar. Prominent themes that mothers and fathers in this sample encouraged children to talk about in their joint narratives included family, gender roles, and educa-

tional achievement. These findings suggest that such topics may be fertile ground for kindergarten teachers hoping to elicit Latino children's optimal performance in producing personal narratives.

Implications and Future Directions

The EHSRE has demonstrated something of the enormous variability in language skills and literacy environments of children from low-income U.S. homes as early as the second year of life and has identified key factors associated with that variability. In addition, it has provided a longitudinal, developmental look at the trajectories of children's language development and their emergent literacy skills through PreK. Future studies will provide further information on many of these same children in grade 5.

Experimental comparisons of families who did and did not receive EHS services have shown that EHS can make a difference in children's language skills by age 3, even though the intervention is not focused specifically or exclusively on language or literacy. Such intervention in the infant and toddler years need not be exclusively in out-of-home day-care settings; in fact, the best outcomes were found for children whose families were in mixed-model programs that included home- and center-based components (ACF, 2002a). Furthermore, fathers, as well as mothers, have an important role to play in children's early language and literacy experiences.

The EHSRE has also shown that intervention from birth to age 3, while powerful, is not the complete boost at-risk children need. Those children who experienced EHS followed by formal, higher-quality preschool settings were better prepared academically for kindergarten than those who received only EHS (ACF, 2006). Future research with these data may shed further light on cultural, logistical, and other factors that influence parents' choices about care for their 3- and 4-year-old children.

All of these findings have critical implications for providers, classroom teachers, intervention programs, and policymakers as each seeks to understand what types of support and intervention should be targeted to whom, and how that support can be early, intensive, and seamless enough to produce optimal language and literacy outcomes for children from at-risk families.

Notes

1. Sample composition differs slightly across studies. See cited studies for details.
2. Demographic variables entered in the first step in hierarchical multiple regression analyses included child gender; birth order (firstborn or later born); mother's teen status at birth of child; mother's highest level of education (i.e., high school graduate or GED diploma, greater than high school or GED diploma); mother's employment status; whether mother was living with a spouse or partner; and mother's race/ethnicity. Children's Bayley MDI scores at 14 months served as an additional control. Preliminary analyses examining children in the program and comparison groups separately showed similar results; thus, program status was not included as a control variable.
3. As in Rodriguez et al. (2009), separate preliminary analyses of program and comparison groups showed no difference in trajectory patterns; thus, program status was not included as a control variable.

References

Administration for Children and Families (ACF). (2002a). *Making a difference in the lives of infants and toddlers and their families: The impacts of Early Head Start*. Washington, DC: U.S. Department of Health and Human Services.

Administration for Children and Families (ACF). (2002b). *A descriptive study of Head Start families: FACES 1997* (Technical Report I). Washington, DC: Author.

Administration for Children and Families (ACF). (2003). *Head Start FACES (2000): A whole child perspective on program performance: Fourth progress report*. Washington, DC: U.S. Department of Health and Human Services.

Administration for Children and Families (ACF). (2006). *Research to practice: Preliminary findings from the Early Head Start pre-kindergarten follow-up*. Washington, DC: U.S. Department of Health and Human Services.

Alexander, K., Entwisle, D., & Horsey, C. (1997). From first grade forward: Early foundations of high school dropout. *Sociology of Education, 70*, 87–107.

Bayley, N. (1993). *Manual for the Bayley Scales of Infant Development*. New York: Psychological Corporation.

Berlin, L., Ispa, J., Fine, M., Malone, P., Brooks-Gunn, J., Brady-Smith, C., et al. (2009). Correlates and consequences of spanking and verbal punishment for low-income white, African American, and Mexican American toddlers. *Child Development, 80*, 1403–1420.

Boller, K., Bradley, R., Cabrera, N., Raikes, H., Pan, B., Shears, J., et al. (2006). The Early Head Start father studies: Design, data collection, and summary of father presence in the lives of infants and toddlers. *Parenting: Science and Practice, 6*, 117–143.

Brady-Smith, C., O'Brien, C., Berlin, L., Ware, A., & Fauth, R. (2000). *Child–Parent Interaction Rating Scales for the Three-Bag Assessment* (Early Head Start Research and Evaluation Project). Unpublished manuscript, Columbia University.

Brooks-Gunn, J., & Duncan, G. (1997). The effects of poverty on children. *The Future of Children, 7*, 55–71.

Brooks-Gunn, J., Gross, R. T., Kraemer, H. C., Spiker, D., & Shapiro, S. (1992). Enhancing the cognitive outcomes of low birth weight, premature infants: For whom is the intervention most effective? *Pediatrics, 89*, 1209–1215.

Bus, A. G., van IJzendoorn, M. H., & Pellegrini, A. D. (1995). Joint book reading makes for success in learning to read: A meta-analysis on intergenerational transmission of literacy. *Review of Educational Research, 65*, 1–21.

Cabrera, N., & Bradley, R. H. (in press). Low-income mother and father interactions with their children. *Child Development*.

Caldwell, B. M., & Bradley, R. H. (1984). *Home Observation for Measurement of the Environment: Administration manual* (rev. ed.). Unpublished manuscript, University of Arkansas at Little Rock, Center for Applied Studies in Education.

Campbell, F. A., & Ramey, C. T. (1994). Effects of early intervention on intellectual and academic achievement: A follow-up study of children from low-income families. *Child Development, 65*, 684–698.

Carle, E. (1983). *The very hungry caterpillar*. New York: Putnam.

Chazen-Cohen, R., Ayoub, C., Pan, B. A., Roggman, L., Raikes, H., McKelvey, L., et al. (2007). It takes time: Impacts of Early Head Start that lead to reductions in maternal depression two years later. *Infant Mental Health Journal, 28*, 151–170.

Christofaro, T. N., & Tamis-LeMonda, C. S. (2008). Lessons in mother–child and father–child personal narratives in Latino families. In A. Bailey, A. McCabe, & G. Melzi (Eds.), *Spanish-language narration and literacy: Culture, cognition, and emotion* (pp. 54–91). New York: Cambridge University Press.

Dickinson, D. K., & Tabors, P. O. (2001). *Beginning literacy with language: Young children's experiences at home and at school*. Baltimore: Brookes.

Dunn, L. M., & Dunn, L. M. (1997). *Peabody Picture Vocabulary Test* (3rd ed.). Circle Pines, MN: American Guidance Service.

Duursma, E. (2007). *Parental bookreading in low income families: Differences and similarities between fathers and mothers in frequency and style of reading and the impact on children's language and literacy development.* Unpublished doctoral dissertation, Harvard Graduate School of Education, Cambridge, MA.

Duursma, E., Pan, B. A., & Raikes, H. (2008). Predictors and outcomes of low-income fathers' reading with their toddlers. *Early Childhood Research Quarterly, 23,* 351–365.

Farkas, G., & Beron, K. (2004). The detailed age trajectory of oral vocabulary knowledge: Differences by class and race. *Social Science Research, 33,* 464–497.

Fenson, L., Dale, P., Reznick, J., Bates, E., Thal, D., & Pethick, S. (1994). Variability in early communicative development. *Monographs for the Society for Research in Child Development, 59*(5, Serial No. 242).

Fenson, L., Pethick, S., Renda, C., Cox, J. L., Dale, P. S., & Reznick, J. S. (2000). Short-form versions of the Mac-Arthur Communicative Development Inventories. *Applied Psycholinguistics, 21,* 95–116.

Guerra, A. W. (2008). The intersection of language and culture among Mexican-heritage children 3 to 7 years old. In A. Bailey, A. McCabe, & G. Melzi (Eds.), *Spanish-language narration and literacy: Culture, cognition, and emotion* (pp. 146–174). New York: Cambridge University Press.

Hart, B., & Risley, T. R. (1995). *Meaningful differences in the everyday experience of young American children.* Baltimore: Brookes.

Hoff, E. (2003). The specificity of environmental influence: Socioeconomic status affects early vocabulary development via maternal speech. *Child Development, 74,* 1368–1378.

Huttenlocher, J., Haight, W., Bryk, A., Seltzer, M., & Lyons, T. (1991). Early vocabulary growth: Relation to language input and gender. *Developmental Psychology, 27,* 236–248.

Ispa, J. M., Fine, M. A., Halgunseth, L. C., Harper, S., Robinson, J., Boyce, L., et al. (2004). Maternal intrusiveness, maternal warmth, and mother–toddler relationship outcomes: Variations across low-income ethnic and acculturation groups. *Child Development, 75,* 1613–1631.

Kang, J. Y., Kim, Y., & Pan, B. A. (2009). Five-year-olds' book talk and story retelling: Contributions of mother–child joint bookreading. *First Language, 29,* 253–275.

Kim, Y., Kang, J. Y., & Pan, B. A. (in press). The relationship of children's spontaneous utterances during joint bookreading to their retellings. *Journal of Early Childhood Literacy.*

Lee, V. E., & Burkam, D. T. (2002). *Inequity at the starting gate: Social background differences in achievement as children begin school.* Washington, DC: Economic Policy Institute.

MacWhinney, B. (2000). *The CHILDES Project: Tools for analyzing talk* (3rd ed.). Mahwah, NJ: Erlbaum.

McCarton, C. M., Brooks-Gunn, J., Wallace, I. F., Bauer, C. R., Bennett, F. C., Bernbaum, J. C., et al. (1997). Results at 8 years of intervention for low birth weight premature infants: The Infant Health and Development Program. *Journal of the American Medical Association, 267,* 2204–2208.

Nagin, D. S., & Land, K. (1993). Age, criminal careers, and population heterogeneity: Specification and estimation of a nonparametric, mixed Poisson model. *Criminology, 31,* 327–362.

National Center for Education Statistics. (2009). Early Childhood Longitudinal Study, Birth Cohort (ECLS-B). Retrieved October 6, 2009, from *nces. ed.gov/ecls/birthinstruments.asp.*

NICHD Early Child Care Research Network. (1994). Child care and child development: The NICHD study of early child care. In S. L. Friedman & H. C. Haywood (Eds.), *Developmental followup: Concepts, domains and methods* (pp. 377–396). New York: Academic Press.

NICHD Early Child Care Research Network. (2001). Before Head Start: Income and ethnicity, family characteristics, child care experiences, and child development. *Early Education and Development, 12,* 545–576.

NICHD Early Child Care Research Network. (2005). Pathways to reading: The role of oral language in the transition to reading. *Developmental Psychology, 41,* 428–442.

Pan, B. A., Rowe, M. L., Singer, J., & Snow, C. E. (2005). Maternal correlates of toddler vocabulary production in low-income families. *Child Development, 76,* 763–782.

Payne, A. C., Whitehurst, G. J., & Angell, A. L. (1994). The role of home literacy environment in the development of language ability in preschool children from low-income families. *Early Childhood Research Quarterly, 9,* 427–440.

Peterson, C. A., Wall, S., Raikes, H. A., Kisker, E. E., Swanson, M. E., Jerald, J., et al. (2004). Early Head Start: Identifying and serving children with disabilities. *Topics in Early Childhood Special Education, 24,* 76–88.

Radloff, L. S. (1977). The CES-D scale: A self-report depression scale for research in the general population. *Applied Psychological Measurement, 1,* 385–401.

Raikes, H., Pan, B. A., Luze, G., Tamis-LeMonda, C. S., Brooks-Gunn, J., Constantine, J., et al. (2006). Mother–child bookreading in low-income families: Correlates and outcomes during the first three years of life. *Child Development, 77*(4), 924–953.

Ramey, C. T., & Campbell, F. (1991). Poverty, early childhood education, and academic competence: The Abecedarian experiment. In A. Huston (Ed.), *Children in poverty: Child development and public policy* (pp. 190–221). New York: Cambridge University Press.

Rodriguez, E. T., & Tamis-LeMonda, C. S. (2009). Trajectories of the home literacy environment over the first five years: Associations with children's cognitive skills at pre-kindergarten. New York: New York University.

Rodriguez, E. T., Tamis-LeMonda, C. S., Spellmann, M. E., Pan, B. A., Raikes, H., Lugo-Gil, J., et al. (2009). The formative role of home literacy experiences across the first three years of life in children from low-income families. *Journal of Applied Developmental Psychology, 30,* 677–694.

Roth, F. P., Speece, D. L., & Cooper, D. H. (2002).

A longitudinal analysis of the connection between oral language and early reading. *Journal of Educational Research, 95,* 259–272.

Rowe, M., Coker, D., & Pan, B. (2004). A comparison of fathers' and mothers' talk to toddlers in low-income families. *Social Development, 2,* 278–291.

Sénéchal, M., & Cornell, E. (1993). Vocabulary acquisition through shared reading experiences. *Reading Research Quarterly, 28,* 360–375.

Shonkoff, J., & Phillips, D. (2000). *From neurons to neighborhoods.* Washington, DC: National Academy Press.

Snow, C. E., Porche, M. V., Tabors, P. O., & Harris, S. R. (2007). *Is literacy enough?: Pathways to academic success for adolescents.* Baltimore: Brookes.

Spieker, S. J., Nelson, D. C., Petras, A., Jolley, S. N., & Barnard, K. E. (2003). Joint influence of child care and infant attachment security for cognitive and language outcomes of low-income toddlers. *Infant Behavior and Development, 26,* 326–344.

Storch, S. A., & Whitehurst, G. J. (2002). Oral language and code-related precursors to reading: Evidence from a longitudinal structural model. *Developmental Psychology, 38,* 934–947.

Wechsler, D. (1981). *Manual for the Wechsler Adult Intelligence Scale—Revised.* San Antonio, TX: Psychological Corporation.

Woodcock, R. (1978). *Development and standardization of the Woodcock–Johnson Psycho-Educational Battery.* Hingham, MA: Teaching Resources.

Woodcock, R., & Johnson, M. (1989). *Woodcock–Johnson Psycho-Educational Test Battery—Revised.* Chicago: Riverside.

Woodcock, R. W., & Johnson, M. B. (1990). *Woodcock–Johnson Psychoeducational Battery—Revised.* Allen, TX: DLM Teaching Resources.

APPENDIX 26.1. Items Comprising Early Home Literacy Experiences (Rodriguez et al., 2009)

Literacy activities (based on maternal interview). Frequency of shared book reading, storytelling, and singing nursery rhymes; engagement in shared book reading and/or storytelling as part of child's regular bedtime routine. Items added at 36 months: frequency of shared book reading with other family members; visits to children's museum with mother and/or other family members; mother's or other household adult's help with learning the alphabet, numbers, shapes and sizes, and colors.

Quality of maternal engagement (based on selected observational items from the HOME scale [Caldwell & Bradley, 1984] and on coding of videotaped mother–child interaction [Child–Parent Interaction Rating Scales for the Three-Bag Assessment; Brady-Smith et al., 2000]). HOME items at 14 and 24 months were whether or not mother spontaneously vocalized to child at least twice, whether she responded verbally to child's vocalizations, whether she labeled an object or person in the environment, and whether she used speech that was clear and audible. HOME items at 36 months were whether or not mother conversed with child at least twice, answered child's questions or requests, recognized and acknowledged child's vocalizations, and used complex sentence structure in conversing.

Two mother behaviors based on coding of mother–child play interaction were used: sensitivity and stimulation of cognitive development. Sensitivity assessed the degree to which the mother responded to child's cues (e.g., gestures, expressions, and signals) during times of both distress and nondistress, and the extent to which she demonstrated a child-centered focus. Stimulation of cognitive development measured the quality and quantity of maternal effortful teaching to enhance the child's perceptual, cognitive, and linguistic development (for further details, see Brady-Smith et al., 2000; Rodriguez et al., 2009).

Provision of learning materials (based on combination of interview and observational items from the HOME scale [Caldwell & Bradley, 1984]). At 14 and 24 months: number of accessible children's books in the home; availability of toys supporting complex eye–hand coordination (e.g., crayons or alphabet blocks); availability of role-playing toys (e.g., doll or teddy bear); and availability of musical toys that allow child to make music (e.g., play a musical jingle). At 36 months: number of accessible children's books in the home; presence and accessibility of materials for play and leisure; child access to a record player, tape deck, or CD player and at least five children's tapes.

27

Professional Development for Early Childhood Educators: Reviewing and Revising Conceptualizations

MARTHA ZASLOW
KATHRYN TOUT
TAMARA HALLE
REBECCA STARR

There are many indications that the field of early childhood education is in the midst of a period of active review and revision of underlying conceptualizations for how professional development affects both practice within early childhood care and education settings, and child outcomes. In this chapter, we focus specifically on professional development aimed at strengthening young children's language and literacy development. We argue that the period of active review and reconceptualization in this area is still in process. The accumulating evidence on how early childhood professional development comes to affect key language and literacy outcomes will have important implications for investments in professional development programs and systems. While we cannot yet identify a full set of implications, we are beginning to be able to articulate ways in which the emerging research can be applied as communities, states, and the federal government increase their focus on strengthening the quality of early childhood education settings.

This chapter begins with a description of a long-held conceptualization of how early childhood professional development affects practice and child outcomes, and why new

evidence is provoking a reevaluation of this conceptualization. We then go on to describe the new conceptualizations that are emerging from multiple projects funded by the U.S. Department of Education to improve access to and quality of professional development for early educators working in low-income communities: the Early Childhood Educator Professional Development (ECEPD) programs. These projects have been described as a national laboratory, and are a valuable source for recent thinking on how professional development comes to strengthen educational practices and improve gains in children's early achievement, especially in the area of emergent literacy. We then describe a small set of ongoing research projects that promise to provoke yet further reevaluation. We conclude by noting the implications that can be gleaned for professional development programs and systems even while this period of reconceptualization is still ongoing.

Two key terms recur throughout this chapter, and it is important, before turning to a summary of relevant research, to define them. The terms *knowledge-focused* and *practice-focused* professional development approaches were introduced in the work of Neuman and Cunningham (2009) to distinguish between approaches that aim to increase the educator's understanding about young children's development (either across domains of development, or in specific domains such as language and literacy development), and those that focus directly on practices in working with young children in early childhood settings.

Knowledge-focused approaches occur most often in group settings and involve coursework providing credits toward a college degree, or training that does not build toward a college degree but for which credits may be earned toward attaining or maintaining licensure (both preservice and inservice training). In contrast, practice-focused approaches occur one-on-one or in small teams within the early educator's own classroom or home-based group (though in some recent work Internet linkages have been used). Practice-focused approaches involve observing, modeling, reflecting on, and discussing interactions between educators and children, and how space, materials, and routines are structured and used in the early childhood setting. They also involve the provision of feedback on these elements of the quality of the early childhood setting. The terminology for the staff member providing the professional development varies, with some programs using the label *coach*, while others use the term *mentor* or *provider of technical assistance*. For simplicity, we use the term *coach* in this chapter.

Traditional Conceptualization

A long-held assumption in the field of early childhood has been that knowledge-focused approaches, undertaken through college coursework or through training, improve knowledge about children's development.

Greater knowledge, in turn, is assumed to result in improvements in the quality of the early childhood environment and in strengthened child outcomes. The traditional conceptualization for improving child outcomes through strengthening early childhood professional development and practice is illustrated in Figure 27.1. In the area of language and literacy development, this conceptualization holds that it is essential to have an understanding of the key components of early literacy development and of educational practices that support the development of each, including the areas of *phonemic awareness* (the ability to isolate and manipulate the sounds of spoken words), *phonics* (the ability to link speech sounds to alphabet letters and letter combinations), *vocabulary* (the meanings of words), *fluency* (the rate of reading), and *comprehension* (understanding sentences and the overall meaning of a passage) (National Early Literacy Panel, 2008; National Reading Panel, 2000). In this conceptualization, knowledge of the key components of early literacy development, and the practices that foster their development, can in and of themselves improve early educators' practice in the early childhood setting and thereby strengthen child outcomes.

The prevalence of this conceptualization is suggested by the fact that nearly half of the states in the United States have preservice education or training requirements, and nearly all states have inservice requirements for education or training for teachers in center-based child-care programs (LeMoine, 2005). The preservice and inservice requirements are not combined with a requirement for the early educator to demonstrate pedagogical practice in the early childhood setting. This is implicit recognition of the assumption that education or training will result in improve-

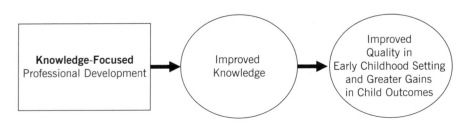

FIGURE 27.1. Traditional conceptualization.

ments in practice. Hyson, Tomlinson, Biggar, and Morris (2009) estimated that there are 1,200 institutions of higher education with programs in early childhood education, with 60% of these providing an associate's degree and 40% providing a bachelor's degree. There has been a great deal of concern about the lack of capacity in such educational institutions to address the growing need for early educators with appropriate educational credentials in state-funded PreK and given the increasing emphasis on educational credentials for Head Start and in state quality rating and improvement systems. Legislation and regulations requiring certain levels of educational attainment, again without a requirement to demonstrate practices, also reflect the traditional conceptualization that knowledge-focused professional development can be assumed to translate into improved pedagogical practices and quality in early childhood settings.

The assumed linkages between knowledge-focused professional development and practices in early childhood classrooms, as well as children's development, have recently come under scrutiny. A series of earlier literature reviews concluded that the quality of early childhood settings increases as educational credentials of teachers and caregivers increase (Barnett, 2003; Tout, Zaslow, & Berry, 2006; Whitebook, 2003). However, when careful analyses of the National Center for Early Learning and Development data on PreK programs in multiple states did not support an association between educational attainment of the early educator and these key outcomes (Early et al., 2006), a consortium of researchers decided this was a critical issue and determined to conduct parallel analyses in seven major early childhood datasets to examine further the pattern of associations.

The coordinated secondary data analyses were carried out with data from the Early Head Start Follow-Up Study, the Head Start Family and Child Experiences Survey, the Georgia Early Care Study, the More at Four Evaluation, the National Center for Early Development and Learning studies of PreK (the Multistate Study of PreK and the Study of Statewide Early Education Programs), the Study of Early Child Care and Youth Development (the National Institute of Child Health and Human Development [NICHD]

study), and the Preschool Curriculum Evaluation Research (PCER) program (Early et al., 2007). Three different measures of educational attainment were examined in relation to observed classroom quality and gain scores on measures of achievement during the year prior to kindergarten: highest level of education attained by the lead teacher/caregiver, whether the early childhood educator or caregiver had a bachelor's degree, and major for the highest degree attained (in child development or early childhood education, any other education major, or a non-education-related major). A common set of carefully selected control variables was used across analyses of the different datasets.

Findings from the coordinated secondary analyses challenged the assumption that highest level of educational attainment, highest education level among those with an early childhood education major, or having an early childhood education major among those with a bachelor's degree were related either to observed classroom quality or to children's gain scores on measures of academic achievement:

> Using seven recent major studies of classroom-based educational programs for 4-year-olds, these analyses, taken together, do not provide convincing evidence of an association between teachers' education or major and either classroom quality or children's academic gains. Most of the analyses yielded null findings. Although there were some statistically significant associations, no clear pattern emerged. (Early et al., 2007, p. 573)

There are multiple interpretations for the lack of consistent associations between early childhood educator educational attainment, classroom quality, and gains in children's achievement (Burchinal, Hyson, & Zaslow, 2008). One major interpretation is that the higher education programs in which the early childhood educators participated were of inconsistent quality or did not convey knowledge that is current in terms of recent research. Of 450 institutions of higher education that offer a bachelor's degree in early childhood education, fewer than half are recognized for quality by the National Association for the Education of Young Children through the National Council for the Accreditation of Teacher Education (Hyson et al., 2009). Hyson and colleagues (2007) report that while some do not apply for accreditation, among those that do, 25% of applications are not approved upon first submission, and that there are some recurring patterns among rejected applications. These include issues such as student assessments that focus on general teacher knowledge rather than knowledge of early childhood education, faculty without appropriate background in early childhood development and education, and field placements without appropriate supervision.

Another possibility is that some early childhood educators may struggle with the written materials provided in college coursework because of low literacy levels. For example, the National Adult Literacy Survey (Kaestle, Campbell, Finn, Johnson, & Mikulecky, 2001) found that a substantial proportion of child-care workers (between 44 and 57%) had scores indicating low levels of proficiency on a standardized assessment of literacy (see Zaslow, Tout, Halle, Whittaker, & Lavelle, 2010, for a review of this evidence).

A further major possibility, however, is that the traditional conceptualization may fail to capture how professional development can lead to improved practices and child outcomes. Knowledge-focused professional development may not suffice to bring about changes in practice and child outcomes. This further possibility is clearly suggested by a recent study by Neuman and Cunningham (2009), in which early educators working in center-based and home-based early childhood care and education settings were randomly assigned to receive a three-credit college course reflecting the most recent research in early language and literacy development, a combination of this course with on-site coaching in early language and literacy practices closely reflecting the content of the academic course, or "business as usual." Findings indicated no differences across groups on postintervention scores on a measure of knowledge of language and literacy development. However differences were found on observed language and literacy stimulation that the early educators were providing at posttest. Significant improvements were found only for the group that received the college course together with the onsite coaching. Effect sizes were large and educationally meaningful for early educators

in both center-based and home-based settings (and somewhat larger for home-based early childhood educators).

This study raises the question of whether knowledge-focused approaches alone suffice to bring about changes in practice within early childhood settings. Indeed, the results question whether coursework can be assumed to bring about changes in knowledge. We turn now to a body of work that provides a different conceptualization of how early childhood professional development brings about improvements in practice and child outcomes.

Emerging Conceptualizations

The study by Neuman and Cunningham (2009) is one of multiple demonstration and evaluation projects that were funded by the U.S. Department of Education as part of the ECEPD program, a federal discretionary program described in Title II, Part A, Subpart 5 Section 2151 (e) of the Elementary and Secondary Education Act (ESEA) as amended by the No Child Left Behind Act of 2001. The purpose of these projects was to enhance the school readiness of young children, particularly those who are disadvantaged, by increasing access to and quality of professional development available to early childhood educators working in areas with high concentrations of poverty. There was a particular emphasis on strengthening practices to support young children's language and literacy development.

As noted earlier, the ECEPD projects have been called a "national laboratory" for identifying effective professional development approaches for early educators. In order to increase what was learned from the multiple grants, a cross-site evaluation reviewed the documentation about the programs and evaluations of the 18 ECEPD programs funded in 2003, 2004 and 2005, and collected consistent interview data from the program directors.

The final report summarizing both the professional development initiatives and the evaluations for these 18 programs makes it clear that all, without exception, were working from a different conceptualization than the traditional one for how professional development for early childhood educators can bring about changes in knowledge and practice, and benefit young children's development (Tout, Halle, Zaslow, & Starr, 2009). In particular, all 18 projects, like the one by Neuman and Cunningham (2009) summarized earlier, involved a combination of knowledge-focused and practice-focused professional development.

Figure 27.2 provides a visual representation of the emerging conceptualization. We note that these projects generally tested *whether* improvements in knowledge, practice, and child outcomes occurred. However, they did not provide empirical examinations of *how* effects came about. While it is clear that all 18 ECEPD projects included in the cross-site evaluation included both knowledge- and practice-focused professional development, they did not use analytic approaches such as structural equation modeling to examine the mediating process through which knowledge, quality, and child outcomes were improved. The arrows in Figure 27.2 provide one set of hypotheses in which both the knowledge- and practice-focused components of professional development influence knowledge, and through knowledge influence quality and child outcomes. The model also reflects the hypothesis that there are direct, as well as indirect, effects from each of the professional development components to quality and child outcomes.

One of the interesting differences across the multiple ECEPD projects was the extent of coordination between the knowledge-focused and practice-focused components of the programs. At one extreme, the two were only loosely coordinated through content, especially a strong focus in each component on early language and literacy development. However in some programs, an iterative process was involved, in which an initial course session was followed by an onsite practice-focused session aimed at supporting the implementation of practices discussed during the coursework. The staff for the practice-based component then provided feedback to the staff of the knowledge-focused component to help shape the subsequent course session around the content that seemed to need clarification or emphasis. In some instances, the same staff members attended both the knowledge-focused and practice-focused components of the professional development to ensure that this iterative process was occurring. A more elaborated version of Figure 27.2, showing this intentional iterative linking of the knowledge- and practice-focused components of professional development, is shown in Figure 27.3.

One of the important conclusions of the cross-site evaluation of the ECEPD programs is that while all 18 sites included both knowledge- and practice-focused components, the 18 programs did not uniformly show evidence of positive effects. A preliminary review of the characteristics of the evaluations for the 18 programs found that only

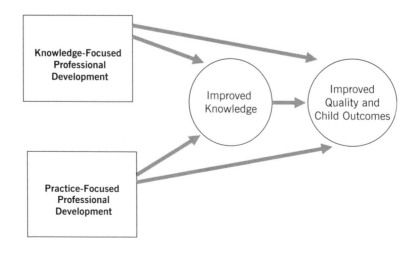

FIGURE 27.2. Emerging conceptualization.

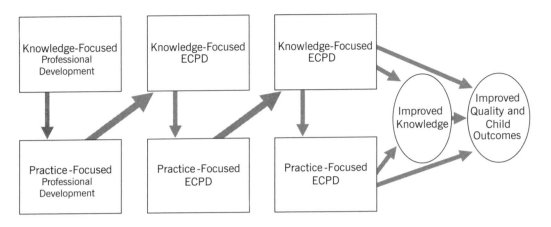

FIGURE 27.3. Iterative linkages.

10 met articulated standards for rigor in conducting the evaluation and in providing information on the evaluation. Criteria for rigor in conducting the evaluation included use of a comparative research design, with evidence of baseline equivalence of groups or adequate controls for differences, adequate cell sizes, and attrition at posttest that did not exceed specified limits. Criteria for rigor in reporting included providing information about the reliability and validity of measures used (see Tout et al., 2009, for a complete listing of criteria).

Of the 10 programs found to meet criteria for rigor in conducting and reporting on the evaluation, eight reported some evidence of statistically significant effects on the outcomes of interest. Thus, while joint use of knowledge-focused and practice-focused components in a professional development initiative shows promise in terms of improving knowledge, quality, and/or child outcomes in the area of language and literacy development, it is important to underscore that use of an approach in alignment with the emerging conceptualization does not ensure positive effects. Furthermore, the study designs to date have not made it possible to test whether the combination of knowledge- and practice-focused components underlies the positive effects, or whether the practice-focused component alone would suffice to bring about positive effects. We return to this possibility in a subsequent section.

With the "national laboratory" of this set of programs pointing very strongly to the emerging conceptualization, we need now to dispel the assumption that all programs involving this combination of knowledge-focused and practice-focused components will be effective, and begin to examine in greater detail the specific features present in programs following this conceptualization that do show evidence of positive effects. To lay the foundation for the testing of more specific program elements, Tout and colleagues (2009) identified the features on which the programs reviewed varied. These features are summarized in Table 27.1.

As can be seen in Table 27.1, there were multiple features on which the ECEPD programs varied even when they combined knowledge- and practice-focused components. To select just a few examples, professional development programs with both major components nevertheless differed in the extent of supervision and monitoring provided to the onsite staff. In some programs, coaches themselves were observed in a regularly occurring sample of onsite visits to ensure that they were adhering to the planned approach, while in others there was much more limited reporting and monitoring.

The professional development programs with both major components differed in terms of whether the focus of each onsite visit was predetermined (e.g., coordinated with the coursework to focus on a particular topic, such as phonological awareness activities), left open so that the early childhood educator him- or herself could provide input

TABLE 27.1. Specific Features of Programs

Features pertaining to the coaches
- Qualifications and personal characteristics of coaching staff
- Preparation and supervision of the coaching staff

Features pertaining to the coaching approach
- Whether a specific theoretical model was used in the coaching approach
- Whether the content focused on in the coaching was broad (e.g., improvement of overall quality) or specific (e.g., focusing specifically on early literacy development)
- Whether and how individualization in keeping with initial knowledge, practice, or attitudes of the early educators occurred
- Specific activities undertaken during coaching and whether these were sequenced (e.g., observation, modeling, discussion)
- Whether goals for each coaching session were predetermined (e.g., focused on implementing a particular curriculum) or flexible (e.g., goals for each session jointly set by the coach and early educator)

Coordination between coaching and coursework or training
- Whether the onsite work was coordinated with group coursework or training
- If there was coordination between coursework or training and coaching sessions, whether these were sequenced or interspersed
- Whether coaches also attended coursework or training
- Were there feedback loops across the coursework or training and coaching, for example, with coaches helping to inform those providing the coursework or training of what needed further focus based on their onsite work?

Dosage
- How often coaching sessions occurred and how long each lasted
- The period of months or years over which coaching occurred
- Whether the "dosage" of coaching was the same across educators or varied according to their starting point or needs

How progress was documented
- Whether documentation was required regarding the focus of each coaching session
- Whether supervisory staff observed coaching as it was occurring
- Whether observational measures of quality were used to document progress, and if so, which ones
- Whether child progress was assessed as part of documenting progress

into the focus, or included both planned and open elements. The dosage of professional development differed across programs, in terms of both how often coursework and onsite individualized professional development occurred and over how many months or years each component occurred. Programs also differed in terms of whether and how progress was documented in terms of both the practices in which the early childhood educator engaged and the development of the children.

To summarize, while it is exciting to document the emergence of a new conceptualization regarding early childhood professional development, the cross-site evaluation of the ECEPD programs underscores the importance of differentiating among programs following this emerging conceptualization, so as to identify the more specific features of effective programs. Within the programs included in the cross-site evaluation, the program features occur together in clusters. It will be important in future work to test the importance of particular elements considered to be of high priority through planned variation approaches.

Further Possibilities

It is striking how consistently the multiple ECEPD programs have followed the emerging conceptualization in which positive effects rely on a joint knowledge-focused and practice-focused approach. Yet we would be remiss ending this chapter without noting that further conceptualizations are also emerging; some have even challenged the emerging conceptualization that is becoming so widespread.

Neuman and Cunningham (2009) were not able fully to separate out the role of the knowledge- and practice-focused professional development in their contrast of coursework alone, coursework with coaching, and "business as usual." The lack of a group receiving coaching alone precluded this. However, in very recent work reported at a conference, Neuman and Wright (2010) took this further step, randomly assigning early educators to receive college coursework, onsite coaching, or no professional development (a waiting-list control). Findings point to improvements in the language and literacy environment of the classroom only for the group that received onsite coaching. Neither treated group improved on an assessment of knowledge of language and literacy.

This study raises the possibility that practice-focused professional development is the "active ingredient," and may be so even when both practice- and knowledge-focused components are present in a professional development program. Two other recent studies also point to effects on observed quality and children's achievement when a professional development approach focuses only on practice. The Quality Interventions for Early Care and Education (QUINCE) evaluation randomly assigned entry-level center teachers and home-based providers to receive onsite individualized professional development following the Partners for Inclusion model of onsite consultation. This model trains the early educator to be able to conduct an assessment of quality on his or her own early childhood classroom or home-based setting, using the appropriate environmental rating scale, and to set goals for quality improvement. Progress toward quality improvement is then supported by onsite consultation. This study found impacts of the intervention for home-based providers, and on some measures for center teachers as well (QUINCE, 2009).

Pianta, Mashburn, Downer, Hamre, and Justice (2008) used a Web-based approach to individualized consultation rather than providing the consultation onsite. In this study, early educators were randomly assigned to have access to videotaped examples of positive practice, or to have access to these videos online while also receiving detailed and specific feedback on a video of their own classroom practices sent to the consultant every 2 weeks. Teachers in the consultation group showed significantly greater improvement than those in the video-only condition on specific observational measures of quality.

The conceptual model suggested by these studies is one in which practice-focused professional development influences quality and child outcomes directly. This model might also show the possibility that early educators may actually derive improved knowledge from the practice-focused professional development; that is, rather than knowledge being gleaned from primarily didactic classroom approaches, it may be that knowledge is consolidated through repeated exposure to positive models and feedback on one's own practice.

Finding that practice-focused professional development is effective in bringing about improvements in practice does not preclude the possibility that specific models integrating practice- and knowledge-focused professional development may have positive effects. For example, it may be that starting with the opportunity to observe positive models and to receive feedback on one's practice provides a valuable starting point for classroom discussions that provide a theoretical framework for consolidating the practice-based knowledge.

Finally, recent research reported by Hamre, Pianta, Burchinal, and Downer (2010) begins to remove strict barriers between practice-focused and knowledge-focused professional development. This intervention involved college coursework focusing on early language and literacy development; thus, by our definition, it fits into knowledge-focused professional development. However, the coursework involved exposure to video exemplars of classroom practice with the aim of increasing teachers' ability to reflect on what they were seeing and identify specific practices with greater accuracy. Thus, the coursework specifically targeted understanding of pedagogical practice and could be called practice-focused. Preliminary results show positive effects on a knowledge measure that involves accurate identification of specific pedagogical practices. Results also show improvement in observed classroom quality (assessed through videotapes submitted by participating teachers). It is important to note that improvements in practice occurred without the provision of feedback to the early educators on their practices within the classroom.

Final results from this study are anticipated, with a full sample and further outcome measures. However, in the present context, the preliminary results suffice to indicate that there may be professional development approaches involving coursework very heavily focused on identification of positive practices, which teachers then imitate in their classrooms without receiving individualized feedback. We have not yet determined how to represent visually this intersection between the major components of professional development. Perhaps this might involve a box in which practice-focused professional development is nested within a larger box for knowledge-focused professional development.

Implications

We are in an active period of reviewing and revising conceptualizations that have guided early childhood professional development for decades. Recent research results challenge previous assumptions that investments in knowledge-focused professional development will suffice to bring about changes in practice and improvements in child outcomes.

How is it possible to reconcile these exciting but also challenging results, with the growing emphasis placed on professionalism of the early childhood workforce as signaled by increasing requirements for educational attainment in Head Start, PreK, and in the higher rating levels of state quality rating and improvement systems? We underscore that the emerging body of research pointing to the effectiveness of some, though not all, practice-focused professional development approaches does not preclude integrating such approaches into the infrastructures that already exist for education (through institutions of higher education) and training (e.g., through resource and referral agencies).

Earlier in this chapter, we noted findings that suggested that quality may be an issue for some programs granting degrees in early childhood education. One important possibility for improving the quality of higher education programs in early childhood is structuring coursework to focus heavily on practice, as in the recently reported study by Hamre and colleagues (2010). Another important possibility is to provide college credit for courses conducted in the format of onsite individualized coaching. Such coursework, instead of a written final exam, might require completion of an observational measure in the participant's early childhood classroom or home-based group. Early educators might be required to attains certain ratings on observational measures of language and literacy stimulation in the classroom or home-based group.

Finally, we have noted the possibility that professional development could be structured to start with practice-focused work but then include group coursework, providing an opportunity to reflect on the individualized work and place it in a theoretical context. However, if steps are taken to integrate practice-focused professional development into coursework or training, it will be important to keep in mind that not all evaluations of practice-focused approaches show evidence of positive effects. It would be easy, and also dangerous, to reify the emerging conceptualizations as showing that practice-focused professional development invariably show positive effects. We need to move toward a more differentiated description of such approaches, and toward an understanding of the specific features that underlie positive effects.

In summary, we can build on and strengthen the infrastructure for knowledge-focused professional development by systematically building into courses the practice-focused approaches that have been demonstrated to be effective.

References

Barnett, W. S. (2003). Better teachers, better preschools: Student achievement linked with teacher qualifications, *Preschool Policy Matters, 2.*

Burchinal, M., Hyson, M., & Zaslow, M. (2008). Competencies and credentials for early childhood educators: What do we know and what do we need to know? *National Head Start Association Dialog Briefs, 11*(1).

Early, D., Bryant, D., Pianta, R., Clifford, R. M., Burchinal, M., Ritchie, S., et al. (2006). Are teachers' education, major, and credentials related to classroom quality and children's academic gains in pre-kindergarten? *Early Childhood Research Quarterly, 21*(2), 174–195.

Early, D. M., Maxwell, K. L., Burchinal, M., Alva, S., Bender, R. H., Bryant, D., et al. (2007). Teachers' education, classroom quality, and young children's academic skills: Results from seven studies of preschool programs. *Child Development, 78*(2), 558–580.

Hamre, B. K., Pianta, R. C., Burchinal, M., & Downer, J. (2010, March). *A course on supporting early language and literacy development through effective teacher–child interactions: Effects on teacher beliefs, knowledge and practice.* Paper presented at the annual meeting of the Society for Research in Educational Effectiveness, Washington, DC.

Hyson, M., Tomlinson, H. B., Biggar, H., & Morris, C. A. (2009). Quality improvement in early childhood teacher education: Faculty perspectives and recommendations for the future. *Early Childhood Research and Practice, 11(1).*

Kaestle, C. F., Campbell, A., Finn, J. D., Johnson, S. T., & Mikulecky, L. J. (2001). *Adult literacy and education in America: Four studies based on the National Adult Literacy Survey.* Washington, DC: National Center for Education Statistics.

LeMoine, S. (2005). *Center child care licensing requirements: Minimum early childhood education (ECE) preservice qualifications and annual ongoing training hours for teachers and master teachers.* Vienna, VA: National Child Care Information Center. Available online at *nccic.org/pubs/cclicensingreq/cclr-teachers.html.*

National Early Literacy Panel. (2008). *Developing early literacy: Report of the National Early Literacy Panel.* Washington, DC: Nation Institute for Literacy.

National Reading Panel. (2000). *Teaching children to read: An evidence-based assessment of the scientific research literature on reading and its implications for reading instruction.* Washington, DC: National Institute of Health and Human Development.

Neuman, S. B., & Cunningham, L. (2009). The impact of professional development and coaching on early language and literacy instructional practices. *American Educational Research Journal, 46,* 532–566.

Neuman, S. B., & Wright, T. (2010, March). *Promoting language and literacy development for early childhood education: A mixed-method study of coursework and coaching.* Paper presented at the annual meeting of the Society for Research in Educational Effectiveness, Washington, DC.

Pianta, R. C., Mashburn, A. J., Downer, J. T., Hamre, B. K., & Justice, L. (2008). Effects of web-mediated professional development resources on teacher–child interactions in pre-kindergarten classrooms. *Early Childhood Research Quarterly, 23,* 431–451.

QUINCE Research Team. (2009, March). *Delivering and evaluating on-site consultation in a five-state collaborative study.* Paper presented at the annual meeting of the National Association of Child Care Resource and Referral Agencies, Washington, DC.

Tout, K., Halle, T., Zaslow, M., & Starr, R. (2009). *Evaluation of the Early Childhood Educator Professional Development program: Final report* (Prepared for the Policy and Program Studies Service, Office of Planning, Evaluation and Policy Development). Washington, DC: U.S. Department of Education.

Tout, K., Zaslow, M., & Berry, D. (2006). Quality and qualifications: Links between professional development and quality in early care and education settings. In M. Zaslow & I. Martinez-Beck (Eds.), *Critical issues in early childhood professional development* (pp. 77–110). Baltimore: Brookes.

Whitebook, M. (2003). *Early education quality: Higher teacher qualifications for better learning environments—a review of the literature.* Berkeley, CA: Institute of Industrial Relations, Center for the Study of Child Care Employment.

Zaslow, M., Tout, K., Halle, T., Whittaker, J., & Lavelle, B. (2010). *Towards the identification of features of effective professional development for early childhood educators* (Prepared for Policy and Program Studies Service, Office of Planning, Evaluation, and Policy Development). Washington, DC: U.S. Department of Education.

28

Preschool Education's Effects on Language and Literacy

W. STEVEN BARNETT
ELLEN C. FREDE

Most children in the United States today attend a preschool or child-care center prior to kindergarten. Federal and state governments subsidize millions of children so that they can attend programs that better meet their needs for early learning and development. Yet many children make such inadequate progress in language and literacy prior to kindergarten that they are poorly prepared to succeed in school (Hair, Halle, Terry-Humen, Lavelle, & Calkins, 2006). We investigate the reasons for this perplexing problem and find a disparity between the characteristics of the programs most children attend and of programs that have produced large gains in language and literacy. We suggest directions for research and policy designed to improve the effectiveness of preschool participation in promoting the language and literacy development of America's children.

What Are the Preschool Education Experiences of American Children?

The term *preschool* encompasses a diverse array of programs under a variety of names for children who have not yet entered kindergarten and typically refers to programs for 3- and 4-year-olds. The programs generally fall into three broad categories: private child-care centers, Head Start, and state

PreK programs that are often, but not always, provided through the public schools. There is some overlap between these categories. State PreK is increasingly delivered by private programs that receive state PreK funds directly or through school districts that contract for services. A substantial portion of Head Start classrooms are operated by public schools. However, their standards, regulations, and funding are reasonably distinct. All three sectors receive public funding. Additional children are served in preschool special education programs, the vast majority in the public schools (Ackerman, Barnett, Curenton, and Frede (2010).

Overall participation in center-based programs and the distribution of children among the three types of programs vary by age (Barnett & Yarosz, 2007). At age 4, as many as three-fourths of children attend a center-based preschool prior to kindergarten. This declines to no more than half of children at age 3. Children under age 3 are much less likely to attend a center, perhaps 25% between ages 1 and 3, and 12% under age 1. Thus, the vast majority of children in centers are ages 3 and 4. Most state PreK programs primarily or solely serve 4-year-olds, and Head Start serves more children age 4 than age 3, so public programs have a much larger role at age 4 than at age 3. For children age 3 or younger, Head Start and

Early Head Start are the major public direct service programs other than special education and early intervention for children with disabilities. Public funding for all three types is primarily targeted toward children from low-income families, so attendance of children from these families is at much higher rates than if they did not have access to subsidies. However, participation rates remain somewhat below average for children in low-income families because public programs do not have the capacity to reach all of them.

Public funding for private child care comes through various subsidies, including the Child Care and Development Block Grant (CCDBG) and Temporary Assistance to Needy Families (TANF), the U.S. Department of Agriculture's Child and Adult Care Food Program (CACFP), and tax credits. Most of this goes directly to parents, and except for the tax credits, these programs target assistance to low-income families. Child-care standards for private centers vary by state but are minimal due to concerns that higher standards would raise costs and lead to greater use of unlicensed informal care. Standards are particularly low for staff qualifications (National Child Care Information and Technical Assistance Center and National Association for Regulatory Administration, 2009). Some states permit teachers to be as young as 14. In only 30 states is a high school diploma or graduate equivalency degree (GED) required. Most do not require any specialized training. Qualifications requirements are even lower for assistant teachers. Standards are somewhat better for staff–child ratios. For example, the most common required staff–child ratios are 1:10 for 3- and 4-year-olds and 1:4 for infants.

The federal Head Start program directly funds local child development programs for preschool children in poverty. Head Start emphasizes comprehensive services for children and families, not just education in the classroom, and standards are considerably higher than for child care. In recent years, Head Start has increased its focus on language and literacy, and Congress has raised requirements for teachers' qualifications (Administration for Children and Families, n.d.). By the 2011 school year, all Head Start teachers are required to have at least an As-sociate of Arts (AA) degree specializing in early childhood education and all education coordinators must have at least a Bachelor of Arts (BA) degree specializing in early childhood education. By 2013, half of all teachers must have at least a BA degree. Head Start regulations require that each classroom have no more than 18 children and be staffed by a teacher and an assistant. The 2007 reauthorization of Head Start also expanded program eligibility to allow enrollment of more children from families between the poverty line and 130% of the poverty line.

State PreK programs are state and locally funded preschool programs administered primarily through state departments of education and the public schools, though some states jointly administer programs through human services agencies and a few have other administrative arrangements. State and local school-based preschool programs are the largest providers of center-based education to 4-year-olds. Several states have committed to provide access for all 4-year-olds: Florida, Georgia, Illinois, Iowa, New York, Oklahoma, and West Virginia. Of these, only Oklahoma currently approaches universal enrollment (Barnett, Epstein, Friedman, Boyd, & Hustedt, 2008). State PreK programs have higher standards than does child care, and typically have higher standards for teacher qualifications than does Head Start. However, there is wide variation, with some states having very high standards and a few states having PreK standards little better than typical child-care standards. When operated through public education they have an infrastructure that is not available to private programs, including accountability systems, professional development support, and a focus on learning and development broadly in service of their mission to prepare children to succeed in school.

As might be expected from the program descriptions, children who attend preschool programs have widely varying experiences (Early et al., 2005; Karoly, Ghosh-Dastidar, Zellman, Perlman, & Fernyhough, 2008). Even public programs vary considerably in their operating schedules, teacher qualifications, class size and ratio, auxiliary services (e.g., health and social services, or parenting education), monitoring and accountability, and teaching practices. Teacher qualifications in state PreK programs range from little more than a high school diploma to a 4-year college degree with specialized training in early childhood education. Head Start has national standards for program structure, operation, and teacher credentials but does not require all teachers to have college degrees. Head Start's teacher pay is far below that in the public schools. State child-care regulations are weak everywhere, but many centers exceed standards, even as others violate them (Blau, 2007). With programs varying so greatly, widely varied effects on children's language and literacy development are to be expected as well.

What Are Preschool's Effects, and Do They Vary by Type of Program?

A large number of studies have investigated the effects of preschool education on the learning and development of young children. A meta-analysis is a convenient way to summarize findings across such a large number of studies, computing averages and estimating the effects of variations in study rigor, program design, and characteristics of the children served. The most recent comprehensive meta-analyses review effect estimates from 123 studies for cognitive development, a category that includes IQ measures, language, reading, writing, spelling, verbal development, and mathematics. The average effect size is about 0.25 SD, but there is a great deal of explainable variation behind the average (Camilli, Vargas, Ryan, & Barnett, 2010). The rigor of the study matters (randomized trials and strong quasi-experimental designs yielded larger effect sizes), as does how much time has passed from the end of the intervention to the measurement of the effect. Adjusting for study quality and time of measurement provides the most relevant effect sizes for policy purposes. In more rigorous studies, the average effect size is 0.69 SD the end of the intervention (usually about age 5), declining to 0.35 SD at ages 5 to 10, and 0.28 SD beyond age 10.

Effect size also varied somewhat by type of measure, with differences between IQ-type measures and language, literacy, and other achievement measures. Initial effects on language, literacy, and other achievement measures tend to be somewhat smaller, but persistent effects are larger for these domains than for IQ (Jacob, Creps, Boulay, & Goodson, 2004). Effects on reading and other literacy and achievement measures tend to be smaller at the end of intervention but decline less long term compared to IQ.

Meta-analysis can be a blunt instrument for investigating details beyond average effects because it is difficult to account for subtle and idiosyncratic differences among studies. Nevertheless, some additional important findings emerge from these meta-analyses (Camilli et al., 2010; Jacob et al., 2004). Finetuning program design appears to have the potential to increase estimated effects substantially. Simulating moderate improvements in program design raised estimated effect sizes to 0.90 SD at program end and 0.45 SD after age 10. What mattered? Preschool programs using intentional teaching had effect sizes more than 0.20 SD greater than those that did not on average. Programs that provided more individualization of instruction had effect sizes that were more that 0.15 SD larger than other programs. To move beyond these general statements regarding program effectiveness it is necessary to examine more closely individual studies, as we do in the next section of this chapter.

Child Care

Typical child care has been found to have modest effects on children's language and literacy development. Effect sizes tend to be considerably smaller in studies of child care (about 0.10 SD) than in the meta-analyses reported earlier. Private center-based programs have been found to have somewhat larger effects than home-based child care on language and literacy development (Bernal & Keane, 2006; National Institute of Child Health and Human Development [NICHD] Early Child Care Research Network, 2002b). Bernal and Keane (2006) find negative effects of informal care in contrast to positive effects of center-based care for children of poorly educated mothers in particular. To some extent this may be due to higher quality in centers, with quality having more robust effects, particularly on long-term measures of language and literacy (Burchinal & Cryer, 2003; McCartney, Dearing, Taylor, & Bub, 2007; NICHD Early Child Care Research

Network & Duncan, 2003; Peisner-Feinberg & Burchinal, 1997; Ruopp, Travers, Glantz, & Coelen, 1979; Vandell, 2004). One indicator is that young children watch much more television each day in home-based than in center-based care (Christakis & Garrison, 2009). In one of the more rigorous studies, higher child-care quality is associated with slightly higher (0.05 *SD*) vocabulary scores through grade 5 (Belsky et al., 2007). Overall, long-term positive effects on literacy appear to be strengthened by higher quality, and to be larger for children from low-income families (Huston, Walker, Dowsett, Imes, & Ware, 2008; Peisner-Feinberg et al., 2001; Sylva et al., 2008).

Experimental studies conducted with very high-quality educational child care indicate that better results can be produced from child care when standards are raised and the program is more educational. The Abecedarian Study employed a randomized trial to evaluate the effects of a full-day (6–8 hours) year-round educational program from about 4 months of age to kindergarten entry (Campbell & Ramey, 2007). The Abecedarian Study found large positive effects on reading achievement (about 0.45) from ages 8 to 21, with only a very slight decrease in magnitude over that time. Findings from other randomized trials providing very high-quality educational child care continuously from birth to age 5 have findings consistent with those of the Abecedarian Study, but when intervention ceased at age 3, long-term effects were not found for reading (Campbell et al., 2008; Garber, 1988; McCormick et al., 2008; Wasik, Ramey, Bryant, & Sparling, 1990). Considering the evidence from child-care studies together, it appears that very high-quality child care over a substantial period of time up to school entry can have large positive effects on language and literacy development when it is intensively educational, but a vast majority of current child-care programs do not provide an intensive education program, nor do they have well-paid, highly trained, expertly supervised teachers. One caveat is that the educationally effective child-care programs in randomized trials enrolled children continuously for years. By contrast, most subsidized child care ends when the parent's eligibility status changes, and eligibility re-

determination is frequent, making it much more difficult for child care to have a large positive effect, regardless of the quality of the program.

Head Start

The most rigorous Head Start study to date is the National Impact Study (NIS) of a large sample of children across the country, randomly assigned to attend Head Start or not at ages 3 and 4 (Puma et al., 2010). Initial effects on letter–word identification and letter naming were 0.20 to 0.25 *SD* after 9 months of Head Start. Initial effects on language development (i.e., receptive vocabulary) were smaller, about 0.10 *SD*. Effects on "prewriting" measures were in the 0.10–0.15 range. The program had very small impacts on the frequency with which parents reported reading to children. Adjustments for children whose actual experience did not correspond to their assignment (e.g., they did not actually go to Head Start even though they were assigned) or who had other preschool education experiences increase the estimated effects, though we would expect this to be less than a 50% increase (Ludwig & Phillips, 2007).

At the beginning of 2010, the NIS released findings through first grade (Puma et al., 2010). With the exception of two weak effects on language (a different one for each age group) no persistent effects were found on literacy-related measures. Little evidence was found of substantive persistent effects in other domains or in parenting behavior. This does not necessarily mean that effects degraded over time. The NIS study provides evidence that public kindergarten greatly accelerated literacy development for both groups, and that initial gains were so slight as to be overwhelmed by literacy instruction in kindergarten and first grade. These results cast doubt on estimates from nonexperimental studies of moderate to large long-term effects from Head Start on educational attainment and other outcomes (e.g., Zill, Resnick, Kim, O'Donnell, & Sorongon, 2003).

Other studies add to our knowledge about possible effects of Head Start. A small, randomized trial of Head Start for 4-year-olds in one program found gains in language, phonemic awareness, and print concepts that were somewhat larger than those in the NIS (Abbott-Shim, Lambert, & McCarty, 2003). A rigorous quasi-experimental study of Head Start in Tulsa, Oklahoma (where public school teachers are in Head Start classrooms), found standardized effect sizes of 0.50 SD for letter identification and over 0.30 SD for spelling (Gormley, Phillips, & Gayer, 2008). The Tulsa estimates may be less affected by control group participation in other programs, but it seems likely that teacher qualifications and compensation play a role in the differences in outcomes, as we discuss later in the chapter. Several other studies produced smaller estimates of Head Start effects than the NIS, but their designs and estimates that are negative (not found in the NIS) suggest that they are susceptible to downward bias (Larzelere, Kuhn, & Johnson, 2004; Loeb, Bridges, Bassok, Fuller, & Rumberger, 2007; Magnuson, Meyers, Ruhm, & Waldfogel, 2004; Magnuson, Ruhm, & Waldfogel, 2007). Overall, these studies offer hope that Head Start could have larger effects if it employed more qualified teachers, though this seems unlikely to be the only change needed. Studies focused on improving the outcomes of Head Start should be a high national priority.

State and Local PreK Programs

As state and local PreK programs vary tremendously in funding, standards, and practices, generalizations about their effectiveness may conceal as much as they reveal. To further complicate matters, state PreK programs often deliver services through Head Start agencies and private child-care centers. Because some of the most rigorous studies have been conducted on PreK programs funded by state and local government, it is useful to review them. In general, state and local PreK programs should be expected to be no more effective than other programs with similar features, including child care, or, if quality is somewhat higher, Head Start. The interesting question is whether programs that clearly differ in key respects from child care and Head Start are more educationally effective.

Two randomized trials with long-term follow-up were conducted with public school PreK programs that share important features with some of today's better state programs (Consortium for Longitudinal Studies, 1983; Lazar & Darlington, 1982). Both employed public school teachers who received intensive coaching and supervision, with regular in-depth discussion and feedback regarding teaching practices. Other preschool programs with strong evidence of effectiveness have also had such teacher support, and it has been suggested that strong teacher support and supervision is likely to be important to replicating positive results (Frede, 1998). Teachers in both programs also conducted home visits.

The well-known High/Scope Perry Preschool Study evaluated the effects over nearly 40 years of a half-day preschool program with home visits by the teachers (Schweinhart et al., 2005). Children attended the preschool program for 2 school years beginning at age 3 (except for a few who entered at age 4). Ratios were much better than is typical of most public programs: six or seven children to each certified teacher (assistant teachers were not used). The program had large initial effects on IQ and receptive vocabulary that disappear over time, in part because public school helped the control group catch up once the children entered kindergarten. Yet moderate effects on reading and language achievement appear in the early grades and are clearly evident through adolescence. On reading at ages 14 and 19, the effect is one-third of a standard deviation. Significant advantages in literacy skills do not appear to have persisted to ages 27 and 40.

Somewhat less well-known is a study of public school preschool education by the Institute for Developmental Studies (IDS). It included 402 children who were randomly assigned to either the PreK program or to a control group (Deutsch, Deutsch, Jordan, & Grallow, 1983; Deutsch, Taleporos, & Victor, 1974). Children attended for 1 year at age 4 and afterward entered an IDS kindergarten program. A teacher and an aide staffed each preschool classroom of 17 children. The program had large effects on receptive vocabulary that continued to be substantial through at least third grade. The IDS study also found some persistent effects to adulthood on achievement, but severe sample attrition limits the confidence that can be placed in the adult findings (Deutsch et al., 1983; Jordan, Grallo, Deutsch, & Deutsch, 1985).

Although not a public school program, a half-day, university-based preschool education program at age 4 for 291 children, whose parents were mostly students at Brigham Young University, warrants discussion here. Classrooms of 20 students were staffed by a qualified teacher and two or three assistants. The curriculum offered a balance of activities, including discovery learning and play, group discussion and learning activities, and opportunities for creative expression. Parent participation in home activities for the children was required. In these respects it resembles a variety of higher-quality programs. However, it is quite dissimilar to most other programs studied, in that the children had an average IQ at study entry of 130 (the 97th percentile). Initial effects were found on a measure of school readiness (Larsen, Hite, & Hart, 1983). In second and third grade, the study found statistically significant gains for reading, spelling, and language achievement for boys of half a standard deviation or more, but effects were not significant for girls (though all seven comparisons on reading and language scores favored the preschool girls) (Larsen & Robinson, 1989).

More recently, studies have employed a regression discontinuity design that emulates the results of a randomized trial under reasonable assumptions (Cook, 2008; Cook, Shadish, & Wong, 2008; Hahn, Todd, & van der Klaauw, 2001). Very large studies of universal PreK in Tulsa, Oklahoma, find effects of nearly a full standard deviation on letter identification and three-fourths of a standard deviation on spelling at kindergarten entry (Gormley, Gayer, Phillips, & Dawson, 2005; Gormley et al., 2008). Effects are found for all children regardless of gender, ethnicity, and family income (Gormley et al., 2005, 2008). Effects are somewhat larger for minority children (Gormley et al., 2005, 2008). Effects on letter recognition and spelling are much larger for children in the public schools than for those in Head Start when researchers control for family background. As public school PreK and Head Start classrooms both employ fully qualified public school teachers, it may be that peer learning effects for disadvantaged children are larger when they have more advantaged classmates.

Similar regression discontinuity studies have been conducted for eight state PreK programs (Arkansas, California, Michigan, New Jersey, New Mexico, Oklahoma, South Carolina, and West Virginia) (Barnett, Howes, & Jung, 2008; Frede, Jung, Barnett, Lamy, & Figueras, 2009; Hustedt, Barnett, Jung, & Figueras, 2008; Hustedt, Barnett, Jung, & Thomas, 2007; Wong, Cook, Barnett, & Jung, 2008). Average effects were 0.26 *SD* on receptive vocabulary and 0.96 *SD* on print awareness (Barnett, Howes, et al., 2008; Hustedt, Barnett, Jung, & Goetze, 2009; Hustedt et al., 2007; Wong et al., 2008). These eight state programs are not representative of all state PreK programs, and they vary somewhat in population served and program standards. However, they are a broad sample of state PreK programs with reasonably high standards. As in the Tulsa study, effects are modestly larger for children from lower-income families. The regression discontinuity approach cannot be used for long-term follow-up, but some of these state PreK studies have been supplemented with follow-up studies using other designs. The less rigorous approaches tend to underestimate program effects but still find persistent effects on vocabulary and reading. Effects on print awareness disappear as virtually all children master this skill during kindergarten (Frede, Jung, Barnett, Lamy, & Figueras, 2009; Hustedt et al., 2007, 2008). Some additional support for these findings comes from studies using national data (Grissmer, Flannagan, Kawata, & Williamson, 2000; Magnuson et al., 2007).

The longest follow-up study of large-scale public school pre-K is the Chicago Child–Parent Centers (CPC) study (Reynolds, 2000). CPC provided low-income children with half-day preschool, kindergarten, and enhanced elementary school experiences. Just over half of CPC study students attended preschool for 2 years, beginning at age 3; the rest attended for 1 year at age 4. Each classroom had a licensed teacher and an assistant for 18 children, with extensive parent outreach and support. Estimated effect sizes for reading achievement were about 0.45 at kindergarten entry and 0.35 through elementary school, falling to 0.20–0.25 in high school. Effects of just 1 year of CPC attendance were somewhat smaller than the average because many children attended 2 years (Reynolds, 2000).

Why Do Effects Vary across Types of Programs, and How Can Effects Be Increased?

As should be clear by now, a review of the literature indicates the effects of preschool programs on children's language and literacy development, while positive, vary across the three major types of programs. On average, private child-care programs have the smallest effects. Head Start is better, but effects are modest and may have little lasting impact. State PreK programs are a mixed bag, but the better programs have larger effects that are more consistent with the substantial effects demonstrated in tightly controlled research studies. The state programs found to produce larger effects more similar in their structural features to the programs research has found to produce large effects.

The evidence reviewed here suggests that it is not program auspice per se but program features, varying by auspice, that account for key differences in effectiveness. The evidence for this view is provided by studies beyond the meta-analyses and other research reviewed earlier. In this section we review the evidence related to four aspects of program design and implementation: program structural features, curriculum and teaching practices, family involvement, and the population served.

Program Structural Features: Ratio and Teacher Qualifications

Findings from studies regarding the effects of structural features of programs on children's language and literacy development are mixed. While many studies have found links between program structure and either teaching practices or children's learning, some have failed to find these links (Barnett, 2004; Barnett, Schulman, & Shore, 2004; Mashburn et al., 2008; Pianta et al., 2005). This is expected given findings from the long history of such research in K–12 education and the nature of the relationships (Hanushek, 2006). Resources make higher-quality education possible; they do not guarantee better outcomes. If structural features

facilitate but do not guarantee better results, then the links between structure and outcomes may not always be observable. In addition, the educational production functions estimated in many studies are misspecified, often omitting important inputs and neglecting simultaneity, which can be expected to bias results (Todd & Wolpin, 2003). Use of parental education and other family background variables as proxies is not sufficient to account for home learning experiences (particularly if parents base their own efforts in part on how much they believe the preschool program is accomplishing), and sorting of children among teachers and programs may be far from random (Rothstein, 2009; Todd & Wolpin, 2007). For these and other reasons, experiments produce quite different results from correlational studies relying on natural variation, and their findings of positive relationships should be given more weight (Krueger, 1999).

Unfortunately, there are few experimental studies of the impacts of preschool program structure on children's learning and development. However, the large-scale Tennessee class size experiment finds that smaller class sizes in kindergarten lead to larger learning gains, with larger gains for disadvantaged children (Krueger, 1999). It seems plausible that this result for 5-year-olds would apply to the education of 3- and 4-year-olds as well. When we combine these results with the finding from the meta-analysis discussed earlier that individual and small-group instruction is associated with larger learning gains, it seems highly unlikely that any large-scale preschool program could reproduce the results of programs that research has found to be highly effective so long as class sizes and student–teacher ratios are much higher than those in the programs with demonstrated effectiveness. Similarly, programs that depart from models that have proven effective with respect to other structural features, such as teacher education, training, and expert supervision, have produced weak effects, while those that have replicated these features have been more effective, providing "demonstration proofs," as we discuss below.

In the absence of randomized trials, we must look elsewhere for evidence regarding the effects of teacher qualifications and professional development. Clearly, some studies find evidence that teachers with higher levels of education and more specialized training in early childhood education teach better and produce larger learning gains (Barnett, 2004). Other studies find that behaviors associated with education levels matter. For example, children experience greater syntactic growth over a year in preschool classes where teachers use more syntactically complex speech (Huttenlocher, Vasilyeva, Cymerman, & Levine, 2002). However, some studies do not find that any level of teacher education matters (Early et al., 2007; Mashburn et al., 2008). As discussed earlier, there is reason to suspect misspecification error as the source of null findings. One study that addresses this issue and provides relatively strong evidence, though it is not a randomized trial, is the NICHD study of Early Child Care, which incorporates unusually detailed information on home learning, as well as preschool program experiences, and in one pertinent analysis attends carefully to issues in correctly modeling the production function. Employing structural models, the NICHD study finds that both teacher education level and ratio appear to influence teaching practices and, thereby, cognitive abilities (including language and literacy) (NICHD Early Care Research Network, 2002a).

Unfortunately, we do not yet have randomized trials to help settle debates over teacher qualifications. In the meantime, we suggest relying on what we call "demonstration proofs." What structural features of programs have produced large gains in language and literacy, and, in particular, large long-term gains in reading achievement? One apparent difference is that the highly effective programs have highly educated, well-paid teachers compared to typical early childhood programs (Barnett, 1998). No programs with poorly educated, poorly paid teachers have been found to produce large, lasting learning gains even when substantial investments are made in inservice teacher training. Of course, this is not to say that real gains cannot be made by providing inservice training alone to teachers who are poorly prepared and do not receive regular expert feedback as part of their program's ongoing supervision and administration. However, we do not find evidence that this alone would result in large, lasting gains in language and literacy for children.

Another sort of demonstration proof is provided by a "natural experiment" in New Jersey, where the state's Supreme Court ordered the transformation of preschool education in 31 high-poverty school districts: All teachers were required to have a 4-year degree and certification in early childhood education; class size was limited to 15 students; and professional development was provided regularly and intensively. The result was a dramatic improvement in program quality, and the program produces gains in language and literacy (Frede et al., 2009).

Curriculum

Overall, the research relating to curriculum provides one conclusion that may seem obvious. Children's learning depends greatly on their opportunities to learn, and there is much to learn beyond literacy, including other cognitive abilities, self-regulation, and a variety of social skills. Together with other research, this suggests that an important principle for curriculum is balance—between teacher-initiated and child-initiated activities, between direct instruction and play, between language and simple literacy skills, and between literacy and other subject areas. As discussed earlier, long-term success in reading may depend as much or more on preschool's contribution to vocabulary and general knowledge than on its contribution to simple literacy skills because the latter can be rapidly acquired by most children in kindergarten. The meta-analysis identified an association between intentional teaching, and individual and small-group work and greater cognitive gains. These results should not be interpreted to mean that 3- and 4-year-old children should spend large amounts of time being drilled in discrete, academic skills in small groups or one-on-one. For example, one of the most widely cited studies of the positive effect of preschool for reading achievement is the High/Scope Perry Preschool Study (Schweinhart et al., 2005). The High/Scope curriculum (Hohmann, Weikart, & Epstein, 2008) used in this study emphasized child-initiated activities and play; however, we know that it also incorporated large amounts of teacher-directed activity (Schweinhart, Weikart, & Larner, 1986). These effective teacher-directed activities cannot be characterized as drilling children on discrete literacy skills even though acquisition of these skills may be one focus of the teacher in conducting these activities. Small-group activities and individual interactions in the High/Scope curriculum model, as with many of the popular curriculum models, incorporate literacy skills learning in the context of functional activities such as play planning, following recipes or dictating captions for artwork (Riley-Ayers & Frede, 2009).

There is a long history of curriculum comparison studies in which few important differences in outcomes are found across curricula (Karnes, Schwedel, & Williams, 1983; Marcon, 1994; Miller & Bizzell, 1984; Weissberg & Haney, 1997). The Preschool Curriculum Evaluation Research Study (PCERS) continues this tradition (Preschool Curriculum Evaluation Research Consortium, 2008). These studies find that differences between curricula in their effects on language and literacy are relatively small. This is not to say that there are not differences, but the sample size in most curriculum studies is under 150 children per group, divided among a much smaller number of classrooms. Given that the average Head Start program produces gains on measures of language and literacy of only 0.10 and 0.20 *SD*, a curriculum that increased the average effect of the program would produce gains far smaller than the minimal detectable effect size found in most curriculum comparison studies. Even a doubling of the effect size would be difficult to detect with the sample sizes common to most studies.

If we are to learn more about curriculum effects, we are likely to need much larger sample sizes in randomized trials. In addition, if these studies are to compare very different curricula adequately, they will need to improve upon the past in other ways. They must be longer term and provide adequate technical assistance and time for teachers to master the curricula. Simple, scripted curricula may be implemented well after a short introduction. More complex curricula that require a great deal of teacher judgment are likely to require several years before teachers become proficient, but they may offer the promise of more sensitive individualization. Also, these studies need to move beyond comparisons with local "business as usual," which provides an overly vague comparison

about which it is difficult to generalize. One interesting approach might be to have opposing teams, representing the curricula to be compared, conduct studies jointly to reduce the chance that a bias toward one approach or the other influences studies in selection of measures, data collection, analysis, and interpretation. When studies are conducted by research teams with no prior opinions about what curriculum works best, these research teams may be insufficiently familiar with the curricula to conduct an adequate study. More importantly, measuring how time is spent in the classroom, fidelity of curriculum implementation, and choosing appropriate outcome measures are critical features of studies if we are to understand how to vary teaching practices. For example, one curriculum model could provide regular scripted lessons on easily taught skills, such as letter naming, while the comparison curriculum focuses large amounts of effort on language-rich vocabulary-building activities. The first curriculum would be expected to have effects on a measure of letter naming, while the second would perform better on a measure of receptive vocabulary. However, letter naming is a fairly finite skill, and oral language acquisition is not; thus, the effects sizes will be larger for letter naming. Without following the children to at least third grade, the long-term benefits cannot be compared. Letter naming may better predict literacy scores in the short run than in the long run, when virtually all children have acquired this skill, and vocabulary and content knowledge play a stronger role. Without knowledge of how time is spent in the classroom, combined with both appropriate outcome measures and long-term follow-up, we could make incomplete and possibly incorrect assumptions about the value of particular curricular approaches, content, and teaching strategies.

The report of the National Early Literacy Panel (NELP) provides some guidance regarding productive directions for future research. The NELP report found that preschool and kindergarten programs could have moderate to large effects on spelling and reading readiness, and that the following program practices contribute to literacy achievement: (1) code-focused instruction, (2) book-sharing interventions, (3) home and parent programs, and (4) language enhanced interventions. We have measured preschool literacy classroom practices in five state studies and two large school districts using a criterion-referenced observation tool, the Supports for Early Literacy Assessment (SELA; Smith, Davidson, & Weisenfeld, 2001). The factor structure of the SELA that emerges from analyses of these multiple datasets breaks down into the following four factors that are remarkably similar to the practices identified by NELP: (1) environmental supports for literacy; (2) support for oral language acquisition; (3) support for parental engagement in early literacy; and (4) explicit early reading and writing skills development (Frede & Jung, 2009). The data reflect practices only in state-funded preschool programs and are not necessarily representative even of all state PreK, much less the landscape of early childhood education settings. However, the dataset contains 650 classrooms selected randomly to represent a much larger universe of relatively high-quality PreK programs. Language and literacy practices in these classrooms were on average good or better at providing a literacy-rich environment (Factor 1) and supporting oral language acquisition (Factor 2); however, classroom practices that enhance parental involvement in literacy support (Factor 3) and explicitly support early reading and writing skills development (Factor 4) can best be characterized as mediocre. We do not have comparable information about child-care and Head Start literacy practices.

Parent Involvement

It is well-known that parents have strong effects on children's language and literacy development. Many of the programs known for having produced large literacy effects, including lasting effects on reading, had significant parent involvement components. Efforts to promote literacy through parents are common and reported to be successful (Zuckerman, 2009). Nevertheless, randomized trials of parenting programs, the Even Start multigenerational approach, and the addition of home visits and other parent involvement activities to center-based programs have failed to find evidence of the educational effectiveness of these efforts to enhance parent involvement (Barnett, 1998; St. Pierre et al., 2003). Head Start's impact on self-reported reading with children is statistically significant but trivial in a practical sense (Puma et al., 2005). If parent education and involvement in the literacy development of their children is to play an important role in improving children's language and literacy, we will need a good deal more rigorous research and development to identify effective models.

Populations Served: Targeted versus Universal Approaches

There is a long history of research on peer effects in education. In the preschool field a few studies can inform us directly about the effects of the socioeconomic mix of the classroom on children's language and literacy development. Given the critical role that language models play in language acquisition, it seems likely that peers would have an effect (Hart & Risley, 1995). Indeed, at least two recent studies suggest that the field should pay attention to this issue. One is the Tulsa study described earlier, in which Head Start produced nearly identical gains to those produced by the public schools in math, but Head Start produced smaller gains in literacy than the public schools, despite having equivalent teachers and teacher pay. This pattern suggests peer effects on learning. Another recent study, this one from England, found that having more advantaged peers in the classroom was associated with greater cognitive gains by disadvantaged children in preschool programs (Sylva, Melhuish, Sammons, Siraj-Blatchford, & Taggart, 2004). More general evidence on preschool peer effects in the United States is provided by Neidell and Waldfogel (2008).

Conclusions and Recommendations

Research clearly establishes that preschool programs produce lasting positive effects on young children's language and literacy. The evidence comes from studies of child care, Head Start, and state and local public education programs. Lasting positive impacts have been found for large-scale public programs, as well as intensive programs implemented on a small scale. All children have been found to receive these benefits—boys and girls, all major ethnic groups, and children from the full range of economic backgrounds. Children from lower-income families do tend to have larger learning gains compared to more advantaged children. However, differences are relatively small, and advantaged peers may well contribute to greater gains for disadvantaged children.

The state of knowledge regarding why some preschool programs are more effective than others is not as fully developed as it should be, but some conclusions can be drawn. Typical child care has smaller short- and long-term effects than more educationally focused programs such as Head Start and higher-quality preschool programs linked to public education (Barnett, 2008; Winsler et al., 2008). Head Start, in turn, has smaller effects on learning and development than other public programs with higher standards. However, state and local PreK programs also vary considerably in their standards and effectiveness (Barnett et al., 2008). As a result, few American children attend high-quality, educational programs that produce substantive lasting effects (Blau & Currie, 2006; Clifford et al., 2005; Karoly et al., 2008). Even fewer children attend programs of consistently high quality over multiple years (Hynes & Havbasevich-Brooks, 2008). Hispanic children are among the least likely to attend effective programs, even though studies reveal that they make especially large learning gains when they do attend (Gormley, 2008).

The discrepancy between what can be accomplished and what is currently accomplished calls for major changes in public policy. What should change? First, policymakers should set goals for program effects on disadvantaged children's learning and development. Reasonable goals are to raise general cognitive, vocabulary, and mathematics abilities at kindergarten entry by half a standard deviation, or the equivalent of 7.5 points on an IQ test. The most basic literacy skills, such as print awareness, should be raised to the population average. In addition, a goal could be set to improve kindergarten teacher ratings of children's social skills, including self-regulation, by half a standard deviation. Goals for the general population should be gains at least half as large as those for disadvantaged children, with the exception of basic literacy skills, which most children already have mastered. To avoid problems that accompany high-stakes testing, these goals should be viewed

as targets for programs on a large scale—citywide, statewide, and nationwide—rather than for individual classrooms. Progress toward the goals should be measured by carefully assessing samples of children rather than testing all students. Policymakers should recognize that these goals for disadvantaged children may not be achievable with just 9 months of preschool education the year before kindergarten.

Second, policymakers should reconfigure programs to replicate more closely those that have produced positive results in the past. Such programs had smaller class sizes and ratios, with more highly qualified, better paid teachers than is common today. Other key features of these highly effective programs include reflective teaching practices, a well-specified curriculum, and parent involvement (Frede, 1998). Reflective teaching practices can be supported through regular teacher participation in planning with other teachers and supervisors, and systematic in-class coaching. Unfortunately, this cannot be a simple replication of yesterday's half-day school-year programs. Most mothers of young children work outside the home, and programs do not have the resources required to replicate yesterday's education models, while meeting today's child-care needs.

Third, policymakers should coordinate and integrate policies across child care, Head Start and public PreK so that their resources can be combined better to meet child development and child-care needs together. How might this work? State and local PreK can be merged with child care to provide an educational school day of 3–6 hours supplemented with wraparound care for a longer day and the remaining work days for families who need and want such care. Head Start could be integrated with public education to provide more intensive services for disadvantaged children, with class sizes and ratios linked to the percentage of children served who are in poverty, providing children in poverty with more extensive family services, and providing mental health, health, and other supportive services. Intensive services for disadvantaged children would start earlier, and Early Head Start would be integrated with subsidized child care. Public schools would provide an infrastructure for all programs, including assessment and accountability systems, supports for English language learners and for children with special needs, and alignment with the K–12 system. This integrated system could expand choice and competition through widespread participation of private providers, as is already done by many state PreK programs.

The integration of policies and standards across child care, Head Start, and the public schools will require more than simply allowing providers to tap multiple funding streams. For example, child-care subsidy policies may set such a low threshold for quality that increased subsidy use could harm the development of some children. Policies that expand child-care availability or raise standards without providing adequate funding could have perverse consequences for child development, particularly for disadvantaged children (Baker, Gruber, & Milligan, 2008; Bernal & Keane, 2006; Blau, 2007). If child-care subsidy eligibility is recertified every few months, many children will not receive the continuity of service required for effective education, unless this recertification applies only to wraparound care. Head Start and state PreK standards should be made be consistent with each other by raising standards, not lowering them. New data systems are required that recognize "enrollment" in multiple programs as desirable and are independent of the physical location of the child's classroom.

Finally, the nation should commit to a systematic program of research and development designed to improve practice and policy. This effort will require substantially more funds than are currently devoted to research on early care and education. It should include creation and testing of new practices and program models. For example, it is widely recognized that parents are powerful influences on their children's learning and development. However, programs have not been successful in harnessing that power on a large scale. Research that identifies successful approaches would have great value. How child care, Head Start, and state PreK programs should be changed to increase their effectiveness is sure to be hotly debated. Systematic experiments will help to decide those debates based on solid evidence. Such experiments may have to take place at the state and county or city levels, as well classroom or student levels, to provide the information needed to develop better policies, as well as better practices.

References

Abbott-Shim, M., Lambert, R., & McCarty, F. (2003). A comparison of school readiness outcomes for children randomly assigned to a Head Start program and program's waiting list. *Journal of Education for Students Placed at Risk, 8*(2), 191–214.

Ackerman, D., Barnett, W. S., Curenton, S., & Frede, E. (2010). *What do we know about the current state of mixed delivery early care and education systems?* (NIEER Policy Brief). New Brunswick, NJ: National Institute for Early Education Research.

Administration for Children and Families, U.S. Department of Health and Human Services. (n.d.). *Statutory degree and credentialing requirements for Head Start teaching staff* (ACF-IM0HS-08-12). Retrieved February 25, 2010, from *www.acf.hhs. gov/programs/ohs/policy/im2008/acfimhs_08_12. html*.

Baker, M., Gruber, J., & Milligan, K. (2008). Universal child care, maternal labor supply, and family well being. *Journal of Political Economy, 116*(4), 709–745.

Barnett, W. S. (1998). Long-term effects on cognitive development and school success. In W. S. Barnett & S. S. Boocock (Eds.), *Early care and education for children in poverty: Promises, programs, and long-term results* (pp. 11–44). Albany: State University of New York Press.

Barnett, W. S. (2004). *Better teachers, better preschools: Student achievement linked to teacher qualifications* (NIEER Policy Brief, Issue 2). New Brunswick, NJ: National Institute for Early Education Research.

Barnett, W. S. (2008). *Preschool education and its lasting effects: Research and policy implications.* Boulder, CO and Tempe, AZ: Education and Public Interest Center and Education Policy Research Unit. Retrieved February 12, 2010, from *nieer.org/ resources/research/preschoollastingeffects.pdf*.

Barnett, W. S., Epstein, D. J., Friedman, A. H., Boyd, J. S., & Hustedt, J. T. (2008). *The state of preschool 2008: State preschool yearbook.* New Brunswick, NJ: National Institute for Early Education Research, Rutgers University.

Barnett, W. S., Howes, C., & Jung, K. (2008). *California's state preschool program: Quality and effects on children's cognitive abilities at kindergarten entry.* New Brunswick, NJ: National Institute for Early Education Research, Rutgers University.

Barnett, W. S., Schulman, K., & Shore, R. (2004). *Class size: What's the best fit?* (NIEER Policy Brief, Issue 9). New Brunswick, NJ: National Institute for Early Education Research.

Barnett, W. S., & Yarosz, D. J. (2007). *Who goes to preschool and why does it matter?* New Brunswick, NJ: National Institute for Early Education Research.

Belsky, J., Vandell, D. L., Burchinal, M., Clarke-Stewart, K. A, McCartney, K., Owen, M. T., et al. (2007). Are there long-term effects of early child care? *Child Development, 78*(2), 681–701.

Bernal, R., & Keane, M. P. (2006). *Child care choices and children's cognitive achievement: The case of single mothers* (Working Paper No. 06-09). Evanston, IL: Institute for Policy Research, Northwestern University.

Blau, D. (2007). Unintended consequences of child care regulation. *Labour Economics, 14*, 513–538.

Blau, D., & Currie, J. (2006). Preschool, daycare and after-school care: Who's minding the kids? In E. Hanushek & F. Welch (Eds.), *Handbook of the economics of education* (Vol. 2, pp. 1163–1278). Amsterdam: North Holland.

Burchinal, M. R., & Cryer, D. (2003). Diversity, child care quality, and developmental outcomes. *Early Childhood Research Quarterly, 18*, 401–426.

Camilli, G., Vargas, S., Ryan, S., & Barnett, W. S. (2010). Meta-analysis of the effects of early education interventions on cognitive and social development. *Teachers College Record, 112*(3). Retrieved February 12, 2010, from *www.tcrecord.org/content.asp?contentid=15440.*

Campbell, F. A., & Ramey, C. T. (2007, December). *Carolina Abecedarian project.* Paper presented at the Conference on Critical Issues in Cost Effectiveness in Children's First Decade, Minneapolis, MN.

Campbell, F. A., Wasik, B. H., Pungello, E. P., Burchinal, M., Barbarin, O., Kainz, K., et al. (2008). Young adult outcomes from the Abecedarian and CARE early childhood educational interventions. *Early Childhood Research Quarterly, 23*(4), 452–466.

Christakis, D. A., & Garrison, M. M. (2009). Preschool-aged children's television viewing in child care settings. *Pediatrics, 124*, 1627–1632.

Clifford, R. M., Barbarin, O., Chang, F., Early, D. M., Bryant, D., Howes, C., et al. (2005). What is prekindergarten?: Characteristics of public prekindergarten programs. *Applied Developmental Science, 9*(3), 126–143.

Consortium for Longitudinal Studies (Ed.). (1983). *As the twig is bent: Lasting effects of preschool programs.* Hillsdale, NJ: Erlbaum.

Cook, T. D. (2008). Waiting for life to arrive: A history of the regression-discontinuity design in psychology, statistics and economics. *Journal of Econometrics, 14*, 636–654.

Cook, T. D., Shadish, W. R., & Wong, V. C. (2008). Three conditions under which experiments and observational studies produce comparable causal estimates: New findings from within-study comparisons. *Journal of Policy Analysis and Management, 27*, 724–750.

Deutsch, M., Deutsch, C. P., Jordan, T. J., & Grallow, R. (1983). The IDS program: An experiment in early and sustained enrichment. In Consortium for Longitudinal Studies (Ed.), *As the twig is bent: Lasting effects of preschool programs* (pp. 377–410). Hillsdale, NJ: Erlbaum.

Deutsch, M., Taleporos, E., & Victor, J. (1974). A brief synopsis of an initial enrichment program in early childhood. In S. Ryan (Ed.), *A report on longitudinal evaluations of preschool programs: Vol. 1. Longitudinal evaluations* (pp. 49–60). Washington, DC: Office of Child Development, US Department of Health, Education, and Welfare.

Early, D. M., Barbarin, O., Bryant, D., Burchinal, M., Chang, F., Clifford, R., et al. (2005). *Prekindergarten in eleven states: NCEDL's multi-state study of pre-kindergarten and study of State-Wide Early Education Programs (SWEEP).* Chapel Hill, NC: National Center for Early Development and Learning.

Early, D. M., Maxwell, K. L., Burchinal, M., Alva, S., Bender, R. H., Bryant, D., et al. (2007). Teachers' education, classroom quality, and young children's academic skills: Results from seven studies of preschool programs. *Child Development, 78*(2), 558–580.

Frede, E., & Jung, K. (2009). [Unpublished raw data analyses]. New Brunswick, NJ: National Institute for Early Education Research.

Frede, E. C. (1998). Preschool program quality in programs for children in poverty. In W. S. Barnett & S. S. Boocock (Eds.), *Early care and education for children in poverty* (pp. 77–98). Albany: State University of New York Press.

Frede, E. C., Jung, K., Barnett, W. S., Lamy, C. E., & Figueras, A. (2009). *The APPLES blossom: Abbott Preschool Program Longitudinal Effects Study (APPLES) preliminary effects through second grade* (Report to the New Jersey Department of Education). New Brunswick, NJ: National Institute for Early Education Research.

Garber, H. L. (1988). *The Milwaukee Project: Preventing mental retardation in children at risk.* Washington, DC: American Association on Mental Retardation.

Gormley, W. T. (2008). The effects of Oklahoma's universal pre-kindergarten program on Hispanic children (Center for Research on Children in the U.S. [CROCUS] Policy Brief). Washington, DC: CROCUS, Georgetown University.

Gormley, W. T., Gayer, T., Phillips, D., & Dawson, B. (2005). The effects of universal pre-K on cognitive development. *Developmental Psychology, 41*(6), 872–884.

Gormley, W. T., Phillips, D., & Gayer, T. (2008). Preschool programs can boost school readiness. *Science, 320*, 1723–1724.

Grissmer, D., Flannagan, A., Kawata, J., & Williamson, S. (2000). *Improving student achievement: What state NAEP scores tell us.* Santa Monica, CA: RAND Corporation.

Hahn, H., Todd, P., & van der Klaauw, W. (2001). Identification and estimation of treatment effects with a regression-discontinuity design. *Econometrica, 69*(3), 201–209.

Hair, E., Halle, T., Terry-Humen, E., Lavelle, B., & Calkins, J. (2006). Children's school readiness in the ECLS-K: Predictions to academic, health, and social outcomes in first grade. *Early Childhood Research Quarterly, 21*, 431–454.

Hanushek, E. (2006). School resources. In E. Hanushek & F. Welch (Eds.). *Handbook of the economics of education* (pp. 865–908). Amsterdam: North Holland.

Hart, B. M., & Risley, R. (1995). *Meaningful differences in the everyday experience of young American children.* Baltimore: Brookes.

Hohmann, M., Weikart, D. P., & Epstein, A. S. (2008). *Educating young children: Active learning practices for preschool and child care programs* (3rd ed.). Ypsilanti, MI: High/Scope Press.

Hustedt, J. T., Barnett, W. S., Jung, K., & Figueras, A.

(2008). *Impacts of New Mexico PreK on children's school readiness at kindergarten entry: Results from the second year of a growing initiative.* New Brunswick, NJ: National Institute for Early Education Research, Rutgers University.

Hustedt, J. T., Barnett, W. S., Jung, K., & Goetze, L. D. (2009). *The New Mexico PreK evaluation: Results from the initial four years of a new state preschool initiative.* New Brunswick, NJ: National Institute for Early Education Research, Rutgers University.

Hustedt, J. T., Barnett, W. S., Jung, K., & Thomas, J. (2007). *The effects of the Arkansas Better Chance Program on young children's school readiness.* New Brunswick, NJ: National Institute for Early Education Research, Rutgers University.

Huston, A. C., Walker, J. T., Dowsett, C. J., Imes, A. E., & Ware, A. (2008). Long-term effects of New Hope on children's academic achievement and achievement motivation (MDRC Working Paper). New York: Manpower Demonstration Research Corporation.

Huttenlocher, J., Vasilyeva, M., Cymerman, E., & Levine, S. (2002). Language input and child syntax. *Cognitive Psychology, 45*(3), 337–374.

Hynes, K., & Havbasevich-Brooks, T. (2008). The ups and downs of child care: Variations in child care quality and exposure across the years. *Early Childhood Research Quarterly, 23,* 559–574.

Jacob, R. T., Creps, C. L., Boulay, B., & Goodson, B. (2004). *Meta-analysis of research and evaluation studies in early childhood education.* Cambridge, MA: Abt Associates.

Jordan, T. J., Grallo, R., Deutsch, M., & Deutsch, C. P. (1985). Long-term effects of early enrichment: A 20-year perspective on persistence and change. *American Journal of Community Psychology, 13*(4), 393–415.

Karnes, M. B., Schwedel, A. M., & Williams, M. B. (1983). A comparison of five approaches for educating young children from low-income homes. In Consortium for Longitudinal Studies (Ed.), *As the twig is bent: Lasting effects of preschool programs* (pp. 133–170). Hillsdale, NJ: Erlbaum.

Karoly, L. A., Ghosh-Dastidar, B., Zellman, G., Perlman, M., & Fernyhough, L. (2008). *Nature and quality of early care and education for California's preschool-age children: Results from the California Preschool Study.* Santa Monica, CA: RAND Corporation.

Krueger, A. B. (1999). Experimental estimates of education production functions. *Quarterly Journal of Economics, 114,* 497–532.

Larsen, J. M., & Robinson, C. C. (1989). Later effects of preschool on low-risk children. *Early Childhood Research Quarterly, 4,* 133–144.

Larsen, J. M., Hite, S. J., & Hart, C. H. (1983). The effects of preschool on educationally advantaged children: First phases of a longitudinal study. *Intelligence, 7,* 345–352.

Larzelere, R. E., Kuhn, B. R., & Johnson, B. (2004). The intervention selection bias: An under-recognized confound in intervention research. *Psychological Bulletin, 130*(2), 289–303.

Lazar, I., & Darlington, R. (1982). Lasting effects of early education: A report from the Consortium for Longitudinal Studies. *Monographs of the Society for Research in Child Development, 47*(2–3, Serial No. 195).

Loeb, S., Bridges, M., Bassok, D., Fuller, B., & Rumberger, R. W. (2007). How much is too much?: The influence of preschool centers on children's social and cognitive development. *Economics of Education Review, 26,* 52–66.

Ludwig, J., & Phillips, D. (2007). The benefits and costs of Head Start. *Social Policy Report, 21*(3), 3–13.

Magnuson, K., Meyers, M., Ruhm, C., & Waldfogel, J. (2004). Inequality in preschool education and school readiness. *American Education Research Journal, 41,* 115–157.

Magnuson, K. A., Ruhm, C., & Waldfogel, J. (2007). Does prekindergarten improve school preparation and performance? *Economics of Education Review, 26,* 33–51.

Marcon, R. A. (1994). *Early learning and early identification follow-up study: Transition from the early to the later grades* (A report prepared for the District of Columbia Public Schools). Washington, DC: District of Columbia Public Schools.

Mashburn, A. J., Pianta, R. C., Hamre, B. K., Downer, J. T., Barbarin, O. A., Bryant, D., et al. (2008). Measures of classroom quality in prekindergarten and children's development of academic, language, and social skills. *Child Development, 79*(3), 732–749.

McCartney, K., Dearing, E., Taylor, B. A., & Bub, K. L. (2007). Quality child care supports the achievement of low-income children: Direct and indirect pathways through caregiving and the home environment. *Journal of Applied Developmental Psychology, 28,* 411–426.

McCormick, M. C., Brooks-Gunn, J., Buka, S. L., Goldman, J., Yu, J., Salganik, M., et al. (2008). Early intervention in low birth weight premature infants: Results at 18 years of age for the Infant Health and Development Program. *Pediatrics, 117*(3), 771–780.

Miller, L. B., & Bizzell, R. P. (1984). Long-term effects of four preschool programs: Ninth and tenth grade results. *Child Development, 55,* 1570–1587.

National Child Care Information and Technical Assistance Center and National Association for Regulatory Administration. (2009). *The 2007 Child Care Licensing Study.* Lexington, KY: National Association for Regulatory Administration.

National Early Literacy Panel. (2008). *Developing early literacy: Report of the National Early Literacy Panel.* Retrieved February 12, 2010, from *www.nifl.gov/publications/pdf/nelpreport09.pdf.*

Neidell, M., & Waldfogel, J. (2008). *Cognitive and non-cognitive peer effects in early education* (NBER Working Paper No. 14277). Cambridge, MA: National Bureau of Economic Research.

NICHD Early Child Care Research Network. (2002a). Child-care structure, process, outcome: Direct and indirect effects of child-care quality on young children's development. *Psychological Science, 13,* 199–206.

NICHD Early Child Care Research Network. (2002b). Early child care and children's development prior to school entry: Results from the NICHD Study of Early Child Care. *American Educational Research Journal, 39*(1), 133–164.

NICHD Early Child Care Research Network & Duncan, G. J. (2003). Modeling the impacts of child care quality on children's preschool cognitive development. *Child Development, 74*, 1454–1475.

Peisner-Feinberg, E. S., & Burchinal, M. R. (1997). Relations between preschool children's child-care experiences and concurrent development: The Cost, Quality, and Outcomes Study. *Merrill–Palmer Quarterly, 43*(3), 451–477.

Peisner-Feinberg, E. S., Burchinal, M. R., Clifford, R. M., Culkin, M. L., Howes, C., Kagan, S. L., et al. (2001). The relation of preschool child-care quality to children's cognitive and social developmental trajectories through second grade. *Child Development, 72*(5), 1534–1553.

Pianta, R. C., Howes, C., Burchinal, M., Bryant, D., Clifford, R., Early, D., et al. (2005). Features of prekindergarten programs, classrooms, and teachers: Do they predict observed classroom quality and child–teacher interactions? *Applied Developmental Science, 9*, 144–159.

Preschool Curriculum Evaluation Research Consortium. (2008). *Effects of preschool curriculum programs on school readiness* (NCER 2008–2009, U.S. Department of Education, National Center for Education Research). Washington, DC: U.S. Government Printing Office.

Puma, M., Bell, S., Cook, R., Heid, C., Lopez, M., Zill, N., et al. (2005). *Head Start impact study: First year findings*. Washington, DC: U.S. Department of Health and Human Services, Administration for Children and Families.

Puma, M., Bell, S., Cook, R., Heid, C., Shapiro, G., Broene, P., et al. (2010). *Head Start Impact Study: Final report*. Washington, DC: U.S. Department of Health and Human Services, Administration for Children and Families.

Reynolds, A. J. (2000). *Success in early intervention: The Chicago Child–Parent Centers*. Lincoln: University of Nebraska Press.

Riley-Ayers, S., & Frede, E. (Guest Eds.). (2009). What works in early childhood curriculum [A special issue on early childhood services]. *An Interdisciplinary Journal of Effectiveness, 3*(1).

Rothstein, J. (2009). Student sorting and bias in value-added estimation: Selection on observables and unobservables. *Education Finance and Policy, 4*(4), 537–571.

Ruopp, R., Travers, R. J., Glantz, F., & Coelen, C. (1979). *Children at the center: Final report of the National Day Care Study* (Vol. 1). Cambridge, MA: Abt Associates.

Schweinhart, L. J., Montie, J., Xiang, Z., Barnett, W. S., Belfield, C. R., & Nores, M. (2005). *Lifetime effects: The High/Scope Perry Preschool study through age 40* (Monographs of the High/Scope Educational Research Foundation No. 14). Ypsilanti, MI: High/Scope Press.

Schweinhart, L. J., Weikart, D. P., & Larner, M. B. (1986). Consequences of three preschool curriculum models through age 15. *Early Childhood Research Quarterly, 1*(1), 15–46.

Smith, S., Davidson, S., & Weisenfeld, G. (2001). *Supports for early literacy assessment for early childhood programs serving preschool-age children*. New York: New York University.

St. Pierre, R., Ricciuti, A., Tao, F., Creps, C., Swartz, J., Lee, W., et al. (2003). *Third national Even Start evaluation: Program impacts and implications for improvement*. Washington, DC: U.S. Department of Education, Planning and Evaluation Service, Elementary and Secondary Education Division.

Sylva, K., Melhuish, E., Sammons, P., Siraj-Blatchford, I., & Taggart, B. (2004). *The Effective Provision of Pre-School Education (EPPE) project: Final report* (A longitudinal study funded by the DfES 1997–2004). Retrieved February 12, 2010, from *www.dcsf.gov.uk/everychildmatters/publications/0/1160.*

Sylva, K., Melhuish, E., Sammons, P., Siraj-Blatchford, I., Taggart, B., Hunt, S., et al. (2008). *Effective preschool and primary education 3-11 Project: Final report from the primary phase: Pre-school, school and family influences on children's development during key stage 2* (age 7–11) (Research Brief No. 61). Nottingham, UK: Department for Children Schools and Families.

Todd, P. E., & Wolpin, K. I. (2003). On the specification and estimation of the production function for cognitive achievement. *Economic Journal, 113*(485), 3–33.

Todd, P. E., & Wolpin, K. I. (2007). The production of cognitive achievement in children: Home, school, and racial test score gaps. *Journal of Human Capital, 1*(1), 91–136.

Vandell, D. L. (2004). Early child care: The known and unknown. *Merrill–Palmer Quarterly, 50*(3), 387–414.

Wasik, B. H., Ramey, C. T., Bryant, D. M., & Sparling, J. J. (1990). A longitudinal study of two early intervention strategies: Project CARE. *Child Development, 61*(6), 1682–1696.

Weissberg, H. I., & Haney, W. (1997). *Longitudinal evaluation of Head Start Planned Variation and Follow Through*. Cambridge, MA: Huron Institute.

Winsler, A., Tran, H., Hartman, S. C., Madigan, A. L., Manfra, L., & Bleiker, C. (2008). School readiness gains made by ethnically diverse children in poverty attending center-based childcare and public school pre-kindergarten programs. *Early Childhood Research Quarterly, 23*, 314–329.

Wong, V. C., Cook, T. D., Barnett, W. S., & Jung, K. (2008). An effectiveness-based evaluation of five state pre-kindergarten programs. *Journal of Policy Analysis and Management, 27*(1), 122–154.

Zill, N., Resnick, G., Kim, K., O'Donnell, K., & Sorongon, A. (2003). *Head Start FACES 2003: A whole-child perspective on program performance*. Washington, DC: Administration for Children, Youth and Families, U.S. Department of Health and Human Services.

Zuckerman, B. (2009). Promoting early literacy in pediatric practice: Twenty years of Reach Out and Read. *Pediatrics, 124*, 1660–1665.

Index

Page numbers followed by *f* indicate figure; *n*, note; and *t*, table